GLEIM®

2016 EDITION

CPA Review

Business Environment and Concepts

by

Irvin N. Gleim, Ph.D., CPA, CIA, CMA, CFM

with the assistance of
Grady M. Irwin, J.D.

The AICPA formal title of this section is *Business Environment and Concepts*, and the AICPA acronym is BEC.

Gleim Publications, Inc.
P.O. Box 12848
University Station
Gainesville, Florida 32604
(800) 87-GLEIM or (800) 874-5346
(352) 375-0772
Fax: (352) 375-6940
Internet: www.gleim.com
Email: admin@gleim:com

For updates to this 2016 edition of *CPA Review: Business Environment and Concepts*

Go To: www.gleim.com/CPAupdate

Or: Email update@gleim.com with **CPA BEC 2016-1** in the subject line. You will receive our current update as a reply.

Updates are available until the next edition is published.

ISSN: Pending

ISBN: 978-1-61854-002-7 *CPA Review: Auditing and Attestation*
ISBN: 978-1-61854-003-4 *CPA Review: Business Environment and Concepts*
ISBN: 978-1-61854-004-1 *CPA Review: Financial Accounting and Reporting*
ISBN: 978-1-61854-005-8 *CPA Review: Regulation*
ISBN: 978-1-61854-010-2 *How to Pass the CPA Exam: A System for Success*

ACKNOWLEDGMENTS

Material from *Uniform CPA Examination, Selected Questions and Unofficial Answers*, Copyright © 1974-2015 by the American Institute of Certified Public Accountants, Inc., is reprinted and/or adapted with permission. Visit the AICPA's website at www.aicpa.org for more information.

The author is indebted to the Institute of Certified Management Accountants for permission to use problem materials from past CMA examinations. Questions and unofficial answers from the Certified Management Accountant Examinations, copyright by the Institute of Certified Management Accountants, are reprinted and/or adapted with permission.

The author is grateful for permission to reproduce Certified Internal Auditor Examination Questions, Copyright © 1991-2015 by The Institute of Internal Auditors, Inc.

Environmental Statement -- This book is printed on recyclable, environmentally friendly groundwood paper, sourced from certified sustainable forests and produced either TCF (totally chlorine-free) or ECF (elementally chlorine-free).

ABOUT THE AUTHOR

Irvin N. Gleim is Professor Emeritus in the Fisher School of Accounting at the University of Florida and is a member of the American Accounting Association, Academy of Legal Studies in Business, American Institute of Certified Public Accountants, Association of Government Accountants, Florida Institute of Certified Public Accountants, The Institute of Internal Auditors, and the Institute of Management Accountants. He has had articles published in the *Journal of Accountancy*, *The Accounting Review*, and *The American Business Law Journal* and is author/ coauthor of numerous accounting books, aviation books, and CPE courses.

REVIEWERS AND CONTRIBUTORS

Garrett W. Gleim, B.S., CPA (not in public practice), received a Bachelor of Science degree from The Wharton School at the University of Pennsylvania. Mr. Gleim coordinated the production staff, reviewed the manuscript, and provided production assistance throughout the project.

William A. Hillison, Ph.D., CPA, CMA, is a Professor Emeritus of Accounting at Florida State University. His primary teaching duties included graduate and undergraduate auditing and systems courses. Dr. Hillison provided substantial editorial assistance throughout the project.

Grady M. Irwin, J.D., is a graduate of the University of Florida College of Law, and he has taught in the University of Florida College of Business. Mr. Irwin provided substantial editorial assistance throughout the project.

Michael Kustanovich, M.A., CPA, is a graduate of Ben-Gurion University of the Negev in Israel. He is a Lecturer of Accountancy in the Department of Accountancy at the University of Illinois at Urbana-Champaign. He has worked in the audit departments of KPMG and PWC and as a financial accounting lecturer in the Department of Economics of Ben-Gurion University of the Negev. Mr. Kustanovich provided substantial editorial assistance throughout the project.

A PERSONAL THANKS

This manual would not have been possible without the extraordinary effort and dedication of Jacob Brunny, Julie Cutlip, Courtney McAllister, Kelsey Olson, Teresa Soard, Justin Stephenson, Joanne Strong, and Elmer Tucker, who typed the entire manuscript and all revisions and drafted and laid out the diagrams and illustrations in this book.

The authors also appreciate the production and editorial assistance of Jacob Bennet, Jessica Felkins, James Harvin, Blaine Hatton, Kristen Hennen, Jeanette Kerstein, Katie Larson, Josh Lehr, Diana León, Jake Pettifor, Shane Rapp, Drew Sheppard, and Martha Willis.

The authors also appreciate the critical reading assistance of Coryn Brewer, Paul Davis, Solomon Gonite, Aitang Guan, Nathan Kaplan, Melissa Leonard, Jerry Mathis, Monica Metz, Sunny Shang, Daniel Sinclair, Tingwei Su, Diana Weng, Samantha Wiley, Madison Willis, and Josie Zhao.

Finally, we appreciate the encouragement, support, and tolerance of our families throughout this project.

TABLE OF CONTENTS

DETAILED TABLE OF CONTENTS

PREFACE FOR CPA CANDIDATES

The purpose of this Gleim CPA Review study book is to help YOU prepare to pass the 2016 Business Environment and Concepts (also referred to throughout the rest of this text as Business or BEC) section of the CPA examination. Our overriding consideration is to provide a comprehensive, effective, and easy-to-use study program. This book

1. Explains how to optimize your grade by focusing on the BEC section of the CPA exam.
2. Defines the subject matter tested on the BEC section of the CPA exam.
3. Outlines all of the subject matter tested on the BEC section in 20 easy-to-use-and-complete study units.
4. Presents multiple-choice questions from recent CPA examinations to prepare you for questions in future CPA exams. Our answer explanations are presented to the immediate right of each question for your convenience. Use a piece of paper to cover our answer explanations as you study the questions.
5. Presents one written communication task in each study unit to acquaint you with the written communication format. Answer the written communication task in your book. A suggested answer follows each task.

The outline format, the spacing, and the question and answer formats in this book are designed to facilitate readability, learning, understanding, and success on the CPA exam. Our most successful candidates use the Gleim Premium CPA Review System,* which includes Gleim Instruct videos; our Access Until You Pass Guarantee; expertly authored books; the largest test bank of multiple-choice questions (presented with NEW adaptive learning technology), Task-Based Simulations, and Written Communications; Audio Lectures; and the support of our team of accounting experts. This review book and all Gleim CPA Review materials are compatible with other CPA review materials and courses that follow the AICPA Content and Skill Specification Outlines (CSOs/SSOs).

To maximize the efficiency and effectiveness of your CPA review program, augment your studying with *How to Pass the CPA Exam: A System for Success*. This booklet has been carefully written and organized to provide important information to assist you in passing the CPA examination.

Thank you for your interest in the Gleim CPA Review materials. We deeply appreciate the thousands of letters and suggestions received from CPA, CIA, CMA, and EA candidates during the past 5 decades.

If you use the Gleim materials, we want YOUR feedback immediately after the exam and as soon as you have received your grades. The CPA exam is NONDISCLOSED, and you will sign an attestation including, "I hereby agree that I will maintain the confidentiality of the Uniform CPA Examination. In addition, I agree that I will not divulge the nature or content of any Uniform CPA Examination question or answer under any circumstance . . ." We ask only for information about our materials, i.e., the topics that need to be added, expanded, etc. Our approach has AICPA approval.

Please go to www.gleim.com/feedbackBEC to share your suggestions on how we can improve this edition.

Good Luck on the Exam,

Irvin N. Gleim

November 2015

* Visit www.gleimcpa.com or call (800) 874-5346 to order.

OPTIMIZING YOUR BUSINESS ENVIRONMENT AND CONCEPTS SCORE

CBT-e Exam

CPA Exam Section	Auditing & Attestation	**Business Environment & Concepts**	Financial Accounting & Reporting	Regulation
Acronym	AUD	**BEC**	FAR	REG
Exam Length	4 hours	**3 hours**	4 hours	3 hours
Testlets:				
Multiple-Choice	3, 30 questions each (60%)	**3, 24 questions each (85%)**	3, 30 questions each (60%)	3, 24 questions each (60%)
Simulations	1 with 7 tasks (40%)	**0**	1 with 7 tasks (40%)	1 with 6 tasks (40%)
Written Communication	0	**1 with 3 tasks (15%)**	0	0

READ *HOW TO PASS THE CPA EXAM: A SYSTEM FOR SUCCESS*

Scan the Gleim *How to Pass the CPA Exam: A System for Success* booklet and note where to revisit later in your studying process to obtain a deeper understanding of the CPA exam.

1. *How to Pass the CPA Exam: A System for Success* has seven study units:

   Study Unit 1: The CPA Examination: An Overview and Preparation Introduction
   Study Unit 2: AICPA Content Specification Outlines and Skill Specification Outlines
   Study Unit 3: Content Preparation, Test Administration, and Performance Grading
   Study Unit 4: Multiple-Choice Questions
   Study Unit 5: Task-Based Simulations and Written Communications
   Study Unit 6: Preparing to Pass the CPA Exam
   Study Unit 7: How to Take the CPA Exam

2. *How to Pass the CPA Exam: A System for Success* is available as an e-book at www.gleim.com/PassCPA.

OVERVIEW OF BUSINESS ENVIRONMENT AND CONCEPTS

BEC is scheduled for 3 hours (180 minutes).

AICPA title:	Business Environment and Concepts
AICPA acronym:	BEC
Question format:	72 multiple-choice questions (including 12 ungraded pretest questions) in three testlets of 24 questions each
	Three written communication tasks (including one ungraded pretest task)

SUBJECT MATTER FOR BUSINESS ENVIRONMENT AND CONCEPTS

Below, we have provided the AICPA's abbreviated Content Specification Outlines (CSOs) for Business. The percentage of coverage for each topic is indicated. Appendix A contains the CSOs in their entirety as well as cross-references to the subunits in our text where topics are covered. Remember that we have studied and restudied the CSOs in developing our CPA Review materials. Accordingly, you do not need to spend time with Appendix A. Rather, it should give you confidence that Gleim CPA Review is the best review source available to help you PASS the CPA exam.

- I. (18%) Corporate Governance
- II. (18%) Economic Concepts and Analysis
- III. (21%) Financial Management
- IV. (17%) Information Systems and Communications
- V. (12%) Strategic Planning
- VI. (14%) Operations Management

The Business Environment and Concepts section tests knowledge and skills necessary to demonstrate an understanding of the general business environment and business concepts. The topics in this section include knowledge of corporate governance; economic concepts essential to understanding the global business environment and its impact on an entity's business strategy; financial risk management; financial management processes; information systems and communications; strategic planning; and operations management. In addition to demonstrating knowledge and understanding of these topics, candidates are required to apply that knowledge in performing audit, attest, financial reporting, tax preparation, and other professional responsibilities as certified public accountants.

According to the AICPA, candidates will be expected to perform the following inclusive list of tasks to demonstrate such knowledge and skills:

- Demonstrate an understanding of globalization on the business environment.
- Distinguish between appropriate and inappropriate governance structures within an organization (e.g., tone at the top, policies, steering committees, strategies, oversight, etc.).
- Assess the impact of business cycles on an entity's industry or business operations.
- Apply knowledge of changes in the global economic markets in identifying the impact on an entity in determining its business strategy and financial management policies, including managing the risks of: inflation, deflation, commodity costs, credit defaults, interest rate variations, currency fluctuation, and regulation.
- Assess the factors influencing a company's capital structure, including risk, leverage, cost of capital, growth rate, profitability, asset structure, and loan covenants.
- Evaluate assumptions used in financial valuations to determine their reasonableness (e.g., investment return assumptions, discount rates, etc.).

- Determine the business reasons for and explain the underlying economic substance of transactions and their accounting implications.
- Identify the information systems within a business that are used to process and accumulate transactional data, as well as provide monitoring and financial reporting information.
- Distinguish between appropriate and inappropriate internal control systems, including system design, controls over data, transaction flow, wireless technology, and internet transmissions.
- Evaluate whether there is appropriate segregation of duties, levels of authorization, and data security in an organization to maintain an appropriate internal control structure.
- Obtain and document information about an organization's strategic planning processes to identify key components of the business strategy and market risks.
- Develop a time-phased project plan showing required activities, task dependencies, and required resources to achieve a specific deliverable.
- Identify the business and operational risks inherent in an entity's disaster recovery (business continuity plan).
- Evaluate business operations and quality control initiatives to understand its use of best practices and the ways to measure and manage performance and costs.

WHICH PRONOUNCEMENTS ARE TESTED?

Following is the section of the AICPA's pronouncement policy that is relevant to the Business section:

For all other materials covered in the Regulation and Business Environment and Concepts sections, material eligible to be tested includes federal laws in the window beginning six months after their **effective** *date and uniform acts in the window beginning one year after their adoption by a simple majority of the jurisdictions.*

AICPA's NONDISCLOSURE AGREEMENT

The following is taken verbatim from the Uniform CPA Examination: Candidate Bulletin dated October 2015. It is reproduced here to remind all CPA candidates about the AICPA's strict policy of nondisclosure, which Gleim consistently supports and upholds.

Policy Statement and Agreement Regarding Exam Confidentiality and the Taking of Breaks

I hereby agree that I will maintain the confidentiality of the Uniform CPA Examination. In addition, I agree that I will not:

- *Divulge the nature or content of any Uniform CPA Examination question or answer under any circumstance*
- *Engage in any unauthorized communication during testing*
- *Refer to unauthorized materials or use unauthorized equipment during testing; or*
- *Remove or attempt to remove any Uniform CPA Examination materials, notes, or any other items from the examination room*

I understand and agree that liability for test administration activities, including but not limited to the adequacy or accuracy of test materials and equipment, and the accuracy of scoring and score reporting, will be limited to score correction or test retake at no additional fee. I waive any and all right to all other claims.

I further agree to report to the AICPA any examination question disclosures, or solicitations for disclosure of which I become aware.

I affirm that I have had the opportunity to read the Candidate Bulletin and I agree to all of its terms and conditions.

I understand that breaks are only allowed between testlets. I understand that I will be asked to complete any open testlet before leaving the testing room for a break.

In addition, I understand that failure to comply with this Policy Statement and Agreement may result in invalidation of my grades, disqualification from future examinations, expulsion from the testing facility and possible civil or criminal penalties.

HOW TO USE THE GLEIM REVIEW SYSTEM

To ensure that you are using your time effectively, we have formulated a three-step process to apply to each study unit that includes all components together. You will be guided through these steps when you access your online course.

Step 1: Diagnostic

a. Multiple-Choice Quiz #1 (30 minutes, plus 10 minutes for review) – Complete Multiple-Choice Quiz #1 in 30 minutes. This is a diagnostic quiz, so it is expected that your scores will be lower.

   1) Immediately following the quiz, review the questions you marked and/or answered incorrectly. This step is essential to identifying your weak areas. Refer to "Learning from Your Mistakes" on page 7 for tips.

Step 2: Comprehension

a. Audiovisual Presentation (30 minutes) – This presentation provides an overview of the study unit. (Use the Gleim CPA Audio Lectures instead if you're on the go!)

b. Gleim Instruct – CPA Video Series (30-90 minutes) – These videos are for customers who prefer live instruction to the slide-show style of the Audiovisual Presentations. Gleim Instruct videos include lectures featuring professors from accredited universities, multiple-choice questions, and detailed examples.

c. Focus Questions (45 minutes) – Complete the Focus Questions and receive immediate feedback.

d. Knowledge Transfer Outline (60-90 minutes) – Study the Knowledge Transfer Outline, particularly the troublesome areas identified from your Multiple-Choice Quiz #1 in Step 1. The Knowledge Transfer Outlines can be studied either online or in the books.

e. Multiple-Choice Quiz #2 (30 minutes, plus 10 minutes for review) – Complete Multiple-Choice Quiz #2 in Gleim Online.

   1) Immediately following the quiz, review the questions you marked and/or answered incorrectly. This step is an essential learning activity. Refer to "Learning from Your Mistakes" on page 7 for tips.

Step 3: Application

a. Written Communication Tasks (60 minutes, including 10 minutes for review) – Complete and review the simulation section.

b. CPA Test Prep (60 minutes, plus 20 minutes for review) – Complete two 20-question quizzes in CPA Test Prep, a component of the Mega Test Bank, using the Practice Exam feature. Spend 30 minutes taking each quiz and then spend about 10 minutes reviewing each quiz as needed.

Additional Assistance

1. Gleim Simulation Bank– For additional practice, complete written communication tasks from the Simulation Bank, a component of the Mega Test Bank, as needed.

2. Core Concepts – These consolidated documents provide an overview of the key points of each subunit that serve as a foundation for learning.

Final Review

1. CPA Exam Rehearsal (3 hours/180 minutes) – Take the Exam Rehearsal at the beginning of your final review stage. It contains three testlets with 24 multiple-choice questions each and one testlet with three written communication tasks, just like the BEC section of the CPA exam. This will help you identify where you should focus during the remainder of your final review.

2. CPA Mega Test Bank (10-20 hours) – Use the Mega Test Bank to focus on your weak areas identified from your Exam Rehearsal. This software features adaptive learning technology and gives you access to the largest test bank of multiple-choice and task-based simulations so you can work on the topics and question-answering techniques you struggle with the most. Also, be sure to do a cumulative review to refresh yourself with topics you learned at the beginning of your studies. View your performance chart to make sure you are scoring 75% or higher.

The times mentioned above and on the previous page are recommendations based on prior candidate feedback and how long you have to answer questions on the actual exam. Each candidate's time spent in any area will vary depending on proficiency and familiarity with the subject matter.

GLEIM KNOWLEDGE TRANSFER OUTLINES

This edition of the CPA Review book has the following features to make studying easier:

1. **Backgrounds:** In certain instances, we have provided historical background or supplemental information. This information is intended to illuminate the topic under discussion and is set off in bordered boxes with shaded headings. This material does not need to be memorized for the exam.

Background
Because ERP software is costly and complex, it is usually installed only by the largest enterprises, although mid-size organizations are increasingly likely to buy ERP software. Major ERP packages include R/3 from SAP AG and Oracle e-Business Suite, PeopleSoft, and JD Edwards EnterpriseOne, all from Oracle Corp.

2. **Examples:** Illustrative examples, both hypothetical and those drawn from actual events, are set off in shaded, bordered boxes.

EXAMPLE
If the Fed requires reserves of 4% on all deposits, a bank with $10 million on deposit can create $250 million of new money [$10,000,000 × (1.0 ÷ .04)].

3. **Gleim Success Tips:** These tips supplement the core exam material by suggesting how certain topics might be presented on the exam or how you should prepare for an issue.

 Because of numerous accounting scandals, CPA candidates can expect to be tested on the responsibilities imposed by SOX on both the company's audit committee and its management.

4. **Memory Aids:** These mnemonic devices are designed to assist you in memorizing important concepts. For example, a useful memory aid for the COSO classes of objectives is

> **O** = **O**perations
> **R** = **R**eporting
> **C** = **C**ompliance

5. **Detailed Table of Contents:** This information at the beginning of the book is a complete listing of all study units and subunits in the Gleim CPA BEC Review program. Use this list as a study aid to mark off your progress and to provide jumping-off points for review.

6. We have also provided additional study materials to supplement the Knowledge Transfer Outlines within Gleim Online. For example, you will find Core Concepts for each study unit. These consolidated documents provide an overview of the key points of each subunit that serve as the foundation for learning. As part of your review, you should make sure that you understand each of them.

TIME BUDGETING AND QUESTION-ANSWERING TECHNIQUES FOR BEC

Expect three testlets of 24 multiple-choice questions each and one testlet with three written communication tasks on the Business section with a 180-minute time allocation. Study Units 4 and 5 in *How to Pass the CPA Exam: A System for Success* contain additional discussion of how to maximize your score on multiple-choice questions and written communications.

1. **Budget your time.** We make this point with emphasis. Just as you would fill up your gas tank prior to reaching empty, so too would you finish your exam before time expires.

    a. Here is our suggested time allocation for BEC:

	Minutes	Start Time	
Testlet 1 (MC)	35	3 hours	00 minutes
Testlet 2 (MC)	35	2 hours	25 minutes
Testlet 3 (MC)	35	1 hour	50 minutes
Testlet 4 (WC)	60	1 hour	15 minutes
***Extra time	15	0 hour	15 minutes

    b. Before beginning your first testlet of multiple-choice questions, prepare a Gleim Time Management Sheet as recommended in Study Unit 7 of *How to Pass the CPA Exam: A System for Success.*

    c. As you work through the individual items, monitor your time. In BEC, we suggest 35 minutes for each testlet of 24 questions. If you answer five items in 7 minutes, you are fine, but if you spend 10 minutes on five items, you need to speed up.

    ***Remember to allocate your budgeted extra time, as needed, to each testlet. Your goal is to answer all of the items and achieve the maximum score possible.

2. **Answer the questions in consecutive order.**

    a. Do **not** agonize over any one item. Stay within your time budget.

    b. Flag for review any questions you are unsure of and return to them later as time allows.

        1) Once you have selected either the Continue or Quit option, you will no longer be able to review or change any answers in the completed testlet.

    c. Never leave a multiple-choice question unanswered. **Make your best educated guess in the time allowed.** Remember that your score is based on the number of correct responses. You will not be penalized for guessing incorrectly.

3. **For each multiple-choice question,**

    a. **Try to ignore the answer choices.** Do not allow the answer choices to affect your reading of the question.

        1) If four answer choices are presented, three of them are incorrect. These choices are called **distractors** for good reason. Often, distractors are written to appear correct at first glance until further analysis.

        2) In computational items, the distractors are carefully calculated such that they are the result of making common mistakes. Be careful, and double-check your computations if time permits.

    b. **Read the question** carefully to determine the precise requirement.

        1) Focusing on what is required enables you to ignore extraneous information, to focus on the relevant facts, and to proceed directly to determining the correct answer.

            a) Be especially careful to note when the requirement is an **exception**; e.g., "Which of the following is **not** valid acceptance of an offer?"

    c. **Determine the correct answer** before looking at the answer choices.

    d. **Read the answer choices carefully.**

       1) Even if the first answer appears to be the correct choice, do **not** skip the remaining answer choices. Questions often ask for the "best" of the choices provided. Thus, each choice requires your consideration.

       2) Treat each answer choice as a true/false question as you analyze it.

    e. **Click on the best answer.**

       1) You have a 25% chance of answering the question correctly by guessing blindly; improve your odds with educated guessing.

       2) For many multiple-choice questions, two answer choices can be eliminated with minimal effort, thereby increasing your educated guess to a 50-50 proposition.

4. After you have answered all the items in a testlet, consult the question status list at the bottom of each multiple-choice question screen **before** clicking the "Exit" button, which permanently ends the testlet.

    a. Go back to the flagged questions and finalize your answer choices.

    b. Verify that all questions have been answered.

5. **If you don't know the answer,**

    a. Make an educated guess, which means selecting the best possible answer. First, rule out answers that you think are incorrect. Second, speculate on what the AICPA is looking for and/or the rationale behind the question. Third, select the best answer or guess between equally appealing answers. Your first guess is usually the most intuitive. If you cannot make an educated guess, read the stem and each answer and pick the most intuitive answer.

    b. Make sure you accomplish this step within your predetermined time budget per testlet.

LEARNING FROM YOUR MISTAKES

Learning from questions you answer incorrectly is very important. Each question you answer incorrectly is an **opportunity** to avoid missing actual test questions on your CPA exam. Thus, you should carefully study the answer explanations provided until you understand why the original answer you chose is wrong as well as why the correct answer indicated is correct. This learning technique is the difference between passing and failing for many CPA candidates.

Also, you **must** determine why you answered questions incorrectly and learn how to avoid the same error in the future. Reasons for missing questions include

1. Misreading the requirement (stem)
2. Not understanding what is required
3. Making a math error
4. Applying the wrong rule or concept
5. Being distracted by one or more of the answers
6. Incorrectly eliminating answers from consideration
7. Not having any knowledge of the topic tested
8. Using a poor educated guessing strategy

It is also important to verify that you answered correctly for the right reasons (i.e., read the discussion provided for the correct answers). Otherwise, if the material is tested on the CPA exam in a different manner, you may not answer it correctly.

HOW TO BE IN CONTROL

Remember, you must be in control to be successful during exam preparation and execution. Perhaps more importantly, control can also contribute greatly to your personal and other professional goals. Control is the process whereby you

1. Develop expectations, standards, budgets, and plans
2. Undertake activity, production, study, and learning
3. Measure the activity, production, output, and knowledge
4. Compare actual activity with expected and budgeted activity
5. Modify the activity, behavior, or study to better achieve the expected or desired outcome
6. Revise expectations and standards in light of actual experience
7. Continue the process or restart the process in the future

Exercising control will ultimately develop the confidence you need to outperform most other CPA candidates and PASS the CPA exam! Obtain our *How to Pass the CPA Exam: A System for Success* booklet for a more detailed discussion of control and other exam tactics.

IF YOU HAVE QUESTIONS ABOUT GLEIM MATERIALS

Gleim has an efficient and effective way for candidates who have purchased the Premium CPA Review System to submit an inquiry and receive a response regarding Gleim materials **directly through their course**. This system also allows you to view your Q&A session in your Gleim Personal Classroom.

Questions regarding the information in this Introduction (study suggestions, studying plans, exam specifics) should be emailed to personalcounselor@gleim.com.

Questions concerning orders, prices, shipments, or payments should be sent via email to customerservice@gleim.com and will be promptly handled by our competent and courteous customer service staff.

For technical support, you may use our automated technical support service at www.gleim.com/support, email us at support@gleim.com, or call us at (800) 874-5346.

FEEDBACK

Please fill out our online feedback form (www.gleim.com/feedbackBEC) IMMEDIATELY after you take the CPA Business section so we can adapt our material based on where candidates say we need to increase or decrease coverage. Our approach has been approved by the AICPA.

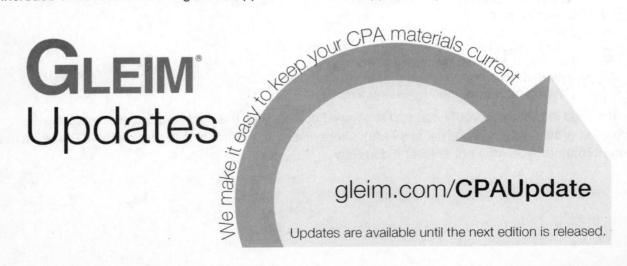

STUDY UNIT ONE
CORPORATE GOVERNANCE

(23 pages of outline)

Accounting scandals and concerns about the functioning of financial markets have resulted in greater attention to the means of directing the actions of a corporation (corporate governance). Significant governance tools are (1) the governance hierarchy, (2) regulatory requirements, (3) internal control, and (4) enterprise risk management.

1.1 ROLES IN THE GOVERNANCE HIERARCHY

1. **Definition of Corporate Governance**

   a. **Governance** is a combination of people, policies, procedures, and processes (including internal control). It helps to ensure that an entity effectively and efficiently directs its activities toward meeting the objectives of its stakeholders.

      1) **Stakeholders** are persons or other entities who are affected by the activities of the entity. Examples are shareholders, employees, suppliers, customers, neighbors of the entity's facilities, and government regulators.

   b. Corporate governance can be either internal or external.

      1) Corporate charters and bylaws, boards of directors, and internal audit functions are internal.

      2) The requirements of the Securities Act of 1933 and the Securities Exchange Act of 1934 administered by the Securities and Exchange Commission (SEC) are external.

2. **Basic Corporate Documents**

   a. Corporations are formed under the laws of the state of incorporation (very few corporations are incorporated under federal law).

   b. A corporation comes into being when the **articles of incorporation** are filed with the secretary of state of the relevant state. The secretary in turn issues a certificate of incorporation.

      1) The articles ordinarily must include the following:

         a) Corporation's name
         b) Number of authorized shares of stock
         c) Street address of the corporation's initial registered office
         d) Name of the registered agent at that office
         e) Name and address of each incorporator

      2) The articles also may contain optional provisions, such as

         a) Purpose and powers of the corporation,
         b) Internal management, and
         c) Any subject required or allowed to be addressed in the bylaws.

    c.   The **bylaws** of a corporation may contain any provision for managing its business and affairs that does not conflict with the law or the articles of incorporation.

        1)   The bylaws state such matters as the authority of officers and directors, how they are selected, the lengths of their terms, their compensation, and how the decision to issue new stock will be made.

3.   **Shareholders**

    a.   The **common** shareholders are those who have contributed the basic capital for the corporation to carry on its business.

        1)   **Preferred** shareholders have the contractual right to receive dividends and liquidation distributions before common shareholders but usually do not have voting rights.

    b.   Generally, shareholders are permitted to act only at a meeting.

        1)   They are required to hold an annual meeting. Special meetings may be held for important purposes, such as to approve a merger or other fundamental change.

        2)   The most important acts performed by the shareholders at the annual meeting are

            a)   Amending the articles of incorporation,
            b)   Voting on any matters requiring a general vote, and
            c)   Electing or removing directors.

    c.   Many states permit shareholders to change, by unanimous agreement, the provisions for corporate governance. This flexibility may allow a closely held corporation to function more nearly as a partnership without loss of corporate status.

        1)   For example, a shareholder agreement may (a) eliminate the board or restrict its powers, (b) determine who will be officers and directors, or (c) set voting requirements for directors and shareholders.

4.   **Board of Directors**

    a.   All major corporate decisions are made or approved by the board.

        1)   Directly managing the day-to-day operations of the entity is management's responsibility. The board has an oversight role.

    b.   The board has the following duties:

        1)   Selection and removal of officers

        2)   Decisions about capital structure (mix of debt and equity, consideration to be received for shares, etc.)

        3)   Adding, amending, or repealing bylaws (unless this authority is reserved to the shareholders)

        4)   Initiation of fundamental changes (mergers, acquisitions, etc.)

        5)   Decisions to declare and distribute dividends

        6)   Setting of management compensation (sometimes performed by a subcommittee called the compensation committee)

        7)   Coordinating audit activities (most often performed by a subcommittee called the audit committee)

        8)   Evaluating and managing risk (sometimes performed by a subcommittee called the risk committee)

    c.   Directors owe a **fiduciary duty** to the corporation.

 Because of the legislation passed in response to major accounting scandals, Dr. Gleim believes that the AICPA will test CPA candidates on the actions required of directors and officers to meet their fiduciary duties.

        1)   A fiduciary has a legal duty to act primarily for the benefit of another person (e.g., a corporation) in matters related to the undertaking.

            a)   A fiduciary is held to a higher standard of care than in the management of his or her own affairs.

            b)   Examples of fiduciaries include an attorney in relation to a client, the trustee of a trust, the personal representative of a decedent's estate, and the conservator (legal guardian) of someone legally determined not to be able to manage his or her own affairs.

        2)   Fiduciary duty requires directors and officers to

            a)   Act in the corporation's best interests,
            b)   Be loyal,
            c)   Use due diligence in carrying out their responsibilities, and
            d)   Disclose conflicts of interest.

        3)   Controlling or majority shareholders owe similar duties.

            a)   However, a **conflicting interest transaction** (e.g., a personal loan by the corporation to a director or officer) is acceptable if it is

                i)   Fair to the corporation and
                ii)   Approved by informed directors who do not have a conflict of interest.

        4)   The Sarbanes-Oxley Act of 2002 generally prohibits personal loans to executives or directors of public companies.

    d.   The **business judgment rule** protects an officer or a director from personal liability for honest mistakes of judgment if (s)he

        1)   Acted in good faith;
        2)   Was not motivated by fraud, conflict of interest, or illegality; and
        3)   Was not grossly negligent.

            a)   To avoid personal liability, directors and officers must

                i)   Make informed decisions (educate themselves about the issues),
                ii)   Be free from conflicts of interest, and
                iii)   Have a rational basis to support their position.

            b)   Furthermore, a director is entitled to rely on information provided by an officer (or professional specialist) if the director reasonably believes the officer (or specialist) has the relevant competence.

e.   A director who has a **corporate opportunity** must give the corporation the right of first refusal.

    1)   The corporation has a right, property interest, or expectancy in a corporate opportunity.

    2)   A corporate opportunity arises when

        a)   A director becomes aware of the opportunity in his or her corporate capacity;

        b)   The opportunity is within the scope of corporate activity; or

        c)   Corporate capital, equipment, personnel, or facilities were used to develop the opportunity.

    3)   Generally, a corporate opportunity does not exist if

        a)   Action by the corporation would be beyond its powers,

        b)   The corporation cannot obtain necessary financing or capital to take advantage of the opportunity, or

        c)   The opportunity is rejected by a majority vote of disinterested directors.

f.   Directors may be held liable for **unlawful distribution** made if the corporation was unable to pay its debts or the corporation's total assets are less than total liabilities.

5.   **Officers**

a.   The corporation's officers (i.e., executive management) are responsible for carrying out the entity's day-to-day operations.

b.   The **chief executive officer (CEO)** is directly selected by, and reports to, the board of directors.

c.   The CEO in turn usually selects other executives such as the chief financial officer (CFO) and chief information officer (CIO). These executives oversee the various functional areas of the entity.

d.   Officers are agents of the corporation and as such may enter the corporation into legally binding contracts.

e.   Corporate officers owe a fiduciary duty to the corporation similar to the duties owed by a director.

6.   **Internal Auditors**

a.   The internal audit function should assess, and make appropriate recommendations for, improving governance to achieve the following objectives:

    1)   Promoting appropriate ethics and values within the organization

    2)   Ensuring effective organizational performance management and accountability

    3)   Communicating risk and control information to appropriate areas of the organization

    4)   Coordinating the activities of, and communicating information among, the board, external and internal auditors, and management

7.   Corporate Governance Structure

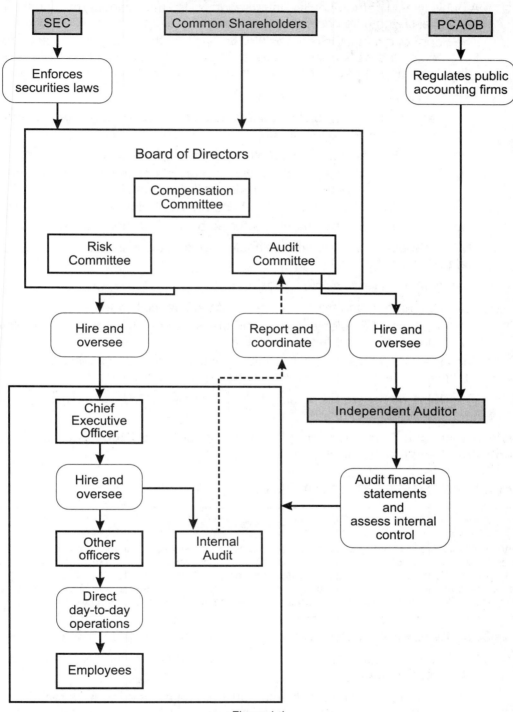

Figure 1-1

8. **Financial Reporting**

    a. A publicly held corporation's annual report to its shareholders must contain audited financial statements and other specified information.

    b. The board of directors is responsible for hiring, setting the compensation for, and overseeing the work of the independent auditor. In large corporations, a group of directors forms an **audit committee** to perform these functions.

        1) The audit committee also must

            a) Address complaints about accounting and auditing matters and
            b) Receive reports about

                i)   All critical accounting polices and practices to be used,
                ii)   All material alternative treatments of financial information within GAAP discussed with management,
                iii) Effects of the use of alternative disclosures and treatments, and
                iv)   The treatments preferred by the external auditors.

        NOTE: Subunit 1.2 states other requirements of the Sarbanes-Oxley Act of 2002 related to audit committees.

    c. Management is responsible for the

        1) Preparation and fair presentation of the financial statements and
        2) The design, implementation, and maintenance of internal control relevant to their preparation and fair presentation.

    d. The independent auditor's responsibility is to express an opinion on whether the financial statements are fairly presented in accordance with GAAP.

        1) If the corporation is publicly held, the auditor also must assess internal control over financial reporting.

Stop and review! You have completed the outline for this subunit. Study multiple-choice questions 1 through 5 beginning on page 32.

1.2 THE SARBANES-OXLEY ACT OF 2002 (SOX)

Background
In late 2001 and 2002, massive accounting scandals were reported in the media. They involved such large firms as Enron (hid debt of over $1 billion in improper off-the-books partnerships), Global Crossing (inflated revenues; shredded accounting-related documents), and WorldCom (booked operating expenses as capital assets; made large off-the-books payments to founder). In response to these and many other fraudulent practices, Congress passed the Sarbanes-Oxley Act of 2002, named for its sponsors, Democratic Senator Paul Sarbanes of Maryland and Republican Representative Mike Oxley of Ohio.

1. **Applicability to Publicly Held Companies (Issuers) and Their Auditors**

    a. Each member of the issuer's audit committee must be an independent member of the board of directors.

        1) To be independent, a director must not be affiliated with, or receive any compensation (other than for service on the board) from, the issuer.

            a) At least one member of the audit committee must be a financial expert.

        2) The audit committee must be directly responsible for appointing, compensating, and overseeing the work of the independent auditor.

            a) The independent auditor must report directly to the audit committee, not to management.

    b.   SOX established the **Public Company Accounting Oversight Board (PCAOB)** as a private-sector body to regulate the accounting profession.

        1) The PCAOB

            a) Issues auditing and related standards;

            b) Inspects and investigates accounting firms; and

            c) Enforces compliance with its rules, professional standards, the act, and relevant securities laws.

        2) Public accounting firms that act as independent auditors must register with the PCAOB.

    c.   A public accounting firm is prohibited from performing consulting, legal, and internal auditing services (with some exceptions) for the audit client.

        1) But audit firms may provide conventional tax planning and certain other nonaudit services if preapproved by the audit committee.

2. **Section 302 -- Reporting**

    a.   In every annual or quarterly filing with the SEC, the CEO and CFO must certify the following:

        1) To the best of their knowledge, the financial statements are free of material misstatements.

        2) They are responsible for the system of internal control and have evaluated its effectiveness.

        3) They have informed the audit committee and the independent auditors of all significant control deficiencies and any fraud, whether or not material.

        4) Significant changes were (or were not) made in internal controls, including corrective actions.

    b.   Intentional violations of this section of SOX can result in the forfeiture of

        1) Any bonus or other incentive-based compensation received during the previous 12 months and

        2) Any profits received from the sale of stock during the previous 12 months.

3. **Section 404 -- Reporting**

    a.   Under current regulations, the annual report must contain a statement by the CEO and CFO that includes the following:

        1) A statement that management has taken responsibility for establishing and maintaining an adequate system of internal control over financial reporting

        2) The name of the internal control model, if any, used to design and assess the effectiveness of the internal control system (COSO's *Internal Control – Integrated Framework* is the most widely used model in the United States)

        3) An assessment of whether internal control over financial reporting is effective

        4) A statement that an independent public accounting firm that is registered with the PCAOB also has assessed the system

4. **Section 407 -- Financial Expert**

    a. An issuer must disclose whether its audit committee has at least one financial expert.

        1) If the audit committee lacks a financial expert, the issuer must disclose the reason(s).

    b. To be considered a financial expert, the director must have

        1) An understanding of generally accepted accounting principles and financial statements;

        2) Experience in

            a) The preparation or auditing of financial statements of generally comparable issuers and

            b) The application of such principles in connection with the accounting for estimates, accruals, and reserves;

        3) Experience with internal accounting controls; and

        4) An understanding of audit committee functions.

5. **Section 802 -- Criminal Penalties**

    a. This section of SOX contains the following wording:

        Whoever knowingly alters, destroys, mutilates, conceals, covers up, falsifies, or makes a false entry in any record, document, or tangible object with the intent to impede, obstruct, or influence the investigation or proper administration of any matter within the jurisdiction of any department or agency of the United States or any case filed under title 11, or in relation to or contemplation of any such matter or case, shall be fined under this title, imprisoned not more than 20 years, or both.

Background

The statutory provision above was a direct response to the shredding of documentation by Enron Corporation, an action specifically intended to impede investigation of the company's massive fraud. Enron's independent auditor, Arthur Andersen, also was indicted for shredding literally tons of documents and deleting thousands of emails. Enron eventually declared bankruptcy, and Andersen surrendered its licenses to practice before the SEC.

---

6. **Section 906 -- Corporate Responsibility for Financial Reports**

    a. This section of the act incorporates into the U.S. Code the requirement that CEOs and CFOs certify financial filings.

    b. Separate criminal penalties are provided for unknowingly certifying noncomplying filings and for knowingly certifying such filings.

        1) Unknowingly certifying filings that do not meet the requirements of the Act can result in fines of up to $1,000,000 or up to 10 years imprisonment.

        2) Knowingly certifying filings that do not meet the requirements of the Act can result in fines of up to $5,000,000 or up to 20 years imprisonment.

7. **Section 1103 -- Temporary Freeze Authority for the Securities and Exchange Commission**

    a. This section empowers the SEC to petition a federal district court for a temporary order requiring the issuer to place in escrow for 45 days any monies that appear likely to be used to make extraordinary payments to executives.

8. **Section 1107 -- Retaliation against Informants**

   a. This section of SOX contains the following wording:

> *Whoever knowingly, with the intent to retaliate, takes any action harmful to any person, including interference with the lawful employment or livelihood of any person, for providing to a law enforcement officer any truthful information relating to the commission or possible commission of any Federal offense, shall be fined under this title or imprisoned not more than 10 years, or both.*

9. **Whistleblowers**

   a. Under SOX and the Dodd-Frank Wall Street Reform Act, the SEC may compensate whistleblowers who provide information other than that from an audit or investigation.

     1) Whistleblowers may sue retaliating employers.

     2) Whistleblower claims may be asserted for up to 180 days.

     3) Trial by jury is allowed.

     4) Whistleblower rights and remedies may not be waived, for example, in an employment contract.

10. **Stock Exchanges**

   a. A stock exchange is a market where owners of shares in corporations can buy and sell shares with other investors.

     1) A corporation's stock is first sold through an initial public offering (IPO) to an initial set of public shareholders.

     2) These shares can then be sold and purchased by other investors in the secondary market using the stock exchanges.

   b. One of the primary ways that corporations can raise capital is through issuing securities.

     1) The major stock exchanges in the United States include the New York Stock Exchange and NASDAQ.

   c. To be listed on one of the major stock exchanges in the United States, a corporation must be in compliance with federal securities laws and any requirements established by the stock exchange.

     1) Corporations may be required to maintain certain capital levels and to have a certain number of independent directors on the board of directors.

     2) Companies may face large compliance costs to qualify to issue securities on one of the major public exchanges.

 Because of numerous accounting scandals, CPA candidates can expect to be tested on the responsibilities imposed by SOX on both the company's audit committee and its management.

Stop and review! You have completed the outline for this subunit. Study multiple-choice questions 6 through 12 beginning on page 33.

1.3 COSO MODEL -- INTERNAL CONTROL

1. **COSO Framework**

   a. *Internal Control – Integrated Framework* is widely accepted as the standard for the design and operation of internal control systems.

      1) However, regulatory or legal requirements may specify another control model or design.

Background

The Watergate investigations of 1973-74 revealed that U.S. companies were bribing government officials, politicians, and political parties in foreign countries. The result was the Foreign Corrupt Practices Act of 1977. The private sector also responded by forming the National Commission on Fraudulent Financial Reporting (NCFFR) in 1985. The NCFFR is known as the Treadway Commission because James C. Treadway was its first chair.

The Treadway Commission was originally sponsored and funded by five professional accounting organizations based in the United States. This group of five became known as the Committee of Sponsoring Organizations of the Treadway Commission (COSO). The Commission recommended that this group of five organizations cooperate in creating guidance for internal control. The result was *Internal Control – Integrated Framework*, published in 1992, which was modified in 1994 and again in 2013.

The executive summary is available at www.coso.org/documents/990025P_Executive_Summary_final_may20_e.pdf.

---

2. **Definition of Internal Control**

   a. The COSO model defines internal control as follows:

      Internal control is a process, effected by an entity's board of directors, management, and other personnel, designed to provide reasonable assurance regarding the achievement of objectives relating to operations, reporting, and compliance.

   b. Thus, internal control is

      1) Intended to achieve three classes of objectives
      2) An ongoing process
      3) Effected by people at all organizational levels, e.g., the board, management, and all other employees
      4) Able to provide reasonable, but not absolute, assurance
      5) Adaptable to an entity's structure

3. **Objectives**

   a. The three classes of objectives direct organizations to the different (but overlapping) elements of control.

      1) **Operations**

         a) Operations objectives relate to achieving the entity's mission.

            i) Appropriate objectives include improving (a) financial performance, (b) productivity, (c) quality, (d) innovation, and (e) customer satisfaction.

         b) Operations objectives also include **safeguarding of assets**.

            i) Objectives related to protecting and preserving assets assist in risk assessment and development of mitigating controls.

            ii) Avoidance of waste, inefficiency, and bad business decisions relates to broader objectives than safeguarding of assets.

    2) **Reporting**

       a) To make sound decisions, stakeholders must have reliable, timely, and transparent financial information.

       b) Reports may be prepared for use by the organization and stakeholders.

       c) Objectives may relate to

          i) Financial and nonfinancial reporting and

          ii) Internal or external reporting.

    3) **Compliance**

       a) Entities are subject to laws, rules, and regulations that set minimum standards of conduct.

          i) Examples include taxation, environmental protection, and employee relations.

          ii) Compliance with internal policies and procedures is an operational matter.

    4) The following is a useful memory aid for the COSO classes of objectives:

          O = **O**perations
          R = **R**eporting
          C = **C**ompliance

  b. Overlap of Objectives

    1) An objective in one category may overlap or support an objective in another.

       a) An example is a policy to close the monthly books by the fifth working day of the following month.

          i) This objective applies to operations and reporting.

    2) Entity-level objectives relate to more specific **sub-objectives** for the entity's subunits and functions (sales, production, marketing, IT, etc.).

  c. Linkage

    1) The entity's overall objectives must connect its particular capabilities and prospects with the objectives of its business units.

    2) As conditions change, the objectives (and related internal controls) of subunits must be altered to adapt to changes in the objectives of the entity as a whole.

  d. Achievement of Objectives

    1) An internal control system is more likely to provide reasonable assurance of achieving the reporting and compliance objectives than the operational objectives.

    2) Reporting and compliance objectives are responses to standards established by external parties, such as regulators.

       a) Thus, achieving these objectives depends on actions almost entirely within the entity's control.

    3) However, operational effectiveness may not be within the entity's control because it is affected by human judgment and many external factors.

4.   **Reasonable Assurance**

   a.   Internal control can increase the probability of achieving objectives. But it cannot provide absolute assurance because any system of internal control has the following **inherent limitations**:

   1)   Established objectives must be **suitable** for internal control.

   a)   For example, if an entity establishes unrealistic objectives, the system of internal controls will be ineffective.

   2)   Human **judgment** is faulty, and controls may fail because of simple errors or mistakes.

   3)   Controls may fail due to **breakdowns** (e.g., employee misunderstanding, carelessness, or fatigue).

   4)   **Management** may inappropriately **override** internal controls, e.g., to fraudulently achieve revenue projections or hide liabilities.

   5)   Manual or automated controls can be circumvented by **collusion**.

   6)   **External events** are beyond an organization's control.

 The AICPA frequently tests the inherent limitations of internal control. Be able to identify the six basic limitations.

---

5.   **Components of Internal Control**

   a.   Supporting the organization in its efforts to achieve objectives are the following five components of internal control:

   1)   Control environment
   2)   Risk assessment
   3)   Control activities
   4)   Information and communication
   5)   Monitoring

6.   **Control Environment**

   a.   The control environment is a set of standards, processes, and structures that pervasively affects the system of internal control.

   1)   The organization demonstrates a commitment to **integrity** and **ethical values** by (a) communicating its attitude toward integrity and ethical values, (b) establishing standards of conduct, (c) evaluating performance based on the standards, and (d) correcting deviations in a timely and consistent manner.

   2)   The board demonstrates **independence** from management and exercises **oversight** of internal control.

   3)   Management establishes, with board oversight, structures, reporting lines, and authorities and responsibilities.

   4)   The organization demonstrates a commitment to attract, develop, and retain competent individuals in alignment with objectives.

   5)   The organization holds **individuals accountable** for their internal control responsibilities in pursuit of objectives.

7. **Risk Assessment**

    a. This process assesses risks and the need to manage organizational change. It is a basis for determining how risks should be managed.

        1) The organization specifies **objectives** to enable the identification and assessment of risks relating to objectives.

            a) **Operations** objectives

                i) Reflect management's choices,
                ii) Must consider risk tolerances,
                iii) Include operations and financial performance goals, and
                iv) Form a basis for committing resources.

            b) **External financial reporting** objectives

                i) Must comply with applicable accounting standards,
                ii) Consider materiality, and
                iii) Reflect entity activities.

            c) **External nonfinancial reporting** objectives

                i) Must comply with externally established standards and frameworks,
                ii) Consider the required level of precision, and
                iii) Reflect entity activities.

            d) **Internal reporting** objectives

                i) Reflect management choices,
                ii) Consider the required level of precision, and
                iii) Reflect entity activities.

            e) **Compliance** objectives

                i) Reflect external laws and regulations and
                ii) Consider risk tolerances.

        2) The organization **identifies** all risks (internal and external) to the achievement of its objectives across the entity and **analyzes** risks to determine how the risks should be managed.

            a) Examples of internal risk factors at the entity level include interruptions of IT systems and the quality of personnel hired.

            b) Examples of external risk factors at the entity level include technological changes and changes in customer wants.

            c) The appropriate management should analyze risks.

                i) The analysis generally involves (a) estimating the significance of an event, (b) assessing its likelihood, and (c) considering the risk response.
                ii) Inherent and residual risk (the post-response) must be considered.

                    • In general, the seriousness of a risk and its likelihood are inversely related.

            d) The **risk response** considers (1) how each risk should be managed; (2) whether to accept, avoid, reduce, or share the risk; and (3) the design of controls.

        3) The organization should consider the potential for **fraud**. It not only must consider various types of fraud but also must assess (a) incentives and pressures, (b) opportunities, and (c) attitudes and rationalizations.

        4) The organization identifies and assesses **changes** (internal or external) that could significantly affect the system of internal control and adopts appropriate controls.

8. **Control Activities**

a. These policies and procedures help ensure that management directives are carried out. Whether automated or manual, they are applied at various levels of the entity and stages of processes. They may be preventive or detective, and segregation of duties is usually present. Three principles relate to control activities:

1) The organization **selects and develops** control activities that contribute to the mitigation of risks to the achievement of objectives to acceptable levels.

a) Control activities are **integrated** with the risk assessment.

b) Management considers how **entity-specific** factors affect control activities.

c) Management determines which **processes** require control activities.

d) The entity evaluates a **mix** of control activities, of which transactional controls are the most basic.

i) Authorizations and approvals
ii) Verifications
iii) Physical controls
iv) Controls over standing data
v) Reconciliations
vi) Supervisory controls

e) Control activities are selected and developed for application at **different levels**.

f) **Segregation of duties** divides responsibility for the recording, authorization, approval, and cash custody functions when feasible.

2) The organization selects and develops **general** control activities over technology to support the achievement of objectives.

3) The organization **deploys** control activities through **policies** that establish what is expected and **procedures** that put policies into action.

9. **Information and Communication**

a. Information systems enable the organization to obtain, generate, use, and communicate information to (1) maintain accountability and (2) measure and review performance.

1) The organization obtains or generates and uses **relevant, quality** information to support the functioning of internal control.

a) Information can include both internal and external sources of data.
b) Only high-quality information is appropriate.
c) The cost and the benefit of obtaining the information are considered.

2) The organization **internally** communicates information, including objectives and responsibilities for internal control, necessary to support the function of internal control.

a) A process enables all personnel to perform their control responsibilities.
b) Management and the board communicate.
c) Alternative internal (and external) communication lines, e.g., hotlines, are provided.
d) The method of internal (and external) communication depends on the timing, audience, and nature of the information.

3) The organization communicates with **external parties** about matters affecting internal control.

    a) Relevant and timely information is communicated to shareholders, regulators, customers, etc.

    b) Input from external sources provides relevant information.

    c) External assessments are communicated to the board.

    d) Legal requirements are considered.

10. **Monitoring**

  a. Controls and their application change. Monitoring assesses the quality of internal control performance over time to ensure that controls continue to meet the needs of the organization.

    1) The organization selects, develops, and performs **ongoing or separate evaluations (or both)** to determine whether the components of internal control are present and functioning.

      a) Ongoing Evaluations

        i) Routine activities that are control-oriented include (a) the periodic reconciliation of operational division data with enterprise-wide financial data, (b) the presence or absence of customer complaints about billing, (c) the reports of internal and external auditors, and (d) training seminars.

      b) Separate Evaluations

        i) The significance of risks determines the scope and frequency of separate evaluations of internal control.

        ii) In some environments, control self-assessment is appropriate. In others, the internal audit function should perform a thorough review.

        iii) The evaluator must understand how the system should work and its objectives and must test whether the system is working as designed.

    2) The organization evaluates and communicates **control deficiencies** in a timely manner.

      a) Whether deficiency is reportable depends on its effect on the entity's ability to achieve its objectives.

        i) Reporting should be to a level of the organization with sufficient authority to correct the deficiency.

11. **Relationship of Objectives, Components, and Organizational Structure**

   a.   The COSO model may be represented by a cube with rows, slices, and columns. (1) The rows are the five components, (2) the slices are the three objectives, and (3) the columns are an entity's organizational structure.

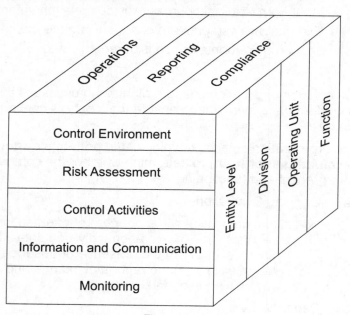

Figure 1-2

12. **Roles and Responsibilities Regarding Internal Control**

   a.   **Responsible Parties**

       1)   Board of Directors and Its Committees

          a)   The entity's commitment to integrity and ethical values is reflected in the board's selections for the CEO and senior vice president positions.

          b)   To be effective, board members should be objective, have knowledge of the organization's industry, and be willing to ask the relevant questions about management's decisions.

          c)   Important committees of the board include

              i)   Audit
             ii)   Compensation
           iii)   Nomination or governance
           iv)   Finance
            v)   Risk

       2)   Senior Management

          a)   The CEO establishes the tone at the top, which means that organizations reflect the ethical values and control consciousness of the CEO.

          b)   The chief accounting officer and accounting staff understand activities across all levels of the organization.

       3)   Internal Auditors

          a)   Internal audit evaluates the adequacy and effectiveness of internal control in response to risks in the entity's oversight, operations, and information systems. For example, internal audit evaluates controls over

              i)   Achievement of the organization's strategic objectives
             ii)   Reliability and integrity of financial and operational information

          iii)   Effectiveness and efficiency of operations and programs

          iv)   Safeguarding of assets

          v)   Compliance with laws, regulations, standards, policies, procedures, and contracts

      b)   To remain independent in the conduct of these reviews, the internal audit cannot be responsible for selecting and executing controls.

   4)   Other Entity Personnel

      a)   Everyone in the organization is expected to (1) perform his or her appropriate control activities and (2) inform those higher in the organization about poor control.

b. **External Parties**

   1)   External Auditors

      a)   Independent accountants have been required to consider the auditee's system of internal control as part of their audit of the financial statements.

      b)   The PCAOB also requires auditors of public companies to examine and report on internal control.

   2)   Legislators and Regulators

      a)   The Foreign Corrupt Practices Act and the Sarbanes-Oxley Act set legal requirements regarding internal control.

   3)   Parties Interacting with the Entity

      a)   The following are examples of control-related information received from outside sources:

          i)   A major customer informs management that a sales representative attempted to arrange a kickback scheme in return for the customer's business.

          ii)   A supplier reveals inventory and shipping problems by complaining about incomplete orders.

      b)   Parties without a supplier or customer relationship with the entity also may provide insight into the functioning of controls.

          i)   As a condition for granting a loan, a bank may require that certain ratios be kept above or below specified levels. As a result, management may need to pay closer attention to controls over cash and inventory levels than it did previously.

   4)   Financial Analysts, Bond Rating Agencies, and the News Media

      a)   The actions of these parties can inform an entity about how it is perceived by the world at large.

   5)   Outsourced Service Providers

      a)   Some of an entity's business functions, e.g., IT, human resources, or internal audit, may be performed by external service providers.

          i)   Accordingly, management must manage the risks of outsourcing.

Stop and review! You have completed the outline for this subunit. Study multiple-choice questions 13 through 20 beginning on page 35.

1.4 COSO MODEL -- ENTERPRISE RISK MANAGEMENT

1. **COSO Risk Management Framework**

    a. *Enterprise Risk Management – Integrated Framework* describes a model that extends the COSO internal control framework to enterprise risk management (ERM).

        1) It is a basis for coordinating and integrating all of an entity's risk management activities.

2. **ERM Definition**

    a. ERM is based on key concepts applicable to many types of entities. The emphasis is on (1) the objectives of a specific entity and (2) establishing a means for evaluating the effectiveness of ERM.

        > *Enterprise risk management is a process, effected by an entity's board of directors, management, and other personnel, applied in strategy setting and across the enterprise, designed to identify potential events that may affect the entity, and manage risk to be within its risk appetite, to provide reasonable assurance regarding the achievement of entity objectives.*

3. **Definitions of Risk and Risk Management**

    a. Risk is the possibility that an event will occur and adversely affect the achievement of objectives.

    b. Risk management, at any level, consists of

        1) Identifying potential events that may affect the entity and
        2) Managing the associated risk to be within the entity's risk appetite.

    c. Ultimately, risk management should provide reasonable assurance of the achievement of entity objectives.

4. **Responsibilities**

    a. Senior Management

        1) The CEO sets the **tone at the top** and has ultimate responsibility for ERM.
        2) Senior management should ensure that sound risk management processes are in place and functioning.
        3) Senior management also determines the entity's risk management philosophy.

            a) For example, some managers (1) issue definitive policy statements, (2) insist on written procedures, and (3) closely monitor performance indicators.
            b) Others take a relaxed approach to performance monitoring.
            c) If senior management establishes a consistent risk management philosophy, all parts of the entity can respond to risk appropriately.

    b. Board of Directors

        1) The board has an **oversight role**. It should determine that risk management processes are in place, adequate, and effective.
        2) Directors must possess certain qualities for them to be effective.

            a) A majority of the board should be outside directors.
            b) Directors generally should have years of experience.
            c) Directors must be willing to challenge management's choices.

    c.   Risk Committee and Chief Risk Officer

        1)   Larger entities may wish to establish a **risk committee** composed of directors that also includes managers.

            a)   A chief risk officer (CRO) may coordinate risk management activities. The CRO is a member of, and reports to, the risk committee.

    d.   Internal Auditing

        1)   Internal auditors may be directed by the board to evaluate the effectiveness and contribute to the improvement of risk management processes.

        2)   The internal auditors' determination of whether risk management processes are effective is a judgment resulting from the assessment that

            a)   Entity objectives support and align with its mission
            b)   Significant risks are identified and assessed
            c)   Appropriate risk responses are selected that align risks and the entity's risk appetite
            d)   Relevant risk information is captured and timely communicated across the entity

5.   **ERM Capabilities**

    a.   ERM allows management to optimize stakeholder value by coping effectively with uncertainty and the risks and opportunities it presents. ERM helps management to

        1)   Reach objectives,
        2)   Prevent loss of reputation and resources,
        3)   Report effectively, and
        4)   Comply with laws and regulations.

    b.   The following are the capabilities of ERM:

        1)   Consideration of risk appetite and strategy

            a)   **Risk appetite** is the degree of willingness of senior management to accept risk. It should be considered in

                i)   Evaluating strategic options,
                ii)   Setting objectives, and
                iii)   Developing risk management techniques.

        2)   Risk response decisions

            a)   ERM permits identification and selection of such responses to risk as

                i)   Avoidance,
                ii)   Reduction,
                iii)   Sharing, and
                iv)   Acceptance.

        3)   Reduction of operational surprises and losses

            a)   These are reduced by an improved ability to anticipate potential events and develop responses.

        4)   Multiple and cross-enterprise risks

            a)   Risks may affect different parts of the entity. ERM allows

                i)   Effective responses to interrelated effects and
                ii)   Integrated responses to multiple risks.

        5)   Response to opportunities

            a)   By facilitating the identification of potential events, ERM helps management to respond quickly to opportunities.

      6)   Deployment of capital

         a)   The risk information provided by ERM permits

            i)   Assessment of capital needs and
            ii)   Better capital allocation.

6. **Events**

    a.   Events with a potential negative effect are risks. Events with a potential positive effect offset risks or create opportunities.

      1)   An **opportunity** is the possibility that an event will occur and positively affect the achievement of objectives, supporting value creation or preservation.

      2)   Management makes plans to exploit opportunities, subject to the entity's adopted strategies and objectives.

    b.   The event identification process should consider past events (looking for trends) as well as future possibilities.

    c.   Specific event identification methods include the following:

      1)   Software is available that provides **event inventories** to be used as a starting point for event identification.

      2)   **Internal analysis** considers experience with similar risks in the past when planning a response for future occurrences.

      3)   A certain risk response may be designed for an **escalation or threshold trigger**, such as a decline in cash on hand or a price cut by a competitor.

      4)   **Facilitated workshops and interviews** take discussion groups consisting of management and other stakeholders through structured conversation and exploration of potential events.

      5)   **Process flow analysis** studies a single business process, such as vendor authorization and payment.

      6)   **Leading event indicators** may predict adverse events. An example is avoiding debtor default by intervention upon the occurrence of a late payment.

      7)   **Loss event data methodologies** can be used to build a predictive model based on past events. An example is matching workers' compensation claims against the frequency of accidents.

7. **Entity Objectives**

    a.   Four categories of objectives apply to all entities:

      1)   Strategic objectives align with and support the entity's mission.
      2)   Operations objectives address effectiveness and efficiency.
      3)   Reporting objectives apply to reliability.
      4)   Compliance objectives relate to adherence to laws and regulations.

    b.   The following is a useful memory aid for the COSO ERM categories of objectives:

> **O** = **O**perations
> **R** = **R**eporting
> **C** = **C**ompliance
> **S** = **S**trategies

    c.   The categories overlap but are distinct. They relate to different needs, and different managers may be assigned responsibility for them.

      1)   Safeguarding of resources is another category that may be appropriate for some entities.

    d. Strategic and operational matters are affected by external events that the entity may not control.

        1) Thus, ERM should provide reasonable assurance that management and the board receive timely information about achievement of objectives.

    e. Reporting and compliance are within the entity's control.

        1) ERM should provide reasonable assurance of achieving those objectives.

8. **Components of COSO ERM**

    a. The components of ERM are integrated with the management process and may mutually influence each other.

        1) The **internal environment** sets the tone of the entity and reflects its

            a) Risk management philosophy,
            b) Risk appetite,
            c) Integrity,
            d) Ethical values, and
            e) Overall environment.

        2) **Objective setting** must be completed before risk events can be identified. ERM ensures that

            a) A process is established and
            b) Objectives align with the mission and the risk appetite.

        3) **Event identification** relates to internal and external events affecting the entity. It differentiates between opportunities and risks.

            a) Opportunities are referred to the strategy or objective-setting processes.

        4) **Risk assessment** considers likelihood and impact as a basis for risk management. The assessment considers the inherent risk and the residual risk.

            a) Inherent risk is the risk resulting from an activity itself. It is the risk in the absence of a risk response.
            b) Residual risk is what remains after risk responses.

        5) **Risk responses** should be consistent with the organization's risk tolerances and appetite.

        6) **Control activities** are policies and procedures to ensure the effectiveness of risk responses.

        7) The **information and communication** component identifies, captures, and communicates relevant and timely information.

        8) **Monitoring** involves ongoing management activities or separate evaluations. The full ERM process is monitored.

    b. The following is a useful memory aid for the components of COSO ERM:

> **C** = **C**ontrol activities
> **R** = **R**isk assessment
> **I** = **I**nformation and communication
> **M** = **M**onitoring
> **E** = **E**vent identification
>
> **R** = **R**isk responses
> **O** = **O**bjective setting
> **I** = **I**nternal environment

9.   **COSO ERM Framework**

    a.   The interaction of the various elements of the framework may be represented by a cube with rows, slices, and columns. (1) The rows are the eight components, (2) the slices are the four objectives, and (3) the columns are an entity's organizational structure.

COSO ERM Framework

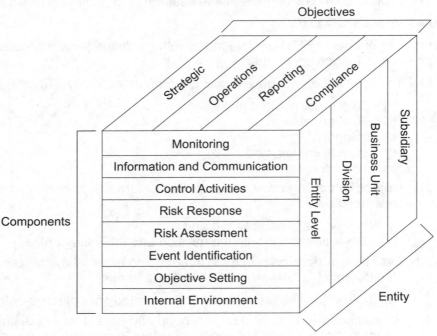

Figure 1-3

    b.   Components should be present and functioning effectively. Consequently, the components are criteria for the effectiveness of ERM.

        1)   A component is present and functioning effectively if

            a)   No material weaknesses exist and
            b)   Risk is within the risk appetite.

        2)   When ERM is effective regarding all of the objectives, the board and management have reasonable assurance that

            a)   Reporting is reliable,
            b)   Compliance is achieved, and
            c)   They know the extent of achievement of strategic and operations objectives.

        3)   The components operate differently in different organizations. For example, they may be applied in a less formal way in smaller organizations.

10. **ERM Limitations**

    a.   Limitations of ERM result from the possibility of

        1)   Faulty human judgment,
        2)   Cost-benefit considerations,
        3)   Simple errors or mistakes,
        4)   Collusion, and
        5)   Management override of ERM decisions.

11. **Strategies for Risk Response**

 a. Risk **avoidance** ends the activity from which the risk arises.

  1) For example, the risk of having a pipeline sabotaged in an unstable region can be avoided by simply selling the pipeline.

 b. Risk **retention** accepts the risk of an activity. This term is a synonym for self insurance.

 c. Risk **reduction** (mitigation) lowers the level of risk associated with an activity.

  1) For example, the risk of systems penetration can be reduced by maintaining a robust information security function within the organization.

 d. Risk **sharing** transfers some loss potential to another party.

  1) Examples are purchasing insurance, hedging, and entering into joint ventures.

 e. Risk **exploitation** seeks risk to obtain a high return on investment.

12. **The Risk Management Process**

 a. Step 1 – <u>I</u>dentify risks.

  1) Every risk that could affect achievement of objectives must be considered.

  2) Risk identification must be performed for the entire entity. Some occurrences may be inconsequential for the entity but disastrous for an individual unit.

 b. Step 2 – <u>A</u>ssess risks.

  1) Every risk identified must be assessed as to its probability and potential effect.

 c. Step 3 – <u>P</u>rioritize risks.

  1) In large or complex entities, senior management may appoint a risk committee to review the risks identified by the various operating units and create a coherent response plan.

 d. Step 4 – <u>F</u>ormulate risk responses.

  1) The risk committee proposes adequate response strategies.

  2) All personnel must be aware of the importance of the risk response appropriate to their levels of the entity.

 e. Step 5 – <u>M</u>onitor risk responses.

  1) The two most important sources of information for ongoing assessments of the adequacy of risk responses are

   a) Those closest to the activities. The manager of an operating unit is in the best position to monitor the effects of the chosen risk response strategies.

   b) The audit function. Operating managers may not be objective about risks, especially if they were involved in designing a response strategy. Analyzing risks and responses are normal duties of internal auditors.

 f. The following is a useful memory aid for the components of the risk management process:

 I = **I**dentify risks
 Ate = **A**ssess risks
 Pie = **P**rioritize risks
 For = **F**ormulate risk responses
 Money = **M**onitor risk responses

Stop and review! You have completed the outline for this subunit. Study multiple-choice questions 21 through 28 beginning on page 37.

QUESTIONS

1.1 Roles in the Governance Hierarchy

1. Davis, a director of Active Corp., is entitled to

   A. Serve on the board of a competing business.
   B. Take sole advantage of a business opportunity that would benefit Active.
   C. Rely on information provided by a corporate officer.
   D. Unilaterally grant a corporate loan to one of Active's shareholders.

Answer (C) is correct.
   REQUIRED: The action not a breach of a director's duties.
   DISCUSSION: In the course of exercising good business judgment and reasonable care, a director is entitled to rely on information provided by an officer (or professional specialist) if the director reasonably believes the officer has competence in the relevant area.
   Answer (A) is incorrect. Serving as a director of a competing business is a conflict of interest. Answer (B) is incorrect. Usurping a business opportunity of the corporation is a breach of the director's fiduciary duty of loyalty. Answer (D) is incorrect. A director is not an agent of the corporation, and directors authorize corporate transactions by approving resolutions as a board.

2. Which of the following provisions must a for-profit corporation include in its articles of incorporation to obtain a corporate charter?

   I.   Provision for the issuance of voting stock
   II. Name of the corporation

   A. I only.
   B. II only.
   C. Both I and II.
   D. Neither I nor II.

Answer (C) is correct.
   REQUIRED: The provisions a for-profit corporation must include in its articles of incorporation.
   DISCUSSION: A corporation comes into being when the articles of incorporation are filed with the secretary of state of the relevant state. Among the items that the articles ordinarily must include are the corporation's name and the number of authorized shares of stock. Because the articles must include the number of authorized shares of stock, the provision for issuance of voting stock is an implicit requirement.
   Answer (A) is incorrect. The name of the corporation must be included in the articles. Answer (B) is incorrect. The articles must include the number of shares authorized to be issued. Thus, provision for issuance of voting stock is an implicit requirement. Answer (D) is incorrect. Both the name of the corporation and the provision for issuance of voting stock must be included in the articles.

3. In general, which of the following must be contained in articles of incorporation?

   A. Names of states in which the corporation will be doing business.
   B. Name of the state in which the corporation will maintain its principal place of business.
   C. Names of the initial officers and their terms of office.
   D. Number of shares of stock authorized to be issued by the corporation.

Answer (D) is correct.
   REQUIRED: The information required in articles of incorporation.
   DISCUSSION: Articles of incorporation must contain the name of the corporation, the number of authorized shares, the address of the initial registered office of the corporation, the name of its first registered agent at that address, and the names and addresses of the incorporators. The articles may also include names and addresses of the initial directors, purpose and duration of the corporation, and any provision that may be set forth in the bylaws.
   Answer (A) is incorrect. The names of states in which the corporation will be doing business need not be included in the articles. Answer (B) is incorrect. The name of the state in which the corporation will maintain its principal place of business need not be included in the articles. Answer (C) is incorrect. The names of initial officers and their terms of office need not be included in the articles.

4. The board of directors performs all of the following duties **except**

   A. Managing day-to-day operations.
   B. Selection and removal of officers.
   C. Adding or repealing bylaws.
   D. Initiation of fundamental changes.

Answer (A) is correct.
   REQUIRED: The duty not performed by the board of directors.
   DISCUSSION: The board of directors guides management. It does not directly manage day-to-day operations of the entity. That is management's responsibility, with the board having an oversight role. All major corporate decisions are made or approved by the board.
   Answer (B) is incorrect. The board has the duty of selection and removal of officers. Answer (C) is incorrect. Adding, amending, or repealing bylaws is a duty of the board. Answer (D) is incorrect. Initiation of fundamental changes, such as mergers or acquisitions, is a duty of the board.

5. A corporate director commits a breach of duty if

    A. The director's exercise of care and skill is minimal.

    B. A contract is awarded by the company to an organization owned by the director.

    C. An interest in property is acquired by the director without prior approval of the board.

    D. The director's action, prompted by confidential information, results in an abuse of corporate opportunity.

Answer (D) is correct.
    REQUIRED: The breach of a corporate director's duty.
    DISCUSSION: Corporate directors have a fiduciary duty to provide the corporation with business opportunities that come to them in their positions as directors of the corporation. A director who personally takes such a business opportunity has breached his or her duty of loyalty.
    Answer (A) is incorrect. A director is under a duty to use good business judgment, but (s)he is not responsible for the highest standard of care and skill. Moreover, a director may reasonably rely on information from competent officers, employees, and experts. Answer (B) is incorrect. A director is not prohibited from entering into a conflicting interest transaction if it is (1) fair to the corporation or (2) approved after required disclosure by a majority of disinterested directors or of shares voted by disinterested parties. Answer (C) is incorrect. A director has no duty to report personal property investments unless they relate to corporate business.

1.2 The Sarbanes-Oxley Act of 2002 (SOX)

6. The Sarbanes-Oxley Act of 2002 limits the nonaudit services that an audit firm can provide to public company audit clients. Which of the following is most likely to be a service that an auditor may provide to a public client?

    A. Internal audit outsourcing.

    B. Legal services.

    C. Management consulting services.

    D. Tax compliance services.

Answer (D) is correct.
    REQUIRED: The type of service that an audit firm may provide to an audit client.
    DISCUSSION: The Sarbanes-Oxley Act prohibits audit firms from providing consulting, legal, and internal auditing services to public audit clients. Audit firms may, however, provide conventional tax planning and certain other nonaudit services to public audit clients if they are preapproved by the audit committee.
    Answer (A) is incorrect. Internal audit outsourcing is a service that may not be provided to public audit clients. Answer (B) is incorrect. Legal and other expert services may not be provided to public audit clients if they do not pertain to the audit. Answer (C) is incorrect. Management consulting services are services that may not be provided to public audit clients.

7. Which of the following is most likely a violation of the rules of the Public Company Accounting Oversight Board (PCAOB)?

    A. An issuer's independent auditor also performs consulting work for the issuer on the design and operation of its internal controls.

    B. An issuer offers its common shares and preferred shares on different stock exchanges.

    C. An issuer's management is not independent of its board of directors.

    D. An issuer uses the same independent auditor in 2 consecutive years.

Answer (A) is correct.
    REQUIRED: The action prohibited by SOX.
    DISCUSSION: The PCAOB prohibits a public accounting firm from performing consulting, legal, and internal auditing services (with some exceptions) for an audit client.
    Answer (B) is incorrect. The PCAOB regulates public accounting firms, not stock offerings. Answer (C) is incorrect. The PCAOB cannot dictate terms of internal corporate governance. Answer (D) is incorrect. The PCAOB's rules do not prohibit issuers from using the same independent auditor in 2 consecutive years.

8. Under the Sarbanes-Oxley Act of 2002 (SOX),

    A. At least one member of the audit committee must be a financial expert.

    B. The chairman of the board of directors must be a financial expert.

    C. The audit committee must rotate at least one seat on an annual basis.

    D. All members of the audit committee must be financial experts.

Answer (A) is correct.
    REQUIRED: The SOX requirement relevant to the audit committee.
    DISCUSSION: Under the terms of SOX, at least one member of the audit committee must be a financial expert. If the audit committee lacks a financial expert, the issuer must disclose the reason(s).
    Answer (B) is incorrect. The SOX requirement regarding a financial expert does not refer to the chairman of the board. Answer (C) is incorrect. SOX imposes no requirements regarding membership rotation of the audit committee. Answer (D) is incorrect. Under the terms of SOX, only one member of the audit committee need be a financial expert.

9. When Congress passed the Sarbanes-Oxley Act of 2002, it imposed greater regulation on public companies and their auditors and required increased accountability. Which of the following is **not** a provision of the act?

    A. Certain executives must certify the fair presentation of the financial statements.

    B. Management must establish and document internal control procedures.

    C. The act created the Public Company Accounting Oversight Board (PCAOB).

    D. One of the company's officers may serve on the audit committee.

Answer (D) is correct.
    REQUIRED: The choice that is not a provision of the Sarbanes-Oxley Act of 2002.
    DISCUSSION: The act requires that all members of the audit committee be independent of the corporation, meaning they can receive no compensation other than what they receive for serving on the board. Thus, no officers or employees of the corporation may serve on the audit committee.
    Answer (A) is incorrect. The CEO and CFO of a public company must provide a statement to accompany the audit report. This statement certifies the fair presentation of the financial statements and disclosures. However, a violation of this requirement must be knowing and intentional. Answer (B) is incorrect. Section 404 of the act requires management to establish and document internal control procedures, and to include in annual reports a report on the entity's internal control over financial reporting. Answer (C) is incorrect. The PCAOB was created by the act as a private sector, nonprofit corporation to oversee the conduct of accounting firms in the performance of financial statement audits of issuers.

10. Under the reporting requirements of Section 404 of the Sarbanes-Oxley Act of 2002 (SOX), the CEO and CFO must include a statement in the annual report to the effect that

    A. The system of internal control has been assessed by an independent public accounting firm that is registered with the PCAOB.

    B. The system of internal control has been assessed by an independent public accounting firm that is not currently the subject of any PCAOB investigation.

    C. The board of directors has taken responsibility for establishing and maintaining an adequate system of internal control over financial reporting.

    D. The issuer has used the COSO model to design and assess the effectiveness of its system of internal control.

Answer (A) is correct.
    REQUIRED: The statement required by Sarbanes-Oxley.
    DISCUSSION: The CEO and CFO must include a statement in the annual report to the effect that the system of internal control has been assessed by an independent public accounting firm that is registered with the PCAOB.
    Answer (B) is incorrect. Section 404 of SOX does not require that the independent auditor not be under investigation by the PCAOB. Answer (C) is incorrect. Section 404 of SOX requires the CEO and CFO to state that they, not the board, have taken responsibility for internal controls. Answer (D) is incorrect. Section 404 of SOX requires that if the issuer used an internal control model, it must be named; it does not have to be the COSO model.

11. Section 302 of the Sarbanes-Oxley Act of 2002 (SOX) requires the CEO and CFO, in every annual or quarterly filing with the SEC, to certify all of the following **except**

    A. That they have taken every practical step to correct significant control deficiencies identified in the previous audit.

    B. That they have evaluated the effectiveness of the system of internal control.

    C. That they have taken responsibility for the system of internal control.

    D. That to the best of their knowledge, the financial statements are free of material misstatements.

Answer (A) is correct.
    REQUIRED: The required certification in SEC filings by the CEO and CFO.
    DISCUSSION: Whether the issuer has taken sufficient steps to correct significant control deficiencies is a matter of the auditor's professional judgment.

12. The Sarbanes-Oxley Act of 2002 (SOX) imposes which of the following requirements?

    A. The board of directors must be composed entirely of independent shareholders.

    B. At least one member of the audit committee must be a former partner of the independent public accounting firm.

    C. The audit committee must be composed entirely of independent members of the board.

    D. Once the audit committee has selected the independent public accounting firm, the committee must not interfere with the firm's conduct of the financial statement audit.

Answer (C) is correct.
    REQUIRED: The provision required by SOX.
    DISCUSSION: Under SOX, each member of the issuer's audit committee must be an independent member of the board of directors. To be independent, a director must not be affiliated with, or receive any compensation (other than for service on the board) from, the issuer.
    Answer (A) is incorrect. The SOX requirement regarding independent members refers to the audit committee, not the entire board. Answer (B) is incorrect. SOX does not impose a requirement regarding mandatory former employment with the independent public accounting firm. Answer (D) is incorrect. The audit committee must be directly responsible for appointing, compensating, and overseeing the work of the independent auditor.

1.3 COSO Model -- Internal Control

13. Internal control is a process designed to provide reasonable assurance regarding the achievement of objectives related to

    A. Reporting.

    B. Operations.

    C. Compliance

    D. All of the answers are correct.

Answer (D) is correct.
    REQUIRED: The true statement regarding COSO's objectives in relation to internal control.
    DISCUSSION: The COSO model for internal control establishes control objectives for operations, reporting, and compliance.
    Answer (A) is incorrect. Operations and compliance also are control objectives. Answer (B) is incorrect. Reporting and compliance also are control objectives. Answer (C) is incorrect. Reporting and operations also are control objectives.

14. Which of the following is the control component that reflects the attitude and actions of the board and management regarding the significance of control within the organization?

    A. Risk assessment.

    B. Control activities.

    C. Control environment.

    D. Monitoring.

Answer (C) is correct.
    REQUIRED: The control component that reflects the attitude and actions of the board and management regarding control.
    DISCUSSION: According to the COSO model for internal control, the control environment reflects the attitude and actions of the board and management regarding the significance of control within the organization.
    Answer (A) is incorrect. Risk assessment identifies and analyzes external or internal risks to achievement of the objectives at the activity level as well as the entity level. Answer (B) is incorrect. Control activities are the policies and procedures helping to ensure that management directives are executed and actions are taken to address risks achievement of objectives. Answer (D) is incorrect. Monitoring is a process that assesses the quality of the system's performance over time.

15. Which of the following are elements included in the control environment as described by the COSO model for internal control?

    A. Organizational structure, management philosophy, and planning.

    B. Integrity and ethical values, assignment of authority, and human resource policies.

    C. Competence of personnel, backup facilities, laws, and regulations.

    D. Risk assessment, assignment of responsibility, and human resource practices.

Answer (B) is correct.
    REQUIRED: The elements of the control environment.
    DISCUSSION: According to the COSO model, the control environment includes the attitude and actions of the board and management regarding the significance of control within the entity. The control environment provides the discipline and structure for the achievement of the primary objectives of the system of internal control. The control environment includes the following elements:

- Human resource policies and practices
- Integrity and ethical values
- Organizational structure
- Commitment to competence
- Management's philosophy and operating style
- Board of directors or audit committee
- Assignment of authority and responsibility

    Answer (A) is incorrect. Planning is not an element of the control environment. Answer (C) is incorrect. Backup facilities, laws, and regulations are not elements of the control environment. Answer (D) is incorrect. Risk assessment is part of planning the internal audit activity and specific engagements.

16. Internal control can provide only reasonable assurance that the entity's objectives and goals will be met efficiently and effectively. One factor limiting the likelihood of achieving those objectives is that

    A. The internal auditor's primary responsibility is the detection of fraud.

    B. The audit committee is active and independent.

    C. The cost of internal control should not exceed its benefits.

    D. Management monitors performance.

Answer (C) is correct.
    REQUIRED: The true statement about the limitation of internal control.
    DISCUSSION: A limiting factor is that the cost of internal control should not exceed the benefits that are expected to be derived. Thus, the potential loss associated with any exposure or risk is weighed against the cost to control it. Although the cost-benefit relationship is a primary criterion that should be considered in designing and implementing internal control, the precise measurement of costs and benefits usually is not possible.
    Answer (A) is incorrect. The internal audit activity's responsibility regarding controls is to evaluate effectiveness and efficiency and to promote continuous improvement. Answer (B) is incorrect. An effective governance function strengthens the control environment. Answer (D) is incorrect. Senior management's role is to oversee the establishment, administration, and assessment of the system of risk management and control processes. Among the responsibilities of the organization's line managers is the assessment of the control processes in their respective areas. Internal auditors provide varying degrees of assurance about the effectiveness of the risk management and control processes in select activities and functions of the organization.

17. The COSO model for internal control lists seven specific areas encompassed by the control environment component. Which of the following are elements of the control environment?

    A. Integrity and ethical values.

    B. Organizational structure.

    C. Assignment of authority and responsibility.

    D. All of the answers are correct.

Answer (D) is correct.
    REQUIRED: The elements of the control environment.
    DISCUSSION: The elements of the control environment are: (1) human resource policies and practices, (2) integrity and ethical values, (3) organizational structure, (4) commitment to competence, (5) philosophy and operating style of management, (6) board of directors or audit committee participation, and (7) assignment of authority and responsibility.
    Answer (A) is incorrect. Organizational structure and assignment of authority and responsibility are also part of the control environment. Answer (B) is incorrect. Integrity and ethical value and assignment of authority and responsibility are also part of the control environment. Answer (C) is incorrect. Integrity and ethical value and organizational structure are also part of the control environment.

18. An adequate system of internal controls is most likely to detect a fraud perpetrated by a

    A. Group of employees in collusion.

    B. Single employee.

    C. Group of managers in collusion.

    D. Single manager.

Answer (B) is correct.
    REQUIRED: The fraud most likely to be detected by an adequate system of internal controls.
    DISCUSSION: Segregation of duties and other control processes serve to prevent or detect a fraud committed by an employee acting alone. One employee may not have the ability to engage in wrongdoing or may be subject to detection by other employees in the course of performing their assigned duties. However, collusion may circumvent controls. For example, comparison of recorded accountability for assets with the assets known to be held may fail to detect fraud if persons having custody of assets collude with record keepers.
    Answer (A) is incorrect. A group has a better chance of successfully perpetrating a fraud than does an individual employee. Answer (C) is incorrect. Management can override controls. Answer (D) is incorrect. Even a single manager may be able to override controls.

19. Control activities constitute one of the five components of internal control described in the COSO model. Control activities do **not** encompass

    A. Performance reviews.

    B. Information processing.

    C. Physical controls.

    D. An internal auditing function.

Answer (D) is correct.
    REQUIRED: The item not belonging to the control activities component.
    DISCUSSION: The COSO model describes control activities as policies and procedures that help ensure that management directives are carried out. They are intended to ensure that necessary actions are taken to address risks to achieve the entity's objectives. Control activities have various objectives and are applied at various organizational and functional levels. However, an internal auditing function is part of the monitoring component.
    Answer (A) is incorrect. Performance reviews is a category of control activities. Answer (B) is incorrect. Information processing is a category of control activities. Answer (C) is incorrect. Physical controls is a category of control activities.

20. An organization's directors, management, and internal auditors all have important roles in creating a proper control environment. Senior management is primarily responsible for

    A. Establishing a proper ethical culture.

    B. Designing and operating a control system that provides reasonable assurance that established objectives and goals will be achieved.

    C. Ensuring that external and internal auditors adequately monitor the control environment.

    D. Implementing and monitoring controls designed by the board of directors.

Answer (A) is correct.
    REQUIRED: The best description of senior management's responsibility.
    DISCUSSION: The COSO model treats internal control as a process, effected by an entity's board of directors, management, and other personnel, designed to provide reasonable assurance regarding the achievement of entity objectives. The control environment component of internal control reflects the attitude and actions of the board and management regarding the significance of control within the organization. It sets the organization's tone and influences the control consciousness of its personnel. Moreover, the control environment provides discipline and structure for the achievement of the primary objectives of internal control. The control environment includes, among other elements, integrity and ethical values. Thus, standards should be effectively communicated, e.g., by management example. Management also should remove incentives and temptations for dishonest or unethical acts.
    Answer (B) is incorrect. Senior management is not likely to be involved in the detailed design and day-to-day operation of a control system. Answer (C) is incorrect. Management administers risk and control processes. It cannot delegate this responsibility to the external or internal auditors. Answer (D) is incorrect. The board has oversight governance responsibilities but ordinarily does not become involved in the details of operations.

1.4 COSO Model -- Enterprise Risk Management

21. Enterprise risk management (ERM) helps management achieve all of the following **except**

    A. Reaching objectives.

    B. Reporting on a timely basis.

    C. Preventing loss of reputation and resources.

    D. Complying with laws and regulations.

Answer (B) is correct.
    REQUIRED: The item not a purpose of ERM.
    DISCUSSION: Enterprise risk management (ERM) helps management

1. Reach objectives
2. Prevent loss of reputation and resources
3. Report effectively
4. Comply with laws and regulations

ERM allows management to report effectively, not necessarily on a timely basis.
    Answer (A) is incorrect. ERM helps management reach objectives. Answer (C) is incorrect. ERM helps management prevent loss of reputation and resources. Answer (D) is incorrect. ERM helps management comply with laws and regulations.

22. ERM allows management greater capabilities. Which of the following is **not** a capability of ERM?

A. Reduced operational surprises and losses.

B. Better deployment of capital.

C. Increased productivity.

D. Improved risk response decisions.

Answer (C) is correct.
REQUIRED: The item not a capability of ERM.
DISCUSSION: The following are the categories of the capabilities of ERM:

1. Risk appetite and strategy
2. Risk response decisions
3. Operational surprises and losses
4. Multiple and cross-enterprise risks
5. Opportunities
6. Deployment of capital

Although increased productivity may result from ERM, it is not directly a capability provided by ERM.
Answer (A) is incorrect. Reduction of operational surprises and losses is a capability of ERM. Answer (B) is incorrect. Better deployment of capital is a capability of ERM. Answer (D) is incorrect. Improvement of risk response decisions is a capability of ERM.

23. The components of ERM should be present and functioning effectively. What does "present and functioning effectively" mean?

I. No material weaknesses exist.
II. Risk is within the risk appetite.

A. I only.

B. II only.

C. Both I and II.

D. Neither I nor II.

Answer (C) is correct.
REQUIRED: The definition of "present and functioning effectively."
DISCUSSION: A component is present and functioning effectively if (1) no material weaknesses exist, and (2) risk is within the risk appetite.

24. Inherent risk is

A. A potential event that will adversely affect the organization.

B. Risk response risk.

C. The risk after management takes action to reduce the impact or likelihood of an adverse event.

D. The risk when management has not taken action to reduce the impact or likelihood of an adverse event.

Answer (D) is correct.
REQUIRED: The definition of inherent risk.
DISCUSSION: Inherent risk is the risk when management has not taken action to reduce the effect or likelihood of an adverse event. Thus, it is risk in the absence of a risk response.
Answer (A) is incorrect. A risk event is a potential event that will affect the entity adversely. Answer (B) is incorrect. A risk response is an action taken to reduce the impact or likelihood of an adverse event, including a control activity. Risk response risk is not meaningful in this context. Answer (C) is incorrect. The risk after management takes action to reduce the impact or likelihood of an adverse event, including control activities, in responding to a risk is residual risk.

25. Which risk response reflects a change from acceptance to sharing?

A. An insurance policy on a manufacturing plant was not renewed.

B. Management purchased insurance on previously uninsured property.

C. Management sold a manufacturing plant.

D. After employees stole numerous inventory items, management implemented mandatory background checks on all employees.

Answer (B) is correct.
REQUIRED: The risk response reflecting a change from acceptance to sharing.
DISCUSSION: The categories of risk responses under the COSO ERM model are avoidance, acceptance, reduction, and sharing. If management does not insure a building, the response is acceptance. Ordinarily, acceptance is based on a judgment that the cost of another response is excessive. However, once management purchases insurance, the risk is shared with an outside party.
Answer (A) is incorrect. Not renewing insurance represents a change from risk sharing to risk acceptance. Answer (C) is incorrect. Selling property avoids all the risks of ownership. Answer (D) is incorrect. Management originally accepted the risk of employee theft by not implementing pre-hire investigation. Conducting background checks on all employees reduces the risk of theft.

26. Under the COSO's ERM framework, which of the following most accurately describes risk management responsibilities?

    A. In practice, management has primary responsibility.

    B. The internal audit activity has an oversight role.

    C. The board provides assurance about the effectiveness of ERM.

    D. The chief audit executive should serve as chief risk officer.

Answer (A) is correct.

    REQUIRED: The most accurate description of ERM responsibilities.

    DISCUSSION: The board has overall responsibility. However, in practice, the board delegates responsibility for ERM to senior management, which ensures that sound processes are in place and functioning.

    Answer (B) is incorrect. The internal audit activity provides objective assurance that (1) ERM processes are effective and (2) key risks are managed at an acceptable level. Answer (C) is incorrect. The board has overall responsibility. Answer (D) is incorrect. The CAE must not be the CRO because of the impairment of independence and objectivity.

27. A recent inventory shortage at XYZ Corp., an unaffiliated supplier, contributed to production failures at OPS Corp. in the current period. To avoid future production failures because of supplier inventory shortages, the most appropriate method is for OPS to

    A. Establish an inventory control framework at XYZ.

    B. Increase the size of orders.

    C. Produce the inventory items instead of purchasing from suppliers.

    D. Inform XYZ about its risk appetite regarding supply failures.

Answer (D) is correct.

    REQUIRED: The most effective method to prevent accepting excessive risk of supplier failure.

    DISCUSSION: The risk appetite is the level of risk that an organization is willing to accept. In an enterprise risk management (ERM) system, the risk appetite is considered in (1) evaluating strategic options, (2) setting objectives, and (3) developing risk management techniques. Thus, communicating about the risk appetite with external parties is an important aspect of risk management. It allows the organization to develop strategies to work with suppliers who may have different objectives.

    Answer (A) is incorrect. OPS has no authority to establish an inventory control framework at XYZ. Answer (B) is incorrect. Increasing order size does not address the cause of supplier failures. Answer (C) is incorrect. Although in-house production will eliminate the external parties, it may not be the most cost effective method. The external party may have cost advantages the organization does not.

28. Which of the following members of an organization has ultimate ownership responsibility of the enterprise risk management, provides leadership and direction to senior managers, and monitors the entity's overall risk activities in relation to its risk appetite?

    A. Chief risk officer.

    B. Chief executive officer.

    C. Internal auditors.

    D. Chief financial officer.

Answer (B) is correct.

    REQUIRED: The member of the organization with the stated responsibilities.

    DISCUSSION: The chief executive officer (CEO) sets the tone at the top of the organization and has ultimate responsibility for ownership of the ERM. The CEO will influence the composition and conduct of the board, provide leadership and direction to senior managers, and monitor the entity's overall risk activities in relation to its risk appetite. If any problems arise with the organization's risk appetite, the CEO will also take any measures to adjust the alignment to better suit the organization.

    Answer (A) is incorrect. The risk officer works in assigned areas of responsibility in a staff function. The work of a risk officer often extends beyond one specific area because the officer will have the necessary resources to work across many segments or divisions. Answer (C) is incorrect. The internal auditors evaluate the ERM and may provide recommendations. Answer (D) is incorrect. The CFO is subordinate to the CEO.

1.5 PRACTICE WRITTEN COMMUNICATION

Business Environment and Concepts
Testlet 4 of 4

Time Remaining
1 hour - 15 minutes

Unsplit   Split Horiz   Split Vertical   Exit

DIRECTIONS

Note: If you believe you have encountered a software malfunction, report it to the test center staff immediately.

Navigation

To navigate from task to task, use the controls at the bottom of the screen. Click on the **Next** button to advance to the next task, or the **Previous** button to go to the previous task. To go directly to any task, click on its number.

If you would like a reminder to revisit a task, or want to indicate that you are finished with it, click on the reminder flag below the task number. To clear the flag, click on it again. Reminder flags are for your use only – they do not contribute to your score.

Tabs

In this part of the examination, you will be asked to complete various tasks. Every task has one or more **Work Tabs**. Every task also has a **Help** tab.

Work tab   Help tab

Work Tabs:

- **Work Tabs** are identified with a pencil icon. This is where your responses are expected.
- Each task has one or more **Work Tabs**.
- **Work Tabs** contain directions for completing the task - be sure to read these directions carefully.
- The **Work Tab** name in the example above is for illustration only - yours will differ.
- You must complete all of the **Work Tabs** in each task to receive full credit.

Help Tab:

- The **Help Tab** provides assistance with the exam software that is used in this task. For example, if the task is to compose a memorandum, **Help** will provide information about the word processor.

The Toolbar

The toolbar at the top of the screen shows the amount of time remaining for you to complete the tasks. In addition, the following tools are available. Note that only the **Exit** button is displayed when Directions are visible - the others will appear when you begin the tasks.

Click on these buttons to split or unsplit the screen. You can split the screen vertically or horizontally.

Click on this button to go on to the next part of the examination. You must complete all of the tasks to receive full credit. Once you click on **Exit** and confirm the action, you will NOT be able to return to this testlet.

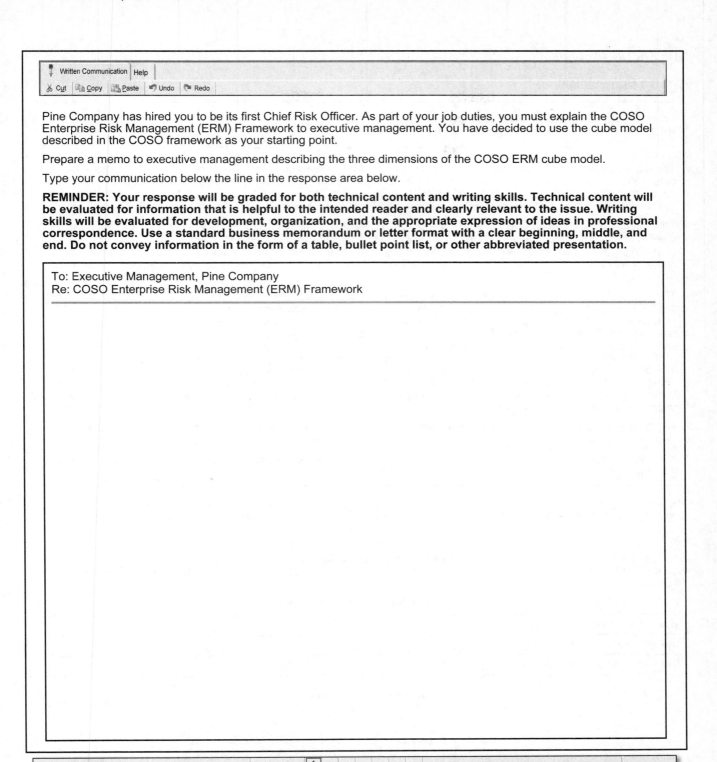

NOTE: Your Written Communications on the actual CPA exam may cover topics outside the scope of the BEC CSO (i.e., they may relate to topics from the AUD, FAR, and/or REG CSOs instead). Answer to the best of your ability, and remember that graders are mainly evaluating your writing ability and will overlook minor technical mistakes.

Unofficial Answer

Written Communication

To: Executive Management, Pine Company
Re: COSO Enterprise Risk Management (ERM) Framework

The COSO Enterprise Risk Management Framework depicts the interaction of the various elements of an ERM program as a matrix in the form of a cube. The four categories of objectives are on one side, the eight interrelated components are on another, and the organizational units of the entity are on a third. The organization can apply the appropriate approach to each intersection of the three elements, such as control activities for reporting objectives at the division level.

The four categories of objectives are strategic, operations, reporting, and compliance. They apply to all entities. Strategic objectives align with and support the entity's mission. Operations objectives address effectiveness and efficiency. Reporting objectives concern reliability. Compliance objectives relate to adherence to laws and regulations. These categories overlap but are distinct. They concern different needs, and different managers may be assigned responsibility for them.

The eight components of ERM are integrated with the management process and may mutually influence each other. They are the internal environment, objective setting, event identification, risk assessment, risk response, control activities, the information and communication component, and monitoring. The internal environment reflects the entity's risk management philosophy, risk appetite, integrity, ethical values, and overall environment. It sets the tone of the entity. Objective setting precedes event identification. Event identification relates to internal and external events affecting the entity. Risk assessment considers likelihood and impact as a basis for risk management. The assessment considers the inherent risk and the residual risk. Risk responses should be consistent with the organization's risk tolerances and appetite. Control activities are policies and procedures to ensure the effectiveness of risk responses. The information and communication component identifies, captures, and communicates relevant and timely information. Monitoring involves ongoing management activities or separate evaluations.

The third dimension is the enterprise's organizational units, for example, subsidiary, business unit, division, and entity level. The structure depends on the unique characteristics of the entity.

In summary, the cube provides a model demonstrating the relationship among the objectives, components, and units of the organization.

The above depicts a Level 5 answer. Consult your booklet, *How to Pass the CPA Exam: A System for Success*, for a description of the three writing skills criteria. You may also access this booklet online by visiting www.gleim.com/PassCPA.

Self-Grade

Below, grade your response on technical content and writing skills. Bubble in the circle next to the most appropriate score for your response based on the criteria given. Your **total** score is the sum of your scores on all six items. The maximum score is 19 points.

Technical Content Evaluation

Was your response on topic?	O No [0]	O Mostly [1]	O Yes [2]
Did your response have any *significant* errors?	O 0 errors [1]	O 1 major error [−1]	O 2 or more major errors [−2]
Did your response contain any illegal advice?	O No [1]	O Yes [0]	

Writing Skills Evaluation

	Poor	Below Average	Average	Above Average	Outstanding
Organization	O 1	O 2	O 3	O 4	O 5
Development	O 1	O 2	O 3	O 4	O 5
Expression	O 1	O 2	O 3	O 4	O 5

Disclaimer: This scoring schedule was developed by Gleim Publications as a guideline only. The AICPA has not released specific information on how the Written Communications are graded.

Practice even more Written Communications with the Gleim Mega Test Bank.
Learn more: gleim.com/CPAmega | 800.874.5346

STUDY UNIT TWO
MICROECONOMICS

(27 pages of outline)

This study unit provides the foundation of economic theory and is important to understand before studying the remaining study units covering economics. **Microeconomics** is the study of economic activity at the "atomic" level, that is, the actions of individual actors in the marketplace. CPA candidates must understand the basics of microeconomics before they can understand more challenging areas of economics, including market influences, business cycles, and the global economy.

2.1 DEMAND, SUPPLY, AND EQUILIBRIUM

1. **Demand -- the Buyer's Side of the Market**

   a. Demand vs. Quantity Demanded

      1) Demand is a schedule of the amounts of a good or service that consumers are willing and able to purchase at various prices during a period of time. Quantity demanded is the amount that will be purchased at a specific price during a period of time.

Demand Schedule

Price per Unit	Quantity Demanded
$10	0
$9	1
$8	2
$7	3
$6	4
$5	5
$4	6
$3	7
$2	8
$1	9
$0	10

      2) A demand schedule can be graphically depicted as a relationship between the prices of a commodity (on the vertical axis) and the quantity demanded at the various prices (horizontal axis), if other determinants of demand are constant.

b. **The Law of Demand**

    1)   If all other factors are constant, the price of a product and the quantity demanded are inversely (negatively) related. The higher (lower) the price, the lower (higher) the quantity demanded. The result is a movement along a demand curve.

Movement Along a Demand Curve

Figure 2-1

c. Factors Other than Price

    1)   A change in any of the determinants of demand (factors other than price) results in a change in demand (shift of the demand curve).

Change in Demand

Figure 2-2

    2)   The determinants of demand are

       a)   Consumer incomes

          i)   As consumers (or the population) become more (less) wealthy, the demand curve shifts to the right (left).

          ii)   Most goods are **normal goods**, that is, commodities for which demand is positively (directly) related to income (e.g., steak, new clothes, and airline travel). Thus, demand shifts to the right as incomes rise.

          iii)   However, a few goods are **inferior goods**, that is, commodities for which demand is negatively (inversely) related to income (e.g., potatoes, used clothing, and bus transportation). In this situation, demand shifts to the left as income rises.

    b) Consumer taste and preference

        i) If a product becomes more (less) popular, the demand curve shifts to the right (left).

    c) Prices of related goods

        i) If a price increase in Product A results in an increase in demand for Product B, Products A and B are **substitutes**. For example, when beef prices rise, the demand for chicken increases.

        ii) If a price increase in Product A results in a decrease in demand for Product B, Products A and B are **complements**. For example, if the price of bread increases, the demand for grape jam decreases.

    d) Consumer expectations

        i) For example, as a hurricane approaches Florida, the increased demand for chainsaws and power generators shifts their demand curves to the right due to the expectation of a natural disaster.

    e) Number of consumers

        i) An increase in the number of consumers shifts the demand curve to the right (increase in demand).

        ii) A decrease in the number of consumers shifts the demand curve to the left (decrease in demand).

2. **Supply -- the Seller's Side of the Market**

  a. Supply vs. Quantity Supplied

    1) Supply is a schedule of the amounts of a good that producers are willing and able to offer to the market at various prices during a specified period. Quantity supplied is the amount that will be offered at a specific price during a period.

    2) A supply schedule can be graphically depicted as a relationship between the prices of a commodity (on the vertical axis) and the quantity offered at the various prices (horizontal axis) if other determinants of supply are constant.

  b. **The Law of Supply**

    1) If all other factors are constant, the price of a product and the quantity supplied are directly (positively) related. The higher (lower) the price, the greater (lower) the quantity supplied. The result is a movement along a supply curve.

Movement Along a Supply Curve

Figure 2-3

c.   Factors Other than Price

1)   A change in any of the determinants of supply (factors other than price) results in a change in supply (shift of the supply curve).

Change in Supply

Figure 2-4

2)   The determinants of supply are

a)   Costs of inputs

i)   An increase in the costs of inputs, such as employees' wages and materials, shifts the supply curve to the left.

ii)   A decrease in the costs of inputs shifts the supply curve to the right.

b)   A change in efficiency of the production process, e.g., better technology

i)   Better technology that improves the production process (e.g., automated manufacturing) shifts the supply curve to the right.

c)   Expectations about price changes

i)   If a product's price is expected to decrease, firms will increase supply before the decrease in prices to sell as much as possible now at the higher price. The supply curve shifts to the right. Production then is decreased when prices fall.

d)   Taxes and subsidies

i)   An increase in taxes or a decrease in subsidies shifts the supply curve to the left.

ii)   A decrease in taxes or an increase in subsidies shifts the supply curve to the right.

3.   **Market Equilibrium**

a.   Market demand is the sum of the individual demand curves of all buyers. Market supply is the sum of the individual supply curves of all sellers.

1)   Market equilibrium is the combination of price and quantity at which the market demand and market supply curves intersect.

Market Equilibrium

P_e = Equilibrium Price
Q_e = Equilibrium Quantity

Figure 2-5

b. At the intersection of the supply and demand curves, anyone wishing to purchase economic goods at the market price can do so. Anyone offering the goods can sell everything they bring to market.

    1) **Equilibrium** is at the market-clearing price and the market-clearing quantity.

c. The market forces of supply and demand create an automatic, efficient rationing system.

    1) When the market price exceeds the equilibrium price, the quantity supplied exceeds the quantity demanded by consumers. A surplus results.

        a) The competition among sellers to eliminate excess inventories causes price cuts and lower production.

        b) As the price falls, more buyers enter the market. Eventually, the price settles at the equilibrium price, and the surplus is eliminated.

        c) Government intervention can create a market surplus. An example is a price floor for an agricultural commodity. If the price is above equilibrium, supply exceeds demand.

    2) When the market price is lower than the equilibrium price, the quantity demanded by consumers is greater than the quantity supplied. A shortage results.

        a) Consumers compete for scarce goods by bidding up prices.

        b) As the price rises, new suppliers enter the market. Eventually, the price settles at the equilibrium price, and the shortage is eliminated.

        c) Government intervention also can create shortages. An example is a price ceiling for apartment rents. If the price is below equilibrium, demand exceeds supply.

d. The effects on equilibrium of shifts in the supply and demand schedules are shown below:

	Demand increase	Demand constant	Demand decrease
Supply increase	P_e unknown Q_e increase	P_e decrease Q_e increase	P_e decrease Q_e unknown
Supply constant	P_e increase Q_e increase	– –	P_e decrease Q_e decrease
Supply decrease	P_e increase Q_e unknown	P_e increase Q_e decrease	P_e unknown Q_e decrease

Stop and review! You have completed the outline for this subunit. Study multiple-choice questions 1 through 5 beginning on page 69.

2.2 ELASTICITY

1. **Elasticity of Demand**

    a. Price elasticity of demand (E_d) measures the sensitivity of the quantity demanded of a product to a change in its price.

    $$E_d = \frac{Percentage\ change\ in\ quantity\ demanded}{Percentage\ change\ in\ price} = \frac{\%\Delta Q}{\%\Delta P}$$

    b. Elasticity is the reaction of demand to a change in price. The two common methods to calculate the price elasticity of demand are the point method and the midpoint method.

    1) The **point method** measures the price elasticity of demand for a specific change in the product's price.

    $$\%\Delta Q = \frac{Quantity\ demanded\ \textbf{after}\ the\ change - Quantity\ demanded\ \textbf{before}\ the\ change}{Quantity\ demanded\ \textbf{before}\ the\ change}$$

    $$\%\Delta P = \frac{Price\ \textbf{after}\ the\ change - Price\ \textbf{before}\ the\ change}{Price\ \textbf{before}\ the\ change}$$

2. **Midpoint Method (Arc Method)**

    a. The midpoint method measures the price elasticity of demand of a range for a specific change in the product's price. This method uses averages of the quantities and prices to measure elasticity. The following is the algebraically simplified version of the formula:

    $$E_d = \frac{\%\Delta Q}{\%\Delta P} = \frac{(Q_1 - Q_2) \div (Q_1 + Q_2)}{(P_1 - P_2) \div (P_1 + P_2)}$$

    1) Absolute value is used when calculating the coefficient of elasticity.

EXAMPLE

Roxy's Ice Cream Shoppe sells 100 quarts of chocolate a day at $6 each. If it lowers the price to $3 per quart, it will sell 300 quarts a day.

Point Method

$$\%\Delta Q = \frac{300 - 100}{100} = 2 = 200\%$$

$$\%\Delta P = \frac{3 - 6}{6} = 0.5 = 50\%$$

$$E_d = \frac{\%\Delta Q}{\%\Delta P} = \frac{200\%}{50\%} = 4$$

The elasticity absolute value of 4 indicates that the specific change of the product's price by 50% (from $6 to $3) will increase the demand for the product by 200% (from Q = 100 to Q = 300).

Midpoint (Arc) Method

	Num.	Denom.		Num.	Denom.		Num.	Denom.		Elasticity
$E_d =$	$\frac{(100 - 300)}{(100 + 300)}$	$\div$	$\frac{(\$6 - \$3)}{(\$6 + \$3)}$	$=$	$\frac{200}{400}$	$\div$	$\frac{\$3}{\$9}$	$=$	0.500 $\div$ 0.333 $=$	**1.50**

The elasticity absolute value of 1.5 indicates that the range on the demand curve between P = 6 and P = 3 is relatively elastic.

b. When the demand elasticity coefficient is

1) **Greater than one**, demand is in a **relatively elastic** range. The percentage change in the quantity demanded is higher than the percentage change in the price.

$$\%\Delta Q \; > \; \%\Delta P$$

a) For example, a 10% decline in the price of ice cream results in a 20% increase in ice cream demanded.

2) **Equal to one**, demand has **unitary elasticity** (usually a very limited range). The percentage change in the quantity demanded is equal to the percentage change in the price.

$$\%\Delta Q \; = \; \%\Delta P$$

3) **Less than one**, demand is in a **relatively inelastic** range. The percentage change in the quantity demanded is lower than the percentage change in the price.

$$\%\Delta Q \; < \; \%\Delta P$$

a) For example, a 20% decline in the price of ice cream results in a 10% increase in ice cream demanded.

4) **Infinite**, demand is **perfectly elastic** (depicted as a horizontal line).

a) In pure competition, the number of firms is so great that one cannot influence the market price. The demand curve faced by a single seller in such a market is perfectly elastic (although the demand curve for the market as a whole has the normal downward slope).

EXAMPLE

Consumers will buy a farmer's total output of soybeans at the market price but will buy none at a slightly higher price. Moreover, the farmer cannot sell below the market price without incurring losses.

---

5) **Equal to zero**, demand is **perfectly inelastic** (depicted as a vertical line).

a) Some consumers' need for a certain product is so high that they will pay whatever price the market sets. The number of these consumers is limited, and the amount they desire is relatively fixed.

EXAMPLE

Drug addiction tends to result in demand that is unresponsive to price changes. Existing buyers (addicts) are not driven out of the market by a rise in price, and no new buyers are induced to enter the market by a reduction in price.

---

c. The price elasticity of demand of a product can be affected by the availability of substitute products in the market.

1) As more substitute products become available, the demand for the product becomes more elastic. A small increase in the product's price causes a proportionally larger decrease in the quantity demanded because substitutes are available.

2) As fewer substitute products become available in the market, the demand for the product becomes more inelastic.

d. Price elasticity of demand is useful for determining how a change in the price of a product will affect total revenue.

Effect on Total Revenue

	Elastic Range	Unitary Elasticity	Inelastic Range
Price increase	Decrease	No change	Increase
Price decrease	Increase	No change	Decrease

3. **Elasticity of Supply**

a. Price elasticity of supply (E_s) measures the sensitivity of the quantity supplied of a product to a change in its price.

$$E_s = \frac{Percentage\ change\ in\ quantity\ supplied}{Percentage\ change\ in\ price}$$

1) The same formulas used in the calculation of price elasticity of demand are used to calculate the price elasticity of supply.

2) When the supply elasticity coefficient is

a) **Greater than one**, supply is in a **relatively elastic** range. The percentage change in the quantity supplied is higher than the percentage change in the price.

$$\%\Delta Q > \%\Delta P$$

b) **Equal to one**, supply has **unitary elasticity** (usually a very limited range). The percentage change in the quantity supplied is equal to the percentage change in the price.

$$\%\Delta Q = \%\Delta P$$

c) **Less than one**, supply is in a **relatively inelastic** range. The percentage change in the quantity supplied is lower than the percentage change in the price.

$$\%\Delta Q < \%\Delta P$$

d) **Infinite**, supply is **perfectly elastic** (depicted as a horizontal line).

e) **Equal to zero**, supply is **perfectly inelastic** (depicted as a vertical line).

i) A perfectly inelastic supply curve indicates that, in the very short run, a seller cannot change the quantity supplied.

EXAMPLE

A farmer offering a perishable good with no means of storage must sell the entire crop regardless of the price buyers offer. The farmer cannot offer a larger quantity because the harvest has ended for the season.

Stop and review! You have completed the outline for this subunit. Study multiple-choice questions 6 through 8 on page 71.

2.3 GOVERNMENT ACTION IN THE MARKET

1. **Price Controls**

   a. Price controls are attempts by government to remedy perceived imbalances of power between economic actors, i.e., sellers and buyers in the marketplace.

2. **Price Ceilings**

   a. To keep essential goods and services affordable to all, sellers sometimes are prohibited from charging the equilibrium price.

   b. Shortages result because the market is unwilling to supply all that is demanded at the (government-mandated) artificially low price.

Price Ceiling and Resulting Shortage

P_C = Artificial ceiling set by government (price not allowed to rise above this ceiling)

Q_S = Quantity supplied at P_C

Q_D = Quantity demanded at P_C

$Q_D - Q_S$ = Amount of shortage

Figure 2-6

   c. Rent controls and usury laws are examples.

3. **Price Floors**

   a. To compensate certain suppliers perceived to be treated adversely by market forces, buyers sometimes are required to pay above the equilibrium price for certain products or services.

   b. Surpluses result because sellers are encouraged by the artificially high price to produce more than the market is willing to buy.

Price Floor and Resulting Surplus

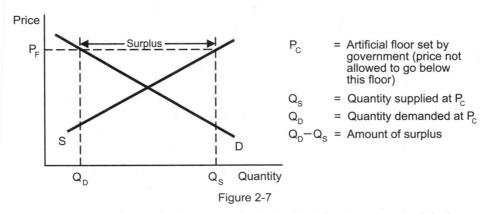

P_C = Artificial floor set by government (price not allowed to go below this floor)

Q_S = Quantity supplied at P_C

Q_D = Quantity demanded at P_C

$Q_D - Q_S$ = Amount of surplus

Figure 2-7

   c. Price supports for agricultural products and minimum wage legislation are examples.

Stop and review! You have completed the outline for this subunit. Study multiple-choice questions 9 through 11 beginning on page 71.

2.4 PROFITS AND COSTS

1. **Explicit vs. Implicit Costs**

   a. **Explicit costs** require actual cash payments. For this reason, they also are known as out-of-pocket or outlay costs.

      1) Explicit costs are **accounting costs**. They are recognized in formal accounting records.

EXAMPLE

An entrepreneur opening a gift shop has to make certain cash payments to start the business.

Inventory	$59,000
Rent	4,000
Utilities	1,000
Total explicit costs	**$64,000**

---

   b. **Implicit costs** are not recognized in formal accounting records.

      1) An implicit cost is an **opportunity cost**, i.e., the maximum benefit forgone by using a scarce resource for a given purpose instead of the next-best alternative.

      2) To measure the true economic success or failure of the venture, the entrepreneur in the example above must consider more than the explicit costs in the accounting records.

         a) The entrepreneur's opportunity costs often are important implicit costs. For example, (s)he could have worked for another firm rather than open the gift shop.

         b) Startup costs are resources that could have been invested in financial instruments.

         c) A **normal profit** is an implicit cost.

EXAMPLE

The normal profit is the income that the entrepreneur could have earned by applying his or her skill in another venture.

Salary forgone	$35,000
Investment income forgone	3,600
Total implicit costs	**$38,600**

---

   c. **Economic costs** are total costs (explicit and implicit).

      1) The standard for an economic decision is whether the revenues from the venture cover all costs, both explicit and implicit.

EXAMPLE

Economic costs = Total costs
= Explicit costs + Implicit costs
= $64,000 + $38,600
= **$102,600**

---

2.   **Accounting vs. Economic Profit**

    a.   **Accounting profits** are earned when the income of an organization exceeds its expenses.

EXAMPLE		
After the first year of operation, the gift shop owner made an accounting profit.		
	Sales revenue	$100,000
	Explicit costs	(64,000)
	Accounting profit	**$ 36,000**

    b.   **Economic profits** are a significantly higher standard. They are not earned until the income exceeds not only costs recorded in the accounting records but also its implicit costs. Economic profit also is called pure profit.

EXAMPLE		
After total costs are considered, the result is different.		
	Accounting profit	$ 36,000
	Implicit costs	(38,600)
	Economic loss	**$ (2,600)**

3.   **Short- vs. Long-Run Costs**

    a.   The **short run** is a period so brief that a firm cannot vary its fixed costs.

    b.   The **long run** is a period long enough that all inputs, including those incurred as fixed costs, can be varied.

        1)   Investment in new, more productive equipment results in higher total fixed costs but may result in lower total and per-unit variable costs.

Stop and review! You have completed the outline for this subunit. Study multiple-choice questions 12 through 15 beginning on page 72.

2.5 MARGINAL ANALYSIS

1.   **Marginal Analysis**

    a.   Marginal analysis allows economic decisions to be made based on projecting the results of varying the levels of resource consumption and output production.

        1)   **Total product** is the entire production of a good or service for a given period.

        2)   **Marginal product** is the additional output obtained by adding one extra unit of input. It is calculated by dividing the change in total output at a given input by the change in inputs.

b. As inputs are added to a process, each additional unit of input results in increased production. However, past the point of diminishing marginal returns, the increase is smaller with each unit. That is, the benefit of adding input units decreases.

1) This principle is the **law of diminishing returns**.

2) Eventually, so many inputs enter the process that it becomes inefficient, and total output actually decreases. This is the point of negative marginal returns.

EXAMPLE

The table below reflects the changes in total product and marginal product as additional units of input are added to the production process.

Units of Input	Total Product	Marginal Product
1	2	2
2	6	4
3	12	6
4	20	8
5	29	9
6	39	10
7	48	9
8	56	8
9	62	6
10	66	4
11	68	2
12	66	−2

At the sixth unit of input, marginal product peaks and then begins to decrease. This is the point of diminishing marginal returns. When the twelfth unit is added, the production process is receiving so much input that the efficiency of the process is actually decreased, and total output also decreases.

---

c. These relationships can be depicted graphically as follows:

Marginal Returns

Figure 2-8

2. **Marginal Revenue**

    a. Marginal revenue is the additional (incremental) revenue produced by generating one additional unit of output. It is the difference in total revenue at each level of output.

        1) If the product is sold in a competitive market (the seller does not have monopoly power), the seller must reduce its price to sell additional units.

        2) Thus, as total revenue increases with the sale of each additional unit, it increases by a smaller amount. The result is constantly decreasing marginal revenue.

EXAMPLE

A company has the following revenue data for one of its products:

Units of Output		Unit Price		Total Revenue	Marginal Revenue
1	×	$580	=	$ 580	$580
2	×	575	=	1,150	570
3	×	570	=	1,710	560
4	×	565	=	2,260	550
5	×	560	=	2,800	540
6	×	555	=	3,330	530
7	×	550	=	3,850	520
8	×	545	=	4,360	510
9	×	540	=	4,860	500
10	×	535	=	5,350	490
11	×	530	=	5,830	480
12	×	525	=	6,300	470

---

    b. Revenue by itself cannot determine the proper level of output. Cost also must be considered.

3. **Marginal Cost**

    a. Marginal cost is the additional (incremental) cost incurred by generating one additional unit of output. It is the difference in total cost at each level of output.

        1) Unit cost tends to decrease as the process becomes more efficient. However, beyond a certain point, the process becomes less efficient, and unit cost increases.

        2) Thus, total cost initially increases gradually, but eventually it increases at a higher rate. This is reflected in a decreasing, then increasing, of marginal cost.

EXAMPLE

The following are cost data for a product, assuming each unit of output requires exactly one unit of input:

Units of Output		Unit Cost		Total Cost	Marginal Cost
1	×	$570.00	=	$ 570	$570
2	×	405.00	=	810	240
3	×	340.00	=	1,020	210
4	×	305.00	=	1,220	200
5	×	287.00	=	1,435	215
6	×	279.17	=	1,675	240
7	×	279.29	=	1,955	280
8	×	284.38	=	2,275	320
9	×	295.00	=	2,655	380
10	×	309.50	=	3,095	440
11	×	326.82	=	3,595	500
12	×	347.08	=	4,165	570

4.   Profit Maximization

a.   The firm's goal is to maximize profits, not revenues. Thus, marginal revenue must be compared with marginal cost to determine the point of profit maximization.

1)   Profit maximization occurs at the output at which **marginal revenue equals marginal cost**. Beyond this point, increasing production results in costs so high that total profit is diminished.

EXAMPLE

Comparing marginal revenue and marginal cost data allows determination of the point of profit maximization.

Units of Output	Marginal				Total			
	Revenue		Cost		Profit	Revenue	Cost	Profit
1	$580	–	$570	=	$ 10	$ 580	– $ 570 =	$ 10
2	570	–	240	=	330	1,150	– 810 =	340
3	560	–	210	=	350	1,710	– 1,020 =	690
4	550	–	200	=	350	2,260	– 1,220 =	1,040
5	540	–	215	=	325	2,800	– 1,435 =	1,365
6	530	–	240	=	290	3,330	– 1,675 =	1,655
7	520	–	280	=	240	3,850	– 1,955 =	1,895
8	510	–	320	=	190	4,360	– 2,275 =	2,085
9	500	–	380	=	120	4,860	– 2,655 =	2,205
10	**490**	–	**440**	=	**50**	**5,350**	**– 3,095 =**	**2,255**
11	480	–	500	=	(20)	5,830	– 3,595 =	2,235
12	470	–	570	=	(100)	6,300	– 4,165 =	2,135

Beyond an output of 10 units, marginal profit is negative. By definition, this output is the point of highest total profit.

Figure 2-9

5. **Marginal Cost (MC) and Average Total Cost (ATC)**

   a. Total costs of production (TC) consist of total fixed costs (FC) and total variable costs (VC).

   $$TC = FC + VC$$

   b. Average total cost (ATC = TC ÷ Q) equals the sum of average fixed costs (AFC = FC ÷ Q) and average variable costs (AVC = VC ÷ Q).

   c. An increase in fixed costs results in the following:

      1) An increase in FC and AFC
      2) An increase in TC and ATC
      3) No effect on VC or AVC

   d. The marginal cost curve (MC) always intersects the ATC curve and the AVC curve at their minimum points.

Cost Relationships in the Short Run

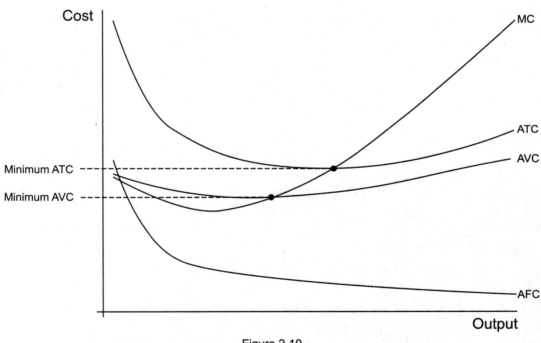

Figure 2-10

6. **Long-Run Cost Relationships**

a. The shape and position of the short-run average total cost (SRATC) curve is determined by productivity.

1) The number of SRATC curves equals the possible variations of production processes. The long-run average total cost (LRATC) curve therefore is extrapolated from all possible SRATC curves. It represents the lowest average total cost for any output that can be produced.

Long-Run ATC Curve

Figure 2-11

b. The LRATC curve derives its shape from the phenomenon of economies and diseconomies of scale.

1) **Economies of scale** (increasing returns to scale). Initially, as production increases, average costs of production tend to decline. Some of the reasons are

a) Increased specialization and division of labor,
b) Better use and specialization of management, and
c) Use of more efficient machinery and equipment.

2) **Constant returns to scale.** For a certain range of output, an increase in production results in no change in average costs.

3) **Diseconomies of scale** (decreasing returns to scale). Eventually, as output continues to increase, the marginal cost of production tends to increase.

a) The most frequent reason for diseconomies of scale is the difficulty of managing a large-scale entity.

Stop and review! You have completed the outline for this subunit. Study multiple-choice questions 16 through 19 beginning on page 73.

2.6 MARKET STRUCTURES -- PURE COMPETITION

1. **Defining Characteristics**

    a. A very large number of buyers and sellers act independently. Examples are the stock market and agricultural markets.

    b. The product is homogeneous or standardized. Thus, the product of one seller is a perfect substitute for that of any other. The only basis for competition is price.

    c. Each seller produces an immaterial amount of the industry's total output and thus cannot influence the market price.

    d. No barriers to entry or exit from the market exist.

    e. Every seller or buyer has perfect information.

        1) Pure competition exists only in theory. However, the model is useful for understanding basic economic concepts. It also provides a standard of comparison with real-world markets.

2. **Industry Demand and Firm Demand**

    a. The demand curve for a normal good in perfect competition is downward sloping.

        1) However, each seller can satisfy only a small part of the demand and must accept the market price. Thus, the demand curve from the seller's perspective is perfectly elastic (horizontal).

Pure Competition

Figure 2-12

        2) The small segment of the industry's demand curve occupied by each seller necessarily is at the point of market equilibrium.

        3) Sellers in perfect competition therefore are price takers because they must sell at the market price.

EXAMPLE

The seller's perfectly elastic demand curve means that marginal revenue, average revenue, and market price are equal.

Units of Output		Unit Price (Average Revenue)		Total Revenue	Marginal Revenue
1	×	$960	=	$ 960	$960
2	×	960	=	1,920	960
3	×	960	=	2,880	960
4	×	960	=	3,840	960
5	×	960	=	4,800	960
6	×	960	=	5,760	960
7	×	960	=	6,720	960
8	×	960	=	7,680	960

3. **Short-Run Profit Maximization in Pure Competition**

    a. In the short run, a seller should produce (continue to operate) when it can earn a profit or incur a loss smaller than fixed costs.

        1) In the short run, operating at a loss may be preferable to closure. This option is indicated when revenues cover all variable costs and some fixed costs (costs incurred even if a firm closes).

    b. For all market structures, a seller that does not close should produce the output at which marginal revenue equals marginal cost **(MR = MC)**.

EXAMPLE

If the next unit of output adds more in revenue (MR) than in cost (MC), the seller increases total profit or decreases total losses. For a purely competitive seller, price equals MC is the same as MR equals MC. MR equals MC at an output of 7 units in the table below.

Units of Output	Revenue		Cost		Profit	
	Total	Marginal	Total	Marginal	Total	Marginal
1	$ 960	$960	$1,800	$1,800	$(840)	$(840)
2	1,920	960	2,500	700	(580)	260
3	2,880	960	3,100	600	(220)	360
4	3,840	960	3,600	500	240	460
5	4,800	960	4,200	600	600	360
6	5,760	960	4,980	780	780	180
7	**6,720**	**960**	**5,940**	**960**	**780**	**0**
8	7,680	960	7,060	1,120	620	(160)

Figure 2-13

4. **Long-Run Equilibrium in Pure Competition**

    a. Because sellers are earning a normal profit, the industry attracts new entrants.

        1) New competitors move the supply curve to the right. The reason is that the industry's additional output will not be purchased unless price is reduced.

        2) The lower price results in losses for sellers with high costs, and they leave the market. Their exit shifts the supply curve to the left.

        3) The output generated by the industry returns to the previous level, and the price can rise again. Equilibrium is restored.

    b. The surviving sellers have the lowest average total cost. Price and quantity are at the intersection of the MR and MC curves.

Long-Run Equilibrium for a Purely Competitive Firm

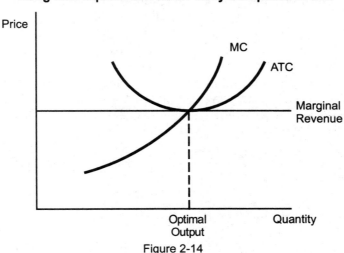

Figure 2-14

Stop and review! You have completed the outline for this subunit. Study multiple-choice questions 20 through 22 beginning on page 74.

2.7 MARKET STRUCTURES -- MONOPOLY

1. **Characteristics**

    a. The industry consists of one seller.
    b. The product has no close substitutes.
    c. The seller can strongly influence price because it is the sole supplier of the product.
    d. Entry by other sellers is completely blocked.

2. **Natural Monopolies**

    a. A natural monopoly exists when economic or technical conditions permit only one efficient supplier.

        1) Very large operations are needed to achieve low unit costs and prices (economies of scale are great). Thus, the long-term average cost of meeting demand is minimized when the industry has one seller. Examples are utilities, such as electricity and gas distribution.

3. **Pricing Power**

    a. Economists use two terms to describe a monopolist's pricing behavior:

        1) A **price maker** sets prices as high as it wants because it is not limited by competition.

        2) A **price searcher** does not set prices arbitrarily high but seeks the price that maximizes its profits.

4. **Demand**

    a. Unlike the horizontal demand curve in pure competition covered in Subunit 2.6, the demand curve is downward sloping because a monopolist can sell more units only by lowering price.

        1) Furthermore, the monopolist's demand curve is the industry's demand curve, not a small part as in pure competition.

        2) A monopolist's price decrease affects all the units sold, not just the additional unit(s). Thus, a monopolist's marginal revenue curve is below the demand curve.

        3) A monopolist's marginal revenue continuously decreases as output increases. Total revenue decreases if marginal revenue is less than $0.

EXAMPLE

Units of Output		Unit Price (Average Revenue)		Total Revenue	Marginal Revenue
1	×	$960	=	$ 960	$960
2	×	910	=	1,820	860
3	×	860	=	2,580	760
4	×	810	=	3,240	660
5	×	760	=	3,800	560
6	×	710	=	4,260	460
7	×	660	=	4,620	360
8	×	610	=	4,880	260

---

5. **Profit Maximization**

    a. Unlike a firm in pure competition, the monopolist can set output at the level at which profits are maximized **(MR = MC)**.

        1) The corresponding price is based on a downward-sloping demand curve.

            a) Monopoly does **not** result in the highest possible price, and the monopolist does **not** produce at the lowest average total cost.

EXAMPLE

Price Searching for a Monopolist

Units of Output	Selling Price per Unit	Revenue		Cost		Profit	
		Total	Marginal	Total	Marginal	Total	Marginal
1	$960	$ 960	$960	$ 800	$800	$ 160	$ 160
2	910	1,820	860	1,480	680	340	180
3	860	2,580	760	1,980	500	600	260
4	810	3,240	660	2,320	340	920	320
5	**760**	**3,800**	**560**	**2,800**	**480**	**1,000**	**80**
6	710	4,260	460	3,480	680	780	(220)
7	660	4,620	360	4,420	940	200	(580)
8	610	4,880	260	5,720	1,300	(840)	(1,040)

The monopolist produces 5 units and sells them at $760 each.

6. **Economic Consequences**

   a. Given sufficiently low costs and adequate demand, a monopolist earns an economic profit in the long run. In the graph below, D is the industry demand curve, and MC is the industry supply curve. (The monopolist is the industry.)

Figure 2-15

   b. In a purely competitive industry, the market price and quantity are P_C and Q_C, respectively.

      1) However, a monopolist restricts output to the profit-maximizing level (Q_M for MR = MC). The resulting price is therefore P_M. MR for the monopolist is less than price, and the MR curve is below the demand curve.

         a) Accordingly, output is lower ($Q_M < Q_C$), and prices are higher ($P_M > P_C$) than under pure competition.

   c. Allocation of resources is not efficient because fewer resources are used in the production process than is justified by society's interests.

Stop and review! You have completed the outline for this subunit. Study multiple-choice questions 23 and 24 on page 75.

2.8 MARKET STRUCTURES -- MONOPOLISTIC COMPETITION

1. **Characteristics**

   a. The industry has a large number of firms. The number is fewer than in pure competition, but it suffices to prevent firms from colluding to restrict output and fix prices.

   b. Products are **differentiated**. In pure competition, products are standardized, so price is the only basis for competition. In monopolistic competition, products can be differentiated on a basis other than price, such as quality, brands, and styles. Thus, advertising may be crucial.

   c. Few **barriers** to entry and exit exist. Because firms tend not to be large, great economies of scale do **not** exist. The cost of product differentiation is the most significant barrier to entry.

2.   Short-Run Profit Maximization

a.   Profit is maximized when marginal revenue (MR) equals marginal cost (MC). The price is the point on the demand curve corresponding to this quantity.

Short-Run Profits in Monopolistic Competition

A = profit-maximizing price and quantity
B = lowest point on ATC curve
C = profit-maximizing quantity (MR = MC)

Figure 2-16

1)   If the profit-maximizing price (P_{MC}) is higher than the minimum average total cost, the firm earns an **economic profit** in the short run.

2)   If the profit-maximizing price (P_{MC}) is lower than the minimum average total cost, the firm incurs a loss in the short run and leaves the industry in the long run.

3.   Long-Run Equilibrium

a.   In the long run, the economic profit of all firms is $0 because firms will enter a profitable industry and leave an unprofitable one.

1)   In a profitable monopolistically competitive industry, the possibility of earning economic profits attracts new entrants.

2)   The presence of new firms requires all firms to differentiate their products further, increasing average total costs.

3)   Higher costs eliminate the economic profits that attracted the new entrants. The firms least able to absorb the higher costs leave the market.

4)   The remaining firms now have higher costs and steady demand. The economic profits generated earlier are replaced with normal profits.

Stop and review! You have completed the outline for this subunit. Study multiple-choice questions 25 and 26 on page 76.

2.9   MARKET STRUCTURES -- OLIGOPOLY

1.   Characteristics

a.   The industry has few large firms. Firms operating in an oligopoly are mutually aware and mutually interdependent. Their decisions as to price, advertising, etc., are significantly dependent on the actions of the other firms.

b.   Products can be differentiated (e.g., autos) or standardized (e.g., steel).

c.   Each firm sets price and production level after considering mutual interdependence.

d.   Entry is difficult because of barriers that can be natural, e.g., an absolute cost advantage, or created, e.g., ongoing advertising or ownership of patents.

2.   **Industry Demand**

   a.   The price rigidity normally found in oligopolistic markets can be explained in part by the **kinked demand curve** theory. Its essence is that firms will follow a price decrease by a competitor but not a price increase.

   1)   If price and quantity for the industry are at P and Q, a firm that raises its price will move into the elastic portion of the demand curve.

   a)   A small increase in price in this portion of the curve leads to a large decline in quantity demanded. Competitors have little incentive to follow, so the price-raising firm loses market share.

   2)   However, if the firm cuts its price, it enters the inelastic portion of the demand curve. A large price decrease is needed to generate even a modest increase in sales.

   a)   More importantly, the discontinuous marginal revenue curve means that marginal revenue falls substantially after a small price cut. Competitors also must reduce their prices so that the first firm gains no market share.

   3)   Price and quantity therefore tend to remain at point A on the demand curve.

Kinked Demand for an Oligopoly

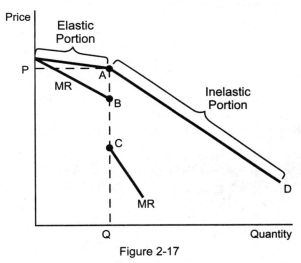

Figure 2-17

   b.   To avoid the hazards of the kinked demand curve, price leadership is typical in oligopolistic industries.

   1)   Price changes are announced first by a major firm in the industry. After the industry leader has acted, other firms match its price.

3.   **Cartels**

   a.   A cartel is a group of oligopolistic firms that agree to set prices. This practice is illegal except in international markets.

   1)   The economic effects are similar to those of a monopoly. Each firm restricts output, charges a higher price, and earns the maximum profit.

   2)   Thus, each firm in effect becomes a monopolist, but only because it is colluding with other members of the cartel.

   b.   Cohesion of the cartel is maintained only if the members maintain their agreed-upon prices and production quotas.

   1)   A cartel fails if one member attempts either to increase profits by producing more or to increase market share by cutting prices.

4.   **Boycotts**

    a.   A boycott is a concerted effort to avoid doing business with a particular supplier, forcing a leftward shift in the demand curve for that supplier.

        1)   Usually, the motivation is moral or ethical rather than purely economic.

Stop and review! You have completed the outline for this subunit. Study multiple-choice questions 27 and 28 beginning on page 76.

2.10   RESOURCE MARKETS AND LABOR

1.   **Resource Planning**

    a.   Resource planning is essential because profit maximization requires production of the optimal output at the least cost. The resources used in production (e.g., labor and materials) are acquired in markets.

        1)   Resource markets also can be structured as pure competition, monopoly, monopolistic competition, and oligopoly.

    b.   **Derived** demand is the demand for the **inputs** to production (factors) derived from the demand for the **outputs** (final goods).

2.   **Factors Affecting Demand for Resources**

    a.   Demand for the final product that the resource produces. Such a change results in a new product price and therefore affects demand.

    b.   Productivity of the resource. As the productivity of an input increases, demand for it increases. This change may occur because

        1)   The proportions of the combination of the resource with other resources shift.
        2)   Technical improvements are made in those combining resources.
        3)   Technical improvements are made in the resource itself.

    c.   Prices of other resources.

        1)   If the price of a resource that can substitute for another resource decreases, the demand for the second resource also decreases. This result is the **substitution** effect.

            a)   For example, as the price of pens decreases, pens are substituted for pencils, and the demand curve for pencils shifts to the left.

        2)   If two resources are **complements**, a decrease in the price of one causes an increase in the demand for the other.

            a)   For example, as the price of computers decreases, the demand curve for computer technicians shifts to the right.

3.   **Elasticity of Resource Demand**

    a.   The elasticity of resource demand applies to movements along, not the shift of, a demand curve. The elasticity of demand for a resource is directly related to the

        1)   Elasticity of demand for the final product. Thus, if the demand for chocolate becomes more elastic, the demand for cocoa beans becomes more elastic.

        2)   Availability of substitutes. For example, as more synthetic chocolates become available, the demand for real chocolate becomes more elastic.

        3)   Proportion of total production cost represented by the resource. For example, if sugar is a large proportion of the total cost of chocolate, an increase in the price of sugar significantly increases the total cost. Accordingly, the firm's demand for sugar becomes more elastic.

4. **Wage Determination**

   a. A wage is the amount paid to the factor of production (labor) that includes the efforts of blue-collar and white-collar workers, professionals, and small business owners. The term "wage" customarily relates to amounts paid per unit of time.

   b. **Nominal wages** are the amounts paid (and received), and **real wages** represent the actual purchasing power (goods and services) of nominal wages.

   c. Real wages are determined by the productivity (real output ÷ hours worked) of labor.

      1) As productivity increases, the demand for labor also increases. Given a certain supply, greater demand results in a higher average real wage.

5. **Labor Supply and Demand in a Competitive Market**

   a. Many firms are competing for a large number of equally skilled workers who provide their services independently, so neither firms nor workers can affect the market rate for labor. Thus, both firms and workers are necessarily price takers.

   b. Market demand for labor is the total of the individual firms' demand curves, i.e., their marginal revenue product (MRP) curves.

   c. The market supply curve has a positive slope because, given little unemployment, firms must raise wages to hire additional workers.

      1) The upward slope reflects the need of firms to match the opportunity costs of workers, such as wages paid in employment alternatives or greater leisure.

   d. The wage rate and the level of employment in the market are determined by the intersection of the market labor demand curve and the market labor supply curve, i.e., labor market equilibrium.

   e. Each firm must accept the market wage rate as determined by the point of labor market equilibrium. Thus, the supply curve for labor facing a single firm is perfectly elastic, and marginal resource cost (MRC) is therefore the same for all amounts of labor hired.

Supply and Demand for Labor in a Purely Competitive Resource Market

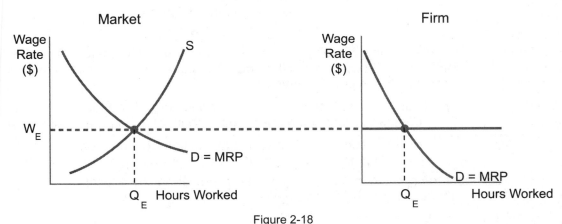

Figure 2-18

6. **Labor Supply and Demand in a Monopsony**

    a. In some labor markets, workers have the option of only a single employer.

        1) A market in which all sellers must sell to a single buyer is a **monopsony**.

    b. For a monopsonist, the marginal resource cost exceeds the current rate for the resource.

        1) The reason is that, given an upward-sloping supply curve, additional units of the resource can be obtained only by paying a higher rate for all resource units (labor hours).

            a) In contrast, a firm in perfect competition pays a constant amount per unit because its consumption is not great enough to influence the rate.

        2) For example, if the first worker may be hired at a rate of $10, but the second must be paid $11, the marginal resource cost (MRC) is $12 ($11 + $1 increase for the first worker), given the need to pay both the same amount to avoid worker dissatisfaction.

        3) To maximize its profits, a buyer of resources in a monopsony uses resources until marginal revenue product equals marginal resource cost.

**Supply and Demand for Labor in
a Monopoly Resource Market**

Figure 2-19

        4) The intersection of the upward-sloping MRC curve and the downward-sloping MRP curve (X) determines the equilibrium quantity. The price is determined by reference to the supply curve (Y).

            a) Thus, a monopsonist pays a lower price (P_M), buys less of the resource (Q_M), and produces a lower output than a firm in pure competition.

                i) For such a firm, MRC is the constant resource price. The result is a higher resource rate (P_C) and a greater quantity demanded (Q_C).

    c. Low-cost transportation reduces monopsony power because local workers can travel more efficiently to distant labor markets.

7. **Minimum Wage Laws**

    a. The federal minimum wage in the United States was established by the Fair Labor Standards Act of 1938. The intent was to provide all workers with a level of pay high enough to avoid poverty by setting a price floor for wages.

    b. Against the Minimum Wage

        1) Because a wage rate above equilibrium is established by law, unemployment is increased. It would be far better for people with marginal skills to have work at some level of pay than to be idle.

        2) The higher labor cost may drive some firms out of business.

c.   For the Minimum Wage

1)   Because many labor markets are monopsonies, minimum wage laws raise pay without increasing unemployment.

2)   The minimum wage may improve productivity.

a)   Because firms cannot pay a substandard wage no matter how menial the task, employers may be encouraged to move workers into productive activities.

b)   A minimum wage may reduce employee turnover, allowing the retention of experienced workers.

Stop and review! You have completed the outline for this subunit. Study multiple-choice questions 29 and 30 on page 77.

QUESTIONS

2.1 Demand, Supply, and Equilibrium

1. Below are the grocers' demand schedules for Palm Valley Grapes. Assuming that John, Towny, and Dorothea are the only three customers of Palm Valley Grapes, which of the following sets of prices and output levels will be on the market demand curve?

Price of Grapes	John Q	Towny Q	Dorothea Q
$6	0	1	0
5	1	2	0
4	2	4	0
3	3	6	1
2	4	8	2
1	5	9	3

A. ($6, 2); ($1, 17)

B. ($5, 3); ($1, 17)

C. ($4, 4); ($2, 12)

D. ($4, 0); ($1, 9)

Answer (B) is correct.

REQUIRED: The points on the demand curve for the product.

DISCUSSION: This type of problem is solved by means of trial and error. Each answer choice should be evaluated to determine whether both points represent demand for a given price. Thus, total demand is 3 at a price of $5 and 17 (5 + 9 + 3) at a price of $1.

Answer (A) is incorrect. Demand is 1 when the price is $6. Answer (C) is incorrect. Demand is 6, not 4, when the price is $4, and demand is 14, not 12, when the price is $2. Answer (D) is incorrect. Demand is 6 when the price is $4 and 17 when the price is $1.

2. If the average household income increases and there is relatively little change in the price of a normal good, then the

A. Supply curve will shift to the left.

B. Quantity demanded will move farther down the demand curve.

C. Demand will shift to the left.

D. Demand curve will shift to the right.

Answer (D) is correct.

REQUIRED: The result of an increase in income given little change in the price of a normal good.

DISCUSSION: The demand schedule is a relationship between the prices of a product and the quantity demanded at each price, holding other determinants of the quantity demanded constant. A movement along an existing demand curve occurs when the price is changed. A shift in the curve itself occurs when any of the determinants changes. Such shifts can be caused by a change in the tastes and preferences of consumers toward a product, for example, as a result of a successful advertising campaign, an increase in consumer income (if a product is a normal good), or changes in the prices of substitute or complementary products. An increase in consumer income would shift the demand curve to the right and result in greater consumption of the product at each price.

Answer (A) is incorrect. The increase in income shifts the demand, not the supply, curve. Answer (B) is incorrect. Moving down an existing demand curve is the effect of a lower price. The change in income shifts the economy to a new demand curve. Answer (C) is incorrect. A shift to the left means that consumers will buy fewer products at each price. This leftward shift in response to increased income is characteristic of an inferior good, not a normal good. The demand for inferior goods is inversely related to income. Hamburger is an inferior good, and steak is a normal good.

3. The demand curve for a normal good is

A. Upward sloping because firms produce more at higher prices.

B. Upward sloping because higher-priced goods are of higher quality.

C. Vertical.

D. Downward sloping because of the income and substitution effects of price changes.

Answer (D) is correct.
  REQUIRED: The true statement about the demand curve for a normal good.
  DISCUSSION: The demand curve for a normal good is downward sloping to the right. At high prices, the amount demanded is relatively low. As prices decrease, the amount demanded increases. The substitution effect is the change in the cost of a good relative to others that will cause a cheaper good to be substituted for more expensive ones. The income effect is the change in purchasing power experienced by consumers as a result of a price change (real income increases or decreases). Both of these effects cause the price of a product and the quantity demanded to be inversely related.
  Answer (A) is incorrect. An upward-sloping demand curve suggests that consumers purchase more of a product if its price is raised. Answer (B) is incorrect. An upward-sloping demand curve suggests that consumers purchase more of a product if its price is raised. Answer (C) is incorrect. A vertical demand curve signifies that the quantity demanded does not change with price.

4. The situation depicted in the graph below could be caused by

A. A price cut by all producers.

B. A price hike by all producers.

C. A rise in the country's population.

D. An improvement in manufacturers' productivity.

Answer (C) is correct.
  REQUIRED: The possible cause of a rightward demand curve shift.
  DISCUSSION: A downward-sloping curve relating price to quantity depicts the demand schedule for a normal good. When a country's population grows, producers can sell more of their products at every price level. This is depicted as a rightward shift in the demand curve.
  Answer (A) is incorrect. A price cut by all producers would be depicted as a downward movement along a fixed curve. Answer (B) is incorrect. A price hike by all producers would be depicted as an upward movement along a fixed curve. Answer (D) is incorrect. An improvement in manufacturers' productivity would be depicted by a shift in the (upward-sloping) supply curve, not the (downward-sloping) demand curve.

5. A decrease in the price of a complementary good will

A. Shift the demand curve of the other commodity to the left.

B. Increase the price paid for a substitute good.

C. Shift the supply curve of the other commodity to the left.

D. Shift the demand curve of the other commodity to the right.

Answer (D) is correct.
  REQUIRED: The effect of a decrease in the price of a complementary good.
  DISCUSSION: A decrease in the price of a good (e.g., gasoline) will cause the demand curve of a complementary good (e.g., automobiles) to shift to the right (increase). The lower price of the first good results in greater demand for the complementary good at each price level.
  Answer (A) is incorrect. A shift to the left (a decrease in demand) would occur if the price of a complementary product increased. Answer (B) is incorrect. Demand for a substitute would decrease, thereby lowering its equilibrium price. Answer (C) is incorrect. The demand curve will shift to the right, but the supply curve will not change.

2.2 Elasticity

6. If the coefficient of elasticity is zero, then the consumer demand for the product is said to be

A. Perfectly inelastic.

B. Perfectly elastic.

C. Unit inelastic.

D. Unit elastic.

Answer (A) is correct.
  REQUIRED: The applicable term when the coefficient of elasticity is zero.
  DISCUSSION: When the coefficient of elasticity (percentage change in quantity ÷ percentage change in price) is less than one, demand is inelastic. When the coefficient is zero, demand is perfectly inelastic.
  Answer (B) is incorrect. Demand is perfectly elastic when the coefficient is infinite. Answer (C) is incorrect. "Unitary inelasticity" is not a meaningful term in this context. Answer (D) is incorrect. Unitary elasticity exists when the coefficient is exactly one.

7. As the price for a particular product changes, the quantity of the product demanded changes according to the following schedule.

Total Quantity Demanded	Price per Unit
100	$50
150	45
200	40
225	35
230	30
232	25

Using the arc method, the price elasticity of demand for this product when the price decreases from $50 to $45 is

A. 0.20

B. 10.00

C. 0.10

D. 3.80

Answer (D) is correct.
  REQUIRED: The price elasticity of demand using the arc method.
  DISCUSSION: A product's price elasticity of demand is measured as the percentage change in quantity demanded divided by the percentage change in price. When price falls from $50 to $45, the coefficient is 3.8, calculated as follows:

$$E_d = [(150 - 100) \div (150 + 100)] \div [(\$50 - \$45) \div (\$50 + \$45)]$$
$$= (50 \div 250) \div (\$5 \div \$95)$$
$$= 20.0\% \div 5.26\%$$
$$= 3.8$$

  Answer (A) is incorrect. The figure of 0.20 equals the 10% decline in price divided by the 50% change in quantity demanded. Answer (B) is incorrect. The figure of 10.00 assumes a 5% change in price. It also does not calculate the change over the sum of the endpoints of the range. Answer (C) is incorrect. The figure of 0.10 is the percentage change in price.

8. Last week, the quantity of apples demanded fell by 6%. If this was a result of a 10% price increase, what is the price elasticity of demand for apples?

A. 1.67

B. 1.06

C. 0.16

D. 0.60

Answer (D) is correct.
  REQUIRED: The price elasticity of demand.
  DISCUSSION: The price elasticity of demand is calculated by dividing the percentage change in quantity demanded by the percentage change in price. Thus, the change in quantity of 6% divided by the 10% price increase produces an elasticity of 0.6.
  Answer (A) is incorrect. The inverse of the elasticity is 1.67. Answer (B) is incorrect. Adding the 6% quantity decline to 1 results in 1.06. Answer (C) is incorrect. The price elasticity of demand is found by dividing the 6% quantity decline by the 10% price increase, not by adding them.

2.3 Government Action in the Market

9. If a rent control law in a competitive housing market establishes a maximum or ceiling rent that is above the market or equilibrium rent,

A. The law has no effect on the rental market.

B. A surplus of rental housing units will result.

C. Supply will decrease as price increases.

D. Demand will increase as price increases.

Answer (A) is correct.
  REQUIRED: The effect of establishing a maximum price above the equilibrium price.
  DISCUSSION: If the market equilibrium rate is less than the maximum allowed, a rent control law will have no effect on the market.
  Answer (B) is incorrect. If the higher price were required to be charged, consumers would demand less housing and a surplus would occur. Answer (C) is incorrect. Price is a determinant of quantity supplied, not supply. Answer (D) is incorrect. Price is a determinant of quantity demanded, not demand.

10. A government price support program will

A. Lead to surpluses.

B. Lead to shortages.

C. Improve the rationing function of prices.

D. Encourage firms to leave the industry.

Answer (A) is correct.
    REQUIRED: The effect of a government price support program.
    DISCUSSION: A government price support program, which sets a price higher than the market price, will cause producers to supply more goods than can be absorbed by the market. The effect will be surpluses because the amount supplied will exceed the amount demanded. In these cases, the government must buy up the surplus and either destroy it or seek other distribution channels; both are highly inefficient outcomes.
    Answer (B) is incorrect. No shortages will occur. Suppliers will be induced by the higher-than-equilibrium price to produce more than the amount demanded. Answer (C) is incorrect. No rationing would occur. Consumers will be able to buy all they desire because supply will exceed demand. Answer (D) is incorrect. Firms will be encouraged to enter the industry by the availability of greater revenue than that provided by consumer demand. In fact, price support programs are often designed with the intention of keeping marginal firms from leaving the industry.

11. Government price regulations in competitive markets that set maximum or ceiling prices below the equilibrium price will in the short run

A. Cause demand to decrease.

B. Cause supply to increase.

C. Create shortages of that product.

D. Produce a surplus of the product.

Answer (C) is correct.
    REQUIRED: The short-run effect of price ceilings that are below the equilibrium price.
    DISCUSSION: A price ceiling lower than the equilibrium price causes shortages to develop. The artificially low price results in an amount supplied less than that at the equilibrium price. It also causes consumers to demand more of the commodity than at the equilibrium price.
    Answer (A) is incorrect. The amount demanded will increase as a result of the artificially low price. Answer (B) is incorrect. The amount supplied will decline as a result of the artificially low price. Answer (D) is incorrect. Surpluses do not occur as a result of price ceilings regardless of whether they are above or below the equilibrium price.

2.4 Profits and Costs

12. A corporation's net income as presented on its income statement is usually

A. More than its economic profits because opportunity costs are not considered in calculating net income.

B. More than its economic profits because economists do not consider interest payments to be costs.

C. Equal to its economic profits.

D. Less than its economic profits because accountants include labor costs, while economists exclude labor costs.

Answer (A) is correct.
    REQUIRED: The true statement about a corporation's net income.
    DISCUSSION: Economic (pure) profit equals total revenue minus economic costs. Economic costs are defined by economists as total costs, which are the sum of outlay costs, and opportunity costs, which are the values of productive resources in their best alternative uses. The return sufficient to induce the entrepreneur to remain in business (normal profit) is an implicit (opportunity) cost. Net income as computed under generally accepted accounting principles considers only explicit costs, not such implicit costs as normal profit and the opportunity costs associated with not using assets for alternative purposes. Thus, net income will be higher than economic profit because the former fails to include a deduction for opportunity costs, for example, the salary forgone by an entrepreneur who chooses to be self-employed.
    Answer (B) is incorrect. Both economists and accountants treat interest as a cost. Answer (C) is incorrect. Economic profits will be less than net income. Answer (D) is incorrect. Economic profits will be less than net income.

13. A normal profit is

A. The same as an economic profit.

B. The same as the accountant's bottom line.

C. An explicit or out-of-pocket cost.

D. A cost of resources from an economic perspective.

Answer (D) is correct.
    REQUIRED: The true statement about normal profit.
    DISCUSSION: Normal profit is the level of profit necessary to induce entrepreneurs to enter and remain in the market. Economists view this profit as an implicit cost of economic activity.
    Answer (A) is incorrect. Economic (pure) profit is the residual return in excess of normal profit. Economic profit equals accounting profit minus implicit costs. These are the sum of explicit and implicit costs, including normal profit. Answer (B) is incorrect. Accounting profit is the excess of total revenue over explicit costs (out-of-pocket payments to outsiders). Answer (C) is incorrect. A normal profit is an implicit cost.

14. The measurement of the benefit lost by using resources for a given purpose is

A. Economic efficiency.

B. Opportunity cost.

C. Comparative advantage.

D. Absolute advantage.

Answer (B) is correct.
    REQUIRED: The measurement of the benefit lost by using resources for a given purpose.
    DISCUSSION: Opportunity cost is the benefit forgone by using scarce resources in a given way. Thus, it is the benefit that could have been obtained from the best alternative use of the resources.
    Answer (A) is incorrect. Economic efficiency is a comparison measured in dollar terms. Answer (C) is incorrect. Comparative advantage compares the costs of producing products within a single country. Answer (D) is incorrect. Absolute advantage compares input costs among countries.

15. In the economic theory of production and cost, the short run is defined to be a production process

A. That spans a time period of less than 1 year in length.

B. In which there is insufficient time to vary the amount of all inputs.

C. That is subject to economies of scale.

D. That always produces economic profits.

Answer (B) is correct.
    REQUIRED: The short run in the economic theory of production and cost.
    DISCUSSION: The short run is defined as a period so brief that a firm has insufficient time to vary the amount of all inputs. Thus, the quantity of one or more inputs is fixed. The long run is a period long enough that all inputs, including plant capacity, can be varied.
    Answer (A) is incorrect. The short run can be more or less than a year depending upon a firm's ability to change its inputs. Answer (C) is incorrect. Economies of scale are associated with the long run. Answer (D) is incorrect. Economic profits may be earned, either in the long or short run, when a firm earns more than the profits needed for it to remain in operation.

2.5 Marginal Analysis

16. Because of economies of scale, as output from production expands,

A. The short-run average cost of production decreases.

B. The long-run average cost of production increases.

C. The long-run total cost decreases.

D. The slope of the demand curve increases.

Answer (A) is correct.
    REQUIRED: The effect of economies of scale.
    DISCUSSION: When a firm experiences economies of scale, the average unit cost of production decreases as production increases. This phenomenon is attributable to spreading fixed costs over a greater number of units of output. Both the short-run and long-run average costs are lower because of economies of scale.
    Answer (B) is incorrect. Long-run unit production costs decline with economies of scale. Answer (C) is incorrect. Total costs increase with increased production; only the average cost per unit declines. Answer (D) is incorrect. Changes in the supply curve do not affect the demand curve.

17. When long-run average cost is declining over a range of increasing output, the firm is experiencing

A. Increasing fixed costs.

B. Technological efficiency.

C. Decreasing returns.

D. Economies of scale.

Answer (D) is correct.
    REQUIRED: The condition experienced when long-run average cost declines over a range of increasing output.
    DISCUSSION: When long-run average cost declines as output increases, the firm is experiencing economies of scale. Average cost falls when marginal cost is below it and rises when marginal cost is above it. Average cost reaches its minimum when it equals marginal cost. Some of the reasons for this phenomenon are increased specialization and division of labor, better use and specialization of management, and use of more efficient machinery and equipment.
    Answer (A) is incorrect. An increase in fixed costs could cause average costs to increase. Also, by definition, all long-run costs are variable. Answer (B) is incorrect. Technological efficiency refers to the ratio of physical output of a given technology and the maximum output that is possible. An increase in technological efficiency is only one of the ways that economies of scale can occur. Answer (C) is incorrect. A decline in average cost means the firm is experiencing increasing returns, not decreasing returns.

18. Because of the existence of economies of scale, business firms may find that

A. Each additional unit of labor is less efficient than the previous unit.

B. As more labor is added to a factory, increases in output will diminish in the short run.

C. Increasing the size of a factory will result in lower average costs.

D. Increasing the size of a factory will result in lower total costs.

Answer (C) is correct.
    REQUIRED: The true statement about economies of scale.
    DISCUSSION: As most firms expand output, average costs of production initially tend to decline. The reasons for this include increased specialization and division of labor, better use and specialization of management, and use of more efficient machinery and equipment. Consequently, increasing the size of a factory often results in lower average costs.
    Answer (A) is incorrect. Economies of scale refer to the savings in costs as production increases; less efficient labor would lead to higher costs. Answer (B) is incorrect. Output should increase, although average productivity may or may not change. Answer (D) is incorrect. Increasing factory size will normally increase total costs but result in lower average costs.

19. The long-run average total cost (ATC) curve

A. Is horizontal and parallel to the demand curve.

B. Is strongly influenced by diminishing returns.

C. Is the same as the rising portion of the marginal cost curve.

D. Is ordinarily U-shaped.

Answer (D) is correct.
    REQUIRED: The true statement about the long-run ATC curve.
    DISCUSSION: The long-run ATC curve is normally U-shaped because the ATC per unit declines as the firm experiences economies of scale. However, beyond the point of intersection with the marginal cost curve, it will begin rising because the amount added (marginal cost) to total cost is greater than the ATC.
    Answer (A) is incorrect. The curve is not horizontal. It varies with changes in production scale. Answer (B) is incorrect. Although returns to incremental input may be diminishing and marginal cost rising, ATC may continue to decline. Answer (C) is incorrect. The ATC curve is a U-shaped curve that is intersected at its minimum point by the rising portion of the marginal cost curve.

2.6 Market Structures -- Pure Competition

20. Mr. Smith is hired as a consultant to a firm in a perfectly competitive industry. At the current output level the price is $20, the average variable cost is $15, average total cost is $22, and marginal cost is $20. In order to maximize profits in the short-run, Mr. Smith will recommend that the firm should

A. Not change output.

B. Decrease production.

C. Increase production.

D. Shut down.

Answer (A) is correct.
    REQUIRED: The action a firm should take when marginal cost equals selling price.
    DISCUSSION: For profit maximization, a firm operating under pure competition should produce the level of output at which price is equal to marginal cost. Since price and marginal cost are both $20, the firm is already at its profit-maximizing position.
    Answer (B) is incorrect. A firm should not decrease output when price is at least equal to marginal cost. Answer (C) is incorrect. There is no incentive to increase production when marginal cost is equal to selling price. Answer (D) is incorrect. A firm should not shut down as long as price exceeds variable cost; any excess of price over variable cost provides a contribution toward the coverage of fixed costs.

21. Which one of the following is **not** a key assumption of perfect competition?

   A. Firms sell a homogeneous product.

   B. Customers are indifferent about which firm they buy from.

   C. The level of a firm's output is small relative to the industry's total output.

   D. Each firm can price its product above the industry price.

Answer (D) is correct.
   REQUIRED: The assumption not made about perfect competition.
   DISCUSSION: Perfect competition is characterized by a market structure with many buyers and sellers acting independently, a homogeneous or standardized product, free entry into and exit from the market, perfect information, no control over the industry price, and the absence of nonprice competition. Moreover, customers are indifferent about which firm they buy from because price is the only difference between one seller and the next.
   Answer (A) is incorrect. A homogeneous product is a key assumption of perfect competition. Answer (B) is incorrect. Customer indifference regarding choice of seller is a key assumption of perfect competition. Answer (C) is incorrect. Small firm output relative to the industry is a key assumption of perfect competition.

22. All of the following are true about perfect competition **except** that

   A. There is free market entry without large capital costs for entry.

   B. There are many firms participating in the market.

   C. In the long run, an increase in profit will have no effect on the number of firms in the market.

   D. Firms are price takers.

Answer (C) is correct.
   REQUIRED: The false statement about perfect competition.
   DISCUSSION: Perfect competition assumes a large number of buyers and sellers that act independently, a homogeneous or standardized product, free entry into and exit from the market, perfect information, no nonprice competition, no control over prices (sellers are price takers rather than price setters), and an equilibrium price equal to the average total cost. Given free entry into the market and perfect information, an increase in profits in the industry will attract new firms. This will have the long-run effect of reducing the price to the level at which no economic profits are earned.
   Answer (A) is incorrect. An absence of barriers to entry is a characteristic of pure competition. Answer (B) is incorrect. A large number of firms is a characteristic of pure competition. Answer (D) is incorrect. Firms in pure competition must accept the market price.

2.7 Market Structures -- Monopoly

23. A characteristic of a monopoly is that

   A. A monopoly will produce when marginal revenue is equal to marginal cost.

   B. There is a unique relationship between the market price and the quantity supplied.

   C. In optimizing profits, a monopoly will increase its supply curve to where the demand curve becomes inelastic.

   D. There are multiple prices for the product to the consumer.

Answer (A) is correct.
   REQUIRED: The characteristic of a monopoly.
   DISCUSSION: A monopoly consists of a single firm with a unique product. Such a firm has significant price control. For profit maximization, it increases production until its marginal revenue equals its marginal cost. In a monopoly, price will be higher and output lower than in perfect competition.
   Answer (B) is incorrect. The monopolist is in control of the quantity supplied. Thus, the supply can be limited to produce the profit-maximizing price. Answer (C) is incorrect. To optimize profits, a monopoly will produce at the point when its marginal revenue equals its marginal cost. Answer (D) is incorrect. There is only one price when a monopoly exists.

24. Any business firm that has the ability to control the price of the product it sells

   A. Faces a downward-sloping demand curve.

   B. Has a supply curve that is horizontal.

   C. Has a demand curve that is horizontal.

   D. Will sell all output produced.

Answer (A) is correct.
   REQUIRED: The true statement about a business firm with the ability to control the price of its product.
   DISCUSSION: A firm that can control the price of its product is a monopolist. In a monopoly, the industry demand curve is also the firm's demand curve. The demand curve is downward-sloping since the lower the price, the higher the demand for a product.
   Answer (B) is incorrect. A horizontal supply curve implies that the company will produce any quantity of output at the constant price. The ability to control one's price implies a changing price level. Answer (C) is incorrect. A horizontal demand curve implies an unchanging price. Answer (D) is incorrect. The firm will not be able to sell all of its output if it sets the price higher than what consumers were willing to pay. Also, a monopolist's incentive is not to sell the maximum that can be produced, but to sell the amount that maximizes profits.

2.8   Market Structures -- Monopolistic Competition

25. All of the following are characteristics of monopolistic competition **except** that

    A. The firms sell a homogeneous product.

    B. The firms tend not to recognize the reaction of competitors when determining prices.

    C. Individual firms have some control over the price of the product.

    D. The consumer demand curve is highly elastic.

Answer (A) is correct.
    REQUIRED: The item not a characteristic of monopolistic competition.
    DISCUSSION: Monopolistic competition assumes a large number of firms with differentiated (heterogeneous) products and relatively easy entry into the market. Sellers have some price control because of product differentiation. Monopolistic competition is characterized by nonprice competition, such as advertising, service after the sale, and emphasis on trademark quality. In the short run, firms equate marginal revenue and marginal cost. In the long run, firms tend to earn normal (not economic) profits, and price exceeds marginal cost, resulting in an underallocation of resources. Firms produce less than the ideal output, and the industry is populated by too many firms that are too small in size. Price is higher and output less than in pure competition.
    Answer (B) is incorrect. Responses to competitors' actions are unnecessary if products are sufficiently differentiated to make price competition meaningless. Answer (C) is incorrect. Product differentiation permits some price control. Answer (D) is incorrect. The availability of close substitutes makes the product demand curve elastic.

26. Entry into monopolistic competition is

    A. Blocked.

    B. Difficult, with significant obstacles.

    C. Rare, as significant capital is required.

    D. Relatively easy, with only a few obstacles.

Answer (D) is correct.
    REQUIRED: The true statement about entry into monopolistic competition.
    DISCUSSION: Monopolistic competition is characterized by the existence of a large number of firms, differentiated products, relative ease of entry, some control of price by the firms, and significant nonprice competition (e.g., by advertising). Entry into monopolistic competition is more difficult than entry into pure competition, but it is relatively easy compared with entry into a monopoly.
    Answer (A) is incorrect. Entry is possible and relatively easy. Blocked entry is typical of monopoly. Answer (B) is incorrect. Difficult entry is typical of oligopoly. Answer (C) is incorrect. Given the large number of firms, most are likely to be small, with correspondingly low economies of scale and capital needs.

2.9   Market Structures -- Oligopoly

27. The distinguishing characteristic of oligopolistic markets is

    A. A single seller of a homogeneous product with no close substitute.

    B. A single seller of a heterogeneous product with no close substitute.

    C. Lack of entry and exit barriers in the industry.

    D. Mutual interdependence of firm pricing and output decisions.

Answer (D) is correct.
    REQUIRED: The distinguishing characteristic of oligopolistic markets.
    DISCUSSION: The oligopoly model is much less specific than the other market structures, but there are typically few firms in the industry. Thus, the decisions of rival firms do not go unnoticed. Products can be either differentiated or standardized. Prices tend to be rigid (sticky) because of the interdependence among firms. Entry is difficult because of either natural or created barriers. Price leadership is typical in oligopolistic industries. Under price leadership, price changes are announced first by a major firm. Once the industry leader has spoken, other firms in the industry match the price charged by the leader. The mutual interdependence of the firms influences both pricing and output decisions.
    Answer (A) is incorrect. Oligopolies contain several firms; a single seller is characteristic of a monopoly. Answer (B) is incorrect. Oligopolies contain several firms; a single seller is characteristic of a monopoly. Answer (C) is incorrect. Oligopolies are typified by barriers to entry; that is the reason the industry has only a few firms.

28. An oligopolist faces a "kinked" demand curve. This terminology indicates that

    A. When an oligopolist lowers its price, the other firms in the oligopoly will match the price reduction, but if the oligopolist raises its price, the other firms will ignore the price change.

    B. An oligopolist faces a non-linear demand for its product, and price changes will have little effect on demand for that product.

    C. An oligopolist can sell its product at any price but, after the "saturation point," another oligopolist will lower its price and therefore shift the demand curve to the left.

    D. Consumers have no effect on the demand curve, and an oligopolist can shape the curve to optimize its own efficiency.

Answer (A) is correct.
    REQUIRED: The meaning of an oligopolist's kinked demand curve.
    DISCUSSION: An oligopoly consists of a few firms. Thus, the decisions of rivals do not go unnoticed. Prices tend to be rigid (sticky) because of the interdependence among firms. Because competitors respond only to certain price changes by one of the firms in an oligopolistic industry, the demand curve for an oligopolist tends to be kinked. Price decreases are usually matched by price decreases, but price increases are often not followed. If other firms do not match a lower price, a price decrease by an oligopolist would capture more of the market. If other firms match the price decrease, less of the market will be captured.
    Answer (B) is incorrect. Price changes will have an effect on demand for an oligopolist's product. Answer (C) is incorrect. An oligopolist must essentially match the price of other firms in the industry. A change in price does not shift the demand curve. Answer (D) is incorrect. An oligopolist cannot shape its demand curve.

2.10 Resource Markets and Labor

29. Derived demand can best be described as

    A. The demand derived purely from the market structure of a particular industry.

    B. The demand for a final product generated by the demand for a complementary good.

    C. The demand for an input generated by the demand for the final product.

    D. The demand for a final product generated by an abundant supply of inputs.

Answer (C) is correct.
    REQUIRED: The definition of derived demand.
    DISCUSSION: Derived demand is the demand for the inputs to the production process (sometimes called factors) derived from the demand for the outputs of the process (i.e., final goods).
    Answer (A) is incorrect. Derived demand is the demand for an input generated by the demand for the final product. Answer (B) is incorrect. The demand for complementary goods is not properly referred to as derived demand. Answer (D) is incorrect. Demand for a final product based on the supply of its inputs is not a meaningful economic concept.

30. The amounts paid to laborers are

    A. Real wages.

    B. Nominal wages.

    C. Productivity wages.

    D. Minimum wages.

Answer (B) is correct.
    REQUIRED: The term for wages actually paid to laborers.
    DISCUSSION: Nominal wages are the amounts actually paid (and received), while real wages represent the purchasing power of goods and services that can be acquired by the nominal wages. The level of real wages is determined by the productivity of labor. As productivity increases, the demand for labor also increases.
    Answer (A) is incorrect. Real wages represent the purchasing power of the wages paid. Answer (C) is incorrect. Productivity wages is a nonsense term. Answer (D) is incorrect. A minimum wage is established by law. It is a nominal wage, but all amounts paid to laborers are not minimum wages.

2.11 PRACTICE WRITTEN COMMUNICATION

Business Environment and Concepts
Testlet 4 of 4

Time Remaining
1 hour - 15 minutes

Unsplit   Split Horiz   Split Vertical   Exit

DIRECTIONS

Note: If you believe you have encountered a software malfunction, report it to the test center staff immediately.

Navigation

To navigate from task to task, use the controls at the bottom of the screen. Click on the **Next** button to advance to the next task, or the **Previous** button to go to the previous task. To go directly to any task, click on its number.

▽ = Reminder   Directions | 1 2 3 4 5 6 7 | ◀ Previous   Next ▶

If you would like a reminder to revisit a task, or want to indicate that you are finished with it, click on the reminder flag below the task number. To clear the flag, click on it again. Reminder flags are for your use only – they do not contribute to your score.

Tabs

In this part of the examination, you will be asked to complete various tasks. Every task has one or more **Work Tabs**. Every task also has a **Help Tab**.

Written Communication | Help

Work tab   Help tab

Work Tabs:

- **Work Tabs** are identified with a pencil icon. This is where your responses are expected.
- Each task has one or more **Work Tabs**.
- **Work Tabs** contain directions for completing the task - be sure to read these directions carefully.
- The **Work Tab** name in the example above is for illustration only - yours will differ.
- You must complete all of the **Work Tabs** in each task to receive full credit.

Help Tab:

- The **Help Tab** provides assistance with the exam software that is used in this task. For example, if the task is to compose a memorandum, **Help** will provide information about the word processor.

The Toolbar

The toolbar at the top of the screen shows the amount of time remaining for you to complete the tasks. In addition, the following tools are available. Note that only the **Exit** button is displayed when Directions are visible - the others will appear when you begin the tasks.

Unsplit   Split Horiz   Split Vertical

Click on these buttons to split or unsplit the screen. You can split the screen vertically or horizontally.

Exit

Click on this button to go on to the next part of the examination. You must complete all of the tasks to receive full credit. Once you click on **Exit** and confirm the action, you will NOT be able to return to this testlet.

▽ = Reminder   Directions | 1 | ◀ Previous   Next ▶

Susan, an individual with primarily consumer debts, has experienced significant financial trouble in the current year. She is considering filing for Chapter 7 bankruptcy but does not know whether she meets the requirements to file. She has asked the managing partner at Accountants LLP, Kristy, to explain to her the requirements that must be met to qualify for this type of bankruptcy. Kristy has asked you, a second-year staff member, to type a memo for Susan with the information requested.

Write a memorandum on the availability of Chapter 7 (liquidation) bankruptcy. The emphasis should be on the eligibility of an individual debtor with primarily consumer debts.

Type your communication below the line in the response area below.

REMINDER: Your response will be graded for both technical content and writing skills. Technical content will be evaluated for information that is helpful to the intended reader and clearly relevant to the issue. Writing skills will be evaluated for development, organization, and the appropriate expression of ideas in professional correspondence. Use a standard business memorandum or letter format with a clear beginning, middle, and end. Do not convey information in the form of a table, bullet point list, or other abbreviated presentation.

To: Susan
Re: Chapter 7 Bankruptcy

NOTE: Your Written Communications on the actual CPA exam may cover topics outside the scope of the BEC CSO (i.e., they may relate to topics from the AUD, FAR, and/or REG CSOs instead). Answer to the best of your ability, and remember that graders are mainly evaluating your writing ability and will overlook minor technical mistakes.

Unofficial Answer

Written Communication

> To: Client
> Re: Chapter 7 Bankruptcy
>
> ---
>
> Chapter 7 is the section of the federal Bankruptcy Code that governs liquidation of an individual's estate. This approach converts a debtor's nonexempt assets into cash. The cash is distributed, and an honest debtor is discharged from most of the remaining debts. Proceedings under Chapter 7 apply to all debtors (persons), including individuals, partnerships, and corporations. Moreover, any person eligible to be a debtor may file a voluntary petition under Chapter 7 without regard to the amount of debt or the number of creditors. This voluntary petition results in an automatic stay of most civil actions against the debtor.
>
> However, a Chapter 7 case may be dismissed or converted to a Chapter 13 case because of abuse by an individual debtor with primarily consumer debts (for example, credit card debt). Abuse is found when (1) the debtor does not pass the means test (if it results in an unrebutted presumption of abuse) or (2) general grounds exist for the finding, for example, bad faith or that the totality of the circumstances indicates abuse.
>
> If the debtor's income exceeds the relevant state median income, any party in interest may seek dismissal for abuse on either basis. Otherwise, only the judge, U.S. Trustee, or bankruptcy administrator may move to dismiss (and then only on general grounds of abuse).
>
> The debtor's income for eligibility purposes equals current monthly income (CMI) times 12. The means test determines the debtor's ability to repay general unsecured claims. CMI is a 6-month average of all income received by the debtor. But Social Security and certain other items are excluded.
>
> Presumed deductions from CMI are allowed for support and payment of higher priority debt. They include (1) living expenses for which allowances are specified by the IRS, (2) actual expenses recognized by the IRS for which it provides no allowances, (3) secured debt coming due within 5 years divided by 60 months, (4) priority debt divided by 60 months, and (5) certain other deductions (e.g., continuing contributions to charity of up to 15% of gross income).
>
> The mandatory trigger point for presumed abuse is when the debtor has more than $207.92 of CMI after deductions ($12,475 ÷ 60 months). If CMI after deductions is less than $124.58 ($7,475 ÷ 60 months), the presumption never arises. For other amounts, abuse is presumed if 5-year income [(CMI − allowed deductions) × 60 months] suffices to pay 25% or more of general unsecured debt. For example, if CMI after deductions is $150, abuse is presumed if general unsecured debt is no more than $36,000 [($150 × 60) ÷ 25].
>
> The presumption of abuse may be rebutted by proof of special circumstances that justify increasing expenses or decreasing CMI.

The above depicts a Level 5 answer. Consult your booklet, *How to Pass the CPA Exam: A System for Success*, for a description of the three writing skills criteria. You may also access this booklet online by visiting www.gleim.com/PassCPA.

Self-Grade

Below, grade your response on technical content and writing skills. Bubble in the circle next to the appropriate score that you may receive based on the criteria given. Your **total** score is the sum of your scores on all six items. The maximum score is 19 points.

Technical Content Evaluation

Was your response on topic?	O No [0]	O Mostly [1]	O Yes [2]
Did your response have any *significant* errors?	O 0 errors [1]	O 1 major error [−1]	O 2 or more major errors [−2]
Did your response contain any illegal advice?	O No [1]	O Yes [0]	

Writing Skills Evaluation

	Poor	Below Average	Average	Above Average	Outstanding
Organization	O 1	O 2	O 3	O 4	O 5
Development	O 1	O 2	O 3	O 4	O 5
Expression	O 1	O 2	O 3	O 4	O 5

Disclaimer: This scoring schedule was developed by Gleim Publications as a guideline only. The AICPA has not released specific information on how the Written Communications are graded.

STUDY UNIT THREE
MACROECONOMICS

(22 pages of outline)

To describe (and manage) the economy, macroeconomists require measurements of an economy's performance. Gross domestic product, the most often-used measure of economic activity, is the aggregate of demand for an economy as a whole (Subunits 3.1 and 3.2). Economic growth in capitalistic economies has not been constant proceeds in cycles of expansion and contraction (Subunit 3.3). Macroeconomics is the study of three interrelated aspects of any economy: growth, inflation, and unemployment (Subunits 3.4 through 3.6). If aggregate demand is either too strong or too weak, the federal government can attempt to stimulate economic activity (Subunit 3.7). Money is created by the banking system. The economic activity in an economy is closely related to the supply of money (Subunit 3.8). The Federal Reserve Board is the body most responsible for managing the supply of money in the United States. To achieve its goals, it uses the tools of monetary policy (Subunit 3.9).

3.1 DOMESTIC OUTPUT -- EXPENDITURES APPROACH

1. **Measuring an Economy's Aggregate Output**

   a. **Gross domestic product (GDP)** is the principal measure of national economic performance.

      1) U.S. GDP is

         a) The total market value
         b) Of all final goods and services
         c) Produced within the boundaries of the U.S.
         d) By domestic- or foreign-owned sources
         e) During a specified period (usually a year)

      2) GDP is calculated without regard to the ownership of productive resources. Thus, the value of the output of a U.S.-owned factory abroad is excluded, but the output of a foreign-owned factory in the U.S. is included.

   b. The two methods of measuring GDP are (1) the expenditures approach (described below and on the next page) and (2) the income approach (described in the next subunit).

2. **Expenditures Approach**

   a. The expenditures approach, the simpler of the two methods, calculates GDP as the sum of all expenditures in the economy.

$$Gross\ domestic\ product = C + I + G + NX$$

b.   Consumer Spending (C)

1)   This measure is by far the largest component of GDP. Its most important determinant is personal incomes.

2)   Changes in incomes do not affect GDP dollar-for-dollar. For every additional dollar consumers receive in income, some portion is spent, and the remainder is saved.

c.   Investment Spending (I)

1)   Business investments create jobs and income. Examples are purchases of equipment and machinery, construction (including construction of leased residences), and changes in inventory.

2)   Business investment is by far the most volatile component. Investment reflects the level of optimism about future demand, and business optimism is subject to wide and sudden variations.

3)   Investment demand has an inverse relationship with the real market interest rate. To determine whether to invest or deposit money in the banking system, the investor compares the real market interest rate and the expected rate of return from the investment. As the interest rate decreases, investment increases.

d.   Government Spending (G)

1)   Government's component of total spending consists of outlays for

a)   Goods and services consumed by the government in providing public services and

b)   Long-lived public infrastructure assets, such as schools, bridges, and military bases.

i)   Transfer payments (e.g., Social Security benefits) to its citizens are not included because they will be spent on final goods and services by consumers.

e.   Net Exports (NX)

1)   GDP reflects all spending on American-made goods, no matter who purchases them, and excludes American spending on goods and services produced abroad (imports).

$$Net\ exports\ (NX) = Exports\ (X) - Imports\ (M)$$

This measure can be positive or negative.

f.   The following is a useful memory aid for the expenditures approach:

Creativity   = **C**onsumer spending
Increases   = **I**nvestment spending
Greenland's = **G**overnment spending
Net   = **N**et
e**X**ports   = **E**xports

EXAMPLE

Expenditures Approach

	In Billions
Consumption by households (C)	$6,000
Investment by businesses (I)	1,200
Government purchases (G)	2,020
Net exports (NX)	(400)
Gross domestic product	**$8,820**

g. A change in any of the four expenditure functions causes equilibrium GDP to rise or fall.

1) Consumer spending (C). If consumers increase their spending, for example, because they expect higher incomes or lower taxes, the consumption function shifts upward to reflect greater national output.

2) Investment spending (I). If businesses increase their spending on productive assets, for example, because new technology is available or real interest rates are lower, the investment function shifts upward to reflect greater national output.

3) Government spending (G). If government increases its spending, for example, because of increased defense spending, the government function shifts upward to reflect greater national output.

4) Net exports (NX). If American firms sell more products abroad, the net exports function shifts upward to reflect greater national output. If exports eventually exceed imports, this measure will be positive.

Stop and review! You have completed the outline for this subunit. Study multiple-choice questions 1 through 3 on page 102.

3.2 DOMESTIC OUTPUT -- INCOME APPROACH

1. **Components of the Income Approach**

a. The income approach determines the same total GDP as the expenditures approach. But the income calculation is more complex.

GDP Calculation -- Income Approach

	In Billions
Salaries and wages	$ x,xxx
Rents	x,xxx
Interest	x,xxx
Proprietor and partnership incomes	x,xxx
Corporate profits	x,xxx
National income	**$xx,xxx**
Indirect business taxes	x,xxx
Net foreign factor income	x,xxx
Net domestic product	**$xx,xxx**
Capital consumption allowance	x,xxx
Gross domestic product	**$xx,xxx**

b. The income approach also produces two intermediate measures that are significant: national income and net domestic product.

1) **National income (NI)** is all income generated by U.S.-owned resources, no matter where located. Employee compensation is by far the largest component.

a) The following is a useful memory aid for national income:

Scholarly = **S**alaries and wages
Research = **R**ents
Interests = **I**nterest
Promote = **P**roprietor and partnership incomes
Competition = **C**orporate profits

2) **Net domestic product (NDP)** measures income generated in the U.S., regardless of the ownership of the productive resources. It is the sum of NI and the following two items:

    a) Indirect business taxes (sales taxes, excise taxes, etc.), are collected by businesses and transmitted to some level of government.

    b) Net foreign-factor income is the excess of (1) income generated in the U.S. from foreign-owned resources over (2) income generated in other countries from U.S.-owned resources.

        i) The following is a useful memory aid for net domestic product:

I	=	Indirect
Bought	=	Business
Two	=	Taxes
Nets	=	Net
For	=	Foreign
Fishing	=	Factor
Income	=	Income

    c) **Gross domestic product (GDP)** is calculated by adding to NDP an allowance for the capital stock consumed or lost in the process of generating income. Thus, GDP equals NDP plus a capital consumption allowance (GDP = NDP + Depreciation of capital).

EXAMPLE

	In Billions
Salaries and wages	$3,200
Rents	500
Interest	500
Proprietor and partnership incomes	200
Corporate profits	2,400
National income	**$6,800**
Indirect business taxes	320
Net foreign factor income	200
Net domestic product	**$7,320**
Capital consumption allowance	1,500
Gross domestic product	**$8,820**

---

2. **Other Income Measures**

    a. **Personal income (PI)** is all income received by individuals.
    b. **Disposable income (DI)** is the after-tax income of individuals.

EXAMPLE

	In Billions
National income (NI)	**$6,800**
Social Security contributions	(600)
Corporate income taxes	(100)
Undistributed corporate profits	(100)
Transfer payments	1,400
Personal income (PI)	**$7,400**
Personal taxes	(1,600)
Disposable income (DI)	**$5,800**

3.   **Graphical Depiction**

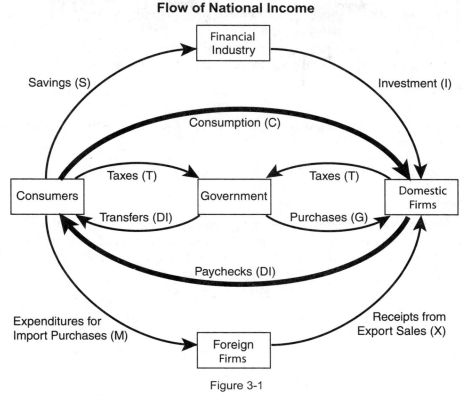

Figure 3-1

4.   **Limitations of GDP**

a.   Calculating GDP requires aggregating an enormous amount of data, some of which may be difficult to acquire, such as information from privately held entities.

b.   Because GDP is calculated in current-year dollars, it is a monetary measure. Thus, comparing GDP over time requires adjustment for changes in the general price level.

c.   GDP includes only final goods and services. Much economic activity involves the trading of intermediate goods, such as when a manufacturer buys materials.

1)   The exchange of intermediate goods is not included in GDP to avoid double-counting some goods.

d.   Increases in GDP often involve environmental damage such as noise, congestion, or pollution. This cost is not considered in the calculation of GDP.

e.   Some economic activity occurs as a result of disasters. For example, after a hurricane, sales by home improvement stores increase. This benefit is reflected in GDP, but the financial loss of the customers is not included in GDP.

f.   Some economic activity, especially in developing countries, occurs in the underground economy. None is captured in GDP.

g.   The value of leisure time to its consumers is not included in GDP.

5.   **Price Level Accounting**

 a.   **Nominal GDP.** The basic GDP calculation includes the total market value of all final goods and services in current dollars.

 b.   **Real GDP.** To facilitate year-to-year comparisons, nominal GDP is adjusted for changes in the general price level so that it can be reported in constant dollars.

$$Real\ GDP = \frac{Nominal\ GDP}{Price\ index\ (in\ hundredths)}$$

Stop and review! You have completed the outline for this subunit. Study multiple-choice questions 4 through 7 on page 103.

3.3 BUSINESS CYCLES

1.   **Overview**

 a.   Over the very long run, economic growth in capitalistic economies has not been steady. The overall trend of growth is periodically interrupted by periods of instability. This tendency toward instability within the context of overall growth is the business cycle.

The Business Cycle

Figure 3-2

1)   At a **peak**, the economy is

 a)   At or near full employment and

 b)   At or near maximum output for the current level of resources and technology.

2)   A **recession** is a period during which real GDP falls and unemployment rises.

 a)   If the recession is severe enough, prices fall and the phase is considered a **depression**.

3)   In a **trough**, economic activity reaches its lowest point.

4)   During a **recovery**, output and employment rise. Eventually, the price level also rises.

In addition to identifying the phases of the business cycle, a candidate should be able to assess the business cycle's effects on an entity's operations and its industry.

b.   Possible Causes of Recessions or Troughs

1)   When consumer confidence declines, i.e., when consumers become pessimistic about the future, they spend less. Unsold inventory increases, and businesses respond by reducing production and laying off workers.

2)   A miscalculation in fiscal or monetary policy by the government may suffice to cause a recession or an expansion.

c.   Economists use leading economic indicators to forecast future economic trends. Lagging indicators report past economic activity.

1)   The best-known sets of economic indicators are those prepared by The Conference Board, a private research group.

2)   These indicators in isolation are not meaningful. It is the composite index that has predictive uses. This index has historically been valuable but not infallible.

2.   **Leading Economic Indicators**

a.   A change in any of the following indicators suggests a future change in real GDP in the same direction:

1)   The average workweek for manufacturing workers
2)   New orders for consumer goods
3)   New orders for nondefense capital goods
4)   Building permits for houses
5)   Stock prices
6)   The money supply
7)   The spread between short- and long-term interest rates
8)   Consumer expectations

b.   A change in either of the following indicators suggests a future change in real GDP in the opposite direction:

1)   Initial claims for unemployment insurance. An increase in unemployment slows business activity.

2)   Vendor performance. Vendors with slack time are holding excess inventory.

You do not need to memorize all of the leading economic indicators. If one of these economic indicators is in the stem of a multiple-choice question, you need to understand how it may affect future growth or contraction of the economy. A written communication question on economic indicators may be required, but your response should be acceptable if you can remember some of them. Most accounting majors should have acquired the necessary knowledge from course work and coverage of business news, e.g., stock prices (such as the S&P 500 and the Dow Jones Industrial Average), unemployment claims, and interest rates.

Stop and review! You have completed the outline for this subunit. Study multiple-choice questions 8 through 10 on page 104.

3.4 GROWTH

1.   **Economic Growth and Prosperity**

a.   The change in real per capita GDP over a period of time is one way to measure economic growth and the accompanying improvement in the standard of living.

1)   If real GDP (adjusted for inflation) rises at a faster rate than the population, the economy has an improved standard of living.

b.   Economic growth also can be measured as an increase in real GDP over a period of time.

2.   **Aggregate Supply and Demand**

   a.   The supply and demand curves used in microeconomics also can be used to analyze an economy.

   b.   Aggregate demand is a schedule reflecting all the goods and services that consumers are willing and able to buy at various price levels. The curve reflects the relationship between the price level and real GDP.

Aggregate Demand

Figure 3-3

   1)   Aggregate demand is downward sloping.

   2)   No distinction is made between a short-run and long-run aggregate demand curve.

   c.   Aggregate supply is a schedule reflecting all the goods and services an economy is willing and able to produce at various price levels.

Aggregate Supply

Figure 3-4

   1)   In the **short run**, changes in the price level induce firms to adjust their output to earn excess profits.

   a)   Unused productive capacity is available, and workers accept the prevailing wage.

   i)   The curve rises as more inputs are added to the production process.

2) In the **long run**, assuming full employment, any change in the price level is matched by a change in wages (and other input prices). Thus, firms' real profits do not change, and no additional output is produced.

    a) Because the change in the price level has no effect on output produced, the long-run aggregate supply curve is a vertical line at the level of full-employment GDP.

3. **Shifts in Aggregate Supply and Demand**

  a. **Growth** is a macroeconomic goal.

    1) When an economy grows, workers ordinarily earn higher real wages and have access to a greater variety and quantity of goods and services. Thus, the standard of living rises.

  b. An important factor that shifts the aggregate supply curve (AS) is a change in productivity.

    1) **Productivity** is usually measured by worker productivity, that is, the total real GDP produced during the year divided by the total number of hours worked in the economy. The more a worker can produce in an hour of work, the more productive (s)he is.

    2) Productivity depends on three factors:

      a) Amount of capital. The more an economy has invested in plant and machinery, the higher its productivity (more automation = higher productivity).

      b) State of technology. The more technologically advanced an economy's plants and machinery, the higher its productivity.

      c) Workforce competence. The more educated and trained an economy's workers, the higher its productivity.

  c. The following is one possibility for economic growth:

    1) An economy is in equilibrium at the intersection of the aggregate demand and aggregate supply curves.

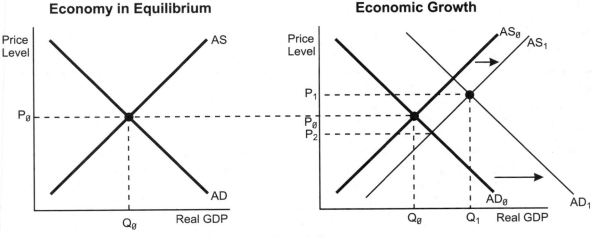

Figure 3-5

    2) New technology increases productivity, shifting the aggregate supply curve to the right (AS_1).

    3) Increased productivity generates additional income for workers and businesses. Additional income shifts the aggregate demand curve to the right (AD_1).

      a) Growth is the increase in real GDP from Q_0 to Q_1.

   4)   A rise in prices may or may not accompany growth.

      a)   The increase in the general price level from P_0 to P_1 depends on the extent to which aggregate demand increases relative to aggregate supply. This change in the price level is inflation.

      b)   If demand does not change, the rightward shift of the aggregate supply curve results in a lowering of the general price level from P_0 to P_2. This change in the price level is deflation.

4. **Factors in Economic Growth**

   a.   Supply Factors

      1)   Increase in productivity
      2)   Increase in the quantity and quality of natural resources

   b.   Demand Factors

      1)   Increase in total spending (Someone has to buy the additional output produced.)

   c.   Efficiency Factor

      1)   Efficient allocation of resources

5. **Policies for Economic Growth**

   a.   **Demand-side policies.** In modern economies, actors in a free market are not the only parties to the determination of aggregate demand.

      1)   The government can use the tools of fiscal policy and monetary policy to either stimulate or suppress demand, depending on whether a recessionary or inflationary environment is expected, respectively.

         a)   To encourage economic growth, stimulative policies are required.

   b.   **Supply-side policies.** The government also can increase the stock of investment capital. Businesses use this capital to increase their productive capacity, thereby increasing aggregate supply.

Stop and review! You have completed the outline for this subunit. Study multiple-choice questions 11 through 13 beginning on page 104.

3.5 INFLATION

1. **Overview**

The AICPA has tested topics related to inflation on recent CPA exams. Multiple-choice questions have asked how inflation is measured and inflation's effects on the economy.

   a.   Inflation is a sustained increase in the general level of prices. The reported rate of inflation is therefore an average of the increase across all prices in the economy. But this definition does not suffice to understand all the effects of inflation.

      1)   The value of any unit of money (e.g., the U.S. dollar) is measured by the goods and services that can be acquired in exchange for it. This measure is money's purchasing power.

b.   The percentage rate of inflation is calculated using a price index.

1)   A **price index** is a measure of the price of a market basket of goods and services in one year compared with the price in a designated base year. By definition, the index for the base year is 100.

a)   The rate of inflation is calculated by using the change in the index.

$$\frac{\textit{Current-year price index } - \textit{ Prior-year price index}}{\textit{Prior-year price index}}$$

EXAMPLE

If the price index of the market basket was 10% higher than the base year in Year 3 and was 15% higher in Year 4, the inflation rate for Year 4 is

$$\frac{115 - 110}{110} = 4.55\%$$

---

2)   The Consumer Price Index (CPI) is the most common price index for adjusting nominal GDP.

$$CPI = \frac{\textit{Cost of market basket in current year}}{\textit{Cost of market basket in base year}} \times 100$$

Background

The CPI is computed monthly by the Bureau of Labor Statistics (an agency of the U.S. Department of Labor). It measures changes in the general price level by a pricing of items on a typical urban household shopping list. According to the agency's website (www.bls.gov/cpi/), prices for the goods and services used to calculate the CPI are collected in 87 urban areas throughout the country and from about 23,000 retail and service establishments. Data on rents are collected from about 50,000 landlords or tenants. The base period for the CPI (i.e., the period for which the index equaled 100) is the period 1982-1984.

---

a)   The CPI also is a relevant tool in business analysis. For example, rising prices can reduce the purchasing power and profit of a business.

b)   To compare two monetary amounts in constant dollars, they must be deflated using the appropriate price index. The difference then must be divided by the prior period's amount.

EXAMPLE

A law firm is analyzing its revenue history. This year's billings were $1,080,000, and last year's were $950,000. This year's CPI is 115, and last year's was 107.

	Nominal Dollars		CPI		Constant Dollars
This year's billings:	$1,080,000	÷	1.15	=	$939,130
Last year's billings:	950,000	÷	1.07	=	887,850
Difference	$ 130,000				$ 51,280

Thus, nominal billings increased by 13.7% ($130,000 ÷ $950,000). But after adjusting for inflation, they increased by only 5.8% ($51,280 ÷ $887,850).

2. **Real Income vs. Nominal Income**

    a.   Nominal income is the money received by a consumer as wages, interest, rent, and profits. For example, a worker might have an annual salary, and therefore a nominal income, of $64,000.

    b.   Real income is the purchasing power of the income received. Purchasing power relates directly to the consumer's standard of living.

    c.   Real income decreases when the rate of increase in nominal income is less than the inflation rate.

3. **Macroeconomic Effects of Inflation**

    a.   Unexpected inflation can cause economic chaos.

    b.   The efficiency of business relationships relies on stable pricing.

4. **Effects on Financial Reporting**

    a.   In financial reporting, the principal effects of inflation are on inventory and depreciation.

    1)   In a last-in, first-out (LIFO) inventory accounting system, the most recently purchased goods are expensed first. In a period of rapidly rising prices, LIFO increases cost of goods sold and decreases operating income, thereby decreasing income tax liability.

    a)   If the entity uses first-in, first-out (FIFO) inventory accounting, cost of goods sold consists of lower inventory costs, thereby increasing operating income.

    2)   The depreciable base of a long-lived asset is its historical cost. During a period of rising prices, depreciation expense is lower than if it were stated in terms of replacement cost. Reported operating income is higher in the current period, but replacing such assets as they are retired is more expensive.

5. **Two Types of Inflation**

    a.   **Demand-pull inflation** is caused by an excess of demand over supply.

Figure 3-6

    1)   If the economy cannot produce enough to meet demand, the prices of existing goods increase.

2) In modern times, demand-pull inflation occurs when an economy approaches full employment and demand continues to increase.

b. **Cost-push inflation** is caused by increased per-unit production costs that are passed on to consumers as higher prices.

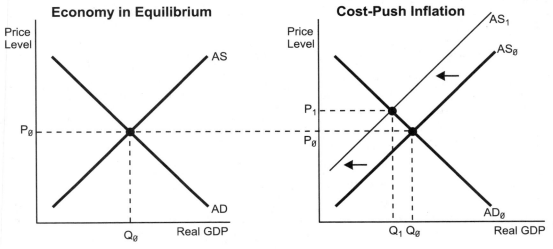

Figure 3-7

1) Increases in materials costs are the principal cause, particularly when they occur suddenly in the form of a **supply shock**.

6. **Deflation**

a. Deflation is a sustained decrease in the general price level. It is caused by conditions that are the opposite of those causing demand-pull and cost-push inflation.

1) A decrease in demand not accompanied by a decrease in supply causes a leftward shift of the aggregate demand curve. Firms sell inventory even if they incur losses. Prices and output fall.

2) An increase in output not accompanied by an increase in demand causes a rightward shift of the aggregate supply curve. Prices fall.

Stop and review! You have completed the outline for this subunit. Study multiple-choice questions 14 through 16 beginning on page 105.

3.6 UNEMPLOYMENT

1. **Overview**

   a. Unemployment is the failure of an economy to employ fully its labor force. The **unemployment rate** is stated in percentage terms.

$$\frac{Number\ of\ unemployed}{Size\ of\ labor\ force} \times 100$$

Background
The unemployment rate is based on the Current Population Survey, a monthly survey of households conducted by the U.S. Census Bureau on behalf of the Bureau of Labor Statistics (www.bls.gov/cps/).

2. **Labor Force**

   a. Understanding the official unemployment rate requires knowledge of its elements.

      1) The first group excluded from the calculation of the labor force (the equation's denominator) consists of those who are (a) under the age of 16 or (b) incarcerated or institutionalized.

      2) The second group excluded consists of the following individuals classified as **not** in the labor force.

         a) Homemakers, full-time students, and retirees.

         b) Discouraged workers. They are unemployed and able to work but are not actively seeking work.

      3) Among those included in the labor force, no distinction is made between full- and part-time workers. They are considered equally employed.

      4) The number of unemployed (the equation's numerator) consists of those who are willing and able to work and are seeking employment.

   b. The official statistics can be distorted by

      1) Workers who falsely claim to be seeking work or

      2) Those employed in the underground economy (e.g., cash-only-basis workers).

3. **Three Types of Unemployment**

   a. **Frictional unemployment** is the amount of unemployment caused by the normal workings of the labor market.

      1) This group can include those (a) moving to another location, (b) stopping work temporarily to obtain further education and training, and (c) who are between jobs.

      2) This definition acknowledges that normal unemployment exists at any given time in a dynamic economy.

   b. **Structural unemployment** results when

      1) The composition of the workforce does not match the need. It can be a result of changes in consumer demand or technology.

         a) The computer revolution has drastically changed the skills required for many jobs and completely eliminated others.

      2) The available jobs are not in the location where unemployed workers live.

    c. **Cyclical unemployment** is directly related to the level of an economy's output. It is likely to occur in the recession phase of the business cycle. For this reason, it is sometimes called **deficient-demand unemployment**.

        1) As consumers spend less, firms reduce production and lay off workers.

        2) The Great Depression of the 1930's was a period of low prices, low demand, and extremely low industrial output. During the worst of this period, as much as 25% of the American labor force was unemployed.

4. **Full Employment**

    a. The **natural rate of unemployment** consists of frictional and structural unemployment combined.

        1) Economists consider the economy to be at full employment when all unemployed workers fall into only these two categories (cyclical unemployment is omitted).

        2) The rate varies over time because of demographic and institutional changes in the economy.

    b. The economy's potential output is the real (i.e., inflation-adjusted) domestic output, or potential national income, that could be achieved if the economy sustained full employment.

        1) This concept illustrates the importance of providing all interested workers with productive jobs.

5. **Macroeconomic Effects of Unemployment**

    a. Lost value to the economy is the primary economic cost of unemployment. The goods not produced and services not provided by idle workers can never be regained.

        1) This loss is called the **GDP gap**. (GDP, or gross domestic product, is a measure of national output covered in Subunit 3.1.)

    b. Unemployment has social costs, including loss of skills, personal and family stress, violence and other crime, and social upheaval.

6. **Inflation and Unemployment**

    a. The theoretical relationship between inflation and employment can be described using the Phillips Curve.

    b. It is based on the historical inverse relationship between the rate of unemployment and the rate of inflation at a specific time.

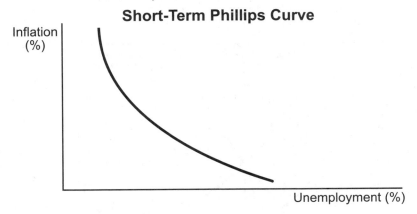

Figure 3-8

        1) The Phillips curve applies only in the short-term.

        2) In the long-term, inflationary policies do not decrease unemployment.

Stop and review! You have completed the outline for this subunit. Study multiple-choice questions 17 and 18 on page 106.

3.7 DEMAND MANAGEMENT THROUGH FISCAL POLICY

1. **Overview**

   a. Government affects the economy through its fiscal and monetary policies.

      1) Fiscal policy is the use of taxation and expenditures to reach macroeconomic objectives, taking in revenues (taxes) and making purchases (the annual budget).

      2) Monetary policy is covered in Subunit 3.9.

   b. Fiscal policies can be discretionary or nondiscretionary.

      1) **Discretionary** fiscal policy involves spending that is under the control of individuals within the government, such as contracting for new weapons systems.

      2) **Nondiscretionary** fiscal policy is enacted in law. Certain outlays, e.g., Social Security, must be made regardless of their consequences or source of funding because Congress has made them a legal requirement. No individual bureaucrat or group can choose to withhold (or increase) these expenditures.

   c. The following tools of fiscal policy are used by the government:

      1) Tax policy

      2) Government spending (highway maintenance, military buildup, etc.)

      3) Transfer payments (welfare, food stamps, unemployment compensation, etc.)

2. **Using Fiscal Policy**

   a. In the graph below, the economy's full employment output is $8.82 trillion.

Recessionary Gap and Demand Stimulus

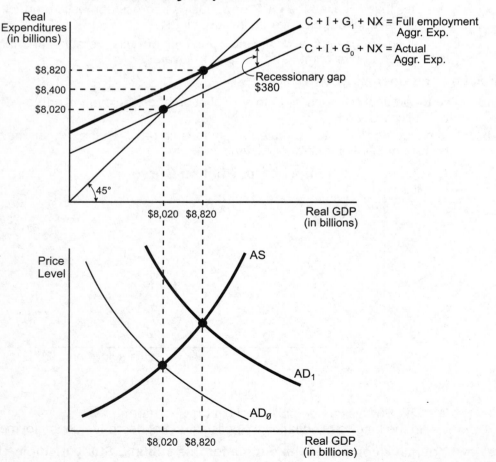

Figure 3-9

1) A change in consumer expectations leads to a decrease in consumption, causing the aggregate demand curve to shift to the left from AD_1 to AD_0 (assuming that prices can go down).

2) Recession and unemployment follow because real GDP decreased from $8,820 billion to $8,020 billion.

    a) The $380 billion recessionary gap causes an $800 billion negative GDP gap.

3) To promote growth and reduce unemployment, the federal government may increase its spending (G_1) by $380 billion ($G_1 = G_0 + \$380$ billion).

    a) Because of the multiplier effect, an increase in government spending of $380 billion suffices to increase real GDP by $800 billion.

    b) The **multiplier effect** occurs because each dollar spent by a consumer in the economy becomes another consumer's income, and so forth. The increase in the consumption for every additional dollar consumers receive in income is the **marginal propensity to consume (MPC)**. The remainder that was not spent is saved.

        i) Spending has a cumulative effect on the economy, greater than the initial amount. The multiplier in the economy is calculated as follows:

$$Multiplier = \frac{1}{(1 - MPC)}$$

        ii) The marginal propensity to consume (MPC) in the example is 0.525. Accordingly, the multiplier in the economy is 2.105 [$1 \div (1 - 0.525)$]. The government needs to increase its expenditures by only $380 billion to increase total GDP by $800 billion ($380 billion × 2.105).

4) The increase in government spending shifts the economy's aggregate demand curve to the right (from AD_0 to AD_1). The recessionary gap of $800 billion ($8,820 billion − $8,020 billion) is closed, and unemployment is reduced.

3. **Issues in Fiscal Policy**

    a. **Keynesian theory** calls for expansionary fiscal policy during times of recession (to stimulate aggregate demand) and contractionary policy during an expansion (to prevent inflation).

    b. If a recessionary gap exists, the government adopts **expansionary policies**.

        1) Taxes can be decreased and transfer payments increased, giving consumers more disposable income.

        2) Government can increase its spending, increasing demand for goods and services from the private sector.

    c. An **inflationary gap** is the amount by which the economy's aggregate expenditures at the full-employment GDP exceed those necessary to achieve full-employment GDP.

    d. If an inflationary gap exists, the government adopts **contractionary policies** to reduce aggregate demand.

        1) Taxes can be increased and transfer payments decreased, giving consumers less disposable income.

        2) Government can decrease its spending, reducing demand for goods and services from the private sector.

Stop and review! You have completed the outline for this subunit. Study multiple-choice questions 19 through 21 on page 107.

3.8 THE CREATION OF MONEY

1. **Three Uses of Money**

   a.   Medium of exchange. The existence of money greatly facilitates the free exchange of goods and services by providing a common means of valuation. Without money, all goods and services would have to be bartered, creating extraordinary inefficiencies.

   b.   Unit of account. Money also provides a convenient basis for bookkeeping. Anything stated in terms of money can be easily compared.

   c.   Store of value. Any society using the barter basis is subject to great inefficiencies. Many objects of great value, such as perishable food, spoil, making them worthless. The value of a unit of money is determined by the quantity of goods and services it can be exchanged for, not by its inherent characteristics.

2. **Interest Rates**

   a.   When money is borrowed, the debtor pays the lender an amount in addition to the sum that was borrowed (interest).

      1)   The two major determinants of the interest rate on a loan are

         a)   Overall economic conditions as reflected in the prime rate, which is the rate to the most credit-worthy customers, and

         b)   The creditworthiness of the borrower.

   b.   Economists distinguish between real and nominal interest rates.

      1)   The **nominal interest rate** is the stated rate on a loan.

      2)   The **real interest rate** equals the nominal rate minus the rate of inflation that the lender expects over the life of the loan.

         a)   The lender must charge this inflation premium to compensate for the purchasing power lost while the loan is at the borrower's disposal.

Figure 3-10

   c.   Misunderstandings over the difference between real and nominal interest rates can lead to distortions in the economy.

      1)   For example, a loan bearing 10% interest may seem excessive to a borrower. But if inflation is 8%, the borrower is paying a real rate of only 2%.

      2)   For example, a loan bearing 6% interest may seem to be a bargain. But if inflation is 1%, the borrower is actually paying 5% real interest.

3. **The Supply of Money**

   a.   The U.S. Federal Reserve System tracks and reports the amount of money in circulation.

      1)   The metrics used by the Fed are called M1 and M2. M1 includes only the most liquid forms of money. M2 includes M1 and less-liquid forms of money.

EXAMPLE

The following is a hypothetical money supply calculation for an economy the approximate size of the U.S.:

	In Billions
Currency (paper money + coins)	$ 600
Checking accounts	700
M1 money supply	**$1,300**
Savings accounts, including	
money market accounts	2,900
Small time deposits (< $100,000)	1,400
Money market mutual funds	800
M2 money supply	**$6,400**

Background

Although they need not be memorized for the CPA exam, the Federal Reserve's latest Money Stock Measures are at www.federalreserve.gov/releases/h6/current/h6.htm.

---

4. **Banks and the Creation of Money**

a. The example M1 money supply calculation illustrates that paper money and coins (currency) are less than half the total.

1) The money in the economy greatly exceeds the currency in circulation because of the creation of money by banks.

EXAMPLE

A bank customer deposits $1,000, and the bank then lends $800. The depositor's statement shows that (s)he has a claim to $1,000 of cash, and the borrower has $800 of cash. Thus, $1,800 exists when only $1,000 existed previously. The bank has created $800.

Background

From its founding, the United States tended to view a central bank as an anti-democratic institution. Thus, instead of having a single central bank like many other countries, the United States has 12 regional Federal Reserve Banks. The Federal Reserve, established in 1913, is independent of the rest of the federal government. This independence, and the long terms of its members, protect the Fed's decisions from political pressures. The Board of Governors is responsible for overseeing the operations of the Federal Reserve System. The Federal Open Market Committee (FOMC) is responsible for administering monetary policy.

In today's world, the actions taken by the Federal Reserve receive extensive media coverage. Be prepared to answer questions about policies pursued of the Federal Reserve for different economic situations.

---

5. **Bank Reserves**

a. Fractional reserve banking is the practice of prohibiting banks from lending all the money they receive on deposit.

b. The required **reserve ratio** is the percentage of each dollar deposited that a bank is required to either (1) keep in its vault or (2) deposit with the Federal Reserve Bank in its district.

1) The minimum that must be held by law is required reserves.

Background

For example, the Fed recently required medium-sized banks to keep 3% in reserve (in the vault or on deposit with the district Fed). An explanation and a complete table of the current reserve requirements are at www.federalreserve.gov/monetarypolicy/reservereq.htm.

---

        a)   The amount of customer deposits that exceeds required reserves is **excess reserves**. It is from excess reserves that the bank makes loans.

    2)   Fractional reserves obviously do not suffice to prevent a bank's collapse in the event customers withdraw excessive amounts. This function is performed by the Federal Deposit Insurance Corporation.

        a)   The actual purpose of required reserves is to provide the Fed with another tool for controlling the money supply.

c.   The amount of money banks potentially can create is approximated using the monetary multiplier.

$$Monetary\ multiplier = \frac{1}{Required\ reserve\ ratio}$$

    1)   The money supply decreases as required reserves are raised.

EXAMPLE

If the Fed requires reserves of 4% on all deposits, a bank with $10 million on deposit can create $250 million of new money [$10,000,000 × (1.0 ÷ .04)].

Stop and review! You have completed the outline for this subunit. Study multiple-choice questions 22 through 25 beginning on page 107.

3.9 MONETARY POLICY

1.   **Goals and Tools of Monetary Policy**

    a.   The Fed balances the goals of gradual, steady economic growth and price stability (manageable inflation).

       1)   The Fed has three tools of monetary policy:

          a)   Open-market operations
          b)   The required reserve ratio
          c)   The discount rate

       2)   Fiscal and monetary policy can be combined to influence aggregate demand.

    b.   **Open-market operations** are the Fed's strongest tool. It can choose potential effects that are immediate and range from large to small.

       1)   U.S. Treasury securities are traded on the open market. The Fed can either purchase them from, or sell them to, commercial banks.

          a)   When the Fed wishes to increase the money supply, it purchases Treasury securities. It removes securities from the market and injects money.

          b)   When the Fed wishes to decrease the money supply, it sells Treasury securities. It removes money from the economy and injects securities.

       2)   The **Federal funds rate** is the rate banks charge each other for overnight loans.

          a)   A bank's excess reserves do not have to be idle. They can be lent on a short-term basis to banks with deficient reserves.

      i)   The following graph depicts the relationship between the money supply (S_0 and S_1) and the interest rate (r):

Figure 3-11

    b)   When the Fed buys Treasury securities, the money supply increases and the Federal funds rate falls. When the Fed sells Treasury securities, the money supply decreases and the Federal funds rate rises.

  3)   The following table summarizes the effects of changes in the money supply resulting from open-market operations:

Increase Money Supply	Decrease Money Supply
1. The Fed expects a **recession**.	1. The Fed expects higher **inflation**.
2. The Fed **buys securities** on the open market.	2. The Fed **sells securities** on the open market.
3. The Fed **credits cash to reserve accounts** of banks selling securities.	3. The Fed **decreases cash in reserve accounts** of banks buying securities.
• The increase in cash **creates excess reserves**. Banks are more willing to lend.	• The decrease in cash **reduces excess reserves**. Banks are less able to lend.
• Greater availability of cash for overnight loans decreases the **Federal funds rate.**	• Lower availability of cash for overnight loans **increases the Federal funds rate.**
4. Lower interest rates stimulate investment spending by businesses.	4. Higher interest rates discourage investment spending by businesses.
5. Greater investment spending increases aggregate demand (a shift to the right), increasing real GDP and decreasing unemployment.	5. Lower investment spending decreases aggregate demand (a shift to the left), decreasing inflation.

  c.   Changes in the required **reserve ratio** are used less frequently. Requiring banks to retain more funds in reserve accounts reduces profits.

    1)   Lowering the reserve ratio increases the money supply.

        a)   If reserves decrease, banks have more money to lend.

    2)   Raising the reserve ratio decreases the money supply.

        a)   If reserves increase, banks have less money to lend.

d.   The **discount rate** is the rate Federal Reserve banks charge for short-term loans to commercial banks.

    1)   Increasing the discount rate reduces borrowing and the money supply.

        a)   Banks are most likely to borrow from the Fed because of temporary shortages of reserves. If such loans are more expensive, banks are more likely to increase reserves to ensure that borrowing is unnecessary.

    2)   Decreasing the discount rate increases borrowing and the money supply.

Background

The widely-held belief is that (1) the Fed is a lender of last resort and (2) borrowing from the Fed is a sign of financial weakness. Thus, banks tend to do so only in emergencies and prefer that the Fed maintain their anonymity.

The direct provision of cash by the Federal Reserve is not publicized. As reported in *Bloomberg Businessweek* on August 22, 2011, the Fed quietly lent $669 billion to the 10 largest U.S. banks during the market crisis of late 2008, an amount that far exceeded the widely discussed $160 billion bailout by the U.S. Treasury. The magazine could only report this information after "compilation of data obtained through Freedom of Information Act requests, months of litigation, and an act of Congress." Including both U.S. and foreign banks (e.g., Royal Bank of Scotland, UBS AG), the Fed had $1.2 trillion in loans outstanding on December 5, 2008.

Stop and review! You have completed the outline for this subunit. Study multiple-choice questions 26 through 30 beginning on page 108.

QUESTIONS
3.1 Domestic Output -- Expenditures Approach

1. Which of the following is **not** included in the gross domestic product (GDP)?

    A.   Purchase of a new home.

    B.   Investment in new computers.

    C.   A doctor's fee.

    D.   Purchase of common stock.

Answer (D) is correct.
    REQUIRED: The transaction not included in GDP.
    DISCUSSION: GDP is the value of all final goods and services produced in the U.S., whether by domestic or foreign-owned sources, during a specified period. A common stock purchase is not a new good or service. It is instead a claim to ownership of property that already exists.
    Answer (A) is incorrect. A new home is a productive good and is included in GDP. Answer (B) is incorrect. An investment in productive assets is part of GDP. Answer (C) is incorrect. The doctor's services were produced during the year. His or her fee is part of GDP.

2. The level of aggregate demand will decline if the level of

    A.   Imports decreases.

    B.   Investment spending decreases.

    C.   Consumption spending increases.

    D.   Government spending increases.

Answer (B) is correct.
    REQUIRED: The activity that causes aggregate demand to decline.
    DISCUSSION: A decrease in investment spending and decreases in consumption or government spending will cause demand to decline.
    Answer (A) is incorrect. A decrease in imports results in an increase in aggregate demand. Answer (C) is incorrect. An increase in consumption spending will result in an increase in aggregate demand. Answer (D) is incorrect. An increase in government spending will increase aggregate demand.

3. Which one of the following components of gross domestic product (GDP) has the greatest fluctuation from year to year?

    A.   Personal consumption expenditures.

    B.   Gross domestic private investment.

    C.   Government spending.

    D.   Net exports.

Answer (B) is correct.
    REQUIRED: The component of GDP fluctuating the most from year to year.
    DISCUSSION: By far the most volatile component of GDP is business investment. Investment reflects the level of businesses' optimism about future demand, and business optimism is subject to sudden variations.
    Answer (A) is incorrect. Personal consumption, while the largest component of GDP, is not the most volatile. Answer (C) is incorrect. Government spending is not as volatile a component of GDP as business investment. Answer (D) is incorrect. Net exports are subject to less variability from year to year than gross domestic private investment.

3.2 Domestic Output -- Income Approach

4. Personal income is equal to

A. Gross domestic product minus net national product.

B. Net domestic product plus transfer payments to individuals.

C. Disposable income minus personal tax payments.

D. Disposable income plus personal tax payments.

Answer (D) is correct.

REQUIRED: The factors calculated in personal income.

DISCUSSION: Personal income is all income received by individuals, whether earned or unearned. It equals disposable income plus taxes.

Answer (A) is incorrect. GDP minus net domestic product equals depreciation (the capital consumption allowance). Answer (B) is incorrect. Net domestic product plus transfer payments to individuals does not define a meaningful national income concept. Answer (C) is incorrect. Disposable income equals personal income minus personal income taxes. Thus, adding personal taxes to disposable income results in personal income.

5. Using the income approach, calculate the national income used to calculate GDP with the information provided below:

Interest:	$ 8,000
Salaries and wages:	50,000
Net foreign factor income:	7,000
Partnership income:	10,000
Rents:	20,000
Indirect business taxes:	1,000
Corporate profits:	25,000
Proprietor income:	4,000

A. $107,000

B. $117,000

C. $118,000

D. $124,000

Answer (B) is correct.

REQUIRED: The calculation of national income using the income approach for measuring GDP.

DISCUSSION: National income is calculated using the following formula: national income = salaries and wages + rents + interest + proprietor and partnership incomes + corporate profits. Thus, national income equals $117,000 ($50,000 + $20,000 + $8,000 + $4,000 + $10,000 + $25,000).

Answer (A) is incorrect. Proprietor and partnership income should be included in national income. Answer (C) is incorrect. National income does not include indirect business taxes. Answer (D) is incorrect. The calculation of national income does not include net foreign factor income.

6. Disposable income is equal to

A. All earned income received.

B. Earned income minus unearned income.

C. Income after taxes have been removed.

D. National income minus personal income.

Answer (C) is correct.

REQUIRED: The definition of disposable income.

DISCUSSION: Disposable income is the personal income of individuals after subtraction of taxes.

Answer (A) is incorrect. Disposable income is not limited to all earned income received. Answer (B) is incorrect. Earned income and unearned income are included in disposable income. Answer (D) is incorrect. National income minus personal income equals transfer payments minus the sum of social security contributions, corporate income taxes, and undistributed corporate profits.

7. Each of the following is a limitation of GDP's usefulness as a measure of a nation's prosperity **except**

A. No practical means are available to compare real GDP from different time periods.

B. GDP leaves out intermediate goods.

C. Increases in GDP often involve environmental damage.

D. Cash-only economic activity is not counted in GDP.

Answer (A) is correct.

REQUIRED: The item not a limitation of GDP's usefulness as a measure of national prosperity.

DISCUSSION: Various price indexes, such as the Bureau of Labor Statistics' Consumer Price Index and the GDP deflator, are suitable for converting nominal GDP amounts from different years to comparable amounts in terms of a base year.

Answer (B) is incorrect. GDP includes only final goods and services. Economic activity that leads to intermediate goods is omitted. Answer (C) is incorrect. Increases in GDP often involve environmental damage, such as noise, congestion, or pollution. Answer (D) is incorrect. Cash-only economic activity is not counted in GDP.

3.3 Business Cycles

8. Which of the following may provide a leading indicator of a future increase in gross domestic product?

    A. A reduction in the money supply.

    B. A decrease in the issuance of building permits.

    C. An increase in the timeliness of delivery by vendors.

    D. An increase in the average hours worked per week of production workers.

Answer (D) is correct.
    REQUIRED: The leading indicator of an increase in GDP.
    DISCUSSION: An economic indicator is highly correlated with changes in aggregate economic activity. A leading indicator changes prior to a change in the direction of the business cycle. The leading indicators included in the Conference Board's index are (1) average weekly hours worked by manufacturing workers, (2) unemployment claims, (3) consumer goods orders, (4) stock prices, (5) orders for fixed assets, (6) building permits, (7) timeliness of deliveries, (8) money supply, (9) consumer confidence, and (10) the spread between the yield on 10-year Treasury bonds and the federal funds rate. An increase in weekly hours worked by production workers is favorable for economic growth.
    Answer (A) is incorrect. A falling money supply is associated with falling GDP. Answer (B) is incorrect. A decline in the issuance of building permits signals lower expected building activity and a falling GDP. Answer (C) is incorrect. An increase in the timeliness of delivery by vendors indicates slacking business demand and a potentially falling GDP.

9. All of the following are stages of the business cycle **except**

    A. Peak.

    B. Trough.

    C. Recovery.

    D. Acceleration.

Answer (D) is correct.
    REQUIRED: The item that is not a stage in the business cycle.
    DISCUSSION: A business cycle has four stages: the trough, recovery, peak, and recession. Acceleration is not one of the stages.
    Answer (A) is incorrect. Peak is one of the stages in the business cycle. Answer (B) is incorrect. Trough is one of the stages in the business cycle. Answer (C) is incorrect. Recovery is one of the stages in the business cycle.

10. Diana has noticed that many of her coworkers at Bubble, Inc., have been laid off over the past year due to low profits. Also, prices were lowered recently due to economic conditions. Even though Diana is worried about her future at Bubble, she has noticed that employment has risen over the past month and that prices are slowly increasing. Because other companies have had the same experience, what phase of the business cycle is the economy currently in?

    A. Peak.

    B. Recession.

    C. Trough.

    D. Recovery.

Answer (D) is correct.
    REQUIRED: The phases of the business cycle.
    DISCUSSION: During a recovery, employment rises. The price level eventually also rises. Employment has been increasing in many companies, and the price level is slowly recovering.
    Answer (A) is incorrect. At a peak, the economy is at or near full employment. Answer (B) is incorrect. A recession is a period during which unemployment rises. Answer (C) is incorrect. In a trough, employment reaches its lowest point.

3.4 Growth

11. One of the measures economists and economic policy makers use to gauge a nation's economic growth is to calculate the change in the

    A. Money supply.

    B. Total wages.

    C. General price level.

    D. Real per capita output.

Answer (D) is correct.
    REQUIRED: The measure used by economists to gauge economic growth.
    DISCUSSION: Real per-capita output is defined as the GDP adjusted for changes in the general price level and divided by the population. It is often used to measure the standard of living.
    Answer (A) is incorrect. The change in the money supply is not a direct measure of the nation's output. Answer (B) is incorrect. The change in total wages is not a direct measure of the nation's output. Answer (C) is incorrect. The change in the general price level is not a direct measure of the nation's output.

12. Which one of the following factors would cause the aggregate supply curve shown below to shift from AS_1 to AS_2?

A. An improvement in technology.

B. A higher resource price.

C. An increase in the expected rate of inflation.

D. A decrease in productivity.

Answer (A) is correct.

REQUIRED: The factor causing a rightward shift in the aggregate supply curve.

DISCUSSION: A shift of the entire aggregate supply curve as opposed to a movement along a given curve is caused by any of three determinants of aggregate demand: a change in input prices, a change in productivity, or a change in the legal-institutional environment in which the industry operates. An improvement in technology leads to greater productivity and thus to an outward shift in aggregate supply.

Answer (B) is incorrect. Higher resource prices lead to a leftward shift of aggregate supply. Answer (C) is incorrect. An increase in the expected rate of inflation causes consumers to purchase more goods before prices increase. This effect is represented as a movement along the aggregate demand curve. Answer (D) is incorrect. A decrease in productivity means a loss of efficiency by businesses, reflected in a leftward shift in aggregate supply.

13. An improvement in technology that in turn leads to improved worker productivity would most likely result in

A. A shift to the right in the supply curve and a lowering of the price of the output.

B. A shift to the left in the supply curve and a lowering of the price of the output.

C. An increase in the price of the output if demand is unchanged.

D. A decrease in real wages.

Answer (A) is correct.

REQUIRED: The result of improved technology and improved worker productivity.

DISCUSSION: Enhanced technology and worker productivity cause the supply curve to shift to the right, where it intersects with the demand curve at a lower price level. The shift is caused by the producer's ability to lower costs and produce more at a given market price.

Answer (B) is incorrect. Increased productivity causes a rightward shift in the supply curve. Answer (C) is incorrect. The rightward shift results in an intersection with the demand curve at a lower price. Answer (D) is incorrect. Improved productivity leads to lower prices, an increase in real wages.

3.5 Inflation

14. Demand-pull inflation occurs when

A. Incomes rise suddenly.

B. There are excessive wage increases.

C. There are rapid increases in raw materials prices.

D. There are substantial changes in energy prices.

Answer (A) is correct.

REQUIRED: The cause of demand-pull inflation.

DISCUSSION: When incomes rise suddenly, consumers demand more of everything, driving up the price level.

Answer (B) is incorrect. Excessive wage increases result in cost-push inflation. Answer (C) is incorrect. A rapid increase in materials prices is a supply shock. It may be the cause of stagflation but not of demand-pull inflation. Answer (D) is incorrect. Changes in the prices of an important input can be increases or decreases. Thus, they do not necessarily predict inflation.

15. Bank is willing to lend a business $1 million at an annual real interest rate of 6%. What is the nominal rate Bank will charge the firm if the rate of inflation is anticipated to be 2%?

A. 2%

B. 4%

C. 6%

D. 8%

Answer (D) is correct.

REQUIRED: The interest rate a bank charges at a given rate of inflation.

DISCUSSION: If the bank requires a real return of 6%, a 2% inflation rate results in an 8% nominal rate.

Answer (A) is incorrect. The expected rate of inflation is 2%. Answer (B) is incorrect. The expected rate of inflation increases, not decreases, the nominal rate. Answer (C) is incorrect. The rate given zero inflation is 6%.

16. Assume that real gross domestic product (GDP), measured in Year 1 dollars, rose from $3,000 billion in Year 1 to $4,500 billion in Year 10. Assume also that the price index rose from 100 to 200 during the same period. The GDP for Year 1 expressed in terms of Year 10 prices is

   A. $1,500 billion.

   B. $3,000 billion.

   C. $4,500 billion.

   D. $6,000 billion.

Answer (D) is correct.
   REQUIRED: The GDP for Year 1 adjusted for inflation.
   DISCUSSION: Between Year 1 and Year 10, the price index doubled (from 100 to 200). Thus, the nominal value of Year 1 GDP ($3,000 billion) also must be doubled when restated in Year 10 terms. The Year 1 GDP in Year 10 prices is $6,000 billion.
   Answer (A) is incorrect. The amount of $1,500 billion assumes deflation rather than inflation from Year 1 to Year 10. Answer (B) is incorrect. The amount of $3,000 billion is the nominal value of the Year 1 GDP. Answer (C) is incorrect. The amount of $4,500 billion is the actual year GDP. The question asks about the restated Year 1 GDP.

3.6 Unemployment

17. The rate of unemployment caused by changes in the composition of employment opportunities over time is referred to as the

   A. Frictional unemployment rate.

   B. Cyclical unemployment rate.

   C. Structural unemployment rate.

   D. Full employment unemployment rate.

Answer (C) is correct.
   REQUIRED: The rate of unemployment caused by changes in the composition of employment opportunities over time.
   DISCUSSION: Economists define full employment as occurring when cyclical unemployment is zero. Thus, the natural rate of unemployment (the full employment unemployment rate) equals the sum of structural and frictional unemployment. Cyclical unemployment is caused by insufficient aggregate demand. Frictional unemployment occurs when both jobs and the workers qualified to fill them are available. This definition acknowledges that workers change jobs, are laid off, abandon paid work temporarily, etc. Structural unemployment exists when aggregate demand is sufficient to provide full employment, but the distribution of the demand does not correspond precisely to the composition of the labor force. This form of unemployment results when the required job skills or the geographic distribution of jobs change.
   Answer (A) is incorrect. Frictional unemployment results from imperfections in the labor market. Answer (B) is incorrect. Cyclical unemployment is caused by a deficiency of aggregate spending. Answer (D) is incorrect. The full employment unemployment rate is the sum of frictional and structural unemployment.

18. Below are the recent monthly unemployment figures for an economy:

Persons moving to a new city and seeking work	100,000
Persons out of work because their industry has just been rendered obsolete by technological change	12,000
Persons in all industries laid off due to general economic slowdown	120,000
Persons taking 2 months off from work to pursue education	100,000

Applying the Bureau of Labor Statistics' guidelines for calculating the official unemployment statistics, what is the "natural" level of unemployment for this economy?

   A. 200,000

   B. 212,000

   C. 232,000

   D. 320,000

Answer (B) is correct.
   REQUIRED: The total number of persons included in the natural level of unemployment.
   DISCUSSION: The natural level of unemployment includes (1) the frictionally unemployed (those moving to another city, those ceasing work temporarily to pursue further education and training, those who are simply between jobs) and (2) the structurally unemployed (those put out of work by changes in consumer demand, technology, and geographical location of industries). The remainder are the cyclically unemployed, that is, those who are out of work because of the generally low output of the economy as a whole (called deficient-demand unemployment for this reason). In this example, frictional unemployment amounts to 200,000 (100,000 + 100,000), and structural unemployment amounts to 12,000, for a total natural level of unemployment of 212,000.
   Answer (A) is incorrect. The amount of 200,000 fails to include the former workers in the obsolete industry who are among the structurally unemployed. Answer (C) is incorrect. The amount of 232,000 improperly includes the 120,000 cyclically unemployed. Answer (D) is incorrect. The amount of 320,000 improperly excludes the 12,000 structurally unemployed former workers in the obsolete industry and improperly includes the 120,000 cyclically unemployed.

3.7   Demand Management through Fiscal Policy

19. What is the recessionary gap if the economy's full-employment real gross domestic product (GDP) is $1.2 trillion and its equilibrium real GDP is $1.0 trillion?

- A. $200 billion.
- B. $200 billion divided by the multiplier.
- C. $200 billion multiplied by the multiplier.
- D. $200 billion times the reciprocal of the marginal propensity to consume.

Answer (B) is correct.
REQUIRED: The amount of the recessionary gap.
DISCUSSION: The $200 billion difference between full-employment GDP and equilibrium GDP can be eliminated by additional consumption, government spending, or exports. Because of the multiplier effect, the amount of the increase can be less than $200 billion. The amount of additional activity necessary to close the gap is ($200 billion ÷ multiplier).
Answer (A) is incorrect. The amount of $200 billion ignores the effect of the multiplier. Answer (C) is incorrect. The amount of $200 billion should be divided by the multiplier. Answer (D) is incorrect. The multiplier is based on the reciprocal of the MPS, not the MPC.

20. If a government were to use only fiscal policy to stimulate the economy from a recession, it would

- A. Raise consumer taxes and increase government spending.
- B. Lower business taxes and government spending.
- C. Increase the money supply and increase government spending.
- D. Lower consumer taxes and increase government spending.

Answer (D) is correct.
REQUIRED: The actions taken if a government were to use only fiscal policy to stimulate the economy.
DISCUSSION: According to Keynesian economics, fiscal policy should be expansionary when the economy is in recession. Increases in government spending, decreases in taxation, or both have a stimulative effect. To achieve this effect, the increase in spending should not be matched by a tax increase, the effect of which is contractionary. Thus, deficit spending is the result of an expansionary fiscal policy.
Answer (A) is incorrect. Raising consumer taxes is contractionary. Answer (B) is incorrect. Lower government spending is contractionary. Answer (C) is incorrect. Increasing the supply of money involves monetary, not fiscal, policy.

21. During a recession, the goal of government fiscal policy is to raise equilibrium output. An appropriate governmental action in this situation is to

- A. Decrease government spending.
- B. Increase government taxes.
- C. Increase government spending.
- D. Increase government taxes and decrease government spending by equal amounts.

Answer (C) is correct.
REQUIRED: The governmental action to increase domestic output.
DISCUSSION: According to Keynesian economics, the sum of personal after-tax consumption expenditures, gross investment, net exports, and government spending equals gross domestic product (GDP) at equilibrium. At this output level, aggregate expenditures equal real aggregate domestic output. Thus, an increase in government spending, with other factors held constant, increases equilibrium GDP, that is, equilibrium output.
Answer (A) is incorrect. A decrease in government spending by itself decreases equilibrium output. Answer (B) is incorrect. An increase in government taxes by itself decreases personal consumption and equilibrium output. Answer (D) is incorrect. An increase in government taxes by itself decreases personal consumption and equilibrium output. A decrease in government spending by itself decreases equilibrium output.

3.8   The Creation of Money

22. The creation of deposit money by U.S. commercial banks increases the

- A. Real wealth of the United States.
- B. Real U.S. national income.
- C. U.S. money supply.
- D. Purchasing power of the U.S. dollar.

Answer (C) is correct.
REQUIRED: The effect of the creation of deposit money by U.S. commercial banks.
DISCUSSION: As money is deposited in banks, the banks lend the money to qualified customers. Banks may lend only a certain percentage of their funds because of the reserve requirement. The more funds they have, the more they can lend. Thus, as the amount of money deposited increases, the amount and number of loans and the money supply increase.
Answer (A) is incorrect. Real wealth is not directly affected by the creation of deposit money. Answer (B) is incorrect. National income is not directly affected by the creation of deposit money. Answer (D) is incorrect. The purchasing power of the dollar (amount of goods that can be bought with a dollar) may well be decreased by the expansion of the money supply.

23. The Federal Reserve System's reserve ratio is the

- A. Specified percentage of a commercial bank's deposit liabilities that must be deposited in the central bank or kept on hand.
- B. Rate that the central bank charges for loans granted to commercial banks.
- C. Ratio of excess reserves to legal reserves that are deposited in the central bank.
- D. Specified percentage of a commercial bank's demand deposits to total liabilities.

Answer (A) is correct.
    REQUIRED: The definition of the reserve ratio.
    DISCUSSION: The reserve ratio is the percentage of the customer deposits that banks must keep on hand or deposit with the Fed. These deposits are required by law to ensure the soundness of the bank and also serve as a tool for monetary policy. Accordingly, changes in the reserve ratio affect the money supply.
    Answer (B) is incorrect. The discount rate is the rate the Fed charges for loans to commercial banks. Answer (C) is incorrect. Excess reserves are amounts in excess of the reserve requirement. Answer (D) is incorrect. The reserve ratio is the ratio of required reserves to demand deposits.

24. A bank with a reserve ratio of 20% and reserves of $1,000,000 can increase its total demand deposits by

- A. $5,000,000
- B. $1,000,000
- C. $800,000
- D. $200,000

Answer (A) is correct.
    REQUIRED: The amount by which a bank can increase its total demand deposits given the reserve ratio and the amount of reserves.
    DISCUSSION: The amount of new money a bank can create equals actual reserves times the monetary multiplier (or divided by the required reserve ratio). This bank therefore can increase total demand deposits by $5,000,000 ($1,000,000 ÷ 0.2).
    Answer (B) is incorrect. Reserves need to be only 20% of deposits. Accordingly, an increase in reserves supports a 500% increase in deposits. Answer (C) is incorrect. The amount of $800,000 equals the increase in net lendable funds, assuming a $1,000,000 increase in deposits. Answer (D) is incorrect. The reserve is 20% of deposits, not the reverse.

25. The money supply in a nation's economy will decrease following

- A. Open-market purchases by the nation's central bank.
- B. A decrease in the discount rate.
- C. An increase in the reserve ratio.
- D. A decrease in the margin requirement.

Answer (C) is correct.
    REQUIRED: The item that causes a decrease in the money supply.
    DISCUSSION: The reserve ratio is the minimum percentage of its deposits that a bank must keep on deposit with the Federal Reserve or in its vault. When the reserve ratio increases, banks must maintain larger reserves, and less money is available for lending and investment. Consequently, the money supply decreases.
    Answer (A) is incorrect. Open-market purchases by the central bank increase the money supply by increasing commercial banks' reserves. Answer (B) is incorrect. A decrease in the rate charged to member banks for loans by the Federal Reserve (the discount rate) increases the money supply by increasing bank reserves. Answer (D) is incorrect. A decrease in the margin requirement decreases the minimum down payment that purchasers of stock must make. This credit control affects the stock market and has no direct impact on the money supply.

3.9 Monetary Policy

26. Providing an adequate supply of money to accommodate the needs of U.S. business is the task of the

- A. United States Treasury.
- B. Controller of the Currency.
- C. Bureau of Printing and Engraving.
- D. Federal Reserve System.

Answer (D) is correct.
    REQUIRED: The entity responsible for providing an adequate money supply.
    DISCUSSION: The Federal Reserve Board (the Fed) controls the money supply independently of the federal government. Any policy implemented by the Fed to affect the money supply, and therefore the economy, is monetary policy. Control of the growth of the money supply by the Fed is essential to control (1) the availability of credit, (2) spending, and (3) inflation. One reason is that the money supply must grow at the same rate as the economy for the economy to be completely healthy.
    Answer (A) is incorrect. The Treasury is responsible for governmental receipts and expenditures. Answer (B) is incorrect. The Controller of the Currency regulates and charters banks. Answer (C) is incorrect. The Bureau of Engraving and Printing prints money as authorized by the Fed.

27. All of the following actions are valid tools that the Federal Reserve Bank uses to control the supply of money **except**

- A. Buying government securities.
- B. Selling government securities.
- C. Changing the reserve ratio.
- D. Printing money when the level of M1 appears low.

Answer (D) is correct.
 REQUIRED: The item that is not a valid tool of the Fed in controlling the money supply.
 DISCUSSION: The amount of money to print is a decision for the Department of the Treasury (an executive branch agency), not the Federal Reserve (an independent agency). Moreover, paper currency and coins make up only about half of the M1 money supply. The Fed has other, more complex tools for implementing monetary policy.
 Answer (A) is incorrect. Buying government securities is one method the Fed uses to control the money supply. Answer (B) is incorrect. Selling government securities is one method the Fed uses to control the money supply. Answer (C) is incorrect. Changing the reserve ratio is one method the Fed uses to control the money supply.

28. The primary mechanism of monetary control of the Federal Reserve System is

- A. Changing the discount rate.
- B. Conducting open market operations.
- C. Changing reserve requirements.
- D. Using moral persuasion.

Answer (B) is correct.
 REQUIRED: The primary mechanism of monetary control used by the Fed.
 DISCUSSION: Open market operations (buying and selling government securities) are the primary means used by the Fed to control the money supply. Fed purchases are expansionary. They increase bank reserves and the money supply. Fed sales are contractional. If money is paid into the Federal Reserve, bank reserves are reduced, and the money supply decreases.
 Answer (A) is incorrect. Changing the discount rate is a less important tool of monetary policy. Answer (C) is incorrect. Changing reserve requirements is a less important tool of monetary policy. Answer (D) is incorrect. Moral persuasion is not a means of controlling the money supply.

29. In order for the Federal Reserve System to increase the money supply, the appropriate policy is to

- A. Encourage banks to increase their holdings of excess reserves.
- B. Increase the discount rate.
- C. Engage in open-market purchases of government securities.
- D. Raise margin requirements on stock market purchases.

Answer (C) is correct.
 REQUIRED: The Fed's policy to increase the money supply.
 DISCUSSION: Open-market purchases of government securities put more money into circulation. Amounts previously unavailable are placed into the hands of the public by the open-market purchase of government securities.
 Answer (A) is incorrect. An increase in excess reserves or reserve requirements means that member banks can make fewer loans. Thus, less money is introduced into the economy. Answer (B) is incorrect. If the discount rate is raised, member banks borrow less from the Fed to lend to their customers. Answer (D) is incorrect. An increase in margin requirements means that investors borrow less.

30. Which of the following results could be expected from an open market operation of the Federal Reserve?

- A. A sale of securities would lower interest rates.
- B. A purchase of securities would raise interest rates.
- C. A purchase of securities would lower security prices.
- D. A sale of securities would raise interest rates.

Answer (D) is correct.
 REQUIRED: The expected result from the given open market operation.
 DISCUSSION: A sale of securities removes money from the economy and reduces bank reserves. Thus, banks cannot lend as much as previously, and higher interest rates follow. Money supply and interest rates are inversely related.
 Answer (A) is incorrect. A sale increases interest rates. Answer (B) is incorrect. A purchase of securities increases reserves, allows banks to make more loans, and results in lower interest rates. Answer (C) is incorrect. A purchase of securities removes securities from the economy, increasing securities prices.

3.10 PRACTICE WRITTEN COMMUNICATION

| Business Environment and Concepts Testlet 4 of 4 | Time Remaining 1 hour - 15 minutes | Unsplit Split Horiz Split Vertical Exit |

DIRECTIONS

Note: If you believe you have encountered a software malfunction, report it to the test center staff immediately.

Navigation

To navigate from task to task, use the controls at the bottom of the screen. Click on the **Next** button to advance to the next task, or the **Previous** button to go to the previous task. To go directly to any task, click on its number.

If you would like a reminder to revisit a task, or want to indicate that you are finished with it, click on the reminder flag below the task number. To clear the flag, click on it again. Reminder flags are for your use only – they do not contribute to your score.

Tabs

In this part of the examination, you will be asked to complete various tasks. Every task has one or more **Work Tabs**. Every task also has a **Help** tab.

Work tab   Help tab

Work Tabs:

- **Work Tabs** are identified with a pencil icon. This is where your responses are expected.
- Each task has one or more **Work Tabs**.
- **Work Tabs** contain directions for completing the task - be sure to read these directions carefully.
- The **Work Tab** name in the example above is for illustration only - yours will differ.
- You must complete all of the **Work Tabs** in each task to receive full credit.

Help Tab:

- The **Help Tab** provides assistance with the exam software that is used in this task. For example, if the task is to compose a memorandum, **Help** will provide information about the word processor.

The Toolbar

The toolbar at the top of the screen shows the amount of time remaining for you to complete the tasks. In addition, the following tools are available. Note that only the **Exit** button is displayed when Directions are visible - the others will appear when you begin the tasks.

 Click on these buttons to split or unsplit the screen. You can split the screen vertically or horizontally.

 Click on this button to go on to the next part of the examination. You must complete all of the tasks to receive full credit. Once you click on **Exit** and confirm the action, you will NOT be able to return to this testlet.

Sunco Corporation (EIN 98-7654321), an accrual-basis, calendar-year taxpayer, timely filed its Year 3 federal income tax return on March 15, Year 4. Sunco is not a member of a controlled group and is exempt from any personal holding company tax. Sunco has no net operating loss, charitable contribution, or foreign tax credit carryovers.

Sunco has over 100 shareholders, none owning more than 5% of the stock. The board of directors holds an annual meeting in New York City. The following lists the members on Sunco's board of directors:

Name	SSN	Address
Bob Smith	123-45-6789	101 Main Street, New York, NY 01234
Anne Johnson	789-01-2345	999 First Street, Chicago, IL 12345
Sam Clark	234-56-7890	234 Ocean Avenue, Los Angeles, CA 23456
Christopher Perry	345-67-8901	789 College Road, Houston, TX 34567
Maria Sanchez	456-78-9012	987 A Street, Atlanta, GA 45678

In a memorandum to Sally Jones, Sunco's controller, discuss the requirements to elect to file a consolidated return.

Type your communication below the line in the response area below.

REMINDER: Your response will be graded for both technical content and writing skills. Technical content will be evaluated for information that is helpful to the intended reader and clearly relevant to the issue. Writing skills will be evaluated for development, organization, and the appropriate expression of ideas in professional correspondence. Use a standard business memorandum or letter format with a clear beginning, middle, and end. Do not convey information in the form of a table, bullet point list, or other abbreviated presentation.

To: Sally Jones, Controller
Re: Election to file consolidated return

NOTE: Your Written Communications on the actual CPA exam may cover topics outside the scope of the BEC CSO (i.e., they may relate to topics from the AUD, FAR, and/or REG CSOs instead). Answer to the best of your ability, and remember that graders are mainly evaluating your writing ability and will overlook minor technical mistakes.

Unofficial Answer

Written Communication

To: Sally Jones, Controller
Re: Election to file consolidated return

A single federal income tax return may be filed by two or more includible corporations that are members of an affiliated group. An affiliated group consists of a chain of corporations connected through stock ownership to a parent that is an includible corporation. The parent must directly own at least 80% of the total voting power and value of at least one other includible corporation. Additionally, stock meeting the 80% test in each includible corporation other than the parent must be owned directly by at least one of the other includible corporations. Includible corporations are all corporations except tax-exempt corporations, S corporations, foreign sales corporations, insurance corporations, real estate investment trusts, regulated investment companies, domestic international sales corporations, and those corporations that claim Sec. 936 possessions tax credit.

An election to file a consolidated tax return may be made only if all corporations that were members of the affiliated group at any given time during the tax year consent. The consent for the election must be made prior to the last day for filing the return. The election to file a consolidated return is made by the act of simply filing the consolidated return. Consolidated financial statements or IRS approval is not required. However, if the group wants to terminate the election, consent of the IRS is required.

Each subsidiary included in a consolidated return must adopt the parent's tax year. One or more members of a controlled group filing a consolidated return may use the cash method, and one or more others may use the accrual method. There is no requirement as to the accounting methods that must be used in order to file a consolidated return.

The above depicts a Level 5 answer. Consult your booklet, *How to Pass the CPA Exam: A System for Success*, for a description of the three writing skills criteria. You may also access this booklet online by visiting www.gleim.com/PassCPA.

Self-Grade

Below, grade your response on technical content and writing skills. Bubble in the circle next to the appropriate score that you may receive based on the criteria given. Your **total** score is the sum of your scores on all six items. The maximum score is 19 points.

Technical Content Evaluation

Was your response on topic?	O No [0]	O Mostly [1]	O Yes [2]
Did your response have any *significant* errors?	O 0 errors [1]	O 1 major error [–1]	O 2 or more major errors [–2]
Did your response contain any illegal advice?	O No [1]	O Yes [0]	

Writing Skills Evaluation

	Poor	Below Average	Average	Above Average	Outstanding
Organization	O 1	O 2	O 3	O 4	O 5
Development	O 1	O 2	O 3	O 4	O 5
Expression	O 1	O 2	O 3	O 4	O 5

Disclaimer: This scoring schedule was developed by Gleim Publications as a guideline only. The AICPA has not released specific information on how the Written Communications are graded.

Practice even more Written Communications with the Gleim Mega Test Bank.
Learn more: gleim.com/CPAmega | 800.874.5346

STUDY UNIT FOUR
GLOBALIZATION

(14 pages of outline)

As the world economy becomes more interconnected, aspects of conducting business across borders grow in importance. This study unit explains why some countries raise barriers to trade (Subunit 4.1) and the inherent difficulties in currency exchange (Subunits 4.2 and 4.3).

Globalization is driven by the **digital revolution** that facilitates international commerce by means that did not exist until recently. It is also driven by such **political events** as (1) the fall of the Soviet Union, (2) the participation of China in the world economic system, (3) the emergence of the European Union, and (4) the creation of other regional free trade zones.

These technological and political factors interact with **social changes**, such as the (1) greater concern for the rights of women and minorities; (2) advance of multilingualism; and (3) convergence of tastes in fashion, music, and other aspects of culture.

Accordingly, these factors favor globalization by (1) reducing trade barriers, (2) reducing costs of coordination, (3) increasing economies of scale, and (4) encouraging standardization and global branding.

4.1 PROTECTIONISM

1. **Overview**

   a. Even though individuals generally are benefited by free trade, governments often establish policies designed to interfere in the workings of the marketplace. **Protectionism** is any measure taken by a government to protect domestic producers.

2. **Forms of Protectionism**

   a. **Tariffs** are taxes imposed on imported goods.

      1) Tariffs can discourage consumption of foreign goods, raise revenue, or both.

      2) To achieve both goals, the government must set the tariff rate very carefully. If the rate is set too high, demand for the good is decreased and revenue declines.

Background

Until the income tax was enacted in 1913, the U.S. government raised most of its revenue from tariffs.

---

   b. **Import quotas** set limits on different products.

      1) In the short run, import quotas improve a country's balance of payments by decreasing foreign outflow payments. But the prices of domestic products increase.

         a) A country's **balance of payments** is the sum of all transactions between domestic and foreign individuals, firms, and governments.

2) An **embargo** is a total ban on some kinds of imports. It is an extreme form of import quota.

3) As a result of import quotas and tariffs, domestic consumers pay higher prices and consume fewer goods. However, the domestic producers are able to sell more goods. Thus, domestic consumers pay a subsidy to domestic producers.

c. Domestic content rules require that at least a portion of any imported product be constructed from parts manufactured in the importing nation.

1) This rule is sometimes used by capital-intensive nations. Parts can be produced using idle capacity and then sent to a labor-intensive country for final assembly.

d. A **trigger price** mechanism automatically imposes a tariff barrier against unfairly cheap imports by levying a duty (tariff) on all imports below a particular reference price.

e. **Antidumping** rules prevent foreign producers from selling excess goods on the domestic market at less than cost to squeeze out competitors and gain control of the market.

f. **Repatriation** is the process of transferring money earned in a foreign location back to the domestic location.

1) Exchange controls limit foreign currency transactions and set exchange rates. The purpose is to limit the ability of a firm selling in a country to repatriate its earnings to its home country.

2) Tax policy can impose additional costs on earnings that are repatriated. For example, the U.S. has a worldwide taxation system that taxes foreign earnings only when they are repatriated.

g. Export subsidies are payments by the government to producers in certain industries in an attempt to increase exports.

1) A government may impose **countervailing duties** on imported goods if those goods were produced in a foreign country with the aid of a governmental subsidy.

h. Certain exports may require licenses. For example, sales of technology with military applications are limited by western nations that are members of the Coordinating Committee for Multilateral Export Controls. The related U.S. legislation is the Export Administration Act of 1979.

3. **Economic Effects of Tariffs and Quotas**

a. Workers are shifted from relatively efficient export industries into less efficient protected industries. Real wages decline as a result, as does total world output.

b. Under a tariff, the excess paid by the customer for an imported good is government revenue that can be spent for domestic purposes.

1) Under a quota, prices also are increased (by the induced shortage), but the excess is paid to the exporter in the foreign country.

c. A tariff is imposed on all importers equally. Thus, the more efficient firms can still charge lower prices.

1) But an import quota does not affect foreign importers equally, and import licenses can be granted based on political favoritism.

4. **Arguments for Protectionism**

    a.   Reducing imports protects domestic jobs.

        1)   This argument is compelling because the costs of cheaper imports are obvious, direct, and concentrated. People lose jobs and firms go out of business. The benefits of unrestricted trade are less noticeable. Lower prices, higher wages, and more jobs in export industries are future effects.

        2)   An argument against protectionism is that many of the ill effects of job loss can be mitigated by government programs to help in displaced-worker transition. Such measures are not protectionist.

    b.   Certain industries are essential to national security.

        1)   This argument is sound for some firms. But firms only peripherally related to national defense can claim that they are crucial to national security.

        2)   The national security concern also may result in the opposite of protectionism. For example, the U.S. government forbids exports of nuclear technology and certain weapons to countries such as Cuba, Iran, and North Korea. Thus, domestic exporters are hurt by government policies.

    c.   Infant industries need protection in the early stages of development.

        1)   An extension of the infant-industry argument is the strategic trade policy argument. It states that a government should use trade barriers strategically to reduce the risk of product development by domestic firms, particularly for products involving advanced technology.

        2)   Two counterarguments are usually offered. One is that, if the firm is promising, venture capitalists will provide financing until the entity becomes profitable. Also, some firms dependent on special government protections never become self-sufficient.

    NOTE: Special-interest groups advocating one or more of these arguments are strong and well organized, and they lobby effectively for legislation that is harmful to free trade.

5. **Global Capital Flow**

    a.   The rise of high-speed electronic communications makes the flow of capital much faster than in earlier eras.

        1)   The Internet and social media also have greatly facilitated **crowdfunding**, which is the funding of a project by raising contributions from a large number of people.

    b.   Emerging-market countries can attract capital with much greater ease than before, thereby exploiting their particular comparative advantages. The economic balance of power can shift rapidly back and forth between developed and developing nations.

6. **Sustainability**

    a.   The sustainability movement is built upon the goal of creating a higher standard of living for the present and the future, with a focus on reducing waste, energy use, and distribution costs and protecting the environment.

    b.   As the sustainability movement has become more important to consumers, major brands are attempting to provide their products and services in a more sustainable manner and to advertise that practice to consumers.

Stop and review! You have completed the outline for this subunit. Study multiple-choice questions 1 through 10 beginning on page 126.

4.2 CURRENCY EXCHANGE RATES

 The AICPA has tested the topic of currency exchange rates on recent CPA exams. Because international standards and international topics in general are now eligible to be tested, CPA candidates should have a solid understanding of currency exchange rates and the effects of globalization on the business environment.

1. **The Market for Foreign Currency**

   a. When an entity buys merchandise, a capital asset, or a financial instrument from another country, the seller wants to be paid in his or her domestic currency.

      1) Thus, in general, when the demand for a country's merchandise, capital assets, and financial instruments rises, demand for its currency rises.

   b. For international exchanges to occur, the two currencies involved must be easily converted at some prevailing exchange rate.

      1) The exchange rate is the price of one country's currency in terms of another country's currency.

2. **Exchange Rate Systems**

   a. **Fixed Exchange Rate System**

      1) In a fixed exchange rate system, the value of a country's currency in relation to another country's currency is either fixed or allowed to fluctuate only within a very narrow range.

      2) The one significant advantage of a fixed exchange rate is that it provides predictability in international trade by eliminating uncertainty about gains and losses on exchange rate fluctuations.

EXAMPLE

Since July 1986, the Saudi government has allowed its currency to trade within an extremely narrow band surrounding the ratio of 3.75 riyals to 1 U.S. dollar. Because the U.S. buys large amounts of petroleum from Saudi Arabia, this system has the advantage of adding stability to the U.S. oil market.

---

      3) A disadvantage is that a government can manipulate the value of its currency.

EXAMPLE

One of the complaints of authorities in the U.S. about the enormous trade deficit with China is the belief that the Chinese government has held the value of the yuan in an artificially low range to make its exports more affordable. (After years of urging by the U.S. government, China allowed its currency to rise almost 18% between 2005 and 2008. After further negotiations, China agreed in April 2012 to allow the value of the yuan to fluctuate by as much as 1.0% against the value of the dollar on any given day. This doubled the size of the previous trading band of 0.5%.)

---

   b. **Freely Floating Exchange Rate System**

      1) In this system, exchange rates are determined entirely by supply and demand.

         a) The advantage is that the system tends to automatically correct any disequilibrium in the balance of payments.

         b) The disadvantage is that a freely floating system makes a country vulnerable to economic conditions in other countries.

c. **Managed Float Exchange Rate System**

1) Under a managed float, market forces determine exchange rates until they move too far in one direction or another. The government then intervenes to maintain the currency within the broad range considered appropriate.

a) The advantage of managed float is that it has the market-response nature of a freely floating system while allowing for government intervention when necessary.

2) The dominant exchange rate system in use among the world's largest economies is the managed float system.

3. **Exchange Rates and Purchasing Power**

a. The graph below depicts the relationship between the supply of, and demand for, a foreign currency by consumers and investors who use a given domestic currency.

Exchange Rate Equilibrium

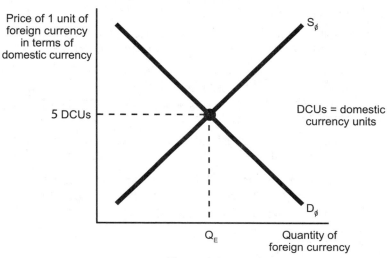

Figure 4-1

1) The demand curve for the foreign currency is downward sloping. When that currency becomes cheaper, goods and services denominated in that currency are more affordable and domestic consumers need more of it.

2) The supply curve for the foreign currency is upward sloping. When that currency becomes more expensive, goods and services denominated in the domestic currency become more affordable to users of the foreign currency. Thus, they inject more of their currency into the domestic market.

b. When one currency can be exchanged for more units of another currency, the first currency **appreciates** in relation to the second currency. The second currency **depreciates** in relation to the first.

1) This phenomenon has definite implications for international trade. The currency that appreciates has greater purchasing power. Any financial instrument denominated in that currency is more valuable (expensive).

EXAMPLE

A U.S. company buys merchandise from an EU company for €1,000,000, due in 60 days. On the day of the sale, $0.795 is required to buy a single euro. By the 60th day, $0.812 is required to buy a euro. The dollar has therefore depreciated in relation to the euro, and the euro has appreciated in relation to the dollar. Accordingly, the dollar has lost purchasing power in relation to the euro. The U.S. firm needed $795,000 to pay a €1,000,000 debt on the date of sale. On the due date, it must pay $812,000.

c.   The five factors that affect currency exchange rates can be classified as three trade-related factors and two financial factors.

1)   Trade-related factors

a)   Relative inflation rates
b)   Relative income levels
c)   Government intervention

2)   Financial factors

a)   Relative interest rates
b)   Ease of capital flow

4.   **Trade-Related Factors that Affect Exchange Rates**

a.   **Relative Inflation Rates**

1)   When the rate of inflation in a given country rises relative to the rates of other countries, the products of that country become relatively expensive and the demand for that country's currency falls.

a)   This leftward shift of the demand curve (from $D_{\emptyset}$ to D_1) results from the reduced purchasing power of that currency.

2)   As investors sell this currency, more of it is available, which is reflected in a rightward shift of the supply curve (from $S_{\emptyset}$ to S_1).

3)   A new equilibrium point is at a lower price in terms of investors' domestic currencies.

a)   Thus, as a result of the higher inflation in a foreign country, the domestic currency has appreciated in relation to that foreign currency.

**Changes in Supply of and Demand
for the Currency of a Foreign Country
with Higher Relative Inflation**

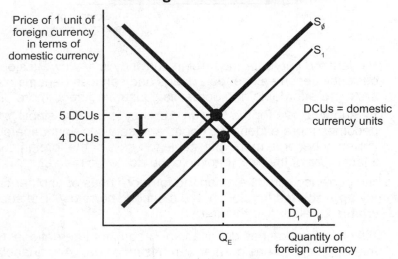

Figure 4-2

b)   The difference between the countries' inflation rates approximately equals the change in the currency exchange rate between the two countries.

i)   For example, X has a 3% inflation rate and Y has a 7% rate. Because of the difference in inflation rates, X's currency appreciates against Y's currency by approximately 4% (7% − 3%).

b. **Relative Income Levels**

1) Persons with higher incomes look for new consumption opportunities in other countries, increasing the demand for those currencies and shifting the demand curve to the right.

   a) Thus, as incomes rise in one country, the prices of foreign currencies also rise and the local currency depreciates.

Changes in Supply of and Demand for the Currency of a Foreign Country When Domestic Incomes Rise

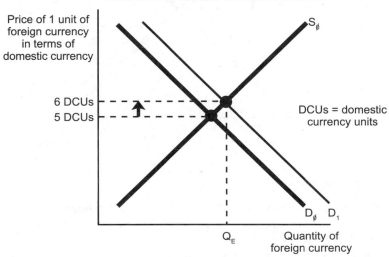

Figure 4-3

c. **Government Intervention**

1) Actions by national governments, such as trade barriers and currency restrictions, complicate the process of exchange rate determination.

5. **Financial Factors that Affect Exchange Rates**

a. **Relative Interest Rates**

1) When the interest rates in a given country rise relative to those of other countries, the demand for that country's currency rises.

   a) This rightward shift of the demand curve (from $D_{\emptyset}$ to D_1) results because holders of other currencies seek the higher returns available in that country.

2) As more investors buy the high-interest country's currency to make investments, less of it is available, which is reflected in a leftward shift of the supply curve (from $S_{\emptyset}$ to S_1).

3) A new equilibrium point is at a higher price in terms of investors' domestic currencies.

   a) An investor's domestic currency has depreciated against the currency of a foreign country with higher interest rates.

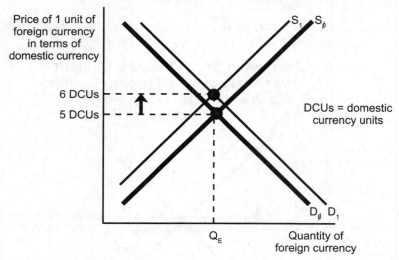

Figure 4-4

b. **Ease of Capital Flow**

1) If a country with high real interest rates removes restrictions on the cross-border movement of capital, the demand for the currency rises as investors seek higher returns.

2) This factor has become by far the most important of those listed.

a) The speed with which capital can be moved electronically and the huge amounts involved in the global economy are more significant than the effects of the trade-related factors.

6. **Graphical Depiction**

Exchange Rate Determination

Figure 4-5

If you can understand the relationship between the value of currency and financial or trade-related factors, you should be able to handle a variety of CPA questions. For example, when the real interest rate increases, the currency value appreciates. Also, when the real interest rate decreases, the currency value depreciates. Therefore, the real interest rate and the currency value have a direct relationship.

Trade-Related Factors that Occur in Domestic Economy	Domestic Currency Value	Foreign Currency Value*
Real interest rate	Direct	Indirect
Inflation rate	Indirect	Direct
Relative income level	Indirect	Direct
Demand for goods (or securities)	Direct	Indirect
Demand for currency	Direct	Indirect
Supply of currency	Indirect	Direct

*Assumes the foreign economy's trade-related factors are constant, i.e., are not changing.

7. Exchange Rates

a. The **spot rate** is the number of units of a foreign currency that can be received today in exchange for a single unit of the domestic currency.

EXAMPLE

A currency trader is willing to give 1.6 Swiss francs today in exchange for one British pound. Today's spot rate for the pound is therefore 1.6 Swiss francs, and today's spot rate for the franc is £0.625 (1 ÷ Ⅎ1.6).

b. The **forward rate** is the number of units of a foreign currency that can be received in exchange for a single unit of the domestic currency at some definite date in the future.

EXAMPLE

The currency trader contracts to provide 1.8 Swiss francs in exchange for one British pound 30 days from now. Today's 30-day forward rate for the pound is therefore 1.8 Swiss francs, and the 30-day forward rate for the franc is £0.555 (1 ÷ Ⅎ1.8).

c. If the exchange rate for the domestic currency is higher in relation to a foreign currency in the forward market than in the spot market, the domestic currency is trading at a **forward premium** in relation to the foreign currency.

EXAMPLE

The pound is currently trading at a forward premium in relation to the Swiss franc (Ⅎ1.8 > Ⅎ1.6). The market believes that the pound is going to appreciate in relation to the Swiss franc.

d. If the exchange rate for the domestic currency is lower in relation to a foreign currency in the forward market than in the spot market, the domestic currency is trading at a **forward discount** in relation to the foreign currency.

EXAMPLE

The Swiss franc is currently trading at a forward discount in relation to the pound (£0.555 < £0.625). The market believes that the Swiss franc is going to depreciate in relation to the pound.

e. The implications of these relationships can be generalized as follows:

If the domestic currency is trading at a forward	Then it is expected to
Premium	Gain purchasing power
Discount	Lose purchasing power

Stop and review! You have completed the outline for this subunit. Study multiple-choice questions 11 through 22 beginning on page 128.

4.3 MITIGATING EXCHANGE RATE RISK

1. **Exchange Rate Fluctuations**

   a. Fluctuations in currency exchange rates can significantly affect a firm's profits.

   b. The settlement date is the future date when the transaction will occur. The settlement amount is the agreed-upon amount of the transaction.

   c. Review the example below of exchange rate and purchasing power interaction reprinted from page 117.

EXAMPLE

A U.S. company buys merchandise from an EU company for €1,000,000, due in 60 days. On the day of the sale, $0.795 is required to buy a single euro. By the 60th day, $0.812 is required to buy a euro. The dollar has therefore depreciated in relation to the euro, and the euro has appreciated in relation to the dollar. Accordingly, the dollar has lost purchasing power in relation to the euro. The U.S. firm needed $795,000 to pay a €1,000,000 debt on the date of sale. On the due date, it must pay $812,000.

---

   d. A firm with a **payable** denominated in a **foreign** currency wants the foreign currency to depreciate by the settlement date so that fewer units of its domestic currency are required to pay the debt.

      1) A firm with a **payable** denominated in the **domestic** currency is indifferent to fluctuations in the exchange rate for the two currencies. The settlement amount is fixed in terms of its domestic currency.

   e. A firm with a **receivable** denominated in a **foreign** currency wants the foreign currency to appreciate by the settlement date. When the firm converts the foreign currency into its domestic currency, the conversion results in more units of the domestic currency.

      1) A firm with a **receivable** denominated in its **domestic** currency is indifferent to fluctuations in the exchange rate for the two currencies. The settlement amount is fixed in terms of its domestic currency.

   f. These effects can be summarized in the following table:

	A Domestic Firm with Foreign Currency	
	Net Inflows	Net Outflows
As of the Settlement Date	Will Experience a	
If the domestic currency has appreciated and the foreign currency has depreciated	(Loss)	Gain
If the domestic currency has depreciated and the foreign currency has appreciated	Gain	(Loss)

2. **Exposures to Exchange Rate Risk**

   a. Transaction Exposure

      1) Transaction exposure is the exposure to fluctuations in exchange rates between the date a transaction is entered into and the settlement date.

   b. Economic Exposure

      1) Economic exposure is the exposure to fluctuations in exchange rates resulting from overall economic conditions.

   c. Translation Exposure

      1) Translation exposure is the exposure to fluctuations in exchange rates between the date a transaction is entered into and the date that financial statements denominated in another currency must be reported.

3. **Transaction Exposure**

   a. Multinational corporations enter into numerous individual cross-border transactions during a year. Each transaction is subject to exchange rate variations between the transaction date and the settlement date.

   b. To address transaction exposure, a firm must

      1) Estimate its net cash flows in each currency for affected transactions.

         a) If inflows and outflows in a given currency are nearly equal, transaction exposure is minimal, even if the currency itself is volatile.

      2) Measure the potential effect of exposure in each currency.

         a) A range of possible rates for each currency must be estimated, reflecting that currency's volatility.

      3) Use hedging methods to mitigate exposure to exchange rate fluctuations.

4. **Hedging in Response to Transaction Exposure**

   a. Hedging and Uncertainty

      1) When hedging, some amount of possible gain is forgone to protect against potential loss.

   b. Basic Hedging Principles

      1) When a debtor is to pay a foreign currency amount at some time in the future, the risk is that the foreign currency will appreciate.

         a) If the foreign currency appreciates, more domestic currency is required to pay the debt.

      2) The hedge is to purchase the foreign currency forward to fix a definite price.

EXAMPLE

A U.S. firm knows that it will need 100,000 Canadian dollars in 60 days to pay an invoice. The firm hedges by purchasing 100,000 Canadian dollars 60 days forward. The firm is buying a guarantee that it will have C $100,000 available for use in 60 days. The 60-day forward rate for a Canadian dollar is US $0.99. Thus, for the privilege of having a guaranteed receipt of 100,000 Canadian dollars, the firm commits now to paying $99,000 in 60 days.

The counterparty to the hedge (the seller of Canadian dollars) also might be hedging, but it could be speculating or simply making a market in the instrument. The two parties are indifferent to each other's goals.

---

      3) When a creditor is to receive a foreign currency amount at some time in the future, the risk is that the foreign currency will depreciate.

         a) If the foreign currency depreciates, the creditor receives less domestic currency in the conversion.

      4) The hedge is to sell the foreign currency forward to fix a definite price.

EXAMPLE

A U.S. firm knows that it will be receiving 5,000,000 pesos in 30 days from the sale of some equipment at one of its facilities in Mexico. The spot rate for a peso is $0.77, and the 30-day forward rate is $0.80. The firm wants to be certain that it can sell the pesos it will receive in 30 days for $0.80 each. The firm hedges by selling 5,000,000 pesos 30 days forward. The firm is buying a guarantee that it can sell 5,000,000 pesos in 30 days and receive $4,000,000 (5,000,000 × $0.80) in return.

The spot rate on day 30 is $0.82. Thus, the U.S. firm could have made more money by forgoing the hedge and simply waiting to convert the pesos on day 30. However, this possibility was not worth the risk that the peso might have fallen below $0.80.

The counterparty to the hedge (the buyer of pesos) also might be hedging, but it could be speculating or simply making a market in the instrument. The two parties are indifferent to each other's goals.

c.   The following are the most common methods for addressing transaction exposure:

1)   **Money Market Hedges**

a)   The least complex method for hedging exchange rate risk is the money market hedge.

b)   A firm with a payable denominated in a foreign currency can buy a money market instrument denominated in that currency that is timed to mature when the payable is due. Exchange rate fluctuations between the transaction date and the settlement date are avoided.

c)   A firm with a receivable denominated in a foreign currency can borrow the amount and convert it to its domestic currency now, then pay the foreign loan when the receivable is collected.

2)   **Forward Contracts**

a)   Large corporations that have close relationships with major banks can enter into contracts for individual transactions in large amounts.

b)   The bank guarantees that it will make available to the firm a given quantity of a certain currency at a definite rate at some time in the future. The price charged by the bank for this guarantee is the premium.

EXAMPLE

A large U.S. firm purchases equipment from a Korean manufacturer for 222,000,000 won, due in 90 days. The exchange rate on the date of sale is $1 to 1,110 won. The U.S. firm suspects that the won may appreciate over the next 90 days and wants to fix a forward rate of 1-to-1,110. The firm negotiates a contract in which its bank promises to deliver 222,000,000 won to the firm in 90 days for $200,000. In return for this guarantee, the firm pays the bank a 2% premium ($200,000 × 2% = $4,000).

---

c)   The use of any mitigation strategy has an opportunity cost. The firm in the example above must execute its part of the contract whether or not the exchange rate with the won has fluctuated.

i)   If the won falls in value or rises less than the 2% premium in relation to the dollar, the firm has incurred an economic loss on the transaction.

3)   **Futures Contracts**

a)   Forward contracts are negotiated individually between the parties on a one-by-one basis. But futures contracts are essentially commodities that are traded on an exchange, making them available to more parties.

i)   The clearinghouse underwrites the contract, removing the risk of nonperformance by either party.

b)   Futures contracts are available only for standard amounts (e.g, 62,500 British pounds, 100,000 Brazilian reals, or 12,500,000 Japanese yen) and with specific settlement dates (typically the third Wednesday in March, June, September, and December).

i)   This rigidity makes them less flexible than forward contracts because forward contracts are customized for the parties.

Background

The largest market in the world for trading currency futures is the Chicago Mercantile Exchange. Information about the sizes and prices of various actively traded futures contracts is available at www.cmegroup.com/trading/fx/.

4) **Currency Options**

   a) A currency option differs from a currency futures contract. A futures contract is a binding contract. Both parties must perform. But an option is exercised only if the party purchasing the option chooses.

   b) Two types of options are available:

      i) A **call option** gives the holder the right to buy (call for) a specified amount of currency at a specified price at a predetermined date in the future. Call options are among the many methods available to **hedge payables**.

      ii) A **put option** gives the holder the right to sell (put onto the market) a specified amount of currency at a specified price at a predetermined date in the future. Put options are among the many methods available to **hedge receivables**.

5. **Economic Exposure**

   a. Economic exposure is the exposure to fluctuations in exchange rates resulting from overall economic conditions.

EXAMPLES

An exporter may require all of its customers to pay their invoices in the exporter's domestic currency. Thus, customers bear all the transaction risk of exchange rate variation. If the exporter's currency appreciates beyond a certain exchange rate, the exporter's products no longer will be price-competitive, and the customers will buy from local firms, reducing the exporter's cash inflows.

A manufacturer establishes operations in a low-wage country. As that country's economy strengthens, its currency appreciates and real wages increase. The manufacturer's cash outflows therefore have increased, eliminating the original cost advantage.

---

   b. Estimating Economic Exposure

      1) The degree of exposure can be estimated using either of two approaches:

         a) Sensitivity of earnings. The entity prepares a pro forma income statement for operations in each country.

         b) Sensitivity of cash flows. The entity performs a regression analysis, weighting each net cash flow by the amount of that currency in the firm's portfolio.

      2) Next, the entity constructs multiple scenarios (performs a sensitivity analysis) using various estimated exchange rates and determines the ultimate effect of each scenario on accrual-basis earnings or cash flows.

   c. Mitigating Economic Exposure

      1) A high level of economic exposure may require restructuring the entity's operations using the following guidelines:

	Actions to Be Taken when Foreign Currency	
Reliance on	Inflows Are Greater	Outflows Are Greater
Sales to foreign customers	Reduce foreign sales	Increase foreign sales
Purchases from foreign suppliers	Increase foreign orders	Reduce foreign orders

6. **Translation Exposure**

   a. Translation exposure is the risk that a foreign subsidiary's balance sheet items and results of operations, denominated in a currency different from the parent's, will change as a result of exchange rate fluctuations.

    b.   The degree of a firm's exposure to translation risk is determined by three factors:

        1)   Proportion of Total Business Conducted by Foreign Subsidiaries

            a)   A firm with half of its revenues derived from overseas subsidiaries has a high degree of exposure to translation risk. A 100% domestic firm has none.

            b)   A 100% domestic firm with foreign customers or suppliers still has transaction and economic risk.

        2)   Locations of Foreign Subsidiaries

            a)   A firm with a subsidiary in a country with a volatile currency has more translation risk than a firm with a subsidiary in a country with a stable currency.

        3)   Applicable Accounting Method

Stop and review! You have completed the outline for this subunit. Study multiple-choice questions 23 through 30 beginning on page 131.

QUESTIONS

4.1 Protectionism

1. Which of the following is a tariff?

    A.   Licensing requirements.

    B.   Consumption taxes on imported goods.

    C.   Unreasonable standards pertaining to product quality and safety.

    D.   Domestic content rules.

Answer (B) is correct.
    REQUIRED: The example of a tariff.
    DISCUSSION: Tariffs are excise taxes on imported goods imposed either to generate revenue or protect domestic producers. Thus, consumption taxes on imported goods are tariffs.
    Answer (A) is incorrect. Licensing requirements limit exports, e.g., of militarily sensitive technology. Answer (C) is incorrect. Unreasonable standards pertaining to product quality and safety are nontariff trade barriers. Answer (D) is incorrect. Domestic content rules require that a portion of an imported good be made in the importing country.

2. Which of the following is an economic reason for government intervention in trade?

    A.   Maintaining spheres of influence.

    B.   Protecting infant industries.

    C.   Preserving national identity.

    D.   Dealing with friendly countries.

Answer (B) is correct.
    REQUIRED: The best economic reason for government intervention in trade.
    DISCUSSION: The infant-industry argument is that protective tariffs are needed to allow new domestic industries to become established. Once such industries reach the maturity stage in their life cycles, the tariffs supposedly can be removed.

3. Which of the following is a direct effect of imposing a protective tariff on an imported product?

    A.   Lower domestic prices on the imported item.

    B.   Lower domestic consumption of the item.

    C.   Reduced domestic production of the item.

    D.   Higher sales revenues for foreign producers of the item.

Answer (B) is correct.
    REQUIRED: The direct effect of imposing a protective tariff on an imported product.
    DISCUSSION: A protective tariff adds to the purchase price of imported goods. If an imported good's sales price is higher than a comparable, less expensive domestic good, consumers will purchase the domestic good. Thus, the direct effect of imposing a protective tariff on an imported good is lower domestic consumption.
    Answer (A) is incorrect. A protective tariff can only increase the domestic price of the imported item. Answer (C) is incorrect. As the imported item's domestic price increases, demand for domestic goods will increase. Thus, domestic production will increase, not decrease. Answer (D) is incorrect. As the imported item's domestic price increases, demand for the item decreases. Lower sales revenues will result.

4. Import restrictions for purposes of creating domestic employment

   A. Are likely to increase the number of export jobs.

   B. May lead to lower prices for consumers.

   C. Will lead to lower sales tax collections.

   D. May lead to retaliation by other countries.

Answer (D) is correct.

   REQUIRED: The true statement about the effect of import restrictions for creating domestic employment.

   DISCUSSION: Protectionism in the form of import restrictions can lead to a variety of economic and social costs, including higher prices to consumers for both domestic and imported goods, higher taxes, and retaliation by other countries.

   Answer (A) is incorrect. Export jobs may decline due to retaliation by other countries. Answer (B) is incorrect. Consumers will have to pay higher prices for the protected domestic goods and may have to pay higher prices for foreign goods as well. Answer (C) is incorrect. Depending on the price elasticity of demand for the product, sales tax revenues may or may not fall.

5. The appropriate remedy for the dumping of products by a foreign firm in the U.S. market would be to

   A. Pass "buy American" laws.

   B. Impose restrictions on U.S. exports to the offending country.

   C. Impose countervailing duties or tariffs.

   D. Deny "most favored nation" treatment to exporters of the offending country.

Answer (C) is correct.

   REQUIRED: The appropriate remedy for the dumping of products by a foreign firm in the U.S. market.

   DISCUSSION: Dumping is the practice of supporting exports by selling products at a lower price in foreign markets than in the domestic market. The result is that foreign goods can be purchased in the U.S. at a price much lower than would be charged by a U.S. manufacturer. Because dumping lowers the price of foreign goods, the appropriate remedy is for the importing nation to impose a tariff that reduces the price differential.

   Answer (A) is incorrect. The passing of laws requiring domestic sourcing could result in a decline in overall domestic consumption, higher prices, and retaliatory foreign action. Answer (B) is incorrect. A country does not benefit from restricting its exports. Answer (D) is incorrect. Denying most favored nation treatment makes trade with a country more difficult and is a more extreme remedy than necessary.

6. Which of the following results in a complete elimination of trade?

   A. Voluntary export restraints.

   B. Domestic content requirements.

   C. Embargoes.

   D. Import quotas.

Answer (C) is correct.

   REQUIRED: The item that results in a complete elimination of trade.

   DISCUSSION: An embargo is a total ban on some kinds of imports. It is an extreme form of the import quota (i.e., the quota is zero).

   Answer (A) is incorrect. A voluntary restraint can be waived. Answer (B) is incorrect. Domestic content rules require that at least a portion of the imported product be constructed from parts manufactured in the importing nation. If this requirement is met, trade is not limited. Answer (D) is incorrect. Import quotas set fixed limits on the quantity of certain goods that can be imported. They limit but do not eliminate trade.

7. Domestic content rules

   A. Tend to be imposed by capital-intensive countries.

   B. Tend to be imposed by labor-intensive countries.

   C. Exclude products not made domestically.

   D. Restrict demand for affected products.

Answer (A) is correct.

   REQUIRED: The description of domestic content rules.

   DISCUSSION: Domestic content rules require that at least a portion of any imported product be constructed from parts manufactured in the importing nation. This rule sometimes is used by capital-intensive nations. Parts can be produced using idle capacity and then sent to a labor-intensive country for final assembly.

   Answer (B) is incorrect. Labor-intensive exporters are more likely to assemble final products. Answer (C) is incorrect. Domestic content rules place limits on, but do not exclude, imports. Answer (D) is incorrect. Supply is restricted.

8. An exemption from U.S. antitrust law is provided by

   A. The Export Trading Company Act of 1982.

   B. The Export Administration Act of 1979.

   C. Antidumping rules.

   D. The Foreign Corrupt Practices Act.

Answer (A) is correct.
   REQUIRED: The source of exemption from U.S. antitrust law.
   DISCUSSION: The Export Trading Company Act of 1982 permits competitors to form export trading companies without regard to U.S. antitrust legislation.
   Answer (B) is incorrect. The Export Administration Act of 1979 requires licensing of certain technology. Answer (C) is incorrect. Antidumping rules prevent foreign producers from dumping excess goods on the domestic market at less than cost to eliminate competitors and gain control of the market. Answer (D) is incorrect. The FCPA prohibits bribery of foreign officials.

9. What is the most likely economic effect of tariffs and quotas?

   A. Workers are shifted into more efficient export industries.

   B. Tariffs but not quotas affect all importers of the affected goods equally.

   C. Total world output increases.

   D. The price increase is received by exporters in foreign countries.

Answer (B) is correct.
   REQUIRED: The effect of tariffs and quotas.
   DISCUSSION: A tariff has an equal effect on all goods on which it is applied. Import licenses, however, may be awarded based on political favoritism.
   Answer (A) is incorrect. The effect is to shift workers into relatively inefficient domestic protected industries. Answer (C) is incorrect. Total world output decreases. Answer (D) is incorrect. A tariff increases the domestic government's general tax revenues.

10. The return to the home country of income earned by a domestic firm in a foreign country is

   A. Expropriation.

   B. Bankruptcy.

   C. Repatriation.

   D. Reinvestment.

Answer (C) is correct.
   REQUIRED: The return to the home country of income earned in a foreign country.
   DISCUSSION: Many firms have business operations abroad. Repatriation is conversion of funds held in a foreign country into another currency and remittance of these funds to another nation. A firm often must obtain permission from the currency exchange authorities to repatriate earnings and investments. Regulations in many nations encourage a reinvestment of earnings in the country.
   Answer (A) is incorrect. Expropriation is a foreign government's seizure (nationalization) of the assets of a business for a public purpose and for just compensation. Answer (B) is incorrect. Bankruptcy occurs when a person's liabilities exceed assets or (s)he cannot meet obligations when they are due. Answer (D) is incorrect. Reinvestment in the foreign country is a purpose of restrictions on repatriation.

4.2 Currency Exchange Rates

11. The U.S. dollar has a freely floating exchange rate. When the dollar has fallen considerably in relation to other currencies, the

   A. Trade account in the U.S. balance of payments is neither in a deficit nor in a surplus because of the floating exchange rates.

   B. Capital account in the U.S. balance of payments is neither in a deficit nor in a surplus because of the floating exchange rates.

   C. Fall in the dollar's value cannot be expected to have any effect on the U.S. trade balance.

   D. Cheaper dollar helps U.S. exporters of domestically produced goods.

Answer (D) is correct.
   REQUIRED: The true statement about the fall in the price of the dollar relative to other currencies.
   DISCUSSION: A decline in the value of the dollar relative to other currencies lowers the price of U.S. goods to foreign consumers. Thus, exporters of domestically produced goods benefit. A low value of the dollar also decreases imports by making foreign goods more expensive.
   Answer (A) is incorrect. Net exports increase as a result of dollar depreciation. Answer (B) is incorrect. The capital account benefits from the cheaper dollar. Foreigners can buy more dollars with fewer yen, euros, etc. Moreover, foreign capital inflow increases because of the federal government's budget deficits. Thus, the U.S. has a net capital inflow. Answer (C) is incorrect. The fall in the dollar has a positive effect on the nation's trade deficit. Exports increase and imports decrease.

12. If the U.S. dollar-peso exchange rate is $1 for 9 pesos, a product priced at 45 pesos will cost a U.S. consumer

   A. $0.20

   B. $5

   C. $45

   D. $405

Answer (B) is correct.
   REQUIRED: The price in dollars of a product for which the price is quoted in pesos.
   DISCUSSION: At a 1-for-9 rate, the price in U.S. dollars is $5, calculated by dividing 45 pesos by 9.
   Answer (A) is incorrect. The amount of $0.20 is based on an inversion of the numerator and denominator in the calculation. Answer (C) is incorrect. The amount of $45 is the price in pesos, not dollars. Answer (D) is incorrect. The amount of $405 is based on multiplying 45 and 9.

13. If a U.S. firm can buy £20,000 for $100,000, the rate of exchange for the pound is

   A. $.20

   B. $5

   C. $20

   D. $50

Answer (B) is correct.
   REQUIRED: The rate of exchange.
   DISCUSSION: An exchange rate of $5 to the pound is produced by dividing $100,000 by £20,000.
   Answer (A) is incorrect. The exchange rate for the dollar, not the pound, is $.20. Answer (C) is incorrect. The exchange rate is $5 to the pound. Answer (D) is incorrect. The exchange rate is $5 to the pound.

14. If the value of the U.S. dollar in foreign currency markets changes from $1 = .75 euros to $1 = .70 euros,

   A. The euro has depreciated against the dollar.

   B. Products imported from Europe to the U.S. will become more expensive.

   C. U.S. tourists in Europe will find their dollars will buy more European products.

   D. U.S. exports to Europe should decrease.

Answer (B) is correct.
   REQUIRED: The effect of a depreciation in the value of the dollar.
   DISCUSSION: The dollar has declined in value relative to the euro. If an American had previously wished to purchase a European product that was priced at 10 euros, the price would have been about $13.33. After the dollar's decline in value, the price of the item has increased to about $14.29. Thus, imports from Europe should decrease and exports increase.
   Answer (A) is incorrect. The euro has appreciated (increased in value) relative to the dollar. Answer (C) is incorrect. Dollars will buy fewer European products. Answer (D) is incorrect. U.S. exports should increase because the euro has appreciated with respect to the dollar.

15. If the U.S. dollar declines in value relative to the currencies of many of the U.S. trading partners, the likely result is that

   A. Foreign currencies will depreciate against the dollar.

   B. The U.S. balance of payments deficit will become worse.

   C. U.S. exports will tend to increase.

   D. U.S. imports will tend to increase.

Answer (C) is correct.
   REQUIRED: The true statement about the decline in the value of the U.S. dollar.
   DISCUSSION: The decline in the value of the dollar reduces the prices of U.S. goods to foreigners and should increase exports. Also, foreign goods will be priced higher (in dollars) and imports from foreign countries should decrease, improving the U.S. balance of payments.
   Answer (A) is incorrect. The dollar has depreciated against foreign currencies. Answer (B) is incorrect. The U.S. trade balance of payments should improve. Answer (D) is incorrect. U.S. imports will decline. Foreign goods will be priced higher than before.

16. If the central bank of a country raises interest rates sharply, the country's currency will likely

   A. Increase in relative value.

   B. Remain unchanged in value.

   C. Decrease in relative value.

   D. Decrease sharply in value at first and then return to its initial value.

Answer (A) is correct.
   REQUIRED: The effect on a country's currency if its central bank raises interest rates sharply.
   DISCUSSION: Exchange rates fluctuate depending upon the demand for each country's currency. If a country raises its interest rates, its currency will appreciate. The demand for investment at the higher interest rates will shift the demand curve for the currency to the right. The reverse holds true for a decrease in interest rates.

17. Given a spot exchange rate for the U.S. dollar against the pound sterling of $1.4925 per pound and a 90-day forward rate of $1.4775 per pound,

    A. The dollar is at a discount against the pound and undervalued in the forward market.

    B. The dollar is at a premium against the pound and overvalued in the forward market.

    C. The forward dollar is at a premium against the pound.

    D. The forward dollar is at a discount against the pound.

Answer (C) is correct.
    REQUIRED: The true statement about the given spot exchange rates.
    DISCUSSION: The exchange rate for the pound sterling is lower in the forward market than the spot market. Thus, the pound sterling is trading at a forward discount relative to the U.S. dollar, which is trading at a forward premium.
    Answer (A) is incorrect. The facts do not indicate whether the rates are over- or undervalued. Answer (B) is incorrect. The facts do not indicate whether the rates are over- or undervalued. Answer (D) is incorrect. The dollar is at a forward premium relative to the pound sterling, not a discount.

18. The spot rate for one Australian dollar is $0.92685 and the 60-day forward rate is $0.93005. Which one of the following statements is consistent with these facts?

    A. The U.S. dollar is trading at a forward discount with respect to the Australian dollar.

    B. The U.S. dollar is trading at a forward premium with respect to the Australian dollar.

    C. The U.S. dollar has lost purchasing power with respect to the Australian dollar.

    D. The U.S. dollar has gained purchasing power with respect to the Australian dollar.

Answer (A) is correct.
    REQUIRED: The conclusion about a forward exchange rate.
    DISCUSSION: The exchange rate for the Australian dollar is higher in the forward market than the spot market. The Australian dollar is therefore trading at a forward premium. Accordingly, the U.S. dollar is trading at a forward discount.
    Answer (B) is incorrect. The U.S. dollar is trading at a forward discount in relation to the Australian dollar. Answer (C) is incorrect. No conclusion about purchasing power changes can be drawn without information about past exchange rates. Answer (D) is incorrect. No conclusion about purchasing power changes can be drawn without information about past exchange rates.

19. The accompanying graph depicts the supply of and demand for U.S. dollars in terms of euros at a moment in time. Currently, the equilibrium exchange rate is $1 to 0.65 €. If inflation of the dollar exceeds that of the euro, the new equilibrium exchange rate would most likely settle at

	Quantity	Price
A.	Indeterminate	0.70 €
B.	Lower than Q_E	0.70 €
C.	Higher than Q_E	0.60 €
D.	Indeterminate	0.60 €

Answer (D) is correct.
    REQUIRED: The graphic depiction of inflation of a base currency against a foreign currency.
    DISCUSSION: The graph depicts the supply of and demand for a particular foreign currency by holders of euros. When the foreign currency inflates faster than the domestic currency (the euro), the foreign currency loses purchasing power. The weakening foreign currency is less attractive, and demand for it falls (its demand curve shifts to the left). Whether the supply curve for dollars remains the same or shifts to the right, the new equilibrium price for it will be lower (fewer euros buy $1). The new equilibrium quantity could be higher, lower, or the same as the old one.
    Answer (A) is incorrect. The new equilibrium price will be lower. Answer (B) is incorrect. The new quantity cannot be determined, and the new price will be lower. Answer (C) is incorrect. The new equilibrium quantity cannot be determined.

20. Which one of the following statements supports the conclusion that the U.S. dollar has gained purchasing power against the Japanese yen?

A. Inflation has recently been higher in the U.S. than in Japan.

B. The dollar is currently trading at a premium in the forward market with respect to the yen.

C. The yen's spot rate with respect to the dollar has just fallen.

D. Studies recently published in the financial press have shed doubt on the interest rate parity (IRP) theory.

Answer (C) is correct.

REQUIRED: The statement that supports the conclusion that the U.S. dollar has gained purchasing power against the Japanese yen.

DISCUSSION: If the yen's spot rate has just fallen, more yen are required to buy a single dollar. The yen has therefore depreciated, i.e., lost purchasing power. At the same time, the dollar has gained purchasing power.

Answer (A) is incorrect. Higher inflation in the U.S. than in Japan reflects a loss, not a gain, of the dollar's purchasing power. Answer (B) is incorrect. No conclusion can be drawn about changes in purchasing power simply from a statement about forward rates. Answer (D) is incorrect. No conclusion can be drawn about changes in purchasing power simply from evidence for or against the interest rate parity (IRP) theory.

21. All of the following are trade-related factors affecting currency exchange rates **except**

A. Relative interest rates.

B. Trade barriers.

C. Relative incomes.

D. Relative inflation rates.

Answer (A) is correct.

REQUIRED: The factor affecting exchange rates that is not trade related.

DISCUSSION: Relative interest rates is a financial, not a trade-related, factor affecting currency exchange rates.

22. A shift of the demand curve for a country's currency to the right could be caused by which of the following?

A. A foreign government placing restrictions on the importation of the country's goods.

B. A fall in the country's interest rates.

C. Domestic inflation worsens.

D. A rise in consumer incomes in another country.

Answer (D) is correct.

REQUIRED: The condition that could cause a rise in demand for a country's currency.

DISCUSSION: Citizens with higher incomes look for new consumption opportunities in other countries, driving up the demand for those currencies. Thus, as incomes rise in one country, the prices of foreign currencies rise as well.

Answer (A) is incorrect. A shift to the right is caused by a foreign government's removal of restrictions on the importation of the country's goods. Answer (B) is incorrect. A shift to the right is caused by a rise, not a fall, in the country's interest rates. Answer (C) is incorrect. As a country's inflation rate rises, its currency loses purchasing power and investors move their capital elsewhere, reducing demand for the country's currency.

4.3 Mitigating Exchange Rate Risk

23. An American importer of English clothing has contracted to pay an amount fixed in British pounds 3 months from now. If the importer worries that the U.S. dollar may depreciate sharply against the British pound in the interim, it would be well advised to

A. Buy pounds in the forward exchange market.

B. Sell pounds in the forward exchange market.

C. Buy dollars in the futures market.

D. Sell dollars in the futures market.

Answer (A) is correct.

REQUIRED: The action to hedge a liability denominated in a foreign currency.

DISCUSSION: The American importer should buy pounds now. If the dollar depreciates against the pound in the next 90 days, the gain on the forward exchange contract offsets the loss from having to pay more dollars to satisfy the liability.

Answer (B) is incorrect. Selling pounds increases the risk of loss for someone who has incurred a liability. However, it is an appropriate hedge of a receivable denominated in pounds. Answer (C) is incorrect. The importer needs pounds, not dollars. Answer (D) is incorrect. Although buying pounds might be equivalent to selling dollars for pounds, this is not the best answer. This choice does not state what is received for the dollars.

24. A U.S. manufacturer sold a piece of equipment to an engineering firm in New Zealand. The New Zealand firm must pay the invoice in U.S. dollars in 30 days and would like to mitigate the risk that the New Zealand dollar will depreciate against the U.S. dollar in the meantime. The type of exchange rate risk contemplated by the New Zealand firm is known as

A. Transition exposure.

B. Economic exposure.

C. Transaction exposure.

D. Translation exposure.

25. A massive inflation across the entire economy of one of a firm's trading partners has benefited the firm greatly by making its fixed amount of payables denominated in that country's currency much cheaper. This exemplifies exchange rate risk stemming from

A. Transition exposure.

B. Economic exposure.

C. Transaction exposure.

D. Translation exposure.

26. A Chinese conglomerate owns a construction subsidiary that is building a port in Mozambique. The firm pays its workers in the Mozambique currency but keeps its books for the project in the South African rand. At the end of the fiscal year, the conglomerate must report consolidated financial statements denominated in the yuan. The exchange rate risk encountered by the conglomerate in the currency conversions leading up to its consolidated financial statements is known as

A. Transition exposure.

B. Economic exposure.

C. Transaction exposure.

D. Translation exposure.

27. A company based in West Palm Beach, Florida, is building a resort in Jamaica. The Jamaican property owners must make a progress payment of US $1 million in 30 days. The spot rate for the U.S. dollar is 88 Jamaican dollars (J $), and the 30-day forward rate is J $90. The most likely hedge in response to the transaction exposure inherent in this situation is

A. The contractor will purchase J $88,000,000 in the spot market.

B. The contractor will sell J $90,000,000 in the 30-day forward market.

C. The property owners will purchase US $1,000,000 in the 30-day forward market.

D. The property owners will sell US $1,000,000 in the 30-day forward market.

Answer (C) is correct.
   REQUIRED: The type of exchange rate exposure embodied in a sale transaction.
   DISCUSSION: Transaction exposure is the exposure to fluctuations in exchange rates between the date a transaction is entered into and the settlement date.
   Answer (A) is incorrect. Transition exposure is not a meaningful term. Answer (B) is incorrect. Economic exposure is the exposure to fluctuations in exchange rates resulting from overall economic conditions. Answer (D) is incorrect. Translation exposure is the risk that a foreign subsidiary's balance sheet items and the results of operations denominated in a currency different from the parent's currency will change in value as a result of exchange rate changes.

Answer (B) is correct.
   REQUIRED: The type of exchange rate exposure embodied in a foreign country's deflation.
   DISCUSSION: Economic exposure is the exposure to fluctuations in exchange rates resulting from overall economic conditions.
   Answer (A) is incorrect. Transition exposure is not a meaningful term. Answer (C) is incorrect. Transaction exposure is the exposure to fluctuations in exchange rates between the date a transaction is entered into and the settlement date. Answer (D) is incorrect. Translation exposure is the risk that a foreign subsidiary's balance sheet items and the results of operations denominated in a currency different from the parent's currency will change in value as a result of exchange rate changes.

Answer (D) is correct.
   REQUIRED: The type of exchange rate exposure embodied in converting the books of foreign subsidiaries.
   DISCUSSION: Translation exposure is the exposure to fluctuations in exchange rates between the date a transaction is entered into and the date that financial statements denominated in another currency must be reported.
   Answer (A) is incorrect. Transition exposure is not a meaningful term. Answer (B) is incorrect. Economic exposure is the exposure to fluctuations in exchange rates resulting from overall economic conditions. Answer (C) is incorrect. Transaction exposure is the exposure to fluctuations in exchange rates between the date a transaction is entered into and the settlement date.

Answer (C) is correct.
   REQUIRED: The most likely hedging transaction in response to a receivable/payable.
   DISCUSSION: This receivable or payable is denominated in the currency of the creditor. Thus, the creditor has no incentive to hedge. The debtors (the property owners) want to hedge against the possibility that their domestic currency will depreciate against the U.S. dollar in the next 30 days. The typical mitigation strategy is to purchase the amount needed to pay the debt so that funds are available when needed.
   Answer (A) is incorrect. The party on the receivable side of this transaction has no need to hedge. The debt is denominated in its domestic currency. Answer (B) is incorrect. The party on the receivable side of this transaction has no need to hedge. The debt is denominated in its domestic currency. Answer (D) is incorrect. The debtors need US $1,000,000 in 30 days to pay the invoice. Thus, they will purchase, not sell, the U.S. dollar in the forward market.

28. A company headquartered in Vancouver, British Columbia, is building a pipeline in Russia. The invoice amount is due in 90 days and is denominated at 28 million rubles. The Canadian dollar is trading for 28 rubles currently and 29 rubles 90 days forward. Which of the following strategies will the Canadian firm most likely pursue in the 90-day forward market to hedge the transaction exposure inherent in this situation?

    A. Sell 29,000,000 rubles.

    B. Purchase 28,000,000 rubles.

    C. Purchase 29,000,000 rubles.

    D. Sell 28,000,000 rubles.

Answer (D) is correct.
    REQUIRED: The most likely hedging transaction in response to a foreign-denominated receivable.
    DISCUSSION: The Canadian company knows that it will be receiving 28,000,000 rubles in 90 days. The firm wants to ensure that it will be able sell these rubles at that time for a certain number of Canadian dollars. The firm therefore hedges by selling 28,000,000 rubles in the 90-day forward market. The company is buying a guarantee that it will be able to sell a definite number of rubles in 90 days and receive a definite number of Canadian dollars in return, regardless of fluctuations in the exchange rate in the meantime.
    Answer (A) is incorrect. The creditor firm will receive only 28 million rubles. Answer (B) is incorrect. The creditor firm wants to sell, not purchase, forward rubles. Answer (C) is incorrect. The creditor firm wants to sell, not purchase, forward rubles. Also, the firm will receive only 28 million rubles.

29. A company with significant sales in a particular foreign country has recently been subjected to extreme variations in the exchange rate with that country's currency. These variations are expected to continue. To mitigate the resulting economic exposure, a likely strategy for the company to implement would be to

    A. Reduce sales to that country.

    B. Increase sales to that country.

    C. Reduce orders from suppliers in other foreign countries.

    D. Increase orders from suppliers in other foreign countries.

Answer (A) is correct.
    REQUIRED: The most likely strategy to mitigate economic exposure to exchange rate variation.
    DISCUSSION: When cash inflows from a country with a volatile currency exceed cash outflows to that country, the appropriate strategy to mitigate economic exposure is to decrease sales to that country.
    Answer (B) is incorrect. The appropriate strategy to mitigate this economic exposure is to decrease, not increase, sales to that country. Answer (C) is incorrect. Reducing orders from suppliers in other foreign countries will not address this economic exposure. Answer (D) is incorrect. Increasing orders from suppliers in other foreign countries will not address this economic exposure.

30. When the U.S. dollar is expected to rise in value against foreign currencies, a U.S. company with foreign currency denominated receivables and payables should

    A. Slow down collections and speed up payments.

    B. Slow down collections and slow down payments.

    C. Speed up collections and speed up payments.

    D. Speed up collections and slow down payments.

Answer (D) is correct.
    REQUIRED: The action a U.S. company with foreign currency denominated receivables should take if the dollar is expected to rise.
    DISCUSSION: The U.S. firm should increase collections and decrease payments. Collections should be made quickly and converted into dollars to sustain the increase in their value as the dollar appreciates. Decreasing payments is profitable because, as the company exchanges dollars for foreign currency at a later date, it will receive more of the foreign currency, thus lowering its real cost.
    Answer (A) is incorrect. Slowing collections and expediting payments increases the company's real cost. Answer (B) is incorrect. Slowing collections does not maximize the amount of U.S. dollars received. Answer (C) is incorrect. Expediting payments does not maximize the amount of U.S. dollars received.

4.4 PRACTICE WRITTEN COMMUNICATION

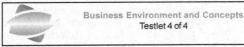

Business Environment and Concepts Testlet 4 of 4	Time Remaining 1 hour - 15 minutes	

DIRECTIONS

Note: If you believe you have encountered a software malfunction, report it to the test center staff immediately.

Navigation

To navigate from task to task, use the controls at the bottom of the screen. Click on the **Next** button to advance to the next task, or the **Previous** button to go to the previous task. To go directly to any task, click on its number.

▼ = Reminder		Directions	1 2 3 4 5 6 7 ▽ ▽ ▽ ▽ ▽ ▽ ▽		◀ Previous	Next ▶

If you would like a reminder to revisit a task, or want to indicate that you are finished with it, click on the reminder flag below the task number. To clear the flag, click on it again. Reminder flags are for your use only – they do not contribute to your score.

Tabs

In this part of the examination, you will be asked to complete various tasks. Every task has one or more **Work Tabs**. Every task also has a **Help** tab.

           Work tab   Help tab

Work Tabs:

- **Work Tabs** are identified with a pencil icon. This is where your responses are expected.
- Each task has one or more **Work Tabs**.
- **Work Tabs** contain directions for completing the task - be sure to read these directions carefully.
- The **Work Tab** name in the example above is for illustration only - yours will differ.
- You must complete all of the **Work Tabs** in each task to receive full credit.

Help Tab:

- The **Help Tab** provides assistance with the exam software that is used in this task. For example, if the task is to compose a memorandum, **Help** will provide information about the word processor.

The Toolbar

The toolbar at the top of the screen shows the amount of time remaining for you to complete the tasks. In addition, the following tools are available. Note that only the **Exit** button is displayed when Directions are visible - the others will appear when you begin the tasks.

Click on these buttons to split or unsplit the screen. You can split the screen vertically or horizontally.

Click on this button to go on to the next part of the examination. You must complete all of the tasks to receive full credit. Once you click on **Exit** and confirm the action, you will NOT be able to return to this testlet.

▼ = Reminder		Directions	1 ▽		◀ Previous	Next ▶

ABC Company has been an audit client of Stellar Accountants, LLP, for many years. As the partner on the engagement, you have assigned two new staff accountants to the audit of ABC Company. Rebecca, one of the new staff members, has asked the engagement manager whether omitting the confirmation of ABC's accounts receivable from the current-year audit is appropriate. She believes that responses will not be timely. The manager has asked you, the partner on the engagement, whether this omission is appropriate.

Write a memorandum to your audit team explaining the specific circumstances under which the confirmation of accounts receivable may be omitted.

Type your communication below the line in the response area below.

REMINDER: Your response will be graded for both technical content and writing skills. Technical content will be evaluated for information that is helpful to the intended reader and clearly relevant to the issue. Writing skills will be evaluated for development, organization, and the appropriate expression of ideas in professional correspondence. Use a standard business memorandum or letter format with a clear beginning, middle, and end. Do not convey information in the form of a table, bullet point list, or other abbreviated presentation.

To: Audit team
Re: Omission of external confirmation of accounts receivable

⚑ = Reminder   Directions   1 ▽   ◀ Previous   Next ▶

NOTE: Your Written Communications on the actual CPA exam may cover topics outside the scope of the BEC CSO (i.e., they may relate to topics from the AUD, FAR, and/or REG CSOs instead). Answer to the best of your ability, and remember that graders are mainly evaluating your writing ability and will overlook minor technical mistakes.

Unofficial Answer

Written Communication

To: Audit team
Re: Omission of external confirmation of accounts receivable

In many circumstances, external confirmation procedures for accounts receivable and performance of other substantive procedures are necessary to reduce the assessed risks of material misstatement to an acceptably low level. The higher the assessed risks of material misstatement, the more persuasive the audit evidence obtained should be. For example, the auditor may decide to obtain more evidence directly from third parties by performing external confirmation procedures. These procedures may provide evidence at the higher level of reliability required for responding to significant RMMs, including those due to fraud.

Audit evidence generally is more reliable (and persuasive) when it is (1) obtained from independent sources external to the entity, (2) obtained directly, or (3) in documentary form (paper, electronic, or other medium). Thus, external confirmations may be more reliable than evidence generated internally by the entity.

Accordingly, auditing standards require the auditor to consider whether external confirmation procedures should be performed as substantive audit procedures. External confirmations provide audit evidence as direct written responses from a third (confirming) party, and they are in documentary form.

External confirmation of accounts receivable is required except when (1) they are immaterial; (2) confirmation would be ineffective; or (3) the assessed RMMs are low, and other substantive procedures address the assessed risks.

An auditor who does not perform external confirmations of material accounts receivable should document the basis for the decisions.

The above depicts a Level 5 answer. Consult your booklet, *How to Pass the CPA Exam: A System for Success*, for a description of the three writing skills criteria. You may also access this booklet online by visiting www.gleim.com/PassCPA.

Self-Grade

Below, grade your response on technical content and writing skills. Bubble in the circle next to the appropriate score that you may receive based on the criteria given. Your **total** score is the sum of your scores on all six items. The maximum score is 19 points.

Technical Content Evaluation

Was your response on topic?	O No [0]	O Mostly [1]	O Yes [2]
Did your response have any *significant* errors?	O 0 errors [1]	O 1 major error [−1]	O 2 or more major errors [−2]
Did your response contain any illegal advice?	O No [1]	O Yes [0]	

Writing Skills Evaluation

	Poor	Below Average	Average	Above Average	Outstanding
Organization	O 1	O 2	O 3	O 4	O 5
Development	O 1	O 2	O 3	O 4	O 5
Expression	O 1	O 2	O 3	O 4	O 5

Disclaimer: This scoring schedule was developed by Gleim Publications as a guideline only. The AICPA has not released specific information on how the Written Communications are graded.

Practice even more Written Communications with the Gleim Mega Test Bank.
Learn more: gleim.com/CPAmega | 800.874.5346

STUDY UNIT FIVE
FINANCIAL RISK MANAGEMENT

(11 pages of outline)

Every investment has an expectation of a return and some amount of risk. An investing entity can receive an adequate return on its investments while minimizing risk by understanding the principles of portfolio management. The prices of derivative financial instruments are based on the price of some other instrument and are used for specialized activities, such as hedging.

5.1 RISK AND RETURN

1. **Rate of Return**

   a. A return is the amount received by an investor as compensation for accepting the risk of the investment.

   $$Return\ on\ investment = Amount\ received - Amount\ invested$$

EXAMPLE

An investor paid $100,000 for an investment that returned $112,000. The investor's return is $12,000 ($112,000 − $100,000).

---

   b. The rate of return is a percentage of the amount invested.

   $$Rate\ of\ return = \frac{Return\ on\ investment}{Amount\ invested}$$

EXAMPLE

The investor's rate of return is 12% ($12,000 ÷ $100,000).

---

2. **Simple Interest vs. Compound Interest**

   a. The interest generated by an investment can either be paid periodically in cash or added to the investment principal in a process known as **compounding**.

EXAMPLE

A mutual fund offers its investors an annual 4% return. It can be received in cash or compounded. The following tables illustrate the difference in cash flows under the two methods.

	Using Simple Interest				Using Compound Interest			
	Beginning Balance	Annual Return	Cash Disbursed	Added to Balance	Beginning Balance	Annual Return	Added to Balance	Cash Disbursed
Year 1	$10,000.00 ×	4% =	$400.00	--	$10,000.00 ×	4% =	$400.00	--
Year 2	10,000.00 ×	4% =	400.00	--	10,400.00 ×	4% =	416.00	--
Year 3	10,000.00 ×	4% =	400.00	--	10,816.00 ×	4% =	432.64	--
Year 4	10,000.00 ×	4% =	400.00	--	11,248.64 ×	4% =	449.95	--
Year 5	10,000.00 ×	4% =	400.00	--	11,698.59 ×	4% =	467.94	--

At the end of 5 years, the investor who received periodic payments had the use of $400 cash every year but has only the original $10,000 principle. An investor who chose compounding received no periodic cash flow but has a principle of $12,166.53 ($11,698.59 Year 5 beginning balance + $467.94 Year 5 return).

---

3. **Two Basic Types of Investment Risk**

    a. All firms have **systematic risk**, also called **market risk**. Changes in the economy, such as inflation or the business cycle, affect all those in the market.

        1) For this reason, systematic risk sometimes is called **undiversifiable risk**. Because all investments are affected, it cannot be reduced by diversification.

    b. **Unsystematic risk**, also called unique risk or company risk, is inherent in a particular investment. Thus, it is the risk of a specific firm. This type of risk is determined by the firm's industry, products, customer loyalty, degree of leverage, management competence, etc.

        1) Unsystematic risk sometimes is called **diversifiable risk**. Because individual investments are affected by the particular strengths and weaknesses of the firm, this risk can be reduced by diversification. (Item 3. in Subunit 5.2 explains diversification.)

4. **Types of Investment Risk**

    a. **Credit default risk** is the risk that the borrower will default and not be able to repay principal or interest. This risk is estimated by credit-rating agencies.

    b. **Liquidity risk** is the risk that a security cannot be sold on short notice for its market value.

    c. **Maturity risk**, also called **interest rate risk**, is the risk that an investment security will fluctuate in value between the time it was issued and its maturity date. The longer the time until maturity, the greater the degree of maturity risk.

    d. **Inflation risk** is the risk that purchasing power will be lost while the loan is at the borrower's disposal. (Study Unit 3, Subunit 5, describes the causes and effects of inflation.)

    e. **Political risk** is the probability of loss from actions of governments, such as changes in tax laws or environmental regulations or expropriation of assets.

    f. **Exchange rate risk** is the risk of loss because of fluctuation in the relative value of a foreign currency.

    g. **Business risk** (or **operations risk**) is the risk of fluctuations in earnings before interest and taxes or in operating income when the firm uses no debt.

        1) It is the risk inherent in operations that excludes **financial risk**, the risk to the shareholders of financial leverage.

        2) Business risk depends on factors such as (a) demand variability, (b) sales price variability, (c) input price variability, and (d) the amount of operating leverage.

    h. **Country risk** is the overall risk of investing in a foreign country.

    i. **Principal risk** is the risk of losing the principal invested.

5. **Relationship Between Risk and Return**

    a. Whether the expected return on an investment suffices to attract an investor depends on (1) its risk, (2) the risks and returns of alternative investments, and (3) the investor's attitude toward risk.

        1) Most investors (and people in general) are **risk averse**. For them, the utility of a gain is less than the disutility of a potential loss of the same amount.

EXAMPLE

Risk aversion is reflected by actions of people in a casino. Many are willing to bet $1 on one of the numbers on a roulette table because the chance of a gain of multiple dollars versus the loss of $1 is acceptable. However, as the minimum amount of a bet increases (from $1 to $100 to $1,000), the number of willing casual gamblers decreases because the chance for earning hundreds or thousands of dollars versus the probability of losing $100 or $1,000 is not acceptable.

a) Because of risk aversion, risky securities must have higher expected returns. These returns induce investors to accept additional risk. In the example on the previous page, if a casino were to provide better odds (i.e., a higher expected return) for higher bet amounts, more casual gamblers may be induced to place higher minimum bets.

2) A **risk-neutral** investor adopts an expected value approach. (S)he regards the utility of a gain as equal to the disutility of a loss of the same amount.

    a) In the case of a roulette gambler, a risk-neutral person is as willing to gamble for a high amount as a low amount.

3) A **risk-seeking** investor has an optimistic attitude toward risk. (S)he regards the utility of a gain as exceeding the disutility of a loss of the same amount.

    a) In the case of a gambler, a risk-seeking person is more willing to play roulette than craps, baccarat, or poker due to the greater risk.

b. The greater the risk of the investment, the higher the rate of return required by the investor. For each type of investment risk, the investor requires an additional risk premium that compensates him or her for bearing that risk.

1) The **risk premium** is the excess of an investment's expected rate of return over the risk-free interest rate.

2) The **risk-free rate** is the interest rate on the safest investment. The stated interest rate on U.S. Treasury bills is considered to be the risk-free interest rate.

    a) A holder of U.S. Treasury bills generally is exposed only to inflation risk. Thus, the market rate of interest on U.S. Treasury bills equals the risk-free rate of interest plus the inflation premium.

3) The **required rate of return** considers all investment risks that relate to a specific security.

EXAMPLE

Real risk-free rate	3%
Inflation premium	1%
Risk-free rate	4%
Liquidity risk premium	1%
Default risk premium	2%
Maturity risk premium	1%
Required rate of return	8%

---

6. **Investment Securities**

a. Financial managers may select from a wide range of financial instruments to raise capital or invest.

1) The safety of an investment and its potential return have an inverse relationship. The following is a short list of widely available investment securities:

Figure 5-1

    b.   The reasons for the varying risks and potential returns of these securities can be summarized as follows:

        1)   Equity securities necessarily are riskier than debt because an entity's owners are not legally guaranteed a return.

            a)   Common shareholders are the residual owners of a corporation. They are last in order of priority during liquidation, but they have the right to receive distributions of excess profits.

            b)   Preferred shareholders have a higher priority than common shareholders in liquidation, but their potential returns are limited by the board of directors.

        2)   Issuers of debt securities are legally obligated to redeem them. Because these returns are guaranteed, their risks and returns are lower than those for equity investments.

            a)   Income bonds pay a return only if the issuer is profitable.

            b)   Debentures are unsecured.

            c)   Mortgage bonds are secured by real property.

            d)   U.S. Treasury bonds are backed by the full faith and credit of the United States government.

        3)   Precious metals normally are considered a risky investment because their prices are highly volatile. During periods of high inflation, however, currency loses purchasing power rapidly, and precious metals may be a safe investment.

Stop and review! You have completed the outline for this subunit. Study multiple-choice questions 1 through 8 beginning on page 147.

5.2 QUANTIFYING INVESTMENT RISK

1.   **Probability and Standard Deviation**

    a.   Probability provides a method for mathematically expressing doubt or assurance about the occurrence of a chance event.

    b.   A **probability distribution** is the set of all possible outcomes of a decision, with a probability assigned to each outcome. For example, a simple probability distribution might be defined for the possible returns on a stock investment. A different return could be estimated for each of a limited number of possible states of the economy, and a probability could be determined for each state. Such a distribution is **discrete** because the outcomes are limited.

2.   **Measures of Risk – Standard Deviation and Variance**

    a.   The **expected rate of return ($\overline{R}$)** on an investment is determined using an expected value calculation. It is an average of the possible outcomes weighted according to their probabilities.

$$\textit{Expected rate of return } (\overline{R}) = \sum (\textit{Possible rate of return} \times \textit{Probability})$$

EXAMPLE

A company is considering investing in the common stock of one of two firms, Xatalan Corp. and Yarmouth Co. The expected rates of return on the two securities based on the weighted averages of their probable outcomes are calculated as follows:

Xatalan Corporation Stock				Yarmouth Company Stock			
Rate of Return %		Probability %	Weighted Average	Rate of Return %		Probability %	Weighted Average
80 %	×	60%	= 48 %	30 %	×	70%	= 21 %
(50)%	×	40%	= (20)%	(10)%	×	30%	= (3)%
Expected rate of return ($\overline{R}$)			28 %	Expected rate of return ($\overline{R}$)			18 %

The expected rate of return on Xatalan stock is higher, but the risk of each investment also should be measured.

---

b. Risk is the probability that the actual return on an investment will differ from the expected return. One measure of risk is the standard deviation (variance) of the distribution of an investment's return.

$$Standard\ deviation\ (\sigma)\ =\ \sqrt{\Sigma[(R_i\ -\ \overline{R})^2 \times Probability]}\ =\ \sqrt{Variance}$$

If: R_i = Possible rate of return
        $\overline{R}$ = Expected rate of return

1) The **standard deviation** measures the tightness of the distribution and the riskiness of the investment.

    a) A large standard deviation reflects a broadly dispersed probability distribution, meaning the range of possible returns is wide. But, the smaller the standard deviation, the tighter the probability distribution and the lower the risk.

    b) Thus, the greater the standard deviation, the riskier the investment.

EXAMPLE

The following are the standard deviations of the returns on the investments from the previous example:

Xatalan Corporation Stock

Standard deviation (σ) = $\sqrt{[(80\% - 28\%)^2 \times 60\%] + [(-50\% - 28\%)^2 \times 40\%]}$ = $\sqrt{4,056}$ = **63.69%**

Yarmouth Company Stock

Standard deviation (σ) = $\sqrt{[(30\% - 18\%)^2 \times 70\%] + [(-10\% - 18\%)^2 \times 30\%]}$ = $\sqrt{336}$ = **18.33%**

The investment in Xatalan stock has a higher expected return than the investment in Yarmouth stock (28% > 18%). It also is riskier because its standard deviation is greater (63.69% > 18.33%). Accordingly, to determine which investment has the preferable risk-return tradeoff, the coefficient of variation (CV) of the expected returns on the two investments is measured.

---

c. The **coefficient of variation (CV)** is useful when the rates of return and standard deviations of two investments differ. It measures the **risk per unit of return**.

$$Coefficient\ of\ variation\ =\ \frac{Standard\ deviation}{Expected\ rate\ of\ return}$$

$$CV\ =\ \sigma \div \overline{R}$$

The lower the ratio, the better the risk-return tradeoff.

EXAMPLE

The coefficients of variation for the expected return of the two potential investments are calculated as follows:

		Coefficient of Variation
Xatalan Corporation Stock:	$\sigma \div \overline{R}$ = 63.69% ÷ 28% =	**2.275**
Yarmouth Company Stock:	$\sigma \div \overline{R}$ = 18.33% ÷ 18% =	**1.018**

The investment in Yarmouth has a better risk-return tradeoff. Its coefficient of variation (CV) is lower than that of the investment in Xatalan (1.018 < 2.275).

---

3. **Diversification**

    a. The measures presented above relate to the risk and return for individual securities. However, few investors hold only one security.

        1) The goal of portfolio management is to hold a group of securities that provides a reasonable rate of return without the risks associated with one security.

            a) Expected portfolio **return** is the weighted average of the returns on the individual securities.

            b) Portfolio **risk** is usually less than a simple average of the standard deviations of the component securities. This is one benefit of diversification.

    b.   Specific risk (also called diversifiable risk, unsystematic risk, residual risk, or unique risk) is associated with one investment security. Specific risk potentially can be eliminated by diversification.

        1)   Diversification reduces aggregate volatility.

            a)   Some stocks move in the same direction as other stocks in the portfolio but by a smaller amount. Some stocks move in the opposite direction from other stocks.

            b)   Thus, by combining imperfectly correlated securities into a portfolio, the risk of the group as a whole is less than the average of their standard deviations.

        2)   In theory, diversifiable risk should continue to decrease as the number of different securities held increases.

            a)   But, in practice, the benefits of diversification become extremely small when more than about 20 to 30 different securities are held. Moreover, commissions and other transaction costs increase with greater diversification.

    c.   Market risk, also called undiversifiable risk and systematic risk, is the risk of the stock market as a whole. For an ideal, well-diversified portfolio, it is the only risk.

    d.   The **coefficient of correlation (r)** measures the degree to which any two variables, e.g., the prices of two stocks, are related.

        1)   The coefficient of correlation has a range from 1.0 to –1.0 (Study Unit 6, Subunit 2, fully covers correlation).

            a)   Perfect positive correlation (1.0) means that the two variables always move together.

            b)   Perfect negative correlation (–1.0) means that the two variables always move in the opposite direction.

            c)   If a pair of securities has a coefficient of correlation of 1.0, the risk of the two together is the same as the risk of each security by itself. If a pair of securities has a coefficient of correlation of –1.0, all specific (unsystematic) risk has been eliminated.

        2)   The ideal portfolio consists of securities with a wide enough variety of coefficients of correlation that only market risk remains.

            a)   The normal range for the correlation of two randomly selected stocks is .50 to .70.

Stop and review! You have completed the outline for this subunit. Study multiple-choice questions 9 through 15 beginning on page 149.

5.3 CAPITAL ASSET PRICING MODEL

    1.   **Capital Asset Pricing Model (CAPM)**

        a.   Investors want to reduce their risk and take advantage of diversification by holding a portfolio of securities. To measure how a particular security contributes to the risk and return of a diversified portfolio, investors can use the **capital asset pricing model (CAPM)**.

        b.   The CAPM quantifies the required return on an equity security by relating the security's level of risk to the average return available in the market.

        c.   The CAPM formula is based on the idea that the investor must be compensated for an investment in two ways: time value of money and risk.

            1)   The time value component is the **risk-free rate** (denoted R_F in the formula). It is the return provided by the safest investments, e.g., U.S. Treasury securities.

2) The risk component consists of

    a) The **market risk premium** (denoted $R_M - R_F$), the return provided by the market over the risk-free rate, weighted by

    b) A measure of the security's risk, called **beta** (β).

        i) The effect of an individual security on the volatility of a portfolio is measured by its sensitivity to movements by the overall market. This sensitivity is stated in terms of a stock's beta coefficient (β).

        ii) Thus, the beta of the market portfolio equals 1, and the beta of U.S. Treasury securities is 0.

    c) The **security risk premium** is $\beta(R_M - R_F)$. Thus, the required rate of return of the security is the risk-free rate of return (R_F) plus the security risk premium.

CAPM Formula

$$Required\ rate\ of\ return\ =\ R_F\ +\ \beta\,(R_M\ -\ R_F)$$

If: R_F = Risk-free return
        R_M = Market return
        β = Measure of the systematic risk or volatility of the individual security in comparison with the market (diversified portfolio)

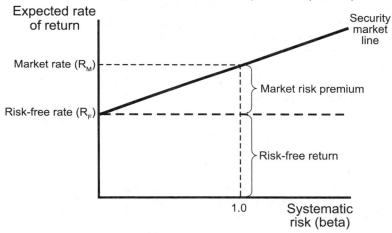

Figure 5-2

d. The market risk premium varies in direct proportion to beta. Consequently, all investments (securities) must lie on the security market line.

EXAMPLE

An investor is considering the purchase of a stock with a beta of 1.2. Treasury bills currently are paying 8.6%, and the average return on the market is 10.1%. (Remember, U.S. Treasuries are considered as close to a risk-free investment as can exist.) To be induced to buy this stock, the return that the investor must receive is calculated as follows:

$$\begin{aligned}
\text{Required rate of return} &= R_F + \beta(R_M - R_F) \\
&= 8.6\% + 1.2(10.1\% - 8.6\%) \\
&= 8.6\% + 1.8\% \\
&= 10.4\%
\end{aligned}$$

Stop and review! You have completed the outline for this subunit. Study multiple-choice questions 16 through 24 beginning on page 151.

5.4 DERIVATIVES

1. **Overview**

    a. A **derivative instrument** is an investment transaction in which the parties' gain or loss is derived from some other economic event, for example, (1) the price of a given stock, (2) a foreign currency exchange rate, or (3) the price of a certain commodity.

        1) One party enters into the transaction to speculate (incur risk) and the other enters into it to hedge (avoid risk).

    b. Derivatives are a type of financial instrument, along with cash, accounts receivable, notes receivable, bonds, preferred shares, etc.

2. **Hedging**

    a. Hedging uses offsetting commitments to minimize or avoid the effect of adverse price movements. To hedge an investment, the entity takes a position in a financial instrument that is almost perfectly correlated with the original asset but in the opposite direction.

    b. An entity has a **long position** in an asset whenever the entity owns the asset. An entity with a long position therefore benefits from a rise in the asset's value.

EXAMPLE

An investor buys 100 shares of Collerup Corporation stock. The investor now has a long position in Collerup Corporation; in financial market terminology, this is referred to as being "long Collerup."

---

    c. An entity has a **short position** in an asset when the entity sells an asset that it does not own at the time of the sale. Entities take short positions when they believe the value of the asset will decrease.

        1) Typically, the entity with the short position must borrow the asset from an entity that owns it before the "short sale" occurs.

EXAMPLE

Money Management Fund A believes that the share price of Collerup Corporation will decrease (perhaps due to a future poor earnings announcement). Fund A therefore borrows a block of Collerup shares from Fund B, which Fund A then sells on the appropriate stock exchange. Fund A is selling short because the fund is selling shares it does not actually own.

•   If the price of Collerup decreases, Fund A can repurchase the shares at the lower price and return them to Fund B, making a profit.

•   If Fund A guessed wrong and the share price of Collerup remains the same or increases, then, to fulfill its obligation to return the borrowed shares to Fund B, Fund A must purchase the shares on the stock exchange (at the higher price), incurring a loss.

---

3. **Options**

    a. A party who buys an option has bought the right to demand that the counterparty (the seller or writer of the option) buy or sell an underlying asset on or before a specified future date. The buyer holds all of the rights, and the seller has all of the obligations. The buyer pays a fee to be able to determine whether the seller buys (sells) the underlying asset from (to) the buyer.

Many CPA candidates become intimidated when studying options. An option is merely a standardized legal contract that requires two parties to comply with its terms. These contracts are no more complicated than the legal contract a person has with his or her cell phone carrier. Individuals pay the cellular phone company money, and in return the cell phone provider is obligated to supply the individual with telephone service when the individual wants to make a phone call. Furthermore, some cell phone carriers charge on the basis of pay-as-you-go while others charge a fixed amount for a fixed amount of minutes. There are many terms associated with cell phone providers, and, similar to cell phones, options have their own terminology. The terms on the next page are useful for people in finance because they indicate how a contract is standardized, allowing people to communicate quickly and succinctly when discussing options.

1) A **call option** gives the buyer (holder) the right to purchase (the right to call for) the underlying asset (stock, currency, commodity, etc.) at a fixed price.

2) A **put option** gives the buyer (holder) the right to sell (the right to put onto the market) the underlying asset (stock, currency, commodity, etc.) at a fixed price.

3) The asset that is subject to being bought or sold under the terms of the option is the **underlying**.

4) The party buying an option is the **holder**. The seller is the **writer**.

5) The exercise of an option always is at the discretion of the option holder (the buyer) who has, in effect, bought the right to exercise the option or not. The seller of an option has no choice. (S)he must perform if the holder chooses to exercise.

6) An option has an expiration date after which it can no longer be exercised.

4. **Valuing an Option**

a. The two best-known models for valuing options are the Black-Scholes formula for call options and the binomial method. The equations are extremely complex and beyond the scope of this text, but some general statements can be made about the factors that affect the outcomes.

   1) **Exercise price.** The exercise price is the price at which the holder can purchase (call option) or sell (put option) the underlying asset in the option contract.

      a) Thus, an increase in the exercise price of an option results in a decrease in the value of a call option and an increase in the value of a put option.

   2) **Price of underlying.** As the price of the underlying increases, the value of a call option also increases.

      a) The value of a put option decreases as the price of the underlying increases. Selling at a lower-than-market price is not advantageous.

   3) **Interest rates.** Buying a call option is similar to buying the underlying on credit. Buying the right to purchase the underlying asset (call option) is much cheaper than buying the underlying asset directly. The holder of the call option may invest the difference between the option premium and the price of the underlying in a savings account and receive interest income. Thus, a rise in interest rates makes call options more attractive to buyers and increases their value.

      a) Instead of receiving interest income from selling the underlying asset and investing the proceeds in a saving account, the holder of a put option needs to hold the underlying asset to deliver it under the put option. Thus, a rise in interest rates makes the put options less attractive to buyers (holders) and decreases the value of the put options.

   4) **Time until expiration.** The longer the term of an option, the greater the chance that the underlying price will change and the option will be in-the-money.

      a) Thus, an increase in the term of an option (both calls and puts) will result in an increase in the value of the option.

   5) **Volatility of price of underlying.** Because the holder's loss on an option is limited to the option premium (amount paid for the option), the holder prefers greater volatility of the price of the underlying. The more volatile the price of the underlying, the greater the chance that it will change and the option will be in-the-money.

      a) An increase in the volatility of the price of the underlying results in an increase in the value of the option (both calls and puts).

b.   These factors and their effects are summarized as follows:

Increase in	Value of call option	Value of put option
Exercise price of option	Decrease	Increase
Price of underlying	Increase	Decrease
Interest rates	Increase	Decrease
Time until expiration	Increase	Increase
Volatility of price of underlying	Increase	Increase

c.   The **intrinsic value of a call option** is the amount by which the exercise price is less than the current price of the underlying.

1)   If an option has a positive intrinsic value, it is in-the-money.

EXAMPLE

An investor holds call options for 200 shares of Locksley Corporation with an exercise price of $48 per share. Locksley stock is currently trading at $50 per share. The investor's options have an intrinsic value of $2 each ($50 – $48).

---

2)   If an option has an intrinsic value of $0, it is out-of-the-money.

EXAMPLE

An investor holds call options for 200 shares of Locksley Corporation with an exercise price of $48 per share. Locksley stock is currently trading at $45 per share. The investor's options are out-of-the-money. They have no intrinsic value.

---

d.   The **intrinsic value of a put option** is the amount by which the exercise price is greater than the current price of the underlying.

1)   If an option has a positive intrinsic value, it is in-the-money.

EXAMPLE

An investor holds put options for 200 shares of Locksley Corporation with an exercise price of $48 per share. Locksley stock is currently trading at $45 per share. The investor's options have an intrinsic value of $3 each ($48 – $45).

---

2)   If an option has an intrinsic value of $0, it is out-of-the-money.

EXAMPLE

An investor holds put options for 200 shares of Locksley Corporation with an exercise price of $48 per share. Locksley stock is currently trading at $50 per share. The investor's options are out-of-the-money. They have no intrinsic value.

---

5.   **Forward Contracts**

a.   One method of mitigating risk is the simple forward contract. The two parties agree that, at a set future date, one of them will perform and the other will pay a specified amount for the performance.

1)   A common example is that of a retailer and a wholesaler who agree in September on the prices and quantities of merchandise to be shipped to the retailer's stores in time for the winter holiday season. The retailer has locked in a price and a source of supply, and the wholesaler has locked in a price and a customer.

b.   The significant difference between a forward contract and an option is that a contract imposes obligations. Both parties must meet those obligations, i.e., to deliver merchandise and to pay. Neither has the option of nonperformance.

1)   Forward contracts are frequently used in transactions to exchange foreign currencies.

6. **Futures Contracts**

    a. A futures contract is a commitment to buy or sell an asset at a fixed price during a specific future period. In contrast with a forward contract, the counterparty is unknown.

    b. Futures contracts are traded actively on futures exchanges.

       1) The clearinghouse randomly matches sellers who will deliver during a given period with buyers who are seeking delivery during the same period.

    c. Because futures contracts are actively traded, the result is a **liquid market** in futures that permits buyers and sellers to net their positions.

    d. Another distinguishing feature of futures contracts is that the market price is posted and netted to each person's account at the close of every business day. This practice is called **mark-to-market**.

       1) A mark-to-market provision minimizes a futures contract's chance of default because profits and losses on the contracts must be received or paid each day through a clearinghouse (and because the clearinghouse guarantees the transactions).

7. **Margin Requirements**

    a. A margin account is a brokerage account in which the investor borrows money (obtains credit) from a broker to purchase securities. The broker charges interest on the credit provided.

    b. A margin requirement (set by the Federal Reserve Board's Regulation T) is the minimum down payment that the purchasers of securities must deposit in the margin account.

Stop and review! You have completed the outline for this subunit. Study multiple-choice questions 25 through 30 beginning on page 154.

QUESTIONS

5.1 Risk and Return

1. A company is evaluating its experience with five recent investments. The following data are available:

Investment	Cost of Investment	Amount Received
A	$ 8,500	$ 8,390
B	4,200	4,610
C	12,100	12,400
D	7,900	8,220
E	11,000	11,400

Rank the investments in order from highest rate of return to lowest.

    A. C, E, A, D, B.

    B. B, D, E, C, A.

    C. B, E, D, C, A.

    D. A, C, D, E, B.

Answer (B) is correct.

    REQUIRED: The order of investments from highest rate of return to lowest.

    DISCUSSION: Rate of return is equal to the return on an investment (the amount received minus the amount invested) divided by the amount invested. The calculation for these five investments can be performed as follows:

Investment	Cost of Investment	Amount Received	Return	Rate of Return
A	$ 8,500	$ 8,390	$(110)	(1.3%)
B	4,200	4,610	410	9.8%
C	12,100	12,400	300	2.5%
D	7,900	8,220	320	4.1%
E	11,000	11,400	400	3.6%

    Answer (A) is incorrect. The ranking C, E, A, D, B is in order by amount received, not rate of return. Answer (C) is incorrect. The ranking B, E, D, C, A is in order by return, not rate of return. Answer (D) is incorrect. The ranking A, C, D, E, B is from lowest rate of return to highest.

2. Dr. G invested $10,000 in a lifetime annuity for his granddaughter Emily. The annuity is expected to yield $400 annually forever. What is the anticipated annual rate of return for the annuity?

    A. Cannot be determined without additional information.

    B. 4.0%

    C. 2.5%

    D. 8.0%

Answer (B) is correct.
    REQUIRED: The internal rate of return.
    DISCUSSION: A return is the amount received by an investor as compensation for taking on the risk of the investment. The rate of return is the return stated as a percentage of the amount invested. In this case, it is 4% ($400 ÷ $10,000).
    Answer (A) is incorrect. The rate of return can be calculated. Answer (C) is incorrect. Reversing the numerator and denominator results in a rate of 2.5%. Answer (D) is incorrect. Treating the return as semi-annual rather than annual results in a rate of 8.0%.

3. Catherine & Co. has extra cash at the end of the year and is analyzing the best way to invest the funds. The company should invest in a project only if the

    A. Expected return on the project exceeds the return on investments of comparable risk.

    B. Return on investments of comparable risk exceeds the expected return on the project.

    C. Expected return on the project is equal to the return on investments of comparable risk.

    D. Return on investments of comparable risk equals the expected return on the project.

Answer (A) is correct.
    REQUIRED: The rule for deciding whether to invest in a project.
    DISCUSSION: Investment risk is analyzed in terms of the probability that the actual return on an investment will be lower than the expected return. Comparing a project's expected return with the return on an asset of similar risk helps determine whether the project is worth investing in. If the expected return on a project exceeds the return on an asset of comparable risk, the project should be pursued.

4. Beginning January 2, Year 1, a company deposited $50,000 in a savings account for 2 years. The account earns 10% interest, compounded annually. What amount of interest did the company earn during the 2-year period?

    A. $10,500

    B. $10,000

    C. $5,500

    D. $5,000

Answer (A) is correct.
    REQUIRED: The amount of interest earned during the 2-year period.
    DISCUSSION: Compounding interest is the practice of adding interest to the carrying amount of the principal rather than paying it in cash. The amount of interest earned in Year 1 ($50,000 × 10% = $5,000) was added to the principal, which was then used to calculate the amount of interest earned in Year 2 [($50,000 + $5,000) × 10% = $5,500]. The total amount of interest earned during the 2-year period was thus $10,500 ($5,000 Year 1 + $5,500 Year 2). This amount also can be calculated as follows: [($50,000 × 1.1 × 1.1) – $50,000].
    Answer (B) is incorrect. The amount of $10,000 is interest that would have been earned using simple, not compound, interest. Answer (C) is incorrect. The amount of $5,500 is the interest earned in the second year. Answer (D) is incorrect. The amount of $5,000 is the interest earned in the first year.

5. The risk of loss because of fluctuations in the relative value of foreign currencies is called

    A. Expropriation risk.

    B. Multinational beta.

    C. Exchange rate risk.

    D. Undiversifiable risk.

Answer (C) is correct.
    REQUIRED: The risk of loss because of fluctuations in the relative value of foreign currencies.
    DISCUSSION: When amounts to be paid or received are denominated in a foreign currency, exchange rate fluctuations may result in exchange gains or losses. For example, if a U.S. firm has a receivable fixed in terms of units of a foreign currency, a decline in the value of that currency relative to the U.S. dollar results in a foreign exchange loss.
    Answer (A) is incorrect. Expropriation risk is the risk that the sovereign country in which the assets backing an investment are located will seize the assets without adequate compensation. Answer (B) is incorrect. The beta value in the capital asset pricing model for a multinational firm is the systematic risk of a given multinational firm relative to that of the market as a whole. Answer (D) is incorrect. Undiversifiable risk is risk that cannot be offset through diversification.

6. Prior to the introduction of the euro, O&B Company, a U.S. corporation, is in possession of accounts receivable denominated in Deutsche marks. To what type of risk are they exposed?

- A. Liquidity risk.
- B. Political risk.
- C. Exchange-rate risk.
- D. Price risk.

Answer (C) is correct.
REQUIRED: The risk to which a business is exposed when accounts receivable are denominated in a foreign currency.
DISCUSSION: Exchange-rate risk is the risk that a foreign currency transaction will be negatively exposed to fluctuations in exchange rates. Because O&B Company sells goods to German customers and records accounts receivable denominated in Deutsche marks, O&B Company is exposed to exchange-rate risk.
Answer (A) is incorrect. Liquidity risk is the possibility that an asset cannot be sold on short notice for its market value. Answer (B) is incorrect. Political risk is the probability of loss from actions of governments. Answer (D) is incorrect. Price risk is a component of interest-rate risk.

7. The marketable securities with the **least** amount of default risk are

- A. Federal government agency securities.
- B. U.S. Treasury securities.
- C. Repurchase agreements.
- D. Commercial paper.

Answer (B) is correct.
REQUIRED: The marketable securities with the least default risk.
DISCUSSION: The marketable securities with the lowest default risk are those issued by the federal government. They are backed by the full faith and credit of the U.S. government and therefore are the least risky form of investment.
Answer (A) is incorrect. Securities issued by a federal agency are backed first by that agency and second by the U.S. government. Agency securities are issued by agencies and corporations created by the federal government, such as the Federal Housing Administration. Answer (C) is incorrect. Repurchase agreements could become worthless if the organization agreeing to make the repurchase goes bankrupt. Answer (D) is incorrect. Commercial paper is unsecured.

8. Which of the following is **not** a political risk of investing in a foreign country?

- A. Rebellions could result in destruction of property.
- B. Assets could be expropriated.
- C. Foreign-exchange controls could limit the repatriation of profits.
- D. A foreign customer might default on its debt.

Answer (D) is correct.
REQUIRED: The item not a political risk of investing in foreign-based assets.
DISCUSSION: Political risks include (1) the threat of expropriation of the firm's assets, (2) destruction of assets in rebellions in third-world nations, and (3) limitations on the repatriation of profits (or even initial investments). Default by a foreign customer is not a political risk, but a risk of doing business either locally or internationally.

5.2 Quantifying Investment Risk

9. City Development, Inc., is considering a new investment project that will involve building a large office block in Frankfurt-am-Main. The firm's financial analysis department has estimated that the proposed investment has the following estimated rate of return distributions:

Rate of Return	Probability
(5%)	30%
10%	50%
20%	20%

Calculate the expected rate of return.

- A. 5.5%
- B. 7.5%
- C. 10.5%
- D. 11.7%

Answer (B) is correct.
REQUIRED: The expected rate of return for an investment project.
DISCUSSION: The expected rate of return on an investment can be calculated by weighting each potential rate of return by its probability of occurrence and summing the results. City Development's expected rate of return for this development is:

Rate of Return	Probability	Expected Rate of Return
(5.0)%	30.0%	(1.5)%
10.0%	50.0%	5.0%
20.0%	20.0%	4.0%
		7.5%

Answer (A) is incorrect. The rate of 5.5% is a nonsense result. Answer (C) is incorrect. The rate of 10.5% results from improperly treating the negative 5% return as a positive number. Answer (D) is incorrect. The rate of 11.7% results from treating the negative return as a positive number and weighting the three possible results equally.

10. Russell, Inc., is evaluating four independent investment proposals. The expected returns and standard deviations for each of these proposals are presented below.

Investment Proposal	Expected Returns	Standard Deviation
I	16%	10%
II	14%	10%
III	20%	11%
IV	22%	15%

Which one of the investment proposals has the **least** risk per unit of return?

- A. Investment I.
- B. Investment II.
- C. Investment III.
- D. Investment IV.

Answer (C) is correct.
 REQUIRED: The investment proposal with the least relative risk.
 DISCUSSION: The coefficient of variation (CV) measures the risk per unit of return by dividing the standard deviation (σ) by the expected return. The investment with the lowest CV has the best risk-return tradeoff. The CVs of Russell's four investment proposals can thus be calculated as follows:

	Standard Deviation		Expected Returns		Coefficient of Variation
Investment I	10%	÷	16%	=	62.5%
Investment II	10%	÷	14%	=	71.4%
Investment III	11%	÷	20%	=	55.0%
Investment IV	15%	÷	22%	=	68.2%

Answer (A) is incorrect. The coefficient of variation for Investment I is 0.625 (10% ÷ 16%), which is not the lowest coefficient of the four. Answer (B) is incorrect. Investment II has the highest relative level of risk with a coefficient of variation of 0.714 (10% ÷ 14%). Answer (D) is incorrect. The coefficient of variation for Investment IV is 0.682 (15% ÷ 22%), which is not the lowest coefficient of the four.

11. Konstans Corp. is considering purchasing an investment security with the following information:

Likelihood	Return on Investment
50%	2%
40%	4%
10%	14%

The expected return on this investment is

- A. 2%
- B. 4%
- C. 25%
- D. 50%

Answer (B) is correct.
 REQUIRED: The expected return on an investment.
 DISCUSSION: The expected return on this investment is 4% [(50% × 2%) + (40% × 4%) + (10% × 14%)].
 Answer (A) is incorrect. The expected return is a weighted average. Answer (C) is incorrect. The return of 25% is not meaningful in this context. Answer (D) is incorrect. An expected return of 50% is a likelihood, not a return.

12. The risk of a single stock is

- A. Interest rate risk.
- B. Unsystematic risk.
- C. Portfolio risk.
- D. Market risk.

Answer (B) is correct.
 REQUIRED: The risk of a single asset.
 DISCUSSION: Unsystematic risk is the risk of a single stock, but portfolio risk is the net risk of holding a portfolio of diversified securities. Portfolio risk therefore includes systematic and unsystematic risk.
 Answer (A) is incorrect. Interest rate risk is the risk of changes in interest rates. Answer (C) is incorrect. Portfolio risk is the net risk of multiple securities. Answer (D) is incorrect. Market risk is systematic risk.

13. The expected rate of return for the stock of Cornhusker Enterprises is 20%, with a standard deviation of 15%. The expected rate of return for the stock of Mustang Associates is 10%, with a standard deviation of 9%. The stock with the worse risk/return relationship is

- A. Cornhusker because the return is higher.
- B. Cornhusker because the standard deviation is higher.
- C. Mustang because the standard deviation is higher.
- D. Mustang because the coefficient of variation is higher.

Answer (D) is correct.
 REQUIRED: The riskier stock.
 DISCUSSION: The coefficient of variation is useful when the rates of return and standard deviations of two investments differ. It measures the risk per unit of return by dividing the standard deviation by the expected return. The coefficient of variation is higher for Mustang (.09 ÷ .10 = .90) than for Cornhusker (.15 ÷ .20 = .75).
 Answer (A) is incorrect. The existence of a higher return is not necessarily indicative of high risk. Answer (B) is incorrect. The level of standard deviation by itself is not enough for determining the stock's risk-return relationship. Answer (C) is incorrect. Mustang does not have the higher standard deviation.

14. If two projects are completely and positively linearly dependent (or positively related), the measure of correlation between them is

A. 0

B. +.5

C. +1

D. −1

Answer (C) is correct.
REQUIRED: The measure of correlation when two projects are positively linearly dependent.
DISCUSSION: The measure of correlation when two projects are linearly dependent in a positive way is +1.
Answer (A) is incorrect. A zero correlation indicates no relationship. Answer (B) is incorrect. The measure +.5 does not indicate linearity. Answer (D) is incorrect. A −1 would indicate a negative correlation.

15. In theory, which of the following coefficients of correlation would eliminate unsystematic risk in an investment portfolio?

A. 1.0

B. 0.0

C. −1.0

D. No theoretical coefficient exists for the elimination of risk in a portfolio context.

Answer (C) is correct.
REQUIRED: The coefficient of correlation that would eliminate risk in an investment portfolio.
DISCUSSION: The correlation coefficient measures the degree to which any two variables, e.g., two stocks in a portfolio, are related. Perfect negative correlation (−1.0) means that the two variables always move in the opposite direction. Given perfect negative correlation, unsystematic risk is, in theory, eliminated.
Answer (A) is incorrect. A coefficient of correlation of 1.0 indicates perfect positive correlation. Given perfect positive correlation, risk for a two-stock portfolio with equal investments in each stock are the same as that for the individual assets. Answer (B) is incorrect. A coefficient of correlation of 0.0 indicates no correlation at all. Answer (D) is incorrect. The coefficient of correlation that, in theory, eliminates unsystematic risk in an investment portfolio is −1.0.

5.3 Capital Asset Pricing Model

16. A market analyst has estimated the equity beta of Modern Homes, Inc., to be 1.4. This beta implies that the company's

A. Systematic risk is lower than that of the market portfolio.

B. Systematic risk is higher than that of the market portfolio.

C. Unsystematic risk is higher than that of the market portfolio.

D. Total risk is higher than that of the market portfolio.

Answer (B) is correct.
REQUIRED: The implications of a beta greater than 1.
DISCUSSION: Systematic risk, also called market risk and undiversifiable risk, is the risk of the stock market as a whole. Some conditions in the national economy affect all businesses, which is why equity prices so often move together. The effect of an individual security on the volatility of a portfolio is measured by its sensitivity to movements by the overall market. This sensitivity is stated in terms of a stock's beta coefficient. An average-risk stock has a beta of 1.0 because its returns are perfectly positively correlated with those on the market portfolio.
Answer (A) is incorrect. A beta of less than 1.0 means that the market, or systematic, risk is lower than that of the market portfolio. Answer (C) is incorrect. Unsystematic risk is the risk that is influenced by an individual firm's policies and decisions. The beta does not concern unsystematic risk. Answer (D) is incorrect. Only a portion of the risk, not the total risk, is higher than that of the market portfolio.

17. If the return on the market portfolio is 10% and the risk-free rate is 5%, what is the effect on a company's required rate of return on its stock of an increase in the beta coefficient from 1.2 to 1.5?

A. 3% increase.

B. 1.5% increase.

C. No change.

D. 1.5% decrease.

Answer (B) is correct.
REQUIRED: The effect on a company's required rate of return on its stock of an increase in the beta coefficient.
DISCUSSION: The required rate of return on equity capital can be estimated with the capital asset pricing model (CAPM). CAPM consists of adding the risk-free rate (i.e., the return on government securities, denoted R_F) to the product of the beta coefficient (a measure of the issuer's risk) and the difference between the market return and the risk-free rate (denoted $R_M − R_F$, referred to as the risk premium). Below is the basic equilibrium equation for the CAPM:

$$\text{Required rate of return} = R_F + \beta(R_M - R_F)$$

In this situation, the risk premium is 5% (10% − 5%). Thus, the required rate of return when the beta coefficient is 1.2 is 11% [5% + (1.2 × 5%)], and the required rate when the beta coefficient is 1.5 is 12.5% [5% + (1.5 × 5%)]. This is an increase of 1.5% (12.5% − 11%).

18. Using the capital asset pricing model (CAPM), the required rate of return for a firm with a beta of 1.25 when the market return is 14% and the risk-free rate is 6% is

A. 6.0%

B. 7.5%

C. 17.5%

D. 16.0%

Answer (D) is correct.
REQUIRED: The required rate of return using the capital asset pricing model.
DISCUSSION: The CAPM adds the risk-free rate to the product of the beta coefficient and the difference between the market return and the risk-free rate. The market-risk premium is the amount above the risk-free rate for which investors must be compensated to induce them to invest in the company. The beta coefficient of an individual stock is the correlation between volatility (price variation) of the stock market and the volatility of the price of the individual stock. Thus, the required rate is 16% [6% + 1.25 (14% − 6%)].

19. If Dexter Industries has a beta value of 1.0, then its

A. Return should equal the risk-free rate.

B. Price is relatively stable.

C. Expected return should approximate the overall market.

D. Volatility is low.

Answer (C) is correct.
REQUIRED: The result when the beta value is 1.0.
DISCUSSION: The effect of an individual security on the volatility of a portfolio is measured by its sensitivity to movements by the overall market. This sensitivity is stated in terms of a stock's beta coefficient. If the beta coefficient is 1.0, the price of that stock tends to move in the same direction and to the same degree as the overall market. The expected return can be calculated from the CAPM model formula.

$$Expected\ return = R_F + \beta\,(R_M - R_F)$$
$$R_F = \text{Risk-free rate}$$
$$R_M = \text{Market return}$$

When $\beta = 1$, expected return is equal to the market return.
Answer (A) is incorrect. Return is equal to the risk-free rate when $\beta = 0$. Answer (B) is incorrect. A beta value of 1.0 only means the price of the stock moves in concert with that of the overall market; if the market is not stable, the stock price will not be either. Answer (D) is incorrect. A beta value of 1.0 only means the price of the stock moves with that of the overall market. If the market is volatile, the stock price also will be.

20. The betas and expected returns for three investments being considered by Sky, Inc., are given below.

Investment	Beta	Expected Return
A	1.4	12%
B	0.8	11%
C	1.5	13%

The return on the market is 11% and the risk-free rate is 6%. If the capital asset pricing model (CAPM) is used for calculating the required rate of return, which investments should the management of Sky make?

A. B only.

B. A and C only.

C. B and C only.

D. A, B, and C.

Answer (A) is correct.
REQUIRED: The investment(s) that should be made based on the CAPM.
DISCUSSION: The required rate of return on equity capital can be estimated with the capital asset pricing model (CAPM). CAPM consists of adding the risk-free rate (i.e., the return on government securities, denoted R_F) to the product of the beta coefficient (a measure of the issuer's risk) and the difference between the market return and the risk-free rate (denoted $R_M - R_F$, referred to as the risk premium). Below is the basic equilibrium equation for the CAPM:

$$Required\ rate\ of\ return = R_F + \beta\,(R_M - R_F)$$

The risk premium is 5% (11% − 6%).

The CAPM can be thus applied to each of the three investments as follows:

Investment A: 6% + (1.4 × 5%) = 13.0%
Investment B: 6% + (0.8 × 5%) = 10.0%
Investment C: 6% + (1.5 × 5%) = 13.5%

These required rates of return can be compared with the expected rates to evaluate which investments should be accepted and which should be rejected.

	Required Rate		Expected Rate	Decision
Investment A:	13.0%	>	12%	Reject
Investment B:	10.0%	<	11%	Accept
Investment C:	13.5%	>	13%	Reject

Answer (B) is incorrect. The required rates of return for Investment A and Investment C exceed their expected returns. Answer (C) is incorrect. R for Investment C exceeds its expected return. Answer (D) is incorrect. The required rates of return for Investment A and Investment C exceed their expected returns.

21. An analyst covering Guilderland Mining Co. common stock estimates the following information for next year:

Expected return on the market portfolio	12%
Expected return on Treasury securities	5%
Expected beta of Guilderland	2.2

Using the CAPM, the analyst's estimate of next year's risk premium for Guilderland's stock is closest to

A. 7.0%

B. 10.4%

C. 15.4%

D. 21.4%

Answer (C) is correct.

REQUIRED: The expected risk-adjusted premium of a stock based on the capital asset pricing model.

DISCUSSION: According to the capital asset pricing model, the risk premium of a particular stock is the excess of the market rate of return over the risk-free rate weighted by the stock's beta coefficient. For Guilderland Mining, this calculation is

$$
\begin{aligned}
\text{Stock's risk premium} &= 2.2 \times (12\% - 5\%) \\
&= 2.2 \times 7\% \\
&= 15.4\%
\end{aligned}
$$

22. Using the capital asset pricing model (CAPM), the required rate of return for a firm with a beta of 1.5 when the market return is 10% and the risk-free rate is 8% is

A. 5%

B. 8%

C. 10%

D. 11%

Answer (D) is correct.

REQUIRED: The required rate of return using the capital asset pricing model.

DISCUSSION: The CAPM quantifies the required rate of return on a security by relating the security's level of risk to the average return available in the market. The required rate of return is calculated as follows:

$$
\begin{aligned}
\text{Required rate of return} &= R_F + \beta(R_M - R_F) \\
&= 8\% + [1.5 \times (10\% - 8\%)] \\
&= 8\% + (1.5 \times 2\%) \\
&= 11\%
\end{aligned}
$$

Answer (A) is incorrect. The required rate of return cannot be lower than the risk-free rate. Answer (B) is incorrect. The required rate of return for the safest investments (U.S. Treasury securities) is the risk-free rate of 8%. Answer (C) is incorrect. The required rate of return is the same as the market return only if beta is equal to 1.

23. According to the capital asset pricing model (CAPM), which of the following statements is true regarding the required rate of return for a security with a beta of 1?

A. The required rate of return is lower than the risk-free rate.

B. The required rate of return is equal to the risk-free rate.

C. The required rate of return is higher than the market return.

D. The required rate of return is equal to the market return.

Answer (D) is correct.

REQUIRED: The true statement regarding a beta value of 1.

DISCUSSION: The CAPM quantifies the required rate of return on a security by relating the security's level of risk to the average return available in the market. When beta equals 1, the required rate of return is equal to the market return, as shown below:

$$
\begin{aligned}
\text{Required rate of return} &= R_F + \beta(R_M - R_F) \\
&= R_F + [1 \times (R_M - R_F)] \\
&= R_F + (R_M - R_F) \\
&= R_M
\end{aligned}
$$

Answer (A) is incorrect. The required rate of return cannot be lower than the risk-free rate. Answer (B) is incorrect. The required rate of return for a security is equal to the risk-free rate when the beta of the security is equal to 0. Answer (C) is incorrect. When the beta of a security is greater than 1, the required rate of return for a security will be higher than the market return.

24. The common stock of Wisconsin's Finest Cheese has a beta coefficient of 1.7. The following information about overall market conditions is available:

Expected return on U.S. Treasury bonds   6%
Expected return on the market portfolio   8.5%

Using the capital asset pricing model (CAPM), what is the risk premium on the market?

    A. 10.3%

    B. 4.3%

    C. 2.5%

    D. 1.7%

Answer (C) is correct.
    REQUIRED: The risk premium on the market using CAPM.
    DISCUSSION: The risk premium on the market is the return on the market portfolio (8.5%) minus the risk-free return as measured by the return on U.S. Treasury securities (6%), or 2.5%.
    Answer (A) is incorrect. The rate of 10.3% is the expected return on the stock. Answer (B) is incorrect. The rate of 4.3% is the risk premium on the stock, not the market. Answer (D) is incorrect. The stock's beta coefficient and the risk premium on the market are not the same in this case.

5.4 Derivatives

25. The use of derivatives to either hedge or speculate results in

    A. Increased risk regardless of motive.

    B. Decreased risk regardless of motive.

    C. Offsetting risk when hedging and increased risk when speculating.

    D. Offsetting risk when speculating and increased risk when hedging.

Answer (C) is correct.
    REQUIRED: The effects on risk of hedging and speculating.
    DISCUSSION: Derivatives, including options and futures, are contracts. Unlike stocks and bonds, they are not claims on business assets. A futures contract is entered into as either a speculation or a hedge. Speculation involves the assumption of risk in the hope of gaining from price movements. Hedging is the process of using offsetting commitments to minimize or avoid the effect of adverse price movements.
    Answer (A) is incorrect. Hedging decreases risk by using offsetting commitments that avoid the impact of adverse price movements. Answer (B) is incorrect. Speculation involves the assumption of risk in the hope of gaining from price movements. Answer (D) is incorrect. Speculating increases risk, while hedging offsets risk.

26. Which one of the following is **not** a determinant in valuing a call option?

    A. Exercise price.

    B. Expiration date.

    C. Forward contract price.

    D. Underlying asset price.

Answer (C) is correct.
    REQUIRED: The item not a determinant in valuing a call option.
    DISCUSSION: The price of an option is equal to its intrinsic value (exercise price – underlying asset price) plus the time premium that depends on the expiration date of an option.
    Answer (A) is incorrect. The exercise price is one of the determinants of the value of a call option. Answer (B) is incorrect. The call option's expiration date is used in determining the call option's value. Answer (D) is incorrect. The underlying asset price is one of the determinants of the value of a call option.

27. A forward contract involves a commitment today to purchase a product

    A. On a specific future date at a price to be determined some time in the future.

    B. At some time during the current day at its present price.

    C. On a specific future date at a price determined today.

    D. Only when its price increases above its current exercise price.

Answer (C) is correct.
    REQUIRED: The terms of a forward contract.
    DISCUSSION: A forward contract is an executory contract in which the parties involved agree to the terms of a purchase and a sale, but performance is deferred. Accordingly, a forward contract involves a commitment today to purchase a product on a specific future date at a price determined today.
    Answer (A) is incorrect. The price of a forward contract is determined on the day of commitment, not some time in the future. Answer (B) is incorrect. Performance is deferred in a forward contract, and the price of the product is not necessarily its present price. The price can be any price determined on the day of commitment. Answer (D) is incorrect. A forward contract is a firm commitment to purchase a product. It is not based on a contingency. Also, a forward contract does not involve an exercise price. (An exercise price is an element of an option contract.)

28. A distinguishing feature of a futures contract is that

   A. Performance is delayed.

   B. It is a hedge, not a speculation.

   C. The parties know each other.

   D. The price is marked to market each day.

Answer (D) is correct.
    REQUIRED: The distinguishing feature of a futures contract.
    DISCUSSION: A characteristic of futures contracts is that their prices are marked to market every day at the close of the day. Thus, the market price is posted at the close of business each day. A mark-to-market provision minimizes a futures contract's chance of default because profits and losses on the contracts must be received or paid each day through a clearinghouse.
    Answer (A) is incorrect. Both a forward contract and a futures contract are executory. Answer (B) is incorrect. A futures contract may be speculative. Answer (C) is incorrect. In a forward contract, the parties know each other. In a future contract, the counterparty is unknown.

29. If on the expiration day a put option is "in-the-money,"

   A. The price of the underlying asset is lower than the exercise price.

   B. The option is not worth exercising.

   C. The exercise price is lower than the price of the underlying asset.

   D. The option has a negative intrinsic value.

Answer (A) is correct.
    REQUIRED: The meaning of a put option being "in-the-money."
    DISCUSSION: A put option gives the holder the right to sell (i.e., put onto the market) the underlying asset at a fixed price, called the exercise or strike. A put option is in-the-money when it has a positive intrinsic value, i.e., when the exercise price is greater than the price of the underlying.
    Answer (B) is incorrect. When an option is in-the-money, its intrinsic value is positive and it is worth exercising. Answer (C) is incorrect. When the exercise price of a put option is lower than the price of the underlying asset, the intrinsic value of the option is $0 and the option is out-of-the-money. Answer (D) is incorrect. A put option is in-the-money when it has a positive intrinsic value, i.e., when the exercise price is greater than the price of the underlying.

30. Which of the following options is(are) worth exercising?

	Exercise Price	Price of Underlying Asset
Put Option A	$30	$27
Call Option B	$29	$26
Put Option C	$25	$25
Call Option D	$20	$24

   A. Options A, B, and C.

   B. Options A and B.

   C. Options A and D.

   D. Option D only.

Answer (C) is correct.
    REQUIRED: The option(s) that is(are) worth exercising.
    DISCUSSION: An option is worth exercising if its intrinsic value is positive. A call option gives the holder the right to purchase (i.e., call for) the underlying asset at a fixed price, called the exercise or strike price. The intrinsic value of a call option is the amount by which the exercise price is less than the market price of the underlying asset. Thus, the intrinsic value of call option D is positive ($24 − $20 = $4). A put option gives the holder the right to sell (i.e., put onto the market) the underlying asset at a fixed price. The intrinsic value of a put option is the amount by which the exercise price is greater than the price of the underlying asset. Thus, the intrinsic value of put option A is positive ($30 − $27 = $3).
    Answer (A) is incorrect. Because their intrinsic values are $0, options B and C are not worth exercising. Answer (B) is incorrect. The intrinsic value of call option B is $0. The holder of this option will prefer to buy the underlying asset at its market price of $26 rather than to exercise the option to buy this asset for $29. Answer (D) is incorrect. Option A is also worth exercising. Its intrinsic value ($30 − $27 = $3) is positive.

5.5 PRACTICE WRITTEN COMMUNICATION

Business Environment and Concepts	Time Remaining				
Testlet 4 of 4	1 hour - 15 minutes	Unsplit	Split Horiz	Split Vertical	Exit

DIRECTIONS

Note: If you believe you have encountered a software malfunction, report it to the test center staff immediately.

Navigation

To navigate from task to task, use the controls at the bottom of the screen. Click on the **Next** button to advance to the next task, or the **Previous** button to go to the previous task. To go directly to any task, click on its number.

If you would like a reminder to revisit a task, or want to indicate that you are finished with it, click on the reminder flag below the task number. To clear the flag, click on it again. Reminder flags are for your use only – they do not contribute to your score.

Tabs

In this part of the examination, you will be asked to complete various tasks. Every task has one or more **Work Tabs**. Every task also has a **Help** tab.

	Written Communication	Help
	Work tab	**Help tab**

Work Tabs:

- **Work Tabs** are identified with a pencil icon. This is where your responses are expected.
- Each task has one or more **Work Tabs**.
- **Work Tabs** contain directions for completing the task - be sure to read these directions carefully.
- The **Work Tab** name in the example above is for illustration only - yours will differ.
- You must complete all of the **Work Tabs** in each task to receive full credit.

Help Tab:

- The **Help Tab** provides assistance with the exam software that is used in this task. For example, if the task is to compose a memorandum, **Help** will provide information about the word processor.

The Toolbar

The toolbar at the top of the screen shows the amount of time remaining for you to complete the tasks. In addition, the following tools are available. Note that only the **Exit** button is displayed when Directions are visible - the others will appear when you begin the tasks.

   Click on these buttons to split or unsplit the screen. You can split the screen vertically or horizontally.

   Click on this button to go on to the next part of the examination. You must complete all of the tasks to receive full credit. Once you click on **Exit** and confirm the action, you will NOT be able to return to this testlet.

Lohmann Co. is beginning its first year of operations as a shoe manufacturer. It has engaged your CPA firm to prepare its financial statements. Unfortunately, the client knows little about the distinctions among the different asset categories. Accordingly, the client has asked you to describe the characteristics of property, plant, and equipment and the relevant basic accounting principles.

Write a memorandum to your client explaining what property, plant, and equipment is and how is it accounted for.

Type your communication in the response area below using the word processor provided.

REMINDER: Your response will be graded for both technical content and writing skills. Technical content will be evaluated for information that is helpful to the intended reader and clearly relevant to the issue. Writing skills will be evaluated for development, organization, and the appropriate expression of ideas in professional correspondence. Use a standard business memo or letter format with a clear beginning, middle, and end. Do not convey information in the form of a table, bullet point list, or other abbreviated presentation.

To: Lohmann Co.
Re: Property, Plant, and Equipment

NOTE: Your Written Communications on the actual CPA exam may cover topics outside the scope of the BEC CSO (i.e., they may relate to topics from the AUD, FAR, and/or REG CSOs instead). Answer to the best of your ability, and remember that graders are mainly evaluating your writing ability and will overlook minor technical mistakes.

Unofficial Answer

Written Communication

To: Lohmann Co.
Re: Property, Plant, and Equipment

Property, plant, and equipment (PPE) are tangible long-term assets that are personal property or real property. PPE are used in ordinary operations and are not held primarily for investment, resale, or inclusion in another product. Types of PPE include land, buildings, land improvements, machinery and equipment, fixtures, vehicles, leaseholds, and leasehold improvements.

PPE also may consist of internally constructed assets, tools, patterns and dies, and returnable containers. Natural resources are sometimes classified among PPE, but they are better treated as long-term inventories. Unlike natural resources, most items treated as PPE are not consumed in ordinary operations.

PPE are reported at their historical cost, including the costs necessarily incurred to bring them to the condition and location necessary for their intended use. Historical cost is adjusted for depreciation and impairment losses. Capital expenditures for acquisition or subsequent enhancement of service potential are included in the historical cost. Other expenditures are excluded because they are deemed to benefit only the period in which they are made.

Depreciation is a crucial element of accounting for PPE. In general, expenses, such as the decline in service potential of PPE, should be recognized at the time related revenues are earned. Because no directly traceable relationship ordinarily exists between the consumption of service potential and specific revenues, the expense (depreciation) must be allocated to the periods expected to be benefited (the estimated useful life) in a systematic and rational manner.

The above depicts a Level 5 answer. Consult your booklet, *How to Pass the CPA Exam: A System for Success*, for a description of the three writing skills criteria. You may also access this booklet online by visiting www.gleim.com/PassCPA.

Self-Grade

Below, grade your response on technical content and writing skills. Bubble in the circle next to the appropriate score that you may receive based on the criteria given. Your **total** score is the sum of your scores on all six items. The maximum score is 19 points.

Technical Content Evaluation

Was your response on topic?	O No [0]	O Mostly [1]	O Yes [2]
Did your response have any *significant* errors?	O 0 errors [1]	O 1 major error [−1]	O 2 or more major errors [−2]
Did your response contain any illegal advice?	O No [1]	O Yes [0]	

Writing Skills Evaluation

	Poor	Below Average	Average	Above Average	Outstanding
Organization	O 1	O 2	O 3	O 4	O 5
Development	O 1	O 2	O 3	O 4	O 5
Expression	O 1	O 2	O 3	O 4	O 5

Disclaimer: This scoring schedule was developed by Gleim Publications as a guideline only. The AICPA has not released specific information on how the Written Communications are graded.

Practice even more Written Communications with the Gleim Mega Test Bank.
Learn more: gleim.com/CPAmega | 800.874.5346

STUDY UNIT SIX
FORECASTING ANALYSIS

(9 pages of outline)

The complex modern organization cannot be administered without forecasts about future activity. The demand for goods, the prices of inputs, the efficiency of a production process, the need for cash, and the trends in interest rates are among the factors about which predictions must be made to prepare for the future, both immediate and long-term. This study unit covers the principal forecasting methods used in business.

Forecasts are the basis for business plans. Forecasts are used to project product demand, inventory levels, cash flow, etc. **Qualitative methods** of forecasting rely on the manager's experience and intuition. **Quantitative methods** use mathematical models and graphs. When some factor in the organization's environment is plotted on the x axis, the method is causal relationship forecasting. When time periods are plotted on the x axis, the method is time-series analysis.

6.1 LINEAR REGRESSION ANALYSIS

1. **Simple Regression**

    a. Regression analysis is the process of deriving the linear equation that describes the relationship between two variables.

        1) Simple regression is used for one independent variable. Multiple regression is used for more than one.

    b. The simple regression equation is the algebraic formula for a straight line.

    $$y = a + bx$$

    If: y = the dependent variable
                a = the y intercept
                b = the slope of the regression line
                x = the independent variable

        1) The best straight line that fits a set of data points is derived using calculus.

    c. Regression analysis is particularly valuable for budgeting and cost accounting purposes.

        1) One extremely common application of simple regression in a business setting is the estimation of a mixed cost function, one with a fixed component and a variable component.

        2) The y axis intercept is the fixed portion, and the slope of the regression line is the variable portion.

EXAMPLE

A firm has performed a linear regression analysis and determined that total manufacturing costs (y) consist of fixed costs of $420,000 and variable costs of $32 per unit of output. This relationship can be stated mathematically as follows:

$$y = \$420{,}000 + \$32x$$

If the firm is planning to produce 12,000 units of output, its forecast for total manufacturing costs is $804,000 ($420,000 + $32 × 12,000).

EXAMPLE

The firm has collected the following observations on units of output (independent variable) and total manufacturing costs (dependent variable) to support its linear regression analysis:

Units of Output (000s)	Total Manufacturing Costs ($000s)
5	$620
8	$640
14	$850
17	$1,010

The observations are graphed as follows:

Figure 6-1

---

2. **Multiple Regression**

    a.   Multiple regression is used for more than one independent variable.

        1)   Multiple regression allows a firm to identify many factors (independent variables) and weight each one according to its influence on the overall outcome.

$$y = a + b_1x_1 + b_2x_2 + b_3x_3 + b_4x_4 + etc.$$

EXAMPLE

Bond traders apply multiple regression to determine the value of bonds. Using the market trading prices of bonds, they can estimate a cost function based on the following independent variables: (1) interest rate, (2) collateral coverage, (3) pro forma coverage, (4) pro forma leverage, and (5) the term of the bonds. Valuing unpriced bonds requires knowledge of these variables and their weights of influence on the equation.

---

3. **Aspects of Regression Analysis**

    a.   The linear relationship established for x and y is valid only across the relevant range, the range from the highest to the smallest measures in the set. The user must identify the relevant range and ensure that (s)he does not project the relationship beyond it.

        1)   In the above example, if the bonds are worth between $1 million and $100 million, the trader should not assume the same equation will produce an accurate valuation of a bond worth $1 billion or $100,000.

    b.   Regression analysis assumes that past relationships are a basis for valid projections.

    c.   Regression does not determine causality.

        1)   Although x and y move together, the apparent relationship may be caused by some other factor. For example, car wash sales volume and sunny weather are strongly correlated, but car wash sales do not cause sunny weather.

4.   **High-Low Method**

   a.   The high-low method generates a regression line using only the highest and lowest of a series of observations.

EXAMPLE

A regression equation for electricity costs can be based on the high-cost month and the low-cost month. If the lowest costs were $400 in April when production was 800 machine hours and the highest costs were $600 in September when production was 1,300 hours, the equation is determined as follows:

High month	$600	for	1,300 hours
Low month	400	for	800 hours
Increase	$200		500 hours

Because costs increased $200 for 500 additional hours, the variable cost is $.40 per machine hour ($200 ÷ 500 hours). For the low month, the total variable portion of that monthly cost is $320 ($.40 × 800 hours). Given that the total cost is $400 and $320 is variable, the remaining $80 must be a fixed cost. The regression equation is $y = 80 + .4x$.

---

   1)   The major criticism of the high-low method is that the high and low points may be abnormalities not representative of normal events.

Stop and review! You have completed the outline for this subunit. Study multiple-choice questions 1 through 6 beginning on page 167.

6.2 CORRELATION ANALYSIS

1.   **Correlation**

   a.   Correlation is the strength of the linear (straight-line) relationship between two variables, expressed mathematically in terms of the **coefficient of correlation** *(r)* (the correlation coefficient).

   1)   The coefficient r can be graphically depicted by plotting the values for the variables on a graph in the form of a scatter diagram.

   b.   The value of r ranges from 1 (perfect direct relationship) to −1 (perfect inverse relationship). The closer the scatter pattern is to a straight line, the greater the absolute value of r.

   1)   Perfect direct relationship ($r = 1$)

Figure 6-2

   2)   Perfect inverse relationship ($r = -1$)

Figure 6-3

3)   Strong direct relationship ($r = 0.7$)

Figure 6-4

4)   No linear relationship ($r = 0$)

Figure 6-5

    a)   A coefficient of correlation of zero does not mean that the two variables are unrelated, only that any relationship cannot be expressed as a linear equation.

    b)   The data points in Figure 6-1 on page 160 have a strong direct relationship, implying an r value close to 1.

2.   **Determination**

    a.   The **coefficient of determination (r^2)**, or the coefficient of correlation squared, is a measure of the fit between the independent and dependent variables.

        1)   The coefficient of determination is the proportion of the total variation in the dependent variable that is accounted for by the independent variable.

        2)   The value of r^2 is from 0 to 1. The closer the value of r^2 to 1, the more useful the independent variable (x) in explaining or predicting the variation in the dependent variable (y).

EXAMPLE

A car dealership determines that new car sales are a function of disposable income with a coefficient of correlation of .8. Thus, 64% ($.8^2$) of the variation of new car sales from the average can be explained by changes in disposable income.

---

3.   **Standard Error**

    a.   The standard error measures how well the linear equation represents the data. It is the vertical distance between the data points in a scatter diagram and the regression line.

        1)   The closer the data points to the regression line, the lower the standard error.

Stop and review! You have completed the outline for this subunit. Study multiple-choice questions 7 through 9 beginning on page 169.

6.3 LEARNING CURVE ANALYSIS

1. **Overview**

    a. Learning curve analysis reflects the increased rate at which people perform tasks as they gain experience.

    1) The time required to perform a given task becomes progressively shorter during the early stages of production.

Figure 6-6

b. The curve is usually expressed as a percentage of reduced time to complete a task for each doubling of cumulative production. The most common percentage used in practice is 80%. The most common assumption is that the learning rate applies to the **cumulative average completion time per unit**.

1) The table below is based on two assumptions: (a) the cumulative average time per unit is reduced by 20% (100% − 80%) for each doubling of production and (b) the first unit required 100 minutes.

Batch	Cumulative Units Produced	Total Time	80% Cumulative Average Time per Unit	The Learning Rate %
1 (Unit 1)	1	100	100	--
2 (Unit 2)	2	160	80 (= 100 × 80%)	80% = [160 ÷ (100 × 2)]
3 (Units 3-4)	4	256	64 (= 80 × 80%)	80% = [256 ÷ (160 × 2)]
4 (Units 5-8)	8	409.6	51.2 (= 64 × 80%)	80% = [409.6 ÷ (256 × 2)]
5 (Units 9-16)	16	655.36	40.96 (= 51.2 × 80%)	80% = [655.36 ÷ (409.6 × 2)]

 Candidates need to be alert to the question's requirement. The question might ask, "What is the average time per unit after two units?" From the table above, the answer is 80. The question also might be, "What is the time to produce the second unit?" The answer is 60. Because the first unit took 100 minutes, and the average for the two units is 80 minutes (a total of 160), the second unit must have taken 60 minutes. Another possible question might ask for the average time for units in a batch. In the table, the average unit time for the third batch (units 3 and 4) is 48 minutes [(256 − 160) ÷ (4 − 2)].

2.   **Limitation**

    a.   The limitation of the learning curve in practice is the difficulty in knowing the shape of the learning curve.

        1)   The existence of the learning curve effect is widely accepted, but the percentage to be used may not be known while the information is still useful. As a result, many simply assume an 80% learning curve and make decisions based on those results.

Stop and review! You have completed the outline for this subunit. Study multiple-choice questions 10 through 15 beginning on page 170.

6.4 EXPECTED VALUE

1.   **Overview**

    a.   Expected value is a means of associating a dollar amount with each possible outcome of a probability distribution. The outcome yielding the highest expected value (which may or may not be the most likely one) is the optimal alternative.

        1)   The decision is under the manager's control.

        2)   The state of nature is the future event whose outcome the manager is attempting to predict.

        3)   The payoff is the financial result of the combination of the manager's decision and the actual state of nature.

    b.   The expected value is calculated by multiplying the probability of each outcome by its payoff and adding the products. This calculation often is called a payoff table.

EXAMPLE

An investor is considering the purchase of two identically priced properties. Their value will change if a road is built. The following are estimates that road construction will occur:

Future State of Nature (SN)	Event	Probability
SN 1	No road is ever built.	.1
SN 2	A road is built this year.	.2
SN 3	A road is built more than 1 year from now.	.7

The following are estimates of the values of the properties (payoffs) for each event:

Property	SN 1	SN 2	SN 3
Bivens Tract	$10,000	$40,000	$35,000
Newnan Tract	$20,000	$50,000	$30,000

The expected value of each property is determined by multiplying the probability of each state of nature (outcome) by its payoff and adding all of the products.

		Expected Value
Bivens Tract:	.1($10,000) + .2($40,000) + .7($35,000) =	$33,500
Newnan Tract:	.1($20,000) + .2($50,000) + .7($30,000) =	$33,000

Thus, the Bivens Tract is the better investment.

---

c.　A criticism is that expected value is based on repetitive trials, but many business decisions ultimately involve only one event.

EXAMPLE

A company wishes to launch a communications satellite. The probability of launch failure is .2, and the payoff is $0. The probability of a successful launch is .8, and the payoff is $25,000,000. The expected value is

.2($0) + .8($25,000,000) = $20,000,000

But $20,000,000 is not a possible payoff. Either the satellite orbits for $25,000,000, or it crashes for $0.

---

d.　The difficulty of constructing a payoff table is the determination of all possible outcomes of decisions and their probabilities. Thus, a probability distribution must be established.

　　1)　The assigned probabilities may reflect prior experience with similar decisions, the results of research, or subjective estimates.

e.　Expected value is likely to be used by a decision maker who is risk neutral. However, other circumstances may cause the decision maker to be risk averse or even risk seeking.

EXAMPLE

A dealer in yachts may order 0, 1, or 2 yachts for inventory.

The dealer projects demand as follows:

Demand	Probability
0 yachts	10%
1 yacht	50%
2 yachts	40%

The cost of carrying an excess yacht is $50,000, and the gain for each yacht sold is $200,000. The profit or loss resulting from each combination of decision and outcome is as follows:

					Expected Value		
Decision	State of Nature Demand = 0				Stock 0 Yachts	Stock 1 Yacht	Stock 2 Yachts
Stock 0 yachts	$　　0 × 10%	=			$0		
Stock 1 yacht	(50,000) × 10%	=				$ (5,000)	
Stock 2 yachts	(100,000) × 10%	=					$ (10,000)
	Demand = 1						
Stock 0 yachts	$　　0 × 50%	=			$0		
Stock 1 yacht	200,000 × 50%	=				$100,000	
Stock 2 yachts	150,000 × 50%	=					$ 75,000
	Demand = 2						
Stock 0 yachts	$　　0 × 40%	=			$0		
Stock 1 yacht	200,000 × 40%	=				$ 80,000	
Stock 2 yachts	400,000 × 40%	=					$160,000
All expected values					**$0**	**$175,000**	**$225,000**

In this example, a risk-averse decision maker may not wish to accept the risk of losing $100,000 by ordering two yachts, even though that decision has the highest expected value.

---

　　1)　Although exact probabilities may not be known, the use of expected value analysis forces managers to evaluate decisions logically. At the least, managers are forced to consider all outcomes of each decision.

Expected value calculations and analysis may appear difficult. However, you are simply multiplying the probability of each outcome by its payoff and summing the products. In the calculation of the net expected value or expected incremental profit from an investment, do not forget to subtract the amount of the initial investment.

Stop and review! You have completed the outline for this subunit. Study multiple-choice questions 16 through 27 beginning on page 172.

6.5 SELECTING THE FORECASTING METHOD

1. **Sensitivity Analysis**

   a. Sensitivity analysis uses trial-and-error to determine the effects of changes in variables or assumptions on final results. It is useful in deciding whether expending additional resources to obtain better forecasts is justified.

   b. The trial-and-error method inherent in sensitivity analysis is greatly facilitated by the use of computer software.

      1) A major use of sensitivity analysis is in capital budgeting. Small changes in interest rates or payoffs can make a significant difference in the profitability of a project.

2. **Simulation**

   a. This method is a sophisticated refinement of probability theory and sensitivity analysis. The computer is used to generate many examples of results based upon various assumptions.

   b. Project simulation is frequently expensive. Unless a project is exceptionally large and expensive, full-scale simulation is usually not worthwhile.

3. **Monte Carlo Simulation**

   a. This method often is used in simulation to generate the individual values for a random variable.

      1) The performance of a quantitative model under uncertainty may be investigated by randomly selecting values for each of the variables in the model (based on the probability distribution of each variable) and then calculating the value of the solution.

   b. Performing this process many times produces the distribution of results from the model.

4. **Delphi Approach**

   a. The Delphi approach solicits opinions from experts, summarizes the opinions, and feeds the summaries back to the experts (without revealing participants to each other).

      1) The process is repeated until the opinions converge on an optimal solution.

5. **Time Series Analysis**

   a. Time series analysis (also called trend analysis) is the process of projecting future trends based on past experience. It is a regression model in which the independent variable is time.

Some of the forecasting-related questions on the CPA exam require the candidate to read about a forecasting situation and then choose the appropriate method. Thus, candidates should be as comfortable recognizing when to use the different forecasting methods as they are in working through the details of applying them.

Stop and review! You have completed the outline for this subunit. Study multiple-choice questions 28 through 30 beginning on page 176.

QUESTIONS

6.1 Linear Regression Analysis

1. In the standard regression equation $y = a + bx$, the letter b is best described as a(n)

A. Independent variable.

B. Dependent variable.

C. Y intercept.

D. Slope of the regression line.

Answer (D) is correct.
  REQUIRED: The meaning of the letter b in the standard regression equation.
  DISCUSSION: In the standard regression equation, b represents the slope of the regression line. For example, in a cost determination regression, y equals total costs, b is the variable cost per unit, x is the number of units produced, and a is fixed cost.
  Answer (A) is incorrect. The independent variable is x. Answer (B) is incorrect. The dependent variable is y. Answer (C) is incorrect. The y intercept is a.

2. In order to analyze sales as a function of advertising expenses, the sales manager of Smith Company developed a simple regression model. The model included the following equation, which was based on 32 monthly observations of sales and advertising expenses with a related coefficient of determination of .90.

  Sales = $10,000 + (2.5 × Advertising expenses)

If Smith Company's advertising expenses in 1 month amounted to $1,000, the related point estimate of sales would be

A. $2,500

B. $11,250

C. $12,250

D. $12,500

Answer (D) is correct.
  REQUIRED: An estimate of expenses using linear regression.
  DISCUSSION: The simple regression equation can be solved as follows:

  Sales = $10,000 + (2.5 × Advertising expenses)
       = $10,000 + (2.5 × $1,000)
       = $10,000 + $2,500
       = $12,500

  Answer (A) is incorrect. The amount of $2,500 includes only the advertising expense. Answer (B) is incorrect. The amount of $11,250 results from improperly multiplying the answer by the coefficient of determination. Answer (C) is incorrect. The amount of $12,250 results from improperly applying the coefficient of determination to the advertising expense.

3. The letter x in the standard regression equation is best described as a(n)

A. Independent variable.

B. Dependent variable.

C. Constant coefficient.

D. Coefficient of determination.

Answer (A) is correct.
  REQUIRED: The meaning of the letter x in the standard regression equation.
  DISCUSSION: The letter x in the standard regression equation is the independent variable. For example, in a regression to determine the total cost of production, x equals units produced.
  Answer (B) is incorrect. The dependent variable is y. Answer (C) is incorrect. The constant coefficient is a. Answer (D) is incorrect. The variable r^2 is the coefficient of determination.

Questions 4 through 6 are based on the following information. Jackson Co. has the following information for the first quarter of this year:

	Machine Hours	Cleaning Expense
January	2,100	$ 900
February	2,600	1,200
March	1,600	800
April	2,000	1,000

4. Using the high-low method, what is Jackson's variable cost of cleaning per machine hour?

A. $.40

B. $.48

C. $2.00

D. $2.50

Answer (A) is correct.
REQUIRED: The variable cost in the high-low method.
DISCUSSION: The high-low method is used to generate a regression line by basing the equation on only the highest and lowest of a series of observations. In this problem, March was the lowest and February the highest.

February	$1,200	for	2,600	hours
March	(800)	for	(1,600)	hours
Increase	$ 400	for	1,000	hours

Thus, it costs $400 for 1,000 hours, or $.40 for an hour.
    Answer (B) is incorrect. The average of the high and low months is $.48. Answer (C) is incorrect. The March machine hours divided by the March cost is $2.00. Answer (D) is incorrect. The increase in hours divided by the increase in cost is $2.50.

5. Using the high-low method, what is Jackson's fixed cost?

A. $160

B. $320

C. $640

D. $1,040

Answer (A) is correct.
REQUIRED: The fixed cost using the high-low method.
DISCUSSION: The high-low method generates a regression equation using only the high-cost month and low-cost month. The variable cost per machine hour is therefore $.40 [($1,200 − $800) ÷ (2,600 hours − 1,600 hours)] for either the high-cost (February) or low-cost (March) month. The fixed costs are calculated as follows:

Total cost in February	$1,200
Minus: Variable cost (2,600 hours × $.40)	(1,040)
Fixed cost	$ 160

    Answer (B) is incorrect. The fixed cost is not $320. Answer (C) is incorrect. The variable cost for 1,600 hours is $640. Answer (D) is incorrect. The variable cost of 2,600 machine hours is $1,040.

6. Jackson's management expects machine hours for the month of May to be 1,400 hours. What is their expected total cost for the month of May using the high-low method?

A. $560

B. $650

C. $720

D. $760

Answer (C) is correct.

REQUIRED: The expected total cost using the high-low method.

DISCUSSION: The expected total cost, using the high-low method, can be found as follows:

First, calculate the variable cost per machine hour.

($1,200 – $800) ÷ (2,600 hours – 1,600 hours) = $.40

Then, using the data from February (or March), calculate the expected fixed costs.

Total cost	$1,200
Less: Variable cost (2,600 hours × $.40)	(1,040)
Fixed cost	$ 160

Finally, calculate the expected total cost.

Expected total cost = Expected fixed cost + Expected variable cost
= $160 + (1,400 hours × $.40 per hour)
= $160 + $560
= $720

Answer (A) is incorrect. The variable cost is $560, not the total cost. Answer (B) is incorrect. The expected total cost for May is not $650. Answer (D) is incorrect. The expected total cost for May is not $760.

6.2 Correlation Analysis

7. The coefficient of correlation that indicates the weakest linear association between two variables is

A. –0.73

B. –0.11

C. 0.12

D. 0.35

Answer (B) is correct.

REQUIRED: The correlation coefficient that indicates the weakest linear association between two variables.

DISCUSSION: The coefficient of correlation can vary from –1 to +1. A –1 coefficient indicates a perfect negative correlation, and a +1 coefficient indicates a perfect positive correlation. A zero coefficient of correlation indicates no linear association between the variables. Thus, the coefficient of correlation that is nearest to zero indicates the weakest linear association. Of the options given in the question, the correlation coefficient that is nearest to zero is –0.11.

Answer (A) is incorrect. The coefficient of -0.73 signifies a strong negative correlation. Answer (C) is incorrect. The coefficient of 0.12 is a slightly stronger correlation. Answer (D) is incorrect. The coefficient of 0.35 is a considerably stronger correlation.

8. Correlation is a term frequently used in conjunction with regression analysis and is measured by the value of the coefficient of correlation, *r*. The best explanation of the value *r* is that it

A. Is always positive.

B. Interprets variances in terms of the independent variable.

C. Ranges in size from negative infinity to positive infinity.

D. Is a measure of the relative relationship between two variables.

Answer (D) is correct.

REQUIRED: The best explanation of the coefficient of correlation *(r)*.

DISCUSSION: The coefficient of correlation *(r)* measures the strength of the linear relationship between the dependent and independent variables. The magnitude of *r* is independent of the scales of measurement of *x* and *y*. The coefficient lies between –1.0 and +1.0. A value of zero indicates no linear relationship between the *x* and *y* variables. A value of +1.0 indicates a perfectly direct relationship, and a value of –1.0 indicates a perfectly inverse relationship.

Answer (A) is incorrect. The coefficient is negative if the relationship between the variables is inverse. Answer (B) is incorrect. The coefficient relates the two variables to each other. Answer (C) is incorrect. The size of the coefficient varies between –1.0 and +1.0.

9. In regression analysis, which of the following coefficients of correlation represents the strongest linear relationship between the independent and dependent variables?

A. 1.03

B. −.02

C. −.89

D. .75

Answer (C) is correct.
    REQUIRED: The correlation coefficient with the strongest relationship between independent and dependent variables.
    DISCUSSION: A coefficient of −1.0 signifies a perfect inverse relationship, and a coefficient of 1.0 signifies a perfect direct relationship. Thus, the higher the absolute value of the coefficient of correlation, the stronger the linear relationship. A coefficient of −.89 suggests a very strong inverse relationship between the independent and dependent variables.
    Answer (A) is incorrect. A coefficient of 1.03 is impossible. Answer (B) is incorrect. A coefficient of −.02 is very weak. Answer (D) is incorrect. A coefficient of .75 is .25 from the maximum, whereas -.89 is only .11 from the minimum.

6.3 Learning Curve Analysis

Questions 10 through 12 are based on the following information. Aerosub, Inc., has developed a new product for spacecraft that includes the production of a complex part. The manufacture of this part requires a high degree of technical skill. Management believes there is a good opportunity for its technical force to learn and improve as they become accustomed to the production process. The production of the first unit requires 10,000 direct labor hours. Management projects an 80% learning curve and wants to produce a total of eight units.

10. After completing the first unit, the estimated total direct labor hours Aerosub will require to produce the seven additional units will be

A. 30,960 hours.

B. 40,960 hours.

C. 56,000 hours.

D. 70,000 hours.

Answer (A) is correct.
    REQUIRED: The total direct labor hours to produce seven incremental units given an 80% learning curve.
    DISCUSSION: The cumulative total hours spent on the units can be calculated as follows:

Batch	Cumulative Units Produced	Cumulative Average Labor Hours	Cumulative Total Labor Hours
1	1	10,000	10,000
2	2	8,000 (10,000 × 80%)	16,000
3	4	6,400 (8,000 × 80%)	25,600
4	8	5,120 (6,400 × 80%)	40,960

Because 40,960 hours were needed to complete eight units and 10,000 to complete the first one, units 2 through 8 needed 30,960 hours (40,960 − 10,000).
    Answer (B) is incorrect. The number of hours to complete all eight units is 40,960. Answer (C) is incorrect. The amount of 56,000 hours results from improperly multiplying the seven units by the 8,000 average labor hours consumed in producing the second batch. Answer (D) is incorrect. The amount of 70,000 hours results from improperly multiplying the seven units by the 10,000 average labor hours consumed in producing the first unit.

11. Upon completion of the eighth unit, Aerosub's cumulative direct labor hours will be

   A. 29,520 hours.

   B. 40,960 hours.

   C. 64,000 hours.

   D. 80,000 hours.

Answer (B) is correct.

   REQUIRED: The cumulative direct labor hours to produce eight units given an 80% learning curve.

   DISCUSSION: The underlying assumption of learning curve analysis is that workers gain productivity at a predictable rate as they gain experience with a new process. A common assumption is that the number of hours required for each doubling of output is 80% of the hours required for the previous doubling. The effects of Aerosub's projected learning curve on this product can be calculated as follows:

Batch	Cumulative Units Produced	Cumulative Average Labor Hours	Cumulative Total Labor Hours
1	1	10,000	10,000
2	2	8,000 (10,000 × 80%)	16,000
3	4	6,400 (8,000 × 80%)	25,600
4	8	5,120 (6,400 × 80%)	40,960

   Answer (A) is incorrect. The amount of 29,520 hours results from improperly summing the cumulative average labor hour figures. Answer (C) is incorrect. The amount of 64,000 hours results from improperly multiplying the cumulative number of units produced by the 10,000 hours spent on the first batch, then multiplying by the learning curve percentage. Answer (D) is incorrect. The amount of 80,000 hours results from improperly multiplying the cumulative number of units produced by the 10,000 hours spent on the first batch.

12. Upon completion of the eighth unit, Aerosub's cumulative average direct labor hours required per unit of the product will be

   A. 5,120 hours.

   B. 6,400 hours.

   C. 8,000 hours.

   D. 10,000 hours.

Answer (A) is correct.

   REQUIRED: The cumulative average hours given an 80% learning curve.

   DISCUSSION: The underlying assumption of learning curve analysis is that workers gain productivity at a predictable rate as they gain experience with a new process. A common assumption is that the number of hours required for each doubling of output is 80% of the hours required for the previous doubling. The effects of Aerosub's projected learning curve on this product can be calculated as follows:

Batch	Cumulative Units Produced	Cumulative Average Labor Hours
1	1	10,000
2	2	8,000 (10,000 × 80%)
3	4	6,400 (8,000 × 80%)
4	8	5,120 (6,400 × 80%)

   Answer (B) is incorrect. The projected number of hours after four units is 6,400. Answer (C) is incorrect. The projected number of hours after two units is 8,000. Answer (D) is incorrect. The number 10,000 results from failing to take the learning curve effect into account at all.

13. Learning curves are most often used to predict

   A. Unit material costs.

   B. Overhead variances.

   C. Total unit costs.

   D. Unit direct labor costs.

Answer (D) is correct.

   REQUIRED: The type of cost best predicted by learning curves.

   DISCUSSION: Learning curves reflect the increased rate at which people perform tasks as they gain experience. Thus, they are useful in predicting unit direct labor costs.

   Answer (A) is incorrect. Unit material costs typically do not decline as workers learn their jobs. Answer (B) is incorrect. Variances are by definition unpredictable. Otherwise, the standards are changed to avoid the variance. Answer (C) is incorrect. Learning curves apply only to labor efficiency and are not effective predictors of total unit costs or unit variable costs.

14. A particular manufacturing job is subject to an estimated 80% learning curve. The first unit required 50 labor hours to complete. If the learning curve is based on a cumulative average time per unit assumption, what is the time required to complete the second unit?

A. 30.0 hours.

B. 40.0 hours.

C. 45.0 hours.

D. 50.0 hours.

Answer (A) is correct.
 REQUIRED: The time required to complete the second unit.
 DISCUSSION: The learning curve reflects the increased rate at which people perform tasks as they gain experience. The time required to perform a given task becomes progressively shorter. Ordinarily, the curve is expressed in a percentage of reduced time to complete a task for each doubling of cumulative production. One common assumption in a learning curve model is that the cumulative average time (and labor cost) per unit is reduced by a certain percentage each time production doubles. Thus, an 80% learning curve indicates that a doubling of production reduces the cumulative average unit completion time by 20%. For example, if the first unit required 50.0 hours to complete, the average completion time after two units will be 40.0 hours (50.0 hours × 80%). If total production time is 80.0 hours (2 × 40 cumulative average time), and the first unit required 50.0 hours, the time to produce the second unit must be 30.0 hours.
 Answer (B) is incorrect. The amount of 40.0 hours is based on the assumption that the time to produce the last unit (the incremental unit-time assumption) is reduced by 20%. Answer (C) is incorrect. The amount of 45.0 hours is based on a 90% learning curve and the incremental unit-time assumption. Answer (D) is incorrect. The completion time for the first unit is 50.0 hours.

15. A learning curve of 80% assumes that direct labor costs are reduced by 20% for each doubling of output. What is the incremental cost of the 16th unit produced as an approximate percentage of the 1st unit produced? All units within a batch are considered to have the average completion time for that batch.

A. 41%

B. 31%

C. 51%

D. 64%

Answer (B) is correct.
 REQUIRED: The cost of the last unit produced.
 DISCUSSION: Given an 80% learning curve, the average cost after eight units is 51.20% of the cost of the first unit (100% × 80% × 80% × 80%). After 16 units, the average cost is 40.96% of the first unit (51.20% × 80%). Thus, the average cost of units in the last batch (units 9 through 16) must have been 30.72% [(40.96% × 2) − 51.20%].
 Answer (A) is incorrect. The average cost after 16 units is 41% of the cost of the first unit. Answer (C) is incorrect. The average cost after 8 units is 51% of the cost of the first unit. Answer (D) is incorrect. The average cost after 4 units is 64% of the cost of the first unit.

6.4 Expected Value

16. Philip Enterprises, distributor of video discs, is developing its budgeted cost of goods sold for next year. Philip has developed the following range of sales estimates and associated probabilities for the year:

Sales Estimate	Probability
$ 60,000	25%
85,000	40
100,000	35

Philip's cost of goods sold averages 80% of sales. What is the expected value of Philip's budgeted cost of goods sold?

A. $85,000

B. $84,000

C. $68,000

D. $67,200

Answer (D) is correct.
 REQUIRED: The expected value of cost of goods sold.
 DISCUSSION: The expected value is calculated by weighting each sales estimate by the probability of its occurrence. Consequently, the expected value of sales is $84,000 [($60,000 × .25) + ($85,000 × .40) + ($100,000 × .35)]. Cost of goods sold is therefore $67,200 ($84,000 × .80).
 Answer (A) is incorrect. The amount of $85,000 is the sales estimate with the highest probability. Answer (B) is incorrect. The amount of $84,000 is the expected value of sales. Answer (C) is incorrect. The amount of $68,000 is 80% of the sales estimate with the highest probability.

17. During the past few years, Wilder Company has experienced the following average number of power outages:

Number per Month	Number of Months
0	3
1	2
2	4
3	3
	12

Each power outage results in out-of-pocket costs of $800. For $1,000 per month, Wilder can lease a generator to provide power during outages. If Wilder leases a generator in the coming year, the estimated savings (or additional expense) for the year will be

A. $(15,200)

B. $(1,267)

C. $3,200

D. $7,200

Answer (C) is correct.
   REQUIRED: The estimated savings or additional expense from leasing the generator, given expected levels of occurrence.
   DISCUSSION: Each outage costs $800, but this expense can be avoided by paying $1,000 per month ($12,000 for the year). The expected-value approach uses the probability distribution derived from past experience to determine the average expected outages per month.

$$3 \div 12 \times 0 = 0.0$$
$$2 \div 12 \times 1 = 0.16667$$
$$4 \div 12 \times 2 = 0.66667$$
$$3 \div 12 \times 3 = \underline{0.75000}$$
$$1.58334$$

The company can expect to have, on average, 1.58334 outages per month. At $800 per outage, the expected cost is $1,266.67. Thus, paying $1,000 to avoid an expense of $1,266.67 saves $266.67 per month, or $3,200 per year.
   Answer (A) is incorrect. The annual amount the company will lose without a generator is $(15,200). Answer (B) is incorrect. The monthly amount the company will lose without a generator is $(1,267). Answer (D) is incorrect. The amount saved if two outages occur per month is $7,200.

Questions 18 and 19 are based on the following information. The probabilities shown in the table below represent the estimate of sales for a new product.

Sales (Units)	Probability
0-200	15%
201-400	45%
401-600	25%
601-800	15%

18. What is the probability of selling between 201 and 600 units of the product?

A. 0%

B. 11.25%

C. 70%

D. 25%

Answer (C) is correct.
   REQUIRED: The probability of selling between 201 and 600 units of the new product.
   DISCUSSION: The probability of selling between 201 and 400 units is 45%, and the probability of selling between 401 and 600 units is 25%. Thus, the probability of selling between 201 and 600 units is the sum of these probabilities, or 70%.

19. Using the midpoint of each range as the best estimate for that range, what is the best estimate of the expected sales of the new product?

A. 480

B. 380

C. 400

D. 800

Answer (B) is correct.
   REQUIRED: The best estimate of the expected sales of the new product.
   DISCUSSION: The expected sales levels should be weighted by the individual probabilities of their occurrence. The midpoint of each sales level is used as the estimate for that level. Thus, sales are expected to be 380 units.

$$100 \times 15\% = 15$$
$$300 \times 45\% = 135$$
$$500 \times 25\% = 125$$
$$700 \times 15\% = \underline{105}$$
$$380$$

   Answer (A) is incorrect. The amount of 480 is based on the maximum value in each range. Answer (C) is incorrect. The maximum value in the modal range is 400. Answer (D) is incorrect. The highest estimate is 800.

20. In decision making under conditions of uncertainty, expected value refers to the

    A. Likely outcome of a proposed action.

    B. Present value of alternative actions.

    C. Probability of a given outcome from a proposed action.

    D. Weighted average of probable outcomes of an action.

Answer (D) is correct.
    REQUIRED: The true statement about expected value.
    DISCUSSION: The expected value of an action is found by multiplying the probability of each possible outcome by its payoff and summing the products. It represents the long-term average payoff for repeated trials. Accordingly, expected value is the weighted average of probable outcomes.
    Answer (A) is incorrect. The expected value is a long-range average; it is likely that the expected value will never be exactly achieved for a particular event. Answer (B) is incorrect. Expected value does not consider present values. Answer (C) is incorrect. Probability is only one component of expected value.

21. A beverage stand can sell either soft drinks or coffee on any given day. If the stand sells soft drinks and the weather is hot, it will make $2,500; if the weather is cold, the profit will be $1,000. If the stand sells coffee and the weather is hot, it will make $1,900; if the weather is cold, the profit will be $2,000. The probability of cold weather on a given day at this time is 60%. The expected payoff for selling coffee is

    A. $1,360

    B. $2,200

    C. $3,900

    D. $1,960

Answer (D) is correct.
    REQUIRED: The expected payoff for selling coffee.
    DISCUSSION: The expected payoff calculation for coffee is

Expected payoff = Prob. hot (Payoff hot) + Prob. cold (Payoff cold)
              = .4($1,900) + .6($2,000)
              = $1,960

    Answer (A) is incorrect. The least the company can make by selling coffee is $1,900. Answer (B) is incorrect. The most the company can make by selling coffee is $2,000. Answer (C) is incorrect. The most the company can make by selling coffee is $2,000.

Question 22 is based on the following information. The Booster Club at Blair College sells hot dogs at home basketball games. The group has a frequency distribution of the demand for hot dogs per game and plans to apply the expected value decision rule to determine the number of hot dogs to stock.

22. The Booster Club should select the demand level that

    A. Is closest to the expected demand.

    B. Has the greatest probability of occurring.

    C. Has the greatest expected opportunity cost.

    D. Has the greatest expected monetary value.

Answer (D) is correct.
    REQUIRED: The demand level that should be selected.
    DISCUSSION: The Booster Club should select the demand level that maximizes profits, that is, the level with the greatest expected monetary value. This level may not include the event with the highest conditional profit because this profit may be accompanied by a low probability of occurrence. Alternatively, the event with the highest probability of occurrence may not be selected because it does not offer a high conditional profit.
    Answer (A) is incorrect. Stocking an amount equal to expected demand (the sum of the products of the possible amounts demanded and their respective probabilities) does not necessarily maximize expected profits. Answer (B) is incorrect. The number of bags to stock is not necessarily the same as the amount demanded with the highest probability. The inventory decision should be based on the relation of the probability distribution to the monetary outcomes. Answer (C) is incorrect. The greatest opportunity cost is not factored into the expected value analysis.

23. Expected value in decision analysis is

A. A standard deviation using the probabilities as weights.

B. An arithmetic mean using the probabilities as weights.

C. The square root of the squared deviations.

D. A measure of the difference between the best possible outcome and the outcome of the original decision.

Answer (B) is correct.
   REQUIRED: The true statement about expected value.
   DISCUSSION: Expected value analysis is an estimate of future monetary value based on forecasts and their related probabilities of occurrence. The expected value is found by multiplying the probability of each outcome by its payoff and summing the products. Expected value is therefore an arithmetic mean using probabilities as weights.
   Answer (A) is incorrect. The standard deviation is a measure of dispersion of a population. Answer (C) is incorrect. The square root of the squared deviations is not meaningful in this context. Answer (D) is incorrect. Expected value is a prospective measure.

24. In decision theory, those uncontrollable future events that can affect the outcome of a decision are

A. Payoffs.

B. States of nature.

C. Probabilities.

D. Nodes.

Answer (B) is correct.
   REQUIRED: The term describing uncontrollable future events.
   DISCUSSION: Applying decision theory requires the decision maker to develop an exhaustive list of possible future events. All possible future events that might occur must be included, even though the decision maker is likely to be uncertain about which specific events will occur. These future uncontrollable events are states of nature.
   Answer (A) is incorrect. Payoffs are outcome measures such as profit or loss. Answer (C) is incorrect. Probabilities are the likelihood of occurrence of the states of nature. Answer (D) is incorrect. Nodes (junction points) are decision points.

Question 25 is based on the following information. The College Honor Society sells hot pretzels at the home football games. The pretzels are sold for $1.00 each, and the cost per pretzel is $.30. Any unsold pretzels are discarded because they will be stale before the next home game.

The frequency distribution of the demand for pretzels per game is presented as follows:

Unit Sales Volume	Probability
2,000 pretzels	.10
3,000 pretzels	.15
4,000 pretzels	.20
5,000 pretzels	.35
6,000 pretzels	.20

25. The estimated demand for pretzels at the next home football game using an expected value approach is

A. 4,000 pretzels.

B. 4,400 pretzels.

C. 5,000 pretzels.

D. Some amount other than those given.

Answer (B) is correct.
   REQUIRED: The estimated demand using an expected value approach.
   DISCUSSION: The calculation using an expected value approach weights each possible sales volume by its probability. Thus, the estimated demand is 4,400 pretzels.

Volume		Probability		Result
2,000	×	.10	=	200
3,000	×	.15	=	450
4,000	×	.20	=	800
5,000	×	.35	=	1,750
6,000	×	.20	=	1,200
	Expected value			4,400

   Answer (A) is incorrect. The amount of 4,000 pretzels assumes each outcome is equally likely. Answer (C) is incorrect. The estimated demand using a deterministic approach based on the most likely outcome is 5,000 pretzels. Answer (D) is incorrect. There is a correct answer among the answers given.

26. Pongo Company's managers are attempting to value a piece of land they own. One potential occurrence is that the old road bordering the land gets paved. Another possibility is that the road does not get paved. A third outcome is that the road might be destroyed and completely replaced by a new road. Based on the following future states of nature, their probabilities, and subsequent values of the land, what is the expected value of the land?

Future States of Nature (SN)	Probability
SN 1: Current road gets paved	.5
SN 2: Road does not get paved	.4
SN 3: Current road destroyed and replaced with new road	.1

Estimates of land value under each possible future state of nature:

Value if SN 1: $200,000
Value if SN 2: $100,000
Value if SN 3: $550,000

A. $133,333

B. $195,000

C. $225,000

D. $283,333

Answer (B) is correct.
   REQUIRED: The expected value of the land.
   DISCUSSION: The expected value of the land is determined by multiplying the probability of each state of nature (outcome) by its payoff and adding all of the products. Thus, the land's expected value is (0.5)($200,000) + (0.4)($100,000) + (0.1)($550,000) = $195,000.
   Answer (A) is incorrect. The amount of $133,333 places too much weight on the second option. Answer (C) is incorrect. The amount of $225,000 gives too much weight to the third option. Answer (D) is incorrect. The amount of $283,333 uses a simple unweighted average of the returns from the three options.

27. The expected monetary value of an event

A. Is equal to the conditional value or profit of the event.

B. Is equal to the payoff of the event times the probability the event will occur.

C. Is the profit forgone by not choosing the best alternative.

D. Is the absolute profit from a particular event.

Answer (B) is correct.
   REQUIRED: The true statement about the expected monetary value of an event.
   DISCUSSION: For decisions involving risk, the concept of expected value provides a rational means for selecting the best alternative. The expected value of a decision is found by multiplying the probability of each outcome by its payoff, and adding the products. The result is the long-term average payoff for repeated trials.
   Answer (A) is incorrect. The conditional value is the return given a certain condition or state of nature. Answer (C) is incorrect. The profit forgone by not choosing the best alternative is the opportunity cost. Answer (D) is incorrect. Expected value is the long-run average profit from an event.

6.5 Selecting the Forecasting Method

28. Through the use of decision models, managers thoroughly analyze many alternatives and decide on the best alternative for the company. Often the actual results achieved from a particular decision are not what was expected when the decision was made. In addition, an alternative that was not selected would have actually been the best decision for the company. The appropriate technique to analyze the alternatives by using expected inputs and altering them before a decision is made is

A. Expected value analysis.

B. Linear programming.

C. Program evaluation review technique (PERT).

D. Sensitivity analysis.

Answer (D) is correct.
   REQUIRED: The technique that involves altering expected inputs during the decision process.
   DISCUSSION: After a problem has been formulated into any mathematical model, it may be subjected to sensitivity analysis. Sensitivity analysis examines how the model's outcomes change as the parameters change.
   Answer (A) is incorrect. Expected value analysis is used to determine an anticipated return or cost based upon probabilities of events and their related outcomes. Answer (B) is incorrect. Linear programming optimizes a function given certain constraints. Answer (C) is incorrect. PERT is a network method used to plan and control large projects.

29. A widely used approach that managers use to recognize uncertainty about individual items and to obtain an immediate financial estimate of the consequences of possible prediction errors is

    A. Expected value analysis.

    B. Learning curve analysis.

    C. Sensitivity analysis.

    D. Regression analysis.

Answer (C) is correct.
    REQUIRED: The approach that gives an immediate financial estimate of the consequences of possible prediction errors.
    DISCUSSION: After a problem has been formulated into any mathematical model, it may be subjected to sensitivity analysis. Sensitivity analysis examines how the model's outcomes change as the parameters change.
    Answer (A) is incorrect. Expected value is the probabilistically weighted average of the outcomes of an action. Answer (B) is incorrect. Learning curve analysis quantifies how labor costs decline as employees learn their jobs through repetition. Answer (D) is incorrect. Regression, or least squares, analysis determines the average change in the dependent variable given a unit change in one or more independent variables.

30. A company experiences both variable usage rates and variable lead times for its inventory items. The probability distributions for both usage and lead times are known. A technique the company could use for determining the optimal safety stock levels for an inventory item is

    A. Queuing theory.

    B. Linear programming.

    C. Decision tree analysis.

    D. Monte Carlo simulation.

Answer (D) is correct.
    REQUIRED: The quantitative technique used to determine safety stock given variable usage rates and lead times.
    DISCUSSION: Simulation is a method for experimenting with mathematical models using a computer. Monte Carlo simulation generates the individual values for a random variable. A random number generator is used to produce numbers with a uniform probability distribution. The second step of the Monte Carlo process then transforms the random numbers into values consistent with the desired distribution. The performance of a model under conditions of uncertainty may be investigated by randomly selecting values for each of the variables in the model based on the probability distribution of each variable and then calculating the value of the solution. Advantages of Monte Carlo simulation are that time can be compressed, alternative policies can be considered, and complex systems can be analyzed.
    Answer (A) is incorrect. Queuing theory is used to minimize the costs of waiting lines. Answer (B) is incorrect. Linear programming is used to minimize a cost function or maximize a profit function given constraints. Answer (C) is incorrect. Decision trees are diagrams that analyze sequences of probabilistic decisions, the events that may follow each decision, and their outcomes.

6.6 PRACTICE WRITTEN COMMUNICATION

DIRECTIONS

Note: If you believe you have encountered a software malfunction, report it to the test center staff immediately.

Navigation

To navigate from task to task, use the controls at the bottom of the screen. Click on the **Next** button to advance to the next task, or the **Previous** button to go to the previous task. To go directly to any task, click on its number.

If you would like a reminder to revisit a task, or want to indicate that you are finished with it, click on the reminder flag below the task number. To clear the flag, click on it again. Reminder flags are for your use only – they do not contribute to your score.

Tabs

In this part of the examination, you will be asked to complete various tasks. Every task has one or more **Work Tabs**. Every task also has a **Help** tab.

Work tab   Help tab

Work Tabs:

- **Work Tabs** are identified with a pencil icon. This is where your responses are expected.
- Each task has one or more **Work Tabs**.
- **Work Tabs** contain directions for completing the task - be sure to read these directions carefully.
- The **Work Tab** name in the example above is for illustration only - yours will differ.
- You must complete all of the **Work Tabs** in each task to receive full credit.

Help Tab:

- The **Help Tab** provides assistance with the exam software that is used in this task. For example, if the task is to compose a memorandum, **Help** will provide information about the word processor.

The Toolbar

The toolbar at the top of the screen shows the amount of time remaining for you to complete the tasks. In addition, the following tools are available. Note that only the **Exit** button is displayed when Directions are visible - the others will appear when you begin the tasks.

Click on these buttons to split or unsplit the screen. You can split the screen vertically or horizontally.

Click on this button to go on to the next part of the examination. You must complete all of the tasks to receive full credit. Once you click on **Exit** and confirm the action, you will NOT be able to return to this testlet.

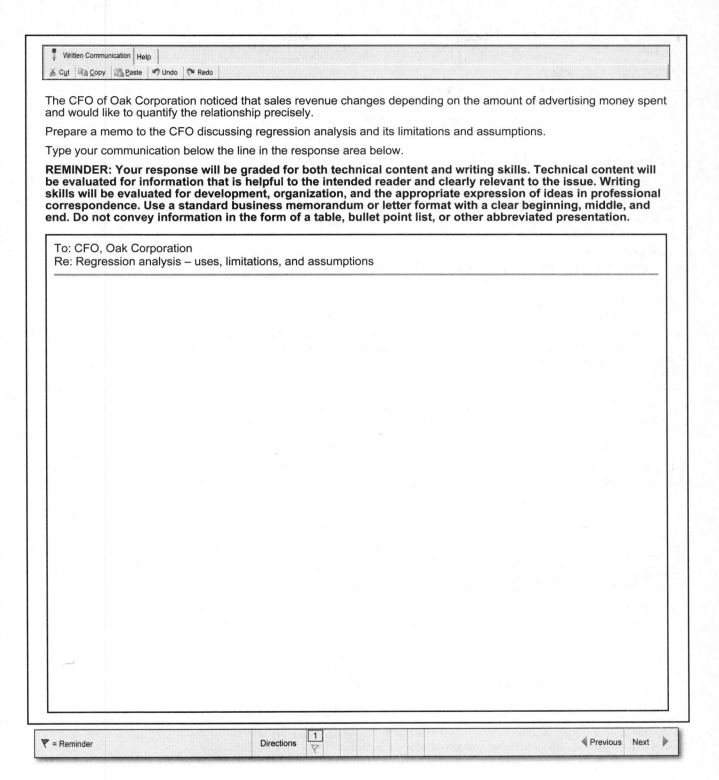

The CFO of Oak Corporation noticed that sales revenue changes depending on the amount of advertising money spent and would like to quantify the relationship precisely.

Prepare a memo to the CFO discussing regression analysis and its limitations and assumptions.

Type your communication below the line in the response area below.

REMINDER: Your response will be graded for both technical content and writing skills. Technical content will be evaluated for information that is helpful to the intended reader and clearly relevant to the issue. Writing skills will be evaluated for development, organization, and the appropriate expression of ideas in professional correspondence. Use a standard business memorandum or letter format with a clear beginning, middle, and end. Do not convey information in the form of a table, bullet point list, or other abbreviated presentation.

To: CFO, Oak Corporation
Re: Regression analysis – uses, limitations, and assumptions

NOTE: Your Written Communications on the actual CPA exam may cover topics outside the scope of the BEC CSO (i.e., they may relate to topics from the AUD, FAR, and/or REG CSOs instead). Answer to the best of your ability, and remember that graders are mainly evaluating your writing ability and will overlook minor technical mistakes.

Unofficial Answer

Written Communication

To: CFO, Oak Corporation
Re: Regression analysis – uses, limitations, and assumptions

Quantitative techniques are available to model information that will help a user determine possible outcomes and preferred courses of action. A common and frequently useful technique is regression analysis. However, it has inherent limitations, and certain assumptions need to be made for it to be effective.

Regression analysis is the process of deriving the linear equation that describes the relationship between two variables, for example, advertising costs and sales revenue. Simple regression is used for one independent variable, and multiple regression is used for more than one. The best straight line that fits a set of data points is derived using calculus.

Regression is particularly valuable for budgeting and cost accounting purposes. For example, one extremely common application of simple regression in a business setting is the estimation of a mixed cost function, i.e., one with a fixed component and a variable component.

However, a limitation of regression analysis is that it does not determine causality. Even if the two variables move together, the apparent relationship may be caused by some other factor.

Furthermore, the linear relationship is valid only across the relevant range, which must be identified by the user. This is a key assumption of the linear regression model. Also, regression analysis assumes that past relationships can be validly projected into the future. Still another assumption is that the distribution of the dependent variable around the regression line is constant for different values of the independent variable. This relationship is constant variance.

The above depicts a Level 5 answer. Consult your booklet, *How to Pass the CPA Exam: A System for Success*, for a description of the three writing skills criteria. You may also access this booklet online by visiting www.gleim.com/PassCPA.

Self-Grade

Below, grade your response on technical content and writing skills. Bubble in the circle next to the appropriate score that you may receive based on the criteria given. Your **total** score is the sum of your scores on all six items. The maximum score is 19 points.

Technical Content Evaluation

Was your response on topic?	O No [0]	O Mostly [1]	O Yes [2]
Did your response have any *significant* errors?	O 0 errors [1]	O 1 major error [–1]	O 2 or more major errors [–2]
Did your response contain any illegal advice?	O No [1]	O Yes [0]	

Writing Skills Evaluation

	Poor	Below Average	Average	Above Average	Outstanding
Organization	O 1	O 2	O 3	O 4	O 5
Development	O 1	O 2	O 3	O 4	O 5
Expression	O 1	O 2	O 3	O 4	O 5

Disclaimer: This scoring schedule was developed by Gleim Publications as a guideline only. The AICPA has not released specific information on how the Written Communications are graded.

Practice even more Written Communications with the Gleim Mega Test Bank.
Learn more: gleim.com/CPAmega | 800.874.5346

STUDY UNIT SEVEN
CORPORATE CAPITAL STRUCTURE

(12 pages of outline)

The balance sheet of a corporation reports the firm's resources and capital structure. Resources consist of the assets used to earn a return. The capital structure consists of the amounts contributed by creditors (Subunit 7.1) and owners (Subunit 7.2).

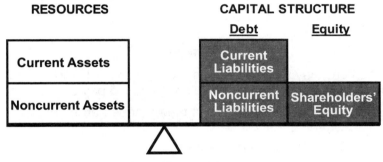

Figure 7-1

Leasing is a means of obtaining the use of plant assets while managing the related liability (Subunit 7.3).

Every corporation must determine the appropriate mix of debt and equity in the capital structure. Each component has a cost that changes as economic conditions vary, and as more or less of a component is used. Finding the right mix is the subject of Subunits 7.4 and 7.5.

7.1 BONDS

1. **Overview**

   a. Bonds are the main form of long-term debt financing for corporations and governments.

      1) A bond is a formal contract to pay an amount of money (par value, maturity amount, or face amount) to the holder at a certain date. Also, most bonds provide for a series of cash interest payments based on a specified percentage (stated rate or coupon rate) of the face amount at specified intervals.

         a) The agreement is included in a document called an **indenture**.

    b.   Issuing bonds requires legal and accounting work. The expense is rarely justified for bonds with maturities of less than 5 years.

        1)   In general, the longer the term of a bond, the higher the return (yield) demanded by investors to compensate for increased risk.

            a)   This relationship is the **term structure of interest rates**. It is depicted by the yield curve.

Positive (Normal) Yield Curve

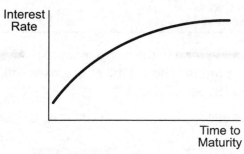

Figure 7-2

    c.   The indenture may require the issuer to maintain a **bond sinking fund**. The objective of the fund is to accumulate sufficient assets to pay the bond principal at maturity.

        1)   The amounts transferred plus the revenue earned on investments provide the necessary funds.

    d.   **Advantages of Bonds to the Issuer**

        1)   Interest paid on debt is tax deductible.
        2)   Control of the firm is not shared with debtholders.

    e.   **Disadvantages of Bonds to the Issuer**

        1)   Unlike returns on equity investments, the payment of interest and principal on debt is a legal obligation. If cash flow is insufficient, the firm could become insolvent.

        2)   The legal requirement to pay interest and principal increases a firm's risk. Shareholders consequently demand increased retained earnings, which may decrease the market price of the stock.

        3)   Bonds may require collateral.

        4)   The amount of debt financing available to the individual firm is limited. Generally accepted standards of the investment community usually require a certain debt-equity ratio for a firm. Beyond this limit, the cost of debt may rise rapidly, or debt may not be available.

2.   **Types of Bonds**

    a.   Maturity Pattern

        1)   A **term bond** has a single maturity date at the end of its term.
        2)   A **serial bond** matures in stated amounts at regular intervals.

    b.   Valuation

        1)   **Variable (or floating) rate bonds** pay interest that is dependent on market conditions.

        2)   **Zero-coupon or deep-discount bonds** have no stated rate of interest and require no periodic cash payments. The interest component consists entirely of the bond's discount.

        3)   **Commodity-backed bonds** are payable at prices related to a commodity such as gold.

    c.   Redemption Provisions

        1)   **Callable bonds** may be repurchased by the issuer at a specified price before maturity. When interest rates are declining, the issuer can replace high-interest debt with low-interest debt.

           a)   Call provisions allow the issuer to repurchase and retire the bonds (or other fixed-income instruments) early. They typically specify when the bond may be called and the price to be paid. Callable bonds have higher interest rates than comparable noncallable bonds.

           b)   If the sum of the interest payments avoided exceeds the premium paid to retire the debt, an advantage to issuers and a disadvantage to investors results.

        2)   **Convertible bonds** may be converted into equity securities of the issuer at the option of the holder under certain conditions. The ability to become equity holders is an inducement to potential investors.

    d.   Securitization

        1)   **Mortgage bonds** are backed by specific assets, usually real estate.
        2)   **Debentures** are backed by the issuer's credit, not specific assets.

    e.   Ownership

        1)   **Registered bonds** are issued in the name of the holder. Only the registered holder may receive interest and principal payments.

        2)   **Bearer bonds** are not individually registered. Interest and principal are paid to whoever presents the bond.

    f.   Priority

        1)   **Subordinated debentures** and second mortgage bonds are junior securities with claims inferior to those of senior bonds.

    g.   Repayment Provisions

        1)   **Income bonds** pay interest contingent on the issuer's profitability.
        2)   **Revenue bonds** are issued by governmental units and are payable from specific revenue sources.

3. **Bond Ratings**

    a.   Credit-rating agencies judge the creditworthiness of bonds. The higher the rating, the more likely the firm will pay the interest and principal.

    b.   The three largest firms are Moody's, Standard & Poor's, and Fitch.

        1)   **Investment-grade bonds** are safe investments and have the lowest yields. The highest rating assigned is AAA. Some fiduciary organizations (such as banks and insurers) are allowed to invest only in investment-grade bonds.

        2)   **Noninvestment-grade bonds**, also called speculative-grade, high-yield, or junk bonds, have high risk.

4. **Bond Valuation**

    a.   A bond issuer's main concern is the cash received from investors.

        1)   This amount equals the **present value** of the cash flows from the bonds (principal at maturity and periodic interest) discounted at the market (effective) interest rate.

        2)   Use of the **effective rate** ensures that the bonds' yield to maturity (ultimate rate of return to the investor) equals the rate of return in the market at the time of sale.

b.   Cash proceeds may be equal to, less than, or greater than the face amount of the bonds, depending on the relationship of the bonds' stated rate of interest to the market rate.

   1)   Bonds are sold **at par** if the stated rate equals the market rate at the time of sale (present value = face amount). But the stated rate seldom equals the market rate at the time the bonds are ready for sale.

   2)   If the bonds' **stated rate is lower than the market rate**, periodic interest payments are lower than those currently available. Thus, the bonds are sold for less than par value (at a **discount**) so that the effective interest rate equals the market rate.

EXAMPLE

On January 1, Year 1, a firm issues 100 bonds at 6% annual interest with a face amount of $1,000 maturing in 5 years. At issuance, the market rate is 8%. The proceeds are calculated as follows:

Face amount:		
Present value of a single payment of		
$100,000 discounted at 8% for 5 years	$100,000 × .68058 =	$68,058
Interest payments:		
Present value of an ordinary annuity of		
$6,000 discounted at 8% for 5 years	$6,000 × 3.99271 =	23,956
Total proceeds		$92,014

The issuer receives cash of $92,014 and records a discount on bonds payable of $7,986 ($100,000 – $92,014).

---

   3)   If the bonds' **stated rate is higher than the market rate**, periodic interest payments are higher than those currently available. Thus, the bonds are sold for more than par value (at a **premium**) so that the effective interest rate equals the market rate.

EXAMPLE

On January 1, Year 1, a firm issues bonds with the same terms as those in the previous example, except that the stated rate is 8% and the effective rate is 6%. The present value of the face amount is $74,726 ($100,000 × .74726) and the present value of the interest payments is $33,699 ($8,000 × 4.21236). The issuer therefore receives cash of $108,425 ($74,726 + $33,699) and records a premium on bonds payable of $8,425.

---

c.   The amortization of discount or premium over the term of the bonds results in a carrying amount at maturity equal to their face amount.

d.   When bonds are traded among investors in the secondary market, the issuer is not a party to the transaction and receives no cash.

   1)   The price of the resold bonds is determined by a risk assessment and the market rate at the time of the trade. Accordingly, the bonds are priced to achieve a new yield.

5.   **Leverage**

a.   Leverage is the relative amount of fixed cost in a firm's cost structure. Leverage creates risk because fixed costs must be paid, regardless of sales.

   1)   A firm's total leverage consists of operating leverage and financial leverage.

b.   **Operating leverage** is the extent to which a firm's costs of operating are fixed. A firm's **degree of operating leverage (DOL)** is a ratio that measures the effect that given fixed operating costs have on earnings.

$$DOL = \frac{\% \text{ change in earnings before interest and taxes (EBIT)}}{\% \text{ change in sales}}$$

1) For example, if the firm's EBIT increases by 24% as a result of an increase in sales of 12%, the firm's DOL is 2 (24% ÷ 12%).

2) The DOL helps the firm to determine the operating leverage that maximizes the firm's EBIT.

3) A firm with a high percentage of fixed costs is more risky than a firm in the same industry that relies more on variable costs. It generates more earnings by increasing sales.

c. **Financial leverage** is the degree of debt (fixed financial costs) in the firm's financial structure. A firm's **degree of financial leverage (DFL)** is a ratio that measures the effect that an amount of fixed financing costs has on earnings per share (EPS).

$$DFL = \frac{\text{\% change in earnings per share (EPS)}}{\text{\% change in earnings before interest and taxes (EBIT)}}$$

1) For example, if the firm's EPS increases by 12% as a result of an increase in EBIT of 6%, the firm's DFL is 2 (12% ÷ 6%).

2) When a firm has a high percentage of fixed financial costs, it must accept more risk to increase its EPS.

d. **The degree of total (combined) leverage (DTL)** is the product of the degrees of operating and financial leverage.

$$DTL = DOL \times DFL = \frac{\text{\% change in EBIT}}{\text{\% change in sales}} \times \frac{\text{\% change in EPS}}{\text{\% change in EBIT}} = \frac{\text{\% change in EPS}}{\text{\% change in sales}}$$

1) For example, if the firm's EPS increases by 10% as a result of an increase in sales of 2%, the firm's DTL is 5 (10% ÷ 2%).

2) A firm with a higher DTL provides a higher return to investors, but it is also more risky.

6. **Debt Covenants**

a. Debt covenants are restrictions imposed on a borrower by the creditor in a formal debt agreement (indenture).

b. The following are examples of debt covenants:

1) Limitations on issuing long-term or short-term debt
2) Limitations on dividend payments
3) Maintenance of certain financial ratios
4) Maintenance of specific collateral that secures the debt

c. The more restrictive the debt covenants, the lower the risk the borrower will not pay. The less risky the investment, the lower the interest rate on the debt (the risk premium is lower).

d. If the debtor violates a covenant, the debt becomes due immediately.

Stop and review! You have completed the outline for this subunit. Study multiple-choice questions 1 through 8 beginning on page 192.

7.2 EQUITY

1. **Common Stock**

a. Common shareholders are the owners of the corporation. But their rights, although reasonably uniform throughout the U.S., depend on the laws of the state of incorporation.

1) Equity ownership involves risk because holders of common stock are not guaranteed a return and are last in priority in a liquidation. Shareholders' capital is a source of funds for payment of creditors if losses occur on liquidation.

b.   **Advantages to the Issuer**

1)   Common stock does not require a fixed dividend. Dividends are paid from profits when available.
2)   Common stock has no fixed maturity date for repayment of capital.
3)   The sale of common stock increases the creditworthiness of the firm by providing more equity.

c.   **Disadvantages to the Issuer**

1)   Cash dividends on common stock are not tax-deductible and are paid from after-tax profits.
2)   New common stock sales dilute EPS available to current shareholders.
3)   Underwriting costs typically are higher for common stock than debt.
4)   Too much equity may raise the average cost of capital of the firm above its optimal level.

d.   Common shareholders ordinarily have a **preemptive right** to purchase additional stock issues in proportion to their current ownership percentages.

e.   Common shareholders have voting rights. They select the board of directors and vote on resolutions.

f.   **Common stock valuation** based on dividend payout models

1)   When the dividend per share of common stock is constant and expected to be paid continuously, the price per share is calculated as follows:

$$P_0 = D \div r$$

P_0 = Current price per share
D = Dividend per share (constant)
r = Required rate of return

2)   The **constant growth model** (dividend discount model) assumes that dividends per share and price per share increase at the same constant rate. The price per share can be calculated as follows:

$$P_0 = \frac{D_0(1 + g)}{r - g} = \frac{D_1}{r - g}$$

P_0 = Current price per share
D_0 = Current dividends per share
D_1 = Dividends per share expected next year
r = Required rate of return
g = Growth rate (constant)

EXAMPLE

A firm currently pays dividends of $10 per common share. The dividends are expected to increase at a constant rate of 5% per year. If investors' required rate of return is 8%, the current market value of a common share is $350.

$$P_0 = \frac{D_0(1 + g)}{r - g} = \frac{\$10(1 + 5\%)}{8\% - 5\%} = \$350$$

---

3)   The required rate of return (the cost of common stock) can be derived from the dividend growth model.

$$r = \frac{D_1}{P_0} + g$$

2. **Preferred Stock**

    a. Preferred stock is a hybrid of debt and equity. It has a fixed payment, but dividends need not be paid.

        1) Also, preferred shareholders have priority over common shareholders in bankruptcy.

    b. **Advantages to the Issuer**

        1) Preferred stock is equity and increases the creditworthiness of the firm.
        2) Control is still held by common shareholders. (Preferred stock rarely has voting rights.)
        3) Superior earnings of the firm benefit the common shareholders.
        4) Preferred stock does not require periodic payments. Thus, nonpayment of dividends does not lead to bankruptcy.

    c. **Disadvantages to the Issuer**

        1) Cash dividends on preferred stock are not tax-deductible and are paid from after-tax profits. The result is a substantially greater cost relative to bonds.
        2) In periods of economic difficulty, accumulated unpaid dividends (dividends in arrears) may create managerial and financial problems for the firm.

    d. **Common Provisions of Preferred Stock Issues**

        1) Priority in assets and earnings. If the firm is bankrupt, the preferred shareholders have priority over common shareholders.
        2) Accumulation of dividends. If preferred dividends are cumulative, dividends in arrears must be paid before any common dividends can be paid.
        3) Convertibility. Preferred stock issues may be convertible into common stock at the option of the shareholder.
        4) Participation. Preferred stock may participate with common stock in excess earnings of the firm. For example, 8% participating preferred stock might pay a dividend each year greater than 8% when the corporation is extremely profitable. But nonparticipating preferred stock receives no more than is required.
        5) Par value. Par value is the liquidation value, and a percentage of par equals the preferred dividend.

    e. **Preferred stock valuation** applies the same method used to value a bond that is described in Subunit 7.1.

        1) Future cash flows associated with the security are discounted at an investor's required rate of return (market rate) used to value preferred stock.
        2) The future cash flows from bonds consist of principal at maturity and periodic interest. But future cash flows from preferred stock are assumed to consist only of the estimated future annual dividends (D_p).

        $$D_p = Par\ value\ of\ preferred\ stock \times Preferred\ dividend\ rate$$

        3) The discount rate used is the investor's required rate of return (r).
        4) Unlike a bond, which has a specific maturity date, preferred stock is assumed to be outstanding in perpetuity.

        $$Preferred\ stock\ price\ (P_p) = \frac{D_p}{r}$$

        a) For example, the value of a share of preferred stock with a par value of $100 and a dividend rate of 5% to an investor with a required rate of return of 10% is $50 [($100 × 5%) ÷ 10%].

3.   **Initial Public Offering (IPO)**

a.   A firm's first issuance of securities to the public is an IPO. The process by which a closely held corporation issues new securities to the public is called **going public**. When a firm goes public, it issues its securities on a new issue or **IPO market** (a primary market).

b.   **Advantages of Going Public**

1)   The ability to raise additional funds
2)   The establishment of the firm's value in the market
3)   An increase in the liquidity of the firm's stock

c.   **Disadvantages of Going Public**

1)   Costs of the reporting requirements of the SEC and other agencies
2)   Access to the firm's operating data by competing firms
3)   Access to net worth information of major shareholders
4)   Limitations on self-dealing by corporate insiders
5)   Pressure from outside shareholders for earnings growth
6)   Stock prices that do not accurately reflect the true net worth of the firm
7)   Loss of control by management as ownership is diversified
8)   Increased shareholder servicing costs

d.   The main differences between debt financing (payment of interest) and equity financing (payment of dividends) can be summarized as follows:

	Equity Financing	Debt Financing
Effect on control of the firm	Yes	No
Cost of issuing	Higher	Lower
Effect on net income	No	Yes
Dilution of EPS	Yes	No
Effect on solvency risk	No	Yes
Tax deductibility of payments	No	Yes

Stop and review! You have completed the outline for this subunit. Study multiple-choice questions 9 through 15 beginning on page 195.

7.3 LEASING

1.   **Overview**

a.   A lease is a long-term contract in which the owner of property (the lessor) allows another party (the lessee) the right to use the property for a stated period in exchange for a stated payment.

1)   The basic issue is whether the lease is (a) a purchase-and-financing arrangement (a capital lease) or (b) a long-term rental contract (an operating lease).

b.   Discounting a lease's cash flows to determine its present value allows a firm to determine the most favorable lease.

c.   Lease financing is analyzed by comparing the cost of owning with the cost of leasing. Leasing also provides tax and other benefits.

1)   If leases are not accounted for as installment purchases (capital leases), they are a form of off-balance-sheet financing. Thus, under an operating lease, the lessee need **not** record an asset or a liability, and rent expense is recognized.

2. **Types of Leases**

   a. A **sale-leaseback** is an alternate method of raising capital. It allows firms to acquire capital from the sale of an asset while retaining the use of the asset.

   b. **Service or operating leases** usually include both financing and maintenance services.

   c. **Financial leases**, which do not provide for maintenance services, are noncancelable and fully amortize the cost of the leased asset over the term of the basic lease contract. They are installment purchases.

3. **Lease Classification**

   a. A **capital lease** is, in substance, the purchase of an asset and should thus be treated as a purchase. For a lease to be classified as a capital lease, it must meet at least one of the following four criteria:

      1) Title passes to the lessee at the end of the lease.
      2) The lease contains a bargain purchase option.
      3) The present value of the minimum lease payments during the lease term equals 90% or more of the fair value of the leased property.
      4) The lease term is 75% or more of the useful economic life of the property.

   b. An **operating lease** (off-balance-sheet financing) is a rental contract and is accounted for as such.

      1) No accounting entry is made to record the lease. Lease payments are expensed as incurred.
      2) Expense is recognized as the services are used. If lease payments are not reasonably aligned with the services obtained, accruals or deferrals must be used.

Stop and review! You have completed the outline for this subunit. Study multiple-choice questions 16 through 18 beginning on page 197.

7.4 COMPONENT COSTS OF CAPITAL

1. **Overview**

   a. Investment in corporations is with the understanding that management will use the capital to provide a return to investors.

      1) If management does not provide required rate of return, investors sell their stock on the secondary market, causing the value of the stock to drop. Creditors then demand higher rates on the firm's debt.
      2) For this reason, investors' required rate of return (also called their opportunity cost of capital) becomes the firm's cost of capital.

   b. A firm's cost of capital is used to discount the future cash flows of long-term projects. Investments with a rate of return higher than the cost of capital will increase the value of the firm and shareholders' wealth. (The cost of capital is **not** relevant to working capital. Short-term needs are met by short-term funds.)

      1) Providers of equity capital are exposed to more risk than are lenders because
         a) The firm is not legally obligated to pay them a return, and
         b) In case of liquidation, creditors have priority.
      2) To compensate for this higher risk, equity investors demand a higher return, making equity financing more expensive than debt.

2.   **Component Costs of Capital**

a.   A firm's financing structure consists of (1) long-term debt, (2) preferred equity, and (3) common equity. (Retained earnings is part of common equity for reasons given below.)

1)   The rate of return demanded by holders of a form of capital is its component cost.

b.   The component cost of **long-term debt** is the after-tax interest rate on the debt. (Interest payments are tax-deductible.)

Effective rate × (1.0 – Marginal tax rate)

c.   The component cost of **preferred stock** is calculated using the dividend yield ratio.

$$\frac{Cash\ dividend\ on\ preferred\ stock}{Market\ price\ of\ preferred\ stock}$$

1)   The market price of preferred stock upon issuance equals the net proceeds (gross proceeds – flotation costs). Flotation costs, also called issuance costs, reduce the net proceeds received, raising the cost of capital.

a)   Thus, the component cost of preferred stock also can be derived by using the following formula:

$$\frac{Cash\ dividend\ on\ preferred\ stock}{Preferred\ stock\ market\ price\ -\ Issuance\ costs}$$

d.   The component cost of **retained earnings** is the same as that for common stock.

1)   If the firm cannot use retained earnings profitably, it should be distributed to the common shareholders as dividends so they can make their own investments.

EXAMPLE

A firm has outstanding bonds with a coupon rate of 7% and an effective rate of 5%. Its 9%, $60 par-value preferred stock currently is trading at $67.50 per share. Its $1 par-value common stock trades at $1.40 per share and pays a 14% dividend. The applicable tax rate is 35%.

The component costs of capital are calculated as follows:

Long-Term Debt	Preferred Equity	Common Equity
Cost = Effective rate × (1.0 – Tax rate)	Cost = Cash dividend ÷ Market price	Cost = Cash dividend ÷ Market price
= 5% × (1.0 – .35)	= ($60 × 9%) ÷ $67.50	= ($1 × 14%) ÷ $1.40
= 5% × .65	= $5.40 ÷ $ 67.50	= $.14 ÷ $1.40
= 3.25%	= 8%	= 10%

Stop and review! You have completed the outline for this subunit. Study multiple-choice questions 19 through 22 beginning on page 198.

7.5 WEIGHTED-AVERAGE COST OF CAPITAL

 The weighted-average cost of capital has been tested recently using general conceptual questions and calculation questions.

1.   **Weighted-Average Cost of Capital (WACC)**

a.   Corporate management usually designates a target capital structure, i.e., the proportion of each component of capital.

b.   A firm's WACC is one composite rate of return on the combined components of capital. The weights are based on the target capital structure.

EXAMPLE

The firm has a target capital structure of 20% long-term debt, 30% preferred equity, and 50% common equity. The weighted-average cost of capital is calculated as follows:

	Target Weight		Cost of Capital		Weighted Cost
Long-term debt	20%	×	3.25%	=	0.65%
Preferred equity	30%	×	8%	=	2.40%
Common equity	50%	×	10%	=	5.00%
					8.05%

   c.   A formula to calculate the WACC given no preferred stock is

$$WACC = \left(\frac{E}{V} \times R_e\right) + \frac{D}{V} \times R_d \times (1 - T)$$

   R_e = Cost of equity
   R_d = Cost of debt
   E   = Market value of the firm's equity
   D   = Market value of the firm's debt
   T   = Corporate tax rate
   V = D + E = Capital used to generate profits

EXAMPLE

The firm provides the following information:

Capital used to generate profits (50% equity and 50% debt)	$1,200
Cost of equity	15%
Cost of debt	5%
Corporate tax rate	40%

$$WACC = \left[\frac{(1,200 \times 50\%)}{1,200} \times 15\%\right] + \frac{(1,200 \times 50\%)}{1,200} \times 5\% \times (1 - 40\%) = 0.09 = 9\%$$

2.   **Optimal Capital Structure**

   a.   Standard financial theory provides a model for the optimal capital structure of every firm. In accordance with this model, shareholder wealth-maximization results from **minimizing the weighted-average cost of capital**. Thus, management should **not** focus only on maximizing earnings per share. (EPS can be increased by assuming more debt, but debt increases risk.)

      1)   The relevant relationships are depicted below:

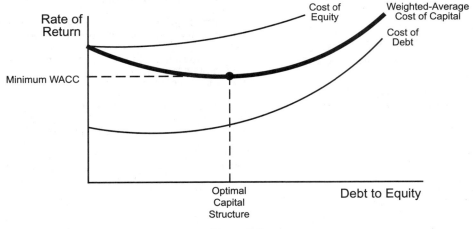

Figure 7-3

Ordinarily, firms cannot identify this optimal point precisely. Thus, they should attempt to find an optimal range for the capital structure.

3.   **Modigliani-Miller and Capital Structure Irrelevance**

a.   The Modigliani-Miller theorem asserts that no optimal capital structure exists for a firm. Thus, whether the firm finances with all debt, all equity, or some combination is irrelevant to shareholders' wealth.

1)   The reasoning is that any increase in expected return from debt financing is exactly offset by an increase in the required rate of return on equity because of the risk related to leverage.

2)   Thus, such measures as degree of leverage and the debt-to-equity ratio should be of no use to shareholders.

Stop and review! You have completed the outline for this subunit. Study multiple-choice questions 23 through 30 beginning on page 199.

QUESTIONS

7.1 Bonds

1. Short-term interest rates are

A.   Usually lower than long-term rates.

B.   Usually higher than long-term rates.

C.   Lower than long-term rates during periods of high inflation only.

D.   Not significantly related to long-term rates.

Answer (A) is correct.
    REQUIRED: The true statement about short-term interest rates.
    DISCUSSION: Historically, a facet of the term structure of interest rates (the relationship of yield and time to maturity) is that short-term interest rates ordinarily have been lower than long-term rates. One reason is that less risk is involved in the short run. Moreover, future expectations about interest rates affect the term structure. Most economists believe that a long-term interest rate is an average of future expected short-term interest rates. For this reason, the yield curve will (1) slope upward if future rates are expected to rise, (2) slope downward if interest rates are anticipated to fall, and (3) remain flat if investors think the rate is stable. Future inflation is incorporated into this relationship. Another consideration is liquidity preference. Investors in an uncertain world accept lower rates on short-term investments because of their greater liquidity.
    Answer (B) is incorrect. Short-term rates are usually lower than long-term rates. Answer (C) is incorrect. Short-term rates are more likely to be greater than long-term rates if current levels of inflation are high. Answer (D) is incorrect. Long-term rates may be viewed as short-term rates adjusted by a risk factor.

2. If Brewer Corporation's bonds are currently yielding 8% in the marketplace, why is the firm's cost of debt lower?

A.   Market interest rates have increased.

B.   Additional debt can be issued more cheaply than the original debt.

C.   There should be no difference; cost of debt is the same as the bonds' market yield.

D.   Interest is deductible for tax purposes.

Answer (D) is correct.
    REQUIRED: The reason a firm's cost of debt is lower than its current market yield.
    DISCUSSION: Because interest is deductible for tax purposes, the actual cost of debt capital is the net effect of the interest payment and the offsetting tax deduction. The actual cost of debt equals the interest rate times the difference of 1 minus the marginal tax rate. Thus, if a firm with an 8% market rate is in a 40% tax bracket, the net cost of the debt capital is 4.8% [8% × (1.0 − .40)].
    Answer (A) is incorrect. The tax deduction always causes the market yield rate to be higher than the cost of debt capital. Answer (B) is incorrect. Additional debt may or may not be issued more cheaply than earlier debt, depending upon the interest rates in the market place. Answer (C) is incorrect. The cost of debt is less than the yield rate given that bond interest is tax deductible.

3. The term structure of interest rates is the relationship of

A. Interest rates over different structures of bonds.

B. Interest rates over different structures of securities.

C. Interest rates over time.

D. The maturity dates of an issuance of bonds.

Answer (C) is correct.
REQUIRED: The relationship in the term structure of interest rates.
DISCUSSION: The term structure of interest rates is the relationship of interest rates and years to maturity. Corporate CFOs use the term structure to decide whether to borrow short-term debt or long-term debt. Investors use the term structure to decide whether to buy short-term or long-term bonds.
Answer (A) is incorrect. Term structure is the relationship of interest rates over time, not different structures of bonds. Answer (B) is incorrect. Term structure is the relationship of interest rates over time, not different structures of securities. Answer (D) is incorrect. Maturity dates refer to the time element, but the interest rate element is missing.

4. This year, Nelson Industries increased earnings before interest and taxes (EBIT) by 17%. During the same period, earnings per share increased by 42%. The degree of financial leverage that existed during the year is

A. 1.70

B. 4.20

C. 2.47

D. 5.90

Answer (C) is correct.
REQUIRED: The degree of financial leverage.
DISCUSSION: If earnings before interest and taxes increased by 17%, and earnings per share income was up 42%, the firm is using leverage effectively. The degree of financial leverage is the percentage change in earnings per share divided by the percentage change in EBIT. Accordingly, Nelson's degree of financial leverage is 2.47 (.42 ÷ .17).

5.

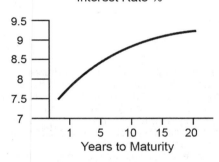

The yield curve shown implies that the

A. Credit risk premium of corporate bonds has increased.

B. Credit risk premium of municipal bonds has increased.

C. Long-term interest rates have a higher annualized yield than short-term rates.

D. Short-term interest rates have a higher annualized yield than long-term rates.

Answer (C) is correct.
REQUIRED: The implication of the yield curve.
DISCUSSION: The term structure of interest rates is the relationship between yield to maturity and time to maturity. This relationship is depicted by a yield curve. Assuming the long-term interest rate is an average of expected future short-term rates, the curve will be upward sloping when future short-term interest rates are expected to rise. Furthermore, the normal expectation is for long-term investments to pay higher rates because of their higher risk. Thus, long-term interest rates have a higher annualized yield than short-term rates.
Answer (A) is incorrect. The yield curve does not reflect the credit risk premium of bonds. Answer (B) is incorrect. The yield curve does not reflect the credit risk premium of bonds. Answer (D) is incorrect. Long-term interest rates should be higher than short-term rates.

6. Serial bonds are attractive to investors because

A. All bonds in the issue mature on the same date.

B. The yield to maturity is the same for all bonds in the issue.

C. Investors can choose the maturity that suits their financial needs.

D. The coupon rate on these bonds is adjusted to the maturity date.

Answer (C) is correct.
REQUIRED: The reason serial bonds are attractive to investors.
DISCUSSION: Serial bonds have staggered maturities. They mature over a period (series) of years. Thus, investors can choose the maturity date that meets their investment needs. For example, an investor who will have a child starting college in 16 years can choose bonds that mature in 16 years.
Answer (A) is incorrect. Serial bonds mature on different dates. Answer (B) is incorrect. Bonds maturing on different dates may have different yields, or they may be the same. Usually, the earlier date maturities carry slightly lower yields than the later maturities. Answer (D) is incorrect. The coupon rate is the same for all bonds; only the selling price and yield differ.

7. If a $1,000 bond sells for $1,125, which of the following statements are true?

I. The market rate of interest is greater than the coupon rate on the bond.

II. The coupon rate on the bond is greater than the market rate of interest.

III. The bond sells at a premium.

IV. The bond sells at a discount.

A. I and III.

B. I and IV.

C. II and III.

D. II and IV.

Answer (C) is correct.
REQUIRED: The true statements about a bond that sells at more than its face value.
DISCUSSION: The excess of the price over the face value is a premium. A premium is paid because the coupon rate on the bond is greater than the market rate of interest. Thus, because the bond is paying a higher rate than other similar bonds, its price is bid up by investors.
Answer (A) is incorrect. If a bond sells at a premium, the market rate of interest is less than the coupon rate. Answer (B) is incorrect. A bond sells at a discount when the price is less than the face amount. Answer (D) is incorrect. A bond sells at a discount when the price is less than the face amount.

8. Debentures are

A. Income bonds that require interest payments only when earnings permit.

B. Subordinated debt and rank behind convertible bonds.

C. Bonds secured by the full faith and credit of the issuing firm.

D. A form of lease financing similar to equipment trust certificates.

Answer (C) is correct.
REQUIRED: The true statement about debentures.
DISCUSSION: Debentures are unsecured bonds. Although no assets are mortgaged as security for the bonds, debentures are secured by the full faith and credit of the issuing firm. Debentures are a general obligation of the borrower. Only a firm with the best credit rating can issue debentures because only its credit rating and reputation secure the bonds.
Answer (A) is incorrect. Debentures must pay interest regardless of earnings levels. Answer (B) is incorrect. Debentures are not subordinated except to the extent of assets mortgaged against other bond issues. Debentures are a general obligation of the borrower and rank equally with convertible bonds. Answer (D) is incorrect. Debentures have nothing to do with lease financing. Debentures are not secured by assets.

7.2 Equity

9. Each share of nonparticipating, 8%, cumulative preferred stock in a company that meets its dividend obligations has all of the following characteristics **except**

A. Voting rights in corporate elections.

B. Dividend payments that are not tax deductible by the company.

C. No principal repayments.

D. A superior claim to common stock equity in the case of liquidation.

Answer (A) is correct.
REQUIRED: The item not characteristic of nonparticipating, cumulative preferred stock.
DISCUSSION: Dividends on cumulative preferred stock accrue until declared. That is, the carrying amount of the preferred stock increases by the amount of any undeclared dividends. Participating preferred stock participates with common shareholders in excess earnings of the firm. Accordingly, 8% participating preferred stock might pay a dividend each year greater than 8% when the corporation is extremely profitable. Thus, nonparticipating preferred stock will receive no more than is stated on the face of the stock. Preferred shareholders rarely have voting rights. Voting rights are exchanged for preferences regarding dividends and liquidation of assets.
Answer (B) is incorrect. A corporation does not receive a tax deduction for making dividend payments on any type of stock. Answer (C) is incorrect. Preferred stock normally need not be redeemed as long as the corporation remains in business. Answer (D) is incorrect. Preferred shareholders do have priority over common shareholders in a liquidation.

10. Unless the shares are specifically restricted, a holder of common stock with a preemptive right may share proportionately in all of the following **except**

A. The vote for directors.

B. Corporate assets upon liquidation.

C. Cumulative dividends.

D. New issues of stock of the same class.

Answer (C) is correct.
REQUIRED: The item not a right of common shareholders.
DISCUSSION: Common stock does not have the right to accumulate unpaid dividends. This right often is attached to preferred stock.
Answer (A) is incorrect. Common shareholders have the right to vote (although different classes of shares may have different privileges). Answer (B) is incorrect. Common shareholders have the right to share proportionately in corporate assets upon liquidation (but only after other claims have been satisfied). Answer (D) is incorrect. Common shareholders have the right to share proportionately in any new issues of stock of the same class (the preemptive right).

11. In general, it is more expensive for a company to finance with equity capital than with debt capital because

A. Long-term bonds have a maturity date and must therefore be repaid in the future.

B. Investors are exposed to greater risk with equity capital.

C. Equity capital is in greater demand than debt capital.

D. Dividends fluctuate to a greater extent than interest rates.

Answer (B) is correct.
REQUIRED: The reason equity financing is more expensive than debt financing.
DISCUSSION: Providers of equity capital are exposed to more risk than are lenders because the firm is not obligated to pay them a return. Also, in case of liquidation, creditors are paid before equity investors. Thus, equity financing is more expensive than debt because equity investors require a higher return to compensate for the greater risk assumed.
Answer (A) is incorrect. The obligation to repay at a specific maturity date reduces the risk to investors and thus the required return. Answer (C) is incorrect. The demand for equity capital is directly related to its greater cost to the issuer. Answer (D) is incorrect. Dividends are based on managerial discretion and may rarely change; interest rates, however, fluctuate daily based upon market conditions.

12. The following excerpt was taken from a company's financial statements: " . . . 10% convertible participating . . . $10,000,000." What is most likely being referred to?

- A. Bonds.
- B. Common stock.
- C. Stock options.
- D. Preferred stock.

Answer (D) is correct.
REQUIRED: The securities that most likely are convertible participating.
DISCUSSION: Preferred shareholders have priority over common shareholders in the assets and earnings of the enterprise. If preferred dividends are cumulative, any past preferred dividends must be paid before any common dividends. Preferred stock also may be convertible into common stock, and it may be participating. For example, 10% fully participating preferred stock will receive additional distributions at the same rates as other shareholders if dividends paid to all shareholders exceed 10%.
Answer (A) is incorrect. Bonds normally have a coupon yield stated in percentage and may be convertible but are not participating. Answer (B) is incorrect. Common stock is not described as convertible or participating on the financial statements. Answer (C) is incorrect. Common stock options are not participating and do not have a stated yield rate.

13. Preferred and common stock differ in that

- A. Failure to pay dividends on common stock will not force the firm into bankruptcy, while failure to pay dividends on preferred stock will force the firm into bankruptcy.
- B. Common stock dividends are a fixed amount, while preferred stock dividends are not.
- C. Preferred stock has a higher priority than common stock with regard to earnings and assets in the event of bankruptcy.
- D. Preferred stock dividends are deductible as an expense for tax purposes, while common stock dividends are not.

Answer (C) is correct.
REQUIRED: The difference between preferred and common stock.
DISCUSSION: In the event of bankruptcy, the claims of preferred shareholders must be satisfied before common shareholders receive anything. The interests of common shareholders are secondary to those of all other claimants.
Answer (A) is incorrect. Failure to pay dividends will not force the firm into bankruptcy, whether the dividends are for common or preferred stock. Only failure to pay interest will force the firm into bankruptcy. Answer (B) is incorrect. Preferred dividends are fixed. Answer (D) is incorrect. Neither common nor preferred dividends are tax deductible.

14. Which of the following is usually **not** a feature of cumulative preferred stock?

- A. Has priority over common stock with regard to earnings.
- B. Has priority over common stock with regard to assets.
- C. Has voting rights.
- D. Has the right to receive dividends in arrears before common stock dividends can be paid.

Answer (C) is correct.
REQUIRED: The item not usually a feature of cumulative preferred stock.
DISCUSSION: Preferred stock usually does not have voting rights. Preferred shareholders have the right to vote for directors only if the firm has not paid the preferred dividend for a specified period of time, such as ten quarters. This provision is an incentive for management to pay preferred dividends.
Answer (A) is incorrect. Preferred stock has priority over common stock with regard to earnings, so dividends must be paid on preferred stock before they can be paid on common stock. Answer (B) is incorrect. Preferred stock has priority over common stock with regard to assets. In the event of liquidation, for example, because of bankruptcy, the claims of preferred shareholders must be satisfied in full before the common shareholders receive anything. Answer (D) is incorrect. Cumulative preferred stock has the right to receive any dividends not paid in prior periods before common stock dividends are paid.

15. Which one of the following statements is correct regarding the effect preferred stock has on a company?

A. The firm's after-tax profits are shared equally by common and preferred shareholders.

B. Control of the firm is now shared by the common and preferred shareholders, with preferred shareholders having greater control.

C. Preferred shareholders' claims take precedence over the claims of common shareholders in the event of liquidation.

D. Nonpayment of preferred dividends places the firm in default, as does nonpayment of interest on debt.

Answer (C) is correct.
REQUIRED: The effect of preferred stock on a firm.
DISCUSSION: Preferred shareholders have priority over common shareholders in relation to dividend and liquidation rights, but payment of preferred dividends, unlike bond interest, is not mandatory. In exchange for these preferences, the preferred shareholders give up the right to vote. Consequently, preferred stock is a hybrid of debt and equity.
Answer (A) is incorrect. The share of profits available to preferred shareholders is normally limited to a percentage of the stock's par value. Thus, they may get more or less than the common shareholders. Answer (B) is incorrect. Preferred shareholders ordinarily do not have voting rights. Answer (D) is incorrect. The nonpayment of preferred dividends does not put the corporation into default. For this reason, preferred stock is sometimes viewed more favorably than debt by corporate management. If the preferred stock is cumulative (most is), the corporation may not pay dividends to common shareholders until the arrearages to preferred shareholders have been paid.

7.3 Leasing

16. Neary Company has entered into a contract to lease computers from Baldwin Company starting on January 1. Relevant information pertaining to the lease is provided below.

Lease term	4 years
Useful life of computers	5 years
Present value of future lease payments	$100,000
Fair value of leased asset on date of lease	$105,000
Baldwin's implicit rate	10%

At the end of the lease term, ownership of the asset transfers from Baldwin to Neary. Neary has properly classified this lease as a capital lease on its financial statements and uses straight-line depreciation on comparable assets. At January 1, the leased equipment would be reported on Neary's books as a(n)

A. Asset only.

B. Asset and a liability.

C. Liability only.

D. Expense and a liability.

Answer (B) is correct.
REQUIRED: The proper classification of leased equipment.
DISCUSSION: A capital lease is, in substance, the purchase of an asset. Thus, the leased asset and the related liability are reported in the balance sheet.
Answer (A) is incorrect. Neary also will report the lease liability. Answer (C) is incorrect. Neary also will report the computers under assets. Answer (D) is incorrect. Neary also will report the computers under assets.

17. If a company uses off-balance-sheet financing, assets have been acquired

A. For cash.

B. With operating leases.

C. With financing leases.

D. With a line of credit.

Answer (B) is correct.
REQUIRED: The nature of off-balance-sheet financing.
DISCUSSION: No liability is reported on the balance sheet for an operating lease other than for the next rental payment.
Answer (A) is incorrect. No liability arises if the assets were paid for with cash. Answer (C) is incorrect. The long-term liability for financing leases must be reported on the balance sheet. Answer (D) is incorrect. The liability associated with a line of credit is reported on the balance sheet.

18. Which one of the following statements with respect to leases is correct?

A. An operating lease is treated as a rental contract between lessor and lessee.

B. A lease that does not transfer ownership from the lessor to the lessee by the end of the lease is automatically an operating lease.

C. Sales and direct financing leases pertain more to lessees than lessors.

D. Unpredictability of lease revenues or expenses can transform what would otherwise be a capital lease for the lessee to an operating lease for the lessee.

Answer (A) is correct.
REQUIRED: The true statement about leases.
DISCUSSION: An operating lease is treated as a rental contract between lessor and lessee.
Answer (B) is incorrect. The transfer of ownership test is only one of four tests that are used to determine whether a lease is classified as a capital lease. Answer (C) is incorrect. Sales-type leases and direct financing leases are reported by lessors, not lessees. Answer (D) is incorrect. The degree of unpredictability of lease revenues or expenses is not a factor in the classification of the lease as a capital or operating lease.

7.4 Component Costs of Capital

19. Maloney, Inc.'s $1,000 par-value preferred stock paid its $100 per share annual dividend on April 4 of the current year. The preferred stock's current market price is $960 a share on the date of the dividend distribution. Maloney's marginal tax rate (combined federal and state) is 40%, and the firm plans to maintain its current capital structure relationship. The component cost of preferred stock to Maloney would be closest to

A. 6%

B. 6.25%

C. 10%

D. 10.4%

Answer (D) is correct.
REQUIRED: The component cost of preferred stock in the firm's capital structure.
DISCUSSION: The component cost of preferred stock is equal to the dividend yield, i.e., the cash dividend divided by the market price of the stock. (Dividends on preferred stock are not deductible for tax purposes; therefore, there is no adjustment for tax savings.) The annual dividend on preferred stock is $100 when the price of the stock is $960. The result is a cost of capital of about 10.4% ($100 ÷ $960).
Answer (A) is incorrect. Preferred dividends are not tax deductible. Answer (B) is incorrect. Preferred dividends are not tax deductible. Answer (C) is incorrect. The denominator is the current market price, not the par value.

20. Global Company Press has $150 par-value preferred stock with a market price of $120 a share. The organization pays a $15 per share annual dividend. Global's current marginal tax rate is 40%. Looking to the future, the company anticipates maintaining its current capital structure. What is the component cost of preferred stock to Global?

A. 4%

B. 5%

C. 10%

D. 12.5%

Answer (D) is correct.
REQUIRED: The cost of preferred stock.
DISCUSSION: The component cost of preferred stock is the dividend divided by the market price (also called the dividend yield). No tax adjustment is necessary because dividends are not deductible. Given that the market price is $120 when the dividend is $15, the component cost of preferred capital is 12.5% ($15 ÷ $120).
Answer (A) is incorrect. The preferred stock dividend is not deductible for tax purposes. Answer (B) is incorrect. The preferred stock dividend is not deductible for tax purposes. Answer (C) is incorrect. The denominator is the market price, not the par value.

21. What is the after-tax cost of preferred stock that sells for $5 per share and offers a $0.75 dividend when the tax rate is 35%?

A. 5.25%

B. 9.75%

C. 10.50%

D. 15%

Answer (D) is correct.
REQUIRED: The after-tax cost of preferred stock.
DISCUSSION: The component cost of preferred stock is the dividend yield, i.e., the cash dividend divided by the market price of the stock ($.75 ÷ $5.00 = 15%). Preferred dividends are not deductible for tax purposes.
Answer (A) is incorrect. Using the complement of the tax rate to reduce the effective cost results in 5.25%. Answer (B) is incorrect. The figure of 9.75% results from reducing the cost by the tax rate, which is not appropriate. Preferred dividends are not deductible for tax purposes. Answer (C) is incorrect. The figure of 10.50% is based on the assumption of a 30% tax rate and deductibility of dividends.

22. Cox Company has sold 1,000 shares of $100 par, 8% preferred stock at an issue price of $92 per share. Stock issue costs were $5 per share. Cox pays taxes at the rate of 40%. What is Cox's cost of preferred stock capital?

A. 8.00%

B. 8.25%

C. 8.70%

D. 9.20%

Answer (D) is correct.
REQUIRED: The cost of preferred equity.
DISCUSSION: Because the dividends on preferred stock are not deductible for tax purposes, the effect of income taxes is ignored. Thus, the relevant calculation is to divide the $8 annual dividend by the quantity of funds received from the issuance. In this case, the funds received equal $87 ($92 proceeds – $5 issue costs). Thus, the cost of capital is 9.2% ($8 ÷ $87).
Answer (A) is incorrect. The figure of 8.00% results from using the par value rather than the selling price and failing to subtract the issue costs. Answer (B) is incorrect. The figure of 8.25% results from adding the issue costs rather than subtracting them. Answer (C) is incorrect. The figure of 8.70% results from failing to subtract the issue costs.

7.5 Weighted-Average Cost of Capital

23. Osgood Products has announced that it plans to finance future investments so that the firm will achieve an optimum capital structure. Which one of the following corporate objectives is consistent with this announcement?

A. Maximize earnings per share.

B. Minimize the cost of debt.

C. Maximize the net worth of the firm.

D. Minimize the cost of equity.

Answer (C) is correct.
REQUIRED: The consistent corporate objective.
DISCUSSION: Financial structure is the composition of the financing sources of the assets of a firm. Traditionally, the financial structure consists of current liabilities, long-term debt, retained earnings, and stock. For most firms, the optimum structure includes a combination of debt and equity. Debt is cheaper than equity, but excessive use of debt increases the firm's risk and drives up the weighted-average cost of capital.
Answer (A) is incorrect. The maximization of EPS may not always suggest the best capital structure. Answer (B) is incorrect. The minimization of debt cost may not be optimal; as long as the firm can earn more on debt capital than it pays in interest, debt financing may be indicated. Answer (D) is incorrect. Minimizing the cost of equity may signify overly conservative management.

24. An accountant for Stability, Inc., must calculate the weighted-average cost of capital of the corporation using the following information.

		Component Cost
Accounts payable	$35,000,000	-0-
Long-term debt	10,000,000	8%
Common stock	10,000,000	15%
Retained earnings	5,000,000	18%

What is the weighted average cost of capital of Stability?

A. 6.88%

B. 8.00%

C. 10.25%

D. 12.80%

Answer (D) is correct.
REQUIRED: The weighted-average cost of capital.
DISCUSSION: Because the effect of income taxes is ignored in this situation, the stated rate on the firm's long-term debt is considered to be its effective rate. The weighted-average cost of capital (WACC) can thus be calculated as follows:

	Carrying Amount	Weight		Cost of Capital		Weighted Cost
Long-term debt	$10,000,000	40%	×	8%	=	3.2%
Common stock	10,000,000	40%	×	15%	=	6.0%
Retained earnings	5,000,000	20%	×	18%	=	3.6%
Totals	$25,000,000	100%				12.8%

Answer (A) is incorrect. The figure of 6.88% results from improperly ignoring the weighted cost of common stock. Answer (B) is incorrect. The figure of 8.00% is the component cost of debt. Answer (C) is incorrect. The figure of 10.25% results from improperly performing a simple average on the four balance sheet items listed.

25. What is the weighted-average cost of capital for a firm with equal amounts of debt and equity financing, a 15% company cost of equity capital, a 35% tax rate, and a 12% coupon rate on its debt that is selling at par value?

    A. 8.775%

    B. 9.60%

    C. 11.40%

    D. 13.50%

Answer (C) is correct.
    REQUIRED: The weighted-average cost of capital.
    DISCUSSION: The 12% debt coupon rate is reduced by the 35% tax shield, resulting in a cost of debt of 7.8% [12% × (1.0 − .35)]. The average of the 15% equity capital and 7.8% debt is 11.4%.
    Answer (A) is incorrect. The figure of 8.775% assumes that dividends on equity capital are tax deductible. Answer (B) is incorrect. Using the complement of the tax rate instead of the tax rate results in 9.60%. Answer (D) is incorrect. The figure of 13.50% overlooks the tax shield on the debt capital.

26. Scrunchy-Tech, Inc., has determined that it can minimize its weighted-average cost of capital (WACC) by using a debt-equity ratio of 2/3. If the firm's cost of debt is 9% before taxes, the cost of equity is estimated to be 12% before taxes, and the tax rate is 40%, what is the firm's WACC?

    A. 6.48%

    B. 7.92%

    C. 9.36%

    D. 10.80%

Answer (C) is correct.
    REQUIRED: The firm's weighted-average cost of capital.
    DISCUSSION: A firm's weighted-average cost of capital (WACC) is derived by weighting the (after-tax) cost of debt of 5.4% [9% × (1 − 40%)] and cost of equity of 12%. The tax rate does not affect the cost of equity. Scrunchy-Tech's WACC can be calculated as follows:

Component	Weight		Component Cost		Totals
Debt	40%	×	5.4%	=	2.16%
Equity	60%	×	12.0%	=	7.20%
	100%				9.36%

    Answer (A) is incorrect. Improperly subtracting the effect of taxes from the cost of equity results in 6.48%. Answer (B) is incorrect. Improperly subtracting the effect of taxes from equity, but not from debt, results in 7.92%. Answer (D) is incorrect. Improperly using the before-tax cost of debt results in 10.80%.

27. Kielly Machines, Inc., is planning an expansion program estimated to cost $100 million. Kielly is going to raise funds according to its target capital structure shown below.

Debt	.30
Preferred stock	.24
Equity	.46

Kielly had net income available to common shareholders of $184 million last year of which 75% was paid out in dividends. The company has a marginal tax rate of 40%.

Additional data

- The before-tax cost of debt is estimated to be 11%.
- The market yield of preferred stock is estimated to be 12%.
- The after-tax cost of common stock is estimated to be 16%.

What is Kielly's weighted-average cost of capital?

    A. 12.22%

    B. 13.00%

    C. 13.54%

    D. 14.00%

Answer (A) is correct.
    REQUIRED: The weighted-average cost of capital.
    DISCUSSION: The effective rate for Kielly's debt is the after-tax cost [11% × (1.0 − .40 tax rate) = 6.6%] The weighted-average cost of capital (WACC) therefore can be calculated as follows:

	Carrying Amount	Weight		Cost of Capital		Weighted Cost
Debt	$ 30,000,000	30%	×	6.6%	=	1.98%
Preferred stock	24,000,000	24%	×	12.0%	=	2.88%
Common equity	46,000,000	46%	×	16.0%	=	7.36%
Totals	$100,000,000	100%				12.22%

    Answer (B) is incorrect. The figure of 13.00% results from performing a simple average cost calculation on the individual components of capital. Answer (C) is incorrect. The figure of 13.54% results from improperly using the before-tax cost of debt. Answer (D) is incorrect. The figure of 14.00% results from performing a simple average on just the preferred stock and common equity components.

28. Following is an excerpt from Albion Corporation's balance sheet.

Long-term debt (9% effective interest rate)	$30,000,000
Preferred stock (100,000 shares, 12% dividend)	10,000,000
Common stock (5,000,000 shares outstanding)	60,000,000

The market value of Albion's debt and equity is equal to the carrying amount. Albion's treasurer estimates that the firm's cost of common equity is 17% and cost of preferred stock is 12%. If Albion's effective income tax rate is 40%, what is the firm's cost of capital?

A. 12.6%

B. 13.0%

C. 13.9%

D. 14.1%

29. Thomas Company's capital structure consists of 30% long-term debt, 25% preferred stock, and 45% common equity. The cost of capital for each component is shown below.

Long-term debt	8%
Preferred stock	11%
Common equity	15%

If Thomas pays taxes at the rate of 40%, what is the company's after-tax weighted-average cost of capital?

A. 7.14%

B. 9.84%

C. 10.94%

D. 11.90%

30. Joint Products, Inc., a corporation with a 40% marginal tax rate, plans to issue $1,000,000 of 8% preferred stock in exchange for $1,000,000 of its 8% bonds currently outstanding. The firm's total liabilities and equity are equal to $10,000,000. The effect of this exchange on the firm's weighted-average cost of capital is likely to be

A. No change, since it involves equal amounts of capital in the exchange and both instruments have the same rate.

B. A decrease, since a portion of the debt payments are tax deductible.

C. A decrease, since preferred stock payments do not need to be made each year, whereas debt payments must be made.

D. An increase, since a portion of the debt payments are tax deductible.

Answer (B) is correct.
   REQUIRED: Calculation of the weighted-average cost of capital.
   DISCUSSION: The effective rate for Albion's debt is the after-tax cost [9% × (1.0 – .40 tax rate) = 5.4%]. The weighted-average cost of capital (WACC) can thus be calculated as follows:

	Market Value	Weight		Cost of Capital		Weighted Cost
Long-term debt	$ 30,000,000	30%	×	5.4%	=	1.6%
Preferred stock	10,000,000	10%	×	12.0%	=	1.2%
Common stock	60,000,000	60%	×	17.0%	=	10.2%
Totals	$100,000,000	100%				13.0%

   Answer (A) is incorrect. The figure of 12.6% results from performing a simple average on the nominal rate of the bonds, the nominal rate of the preferred stock, and the estimated cost of equity. Answer (C) is incorrect. The figure of 13.9% results from using the bonds' yield rather than the after-tax interest cost. Answer (D) is incorrect. The figure of 14.1% results from improperly using the before-tax cost of debt.

Answer (C) is correct.
   REQUIRED: Calculation of the weighted-average cost of capital.
   DISCUSSION: The effective rate for Thomas' debt is the after-tax cost [8% × (1.0 – .40 tax rate) = 4.8%]. The weighted-average cost of capital (WACC) can thus be calculated as follows:

	Weight		Cost of Capital		Weighted Cost
Long-term debt	30%	×	4.8%	=	1.44%
Preferred stock	25%	×	11.0%	=	2.75%
Common equity	45%	×	15.0%	=	6.75%
Totals	100%				10.94%

   Answer (A) is incorrect. The figure of 7.14% results from improperly applying the tax effect to the rates on preferred stock and common equity. Answer (B) is incorrect. The figure of 9.84% results from improperly applying the tax effect to the rate on preferred stock. Answer (D) is incorrect. The figure of 11.90% results from failing to adjust the rate on debt for the tax effect.

Answer (D) is correct.
   REQUIRED: The effect on WACC of the replacement of bonds with preferred stock.
   DISCUSSION: The payment of interest on bonds is tax-deductible, whereas dividends on preferred stock must be paid out of after-tax earnings. Thus, when bonds are replaced in the capital structure with preferred stock, an increase in the cost of capital is likely, because there is no longer a tax shield.
   Answer (A) is incorrect. Although the dollar amounts may be equal, the different effective rates on the two instruments will cause a change in the cost of capital. Answer (B) is incorrect. The cost of capital will increase (debt is being replaced by preferred stock, not the reverse). Answer (C) is incorrect. The preferred stock has a higher effective rate, leading to an increase in the cost of capital.

7.6 PRACTICE WRITTEN COMMUNICATION

| | Business Environment and Concepts
Testlet 4 of 4 | Time Remaining
1 hour - 15 minutes | Unsplit Split Horiz Split Vertical Exit |

DIRECTIONS

Note: If you believe you have encountered a software malfunction, report it to the test center staff immediately.

Navigation

To navigate from task to task, use the controls at the bottom of the screen. Click on the **Next** button to advance to the next task, or the **Previous** button to go to the previous task. To go directly to any task, click on its number.

| ⚐ = Reminder | | Directions | 1 ⚐ | 2 ⚐ | 3 ⚐ | 4 ⚐ | 5 ⚐ | 6 ⚐ | 7 ⚐ | | ◀ Previous | Next ▶ |

If you would like a reminder to revisit a task, or want to indicate that you are finished with it, click on the reminder flag below the task number. To clear the flag, click on it again. Reminder flags are for your use only – they do not contribute to your score.

Tabs

In this part of the examination, you will be asked to complete various tasks. Every task has one or more **Work Tabs**. Every task also has a **Help** tab.

Work tab   Help tab

Work Tabs:

- **Work Tabs** are identified with a pencil icon. This is where your responses are expected.
- Each task has one or more **Work Tabs**.
- **Work Tabs** contain directions for completing the task - be sure to read these directions carefully.
- The **Work Tab** name in the example above is for illustration only - yours will differ.
- You must complete all of the **Work Tabs** in each task to receive full credit.

Help Tab:

- The **Help Tab** provides assistance with the exam software that is used in this task. For example, if the task is to compose a memorandum, **Help** will provide information about the word processor.

The Toolbar

The toolbar at the top of the screen shows the amount of time remaining for you to complete the tasks. In addition, the following tools are available. Note that only the **Exit** button is displayed when Directions are visible - the others will appear when you begin the tasks.

Click on these buttons to split or unsplit the screen. You can split the screen vertically or horizontally.

Click on this button to go on to the next part of the examination. You must complete all of the tasks to receive full credit. Once you click on **Exit** and confirm the action, you will NOT be able to return to this testlet.

| ⚐ = Reminder | | Directions | 1 ⚐ | | | | | ◀ Previous | Next ▶ |

Garfield Enterprises has been your audit client for many years. Every year since its inception, it has declared and distributed either a cash dividend or a property dividend. This year, however, Garfield is considering either a stock dividend or a stock split. Thus, the company has asked you for advice about the relevant accounting treatments and the effects on shareholders.

Write a memorandum to your client discussing the accounting for stock dividends and stock splits. Also include the accounting treatment for the recipient shareholders.

Type your communication below the line in the response area below.

REMINDER: Your response will be graded for both technical content and writing skills. Technical content will be evaluated for information that is helpful to the intended reader and clearly relevant to the issue. Writing skills will be evaluated for development, organization, and the appropriate expression of ideas in professional correspondence. Use a standard business memorandum or letter format with a clear beginning, middle, and end. Do not convey information in the form of a table, bullet point list, or other abbreviated presentation.

To: Garfield Enterprises
Re: Accounting for stock dividends and stock splits

NOTE: Your Written Communications on the actual CPA exam may cover topics outside the scope of the BEC CSO (i.e., they may relate to topics from the AUD, FAR, and/or REG CSOs instead). Answer to the best of your ability, and remember that graders are mainly evaluating your writing ability and will overlook minor technical mistakes.

Unofficial Answer

Written Communication

To: Garfield Enterprises
Re: Accounting for stock dividends and stock splits

Stock dividends and stock splits are distributions of stock to current shareholders in return for no consideration.

A stock dividend is recognized by capitalizing retained earnings in an amount equal to the fair value of the additional shares distributed. Capitalizing retained earnings results in a debit to retained earnings and credits to common stock and additional paid-in capital. Moreover, the par or stated value of each common share is unaffected. Accordingly, a stock dividend increases the aggregate par or stated value of shares outstanding.

A stock split is recognized by a decrease in the par or stated value of each common share, resulting in a proportionate increase in the number of shares outstanding. Accordingly, a stock split does not change the aggregate par or stated value of shares outstanding.

In some circumstances, legal requirements of the state of incorporation may require the capitalization of retained earnings when a stock split in the form of a dividend occurs. Under these circumstances, the par or stated value per share is not changed. Retained earnings should be capitalized in an amount equal to the legal requirement, usually the par or stated value of the additional shares distributed. Furthermore, the term "dividend" should be avoided in referring to a stock split. When this usage is legally required, the transaction should be described as a stock split in the form of a dividend.

The corporation's description of the intent of the distribution normally determines whether the distribution should be accounted for as a stock dividend. However, an issuance of shares of less than 20% or 25% of the previously outstanding shares usually should be recognized as a stock dividend. Moreover, the SEC provides that an issuance of less than 25% by a public company should be treated as a stock dividend.

The recipient of a stock dividend or stock split should not recognize income. After receipt, the shareholder has the same proportionate interest in the corporation and the same total carrying amount as before the declaration of the stock dividend or stock split.

The above depicts a Level 5 answer. Consult your booklet, *How to Pass the CPA Exam: A System for Success*, for a description of the three writing skills criteria. You may also access this booklet online by visiting www.gleim.com/PassCPA.

Self-Grade

Below, grade your response on technical content and writing skills. Bubble in the circle next to the appropriate score that you may receive based on the criteria given. Your **total** score is the sum of your scores on all six items. The maximum score is 19 points.

Technical Content Evaluation

Was your response on topic?	O No [0]	O Mostly [1]	O Yes [2]
Did your response have any *significant* errors?	O 0 errors [1]	O 1 major error [–1]	O 2 or more major errors [–2]
Did your response contain any illegal advice?	O No [1]	O Yes [0]	

Writing Skills Evaluation

	Poor	Below Average	Average	Above Average	Outstanding
Organization	O 1	O 2	O 3	O 4	O 5
Development	O 1	O 2	O 3	O 4	O 5
Expression	O 1	O 2	O 3	O 4	O 5

Disclaimer: This scoring schedule was developed by Gleim Publications as a guideline only. The AICPA has not released specific information on how the Written Communications are graded.

Practice even more Written Communications with the Gleim Mega Test Bank.

Learn more: gleim.com/CPAmega | 800.874.5346

STUDY UNIT EIGHT
WORKING CAPITAL

(17 pages of outline)

All firms must hold a certain amount of current assets to operate day-to-day. Because of different types of inventory, manufacturers and distributors often hold as much as 50% of their total assets in the form of current assets. Thus, the proper management of current assets is crucial to a firm's efficient operation.

Working capital management is the process of determining the optimal level and mix of these assets. The measures used to assess the success achieved also are addressed.

8.1 WORKING CAPITAL MANAGEMENT

1. **Working capital**, as used by accountants, is calculated as follows:

   Working capital = Current assets – Current liabilities

   a. Liquidity is a firm's ability to pay its current obligations as they come due and thus remain in business in the short run. Liquidity measures the ease with which assets can be converted to cash.

   b. **Current assets** are the most liquid assets. They are expected to be converted to cash, sold, or consumed within 1 year or the operating cycle, whichever is longer. Accordingly, ratios involving current assets measure a firm's ability to continue operating in the short run.

      1) Current assets include, in descending order of liquidity, (a) cash and equivalents, (b) marketable securities, (c) receivables, (d) inventories, and (e) prepaid items.

   c. **Current liabilities** are the liabilities with the earliest due dates. They are expected to be settled or converted to other liabilities within 1 year or the operating cycle, whichever is longer.

      1) Current liabilities include (a) accounts payable, (b) notes payable, (c) current maturities of long-term debt, (d) unearned revenues, (e) taxes payable, (f) wages payable, and (g) other accruals.

2. **Permanent and Temporary Working Capital**

   a. In principle, current assets should be financed with current liabilities. But this approach oversimplifies the requirements of working capital management.

      1) Some liquid current assets must be maintained to meet the firm's long-term minimum needs regardless of the firm's level of activity or profitability. This working capital is permanent.

      2) As the firm's needs for current assets change on a seasonal basis, temporary working capital is increased or decreased.

b.   Both elements tend to increase with the growth of the firm.

Working Capital

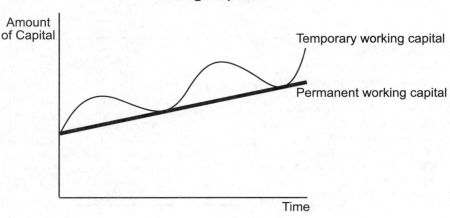

Figure 8-1

3. **Spontaneous Financing**

a.   Financing is spontaneous when current liabilities, such as trade payables and accruals, occur naturally in the ordinary course of business.

b.   Trade credit is created when a firm is offered credit terms by its suppliers.

EXAMPLE

A vendor has delivered goods and charged the firm $160,000 on terms of net 30. The firm effectively has received a 30-day interest-free $160,000 loan.

---

c.   Accrued expenses, such as (1) salaries, (2) wages, (3) interest, (4) dividends, and (5) taxes payable, are another source of (interest-free) spontaneous financing.

1)   For example, employees work 5, 6, or 7 days a week but are paid only every 2 weeks. A firm operates continuously but must remit federal income taxes only every quarter.

2)   Accruals have the additional advantage of fluctuating directly with operating activity, satisfying the matching principle.

d.   The response to capital needs that cannot be satisfied spontaneously must be carefully planned.

4. **Short-Term vs. Long-Term Financing**

a.   The firm's temporary working capital usually cannot be financed by spontaneous financing alone. Thus, the firm must decide whether to use short-term or long-term financing.

1)   The interest rate on long-term debt is higher than the interest rate on short-term debt. Consequently, long-term financing is more expensive.

2)   However, the shorter the maturity schedule of a firm's debt obligations, the greater the risk that the firm will be unable to make principal and interest payments.

b.   In general, short-term financing is more risky and less expensive than long-term financing.

c.   The appropriate financing of the firm's working capital depends on management's attitude toward the tradeoff between profitability and risk.

5. **Maturity Matching**

    a.   A firm ideally should offset each element of its temporary working capital with a short-term liability with the same maturity. For example, a short-term loan could be obtained before the winter season and repaid with the collections from holiday sales.

        1)   This ideal practice is maturity matching or hedging. It is rarely achievable because of uncertainty.

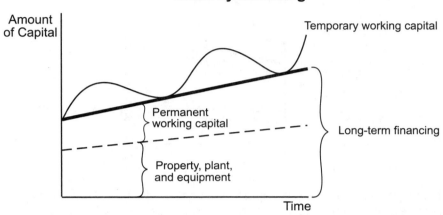

Figure 8-2

6. **Conservative Policy**

    a.   A firm that adopts a conservative financing policy seeks to minimize liquidity risk by financing its temporary working capital mostly with long-term debt.

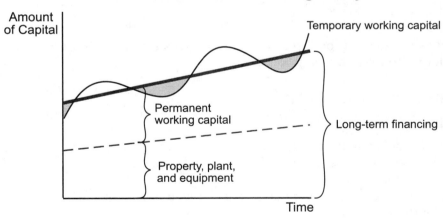

Figure 8-3

    b.   This approach takes advantage of the certainty inherent in long-term debt.

        1)   The locked-in interest rate mitigates interest rate risk (the risk that rates will rise in the short run).

            a)   The long-term maturity date mitigates liquidity risk (the inability to repay a current obligation when due).

    c.   The disadvantages are that

        1)   Working capital is idle during periods when it is not needed, as represented by the shaded areas in Figure 8-3. This inefficiency is mitigated in part by investing in short-term securities. (This issue is covered in Subunit 8.5.)

        2)   Long-term debt is more expensive.

7.   **Aggressive Policy**

a.   To increase profits, an aggressive financing policy reduces liquidity and accepts a higher risk of short-term cash flow shortages.

Aggressive Financing Policy

Figure 8-4

b.   This approach avoids the opportunity cost of idle funds incurred under the conservative policy. But it risks either unexpectedly high interest rates or the total unavailability of financing in the short run.

8.   **Summary**

Risk and Profitability in Relation to Financing

Working	Financed with	
Capital Component	Short-Term Debt	Long-Term Debt
Temporary	Medium	Low
Permanent	High	Medium

Stop and review! You have completed the outline for this subunit. Study multiple-choice questions 1 through 4 beginning on page 221.

8.2 LIQUIDITY RATIOS -- CALCULATION

1.   **Liquidity**

a.   Liquidity is a firm's ability to pay its current obligations as they come due and remain in business in the short run. Liquidity measures the ease with which assets can be converted to cash.

b.   Liquidity ratios measure this ability by relating a firm's liquid assets to its current liabilities.

Figure 8-5

EXAMPLE

The following balance sheet is used in this subunit and Subunits 8.6 and 8.7:

RESOURCES			FINANCING		
CURRENT ASSETS:	**Year 3**	**Year 2**	**CURRENT LIABILITIES:**	**Year 3**	**Year 2**
Cash and equivalents	$ 325,000	$ 275,000	Accounts payable	$ 150,000	$ 75,000
Available-for-sale securities	165,000	145,000	Notes payable	50,000	50,000
Accounts receivable (net)	120,000	115,000	Accrued interest on note	5,000	5,000
Notes receivable	55,000	40,000	Current maturities of L.T. debt	100,000	100,000
Inventories	85,000	55,000	Accrued salaries and wages	15,000	10,000
Prepaid expenses	10,000	5,000	Income taxes payable	70,000	35,000
Total current assets	**$ 760,000**	**$ 635,000**	**Total current liabilities**	**$ 390,000**	**$ 275,000**
NONCURRENT ASSETS:			**NONCURRENT LIABILITIES:**		
Equity-method investments	$ 120,000	$ 115,000	Bonds payable	$ 500,000	$ 600,000
Property, plant, and equipment	1,000,000	900,000	Long-term notes payable	90,000	60,000
Minus: accum. depreciation	(85,000)	(55,000)	Employee-related obligations	15,000	10,000
Goodwill	5,000	5,000	Deferred income taxes	5,000	5,000
Total noncurrent assets	**$1,040,000**	**$ 965,000**	**Total noncurrent liabilities**	**$ 610,000**	**$ 675,000**
			Total liabilities	**$1,000,000**	**$ 950,000**
			SHAREHOLDERS' EQUITY:		
			Preferred stock, $50 par	$ 120,000	$ 0
			Common stock, $1 par	500,000	500,000
			Additional paid-in capital	110,000	100,000
			Retained earnings	70,000	50,000
			Total shareholders' equity	**$ 800,000**	**$ 650,000**
			Total liabilities and		
Total assets	**$1,800,000**	**$1,600,000**	**shareholders' equity**	**$1,800,000**	**$1,600,000**

A candidate should know the formulas used to calculate the various financial ratios and be able to analyze the results. Numerous CPA exams have included questions on both the calculation and analysis of financial ratios. However, the numbers necessary to calculate a ratio often are not given directly. You may have to determine these numbers using information given in the question and then calculate the ratio.

NOTE: This Tip also applies to Subunit 8.7 and Study Unit 10, Subunits 3 and 4.

2. **Liquidity Ratios**

   a. **Net working capital** equals the resources the firm must have to continue operating in the short run if it must liquidate all of its current liabilities.

$$Current\ assets - Current\ liabilities$$

EXAMPLE

Year 3: $760,000 – $390,000 = $370,000
Year 2: $635,000 – $275,000 = $360,000

Although the firm's current liabilities increased, its current assets increased by $10,000 more.

   b. The **current ratio** (working capital ratio) is the most common measure of liquidity.

$$\frac{Current\ assets}{Current\ liabilities}$$

EXAMPLE

Year 3: $760,000 ÷ $390,000 = 1.95
Year 2: $635,000 ÷ $275,000 = 2.31

Although working capital increased in absolute terms ($10,000), current assets now provide less proportional coverage of current liabilities than in the prior year.

---

        1)   A low current ratio indicates a possible lack of liquidity. An overly high ratio indicates that management may not be investing idle assets productively.

   c.   The **quick (acid-test) ratio** excludes inventories and prepaid items from the numerator. Such assets are difficult to liquidate at their carrying amounts. The quick ratio is therefore a more conservative measure than the current ratio.

$$\frac{Cash \ and \ equivalents + Marketable \ securities + Net \ receivables}{Current \ liabilities}$$

EXAMPLE

Year 3:   ($325,000 + $165,000 + $120,000 + $55,000) ÷ $390,000 = 1.71
Year 2:   ($275,000 + $145,000 + $115,000 + $40,000) ÷ $275,000 = 2.09

Despite its increase in total working capital, the firm's position in its most liquid assets deteriorated significantly.

---

        1)   This ratio measures the firm's ability to pay its short-term debts easily. It also avoids the problem of inventory valuation.

Stop and review! You have completed the outline for this subunit. Study multiple-choice questions 5 through 8 beginning on page 222.

8.3 LIQUIDITY RATIOS -- EFFECTS OF TRANSACTIONS

   1.   **Effects of Transactions**

      a.   If a ratio is less than 1.0, the numerator is lower than the denominator.

          1)   A transaction that causes equal changes in the numerator and denominator has a proportionally greater effect on the numerator, resulting in a change in the ratio in the same direction.

             a)   If the current (or quick) ratio is less than 1.0, paying a current liability with current (or quick) assets decreases the numerator and the denominator by the same amount. The effect is to **decrease** the ratio.

$$\text{EXAMPLE:} \quad \frac{3-1}{4-1} = \frac{2}{3} \quad \text{and} \quad \frac{3}{4} > \frac{2}{3}$$

      b.   If a ratio is equal to 1.0, the numerator and denominator are the same.

          1)   A transaction that causes equal changes in the numerator and denominator does not affect the ratio.

$$\text{EXAMPLE:} \quad \frac{4-1}{4-1} = \frac{3}{3} \quad \text{and} \quad \frac{4}{4} = \frac{3}{3}$$

      c.   If a ratio is greater than 1.0, the numerator is higher than the denominator.

          1)   A transaction that causes equal changes in the numerator and denominator has a proportionally greater effect on the denominator, resulting in a change in the ratio in the opposite direction.

a) If the current (or quick) ratio is greater than 1.0, paying a current liability with current (or quick) assets decreases the numerator and denominator by the same amount. The effect is to **increase** the ratio.

$$\text{EXAMPLE: } \frac{4 - 1}{3 - 1} = \frac{3}{2} \quad \text{and} \quad \frac{4}{3} < \frac{3}{2}$$

d.

Ratio range	Effect on ratio of equal increase of numerator and denominator	Effect on ratio of equal decrease of numerator and denominator
< 1.0	Increase	Decrease
= 1.0	No effect	No effect
> 1.0	Decrease	Increase

Stop and review! You have completed the outline for this subunit. Study multiple-choice questions 9 through 12 beginning on page 224.

8.4 CASH MANAGEMENT

1. **Managing the Level of Cash**

    a. The three motives for holding cash are to

        1) Use as a medium of exchange (transactional motive).
        2) Provide for unexpected contingencies (precautionary motive).
        3) Take advantage of unexpected opportunities (speculative motive).

    b. The goal of cash management is to maintain the firm's **optimal** cash balance.

        1) The optimal balance is rarely the largest. Because cash does not earn a return, only the amount needed to pay current obligations as they come due should be held.

    c. The firm's optimal level of cash should be determined by a cost-benefit analysis.

        1) The three motives for holding cash must be balanced against the opportunity cost of missed investments in marketable securities.

    d. A **compensating balance** is a minimum amount that a bank requires the firm to keep in its demand (checking) account.

        1) This noninterest-bearing balance compensates the bank for services rendered, such as unlimited check writing.
        2) The funds are unavailable for short-term investment and incur an opportunity cost.

2. **Speeding Cash Collections**

    a. The period of time from when a payor puts a check in the mail to the availability of the funds in the payee's bank is called float. Firms attempt to decrease float for receipts and increase float for payments.

    b. A **lockbox** system expedites the receipt of funds from cashing checks.

        1) Customers submit their payments to a post office box. Bank personnel remove the envelopes from the mailbox and immediately deposit the checks in the firm's account. The remittance advices then must be transferred to the firm for entry into the accounts receivable system. The bank generally charges a flat monthly fee for this service.
        2) For firms doing business nationwide, a lockbox network is appropriate. The country is divided into regions according to customer population patterns. A lockbox arrangement then is established with a bank in each region.

    c. A firm using a lockbox network also participates in concentration banking. The regional banks that provide lockbox services automatically transfer their daily collections to the firm's principal bank, where they can be used for payments and short-term investment.

3. **Slowing Cash Payments**

    a. A **draft** is a three-party instrument in which one person (the drawer) orders a second person (the drawee) to pay money to a third person (the payee).

        1) A **check** is the most common form of draft. It is an instrument payable on demand by a drawee bank. Consequently, a draft can be used to delay the outflow of cash.

        2) A draft dated on the due date of an invoice is not processed by the drawee until that date. Thus, the outflow is delayed until the check clears the drawee bank. By contrast, an electronic funds transfer (EFT) eliminates float.

    b. A **payable through draft** (PTD) differs from a check. (1) It is not payable on demand, and (2) the drawee is the payor, not a bank. After the payee presents the PTD to a bank, the bank in turn presents it to the issuer. The issuer then must deposit sufficient funds to cover the PTD. Use of PTDs therefore allows a firm to maintain lower cash balances.

        1) Disadvantages are that (a) vendors prefer to receive an instrument that is payable on demand and (b) banks generally impose higher processing fees for PTDs.

    c. A **zero-balance account** (ZBA) has a balance of $0. At the end of each processing day, the bank transfers just enough from the firm's master account to cover all checks presented against the ZBA that day.

        1) This practice allows the firm to maintain higher balances in the master account from which short-term investments can be made. The bank generally charges a fee for this service.

    d. **Disbursement float** is the period of time from when the payor puts a check in the mail to withdrawal of the funds from the payor's account. To increase disbursement float, a firm may mail checks to its vendors despite uncertainty about whether funds suffice to pay them all.

        1) For these situations, some banks offer overdraft protection. The bank guarantees (for a fee) to cover any shortage with a transfer from the firm's master account.

Background

Too *much* cash can create a finance challenge. During the summer of 2011, large U.S. firms held large amounts of cash. They were unwilling to spend in the highly uncertain economic environment, and banks had huge U.S. dollar deposits. This sudden influx of cash greatly increased the banks' interest payouts and made them subject to more stringent ratio and reserve requirements. To compensate, Bank of New York Mellon, the largest custody bank, announced that it would start charging fees to clients whose cash balances exceeded $50 million.

Stop and review! You have completed the outline for this subunit. Study multiple-choice questions 13 through 15 beginning on page 225.

8.5 MARKETABLE SECURITIES MANAGEMENT

1. **Idle Cash and Its Uses**

    a. Idle cash incurs an opportunity cost. To offset this cost, firms invest their idle cash in marketable securities.

    b. Other than earning a modest return, the most important goals of marketable securities management are liquidity and safety.

        1) Marketable securities management applies to low-yield, low-risk instruments (money market instruments) that are traded in highly active markets.

    c.   Firms invest their temporary surpluses of cash in the market for short-term investments (the money market).

        1)   The money market is not formally organized but consists of many financial institutions, firms, and government agencies offering instruments of various risk levels and short- to medium-range maturities.

2.   **Money Market Instruments**

    a.   U.S. Treasury obligations are the safest investment. They are exempt from state and local taxation and are highly liquid.

        1)   **Treasury bills** (T-bills) have maturities of 1 year or less. They do not pay interest but are sold at a discount.

        2)   **Treasury notes** (T-notes) have maturities of 1 to 10 years. They pay the lender interest every 6 months.

        3)   **Treasury bonds** (T-bonds) have maturities of 10 years or longer. They pay the lender interest every 6 months.

Background

The U.S. government stopped issuing the famous 30-year Treasury bond (the long bond) in October 2001 as efforts to pay off the national debt accelerated. The long bond became available again starting in February 2006.

---

    b.   **Repurchase agreements** (repos) are a means for dealers in government securities to finance their portfolios. When a firm buys a repo, it temporarily purchases some of the dealer's government securities. The dealer agrees to repurchase them at a later time for a specific (higher) price. In essence, the firm makes a secured short-term loan. Maturities vary from overnight to a few days.

    c.   **Federal agency securities** are backed (1) by the full faith and credit of the U.S. government or (2) only by the issuing agency.

        1)   Obligations of the Federal Housing Administration (FHA) and the Government National Mortgage Association (Ginnie Mae) are backed by the U.S. Treasury.

        2)   Obligations of such government-sponsored enterprises (GSEs) as the Federal National Mortgage Association (Fannie Mae) and the Federal Home Loan Mortgage Corporation (Freddie Mac), which issue mortgage-backed securities, officially are backed only by the agencies themselves. But they do have an implied guarantee by the federal government.

    d.   **Bankers' acceptances** are drafts drawn by a nonfinancial firm on deposits at a bank. Acceptance by the bank is a guarantee of payment at maturity.

        1)   The payee can rely on the creditworthiness of the bank rather than on that of the (presumably riskier) drawer.

        2)   Because they are backed by the prestige of a large bank, these instruments are highly marketable after acceptance.

    e.   **Commercial paper** consists of short-term, unsecured notes payable issued in large denominations ($100,000 or more) by large corporations with high credit ratings. They are issued to other corporations and institutional investors, such as pension funds, banks, and insurers.

        1)   Maturities of commercial paper are at most 270 days, and no general secondary market exists. It is a lower-cost source of funds than bank loans because it is usually issued at below the prime rate.

    f.   **Certificates of deposit** (CDs) are savings deposits that cannot be withdrawn before maturity without a high penalty. CDs often yield a lower return than commercial paper because they are less risky. Negotiable CDs are traded under the regulation of the Federal Reserve System.

    g.   **Eurodollars** are time deposits of U.S. dollars in banks located abroad.

    h.   Money-market **mutual funds** invest in short-term, low-risk securities. In addition to paying interest, these funds allow investors to write checks on their balances.

    i.   **State and local** governments issue short-term securities exempt from taxation.

Stop and review! You have completed the outline for this subunit. Study multiple-choice questions 16 and 17 on page 226.

8.6 RECEIVABLES MANAGEMENT

1.   **Overview**

    a.   The goal of receivables management is to offer the **terms of credit** that maximize profits, not sales.

        1)   Maximizing sales is easily done by raising discount percentages, offering longer payment periods, and accepting riskier customers. But this strategy could lead to cash flow shortages.

Background

In 1969, in a desperate attempt to increase sales, the department store chain W.T. Grant drastically lowered its credit standards. As a result, sales boomed. However, during the economic downturn of 1970-71, cash inflows dried up as customer accounts began to turn delinquent. The firm finally went bankrupt in 1974. Grant's creditors were completely unaware because its accrual-basis income statement reported consistently positive results, and Grant never stopped paying a dividend. The inadequacy of the traditional income statement for assessing liquidity was made obvious by the Grant bankruptcy. This incident was one of the reasons for the FASB's requirement of a statement of cash flows.

---

        2)   Default risk can be minimized by raising credit standards, but the effect is loss of sales. Thus, the firm must achieve the proper balance.

    b.   Common credit terms are 2/10, net 30. These terms mean that the customer may either (1) subtract 2% of the invoice amount if it is paid within 10 days or (2) pay the entire balance by the 30th day.

    c.   Factoring is an arrangement in which a firm sells its accounts receivable at a discount to a factor, an entity that specializes in collections.

        1)   The seller receives cash and eliminates bad debts. Also, the seller need not maintain a credit department and an accounts receivable staff.

2.   **Receivables Ratios**

EXAMPLE

The following is from an income statement:

	Current Year	Prior Year
Net sales	$1,800,000	$1,400,000
Cost of goods sold	(1,650,000)	(1,330,000)
Gross profit	$ 150,000	$ 70,000

---

    a.   The **accounts receivable turnover ratio** is the number of times in a year the total balance of receivables is converted to cash.

$$\text{Accounts receivable turnover} = \frac{\text{Net credit sales}}{\text{Average balance in receivables}}$$

EXAMPLE

In the example presented in Subunit 8.2, all of the firm's sales are on credit. Net trade receivables at the balance sheet date for Year 1 were $105,000.

Year 3: $1,800,000 ÷ [($120,000 + $115,000) ÷ 2] = 15.3 times
Year 2: $1,400,000 ÷ [($115,000 + $105,000) ÷ 2] = 12.7 times

The firm turned over its trade receivables balance 2.6 more times during Year 3, even as receivables increased. Thus, the firm's collection effectiveness improved.

---

      b.   The **average collection period (days' sales in receivables)** measures the average number of days between the time of sale and receipt of payment.

$$Days'\ sales\ in\ receivables = \frac{Days\ in\ year}{Accounts\ receivable\ turnover\ ratio}$$

EXAMPLE

Year 3:   365 days ÷ 15.3 times = 23.9 days
Year 2:   365 days ÷ 12.7 times = 28.7 days

The denominator (calculated in the preceding example) increased, and the numerator is a constant. Thus, days' sales necessarily decrease. In addition to improving its collection practices, the firm may have better assessed the creditworthiness of potential customers.

Stop and review! You have completed the outline for this subunit. Study multiple-choice questions 18 through 20 on page 227.

8.7 INVENTORY MANAGEMENT -- RATIOS

1. **Inventory Ratios**

    a.   Two ratios measure the efficiency of the management of inventory.

        1)   **Inventory turnover** is the number of times in a year the total balance of inventory is converted to cash or receivables.

            a)   Generally, the higher the inventory turnover rate, the more efficient the inventory management. A high rate may imply that the firm is not carrying excess inventory or inventory that is obsolete.

$$Inventory\ turnover = \frac{Cost\ of\ goods\ sold}{Average\ balance\ in\ inventory}$$

EXAMPLE

The balance in inventories at the balance sheet date of Year 1 was $45,000.

Year 3: $1,650,000 ÷ [($85,000 + $55,000) ÷ 2] = 23.6 times
Year 2: $1,330,000 ÷ [($55,000 + $45,000) ÷ 2] = 26.6 times

The firm did not turn over its inventories as many times during Year 3. This result is expected during a period of increasing sales (and increased inventory). Accordingly, lower turnover does not necessarily indicate poor inventory management.

---

            b)   If business is seasonal, a simple average of beginning and ending balances is inadequate. The monthly balances should be averaged instead.

            c)   Because cost of goods sold is in the numerator, higher sales (and a higher cost of goods sold) without an increase in inventory results in higher turnover.

               i)   Because inventory is in the denominator, reducing inventory results in a higher turnover ratio.

        d)   The ratio of a firm that uses LIFO may not be comparable with that of a firm with a higher inventory measurement.

    2)   **Days' sales in inventory** measures the average number of days between the acquisition of inventory and its sale.

$$Days'\ sales\ in\ inventory = \frac{Days\ in\ year}{Inventory\ turnover\ ratio}$$

EXAMPLE

Year 3:   365 days ÷ 23.6 times = 15.5 days
Year 2:   365 days ÷ 26.6 times = 13.7 days

The numerator is a constant. Thus, the decreased inventory turnover means that days' sales in inventory increased. This phenomenon is common during a period of increasing sales.

Stop and review! You have completed the outline for this subunit. Study multiple-choice questions 21 and 22 on page 228.

8.8 INVENTORY MANAGEMENT -- METHODS

1.   **Overview**

    a.   Minimizing the total cost of inventory involves constant evaluation of the tradeoffs among the four components of total cost.

       Purchase costs + Carrying costs + Ordering costs + Stockout costs

       1)   **Purchase costs** are the actual invoice amounts charged by suppliers. It is the investment in inventory.

       2)   **Carrying costs** is a broad category. It consists of all costs associated with holding inventory: (a) storage, (b) insurance, (c) security, (d) depreciation or rent of facilities, (e) interest, (f) obsolescence, (g) spoilage, and (h) the opportunity cost of funds invested in inventory (percentage investment in inventory).

       3)   **Ordering costs** are the fixed costs of placing an order with a vendor. They are not affected by the number of units ordered. If units are manufactured internally, **setup costs** for production lines are calculated instead.

       4)   **Stockout costs** are the opportunity costs of not being able to fill customer orders. They also include the costs of expediting special shipments required because of insufficient inventory.

    b.   Minimization of total inventory cost is difficult because of the following factors:

       1)   Stockout costs can be minimized only by incurring higher carrying costs.

       2)   Carrying costs can be minimized only by incurring the high fixed costs of placing many small orders.

       3)   Ordering costs can be minimized only by incurring the higher carrying costs of larger inventories.

2.   **Inventory Replenishment Factors**

    a.   **Lead time** is the time between placing an order and receipt of goods from the supplier.

       1)   When lead time is known and demand is uniform, the goods can be timed to arrive just as inventory is eliminated. This is the basis of the just-in-time model discussed later in this subunit.

    b.   **Safety stock** is inventory held as a hedge against contingencies.

       1)   Determining the appropriate safety stock requires a probabilistic calculation that balances the variability of demand with the risk of stockouts the firm is willing to accept.

c. The **reorder point** is the inventory amount indicating that a new order should be placed. It is calculated using the following equation:

(Average daily demand × Lead time in days) + Safety stock

3. **The Economic Order Quantity Model**

a. The economic order quantity (EOQ) model determines the order quantity that minimizes the sum of ordering costs and carrying costs.

$$EOQ = \sqrt{\frac{2OD}{c}}$$

If: O = **o**rdering cost per purchase order
D = periodic **d**emand in units/usage of units
c = periodic **c**arrying costs per uni

Inventory Management

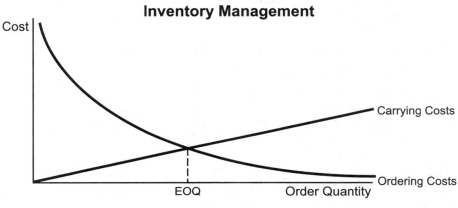

Figure 8-6

b. The assumptions underlying the EOQ model are that

1) Demand or production is uniform.
2) Order (setup) costs and carrying costs are constant.
3) No quantity discounts are allowed.

c. A change in any variable changes the EOQ. If demand or ordering costs increase, each order must contain more units. If carrying costs increase, each order contains fewer units.

EXAMPLE

A firm plans to use 2,500 inventory units (D) during the 180-day period. The ordering cost per order is $30 (O). The carrying costs per inventory unit is $15 (c). In order to minimize the total inventory cost for the 180-day period, the firm should order 100 inventory units (EOQ) in each order.

$$EOQ = \sqrt{\frac{2 \times 2,500 \times 30}{15}} = 100$$

The firm should make 25 orders during that period (2,500 ÷ 100).

---

4. **Periodic Inventory Systems**

a. Under a periodic system, inventory and cost of goods sold are updated only when physical inventory counts are made.

1) Physical inventory counts are time-consuming and costly, so inventory counts are usually only annually or quarterly.

    a) Firms with relatively inexpensive and homogeneous items, such as wheat dealers, that have no need to monitor continuously their inventory and cost of goods sold generally use this system.

5. **Perpetual Inventory Systems**

    a. Under a perpetual system, every item received is individually recorded in the tracking system. Inventory and cost of goods sold are updated after every sale.

      1) A perpetual system is used by a firm that requires accurate inventory information at all times.

      2) However, even in a perpetual system, a full count must be made at least annually to (a) correct errors in the tracking system and (b) determine an ending balance for financial reporting.

      3) A perpetual system requires intensive bookkeeping. But the rapid, continuous increases in computer storage and processing power have made such systems more feasible.

    b. A perpetual system makes the replenishment models such as EOQ more practicable.

      1) Under a periodic system, determining the optimal reorder point is difficult. Item quantities are not continuously monitored, and reordering can be unsystematic.

      2) But the continuous monitoring inherent in a perpetual system allows reorder points for all items to be preprogrammed. The system then can initiate a reorder automatically. Safety stocks and stockout costs can be minimized simultaneously.

    c. Thus, the added expense of a perpetual inventory system is offset by the reduced order and carrying costs made possible by modern technology.

6. **Just-in-Time Inventory**

    a. In a just-in-time (JIT) inventory system, the moving, handling, and storage of inventory are treated as nonvalue-adding activities.

      1) Not just safety stock but all materials inventories (and their associated carrying costs) are reduced or eliminated entirely. Binding agreements with suppliers ensure that materials arrive exactly when they are needed and not before.

      2) JIT is a pull system. Thus, it is demand-driven. In a manufacturing environment, production of goods does not begin until an order has been received. In this way, finished goods inventories also are eliminated.

      3) The purpose of the JIT inventory system is to minimize the cost associated with inventory control and maintenance by reducing the lag time between inventory's arrival and use.

    b. A backflush costing system often is used in a JIT environment. Backflush costing eliminates the traditional sequential tracking of costs. Instead, entries to inventory may be delayed until as late as the end of the period.

      1) For example, all product costs may be charged initially to cost of sales, and costs may be flushed back to the inventory accounts only at the end of the period. Thus, the detail of cost accounting is decreased.

7. **Kanban**

    a. Another method of improving inventory flow is the kanban system developed by Toyota.

      1) Kanban means ticket. Tickets (also described as cards or markers) control the flow of production or parts so that they are produced or obtained in the needed amounts at the needed times.

b. Kanban is essentially a visual workflow management system.

   1) A kanban is an authorization to a worker to release inventory to the next step. Work cannot move to the next stage until a kanban indicates that stage is ready for it.

   2) A basic kanban system includes (a) a withdrawal kanban that states the quantity that a later process should withdraw from its predecessor; (b) a production kanban that states the output of the preceding process; and (c) a vendor kanban that tells a vendor what, how much, where, and when to deliver.

8. **MRP and MRP II**

   a. Materials requirements planning (MRP) is a computerized system for moving materials through a production process according to a predetermined schedule.

      1) MRP embodies the principle of dependent demand (also called derived demand, defined in item 1.b. in Study Unit 2, Subunit 10).

         a) Demand-dependent goods are components of other goods. Their demand is driven by the demand for the final goods of which they are a part.

      2) MRP is a push system. The demand for materials is driven by the forecasted demand for the final product as programmed into the system.

         a) MRP, in effect, creates schedules of when items of inventory are needed in the production departments.

         b) If an outage of a given item is projected, the system automatically generates a purchase order on the proper date (considering lead times) so that deliveries arrive on time.

      3) MRP consists of three essential components:

         a) The master production schedule (MPS) is a table of the projected demand for end products along with the dates they are needed.

         b) The bill of materials (BOM) is a table of every component part required by every end product (and by every subassembly).

         c) Perpetual inventory records must be used to ensure that a true count of every component, subassembly, and finished good is available at all times.

   b. Manufacturing resource planning (MRP II) does not replace, but extends the scope of, an MRP system.

      1) MRP is based on programmed demand, regardless of capacity considerations or changes in the market for the end product.

      2) MRP II is a closed-loop system that adds a feedback loop to allow analysis of capacity, market changes, and other variables.

   c. MRP is a common function contained in enterprise resource planning (ERP) software systems.

      1) Although ERP and MRP are similar, they are not interchangeable. ERP includes many functions not included in MRP.

         a) For example, an ERP system allows a firm to determine what hiring decisions need to be made or whether it should invest in new capital assets.

            i) A firm that only needs to control materials should implement MRP.

      2) An ERP outline is in Study Unit 11, Subunit 4.

Stop and review! You have completed the outline for this subunit. Study multiple-choice questions 23 through 28 beginning on page 229.

8.9 THE OPERATING CYCLE AND CASH CONVERSION CYCLE

1. **Inventory to Receivables to Cash**

    a. A firm's **operating cycle** is the time between the acquisition of inventory and the collection of cash for its sale.

    Operating cycle = Days' sales in receivables + Days' sales in inventory

    ---

    ### EXAMPLE

    Year 3: 23.9 days + 15.5 days = 39.4 days
    Year 2: 28.7 days + 13.7 days = 42.4 days

    The firm has reduced its operating cycle while increasing sales and inventories.

    ---

    b. The following diagram depicts the phases of the operating cycle:

**Operating Cycle
39.4 Days**

Acquire
Inventory

Collect
Receivable

Days' Sales
in Inventory
(15.5 days)

Days' Sales
in Receivables
(23.9 days)

Sell
Inventory

Figure 8-7

2. **Cash Conversion Cycle**

    a. A firm's cash conversion cycle is the time between the payment of cash for inventory and the collection of cash from its sale.

    *Cash conversion cycle = Average collection period + Days' sales in inventory –
    Average payables period*

    1) The accounts payable turnover ratio is the number of times during a period that the firm pays its accounts payable.

    $$Accounts\ payable\ turnover = \frac{Cost\ of\ goods\ sold}{Average\ balance\ in\ accounts\ payable}$$

2) The average payables period (payables turnover in days or payables deferral period) is the average time between the purchase of inventory and the payment of cash.

$$\textit{Average payable period} = \frac{\textit{Days in year}}{\textit{Accounts payable turnover}}$$

b. The operating cycle and the cash conversion cycle differ because the firm's purchases of inventory are made on credit. Thus, the cash conversion cycle equals the operating cycle minus the average payables period.

Stop and review! You have completed the outline for this subunit. Study multiple-choice question 29 on page 231.

8.10 MULTIPLE RATIO ANALYSIS

Some multiple-choice questions require candidates to combine their knowledge of the different categories of ratios. This subunit consists entirely of such questions. If you have not already mastered the ratios presented in Subunits 8.2 and 8.7, you should review those outlines before answering the questions.

Stop and review! You have completed the outline for this subunit. Study multiple-choice question 30 on page 231.

QUESTIONS

8.1 Working Capital Management

1. As a company becomes more conservative in its working capital policy, it tends to have a(n)

A. Decrease in its acid-test ratio.

B. Increase in the ratio of current liabilities to noncurrent liabilities.

C. Increase in the ratio of current assets to current liabilities.

D. Increase in funds invested in common stock and a decrease in funds invested in marketable securities.

Answer (C) is correct.

REQUIRED: The effect of a more conservative working capital policy.

DISCUSSION: A conservative working capital policy minimizes liquidity risk by increasing net working capital (current assets – current liabilities). The result is that the company forgoes the potentially higher returns available from using the additional working capital to acquire long-term assets. A conservative working capital policy is characterized by a higher current ratio (current assets ÷ current liabilities) and acid-test ratio (quick assets ÷ current liabilities). Thus, the firm will increase current assets or decrease current liabilities. A conservative policy finances assets using long-term or permanent funds rather than short-term sources.

Answer (A) is incorrect. A decrease in the acid-test ratio suggests an aggressive policy. A conservative firm wants a higher acid-test ratio, that is, more liquid assets relative to liabilities. Answer (B) is incorrect. A conservative firm wants working capital to be financed from long-term sources. Answer (D) is incorrect. A conservative firm seeks more liquid (marketable) investments.

2. Which one of the following provides a spontaneous source of financing for a firm?

A. Accounts payable.

B. Mortgage bonds.

C. Accounts receivable.

D. Debentures.

Answer (A) is correct.

REQUIRED: The spontaneous source of financing.

DISCUSSION: Trade credit is a spontaneous source of financing because it exists automatically as part of a purchase transaction. Because of its ease in use, trade credit is the largest source of short-term financing for many firms, both large and small.

Answer (B) is incorrect. Mortgage bonds and debentures do not arise automatically as a result of a purchase transaction. Answer (C) is incorrect. The use of receivables as a financing source requires an extensive factoring arrangement and often involves the creditor's evaluation of the credit ratings of the borrower's customers. Answer (D) is incorrect. Mortgage bonds and debentures do not arise automatically as a result of a purchase transaction.

3. Net working capital is the difference between

    A. Current assets and current liabilities.

    B. Fixed assets and fixed liabilities.

    C. Total assets and total liabilities.

    D. Shareholders' investment and cash.

Answer (A) is correct.
    REQUIRED: The definition of net working capital.
    DISCUSSION: Net working capital is defined by accountants as the difference between current assets and current liabilities. Working capital is a measure of liquidity.
    Answer (B) is incorrect. Working capital refers to the difference between current assets and current liabilities; fixed assets are not a component. Answer (C) is incorrect. Total assets and total liabilities are not components of working capital; only current items are included. Answer (D) is incorrect. Shareholders' equity is not a component of working capital; only current items are included in the concept of working capital.

4. Determining the appropriate level of working capital for a firm requires

    A. Changing the capital structure and dividend policy of the firm.

    B. Maintaining short-term debt at the lowest possible level because it is generally more expensive than long-term debt.

    C. Offsetting the benefit of current assets and current liabilities against the probability of technical insolvency.

    D. Maintaining a high proportion of liquid assets to total assets in order to maximize the return on total investments.

Answer (C) is correct.
    REQUIRED: The requirement for determining the appropriate level of working capital.
    DISCUSSION: Working capital finance addresses the determination of the optimal level, mix, and use of current assets and current liabilities. The objective is to minimize the cost of maintaining liquidity while guarding against the possibility of technical insolvency. Technical insolvency is the inability to pay debts as they come due.
    Answer (A) is incorrect. Capital structure and dividends relate to capital structure finance, not working capital finance. Answer (B) is incorrect. Short-term debt is usually less expensive than long-term debt. Answer (D) is incorrect. Liquid assets do not ordinarily earn high returns relative to long-term assets, so holding the former will not maximize the return on total assets.

8.2 Liquidity Ratios -- Calculation

5. Given an acid-test ratio of 2.0, current assets of $5,000, and inventory of $2,000, the value of current liabilities is

    A. $1,500

    B. $2,500

    C. $3,500

    D. $6,000

Answer (A) is correct.
    REQUIRED: The value of current liabilities given the acid-test ratio, current assets, and inventory.
    DISCUSSION: The acid-test, or quick, ratio equals the ratio of the quick assets (cash, net accounts receivable, and marketable securities) divided by current liabilities. Current assets equal the quick assets plus inventory and prepaid expenses. This question assumes that the entity has no prepaid expenses. Given current assets of $5,000, inventory of $2,000, and no prepaid expenses, the quick assets must be $3,000. Because the acid-test ratio is 2.0, the quick assets are double the current liabilities. Current liabilities therefore are equal to $1,500 ($3,000 quick assets ÷ 2.0).
    Answer (B) is incorrect. Dividing the current assets by 2.0 results in $2,500. Current assets includes inventory, which should not be included in the calculation of the acid-test ratio. Answer (C) is incorrect. Adding inventory to current assets rather than subtracting it results in $3,500. Answer (D) is incorrect. Multiplying the quick assets by 2 instead of dividing by 2 results in $6,000.

Questions 6 through 8 are based on the following information.

Tosh Enterprises reported the following account information:

Accounts receivable	$400,000	Inventory	$800,000
Accounts payable	260,000	Land	500,000
Bonds payable, due in 10 years	600,000	Short-term prepaid expense	80,000
Cash	200,000		
Interest payable, due in 3 months	20,000		

6. The current ratio for Tosh Enterprises is

   A. 1.68

   B. 2.14

   C. 5.00

   D. 5.29

Answer (D) is correct.
   REQUIRED: The current ratio.
   DISCUSSION: The current ratio equals current assets divided by current liabilities. Current assets consist of accounts receivable, cash, inventory, and prepaid expenses, a total of $1,480,000 ($400,000 + $200,000 + $800,000 + $80,000). Current liabilities consist of accounts payable and interest payable, a total of $280,000 ($260,000 + $20,000). Hence, the current ratio is 5.29 ($1,480,000 ÷ $280,000).
   Answer (A) is incorrect. The figure of 1.68 includes long-term bonds payable among the current liabilities. Answer (B) is incorrect. The figure of 2.14 is the quick ratio. Answer (C) is incorrect. The figure of 5.00 excludes prepaid expenses from current assets.

7. What is Tosh Enterprises' quick (acid-test) ratio?

   A. 0.68

   B. 1.68

   C. 2.14

   D. 2.31

Answer (C) is correct.
   REQUIRED: The quick ratio.
   DISCUSSION: The quick ratio equals quick assets divided by current liabilities. For Tosh, quick assets consist of cash ($200,000) and accounts receivable ($400,000), a total of $600,000. Current liabilities consist of accounts payable ($260,000) and interest payable ($20,000), a total of $280,000. Thus, the quick ratio is 2.14 ($600,000 ÷ $280,000).

8. Tosh Enterprises' amount of working capital is

   A. $600,000

   B. $1,120,000

   C. $1,200,000

   D. $1,220,000

Answer (C) is correct.
   REQUIRED: The amount of working capital.
   DISCUSSION: Working capital equals current assets minus current liabilities. For Tosh Enterprises, current assets consist of accounts receivable, cash, inventory, and prepaid expenses, a total of $1,480,000 ($400,000 + $200,000 + $800,000 + $80,000). Current liabilities consist of accounts payable and interest payable, a total of $280,000 ($260,000 + $20,000). Accordingly, working capital is $1,200,000 ($1,480,000 − $280,000).
   Answer (A) is incorrect. The amount of $600,000 includes long-term bonds payable among the current liabilities. Answer (B) is incorrect. The amount of $1,120,000 excludes prepaid expenses from current assets. Answer (D) is incorrect. The amount of $1,220,000 excludes interest payable from current liabilities.

8.3 Liquidity Ratios -- Effects of Transactions

9. Bond Corporation has a current ratio of 2 to 1 and a (acid test) quick ratio of 1 to 1. A transaction that would change Bond's quick ratio but **not** its current ratio is the

A. Sale of inventory on account at cost.

B. Collection of accounts receivable.

C. Payment of accounts payable.

D. Purchase of a patent for cash.

Answer (A) is correct.
REQUIRED: The transaction affecting the quick ratio but not the current ratio.
DISCUSSION: The quick ratio is determined by dividing the sum of cash, short-term marketable securities, and accounts receivable by current liabilities. The current ratio is equal to current assets divided by current liabilities. The sale of inventory (a nonquick current asset) on account increases accounts receivable (a quick asset), changing the quick ratio. The sale of inventory on account, however, replaces one current asset with another, and the current ratio is unaffected.
Answer (B) is incorrect. Neither ratio is changed. Answer (C) is incorrect. The current, not the quick, ratio changes. Answer (D) is incorrect. Both ratios decrease.

10. Rice, Inc., uses the allowance method to account for uncollectible accounts. An account receivable that was previously determined uncollectible and written off was collected during May. The effect of the collection on Rice's current ratio and total working capital is

	Current Ratio	Working Capital
A.	None	None
B.	Increase	Increase
C.	Decrease	Decrease
D.	None	Increase

Answer (A) is correct.
REQUIRED: The effect on the current ratio and working capital of collecting an account previously written off.
DISCUSSION: The entry to record this transaction is to debit receivables, credit the allowance, debit cash, and credit receivables. The result is to increase both an asset (cash) and a contra asset (allowance for bad debts). These appear in the current asset section of the balance sheet. Thus, the collection changes neither the current ratio nor working capital because the effects are offsetting. The credit for the journal entry is made to the allowance account on the assumption that another account will become uncollectible. The firm had previously estimated its bad debts and established an appropriate allowance. It then (presumably) wrote off the wrong account. Accordingly, the journal entry reinstates a balance in the allowance account to absorb future uncollectibles.

11. Peters Company has a 2-to-1 current ratio. This ratio would increase to more than 2 to 1 if

A. A previously declared stock dividend were distributed.

B. The company wrote off an uncollectible receivable.

C. The company sold merchandise on open account that earned a normal gross margin.

D. The company purchased inventory on open account.

Answer (C) is correct.
REQUIRED: The transaction increasing a current ratio greater than one.
DISCUSSION: The current ratio is current assets divided by current liabilities. Thus, an increase in current assets or a decrease in current liabilities, by itself, increases the current ratio. The sale of inventory at a profit increases current assets without changing liabilities. Inventory decreases, and receivables increase by a greater amount. Thus, total current assets and the current ratio increase.
Answer (A) is incorrect. The distribution of a stock dividend affects only shareholders' equity accounts (debit common stock dividend distributable and credit common stock). Answer (B) is incorrect. Writing off an uncollectible receivable does not affect total current assets. The allowance account absorbs the bad debt. Thus, the balance of net receivables is unchanged. Answer (D) is incorrect. The purchase of inventory increases current assets and current liabilities by the same amount. The transaction reduces a current ratio in excess of 1.0 because the numerator and denominator of the ratio increase by the same amount.

12. Windham Company has current assets of $400,000 and current liabilities of $500,000. Windham Company's current ratio will be increased by

A. The purchase of $100,000 of inventory on account.

B. The payment of $100,000 of accounts payable.

C. The collection of $100,000 of accounts receivable.

D. Refinancing a $100,000 long-term loan with short-term debt.

Answer (A) is correct.
   REQUIRED: The transaction increasing a current ratio less than 1.0.
   DISCUSSION: The current ratio equals current assets divided by current liabilities. An equal increase in both the numerator and denominator of a current ratio less than 1.0 causes the ratio to increase. Windham Company's current ratio is .8 ($400,000 ÷ $500,000). The purchase of $100,000 of inventory on account would increase the current assets to $500,000 and the current liabilities to $600,000, resulting in a new current ratio of .83.
   Answer (B) is incorrect. The payment of $100,000 of accounts payable decreases the current ratio. Answer (C) is incorrect. The current ratio is unchanged. Answer (D) is incorrect. Refinancing a $100,000 long-term loan with short-term debt decreases the current ratio.

8.4 Cash Management

13. A consultant recommends that a company hold funds for the following two reasons:

Reason #1: Cash needs can fluctuate substantially throughout the year.

Reason #2: Opportunities for buying at a discount may appear during the year.

The cash balances used to address the reasons given above are correctly classified as

	Reason #1	Reason #2
A.	Speculative balances	Speculative balances
B.	Speculative balances	Precautionary balances
C.	Precautionary balances	Speculative balances
D.	Precautionary balances	Precautionary balances

Answer (C) is correct.
   REQUIRED: The classifications of the reasons for a firm to hold cash.
   DISCUSSION: The three motives for holding cash are as a medium of exchange, as a precaution, and as a speculation. Reason #1 can be classified as a precaution, and Reason #2 can be classified as holding cash for speculation.
   Answer (A) is incorrect. Reason #1 is fulfilled by precautionary balances. Answer (B) is incorrect. This combination results from reversing the correct balances. Answer (D) is incorrect. Reason #2 is fulfilled by speculative balances.

14. A lockbox system

A. Reduces the need for compensating balances.

B. Provides security for late night deposits.

C. Reduces the risk of having checks lost in the mail.

D. Accelerates the inflow of funds.

Answer (D) is correct.
   REQUIRED: The true statement about a lockbox system.
   DISCUSSION: A lockbox system is one strategy for expediting the receipt of funds. Customers submit their payments to a mailbox controlled by the bank rather than to the firm's offices. Bank personnel remove the envelopes from the mailbox and deposit the checks to the firm's account immediately. The remittance advices must then be transported to the company for entry into the accounts receivable system. The bank generally charges a flat monthly fee for this service.
   Answer (A) is incorrect. A lockbox system is not related to compensating balances; a compensating balance may be required by a covenant in a loan agreement that requires a company to maintain a specified balance during the term of the loan. Answer (B) is incorrect. A lockbox system is a process by which payments are sent to a bank's mailbox, which is checked during normal post office hours. Answer (C) is incorrect. The use of a lockbox system entails sending checks through the mail to a post office box. Thus, it does not reduce the risk of losing checks in the mail.

15. A working capital method that delays the outflow of cash is

A. Factoring.

B. A draft.

C. A lockbox system.

D. Electronic funds transfer.

Answer (B) is correct.
REQUIRED: The working capital method that delays the outflow of cash.
DISCUSSION: A draft is a three-party instrument in which one person (the drawer) orders a second person (the drawee) to pay money to a third person (the payee). A check is the most common form of draft. It is an instrument payable on demand in which the drawee is a bank. Consequently, a draft can be used to delay the outflow of cash. A draft can be dated on the due date of an invoice and will not be processed by the drawee until that date, thereby eliminating the necessity of writing a check earlier than the due date or using an EFT. Thus, the outflow is delayed until the check clears the drawee bank.
Answer (A) is incorrect. Factoring is the sale of receivables and therefore applies to cash inflows, not outflows. Answer (C) is incorrect. A lockbox system is a means of accelerating cash inflows. Answer (D) is incorrect. An EFT results in an immediate reduction of the payor's bank balance, eliminating float.

8.5 Marketable Securities Management

16. When managing cash and short-term investments, a corporate CFO is primarily concerned with

A. Maximizing rate of return.

B. Minimizing taxes.

C. Investing in Treasury bonds since they have no default risk.

D. Liquidity and safety.

Answer (D) is correct.
REQUIRED: The primary concern when managing cash and short-term investments.
DISCUSSION: Cash and short-term investments are crucial to a firm's continuing success. Sufficient liquidity must be available to meet payments as they come due. But liquid assets have significant risk. Thus, liquidity and safety are the primary concerns of the treasurer regarding highly liquid assets. Cash and short-term investments are held because of their ability to facilitate routine operations. These assets are not held to earn high investment returns.
Answer (A) is incorrect. Most firms are not in business to earn high returns on liquid assets because they are held to facilitate operations. Answer (B) is incorrect. The holding of cash and cash-like assets is not a major factor in controlling taxes. Answer (C) is incorrect. Investments in Treasury bonds do not have sufficient liquidity to serve as short-term assets.

17. All of the following are alternative marketable securities suitable for short-term investment **except**

A. U.S. Treasury bills.

B. Eurodollars.

C. Commercial paper.

D. Convertible bonds.

Answer (D) is correct.
REQUIRED: The item not a marketable security.
DISCUSSION: Marketable securities are near-cash items used primarily for short-term investment. Examples include (1) U.S. Treasury bills, (2) Eurodollars, (3) commercial paper, (4) money-market mutual funds with portfolios of short-term securities, (5) bankers' acceptances, (6) floating rate preferred stock, and (7) negotiable CDs of U.S. banks. A convertible bond is not a short-term investment because its maturity date is usually more than 1 year in the future and its price can be influenced substantially by changes in interest rates or by changes in the investee's stock price.

8.6 Receivables Management

18. The average collection period for a firm measures the number of days

A. After a typical credit sale is made until the firm receives the payment.

B. For a typical check to "clear" through the banking system.

C. Beyond the end of the credit period before a typical customer payment is received.

D. Before a typical account becomes delinquent.

Answer (A) is correct.
   REQUIRED: The firm's average collection period.
   DISCUSSION: The average collection period measures the number of days between the date of sale and the date of collection. It should be related to a firm's credit terms. For example, a firm that allows terms of 2/15, net 30, should have an average collection period of somewhere between 15 and 30 days.
   Answer (B) is incorrect. The time for a typical check to clear the banking system is float. Answer (C) is incorrect. The average collection period includes the total time before a payment is received, including the periods before and after the end of the normal credit period. Answer (D) is incorrect. The period before a typical account becomes delinquent is the normal credit period.

19. The number of days' sales in receivables is a measure of

A. Asset value.

B. Sales performance.

C. Profitability.

D. Collectibility.

Answer (D) is correct.
   REQUIRED: The characteristic measured by the days' sales in receivables.
   DISCUSSION: Turnover ratios are activity ratios that measure management's efficiency in using assets. The number of days' sales in receivables (days in the period divided by the receivables turnover ratio), also known as the average collection period, measures how quickly receivables can be collected.
   Answer (A) is incorrect. Valuation is not measured. Answer (B) is incorrect. Sales performance is measured by profitability ratios. Answer (C) is incorrect. Profitability ratios measure a firm's return on its investment. An example is earnings per share.

20. Yonder Motors sells 20,000 automobiles per year on credit for $25,000 each. The firm's average receivables are $30,000,000 and average inventory is $40,000,000. Yonder's average collection period is closest to which one of the following? Assume a 365-day year.

A. 17 days.

B. 22 days.

C. 29 days.

D. 61 days.

Answer (B) is correct.
   REQUIRED: The average collection period.
   DISCUSSION: The average collection period, also called the days' sales outstanding in receivables, is calculated as the number of days in the year over the receivables turnover ratio. Yonder's can thus be calculated as follows:

Average collection period = Days in year ÷ Accounts receivable turnover
= 365 ÷ (Net credit sales ÷ Average net receivables)
= 365 ÷ [(20,000 × $25,000) ÷ $30,000,000]
= 365 ÷ ($500,000,000 ÷ $30,000,000)
= 365 ÷ 16.667
= 21.9 days

   Answer (A) is incorrect. The amount of 17 days results from improperly using the turnover rate (16.667) as the number of days. Answer (C) is incorrect. The amount of 29 days results from improperly using average inventory instead of average receivables. Answer (D) is incorrect. The amount of 61 days results from improperly adding together the average collection period and the average number of days that inventory is held.

8.7 Inventory Management -- Ratios

21. The selected information below (in thousands) pertains to Devlin Company.

	December 31	
	Year 2	Year 1
Assets		
Current assets		
Cash	$ 45	$ 38
Trading securities	30	20
Accounts receivable (net)	68	48
Inventory	90	80
Prepaid expenses	22	30
Total current assets	$255	$216
Net sales	$480	$460
Costs and expenses		
Costs of goods sold	330	315
Selling, general, and administrative	52	51
Interest expense	8	9
Income before taxes	$ 90	$ 85
Income taxes	36	34
Net income	$ 54	$ 51

Devlin Company's inventory turnover for Year 2 was

A. 3.67 times.

B. 3.88 times.

C. 5.33 times.

D. 5.65 times.

Answer (B) is correct.

REQUIRED: The inventory turnover.

DISCUSSION: Inventory turnover equals cost of goods sold divided by the average balance in inventory. Thus, the inventory turnover is 3.88 times per year {$330 COGS ÷ [($90 + $80) ÷ 2]}.

Answer (A) is incorrect. The ratio of 3.67 times is based on ending inventory. Answer (C) is incorrect. The ratio of 5.33 times equals sales divided by ending inventory. Answer (D) is incorrect. The ratio of 5.65 times is based on sales, not cost of goods sold.

22. Selected information (in thousands) from the statement of financial position for King Products Corporation for the fiscal years ended December 31, Year 2, and Year 1, is presented below. Net credit sales and cost of goods sold for Year 2 were $600,000 and $440,000, respectively.

	December 31	
	Year 2	Year 1
Cash	$ 60	$ 50
Marketable securities (at market)	40	30
Accounts receivable (net)	90	60
Inventories (at lower of cost or market)	120	100
Prepaid items	30	40
Total current assets	$340	$280

King Products Corporation's inventory turnover ratio for Year 2 was

A. 3.7

B. 4.0

C. 4.4

D. 6.0

Answer (B) is correct.

REQUIRED: The inventory turnover ratio for Year 2.

DISCUSSION: The inventory turnover ratio equals cost of goods sold divided by the average balance in inventory. Consequently, the inventory turnover is 4 times per year {$440,000 ÷ [($120,000 + $100,000) ÷ 2]}.

Answer (A) is incorrect. The ratio of 3.7 is based on year-end inventory. Answer (C) is incorrect. The ratio of 4.4 is based on beginning inventory. Answer (D) is incorrect. The ratio of 6.0 is based on sales and beginning inventory.

8.8 Inventory Management -- Methods

23. Which changes in costs are most conducive to switching from a traditional inventory ordering system to a just-in-time ordering system?

	Cost per Purchase Order	Inventory Unit Carrying Costs
A.	Increasing	Increasing
B.	Decreasing	Increasing
C.	Decreasing	Decreasing
D.	Increasing	Decreasing

Answer (B) is correct.
    REQUIRED: The changes in costs most conducive to switching to a JIT ordering system.
    DISCUSSION: A JIT system is intended to minimize inventory. Thus, if inventory carrying costs are increasing, a JIT system becomes more cost effective. Moreover, purchases are more frequent in a JIT system. Accordingly, a decreasing cost per purchase order is a reason to switch to a JIT system.

24. Stewart Co. uses the economic order quantity (EOQ) model for inventory management. A decrease in which one of the following variables would increase the EOQ?

A. Annual sales.

B. Cost per order.

C. Safety stock level.

D. Carrying costs.

Answer (D) is correct.
    REQUIRED: The decrease in a variable that increases the EOQ.
    DISCUSSION: The EOQ model minimizes the total of ordering and carrying costs. The EOQ is calculated as follows:

$$\sqrt{\frac{2 \times Periodic\ demand \times Ordering\ costs\ per\ order}{Carrying\ costs\ per\ unit}}$$

Increases in the numerator (demand or ordering costs) increase the EOQ, but decreases in the numerator decrease the EOQ. Also, a decrease in the denominator (carrying costs) increases the EOQ.
    Answer (A) is incorrect. A decrease in demand (annual sales), which is in the numerator, decreases the EOQ. Answer (B) is incorrect. A decrease in ordering costs, which is in the numerator, encourages more orders, or a decrease in the EOQ. Answer (C) is incorrect. A decrease in safety stock does not affect the EOQ, although it might lead to a different ordering point.

25. Which of the following assumptions is associated with the economic order quantity formula?

A. The carrying cost per unit will vary with quantity ordered.

B. The cost of placing an order will vary with quantity ordered.

C. Periodic demand is known.

D. The purchase cost per unit will vary based on quantity discounts.

Answer (C) is correct.
    REQUIRED: The assumption associated with the EOQ formula.
    DISCUSSION: The economic order quantity (EOQ) model is a mathematical tool for determining the order quantity that minimizes the sum of ordering costs and carrying costs. The following assumptions underlie the EOQ model: (1) Demand is uniform, (2) order (setup) costs and carrying costs are constant, and (3) no quantity discounts are allowed.
    Answer (A) is incorrect. An assumption of the EOQ model is that the carrying cost per unit is constant. Answer (B) is incorrect. The cost of placing an order is constant when using the EOQ formula. Answer (D) is incorrect. An assumption of the EOQ model is that no quantity discounts are allowed.

26. The following information regarding inventory policy was assembled by the TKF Corporation. The company uses a 50-week year in all calculations.

Sales	12,000 units per year
Order quantity	4,000 units
Safety stock	1,500 units
Lead time	5 weeks

The reorder point is

A. 5,500 units.

B. 2,700 units.

C. 1,200 units.

D. 240 units.

Answer (B) is correct.
REQUIRED: The level of inventory at which an order should be placed.
DISCUSSION: The reorder point is the inventory level at which an order should be placed. It can be quantified using the following equation:

Reorder point = (Average weekly demand × Lead time) + Safety stock
= [(12,000 units ÷ 50 weeks) × 5 weeks] + 1,500 units
= 1,200 units + 1,500 units
= 2,700 units

Answer (A) is incorrect. The amount of 5,500 units equals the order size plus the safety stock. Answer (C) is incorrect. The amount of 1,200 units omits safety stock. Answer (D) is incorrect. The average weekly usage is 240 units.

27. In inventory management, the safety stock will tend to increase if the

A. Carrying cost increases.

B. Cost of running out of stock decreases.

C. Variability of the lead time increases.

D. Variability of the usage rate decreases.

Answer (C) is correct.
REQUIRED: The factor that increases safety stocks.
DISCUSSION: A firm maintains safety stocks to protect itself against the losses caused by stockouts. These can take the form of lost sales or lost production time. Safety stock is necessary because of the variability in lead time and usage rates. As the variability in lead time increases, a firm tends to carry larger safety stocks.
Answer (A) is incorrect. An increase in inventory carrying costs makes carrying safety stocks less efficient. Answer (B) is incorrect. If the cost of stockouts declines, the incentive to carry large safety stocks is reduced. Answer (D) is incorrect. A decline in the variability of usage makes planning easier and safety stocks less necessary.

28. A company serves as a distributor of products by ordering finished products once a quarter and using that inventory to accommodate the demand over the quarter. If it plans to ease its credit policy for customers, the amount of products ordered for its inventory every quarter will be

A. Increased to accommodate higher sales levels.

B. Reduced to offset the increased cost of carrying accounts receivable.

C. Unaffected if safety stock is part of the current quarterly order.

D. Unaffected if the JIT inventory control system is used.

Answer (A) is correct.
REQUIRED: The effect on the quantity of products ordered as a result of relaxing credit policy.
DISCUSSION: Relaxing the credit policy for customers leads to increased sales because more people are eligible for more credit. As sales increase, the amount ordered on each purchase order increases to accommodate the higher sales.
Answer (B) is incorrect. Inventory should be increased to accommodate higher sales levels. Answer (C) is incorrect. Safety stock is based on expected sales, which are expected to rise. Answer (D) is incorrect. A just-in-time system is not used when a company orders inventory once a quarter.

8.9 The Operating Cycle and Cash Conversion Cycle

29. To determine the operating cycle for a retail department store, which one of the following pairs of items is needed?

A. Days' sales in accounts receivable and average merchandise inventory.

B. Cash turnover and net sales.

C. Accounts receivable turnover and inventory turnover.

D. Asset turnover and return on sales.

Answer (C) is correct.
REQUIRED: The pair of items needed to determine the operating cycle for a retailer.
DISCUSSION: The operating cycle is the time needed to turn cash into inventory, inventory into receivables, and receivables back into cash. For a retailer, it is the time from purchase of inventory to collection of cash. Thus, the operating cycle of a retailer is equal to the sum of the number of days' sales in inventory and the number of days' sales in receivables. Inventory turnover equals cost of goods sold divided by average inventory. The days' sales in inventory equals 365 (or another period chosen by the analyst) divided by the inventory turnover. Accounts receivable turnover equals net credit sales divided by average receivables. The days' sales in receivables equals 365 (or other number) divided by the accounts receivable turnover.
Answer (A) is incorrect. Cost of sales must be known to calculate days' sales in inventory. Answer (B) is incorrect. These items are insufficient to permit determination of the operating cycle. Answer (D) is incorrect. These items are insufficient to permit determination of the operating cycle.

8.10 Multiple Ratio Analysis

30. Selected data from Sheridan Corporation's year-end financial statements are presented below. The difference between average and ending inventory is immaterial.

Current ratio	2.0
Quick ratio	1.5
Current liabilities	$120,000
Inventory turnover	
(based on cost of goods sold)	8 times
Gross profit margin	40%

Assuming no prepaid expenses are included in current assets, Sheridan's net sales for the year were

A. $800,000

B. $480,000

C. $1,200,000

D. $240,000

Answer (A) is correct.
REQUIRED: The net sales for the year.
DISCUSSION: Net sales can be calculated indirectly from the inventory turnover ratio and the other ratios given. If the current ratio is 2.0, and current liabilities are $120,000, current assets must be $240,000 (2.0 × $120,000). Similarly, if the quick ratio is 1.5, the total quick assets must be $180,000 (1.5 × $120,000). The difference between quick assets and current assets is that inventory is not included in the definition of quick assets. Consequently, ending inventory must be $60,000 ($240,000 – $180,000). The inventory turnover ratio (COGS ÷ average inventory) is 8. Thus, cost of goods sold must be 8 times average inventory, or $480,000, given no material difference between average and ending inventory. If the gross profit margin is 40%, the cost of goods sold percentage is 60%, cost of goods sold equals 60% of sales, and net sales must be $800,000 ($480,000 ÷ 60%).
Answer (B) is incorrect. Cost of goods sold is $480,000. Answer (C) is incorrect. The amount of $1,200,000 is based on a 60% gross profit margin. Answer (D) is incorrect. Current assets equal $240,000.

8.11 PRACTICE WRITTEN COMMUNICATION

| Business Environment and Concepts Testlet 4 of 4 | Time Remaining 1 hour - 15 minutes | Unsplit Split Horiz Split Vertical Exit |

DIRECTIONS

Note: If you believe you have encountered a software malfunction, report it to the test center staff immediately.

Navigation

To navigate from task to task, use the controls at the bottom of the screen. Click on the **Next** button to advance to the next task, or the **Previous** button to go to the previous task. To go directly to any task, click on its number.

| ▼ = Reminder | Directions | 1 ▽ | 2 ▽ | 3 ▽ | 4 ▽ | 5 ▽ | 6 ▽ | 7 ▽ | ◀ Previous | Next ▶ |

If you would like a reminder to revisit a task, or want to indicate that you are finished with it, click on the reminder flag below the task number. To clear the flag, click on it again. Reminder flags are for your use only – they do not contribute to your score.

Tabs

In this part of the examination, you will be asked to complete various tasks. Every task has one or more **Work Tabs**. Every task also has a **Help** tab.

Work tab   Help tab

Work Tabs:

- **Work Tabs** are identified with a pencil icon. This is where your responses are expected.
- Each task has one or more **Work Tabs**.
- **Work Tabs** contain directions for completing the task - be sure to read these directions carefully.
- The **Work Tab** name in the example above is for illustration only - yours will differ.
- You must complete all of the **Work Tabs** in each task to receive full credit.

Help Tab:

- The **Help Tab** provides assistance with the exam software that is used in this task. For example, if the task is to compose a memorandum, **Help** will provide information about the word processor.

The Toolbar

The toolbar at the top of the screen shows the amount of time remaining for you to complete the tasks. In addition, the following tools are available. Note that only the **Exit** button is displayed when Directions are visible - the others will appear when you begin the tasks.

Click on these buttons to split or unsplit the screen. You can split the screen vertically or horizontally.

Click on this button to go on to the next part of the examination. You must complete all of the tasks to receive full credit. Once you click on **Exit** and confirm the action, you will NOT be able to return to this testlet.

| ▼ = Reminder | Directions | 1 ▽ | | | | | ◀ Previous | Next ▶ |

Alexa Corporation loosened its credit policy at the beginning of the current year. Due to the policy change, accounts receivable and uncollectible accounts have increased significantly. The allowance for uncollectible accounts is based on a percentage of the ending accounts receivable balance. But the company's accounting department believes that the percentage-of-sales method should be used. The CFO has approached your CPA firm seeking advice.

Write a memorandum to your new client describing the two basic approaches to estimating uncollectible accounts receivable. Include the rationale for each approach, whether it is acceptable for GAAP purposes, entries, and how it is applied.

Type your communication below the line in the response area below.

REMINDER: Your response will be graded for both technical content and writing skills. Technical content will be evaluated for information that is helpful to the intended reader and clearly relevant to the issue. Writing skills will be evaluated for development, organization, and the appropriate expression of ideas in professional correspondence. Use a standard business memorandum or letter format with a clear beginning, middle, and end. Do not convey information in the form of a table, bullet point list, or other abbreviated presentation.

To: Alexa Corporation
Re: Estimating uncollectible accounts

NOTE: Your Written Communications on the actual CPA exam may cover topics outside the scope of the BEC CSO (i.e., they may relate to topics from the AUD, FAR, and/or REG CSOs instead). Answer to the best of your ability, and remember that graders are mainly evaluating your writing ability and will overlook minor technical mistakes.

Unofficial Answer

Written Communication

To: Alexa Corporation
Re: Estimating uncollectible accounts

The principal valuation issue for accounts receivable is the estimation of uncollectible accounts expense. The two approaches to determining this expense are the direct write-off method and the allowance method.

The direct write-off method debits bad debt expense and credits accounts receivable at the time the uncollectibility of a specific account is established. This method is convenient but is not acceptable under GAAP because it neither (1) matches revenue and expense when the receivable and the write-off are recorded in different periods nor (2) states receivables at net realizable value.

The allowance method attempts both to match bad debt expense with the related revenue and to determine the net realizable value of the accounts receivable. It is acceptable under GAAP. Based on an estimate of uncollectible accounts for a period, bad debt expense is debited and an allowance account is credited. A subsequent write-off results in a debit to the allowance and a credit to accounts receivable. When accounts are written off, no immediate debit is made to expense. The allowance is a contra-asset account, and its balance is subtracted from accounts receivable on the balance sheet. Thus, write-offs do not affect the carrying amount of net accounts receivable because gross accounts receivable and the allowance are reduced by the same amounts.

Under the allowance method, bad debt expense reported on the income statement can be estimated by applying a percentage (usually based on past bad debt losses) to credit sales (also reported on the income statement). This process results in an adjusting entry that debits bad debt expense and credits the allowance without regard to the existing balances. Use of total sales also may be acceptable if the entity has a stable mix of cash and credit sales over the years.

Other allowance methods emphasize the net realizable value of the receivables to be reported on the balance sheet. One way to estimate the allowance is to apply a single percentage to the accounts receivable balance at the end of the period. This approach does not directly estimate bad debt expense. Instead, it indicates the amount to which the existing balance must be adjusted. The adjustment is the bad debt expense. A more sophisticated method of estimating the desired allowance for bad debts is to apply different percentages to blocks of receivables classified according to how long they have been outstanding, a practice known as aging of receivables.

If an entity's estimates of bad debt expense are inaccurate, it may change the percentage(s) used or its method of estimation. In either case, the change should be treated as a change in accounting estimate and accounted for currently and prospectively. No retrospective effect is recognized.

If the entity collects previously written-off accounts, the procedure is to reestablish the account by debiting accounts receivable and crediting the allowance and then to debit cash and credit accounts receivable for the amount recovered.

The above depicts a Level 5 answer. Consult your booklet, *How to Pass the CPA Exam: A System for Success*, for a description of the three writing skills criteria. You may also access this booklet online by visiting www.gleim.com/PassCPA.

Self-Grade

Below, grade your response on technical content and writing skills. Bubble in the circle next to the appropriate score that you may receive based on the criteria given. Your **total** score is the sum of your scores on all six items. The maximum score is 19 points.

Technical Content Evaluation

Was your response on topic?	o No [0]	o Mostly [1]	o Yes [2]
Did your response have any *significant* errors?	o 0 errors [1]	o 1 major error [–1]	o 2 or more major errors [–2]
Did your response contain any illegal advice?	o No [1]	o Yes [0]	

Writing Skills Evaluation

	Poor	Below Average	Average	Above Average	Outstanding
Organization	o 1	o 2	o 3	o 4	o 5
Development	o 1	o 2	o 3	o 4	o 5
Expression	o 1	o 2	o 3	o 4	o 5

Disclaimer: This scoring schedule was developed by Gleim Publications as a guideline only. The AICPA has not released specific information on how the Written Communications are graded.

STUDY UNIT NINE
SHORT-TERM FINANCING
AND CAPITAL BUDGETING I

(11 pages of outline)

All entities finance daily operations with capital from outside sources. These sources include (1) spontaneous financing in the form of trade credit offered by vendors and (2) bank loans. Moreover, firms must decide whether to invest in new product lines or means of production. This process involves (1) identifying investments, (2) determining the resources required, (3) projecting the expected amounts and timing of returns, and (4) ranking the identified investments.

9.1 TYPES AND COSTS OF SHORT-TERM FINANCING

1. **Spontaneous Financing -- Trade Credit**

    a. A supplier may offer an early payment discount. For example, payment terms may be 2/10, n/30. These terms provide a 2% discount if payment is within 10 days. Otherwise, the entire balance is due in 30 days (an interest-free 30-day loan). Taking the discount ordinarily is advantageous. The annualized cost of **not** taking a discount can be calculated using the following formula:

$$\frac{Discount\ \%}{100\% - Discount\ \%} \times \frac{Days\ in\ year}{Total\ payment\ period - Discount\ period}$$

EXAMPLE

A vendor has sold goods to a firm on terms of 2/10, net 30. The firm has chosen to pay on day 30. The effective annual rate paid by forgoing the discount is calculated as follows (using a 360-day year):

Cost of not taking discount = [2% ÷ (100% − 2%)] × [360 days ÷ (30 days − 10 days)]
= (2% ÷ 98%) × (360 days ÷ 20 days)
= 2.0408% × 18
= 36.73%

Only firms with extreme cash-flow problems are willing to pay a 36.73% rate.

---

2. **Formal Financing Arrangements**

    a. Commercial banks offer short-term loans and lines of credit.

        1) A **term loan**, such as a note, must be repaid by a definite time.

        2) A **line of credit** allows the firm to reborrow amounts continuously up to a maximum amount if minimum payments are made each month. This arrangement is similar to a consumer's credit card.

3. **Simple Interest Short-Term Loans**

   a.   Interest on a simple interest loan is paid at the end of the loan term. The amount to be paid is based on the nominal (stated) rate and the principal of the loan (amount needed).

$$Interest\ expense\ =\ Principal\ of\ loan\ \times\ Stated\ rate$$

EXAMPLE

A firm obtained a short-term bank loan of $15,000 at an annual interest rate of 8%. The interest expense on the loan is $1,200 ($15,000 × 8%).

The stated rate of 8% also is the effective rate.

---

   b.   The **effective rate** of any financing arrangement is the ratio of the amount the firm must pay to the amount it can use.

$$Effective\ interest\ rate\ =\ \frac{Interest\ expense\ (interest\ to\ be\ paid)}{Usable\ funds\ (net\ proceeds)}$$

EXAMPLE

A firm obtained a short-term bank loan of $15,000 at an annual interest rate of 8%. The bank charges a loan origination fee of $500.

$$
\begin{aligned}
Effective\ rate\ &= Interest\ paid \div Net\ proceeds \\
&= (\$15,000 \times 8\%) \div (\$15,000 - \$500) \\
&= \$1,200 \div \$14,500 \\
&= 8.27\%
\end{aligned}
$$

The effective interest rate (8.27%) is higher than the stated interest rate (8%) because the net proceeds are lower than the principal.

---

4. **Discounted Loans**

   a.   For a discounted loan, the interest and finance charges are paid at the beginning of the loan term.

$$Total\ borrowings\ =\ \frac{Amount\ needed}{(1.0\ -\ Stated\ rate)}$$

EXAMPLE

A firm needs to pay a $90,000 debt. Its bank has offered to extend this amount at an 8% nominal rate on a discounted basis.

$$
\begin{aligned}
Total\ borrowings\ &= Amount\ needed \div (1.0 - Stated\ rate) \\
&= \$90,000 \div (100\% - 8\%) \\
&= \$90,000 \div 92\% \\
&= \$97,826
\end{aligned}
$$

---

   b.   Because the borrower can use only a smaller amount, the effective rate on a discounted loan is higher than its nominal rate.

EXAMPLE

$$
\begin{aligned}
Effective\ rate\ &= Net\ interest\ expense\ (annualized) \div Usable\ funds \\
&= (\$97,826 \times 8\%) \div \$90,000 \\
&= \$7,826 \div \$90,000 \\
&= 8.696\%
\end{aligned}
$$

c. In all financing arrangements, the effective rate can be calculated without dollar amounts.

$$\text{Effective rate on discounted loan} = \frac{\text{Stated rate}}{(1.0 - \text{Stated rate})}$$

EXAMPLE

The firm calculates the effective rate on this loan without dollar amounts.

Effective rate = Stated rate ÷ (1.0 – Stated rate)
= 8% ÷ (100% – 8%)
= 8% ÷ 92%
= 8.696%

---

5. **Loans with Compensating Balances**

a. To reduce risk, banks may require a borrower to maintain a compensating balance during the term of a financing arrangement.

$$\text{Total borrowings} = \frac{\text{Amount needed}}{(1.0 - \text{Compensating balance \%})}$$

EXAMPLE

A firm has received a loan of $120,000 with terms of 2/10, net 30. The firm's bank will lend the necessary amount for 20 days. Thus, the discount can be taken on the 10th day at a nominal annual rate of 6% and a compensating balance of 10%.

Total borrowings = Amount needed ÷ (1.0 – Compensated balance %)
= ($120,000 × 98%) ÷ (100% – 10%)
= $117,600 ÷ 90%
= $130,667

---

b. As in a discounted loan, the borrower can use a smaller amount than the face amount of the loan and therefore pays an effective rate higher than the nominal rate.

EXAMPLE

Effective rate = Net interest expense (annualized) ÷ Usable funds
= ($130,667 × 6%) ÷ $117,600
= $7,840 ÷ $117,600
= 6.667%

---

c. Again, the effective rate can be determined without dollar amounts.

$$\text{Effective rate with comp. balance} = \frac{\text{Stated rate}}{(1.0 - \text{Compensating balance \%})}$$

EXAMPLE

Effective rate = Stated rate ÷ (1.0 – Compensating balance %)
= 6% ÷ (100% – 10%)
= 6% ÷ 90%
= 6.667%

Stop and review! You have completed the outline for this subunit. Study multiple-choice questions 1 through 5 beginning on page 246.

9.2 CAPITAL BUDGETING -- BASICS

1.   **Capital Budgeting**

  a.   Capital budgeting is the process of planning and controlling investments for long-term projects.

   1)   Most financial and management accounting topics, such as calculating the allowance for doubtful accounts or accumulating product costs, require reporting activity for a single accounting or reporting cycle, such as 1 month or 1 year.

   2)   But capital projects affect multiple accounting periods and limit the firm's future financial planning. Thus, capital budgeting decisions tend to be relatively inflexible.

  b.   A capital project usually involves substantial expenditures. Planning is important because of uncertainties about capital markets, inflation, interest rates, and the money supply.

  c.   The following are capital budgeting applications:

   1)   Buying equipment
   2)   Building facilities
   3)   Acquiring a business
   4)   Developing a product or product line
   5)   Expanding into new markets
   6)   Replacing of equipment

2.   **Relevant Cash Flows**

  a.   The first step in assessing a potential capital project is to identify the relevant cash flows (future revocable cash flows).

   1)   Relevant cash flows do **not** include sunk costs, those already paid or irrevocably committed to be paid.

  b.   The following are relevant cash flows for capital budgeting:

   1)   Cost of new equipment
   2)   Annual after-tax cash savings or inflows
   3)   Proceeds from disposal of old equipment (residual or salvage value)
   4)   Adjustment for depreciation expense on new equipment (the depreciation tax shield that reduces taxable income and cash outflows for tax expense)

EXAMPLE

A firm's annual recurring operating cash income from a new machine is $100,000. The annual depreciation expense on this machine is $20,000. The effective tax rate is 40%. To calculate the after-tax annual cash flows, annual depreciation expense must be considered.

Operating cash inflow	$100,000	Taxable income	$80,000
Depreciation expense	(20,000)	Effective tax rate	× 40%
Annual taxable income	$ 80,000	Income tax payment	$32,000

Operating cash inflow	$100,000
Income tax payment	(32,000)
After-tax cash flow	$ 68,000

After-tax cash flow also can be calculated as follows:

Operating cash flow net of taxes [$100,000 × (1.0 − .40)]	$60,000
Depreciation tax shield [$20,000 × 40%]	8,000
Annual after-tax cash flow	$68,000

NOTE: Depreciation expense affects cash flows only because it reduces tax payments.

3.   **Accounting Rate of Return**

  a.   The accounting rate of return is used to assess potential capital projects. It ignores the time value of money.

$$Accounting\ rate\ of\ return = \frac{Annual\ increase\ in\ GAAP\ net\ income}{Required\ investment} = \frac{Annual\ cash\ inflow - Depreciation}{Initial\ investment}$$

  1)   Shareholders and financial analysts prefer the accounting rate of return because GAAP-based numbers are readily available.

EXAMPLE

A manufacturer considers the purchase of a new machine. It costs $250,000 and will decrease annual after-tax cash payments by $40,000. The machine is expected to have a 10-year useful life, no salvage value, and be depreciated on the straight-line basis. The accounting rate of return on this machine is calculated as follows:

Annual cash savings	$ 40,000
Minus: annual depreciation expense ($250,000 ÷ 10 years)	(25,000)
Annual increase in accounting net income	$ 15,000
Divided by: purchase price of new equipment	÷ 250,000
Accounting rate of return	6%

---

  2)   However, certain characteristics of the accounting rate of return limit its usefulness for selecting capital projects.

  b.   The accounting rate of return is affected by the accounting methods chosen.

  1)   Accountants must choose which expenditures to capitalize and which to expense immediately. They also choose how quickly to depreciate capitalized assets.

  2)   A project's true rate of return cannot be dependent on such decisions.

  c.   Another distortion occurs when comparing a single project's accounting rate of return with the total return for all of the firm's capital projects.

The AICPA has tested the accounting rate of return by asking for its calculation. Questions also have asked for the components of the accounting rate of return.

Stop and review! You have completed the outline for this subunit. Study multiple-choice questions 6 through 10 beginning on page 247.

9.3 CAPITAL BUDGETING -- NET PRESENT VALUE (NPV)

1. **Discounted Cash Flow Analysis**

   a. A more sophisticated method for evaluating potential capital projects than the accounting rate of return is discounted cash flow analysis. It discounts the relevant cash flows using the required rate of return as the rate. (This rate also is called the hurdle rate or opportunity cost of capital.)

2. **NPV**

   a. A capital project's NPV is the difference between the present value of the net cash savings or inflows expected over the life of the project and the required investment.

      1) If the difference is positive, the project should be accepted. If the difference is negative, it should be rejected.

EXAMPLE

Firm is planning to invest $100,000 in new equipment. The equipment is expected to create savings in cash operating expenses of $80,000 in the first year and $60,000 in the second year. The equipment's estimated useful life is 2 years, and Firm expects to resell it at the end of its useful life (salvage value) for $15,000. The equipment is depreciated for tax purposes at a rate of 50% each year. Firm's internal rate of return is 12%, and its effective tax rate is 40%. The present value of $1 for one period at 12% is 0.893, and the present value of $1 for two periods at 12% is 0.8. Firm calculates the NPV of this potential investment as follows:

Annual depreciation shield for Years 1 and 2

Asset's cost	$100,000
Depreciation percentage	× 50%
Annual depreciation charge	$ 50,000
Tax rate	× 40%
Depreciation tax shield	$ 20,000

Resale of equipment (salvage value)

Expected proceeds	$ 15,000
Tax basis of equipment	-- (because fully depreciated)
Gain on expected disposal	$ 15,000
Tax expense ($15,000 × 40%)	(6,000)
Expected cash inflow	$ 9,000

Net annual cash savings	Year 1	Year 2
Annual savings (cash inflow)	$ 80,000	$60,000
Tax expense	× 40%	× 40%
Net annual savings (cash inflow)	$ 48,000	$36,000

NPV	Year 0	Year 1	Year 2
Initial investment in equipment	$(100,000)		
Net annual savings (cash inflow)		$ 48,000	$36,000
Depreciation tax shield		20,000	20,000
Inflow from resale (salvage value)			9,000
After-tax net expected cash flows	$(100,000)	$ 68,000	$65,000
Discount rate	× 1	× 0.893	× 0.8
NPV	$(100,000) +	$ 60,724 +	$52,000 = $12,724

The positive NPV indicates that the project should be accepted.

EXAMPLE

Firm is considering the purchase of a machine for $250,000 that has a useful life of 10 years and no residual (salvage) value. The machine is expected to generate an annual operating cash savings of $60,000 over its useful life. It will be depreciated on the straight-line basis, resulting in annual depreciation expense of $25,000 ($250,000 ÷ 10 years). Firm's internal rate of return is 12%, and its effective tax rate is 40%.

The present value of $1 for 10 periods at 12% is 0.322, and the present value of an ordinary annuity of $1 for 10 periods at 12% is 5.650. Firm calculates the NPV of this investment as follows:

Present value of cash savings		
Annual operating savings (cash inflow)		$ 60,000
Annual tax expense:		
Tax expense ($60,000 × 40%)	$(24,000)	
Depreciation tax shield ($25,000 × 40%)	10,000	(14,000)
After-tax net annual savings (cash inflow)		$ 46,000
Times: PV factor for an ordinary annuity		× 5.650
Present value of net savings (cash inflow)		$259,900
Required investment		
Cost of new equipment		$250,000
NPV of investment		
Present value of net savings (cash inflow)		$259,900
Minus: required investment		(250,000)
NPV of investment		$ 9,900

The positive NPV indicates that the project should be accepted.

---

    b.   Use of the NPV method implicitly assumes cash flows are reinvested at the firm's **required rate of return**.

  3.   **The Hurdle Rate**

    a.   Adjusting for Inflation

        1)   In an inflationary environment, future cash inflows consist of inflated dollars. To compensate for this decline in purchasing power, hurdle rates must be adjusted upward.

    b.   Adjusting for Risk

        1)   Particularly risky projects may be assigned higher hurdle rates to ensure that only those whose potential returns are proportionate to their risks are accepted.

    c.   Division-Specific Rates of Return

        1)   When the divisions of a large, complex firm have specific risk attributes and capital costs, using a single firm-wide hurdle rate may result in bad decisions.

            a)   The managers of high-risk divisions may over-invest in new projects, and managers of low-risk divisions may under-invest.

                i)   Thus, compared with the firm-wide average, high-risk divisions should have slightly higher hurdle rates, and low-risk divisions should have slightly lower hurdle rates.

Stop and review! You have completed the outline for this subunit. Study multiple-choice questions 11 through 16 beginning on page 249.

9.4 CAPITAL BUDGETING -- NPV CALCULATIONS

This subunit consists entirely of questions that require the candidate to perform the detailed calculations involved in applying the NPV method. Please review Subunit 9.3 thoroughly before answering the questions.

Stop and review! You have completed the outline for this subunit. Study multiple-choice questions 17 through 19 beginning on page 250.

9.5 CAPITAL BUDGETING -- INTERNAL RATE OF RETURN (IRR)

1. **IRR**

    a. The IRR of a project is the discount rate at which the investment's NPV equals zero. Thus, the IRR equates the present value of the expected cash inflows with the present value of the expected cash outflows.

        1) If the IRR is higher than the hurdle rate (required rate of return), the investment is accepted. If the IRR is lower, the project should be rejected.

            IRR > Hurdle rate: Accept project = Positive NPV

            IRR < Hurdle rate: Reject project = Negative NPV

EXAMPLE

Firm has a hurdle rate of 12% for all capital projects. It is considering a project with an initial cash outlay of $200,000 that will save $52,000 of after-tax cash costs in each of the next 5 years. The applicable present value factor is 3.846 ($200,000 ÷ $52,000). According to a table of present value factors for an ordinary annuity for five periods, this factor is between 9% and 10%. Because a rate below 10% is less than the hurdle rate, the project should be rejected.

---

2. **Comparing Cash Flow Patterns**

    a. A decision maker may need to choose between two mutually exclusive projects, one with high initial cash flows and one with relatively constant cash flows.

        1) The higher the hurdle rate, the more quickly a project must be profitable.
        2) Firms with low hurdle rates prefer a steady payback.

EXAMPLE

The following are the net cash flows of two projects with the same initial investment:

	Initial Investment	Year 1	Year 2	Year 3	Year 4
Project K	$(200,000)	$140,000	$100,000	–	–
Project L	(200,000)	65,000	65,000	$65,000	$65,000

A graph of the two projects at various discount rates illustrates the factors a decision maker must consider.

-- Continued on next page --

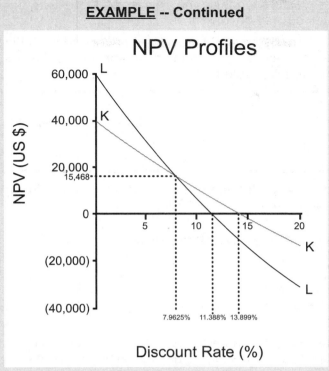

EXAMPLE -- Continued

Figure 9-1

Project K's IRR is 13.899%. Project L's is 11.388%.

The NPV profile helps a manager to determine how sensitive a project's profitability is to changes in the discount rate.

- At a hurdle rate of **exactly** 7.9625%, a decision maker is **indifferent** between the two projects. The NPV of K and L is $15,468 at that discount rate.
- At hurdle rates **below** 7.9625%, the project whose **inflows last longer** into the future is the better investment (L).
- At hurdle rates **above** 7.9625%, the project whose **inflows are received more quickly** is the better choice (K).

3. **Comparing NPV and IRR**

    a.   The reinvestment rate is an important factor in choosing between the NPV and IRR methods. NPV assumes the cash flows from the investment can be reinvested at the project's **required rate of return**.

        1)   The IRR method assumes reinvestment is at the **IRR**.

    b.   The NPV and IRR methods give the same accept or reject decision if projects have unrelated cash flows (are independent). Thus, all acceptable, independent projects can be chosen.

        1)   However, if projects are mutually exclusive, the NPV and IRR methods may rank them differently if

            a)   The cost of one project is greater than the cost of another.

            b)   The timing, amounts, and directions of cash flows differ among projects.

            c)   The projects have different useful lives.

            d)   The cost of capital or desired rate of return varies over the life of a project. The NPV can be determined easily using different desired rates of return for different periods. The IRR determines one rate for the project.

            e)   Multiple investments are involved in a project. NPV amounts are cumulative; IRR rates are not. The IRR for the whole is not the sum of the IRRs for the parts.

2) If the project's funds are not reinvested at the IRR, the ranking calculations obtained may be in error.

a) The NPV method provides a better understanding of the problem in many decision situations because reinvestment is assumed to be at the required rate of return.

For both the NPV and IRR, expect to see questions asking for calculation of these values as well as an understanding of the underlying theory.

Stop and review! You have completed the outline for this subunit. Study multiple-choice questions 20 through 25 beginning on page 252.

9.6 CAPITAL BUDGETING -- PAYBACK METHODS

1. **Payback Period**

    a. The payback period is the number of years required for the net cash savings or inflows to equal the original investment, i.e., the time necessary for an investment to pay for itself.

        1) Firms using the payback method set a maximum length of time within which projects must pay for themselves to be acceptable.

    b. If the cash flows are constant, the formula is

$$Payback\ period = \frac{Initial\ investment}{Annual\ after\text{-}tax\ savings\ (cash\ inflow)}$$

        1) This method ignores the time value of money.

EXAMPLE of Constant Cash Flows

Firm performs a 4-year payback period test on all capital projects. It is considering a project requiring an initial cash outlay of $200,000 that will save a total of $260,000 of after-tax costs. These savings will be in equal amounts for each of the next 5 years.

The first step in the payback method is to determine the annual after-tax cash flow. In this example, it is $52,000 ($260,000 ÷ 5 years).

Payback period = $200,000 ÷ $52,000 = 3.846 years

Judged by this criterion, the project is acceptable because its payback period is less than the firm's maximum.

---

    c. If the cash flows are not constant, the calculation must be in cumulative form.

EXAMPLE of Variable Cash Flows

Assume that Firm's initial investment is $160,000 and that the project's cash flows are expected to vary as shown below. The payback period is calculated as follows:

End of Year	Cash Savings	Initial Investment to be Recovered
Initial investment	$ --	$160,000
Year 1	48,000	112,000
Year 2	54,000	58,000
Year 3	54,000	4,000
Year 4	60,000	--

The project is acceptable because its payback period is between 3 and 4 years and is less than the firm's maximum.

    d.   The advantage of the payback method is its simplicity.

        1)   To some extent, the payback period measures risk. The longer the period, the more risky the investment.

    e.   The payback method has the following two significant disadvantages:

        1)   Weighting all cash flows equally disregards the time value of money.

        2)   All cash inflows after the payback cutoff date are disregarded. Applying a single cutoff date to every project results in accepting marginal projects and rejecting good ones.

2.   **Discounted Payback**

    a.   The discounted payback method is sometimes used to overcome the major disadvantage of the basic payback method.

        1)   The net cash flows in the denominator are discounted to calculate the period required to recover the initial investment.

EXAMPLE

Firm has a 12% cost of capital.

Period	Cash Savings		12% PV Factor		Discounted Cash Savings	Initial Investment to be Recovered
Initial investment	$ --		--		$ --	$160,000
Year 1	48,000	×	0.89286	=	42,857	117,143
Year 2	54,000	×	0.79719	=	43,048	74,095
Year 3	54,000	×	0.71178	=	38,436	35,659
Year 4	60,000	×	0.63552	=	38,132	--

The project is acceptable because its discounted payback period is between 3 and 4 years and is less than the firm's maximum.

EXAMPLE

Firm wants to determine the discounted payback periods in years and assumes that the cash flows are earned evenly throughout each year. The discounted payback period in years is calculated as follows:

1)   Full payback occurs sometime in Year 4. The remaining investment at the beginning of Year 4 is $35,659.

2)   The following is the percentage of Year 4 at which the amount of $35,659 is recovered:

$$\frac{\$35,659}{\$38,132} = 0.935\%$$

3)   The discounted payback period in years is **3.935 years** (3 + 0.935).

---

    b.   The **breakeven time** is the time required for the discounted cash flows of an investment to equal its initial cost.

    c.   The discounted payback method's advantage is that it reflects the time value of money.

        1)   Its disadvantages are (a) its greater complexity and (b) not considering cash flows after the arbitrary cutoff date.

Stop and review! You have completed the outline for this subunit. Study multiple-choice questions 26 through 30 beginning on page 254.

QUESTIONS

9.1 Types and Costs of Short-Term Financing

> Questions 1 through 3 are based on the following information. Skilantic Company needs to pay a supplier's invoice of $60,000 and wants to take a cash discount of 2/10, net 40. The firm can borrow the money for 30 days at 11% per annum plus a 9% compensating balance.

1. The amount Skilantic Company must borrow to pay the supplier within the discount period and cover the compensating balance is

A. $60,000

B. $65,934

C. $64,615

D. $58,800

Answer (C) is correct.
REQUIRED: The amount to borrow to pay the supplier within the discount period and cover the compensating balance requirement.
DISCUSSION: Skilantic's total borrowings on this loan can be calculated as follows:

$$
\begin{aligned}
\text{Total borrowings} &= \text{Amount needed} \div \\
&\quad (1.0 - \text{Compensating balance \%}) \\
&= (\$60,000 \times 98\%) \div (100\% - 9\%) \\
&= \$58,800 \div 91\% \\
&= \$64,615
\end{aligned}
$$

Answer (A) is incorrect. The amount of $60,000 is the invoice amount. Answer (B) is incorrect. The amount of $65,934 assumes the amount paid to the supplier is $60,000. Answer (D) is incorrect. The amount of $58,800 is the amount to be paid to the supplier.

2. Assuming Skilantic Company borrows the money on the last day of the discount period and repays it 30 days later, the effective interest rate on the loan is

A. 11%

B. 10%

C. 12.09%

D. 9.90%

Answer (C) is correct.
REQUIRED: The effective interest rate when borrowing to take a discount.
DISCUSSION: Skilantic's effective rate on this loan can be calculated as follows:

$$
\begin{aligned}
\text{Effective rate} &= \text{Stated rate} \div (1.0 - \text{Compensating balance \%}) \\
&= 11\% \div (100\% - 9\%) \\
&= 11\% \div 91\% \\
&= 12.09\%
\end{aligned}
$$

Answer (A) is incorrect. The contract rate is 11%. Answer (B) is incorrect. The effective rate is greater than the contract rate. The usable funds are less than the face amount of the note. Answer (D) is incorrect. The effective rate is greater than the contract rate. The usable funds are less than the face amount of the note.

3. Skilantic fails to take the discount and pays on the 40th day. Assuming a 360-day year, what effective rate of annual interest does it pay the vendor?

A. 2%

B. 24%

C. 24.49%

D. 36.73%

Answer (C) is correct.
REQUIRED: The effective interest rate paid when a discount is not taken.
DISCUSSION: By failing to take the discount, Skilantic is essentially borrowing $58,800 for 30 days. Thus, at a cost of $1,200, it acquires the use of $58,800, resulting in a rate of 2.0408% ($1,200 ÷ $58,800) for 30 days. Assuming a 360-day year, the effective annual rate is 24.49% [2.0408% × (360 days ÷ 30 days)].

Answer (A) is incorrect. The discount rate for a 30-day period is 2%. Answer (B) is incorrect. The percentage of 24% assumes that the available funds equal $60,000. Answer (D) is incorrect. The percentage of 36.73% assumes a 20-day discount period.

4. A company obtained a short-term bank loan of $250,000 at an annual interest rate of 6%. As a condition of the loan, the company is required to maintain a compensating balance of $50,000 in its checking account. The checking account earns interest at an annual rate of 2%. Ordinarily, the company maintains a balance of $25,000 in its account for transaction purposes. What is the effective interest rate of the loan?

A. 6.44%

B. 7.00%

C. 5.80%

D. 6.66%

Answer (A) is correct.

REQUIRED: The effective interest rate on a loan that requires a compensating balance above the normal working balance.

DISCUSSION: The $50,000 compensating balance requirement is partially satisfied by the practice of maintaining a $25,000 balance for transaction purposes. Thus, only $25,000 of the loan is not available for current use. At 6% interest, the $250,000 loan requires an interest payment of $15,000 per year. This amount is partially offset by the 2% interest earned on the $25,000 incremental balance, or $500. Subtracting the $500 interest earned from the $15,000 of expense results in net interest expense of $14,500 for the use of $225,000 ($250,000 – $25,000). Dividing $14,500 by $225,000 produces an effective interest rate of 6.44%.

Answer (B) is incorrect. The percentage of 7.00% fails to consider that the $25,000 currently being maintained counts toward the compensating balance requirement. Answer (C) is incorrect. The percentage of 5.80% fails to consider the compensating balance requirement. Answer (D) is incorrect. The percentage of 6.66% fails to consider the interest earned on the incremental balance being carried.

5. If a firm purchases raw materials from its supplier on a 2/10, net 40, cash discount basis, the equivalent annual interest rate (using a 360-day year) of forgoing the cash discount and making payment on the 40th day is

A. 2%

B. 18.36%

C. 24.49%

D. 36.72%

Answer (C) is correct.

REQUIRED: The equivalent annual interest charge for not taking the discount.

DISCUSSION: The buyer could satisfy the $100 obligation by paying $98 on the 10th day. By choosing to wait until the 40th day, the buyer is effectively paying a $2 interest charge for the use of $98 for 30 days (40-day credit period – 10-day discount period). The annualized cost of not taking this discount can be calculated as follows:

$$\frac{Discount\ \%}{100\%\ -\ Discount\ \%} \times \frac{Days\ in\ year}{Total\ payment\ period\ -\ Discount\ period}$$

Cost of not taking discount = [2% ÷ (100% – 2%)] ×
           [360 days ÷ (40 days – 10 days)]
           = (2% ÷ 98%) × (360 days ÷ 30 days)
           = 2.0408% × 12
           = 24.49%

Answer (A) is incorrect. The discount rate is 2%. Answer (B) is incorrect. The percentage of 18.36% is based on the 40-day credit period. Answer (D) is incorrect. The percentage of 36.72% is based on a 20-day credit period.

9.2 Capital Budgeting -- Basics

6. Of the following decisions, capital budgeting techniques would **least** likely be used in evaluating the

A. Acquisition of new aircraft by a cargo company.

B. Design and implementation of a major advertising program.

C. Trade for a star quarterback by a football team.

D. Adoption of a new method of allocating nontraceable costs to product lines.

Answer (D) is correct.

REQUIRED: The decision least likely to be evaluated using capital budgeting.

DISCUSSION: Capital budgeting is the process of planning expenditures for investments on which the returns are expected to occur over a period of more than 1 year. Thus, capital budgeting applies to the acquisition or disposal of long-term assets and the financing ramifications of such decisions. The adoption of a new method of allocating nontraceable costs to product lines has no effect on a firm's cash flows, the acquisition of long-term assets, and financing. Thus, capital budgeting is irrelevant to such a decision.

Answer (A) is incorrect. A new aircraft is a long-term investment in a capital good. Answer (B) is incorrect. A major advertising program is a high cost investment with long-term effects. Answer (C) is incorrect. A star quarterback is a costly asset who is expected to have a substantial effect on the team's long-term profitability.

7. The relevance of a particular cost to a decision is determined by

- A. Riskiness of the decision.
- B. Number of decision variables.
- C. Amount of the cost.
- D. Potential effect on the decision.

Answer (D) is correct.
    REQUIRED: The determinant of relevance of a particular cost to a decision.
    DISCUSSION: Relevance is the capacity of information to make a difference in a decision by helping users of that information to predict the outcomes of events or to confirm or correct prior expectations. Thus, relevant costs are expected future costs that vary with the action taken. All other costs are constant and therefore have no effect on the decision.
    Answer (A) is incorrect. The ultimate determinant of relevance is the ability to influence the decision. Answer (B) is incorrect. The ultimate determinant of relevance is the ability to influence the decision. Answer (C) is incorrect. The ultimate determinant of relevance is the ability to influence the decision.

8. Which of the following is irrelevant in projecting the cash flows of the final year of a capital project?

- A. Cash devoted to use in project.
- B. Disposal value of equipment purchased specifically for project.
- C. Depreciation tax shield generated by equipment purchased specifically for project.
- D. Historical cost of equipment disposed of in the project's first year.

Answer (D) is correct.
    REQUIRED: The irrelevant information in projecting the cash flows for the final year of a capital project.
    DISCUSSION: After disposal of an old piece of equipment, its historical cost no longer affects a firm's cash flows.
    Answer (A) is incorrect. The recovery of working capital devoted to a capital project is a relevant cash flow in the final year. Answer (B) is incorrect. The disposal value of equipment acquired for the project is relevant in the final year. Answer (C) is incorrect. The depreciation tax shield generated by equipment acquired for the project is relevant to the final year.

9. The accounting rate of return

- A. Is synonymous with the internal rate of return.
- B. Focuses on income as opposed to cash flows.
- C. Is inconsistent with the divisional performance measure known as return on investment.
- D. Recognizes the time value of money.

Answer (B) is correct.
    REQUIRED: The true statement about the accounting rate of return.
    DISCUSSION: The accounting rate of return is a capital budgeting method that ignores the time value of money. It is calculated by dividing the increase in average annual accounting net income by the required investment. This method focuses on income rather than cash flows.
    Answer (A) is incorrect. The IRR is the rate at which the NPV is zero. Thus, it incorporates time value of money concepts, but the accounting rate of return does not. Answer (C) is incorrect. The accounting rate of return is similar to the divisional performance measure of return on investment. Answer (D) is incorrect. The accounting rate of return ignores the time value of money.

10. Which one of the following items is **least** likely to directly impact an equipment replacement capital expenditure decision?

- A. The net present value of the equipment that is being replaced.
- B. The depreciation rate that will be used for tax purposes on the new asset.
- C. The amount of additional accounts receivable that will be generated from increased production and sales.
- D. The sales value of the asset that is being replaced.

Answer (A) is correct.
    REQUIRED: The item least likely to directly affect an equipment replacement capital expenditure decision.
    DISCUSSION: The only relevant valuation of existing equipment is its salvage value at the time of the decision.
    Answer (B) is incorrect. The depreciation rate for tax purposes on the new asset will determine the depreciation tax shield. Answer (C) is incorrect. The additional working capital associated with the new equipment is relevant to the decision. Answer (D) is incorrect. The salvage value of the existing equipment is relevant to the decision.

9.3 Capital Budgeting -- Net Present Value (NPV)

11. A depreciation tax shield is

    A. An after-tax cash outflow.

    B. A reduction in income taxes.

    C. The cash provided by recording depreciation.

    D. The expense caused by depreciation.

Answer (B) is correct.
    REQUIRED: The definition of a depreciation tax shield.
    DISCUSSION: A tax shield is something that protects income from taxation. Thus, a depreciation tax shield is a reduction in income taxes due to the tax deductibility of depreciation.
    Answer (A) is incorrect. A tax shield is not a cash flow but a means of reducing outflows for income taxes. Answer (C) is incorrect. Cash is not provided by recording depreciation; the shield is a result of deducting depreciation from taxable revenues. Answer (D) is incorrect. Depreciation is recognized as an expense even if it has no tax benefit.

12. The NPV of a project has been calculated to be $215,000. Which one of the following changes in assumptions would decrease the NPV?

    A. Decrease the estimated effective income tax rate.

    B. Decrease the initial investment amount.

    C. Extend the project life and associated cash inflows.

    D. Increase the discount rate.

Answer (D) is correct.
    REQUIRED: The change in assumption that decreases the NPV.
    DISCUSSION: An increase in the discount rate, a decrease in cash flows, or an increase in the initial investment lowers the NPV.
    Answer (A) is incorrect. A decrease in the tax rate would decrease tax expense, thus increasing cash flows and the NPV. Answer (B) is incorrect. A decrease in the initial investment amount would increase the NPV. Answer (C) is incorrect. An extension of the project life and associated cash inflows would increase the NPV.

13. Assume that the interest rate is greater than zero. Which of the following cash-inflow streams should you prefer?

	Year 1	Year 2	Year 3	Year 4
A.	$400	$300	$200	$100
B.	$100	$200	$300	$400
C.	$250	$250	$250	$250
D.	Any of these, since they each sum to $1,000.			

Answer (A) is correct.
    REQUIRED: The cash flows that are most advantageous.
    DISCUSSION: The concept of present value gives greater value to inflows received earlier than later. Thus, the declining inflows are superior to increasing inflows or even inflows.
    Answer (B) is incorrect. The cash flow shown does not produce the greatest present value. Answer (C) is incorrect. The cash flow shown does not produce the greatest present value. Answer (D) is incorrect. Present value of the cash flows must be considered.

14. For capital budgeting purposes, management would select a high hurdle rate of return for certain projects because management

    A. Wants to use equity funding exclusively.

    B. Believes too many proposals are being rejected.

    C. Believes bank loans are riskier than capital investments.

    D. Wants to factor risk into its consideration of projects.

Answer (D) is correct.
    REQUIRED: The reason for selecting a high hurdle rate for certain projects.
    DISCUSSION: Risk analysis measures the likelihood of the variability of future returns from the proposed investment. Risk can be incorporated into capital budgeting decisions in various ways, one of which is to use a hurdle rate (desired rate of return) higher than the firm's cost of capital, that is, a risk-adjusted discount rate. This method adjusts the interest rate used for discounting upward as an investment becomes riskier. The expected flow from the investment must be relatively larger, or the increased discount rate will generate a negative NPV, and the proposed acquisition will be rejected.
    Answer (A) is incorrect. The nature of the funding may not be a sufficient reason to use a risk-adjusted rate. The type of funding is just one factor affecting the risk of a project. Answer (B) is incorrect. A higher hurdle will result in rejection of more projects. Answer (C) is incorrect. A risk-adjusted high hurdle rate is used for capital investments with greater risk.

15. The net present value of an investment project represents the

A. Total actual cash inflows minus the total actual cash outflows.

B. Excess of the discounted cash inflows over the discounted cash outflows.

C. Total after-tax cash flow including the tax shield from depreciation.

D. Cumulative accounting profit over the life of the project.

16. Depreciation is incorporated explicitly in the discounted cash flow analysis of an investment proposal because it

A. Is a cost of operations that cannot be avoided.

B. Is a cash inflow.

C. Reduces the cash outlay for income taxes.

D. Represents the initial cash outflow spread over the life of the investment.

9.4 Capital Budgeting -- NPV Calculations

17. Jackson Corporation uses net present value techniques in evaluating its capital investment projects. The company is considering a new equipment acquisition that will cost $100,000, fully installed, and have a zero salvage value at the end of its 5-year productive life. Jackson will depreciate the equipment on a straight-line basis for both financial and tax purposes. Jackson estimates $70,000 in annual recurring operating cash income and $20,000 in annual recurring operating cash expenses. Jackson's desired rate of return is 12% and its effective income tax rate is 40%.

The present value factors for 12% are as follows:

Present value of $1 at the end of five periods   .567
Present value of an ordinary annuity of $1 for
  five periods   3.605

What is the net present value of this investment on an after-tax basis?

A. $28,840

B. $8,150

C. $36,990

D. $80,250

Answer (B) is correct.
    REQUIRED: The meaning of NPV.
    DISCUSSION: The NPV of an investment project represents the excess of the discounted cash inflows over the discounted cash outflows.
    Answer (A) is incorrect. Actual cash inflows minus actual cash outflows ignores the time value of money. Answer (C) is incorrect. Total after-tax cash flow including the tax shield from depreciation ignores the time value of money. Answer (D) is incorrect. Accounting profit ignores the time value of money.

Answer (C) is correct.
    REQUIRED: The explanation of how depreciation is explicitly incorporated in discounted cash flow analysis.
    DISCUSSION: Depreciation is a noncash expense that is deductible for federal income tax purposes. Thus, it directly reduces the cash outlay for income taxes and is explicitly incorporated in the capital budgeting model.
    Answer (A) is incorrect. Depreciation is not a cost of operations in the capital budgeting model. Also, depreciation can be avoided by not making investments. Answer (B) is incorrect. Depreciation is an allocation of historical cost and as such is not a cash inflow, but it may reduce cash outflows for taxes. Answer (D) is incorrect. Periodic depreciation is determined by spreading the depreciation base, i.e., the cost of the asset minus salvage value, not the initial cash outflow, over the life of the investment.

Answer (C) is correct.
    REQUIRED: The NPV on an after-tax basis.
    DISCUSSION: Annual cash outflow for taxes is $12,000 {[[$70,000 inflows – $20,000 cash operating expenses – ($100,000 ÷ 5) depreciation] × 40%}. The annual net cash inflow is therefore $38,000 ($70,000 – $20,000 – $12,000). The present value of these net inflows for a 5-year period is $136,990 ($38,000 × 3.605 present value of an ordinary annuity for 5 years at 12%), and the NPV of the investment is $36,990 ($136,990 – $100,000 investment).
    Answer (A) is incorrect. The amount of $28,840 is the present value of the depreciation tax savings. Answer (B) is incorrect. The amount of $8,150 ignores the depreciation tax savings. Answer (D) is incorrect. The amount of $80,250 ignores taxes.

18. The Hopkins Company has estimated that a proposed project's 10-year annual net cash benefit, received each year end, will be $2,500 with an additional terminal benefit of $5,000 at the end of the 10th year.

Information on present value factors is as follows:

Present value of $1 at 8% at the end of
  10 periods .... .463
Present value of an ordinary annuity of $1
  at 8% for 10 periods 6.710

Assuming that these cash inflows satisfy exactly Hopkins' required rate of return of 8%, what is the initial cash outlay?

A. $16,775

B. $19,090

C. $25,000

D. $30,000

Answer (B) is correct.
  REQUIRED: The initial cash outlay.
  DISCUSSION: If the 8% return exactly equals the present value of the future flows (the NPV is zero), the present value of the future inflows equals the initial cash outlay. Thus, the initial cash outlay is $19,090 [($2,500)(present value of an ordinary annuity at 8% for 10 periods) + ($5,000)(present value of a single amount at 8% for 10 periods = ($2,500)(6.710) + ($5,000)(.463)].
  Answer (A) is incorrect. The amount of $16,775 failed to include the present value of the $5,000 terminal benefit. Answer (C) is incorrect. The amount of $25,000 is not a result of using present value analysis. Answer (D) is incorrect. The amount of $30,000 is not a result of using present value analysis.

Question 19 is based on the following information. Jorelle Company's financial staff has been requested to review a proposed investment in new capital equipment. Applicable financial data is presented below. There will be no salvage value at the end of the investment's life and, due to realistic depreciation practices, it is estimated that the salvage value and net book value are equal at the end of each year. All cash flows are assumed to take place at the end of each year. For investment proposals, Jorelle uses a 12% after-tax target rate of return.

Investment Proposal

Year	Purchase Cost and Book Value	Annual Net After-Tax Cash Flows	Annual Net Income
0	$250,000	$ 0	$ 0
1	168,000	120,000	35,000
2	100,000	108,000	39,000
3	50,000	96,000	43,000
4	18,000	84,000	47,000
5	0	72,000	51,000

Discounted Factors for a 12% Rate of Return

Year	Present Value of $1.00 Received at the End of Each Period	Present Value of an Annuity of $1.00 Received at the End of Each Period
1	.89	.89
2	.80	1.69
3	.71	2.40
4	.64	3.04
5	.57	3.61
6	.51	4.12

---

19. The net present value for the investment proposal is

A. $106,160

B. $(97,970)

C. $356,160

D. $96,560

Answer (A) is correct.
  REQUIRED: The NPV.
  DISCUSSION: The NPV is the sum of the present values of all cash inflows and outflows associated with the proposal. If the NPV is positive, the proposal should be accepted. The NPV is determined by discounting each expected cash flow using the appropriate 12% interest factor for the present value of $1. Thus, the NPV is $106,160 [(.89 × $120,000) + (.80 × $108,000) + (.71 × $96,000) + (.64 × $84,000) + (.57 × $72,000) – (1.00 × $250,000)].
  Answer (B) is incorrect. The amount of $(97,970) is based on net income instead of cash flows. Answer (C) is incorrect. The amount of $356,160 excludes the purchase cost. Answer (D) is incorrect. The amount of $96,560 equals average after-tax cash inflow times the interest factor for the present value of a 5-year annuity, minus $250,000.

9.5 Capital Budgeting -- Internal Rate of Return (IRR)

20. What is the approximate IRR for a project that costs $50,000 and provides cash inflows of $20,000 for 3 years?

Rate of Return	Present Value of an Annuity of $1 Received at the End of 3 Years
6%	2.673
8%	2.577
10%	2.487
12%	2.402

A. 10%

B. 12%

C. 22%

D. 27%

Answer (A) is correct.
REQUIRED: The approximate IRR.
DISCUSSION: The applicable factor is 2.5, which is found just below 10% on the 3-year line of an annuity table.
Answer (B) is incorrect. Discounting the cash inflows at 12% would not produce a NPV of zero. Answer (C) is incorrect. Discounting the cash inflows at 22% would not produce a NPV of zero. Answer (D) is incorrect. Discounting the cash inflows at 27% would not produce a NPV of zero.

21. Pena Company is considering a project that calls for an initial cash outlay of $50,000. The expected net cash inflows from the project are $7,791 for each of 10 years.

Rate of Return	Present Value of an Annuity of $1 Received at the End of 10 Years
6%	7.360
8%	6.710
9%	6.418
10%	6.145
12%	5.650

What is the IRR of the project?

A. 6%

B. 7%

C. 8%

D. 9%

Answer (D) is correct.
REQUIRED: The IRR.
DISCUSSION: The IRR can be calculated by equating the initial cash outlay with the present value of the net cash inflows:

$7,791 × PV at i for 10 periods = $50,000
= 6.418

Using the present value table, 6.418 is PV at 9% for 10 periods.
Answer (A) is incorrect. Discounting the cash inflows at 6% would not produce a NPV of zero. Answer (B) is incorrect. Discounting the cash inflows at 7% would not produce a NPV of zero. Answer (C) is incorrect. Discounting the cash inflows at 8% would not produce a NPV of zero.

22. The net present value of a proposed investment is negative; therefore, the discount rate used must be

A. Greater than the project's internal rate of return.

B. Less than the project's internal rate of return.

C. Greater than the firm's cost of equity.

D. Less than the risk-free rate.

Answer (A) is correct.
REQUIRED: The true statement about the discount rate when the NPV is negative.
DISCUSSION: The higher the discount rate, the lower the NPV. The IRR is the discount rate at which the NPV is zero. Consequently, if the NPV is negative, the discount rate must exceed the IRR.
Answer (B) is incorrect. If the discount rate is less than the IRR, the NPV is positive. Answer (C) is incorrect. The NPV measures the difference between a firm's discount rate and the IRR. Answer (D) is incorrect. The relationship between the discount rate and the risk-free rate is not a factor in investment analysis under the NPV method.

23. Wilkinson, Inc., which has a cost of capital of 12%, invested in a project with an internal rate of return (IRR) of 14%. The project is expected to have a useful life of 4 years, and it will produce net cash inflows as follows:

Year	Net Cash Inflows
1	$1,000
2	2,000
3	4,000
4	4,000

The present value of $1 is as follows:

	Present Value	
No. of Periods	12%	14%
1	0.893	0.877
2	0.797	0.769
3	0.712	0.675
4	0.636	0.592

The initial cost of this project amounted to

A. $7,483

B. $9,647

C. $11,000

D. $12,540

Answer (A) is correct.

REQUIRED: The NPV of the cash inflows from a capital project.

DISCUSSION: The IRR of a capital project is the rate at which the NPV of its future cash flows equals zero. To find this project's NPV, the cash flows should be discounted at the appropriate rate (14%):

Year	Net Cash Inflows	PV Factor	Present Value
1	$1,000	0.877	$ 877
2	2,000	0.769	1,538
3	4,000	0.675	2,700
4	4,000	0.592	2,368
			$7,483

Answer (B) is incorrect. The amount of $9,647 results from treating the cash inflows as occurring at the beginning of the year instead of at year end. Answer (C) is incorrect. The amount of $11,000 results from failing to take the time value of money into account. Answer (D) is incorrect. The amount of $12,540 results from multiplying times the 14% rate rather than discounting by that rate.

24. Brown and Company uses the internal rate of return (IRR) method to evaluate capital projects. Brown is considering four independent projects with the following IRRs:

Project	IRR
I	10%
II	12%
III	14%
IV	15%

Brown's cost of capital is 13%. Which one of the following project options should Brown accept based on IRR?

A. Projects I and II only.

B. Projects III and IV only.

C. Project IV only.

D. Projects I, II, III and IV.

Answer (B) is correct.

REQUIRED: The acceptable projects given a certain cost of capital.

DISCUSSION: When sufficient funds are available, any capital project whose IRR exceeds the firm's cost of capital should be accepted.

Answer (A) is incorrect. Projects I and II have rates of return lower than the company's cost of capital. Answer (C) is incorrect. The rate of return for Project III also exceeds the company's cost of capital. Answer (D) is incorrect. Projects I and II should be rejected; their rates of return are lower than the company's cost of capital.

25. Which of the following is **not** a shortcoming of the internal rate of return (IRR) method?

A. IRR assumes that funds generated from a project will be reinvested at an interest rate equal to the project's IRR.

B. IRR does not take into account the difference in the scale of investment alternatives.

C. IRR is easier to visualize and interpret than net present value (NPV).

D. Sign changes in the cash flow stream can generate more than one IRR.

Answer (C) is correct.

REQUIRED: The item not a disadvantage of the IRR method.

DISCUSSION: IRR is widely used because of its simplicity.

Answer (A) is incorrect. IRR assumes that funds generated from a project will be reinvested at an interest rate equal to the project's IRR. Answer (B) is incorrect. IRR does not consider the difference in the scale of investment alternatives. Answer (D) is incorrect. Sign changes in the series of cash flows can generate more than one IRR.

9.6 Capital Budgeting -- Payback Methods

26. A characteristic of the payback method (before taxes) is that it

    A. Incorporates the time value of money.

    B. Neglects total project profitability.

    C. Uses accrual accounting inflows in the numerator of the calculation.

    D. Uses the estimated expected life of the asset in the denominator of the calculation.

Answer (B) is correct.
    REQUIRED: The characteristic of the payback method.
    DISCUSSION: The payback method calculates the number of years required to complete the return of the original investment. This measure is determined by dividing the net investment required by the average expected cash flow to be generated, resulting in the number of years required to recover the original investment. Payback is easy to calculate but has two principal problems: (1) It ignores the time value of money, and (2) it does not consider returns after the payback period. Thus, it ignores total project profitability.
    Answer (A) is incorrect. The payback method does not incorporate the time value of money. Answer (C) is incorrect. The payback method uses the net investment in the numerator of the calculation. Answer (D) is incorrect. Payback uses the net annual cash inflows in the denominator of the calculation.

27. Jasper Company has a payback goal of 3 years on new equipment acquisitions. A new sorter is being evaluated that costs $450,000 and has a 5-year life. Straight-line depreciation will be used; no salvage is anticipated. Jasper is subject to a 40% income tax rate. To meet the company's payback goal, the sorter must generate reductions in annual cash operating costs of

    A. $60,000

    B. $100,000

    C. $150,000

    D. $190,000

Answer (D) is correct.
    REQUIRED: The cash savings that must be generated to achieve a targeted payback period.
    DISCUSSION: Given a periodic constant cash flow, the payback period is calculated by dividing cost by the annual cash inflows, or cash savings. To achieve a payback period of 3 years, the annual increment in net cash inflow generated by the investment must be $150,000 ($450,000 ÷ 3-year targeted payback period). This amount equals the total reduction in cash operating costs minus related taxes. Depreciation is $90,000 ($450,000 ÷ 5 years). Because depreciation is a noncash deductible expense, it shields $90,000 of the cash savings from taxation. Accordingly, $60,000 ($150,000 – $90,000) of the additional net cash inflow must come from after-tax net income. At a 40% tax rate, $60,000 of after-tax income equals $100,000 ($60,000 ÷ 60%) of pre-tax income from cost savings, and the outflow for taxes is $40,000. Thus, the annual reduction in cash operating costs required is $190,000 ($150,000 additional net cash inflow required + $40,000 tax outflow).
    Answer (A) is incorrect. The amount of $60,000 is after-tax net income from the cost savings. Answer (B) is incorrect. The amount of $100,000 is the pre-tax income from the cost savings. Answer (C) is incorrect. The amount of $150,000 ignores the impact of depreciation and income taxes.

28. Whatney Co. is considering the acquisition of a new, more efficient press. The cost of the press is $360,000, and the press has an estimated 6-year life with zero salvage value. Whatney uses straight-line depreciation for both financial reporting and income tax reporting purposes and has a 40% corporate income tax rate. In evaluating equipment acquisitions of this type, Whatney uses a goal of a 4-year payback period. To meet Whatney's desired payback period, the press must produce a minimum annual before-tax operating cash savings of

    A. $90,000

    B. $110,000

    C. $114,000

    D. $150,000

Answer (B) is correct.
    REQUIRED: The minimum annual before-tax operating cash savings yielding a specified payback period.
    DISCUSSION: Payback is the number of years required to complete the return of the original investment. Given a periodic constant cash flow, the payback period equals net investment divided by the constant expected periodic after-tax cash flow. The desired payback period is 4 years, so the constant after-tax annual cash flow must be $90,000 ($360,000 ÷ 4). Assuming that the company has sufficient other income to permit realization of the full tax savings, depreciation of the machine will shield $60,000 ($360,000 ÷ 6) of income from taxation each year, an after-tax cash savings of $24,000 ($60,000 × 40%). Thus, the machine must generate an additional $66,000 ($90,000 – $24,000) of after-tax cash savings from operations. This amount is equivalent to $110,000 [$66,000 ÷ (1.0 – .4)] of before-tax operating cash savings.
    Answer (A) is incorrect. The amount of $90,000 is the total desired annual after-tax cash savings. Answer (C) is incorrect. The amount of $114,000 results from adding, not subtracting, the $24,000 of tax depreciation savings to determine the minimum annual after-tax operating savings. Answer (D) is incorrect. The amount of $150,000 assumes that depreciation is not tax deductible.

29. If the present value of expected cash inflows from a project equals the present value of expected cash outflows, the discount rate is the

   A. Payback rate.

   B. Internal rate of return.

   C. Accounting rate of return.

   D. Net present value rate.

Answer (B) is correct.
   REQUIRED: The relationship of NPV and the discount rate.
   DISCUSSION: The IRR is the discount rate at which the NPV of a project's cash flows equals zero.
   Answer (A) is incorrect. "Payback rate" is not a meaningful term in this context. Answer (C) is incorrect. The accounting rate of return is arrived at without reference to present value. Answer (D) is incorrect. The net present value rate is the rate under discussion.

30. Which one of the following methods for evaluating capital projects is the **least** useful from an investment analysis point of view?

   A. Accounting rate of return.

   B. Internal rate of return.

   C. Net present value.

   D. Payback.

Answer (A) is correct.
   REQUIRED: The least useful capital budgeting method.
   DISCUSSION: The accounting rate of return is an unsatisfactory means of evaluating capital projects for two reasons. Because it uses accrual-basis numbers, the calculation is subject to such accounting judgments as how quickly to depreciate capitalized assets. Also, it is an average of all of a firm's capital projects. It reveals nothing about the performance of individual investment choices.
   Answer (B) is incorrect. The IRR, which uses discounted cash flows, can be a useful method for evaluating capital projects. Answer (C) is incorrect. NPV, which uses discounted cash flows, generally is the most useful method for evaluating capital projects. Answer (D) is incorrect. The payback method can be useful for firms that have set a minimum length of time within which projects must pay for themselves.

9.7 PRACTICE WRITTEN COMMUNICATION

Business Environment and Concepts
Testlet 4 of 4

Time Remaining
1 hour - 15 minutes

Unsplit Split Horiz Split Vertical Exit

DIRECTIONS

Note: If you believe you have encountered a software malfunction, report it to the test center staff immediately.

Navigation

To navigate from task to task, use the controls at the bottom of the screen. Click on the **Next** button to advance to the next task, or the **Previous** button to go to the previous task. To go directly to any task, click on its number.

If you would like a reminder to revisit a task, or want to indicate that you are finished with it, click on the reminder flag below the task number. To clear the flag, click on it again. Reminder flags are for your use only – they do not contribute to your score.

Tabs

In this part of the examination, you will be asked to complete various tasks. Every task has one or more **Work Tabs**. Every task also has a **Help** tab.

Work tab   Help tab

Work Tabs:

- **Work Tabs** are identified with a pencil icon. This is where your responses are expected.
- Each task has one or more **Work Tabs**.
- **Work Tabs** contain directions for completing the task - be sure to read these directions carefully.
- The **Work Tab** name in the example above is for illustration only - yours will differ.
- You must complete all of the **Work Tabs** in each task to receive full credit.

Help Tab:

- The **Help Tab** provides assistance with the exam software that is used in this task. For example, if the task is to compose a memorandum, **Help** will provide information about the word processor.

The Toolbar

The toolbar at the top of the screen shows the amount of time remaining for you to complete the tasks. In addition, the following tools are available. Note that only the **Exit** button is displayed when Directions are visible - the others will appear when you begin the tasks.

Click on these buttons to split or unsplit the screen. You can split the screen vertically or horizontally.

Exit

Click on this button to go on to the next part of the examination. You must complete all of the tasks to receive full credit. Once you click on **Exit** and confirm the action, you will NOT be able to return to this testlet.

The CFO of Alachua Corporation asked your firm to analyze two projects that Alachua is considering. The CFO knows only the payback period technique for evaluating capital projects and is unaware that it may have drawbacks.

Prepare a memo to the CFO of Alachua Corporation describing the net present value, internal rate of return, and payback period methods of evaluating capital projects.

Type your communication below the line in the response area below.

REMINDER: Your response will be graded for both technical content and writing skills. Technical content will be evaluated for information that is helpful to the intended reader and clearly relevant to the issue. Writing skills will be evaluated for development, organization, and the appropriate expression of ideas in professional correspondence. Use a standard business memorandum or letter format with a clear beginning, middle, and end. Do not convey information in the form of a table, bullet point list, or other abbreviated presentation.

To: CFO, Alachua Corporation
Re: Evaluation methods for capital projects

NOTE: Your Written Communications on the actual CPA exam may cover topics outside the scope of the BEC CSO (i.e., they may relate to topics from the AUD, FAR, and/or REG CSOs instead). Answer to the best of your ability, and remember that graders are mainly evaluating your writing ability and will overlook minor technical mistakes.

Unofficial Answer

Written Communication

> To: CFO, Alachua Corporation
> Re: Evaluation methods for capital projects
>
> ---
>
> For management to make an effective investment decision when choosing between two projects, the projects must be evaluated. Common methods used for evaluating capital projects include the net present value, the internal rate of return, and the payback period methods.
>
> The net present value (NPV) method expresses a project's returns in monetary terms. It involves netting the expected cash streams (inflows and outflows) related to a project and then discounting them at the desired rate of return. If the NPV of the project is positive, the project is desirable because it has a higher rate of return than the entity's desired rate.
>
> The internal rate of return (IRR) method expresses a project's return in percentage terms. The IRR of an investment is the discount rate at which the investment's NPV equals zero. Thus, it is the rate at which the present value of the expected cash inflows equal the present value of the expected cash outflows. If the IRR is higher than the entity's desired rate of return, the project is desirable.
>
> The payback period method calculates the number of years required to return the original investment, that is, the time necessary for the new project to pay for itself. Entities using the payback period method set a maximum length of time within which the projects must pay for themselves to be considered acceptable. If the project's payback period is less than the entity's maximum, the project is acceptable. The strength of the payback method is its simplicity. Moreover, it also provides a simple measure of risk. The longer the payback period, the more risky the investment. Weaknesses of the payback period are that it disregards (1) the time value of money and (2) all cash flows after the payback cutoff date.

The above depicts a Level 5 answer. Consult your booklet, *How to Pass the CPA Exam: A System for Success*, for a description of the three writing skills criteria. You may also access this booklet online by visiting www.gleim.com/PassCPA.

Self-Grade

Below, grade your response on technical content and writing skills. Bubble in the circle next to the appropriate score that you may receive based on the criteria given. Your **total** score is the sum of your scores on all six items. The maximum score is 19 points.

Technical Content Evaluation

Was your response on topic?	O No [0]	O Mostly [1]	O Yes [2]
Did your response have any *significant* errors?	O 0 errors [1]	O 1 major error [−1]	O 2 or more major errors [−2]
Did your response contain any illegal advice?	O No [1]	O Yes [0]	

Writing Skills Evaluation

	Poor	Below Average	Average	Above Average	Outstanding
Organization	O 1	O 2	O 3	O 4	O 5
Development	O 1	O 2	O 3	O 4	O 5
Expression	O 1	O 2	O 3	O 4	O 5

Disclaimer: This scoring schedule was developed by Gleim Publications as a guideline only. The AICPA has not released specific information on how the Written Communications are graded.

Receive even more exam-emulating Task-Based Simulations in the Gleim Mega Test Bank.
Learn more: gleim.com/CPAmega | 800.874.5346

STUDY UNIT TEN
CAPITAL BUDGETING II
AND CORPORATE PERFORMANCE

(8 pages of outline)

Because investment capital is a scarce resource, potential projects must be ranked (Subunit 10.1). Accountants must be able to recognize the differences among capital budgeting methods (Subunit 10.2).

The success of a firm in achieving the desired return for its stakeholders is the subject of corporate performance measures (Subunits 10.3 and 10.4). A firm's ability to remain in business in the long run is solvency, a measurable condition (Subunit 10.5).

10.1 RANKING CAPITAL PROJECTS

1. **Profitability Index**

    a. When sufficient resources are available, every project with a positive NPV should be accepted.

      1) However, few firms have the resources to accept every capital project with a return exceeding the hurdle rate.

      2) Under **capital rationing**, management determines which investments provide not necessarily the highest total return but the highest per dollar invested.

    b. The **profitability index** (or excess present value index) is a method for ranking projects to ensure that limited resources are allocated to the investments with the highest return per dollar invested.

$$Profitability\ index = \frac{PV\ of\ future\ net\ cash\ flows\ or\ NPV\ of\ project}{Initial\ investment}$$

EXAMPLE

A firm has $200,000 to invest. It can invest either in (1) Project F or (2) Projects G and H:

	Project F	Project G	Project H
Initial investment	$(200,000)	$(150,000)	$(50,000)
Year 1	140,000	50,000	40,000
Year 2	140,000	50,000	30,000
Year 3		50,000	10,000
Year 4		77,453	

The first step in ranking these projects is to calculate their NPVs. The firm uses a 6% hurdle rate.

	Project F		Project G		Project H	
	Undiscounted Cash Flows	Discounted Cash Flows	Undiscounted Cash Flows	Discounted Cash Flows	Undiscounted Cash Flows	Discounted Cash Flows
Year 1	$140,000	$132,076	$ 50,000	$ 47,170	$40,000	$37,736
Year 2	140,000	124,600	50,000	44,500	30,000	26,700
Year 3			50,000	41,980	10,000	8,396
Year 4			77,453	61,350		
PV of cash inflows		$256,676		$195,000		$72,832
Initial investment	(200,000)	(200,000)	(150,000)	(150,000)	(50,000)	(50,000)
NPV		$ 56,676		$ 45,000		$22,832

Each project's profitability index now can be calculated. Note that choice of numerator has no effect on the decision.

PV of cash inflows in numerator	NPV in numerator
Project F: $256,676 ÷ $200,000 = 1.283	Project F: $56,676 ÷ $200,000 = 0.283
Project G: $195,000 ÷ $150,000 = 1.300	Project G: $45,000 ÷ $150,000 = 0.300
Project H: $72,832 ÷ $50,000 = 1.457	Project H: $22,832 ÷ $50,000 = 0.457

Project H provides the highest profitability index, and Project G has the next highest. Thus, the initial decision is to accept Projects G and H.

---

    c.   When the initial investment is the same, the independent project with the higher NPV is the project with the higher profitability index.

Stop and review! You have completed the outline for this subunit. Study multiple-choice questions 1 through 5 beginning on page 266.

10.2 COMPARISON OF CAPITAL BUDGETING METHODS

Some CPA exam questions involve selecting the best capital budgeting method for a given set of facts rather than the mechanics of the calculation. This subunit consists entirely of this type of question. If you have not already mastered the calculations of capital budgets presented in Study Unit 9, Subunits 2 through 6, and Subunit 10.1, you should review the outlines before answering these questions.

Stop and review! You have completed the outline for this subunit. Study multiple-choice questions 6 through 10 beginning on page 268.

10.3 RETURN ON INVESTMENT AND RESIDUAL INCOME

    1.   **Asset Effectiveness and Efficiency**

        a.   The return provided to a corporation's owners most often is assessed using one of two measures:

            1)   Return on investment, stated in percentage terms
            2)   Residual income, stated in dollar terms

        b.   These measures allow an investor to assess how effectively and efficiently the firm is using assets to obtain a return.

2. **Return on Investment -- Basic Version**

    a.   Return on investment (ROI) is calculated as follows:

$$Return\ on\ investment\ (ROI) = \frac{Operating\ income}{Average\ invested\ capital} = \frac{Operating\ income}{Total\ assets}$$

        1)   If the firm's ROI is higher than its cost of capital, its activities are adding to shareholder value.

EXAMPLE

A firm had the following information for the year just ended:

Sales	$100,000
Operating expenses	58,000
Invested capital (total assets)	800,000

Invested capital at the previous year end was $600,000. ROI for the year can be calculated as follows:

Return on investment (ROI) = Operating income ÷ Average invested capital
                    = ($100,000 – $58,000) ÷ [($800,000 + $600,000) ÷ 2]
                    = $42,000 ÷ $700,000
                    = 6%

---

3. **Return on Investment -- Component View**

    a.   ROI can be viewed as the product of two component ratios.

Return on Investment		**Profit Margin**		**Capital (Asset) Turnover**
$\dfrac{Operating\ income}{Average\ invested\ capital}$	$=$	$\dfrac{Operating\ income}{Sales}$	$\times$	$\dfrac{Sales}{Average\ invested\ capital}$

EXAMPLE

Invested capital at the previous year end was $600,000. ROI for the year can be calculated as follows:

    Profit margin*:   Operating income ÷ Sales   = $42,000 ÷ $100,000   = 42%
    Capital turnover: Sales ÷ Average invested capital = $100,000 ÷ $700,000 = 14.286 times

The calculation can be checked by recombining the two ratios to generate ROI.

        Return on investment: Profit margin × Capital turnover = 42% × 14.286 = 6%

*Profit margin also is known as return on sales (ROS).

---

4. **Residual Income**

    a.   Residual income is calculated as follows:

$$Residual\ income = Operating\ income - Target\ return\ on\ invested\ capital$$

        1)   The target return amount equals average invested capital times an imputed interest rate.

EXAMPLE

The firm's capital has an imputed interest rate of 5.5%.

        Residual income = Operating income – Target return on invested capital
                        = $42,000 – ($700,000 × 5.5%)
                        = $42,000 – $38,500
                        = $3,500

---

5. **Comparison of ROI and Residual Income**

    a. ROI is a percentage, and residual income is a monetary amount.

    b. ROI is widely used because it facilitates comparison with other percentage-based measures, such as the firm's cost of capital and the ROIs of competitors.

        1) But a disadvantage of ROI is the potential rejection of projects that decrease the ROI despite increasing shareholder value.

EXAMPLE

A firm assesses divisional performance based solely on ROI. If a division with a current ROI of 12% is considering a project that is estimated to return only 10%, management might reject it because divisional ROI would decrease.

Nevertheless, if the project has a positive NPV, it should be accepted because it increases shareholder value.

---

    c. The example above indicates why residual income often is preferable.

        1) The distinction between ROI and residual income is similar to that between internal rate of return (IRR), a percentage, and net present value (NPV), a monetary amount.

            a) A percentage identifies the highest return per dollar invested. But the firm ultimately is most interested in the total monetary amount of the return.

The AICPA has frequently asked questions about the determination of ROI and residual income as well as questions requiring their comparison.

Stop and review! You have completed the outline for this subunit. Study multiple-choice questions 11 through 25 beginning on page 269.

10.4 OTHER PERFORMANCE MEASURES

1. **Return on Assets**

    a. Return on assets (ROA) is an alternative to return on investment.

$$Return\ on\ assets\ (ROA)\ =\ \frac{Net\ income}{Average\ total\ assets}$$

EXAMPLE

A firm reports the following information for the year just ended:

Operating income	$ 90,000
Income taxes	27,000
Total assets	400,000

Total assets at the previous year end were $500,000. ROA for the year is calculated as follows:

Return on assets (ROA) = Net income ÷ Average total assets
= ($90,000 − $27,000) ÷ [($400,000 + $500,000) ÷ 2]
= $63,000 ÷ $450,000
= 14%

---

2. **Earnings per Share (EPS) and Return on Common Equity**

    a. EPS is a ratio of interest to common shareholders. It is a profitability ratio that measures the amount of current-period earnings that can be associated with a single share of common stock.

    $$EPS = \frac{Net\ income\ -\ Preferred\ dividends}{Common\ shares\ outstanding}$$

        1) The numerator also is known as income available to common shareholders.

    b. Return on common equity (ROCE) measures the amount of income earned per dollar invested by the common shareholders.

    $$ROCE = \frac{Net\ income\ -\ Preferred\ dividends}{Average\ common\ equity}$$

    c. The price-earnings (P-E) ratio measures the amount that investors are willing to pay for $1 of earnings.

    $$P\text{-}E = \frac{P}{E} = \frac{Market\ price\ of\ share}{EPS}$$

        1) Generally, the higher the ratio, the more confidence the market has in the firm's ability to provide higher returns to investors.

3. **Economic Rate of Return on Common Stock**

    a. The economic rate of return on common stock measures the amount of shareholder value generated during a period in relation to the investment.

    $$\frac{Dividends\ paid\ +\ Change\ in\ share\ price}{Beginning\ share\ price}$$

4. **Economic Value Added**

    a. Economic value added (EVA) is the formula for residual income adjusted for the opportunity cost of capital.

    b. The following is the basic formula:

    $$EVA = After\text{-}tax\ operating\ income\ -\ (Initial\ investment\ \times\ Cost\ of\ capital^{1})$$

    [1]The weighted average cost of capital (WACC) is defined in Study Unit 7, Subunit 5.

EXAMPLE

A firm invested $200,000 in a new operating segment. Its current-year net income was $21,000. The cost of capital is 9%.

Net income	$21,000
Investment × Cost of capital ($200,000 × 9%)	(18,000)
EVA	$ 3,000

The EVA is positive. Thus, the investment increased shareholder value.

---

    c. EVA represents a business unit's true economic profit primarily because it is determined by subtracting the cost of equity capital.

        1) The cost of equity is an opportunity cost, i.e., the return on the best alternative investment of similar risk.

        2) Accordingly, EVA measures the marginal benefit obtained by using resources in a specific way.

    d.   EVA also differs from accounting income because it results from certain other adjustments.

        1)   For example, R&D costs may be capitalized and amortized over 5 years for EVA purposes, and true economic depreciation rather than the amount used for accounting or tax purposes may be recognized. Adjustments vary from firm to firm.

A candidate should know the formulas used to calculate the various financial ratios and also should be able to analyze the results. Numerous CPA exams have included questions on both the calculation and analysis of financial ratios. However, the numbers necessary to calculate a ratio often are not given directly.

NOTE: This Tip also applies to Study Unit 8, Subunits 2 and 7, and Subunit 10.3.

Stop and review! You have completed the outline for this subunit. Study multiple-choice questions 26 through 28 beginning on page 273.

10.5 MEASURES OF SOLVENCY

1.   **Solvency**

    a.   Solvency is a firm's ability to pay its noncurrent obligations as they come due and to remain in business in the long run. It should be contrasted with liquidity.

        1)   The ability to service debt from current earnings is part of the effective use of leverage.

$$Times\text{-}interest\text{-}earned\ ratio\ =\ \frac{Earnings\ before\ interest\ and\ taxes\ (EBIT)}{Interest\ expense}$$

    b.   The key elements of solvency are the firm's capital structure and degree of leverage. (The degree of leverage is defined in item 5. in Study Unit 7, Subunit 1.)

2.   **Capital Structure**

    a.   A firm's capital structure includes its sources of financing, both long- and short-term. These sources are debt (external sources) and equity (internal sources).

    b.   **Debt** is the creditor interest in the firm.

        1)   The firm is contractually obligated to repay debtholders. The terms of repayment (timing of interest and principal) are specified in the debt agreement.

        2)   If the return on debt exceeds the interest paid, debt financing is advantageous. The return is increased because interest payments on debt are tax-deductible.

        3)   The disadvantage of debt is that it increases the firm's risk. Debt must be paid regardless of whether the firm is profitable.

    c.   **Equity** is the ownership interest in the firm.

        1)   Equity is permanent capital contributed by the firm's owners to earn a return.

        2)   However, a return on equity is uncertain. Equity is a residual interest in the firm's assets. It is residual because it is a claim only to assets remaining after all debt has been paid.

        3)   Periodic returns to owners of excess earnings are dividends. The firm may be contractually obligated to pay dividends to preferred shareholders but not common shareholders.

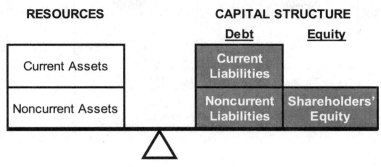

RESOURCES   CAPITAL STRUCTURE

Figure 10-1

d.   Capital structure decisions affect the risk of a firm. For example, a firm with a higher percentage of debt capital is riskier than a firm with a higher percentage of equity capital.

1)   Thus, when the relative amount of debt is high, equity investors demand a higher rate of return on their investments to compensate for the additional risk of financial leverage.

2)   But a firm with a relatively larger proportion of equity capital may be able to borrow at lower rates. Debt holders accept lower interest rates in exchange for lower risk.

3.   **Capital Structure Ratios**

a.   Capital structure ratios report the relative proportions of debt and equity in a firm's capital structure.

b.   The total-debt-to-total-capital ratio measures the percentage of the firm's capital provided by creditors.

$$Total\ debt\ to\ total\ capital\ = \frac{Total\ debt}{Total\ capital}$$

EXAMPLE

The following are a firm's ratios for the current and prior years:

Current year: $1,000,000 ÷ $1,800,000 = 0.556
Prior year: $950,000 ÷ $1,600,000 = 0.594

The firm became slightly less reliant on debt during the current year. Although total debt increased, equity increased by a greater percentage. The firm is therefore less leveraged than before.

---

1)   When total debt to total capital is low, more of the firm's capital is supplied by the shareholders. Thus, creditors prefer this ratio to be low to provide a cushion against losses.

c.   The debt-to-equity ratio is a direct comparison of the firm's debt with its equity.

$$Debt\ to\ equity\ = \frac{Total\ debt}{Shareholders'\ equity}$$

EXAMPLE

Current year: $1,000,000 ÷ $800,000 = 1.25
Prior year: $950,000 ÷ $650,000 = 1.46

The amount by which the firm's debt exceeds its equity declined in the current year.

---

1)   Like the previous ratio, the debt-to-equity ratio reflects long-term debt-payment ability. Again, a low ratio means a lower relative debt and less risk for creditors.

d.   The long-term-debt-to-total-equity ratio reports long-term debt per dollar of equity.

$$\text{Long-term debt to total equity} = \frac{\text{Long-term debt}}{\text{Shareholder's equity}}$$

EXAMPLE

Current year: $610,000 ÷ $800,000 = 0.763
Prior year: $675,000 ÷ $650,000 = 1.038

The firm has reduced its long-term debt. It now has less than one dollar of long-term debt for every dollar of equity.

1)   A firm with a low ratio has a better chance of obtaining new debt financing at a favorable rate.

e.   The debt-to-total-assets ratio (the debt ratio) reports the total debt per dollar of assets.

$$\text{Debt to total assets} = \frac{\text{Total debt}}{\text{Total assets}}$$

EXAMPLE

Current year: $1,000,000 ÷ $1,800,000 = 0.556
Prior year: $950,000 ÷ $1,600,000 = 0.594

Although total liabilities increased in absolute terms, this ratio improved because total assets increased even more.

1)   This ratio is identical to the total-debt-to-total-capital ratio because total capital equals total assets.

Stop and review! You have completed the outline for this subunit. Study multiple-choice questions 29 and 30 on page 275.

QUESTIONS

10.1 Ranking Capital Projects

1. Wood, Inc., is considering four independent investment proposals. Wood has $3 million available for investment during the present period. The investment outlay for each project and its projected net present value (NPV) is presented below.

Project	Investment Cost	NPV
I	$ 500,000	$ 40,000
II	900,000	120,000
III	1,200,000	180,000
IV	1,600,000	150,000

Which of the following project options should be recommended to Wood's management?

A.   Projects I, II, and III only.

B.   Projects I, II, and IV only.

C.   Projects II, III, and IV only.

D.   Projects III and IV only.

Answer (A) is correct.
   REQUIRED: The acceptable capital projects given NPV.
   DISCUSSION: When available funds are limited, potential projects should be ranked by profitability index. The indexes for the potential projects can be calculated as follows:

Project	NPV		Investment Cost		Profitability Index
I	$ 40,000	÷	$ 500,000	=	0.080
II	120,000	÷	900,000	=	0.133
III	180,000	÷	1,200,000	=	0.150
IV	150,000	÷	1,600,000	=	0.094

Ranked in order of desirability, they are III, II, IV, and I. Because only $3 million is available for funding, only III, II, and I will be selected.
   Answer (B) is incorrect. Project III is more desirable than Project IV. Answer (C) is incorrect. Project IV is more desirable than Project I, but funding is not sufficient. Answer (D) is incorrect. Projects I and II also are desirable, and sufficient funding is available.

2. The profitability index approach to investment analysis

A. Fails to consider the timing of project cash flows.

B. Considers only the project's contribution to net income and does not consider cash flow effects.

C. Always yields the same accept/reject decisions for independent projects as the net present value method.

D. Always yields the same accept/reject decisions for mutually exclusive projects as the net present value method.

Answer (C) is correct.
REQUIRED: The true statement about the profitability index.
DISCUSSION: The profitability index is the ratio of a discounted cash flow amount to the initial investment. It is a variation of the net present value (NPV) method and facilitates the comparison of different-sized investments. Because it is based on the NPV method, the profitability index yields the same decision as the NPV for independent projects. However, decisions may differ for mutually exclusive projects of different sizes.
Answer (A) is incorrect. The profitability index, like the NPV method, discounts cash flows based on the cost of capital. Answer (B) is incorrect. The profitability index is cash based. Answer (D) is incorrect. The NPV and the profitability index may yield different decisions if projects are mutually exclusive and of different sizes.

3. Future, Inc., is in the enviable situation of having unlimited capital funds. The best decision rule, in an economic sense, for it to follow would be to invest in all projects in which the

A. Accounting rate of return is greater than the earnings as a percent of sales.

B. Payback reciprocal is greater than the internal rate of return.

C. Internal rate of return is greater than zero.

D. Net present value is greater than zero.

Answer (D) is correct.
REQUIRED: The investment rule given unlimited capital funds.
DISCUSSION: Given unlimited funds, all projects with an NPV greater than zero should be accepted. Thus, it is profitable to invest in any firm if the rate of return is greater than the cost of capital.
Answer (A) is incorrect. Neither the accounting rate of return nor the earnings as a percent of sales is useful in capital budgeting. The accounting rate of return is accounting net income over the required investment; it ignores the time value of money. Earnings as a percentage of sales ignores the amount of required investment. Answer (B) is incorrect. The payback criterion for capital budgeting is not efficient or effective. Answer (C) is incorrect. Capital funds are unlimited, but the cost of capital is not given. Accordingly, projects can be accepted only if the IRR is greater than cost of capital. Thus, the NPV needs to be greater than zero.

4. The profitability index (present value index)

A. Represents the ratio of the discounted net cash outflows to cash inflows.

B. Is the relationship between the net discounted cash inflows less the discounted cash outflows divided by the discounted cash outflows.

C. Is calculated by dividing the discounted profits by the cash outflows.

D. Is the ratio of the discounted net cash flows to initial investment.

Answer (D) is correct.
REQUIRED: The true statement about the profitability index.
DISCUSSION: The profitability index, also known as the excess present value index, is the ratio of discounted net cash flows to the initial investment. It is a variation of the NPV method that facilitates comparison of different-sized investments.
Answer (A) is incorrect. The cash inflows also are discounted in the profitability index. Answer (B) is incorrect. The denominator is the initial investment. Answer (C) is incorrect. The profitability index is based on cash flows, not profits.

5. Mesa Company is considering an investment to open a new banana processing division. The project involves an initial investment of $45,000, and cash inflows of $20,000 can be expected in each of the next 3 years. The hurdle rate is 10%. The present value of an ordinary annuity of 1 discounted at 10% for 3 periods is 2.487. The present value of 1 due in 3 periods discounted at 10% is .751. What is the profitability index for the project?

A. 1.0784

B. 1.1053

C. 1.1379

D. 1.1771

Answer (B) is correct.
REQUIRED: The profitability index.
DISCUSSION: At a 10% hurdle rate, the present value of the future cash inflows is $49,740 (20,000 × 2.487), an NPV for the project of $4,740 ($49,740 – $45,000). The profitability index is therefore 1.1053 ($49,740 ÷ $45,000).

10.2 Comparison of Capital Budgeting Methods

6. Which limitation is common to the calculations of the payback period, discounted payback, internal rate of return (IRR), and net present value (NPV)?

- A. They do not consider the time value of money.
- B. They require multiple trial and error calculations.
- C. They require knowledge of a firm's cost of capital.
- D. They rely on forecasts of future data.

Answer (D) is correct.
REQUIRED: The limitation common to the calculations of the given capital budgeting evaluation methods.
DISCUSSION: The long-term aspect of capital budgeting presents the accountant with specific challenges. A firm must forecast accurately future changes in demand to have the necessary production capacity when demand increases. But it must avoid excess idle capacity when demand decreases. Because capital budgeting requires choosing among investment proposals, a ranking procedure is needed. The ranking procedure also requires reliable estimates of future cost savings or revenues to calculate the estimated cash flows.
Answer (A) is incorrect. Discounted cash flow, IRR, and NPV all consider the time value of money. Answer (B) is incorrect. Multiple trial and error calculations only are required for determining the IRR. Answer (C) is incorrect. The payback period calculation does not require knowledge of the cost of capital.

7. The technique that recognizes the time value of money by discounting the after-tax cash flows for a project over its life to time period zero using the company's minimum desired rate of return is called the

- A. Net present value method.
- B. Payback method.
- C. Average rate of return method.
- D. Accounting rate of return method.

Answer (A) is correct.
REQUIRED: The capital budgeting method that discounts the after-tax cash flows to their present value using the firm's minimum desired rate of return.
DISCUSSION: The NPV method discounts future cash flows using some arbitrary rate of return, which is presumably the firm's cost of capital.
Answer (B) is incorrect. The payback method does not recognize the time value of money. Answer (C) is incorrect. The average rate of return method does not use the firm's cost of capital as a discount rate. Answer (D) is incorrect. The accounting rate of return method does not recognize the time value of money.

8. The method that divides a project's annual after-tax net income by the average investment cost to measure the estimated performance of a capital investment is the

- A. Internal rate of return method.
- B. Accounting rate of return method.
- C. Payback method.
- D. Net present value (NPV) method.

Answer (B) is correct.
REQUIRED: The capital budgeting method that divides annual after-tax net income by the average investment cost.
DISCUSSION: The accounting rate of return uses undiscounted net income (not cash flows) to determine a rate of profitability. Annual after-tax net income is divided by the average carrying amount (or the initial value) of the investment in assets.
Answer (A) is incorrect. The IRR is the rate at which the project's NPV is zero. Answer (C) is incorrect. The payback period is the time required to recover the original investment. This method does not consider the time value of money or returns after the payback period. Answer (D) is incorrect. The NPV method calculates the discounted present value of future cash inflows to determine whether it is greater than the initial cash outflow.

9. The technique that measures the number of years required for the after-tax cash flows to recover the initial investment in a project is called the

- A. Net present value method.
- B. Payback method.
- C. Profitability index method.
- D. Accounting rate of return method.

Answer (B) is correct.
REQUIRED: The capital budgeting method that measures the number of years required for the after-tax cash flows to recover the initial investment.
DISCUSSION: The usual payback formula divides the initial investment by the constant net annual cash inflow. The payback method is unsophisticated because it ignores the time value of money. But it is widely used because of its simplicity and emphasis on recovery of the initial investment.
Answer (A) is incorrect. The NPV method first discounts the future cash flows to their present value. Answer (C) is incorrect. The profitability index method divides the present value of the future net cash inflows by the initial investment. Answer (D) is incorrect. The accounting rate of return divides the annual net income by the average investment in the project.

10. The technique that reflects the time value of money and is calculated by dividing the present value of the future net after-tax cash inflows that have been discounted at the desired cost of capital by the initial cash outlay for the investment is called the

A. Capital rationing method.

B. Average rate of return method.

C. Profitability index method.

D. Accounting rate of return method.

Answer (C) is correct.
    REQUIRED: The method that divides the present value of future net cash inflows by the initial cash outlay.
    DISCUSSION: The profitability index, also called the excess present value index, measures the ratio of the present value of a project's future net cash inflows to the original investment. If capital rationing is necessary, the profitability index allows management to identify the projects with the highest return per investment dollar.
    Answer (A) is incorrect. Capital rationing is not a method but rather a condition that characterizes capital budgeting when insufficient capital is available to finance all profitable investment opportunities. Answer (B) is incorrect. The average rate of return method does not divide the future cash flows by the cost of the investment. Answer (D) is incorrect. The accounting rate of return does not recognize the time value of money.

10.3 Return on Investment and Residual Income

11. Minon, Inc., purchased a long-term asset on the last day of the current year. What are the effects of this purchase on return on investment and residual income?

	Return on Investment	Residual Income
A.	Increase	Increase
B.	Decrease	Decrease
C.	Increase	Decrease
D.	Decrease	Increase

Answer (B) is correct.
    REQUIRED: The effects of a long-term asset purchase.
    DISCUSSION: ROI equals operating income divided by average invested capital. The purchase of a long-term asset on the last day of the fiscal year has little or no effect on net income. But it increases average invested capital, thereby decreasing ROI. Residual income is operating income minus a target return on average invested capital. Given no change in operating income or the required rate of return, an increase in invested capital decreases residual income.

12. The return on investment calculation considers only the following components:

$$S = \text{Sales}$$
$$I = \text{Investment}$$
$$NI = \text{Net income}$$

Which of the following formulas best describes the return on investment calculation?

A. $(I \div S) \times (S \div NI) = I \div NI$

B. $(S \div I) \times (NI \div S) = NI \div I$

C. $(I \div S) \times (NI \div S) = (I \times NI) \times (S \times S)$

D. $(S \div I) \times (S \div NI) = (S \times S) \div (I \times NI)$

Answer (B) is correct.
    REQUIRED: The formula for ROI.
    DISCUSSION: The first term in the formula for return on investment is the number of times investment capital has turned over through sales ($S \div I$). This amount is multiplied by the net income as a percentage of sales ($NI \div S$) to give the return on investment ($NI \div I$). The basic formula for return on investment is therefore

$$(S \div I) \times (NI \div S) = NI \div I$$

Answer (A) is incorrect. $I \div NI$ is the reciprocal of return on investment. Answer (C) is incorrect. Sales must be divided by investment ($S \div I$) to determine the number of times investment capital has turned over, which results in $NI \div I$ as return on investment. Answer (D) is incorrect. Net income must be expressed as a percentage of sales ($NI \div S$), which results in $NI \div I$ as return on investment.

13. Residual income is a better measure for performance evaluation of an investment center manager than return on investment because

A. The problems associated with measuring the asset base are eliminated.

B. Desirable investment decisions will not be neglected by high return divisions.

C. Only the gross book value of assets needs to be calculated.

D. Returns do not increase as assets are depreciated.

Answer (B) is correct.
    REQUIRED: The reason residual income is a better measure of investment center performance than ROI.
    DISCUSSION: A disadvantage of ROI is potential rejection of projects that decrease ROI despite increasing shareholder value. Residual income often is preferable because a firm ultimately is most interested in the total monetary amount of its return.
    Answer (A) is incorrect. The investment base must be determined before calculating the target return. Answer (C) is incorrect. The investment base may be defined in various ways. Answer (D) is incorrect. ROI returns will be affected in the same manner as the target return.

14. Which one of the following statements pertaining to the return on investment (ROI) as a performance measurement is **false**?

A. When the average age of assets differs substantially across segments of a business, the use of ROI may not be appropriate.

B. ROI relies on financial measures that are capable of being independently verified, while other forms of performance measures are subject to manipulation.

C. The use of ROI may lead managers to reject capital investment projects that can be justified by using discounted cash flow models.

D. The use of ROI can make it undesirable for a skillful manager to take on troubleshooting assignments such as those involving turning around unprofitable divisions.

Answer (B) is correct.
REQUIRED: The false statement about ROI as a performance measure.
DISCUSSION: ROI is the key performance measure in an investment center. ROI is a rate calculated by dividing a segment's income by the invested capital. ROI is therefore subject to manipulation of the income and investment amounts. For example, a manager may choose not to invest in a project that yield less than the desired rate of return, or (s)he may defer necessary expenses.
Answer (A) is incorrect. ROI can be misleading when the quality of the investment base differs among segments. Answer (C) is incorrect. Managers may reject projects that are profitable (a return greater than the cost of capital) but decrease ROI. For example, the manager of a segment with a 15% ROI may not want to invest in a new project with a 10% ROI, even though the cost of capital might be only 8%. Answer (D) is incorrect. The use of ROI does not reflect the relative difficulty of tasks undertaken by managers.

15. A firm earning a profit can increase its return on investment by

A. Increasing sales revenue and operating expenses by the same dollar amount.

B. Decreasing sales revenues and operating expenses by the same percentage.

C. Increasing investment and operating expenses by the same dollar amount.

D. Increasing sales revenues and operating expenses by the same percentage.

Answer (D) is correct.
REQUIRED: The means by which a profitable firm can increase its ROI.
DISCUSSION: ROI equals income divided by invested capital. If a firm is profitable, increasing sales and expenses by the same percentage increases ROI. For example, if it has sales of $100 and expenses of $80, its net income is $20. Given invested capital of $100, ROI is 20% ($20 ÷ $100). If sales and expenses both increase 10% to $110 and $88, respectively, net income increases to $22. ROI then is 22% ($22 ÷ $100).
Answer (A) is incorrect. Increasing sales and expenses by the same dollar amount does not change income or ROI. Answer (B) is incorrect. Decreasing revenues and expenses by the same percentage reduces income and ROI. Answer (C) is incorrect. Increasing investment and operating expenses by the same dollar amount reduces ROI. The higher investment increases the denominator, and the increased expenses reduce the numerator.

16. Listed below is selected financial information for the Western Division of the Hinzel Company for last year.

Account	Amount (thousands)
Average working capital	$ 625
General and administrative expenses	75
Net sales	4,000
Average plant and equipment	1,775
Cost of goods sold	3,525

If Hinzel treats the Western Division as an investment center for performance measurement purposes, what is the before-tax return on investment (ROI) for last year?

A. 34.78%

B. 22.54%

C. 19.79%

D. 16.67%

Answer (D) is correct.
REQUIRED: The before-tax ROI for an investment center.
DISCUSSION: An investment center's ROI is its operating income divided by its average invested capital. The Western Division's operating income is $400 ($4,000 sales – $3,525 cost of goods sold – $75 general expenses). Given average plant and equipment of $1,775 and average working capital of $625, the net investment is $2,400. ROI is thus 16.67% ($400 ÷ $2,400).
Answer (A) is incorrect. Subtracting working capital from plant and equipment in calculating the net investment results in 34.78%. Answer (B) is incorrect. The percentage of 22.54% does not include average working capital in the total for the net investment. Answer (C) is incorrect. Not subtracting general and administrative expenses in the calculation of before-tax profit results in 19.79%.

17. One approach to measuring divisional performance is return on investment. Return on investment is expressed as operating income

A. Divided by the current year's capital expenditures plus cost of capital.

B. Minus imputed interest charged for invested capital.

C. Divided by average fixed assets.

D. Divided by average total assets.

Answer (D) is correct.
REQUIRED: The method of calculating ROI.
DISCUSSION: ROI is calculated by dividing income by average invested capital. It is a key performance measure of an investment center. Invested capital may be defined in various ways, such as shareholders' equity, total assets available, or total assets employed, which excludes idle assets. Total assets available is the measure that assumes the manager uses all assets without regard to financing.
Answer (A) is incorrect. ROI is based on all assets, not just current investment expenditures. Answer (B) is incorrect. The calculation of ROI does not adjust for imputed interest on invested capital. Answer (C) is incorrect. The denominator is not limited to fixed assets.

18. Charlie's Service Co. is a service center. For the month of June, Charlie's had the following operating statistics:

Sales	$750,000
Operating income	25,000
Net profit after taxes	8,000
Total assets available	500,000
Shareholders' equity	200,000
Cost of capital	6%

Charlie's has a

A. Return on investment of 3.33%.

B. Residual income of $(5,000).

C. Return on investment of 6%.

D. Residual income of $(20,000).

Answer (B) is correct.
REQUIRED: The true statement about operating performance.
DISCUSSION: Residual income is the excess of operating income (a pretax amount) over a targeted amount equal to an imputed interest charge on invested capital. Using total assets available as the investment base, Charlie's targeted amount is $30,000 ($500,000 total assets × 6% cost of capital). Subtracting this amount from operating income results in residual income of $(5,000).
Answer (A) is incorrect. The return on sales was 3.33%. Answer (C) is incorrect. The cost of capital is 6%. Answer (D) is incorrect. Residual income of $(20,000) results from improperly subtracting weighted sales rather than weighted assets.

19. The imputed interest rate used in the residual income approach to performance evaluation can best be described as the

A. Average lending rate for the year being evaluated.

B. Historical weighted-average cost of capital for the company.

C. Target return on investment set by the company's management.

D. Average return on investments for the company over the last several years.

Answer (C) is correct.
REQUIRED: The true statement about the imputed interest rate used in the residual income approach to performance evaluation.
DISCUSSION: Residual income is the excess of operating income over a targeted amount equal to an imputed interest charge on invested capital. The rate used ordinarily is set as a target return by management but is often equal to the weighted average cost of capital.
Answer (A) is incorrect. The cost of equity capital also must be included in the imputed interest rate. Answer (B) is incorrect. The current weighted-average cost of capital must be used. Answer (D) is incorrect. The rate should be based on cost of capital, not investment returns of preceding years.

20. REB Service Co. is a computer service center. For the month, REB had the following operating statistics:

Sales	$450,000
Operating income	25,000
Net profit after taxes	8,000
Total assets	500,000
Shareholders' equity	200,000
Cost of capital	6%

Based on the above information, which one of the following statements is true? REB has a

A. Return on investment of 4%.

B. Residual income of $(5,000).

C. Return on investment of 1.6%.

D. Residual income of $(22,000).

Answer (B) is correct.
REQUIRED: The true statement about performance.
DISCUSSION: Residual income is the excess of operating income (a pretax amount) over a targeted amount equal to an imputed interest charge on invested capital. Using assets of $500,000 as the investment base and a cost of capital of 6%, REB must earn $30,000 on those assets to cover the cost of capital. Given that operating income was only $25,000, residual income is $(5,000).
Answer (A) is incorrect. Although the firm's return on equity investment was 4%, its return on all funds invested was 5% ($25,000 pretax operating income ÷ $500,000). Answer (C) is incorrect. ROI is commonly based on before-tax income. Answer (D) is incorrect. Residual income of $(22,000) results from improperly using after-tax, rather than pretax, profit.

21. James Webb is the general manager of the Industrial Product Division, and his performance is measured using the residual income method. Webb is reviewing the following forecasted information for his division for next year:

Category	Amount (thousands)
Working capital	$ 1,800
Revenue	30,000
Plant and equipment	17,200

If the imputed interest charge is 15% and Webb wants to achieve a residual income target of $2,000,000, what will costs (cost of goods sold and other operating expenses) have to be in order to achieve the target?

A. $9,000,000

B. $10,800,000

C. $25,150,000

D. $25,690,000

Answer (C) is correct.
   REQUIRED: The maximum costs consistent with meeting a residual income target.
   DISCUSSION: Residual income is the excess of operating income over a targeted amount equal to an imputed interest charge on invested capital. If a manager has $19,000,000 of invested capital ($17,200,000 of plant and equipment + $1,800,000 of working capital), a 15% imputed interest charge equals $2,850,000. Adding $2,000,000 of residual income to the imputed interest results in a target profit of $4,850,000. This profit can be achieved if costs are $25,150,000 ($30,000,000 revenue – $4,850,000 profit).
   Answer (A) is incorrect. Costs of $9,000,000 result in a residual income greater than $2,000,000. Answer (B) is incorrect. Costs of $10,800,000 result in a residual income greater than $2,000,000. Answer (D) is incorrect. Subtracting working capital from plant and equipment in determining invested capital results in $25,690,000.

22. The following forecasted information is available for a manufacturing division for next year:

Category	Amount (thousands)
Working capital	$ 1,800
Revenue	30,000
Plant and equipment	17,200

To establish a standard of performance for the division's manager using the residual income approach, four scenarios are being considered.

	Imputed Interest	Target Residual Income
1	15%	$2,000,000
2	12%	1,500,000
3	18%	1,250,000
4	10%	2,500,000

Which scenario assumes the lowest maximum cost?

A. Scenario 1.

B. Scenario 2.

C. Scenario 3.

D. Scenario 4.

Answer (A) is correct.
   REQUIRED: The lowest maximum cost consistent with meeting a residual income target.
   DISCUSSION: Residual income is the excess of operating income over a targeted amount equal to an imputed interest charge on invested capital. If a manager has $19,000,000 of invested capital ($17,200,000 of plant and equipment + $1,800,000 of working capital), a 15% imputed interest charge equals $2,850,000. Adding $2,000,000 of residual income to the imputed interest results in a target profit of $4,850,000. This profit can be achieved if costs are $25,150,000 ($30,000,000 revenue – $4,850,000 profit).
   Answer (B) is incorrect. Scenario 2 requires maximum costs of $26,220,000 to reach the target. Answer (C) is incorrect. Scenario 3 requires maximum costs of $25,330,000 to reach the target. Answer (D) is incorrect. Scenario 4 requires maximum costs of $25,600,000 to reach the target.

23. Managerial performance can be measured in many different ways, including return on investment (ROI) and residual income. A good reason for using residual income instead of ROI is that

A. Residual income can be computed without regard to identifying an investment base.

B. Goal congruence is more likely to be promoted by using residual income.

C. Residual income is well understood and often used in the financial press.

D. ROI does not take into consideration both the investment turnover ratio and return-on-sales percentage.

Answer (B) is correct.
   REQUIRED: The reason for using the residual income method instead of ROI.
   DISCUSSION: Residual income is the excess of operating income over a targeted amount equal to an imputed interest charge on invested capital. Residual income may be preferable to ROI because a firm benefits from expansion if residual income is earned. Using an ROI criterion, expansion might be rejected if it lowered ROI even though residual income increases. Thus, the residual income method promotes the congruence of a manager's goal with those of the firm. Actions that tend to benefit the firm also tend to improve the measure of the manager's performance.
   Answer (A) is incorrect. An investment base is needed to calculate residual income. Answer (C) is incorrect. ROI is more widely used than residual income. Answer (D) is incorrect. Both measures consider the same items.

24. The basic objective of the residual income approach to performance measurement and evaluation is to have a division maximize its

A. Return on investment rate.

B. Imputed interest rate charge.

C. Cash flows.

D. Income in excess of a desired minimum return.

Answer (D) is correct.
   REQUIRED: The basic objective of the residual income approach to performance measurement and evaluation.
   DISCUSSION: Residual income is the excess of the return on an investment over the targeted amount. This amount may be defined as the imputed interest on invested capital. Some firms prefer to measure managerial performance in terms of the amount of residual income rather than the percentage ROI. The principle is that the firm is expected to benefit from expansion if residual income is earned. Using a percentage ROI approach, expansion might be rejected if it lowered ROI even though residual income increases.
   Answer (A) is incorrect. ROI does not have to be maximized under the residual income approach. Answer (B) is incorrect. Maximizing the imputed interest rate charge decreases the residual return. Answer (C) is incorrect. The residual income method is based on net income rather than cash flows.

25. After investing in a new project, a company discovered that its residual income remained unchanged. Which one of the following must be true about the new project?

A. The net present value of the new project must have been negative.

B. The return on investment of the new project must have been less than the firm's cost of capital.

C. The return on investment of the new project must have been equal to the firm's cost of capital.

D. The net present value of the new project must have been positive.

Answer (C) is correct.
   REQUIRED: The true statement about residual income given that it is unchanged.
   DISCUSSION: Residual income is the excess of the return on an investment over the firm's cost of capital. If residual income is unchanged, the return on the project must have been the same as the firm's cost of capital.
   Answer (A) is incorrect. A negative NPV decreases residual income. Answer (B) is incorrect. A return less than the cost of capital decreases residual income. Answer (D) is incorrect. A positive NPV increases residual income.

10.4 Other Performance Measures

26. Avionics Industrials reported at year end that operating income before taxes for the year equaled $2,400,000. The firm's weighted-average cost of capital (WACC) is 7.24%. The carrying amount of debt is $1,300,000, and the carrying amount of equity capital is $8,800,000. The income tax rate for Avionics is 30%. What is the economic value added (EVA)?

A. $731,240

B. $948,760

C. $1,668,760

D. $1,680,000

Answer (B) is correct.
   REQUIRED: The EVA.
   DISCUSSION: EVA equals after-tax operating income minus the product of the weighted-average cost of capital (WACC) and the investment base. After-tax operating income equals operating income multiplied by 1 minus the tax rate, or $1,680,000. The investment base is $10,100,000, consisting of $1,300,000 of debt and $8,800,000 of equity. Thus, EVA equals $948,760 {($1,680,000) − [$10,100,000 × (0.0724)]}.
   Answer (A) is incorrect. The cost of capital is $731,240. Answer (C) is incorrect. Income taxes must be subtracted from operating income to compute EVA. Answer (D) is incorrect. The after-tax operating income is $1,680,000.

Questions 27 and 28 are based on the following information. The information below pertains to Devlin Company.

Statement of Financial Position as of May 31
(in thousands)

	Year 2	Year 1
Assets		
Current assets		
Cash	$ 45	$ 38
Trading securities	30	20
Accounts receivable (net)	68	48
Inventory	90	80
Prepaid expenses	22	30
Total current assets	$255	$216
Investments, at equity	38	30
Property, plant, and equipment (net)	375	400
Intangible assets (net)	80	45
Total assets	$748	$691
Liabilities		
Current liabilities		
Notes payable	$ 35	$ 18
Accounts payable	70	42
Accrued expenses	5	4
Income taxes payable	15	16
Total current liabilities	$125	$ 80
Long-term debt	35	35
Deferred taxes	3	2
Total liabilities	$163	$117
Equity		
Preferred stock, 6%, $100 par value, cumulative	$150	$150
Common stock, $10 par value	225	195
Additional paid-in capital -- common stock	114	100
Retained earnings	96	129
Total equity	$585	$574
Total liabilities and equity	$748	$691

Income Statement for the year ended May 31
(in thousands)

	Year 2	Year 1
Net sales	$480	$460
Costs and expenses		
Costs of goods sold	330	315
Selling, general, and administrative	52	51
Interest expense	8	9
Income before taxes	$ 90	$ 85
Income taxes	36	34
Net income	$ 54	$ 51

---

27. Assuming there are no preferred stock dividends in arrears, Devlin Company's return on common equity for the year ended May 31, Year 2, was

A. 6.3%

B. 7.5%

C. 7.8%

D. 10.5%

Answer (D) is correct.
REQUIRED: The return on common equity.
DISCUSSION: The return on common equity equals income available to common shareholders divided by average common equity. Net income available to common shareholders is $45 [$54 − ($150 par value of preferred stock × 6%)]. Average common equity is $429.5 {[($574 − $150 preferred stock) + ($585 − $150 preferred stock)] ÷ 2}. Thus, the return is 10.5% ($45 ÷ $429.5).
Answer (A) is incorrect. Net income available to common shareholders divided by average total assets equals 6.3%. Answer (B) is incorrect. Net income divided by average total assets equals 7.5%. Answer (C) is incorrect. Net income divided by beginning total assets equals 7.8%.

28. Devlin Company's rate of return on assets for the year ended May 31, Year 2, was

A. 7.2%

B. 7.5%

C. 7.8%

D. 11.2%

Answer (B) is correct.
REQUIRED: The rate of return on assets.
DISCUSSION: The rate of return on assets equals net income divided by average total assets. Accordingly, the rate of return is 7.5% {$54 ÷ [($748 + $691) ÷ 2]}.
Answer (A) is incorrect. The percentage of 7.2% is based on ending total assets instead of average total assets. Answer (C) is incorrect. Net income divided by beginning total assets equals 7.8%. Answer (D) is incorrect. The return on sales is 11.2%.

10.5 Measures of Solvency

29. The relationship of the total debt to the total equity of a corporation is a measure of

  A. Liquidity.

  B. Profitability.

  C. Creditor risk.

  D. Break even.

Answer (C) is correct.
   REQUIRED: The characteristic measured by the relationship of total debt to total equity.
   DISCUSSION: The debt-to-equity ratio is a measure of risk to creditors. It indicates how much equity is available to absorb losses before the interests of debt holders are impaired. The less leveraged the firm, the safer the creditors' interests.
   Answer (A) is incorrect. Liquidity relates to how quickly cash can be made available to pay debts as they come due. Answer (B) is incorrect. The debt-to-equity ratio evaluates a firm's capital structure and is not oriented toward the balance sheet. It does not measure the use (profits) made of assets. Answer (D) is incorrect. Breakeven relates to profitability, not financing.

30. If the ratio of total liabilities to equity increases, a ratio that must also increase is

  A. Times interest earned.

  B. Total liabilities to total assets.

  C. Return on equity.

  D. The current ratio.

Answer (B) is correct.
   REQUIRED: The ratio that increases if the ratio of total liabilities to equity increases.
   DISCUSSION: Because total assets equal the sum of liabilities and equity, a factor that increases the liabilities-to-equity ratio also increases the liabilities-to-assets ratio.
   Answer (A) is incorrect. No determination can be made of the effect on interest coverage without knowing the amounts of income and interest expense. Answer (C) is incorrect. The return on equity may be increased or decreased as a result of a factor that increases in the liabilities-to-equity ratio. Answer (D) is incorrect. The current ratio equals current assets divided by current liabilities, and additional information is necessary to determine whether it is affected. For example, an increase in current liabilities from short-term borrowing increases the liabilities-to-equity ratio but decrease the current ratio.

10.6 PRACTICE WRITTEN COMMUNICATION

	Business Environment and Concepts Testlet 4 of 4	Time Remaining 1 hour - 15 minutes	Unsplit Split Horiz Split Vertical Exit

DIRECTIONS

Note: If you believe you have encountered a software malfunction, report it to the test center staff immediately.

Navigation

To navigate from task to task, use the controls at the bottom of the screen. Click on the **Next** button to advance to the next task, or the **Previous** button to go to the previous task. To go directly to any task, click on its number.

If you would like a reminder to revisit a task, or want to indicate that you are finished with it, click on the reminder flag below the task number. To clear the flag, click on it again. Reminder flags are for your use only – they do not contribute to your score.

Tabs

In this part of the examination, you will be asked to complete various tasks. Every task has one or more **Work Tabs**. Every task also has a **Help** tab.

Work tab	**Help tab**

Work Tabs:

- **Work Tabs** are identified with a pencil icon. This is where your responses are expected.
- Each task has one or more **Work Tabs**.
- **Work Tabs** contain directions for completing the task - be sure to read these directions carefully.
- The **Work Tab** name in the example above is for illustration only - yours will differ.
- You must complete all of the **Work Tabs** in each task to receive full credit.

Help Tab:

- The **Help Tab** provides assistance with the exam software that is used in this task. For example, if the task is to compose a memorandum, **Help** will provide information about the word processor.

The Toolbar

The toolbar at the top of the screen shows the amount of time remaining for you to complete the tasks. In addition, the following tools are available. Note that only the **Exit** button is displayed when Directions are visible - the others will appear when you begin the tasks.

Click on these buttons to split or unsplit the screen. You can split the screen vertically or horizontally.

Click on this button to go on to the next part of the examination. You must complete all of the tasks to receive full credit. Once you click on **Exit** and confirm the action, you will NOT be able to return to this testlet.

The partners of Packitup Partnership are considering the decision to convert to the corporate form of business organization. During your discussions with them, you determine that they have only the vaguest ideas about the relationship between corporate debt and equity.

Prepare a memo to the partners of Packitup Partnership describing the concept of solvency, the two main components of corporate capital, and how capital structure decisions affect the risk profile of a firm.

Type your communication below the line in the response area below.

REMINDER: Your response will be graded for both technical content and writing skills. Technical content will be evaluated for information that is helpful to the intended reader and clearly relevant to the issue. Writing skills will be evaluated for development, organization, and the appropriate expression of ideas in professional correspondence. Use a standard business memorandum or letter format with a clear beginning, middle, and end. Do not convey information in the form of a table, bullet point list, or other abbreviated presentation.

To: Packitup Partnership
Re: Solvency and capital structure

NOTE: Your Written Communications on the actual CPA exam may cover topics outside the scope of the BEC CSO (i.e., they may relate to topics from the AUD, FAR, and/or REG CSOs instead). Answer to the best of your ability, and remember that graders are mainly evaluating your writing ability and will overlook minor technical mistakes.

Unofficial Answer

Written Communication

To: Packitup Partnership
Re: Solvency and capital structure

Solvency is a firm's ability to pay its noncurrent obligations as they come due and remain in business in the long run. It differs from liquidity, the ability to remain in business in the short run. The key ingredients of solvency are the firm's capital structure and degree of leverage. A firm's capital structure includes its sources of financing, both long- and short-term. These sources can be in the form of debt (external sources) or equity (internal sources).

Debt is the creditor interest in the firm. The firm is contractually obligated to repay debtholders. The terms of repayment (i.e., timing of interest and principal payments) are specified in the debt agreement. If the return on debt capital exceeds the amount of interest paid, debt financing is advantageous. The return is increased because interest payments on debt are tax-deductible. The tradeoff is that increased debt increases the firm's risk. Debt must be paid regardless of whether the firm is profitable. When risk reaches a certain level, either the firm will have to pay a higher interest rate than its return on debt, or creditors will refuse to lend more money.

Equity is the ownership interest in the firm. Equity is permanent capital, contributed by the firm's owners in expectation of a return. However, a return on equity is uncertain because equity is only a residual interest in the firm's assets. It is residual because it is the claim remaining after all debt has been satisfied. Periodic returns to owners of excess earnings are dividends. The firm may be contractually obligated to pay dividends to preferred shareholders but not to common shareholders.

Capital structure decisions affect the risk of a firm. For example, a firm with a higher percentage of debt will be riskier than a firm with a higher percentage of equity. Thus, when the relative amount of debt is high, equity investors will demand a higher rate of return on their investments to compensate for the greater risk. But a firm with a relatively larger proportion of equity will be able to borrow at lower rates because debt holders will accept lower interest in exchange for the lower risk.

The above depicts a Level 5 answer. Consult your booklet, *How to Pass the CPA Exam: A System for Success*, for a description of the three writing skills criteria. You may also access this booklet online by visiting www.gleim.com/PassCPA.

Self-Grade

Below, grade your response on technical content and writing skills. Bubble in the circle next to the appropriate score that you may receive based on the criteria given. Your **total** score is the sum of your scores on all six items. The maximum score is 19 points.

Technical Content Evaluation

Was your response on topic?	O No [0]	O Mostly [1]	O Yes [2]
Did your response have any *significant* errors?	O 0 errors [1]	O 1 major error [−1]	O 2 or more major errors [−2]
Did your response contain any illegal advice?	O No [1]	O Yes [0]	

Writing Skills Evaluation

	Poor	Below Average	Average	Above Average	Outstanding
Organization	O 1	O 2	O 3	O 4	O 5
Development	O 1	O 2	O 3	O 4	O 5
Expression	O 1	O 2	O 3	O 4	O 5

Disclaimer: This scoring schedule was developed by Gleim Publications as a guideline only. The AICPA has not released specific information on how the Written Communications are graded.

Practice even more Written Communications with the Gleim Mega Test Bank.
Learn more: gleim.com/CPAmega | 800.874.5346

STUDY UNIT ELEVEN
IT ROLES, SYSTEMS, AND PROCESSING

(13 pages of outline)

While the use of information technology (IT) was once restricted to financial applications, it has permeated every area of the modern organization over the last 40 years. No entity, whether for-profit or not-for-profit, can fulfill its mission without the use of sophisticated electronic technologies and their accompanying procedures.

This study unit describes the various broad categories of information systems and the functions they perform, the standardized modes of processing transactions, and standardized phases of processing.

11.1 ROLE OF INFORMATION SYSTEMS IN THE MODERN ORGANIZATION

1. **Overview**

    a. Information technology (IT) is an all-encompassing term that refers to the electronic storage, retrieval, and manipulation of data; its conversion into human-usable form (i.e., information); and its transmission from one point to another.

        1) The Information Technology Association of America has defined IT as "the study, design, development, application, implementation, support or management of computer-based information systems."

    b. For the purposes of the CPA exam, IT is a synonym for computers, computer networks, and the use of computer programs (i.e., software).

Block Diagram of Information Technology

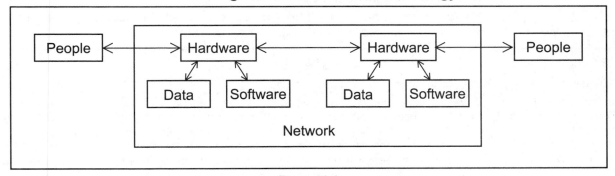

Figure 11-1

2. **Definitions**

    a. **Hardware** is any physical item that comprises a computer system. This could refer to the monitor, keyboard, mouse, microchips, disk drives, etc. In other words, hardware is anything in information technology that can be touched.

    b. **Software** is a combination of computer programs that manipulate data and instruct the hardware on what to do. Software provides instructions to the computer hardware and may also serve as input to other pieces of software. Software is intangible and is anything in the computer system that is not hardware. Examples are Microsoft Word, CCH's TaxWise, or IDEA Data Analysis Software.

    c.   **Network** is a collection of hardware devices that are interconnected so they can communicate among themselves. This allows different hardware to share software and communicate data. The Internet is an example of a network, but many offices have intranets where office computers can communicate with other office computers.

    d.   **Data** are information, not instructions, that are stored in hardware. Data may be financial sales data or could be calculations provided by a software program.

    e.   **People** refers to anyone who uses hardware (i.e., a computer). This could be an IT professional, an accountant, or a young adult who is surfing the Internet.

3.   **Business Information Systems (BIS)**

    a.   A business information system is any combination of hardware, software, data, people, and procedures employed to pursue an organizational objective.

        1)   The first generation of business information systems served the finance and accounting functions, since computing lends itself so readily to quantitative tasks.

        2)   Business information systems have evolved to serve the needs of users at all levels of the organizational hierarchy and, with the advent of fast telecommunications, even users outside the organization.

    b.   Business information systems have three strategic roles:

        1)   Support business processes and operations, such as creating purchase orders.

        2)   Support decision making, such as creating an accounts receivable aging report so a manager can ascertain if a customer's credit is still acceptable.

        3)   Support managers in planning for the future, such as the development of long-range planning and strategies.

    c.   Any information system performs four major tasks:

        1)   **Input.** The system must acquire (capture) data from within or outside of the entity.

        2)   **Processing/Transformation.** Raw materials (data) are converted into knowledge useful for decision making (information).

        3)   **Output.** The ultimate purpose of the system is communication of results to internal or external users.

        4)   **Storage.** Before, during, and after processing, data must be temporarily or permanently stored, for example, in files or databases.

EXAMPLE

All four tasks can be identified in the following description:

A firm collects sales and expense data in its automated accounting system. At year end, adjusting and closing entries are added to the system, and the data are processed into a special format from which the annual report is produced. The firm owns a database server on which all of its transactions and formatted financial statements are kept.

---

    d.   Stakeholders in business information systems are those who affect, or are affected by, the output of the information system. They have an interest in the system's effective and efficient functioning.

        1)   Hence, they include users such as managers, employees, suppliers, and customers.

4.   **Electronic Communication (Networks)**

    a.   Computer-based systems have been woven into almost every facet of the modern organization, from back-office functions, such as human resources and payroll, to instantaneous customer order placement over the Internet.

    b.   The use of high-speed communication networks, such as the Internet, has enabled the growth of the truly global organization.

       1)   Markets can be tapped on any part of the globe.

       2)   Customer support and supply chain functions can be performed around the clock by personnel located on different continents.

    c.   Organizations can make use of social networking sites, such as **Facebook** and **Twitter**, to disseminate information and gather customer feedback.

    d.   **RSS**, which stands for rich site summary, allows the content of a website that changes often to be downloaded and stored automatically to a user's computer. This saves the user the need to constantly revisit the site to get the latest information.

    e.   The newest stage of evolution is **cloud computing**, where organizations are relieved of the need to manage the storage of both applications and data since all the software and data they need are located on the Internet.

       1)   Cloud computing is defined as a standardized IT capability (services, software, infrastructure) delivered via the Internet in a pay-per-use, self-service way.

       2)   Advantages of cloud computing include lower infrastructure investments and maintenance costs, increased mobility, and lower personnel and utility costs.

       3)   Disadvantages of cloud computing include less control than there would be over an internal IT department, more difficulty ensuring data security and privacy, and less compatability with existing tools and software.

Stop and review! You have completed the outline for this subunit. Study multiple-choice question 1 on page 292.

11.2 TRANSACTION PROCESSING

1.   **Overview**

    a.   The most common type of system used in the business information systems (BIS) environment is a **transaction processing system (TPS)**.

       1)   A transaction is a single discrete event that can be stored in an information system.

       2)   Examples include the movement of raw materials from storage to production, the issuance of a purchase order, the recording of a new employee's personal data, or the sale of merchandise.

    b.   A TPS captures the fundamental data that reflect the economic life of an organization. An example of a TPS is an **accounting information system (AIS)**.

2.   **Two Modes of Transaction Processing**

    a.   The phrase "transaction processing modes" refers to the way in which a system is updated with new data. The methods in use can be classified into one of two categories: batch or online.

    b.   **Batch Processing**

       1)   In this mode, transactions are accumulated and submitted to the computer as a single "batch." In the early days of computers, this was the only way a set of transactions could be processed.

       2)   Inherent in batch processing is a **time delay** between the batching of the transactions and the updating of the records. Sometimes this delay can be as long as overnight.

          a)   Thus, errors in a batch processing system caused by incorrect programs or data may not be detected immediately.

c.   **Online Processing**

1)   In this mode, the computer processes each transaction individually as the user enters it. The user is in direct communication with the computer and gets **immediate processing/feedback** on whether the transaction was accepted or not.

a)   A common example is an accounts payable system in which a payables clerk can enter each individual invoice as (s)he verifies the paperwork.

2)   In online systems, having the latest information available at all times is crucial so that users can make immediate decisions. A common example is an airline reservation system, which is constantly updated from moment to moment and must be available all the time.

a)   These are called **real-time systems**. A thermostat is another example, constantly monitoring the temperature in the room and engaging the heating or cooling system accordingly.

d.   Many applications use combined batch and online modes.

1)   In such systems, users continuously enter transactions in online mode throughout the workday, collecting them in batches. The computer can then take advantage of the efficiencies of batch mode overnight when there are fewer users logged on to the system.

e.   The use of batch processing tends to be restricted to TPSs and systems that get their input from TPSs. Systems that support decision making are almost always of the online type.

3.   **IT Infrastructure**

a.   Centralization. During the early days of computer processing, computers were very large and expensive, and only organizations such as large banks and governmental agencies could afford them.

1)   As a result, all processing and systems development were done at a single, central location. Users connected to the mainframe via "dumb terminals," i.e., simple monitor-and-keyboard combinations with no processing power of their own.

2)   Since hardware, information security, and data integrity functions were located in one office, economies of scale were achieved and controls were strong.

b.   Decentralization. As the data processing industry evolved, computers became smaller (so-called minicomputers), and branch offices of large organizations could have their own.

1)   Each branch could store and process its data onsite, transmitting the results overnight to the mainframe at the home office. This was an early form of distributed processing in which parts of an organization's computer operations could be performed in separate physical locations.

Centralization Advantages	Decentralization Advantages
• Better and more efficient security	• Remote locations have increased accountability over their data and processes
• Consistent processing because it occurs at a set time in one location	• Remote locations can get data without concern of bottlenecks of traffic over networks

Stop and review! You have completed the outline for this subunit. Study multiple-choice questions 2 through 11 beginning on page 292.

11.3 APPLICATION PROCESSING PHASES

This subunit explains how data is entered into a transaction processing system (TPS), specifically the accounting information system (AIS). As a future CPA who will hold a license with the ability to perform an audit, you will need to understand how data is entered into a TPS (especially the AIS) as well as how the data in a TPS is processed.

1. **Data Capture**

   a. Data capture is the process of entering data into an information system. Two methods of capture are identical to their respective processing modes, discussed in item 2. in the previous subunit.

      1) **Batch entry** involves loading a group of records at one time.

      2) **Online entry** involves entering single records, usually in an interactive environment where the user gets immediate feedback.

   b. One type of online entry for capturing input is the optical scanner, such as that used in retail checkout lines (called **point-of-sale**, or POS, transactions). Besides instant updating of accounting and inventory records, POS transaction systems can help management

      1) Identify and respond to trends,

      2) Make sales forecasts,

      3) Determine which products are or are not in demand,

      4) Improve customer service,

      5) Target products and promotions to customers with different demographic traits, and

      6) Evaluate the effects of promotions, including coupons.

2. **Processing**

   a. Processing is the act of converting raw data into usable information. This is performed by the combination of hardware and software that makes up the organization's IT infrastructure.

3. **Types of Data Files**

   a. An understanding of the application processing phases requires an explanation of the two types of computer data files, **master files** and **transaction files**. These types are applicable whether the files are stored on tape, disk, flash drive, or other media and whether they are "flat" files or structured databases.

   b. A master file may be fairly static or very volatile.

      1) An example of a fairly static master file is an authorized vendor file containing each vendor's number, name, and address.

EXAMPLE							
Authorized Vendor Master File							
vendor_num	vendor_name	address_1	city	state	zip	credit_limit	last_updated
0187634	Neyland's Nuts	101 Dandridge Av	Knoxville	TN	37915	$10,000	07/19/2010
1264428	Basic Barbecue	2224 Blossom St	Columbia	SC	29201	$50,000	06/25/2008
4552170	Bayou Bakery	10118 Florida St	Baton Rouge	LA	70801	$15,000	03/04/2008
5006321	Bulldog Barcoding	9085 Old West Point Rd	Starkville	MS	39759	$5,000	10/01/2007
8981463	Razorback Restaurant Supply	3510 West Maple St	Fayetteville	AR	72701	$20,000	07/01/2009

2) An example of a volatile master file is a general ledger file, which at any given moment holds the balances of all accounts in the ledger.

EXAMPLE

General Ledger Master File

account_num	account_name	balance	last_transaction_posted
A1209	Cash	$89,580.22	06/10/2011
G6573	Accounts Receivable	$72,024.57	06/10/2011
J0226	Accounts Payable	$(15,156.89)	06/10/2011
K4411	Sales	$(100,558.60)	06/10/2011
M2020	Cost of Goods Sold	$70,005.64	06/10/2011
Y3577	Administrative Expenses	$21,110.33	06/10/2011

---

3) Volatility is the relative frequency with which the records in a file are added, deleted, or changed during a period.

c. A transaction file contains the data that reflect ongoing business activity, such as individual purchases from vendors or general journal entries.

EXAMPLE

General Journal Transaction File

transaction	transaction_date	debit_acct	debit_amt	credit_acct	credit_amt
GL5261904	06/10/2011	A1209	$1,001.56	G6573	$(1,001.56)
GL5261905	06/10/2011	G6573	$660.48	K4411	$(660.48)
GL5261906	06/10/2011	G6573	$898.15	K4411	$(898.15)
GL5261907	06/10/2011	Y3577	$150.75	J0226	$(150.75)

---

d. Transaction files and master files are constantly interacting.

1) Before an invoice can be paid, the payables transaction file must be matched against the vendor master file to see whether the vendor really exists.

2) The general ledger balance file must be updated every day by posting from the general journal transaction file.

4. **REA (Resources, Events, Agents) Processing**

a. REA contrasts with the traditional TPS that uses double entry (debit and credit) by using single entry.

b. It uses a relational database to store and process transactions.

c. Each transaction (event) is stored in a table chronologically and linked to other tables with the details of the transaction (resources, agents, or other attributes). For example, a sales event would be recorded in the sales table and linked to a customer table, inventory table, salesperson table, etc.

d. Processing is accomplished through queries to the tables. Examples include calculating (1) the sales for a period by summing the amounts in the sales table from the beginning of the period to the end of the period and (2) the accounts receivable balance for a period end by summing all sales from the sales table and subtracting the sum of all receipts from the accounts receivable cash collections table.

  e. Advantages include the following:

    1) Debits and credits are not considered.

    2) No general ledger is maintained since all balances are calculated through queries.

    3) Ad hoc reports are easily produced. For example, a report listing all customers who purchased a particular product between certain dates can be produced with a simple query.

  f. A major disadvantage is implementation cost because it is usually so high that it is prohibitive. Reasons for this include the following:

    1) Considerable computer storage and processing power are needed.

    2) Many accountants and auditors are not familiar with REA, so training needs are high and acceptance may be low.

5. **Reporting**

  a. **Reporting in General**

    1) The term "report" in this context does not necessarily refer to a printed hard copy. Advances in technology allow for report viewing on a computer screen or personal data assistant with the option of printing granted to the user.

  b. **Periodic Routine Reports**

    1) Certain reports are required at regular intervals. Examples are monthly trial balances and ledger summaries to assist in closing the books.

  c. **On-Demand and Ad Hoc Reports**

    1) Systems can be designed so that users can generate reports at times they specify. An on-demand report is one whose design is programmed into the system. The user specifies the date and time the report is run.

    2) Advances in processing power and software have given users the ability to design their own reports "on the fly."

      a) These ad hoc (sometimes called "quick-and-dirty") reports can be designed to the user's own specifications without the involvement of IT personnel. Database queries are a common example.

  d. **Exception Reports**

    1) It is a common practice after daily processing to generate reports of transactions or activities that lie outside predefined boundaries. The appropriate personnel can then follow up and determine the reasons for these exceptions.

    2) Examples are batches whose debits and credits do not match and instances of multiple unsuccessful attempts to access the network (which may indicate hacking).

  e. **Electronic Distribution of Reports**

    1) The advent of email and other forms of digital communication has greatly enhanced the ability of organizations to distribute reports. Rather than wait for paper copies to be hand delivered, reports can be sent digitally to the appropriate personnel. This is sometimes referred to as **push reporting**.

  f. **Audit Trail**

    1) An audit trail of activities is a crucial part of monitoring security over a system. The audit trail includes not only the reports described above, but also such reports as logs of system sign-in and sign-out times to monitor who was doing what on the system.

Stop and review! You have completed the outline for this subunit. Study multiple-choice questions 12 through 17 beginning on page 295.

11.4 SYSTEMS THAT SUPPORT ROUTINE PROCESSES

 This subunit will acquaint you with other types of business information systems (BISs) used in the corporate environment to perform transaction type processes. As a CPA candidate, your knowledge level is most likely highest with the accounting information systems (AIS). However, there are many other types of information systems that comprise the BIS and help corporations perform their day-to-day activities. As a future CPA who will hold a license with the ability to perform an audit, you will need to understand how each of these transaction information systems work and how they interrelate to each other and BISs.

1.   **Management Information System (MIS)**

   a.   A MIS typically receives input from a transaction processing system, aggregates it, then reports it in a format useful by middle management in running the business. For this reason, MISs are often classified by function or activity, such as the following:

       1)   Accounting: general ledger, accounts receivable, accounts payable, payroll processing, fixed asset management, and tax accounting; other aspects of accounting information systems are described in item 2. below.

       2)   Finance: capital budgeting, operational budgeting, cash management

       3)   Manufacturing: production planning, cost control, quality control

       4)   Logistics: inventory management, transportation planning

       5)   Marketing: sales analysis, forecasting

       6)   Human resources: projecting payroll, projecting benefits obligations, employment-level planning, employee evaluation tracking

   b.   These single-function systems, often called stovepipe systems because of their limited focus, are gradually being replaced by integrated systems that link multiple business activities across the enterprise. The most comprehensive integrated system is termed an enterprise resource planning (ERP) system (discussed in item 3. below and on the next 2 pages).

2.   **Accounting Information System (AIS)**

   a.   An AIS is a subsystem of a MIS that processes routine, highly structured financial and transactional data relevant to managerial as well as financial accounting. An AIS is concerned with

       1)   Transactions with external parties (e.g., customers, suppliers, governments, owners, and creditors) reflected in financial statements prepared in conformity with GAAP, and

       2)   The internal activities recorded in the cost accounting system and the preparation of related reports and analyses (e.g., production reports, pro forma financial statements, budgets, and cost-volume-profit analyses).

3.   **Enterprise Resource Planning (ERP)**

   a.   ERP is the latest phase in the development of computerized systems for managing organizational resources. ERP is intended to integrate enterprise-wide information systems by creating one database linked to all of an organization's applications.

       1)   ERP subsumes traditional MISs.

2) Figure 11-2 contrasts the less integrated MIS with the more integrated ERP system.

Figure 11-2

b. In the traditional ERP system, subsystems share data and coordinate their activities. Thus, if marketing receives an order, it can quickly verify that inventory is sufficient to notify shipping to process the order.

1) Otherwise, production is notified to manufacture more of the product, with a consequent automatic adjustment of output schedules.

2) If materials are inadequate for this purpose, the system will issue a purchase order.

3) If more labor is needed, human resources will be instructed to reassign or hire employees.

4) The foregoing business processes (and others) should interact seamlessly in an ERP system.

c. The subsystems in a traditional ERP system are internal to the organization. Hence, they are often called **back-office functions**. The information produced is principally (but not exclusively) intended for internal use by the organization's managers.

d. The current generation of ERP software has added **front-office functions**. These connect the organization with customers, suppliers, owners, creditors, and strategic allies (e.g., the members of a trading community or other business association).

1) Moreover, the current generation of ERP software also provides the capability for smooth (and instant) interaction with the business processes of external parties.

2) A newer ERP system's integration with the firm's back-office functions enables supply-chain management (SCM), customer relationship management (CRM), and partner relationship management (PRM).

e.   The disadvantages of ERP are its extent and complexity, which make implementation difficult and costly.

Background

Because ERP software is costly and complex, it is usually installed only by the largest enterprises, although mid-size organizations are increasingly likely to buy ERP software. Major ERP packages include R/3 from SAP AG and Oracle e-Business Suite, PeopleSoft, and JD Edwards EnterpriseOne, all from Oracle Corp.

Background

The tremendous variety of forms that information systems can take and the diverse needs of users have led to the concept of information resources management (IRM), which takes a global view of the information holdings and needs of an organization. This view is promoted by the Information Resources Management Association of Hershey, PA (www.irma-international.org).

Stop and review! You have completed the outline for this subunit. Study multiple-choice questions 18 through 24 beginning on page 296.

11.5 SYSTEMS THAT SUPPORT DECISION MAKING

 This subunit will acquaint you with information systems that support the decision-making process. In contrast to transaction-type processes, these types of programs assist humans with making decisions. As a future CPA who will hold a license with the ability to perform an audit, you will need to understand how these decision-making systems work.

1.   **Data Warehouse**

   a.   A data warehouse is a central database for transaction-level data from more than one of the organization's transaction processing system (TPS).

      1)   A data warehouse is strictly a query-and-reporting system. It is not used to carry on the enterprise's routine operations.

      2)   Rather, a data warehouse gets its input from the various TPSs in the organization.

   b.   Data warehouses store a large quantity of data and require that the transaction records be converted to a standard format.

      1)   The ability of the data warehouse to relate data from multiple systems makes it a very powerful tool for ad hoc queries.

      2)   The data warehouse can also be accessed using analytical and graphics tools, a technique called **online analytical processing (OLAP)**.

         a)   An important component of OLAP is drill-down analysis, in which the user is first presented with the data at an aggregate level and then can display successive levels of detail for a given date, region, product, etc., until finally reaching the original transactions.

    c.   A data warehouse enables **data mining**, i.e., the search for unexpected relationships among data.

          1)   The classic example of the use of data mining was the discovery by convenience stores that diapers and beer often appeared on the same sales transaction in the late evening.

Data Warehouse and Data Mining

Figure 11-3

2. **Decision Support System (DSS)**

    a.   A DSS is an interactive system that is useful in solving semistructured problems, that is, those with a structured portion (which the computer can solve) and an unstructured portion (which requires the manager's insight and judgment).

          1)   This point requires emphasis: A DSS does not automate a decision. It examines the relevant data and presents a manager with choices between alternative courses of action.

b.   A DSS has three basic components:

1)   The **database** consists of the raw data that are relevant to the decision. In this context, a data warehouse is very useful. The data can come from both within and outside of the organization.

2)   The **model** is the set of equations, comparisons, graphs, conditions, assumptions, etc., into which the data will be fed.

3)   The **dialog** is the user interface that allows the user to specify the appropriate model and the particular set of data to which the model should be applied.

Decision Support System

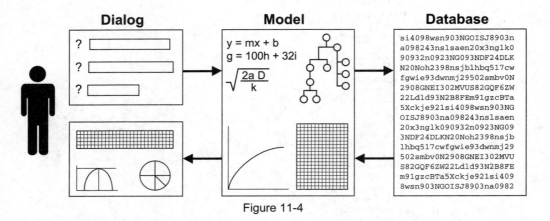

Figure 11-4

EXAMPLE

A manufacturer wishes to improve its inventory management.

- The firm creates a database of the past 5 years of inventory and purchasing history, along with projections for future production, transportation costs, and forecasts of the prices of raw materials.

- The firm creates a model containing the formula for economic order quantity, an algorithm for calculating safety stock, and graphs of inventory levels over time.

- The firm creates a dialog screen allowing the decision maker to specify time periods, particular products, and the variables for displaying on graphs.

---

c.   A group DSS (GDSS) aids in the collaborative solution of unstructured problems. Users in separate areas of the organization can specify parameters pertinent to their functions.

3.   **Artificial Intelligence (AI)**

a.   AI is computer software designed to perceive, reason, and understand.

1)   Historically, computer software works through a series of if/then conditions in which every operation has exactly two possible outcomes (yes/no, on/off, true/false, one/zero).

a)   Human reasoning, on the other hand, is extremely complex, based on deduction, induction, intuition, emotion, and biochemistry, resulting in a range of possible outcomes.

2)   AI attempts to imitate human decision making, which hinges on this combination of knowledge and intuition (i.e., remembering relationships between variables based on experience).

3) The advantage of AI in a business environment is that IT systems

    a) Can work 24 hours a day

    b) Will not become ill, die, or be hired away

    c) Are extremely fast processors of data, especially if numerous rules (procedures) must be evaluated

b. There are several types of AI:

1) **Neural networks** are a collection of processing elements working together to process information much like the human brain, including learning from previous situations and generalizing concepts.

2) **Case-based reasoning systems** use a process similar to that used by humans to learn from previous, similar experiences.

3) **Rule-based expert systems** function on the basis of set rules to arrive at an answer. These cannot be changed by the system itself. They must be changed by an outside source (i.e., the computer programmer).

4) **Intelligent agents** are programs that apply a built-in or learned knowledge base to execute a specific, repetitive, and predictable task, for example, showing a computer user how to perform a task or searching websites for particular financial information.

5) An **expert system** is an interactive system that attempts to imitate the reasoning of a human expert in a given field. It is useful for addressing unstructured problems when there is a local shortage of human experts.

4. **Executive Support System (ESS)**

a. At the strategic level, high-level decision makers get the information they need to set, and monitor progress toward, the organization's long-term objectives from an ESS, also called an executive information system (EIS).

1) An ESS assists senior management in making nonroutine decisions, such as identifying problems and opportunities.

2) An ESS also provides information about the activities of competitors.

b. The information in an ESS comes from sources both within and outside the organization, including information from nontraditional computer sources.

1) An ESS should have the ability to provide overviews, often in graphical format, or to drill down to the detailed data.

2) An ESS can be used on computers of all sizes.

5. **Business Intelligence (BI)**

a. Business intelligence is what gives upper management the information it needs to know where the organization is and how to steer it in the intended direction. BI gives an executive immediate information about an organization's critical success factors.

1) BI is replacing the older ESS model.

b. BI tools display information about the organization as bar graphs, pie charts, columnar reports, or any other format considered appropriate to upper management's decision making. These displays are sometimes grouped by a particular executive's needs into what is termed a **digital dashboard**.

1) Stock price trend, sales by region and date, on-time delivery performance, instantaneous cash balances, and profitability by customer are possible metrics to be included.

c. BI tools use data both from within and outside the organization.

Stop and review! You have completed the outline for this subunit. Study multiple-choice questions 25 through 30 beginning on page 299.

QUESTIONS

11.1 Role of Information Systems in the Modern Organization

1. The four major tasks that any system must perform are

A. Input, transformation, output, and storage.

B. Input, backup, output, and storage.

C. Input, transformation, output, and maintenance.

D. Input, transformation, storage, and feedback.

Answer (A) is correct.

REQUIRED: The four major tasks that any system must perform.

DISCUSSION: The four major tasks that any system must perform are input, transformation, output, and storage.

11.2 Transaction Processing

2. Batch processing

A. Is not used by most businesses because it reduces the audit trail.

B. Allows users to inquire about groups of information contained in the system.

C. Accumulates transaction records into groups for processing against the master file on a delayed basis.

D. Can only be performed on a centralized basis.

Answer (C) is correct.

REQUIRED: The true statement about batch processing.

DISCUSSION: Batch processing is the accumulation and grouping of transactions for processing on a delayed basis. The batch approach is suitable for applications that can be processed against the master file at intervals and involve large volumes of similar items, such as payroll, sales, inventory, and billing.

Answer (A) is incorrect. Batch processing provides as much of an audit trail as any computerized operation. Answer (B) is incorrect. Batch processing refers to the input of data, not inquiry. Answer (D) is incorrect. Batch processing can also be performed on a decentralized basis.

3. An interactive system environment is best characterized by

A. Data files with records arranged sequentially.

B. The processing of groups of data at regular intervals.

C. Sorting the transaction file before processing.

D. The processing of data immediately on input.

Answer (D) is correct.

REQUIRED: The characteristic of an interactive system environment.

DISCUSSION: In an interactive (inquiry) system, users employ interactive devices to converse directly with the system. The system is characterized by online entry and processing, direct access, and time sharing.

Answer (A) is incorrect. An interactive system requires direct-access files. Answer (B) is incorrect. An interactive system permits immediate, online processing of single transactions. Answer (C) is incorrect. The transaction file need not be sorted before processing.

4. Information processing made possible by a network of computers dispersed throughout an organization is called

A. Online processing.

B. Interactive processing.

C. Time sharing.

D. Distributed data processing.

Answer (D) is correct.

REQUIRED: The method of information processing by dispersed computers.

DISCUSSION: Distributed processing is characterized by a merger of computer and telecommunications technology. Distributed systems permit not only remote access to a computer but also the performance of local processing at local sites. The result is greater flexibility in systems design and the possibility of an optimal distribution of processing tasks.

Answer (A) is incorrect. Online processing is a method of processing data that permits both immediate posting (updating) and inquiry of master files as transactions occur. Answer (B) is incorrect. Interactive processing is a method of processing data immediately upon input. Answer (C) is incorrect. Time sharing is the processing of a program by the CPU until an input or output operation is required. In time sharing, the CPU spends a fixed amount of time on each program.

5. A new purchasing system for just-in-time production requirements has been proposed. Users want access to current master file information at all times. To satisfy user needs, master file changes should be implemented with

A. Periodic entry with subsequent batch processing.

B. Periodic entry with immediate batch processing.

C. Online entry with subsequent batch processing.

D. Online entry with immediate processing.

Answer (D) is correct.
REQUIRED: The appropriate system for JIT production.
DISCUSSION: JIT production attempts to minimize inventory by more closely coordinating deliveries of needed materials and production. Thus, inventory data must be current. Online entry with immediate (real-time) processing gives users current master file information because changes are entered and applied to the master file as they occur. However, check printing can still occur in batch mode.
Answer (A) is incorrect. Periodic entry and batch processing do not permit the immediate updating required by JIT production. Answer (B) is incorrect. Periodic entry does not permit immediate updating, and "immediate batch processing" is a contradiction in terms. Answer (C) is incorrect. Online entry and subsequent batch processing do not permit the immediate updating required by JIT production.

6. The concept of timeliness of data availability is most relevant to

A. Computerized systems.

B. Payroll systems.

C. Manual systems.

D. Online systems.

Answer (D) is correct.
REQUIRED: The relevance of the concept of timeliness of data availability.
DISCUSSION: An online processing system is in direct communication with the computer, giving it the capability to handle transactions as they are entered. An online system permits both immediate posting (updating) and inquiry of master files as transactions occur. In an online system, data are immediately available to users upon entry.
Answer (A) is incorrect. Timeliness is not necessarily an element of a computerized system. Answer (B) is incorrect. Timeliness is not necessarily an element of a payroll system. Answer (C) is incorrect. Timeliness is not necessarily an element of a manual system.

7. The relationship between online, real-time database systems and batch processing systems is that

A. A firm will have only one processing mode because a single computer cannot do both.

B. A firm will not use batch processing if it has a large computer.

C. A firm may use both processing modes concurrently.

D. A firm will always prefer an online, real-time processing system because batch processing is slow.

Answer (C) is correct.
REQUIRED: The relationship between online, real-time database systems and batch processing systems.
DISCUSSION: Firms may find it beneficial to incorporate both processing modes into one system. A database may be established for information that must be obtained quickly, for instance, a sales processing system in which credit information must be available to sales personnel on an ongoing basis. However, other processing requirements may take advantage of the speed and control provided in a batch processing system. For example, payroll transactions may be processed quickly and efficiently in a batch mode.
Answer (A) is incorrect. One computer can operate in both modes. Answer (B) is incorrect. Firms with large computers find it both cost effective and efficient to group transactions and process them periodically. Answer (D) is incorrect. A firm will not automatically prefer an online, real-time system. When transactions, e.g., payroll, can be conveniently grouped, processing is extremely fast and efficient in a batch mode.

8. Devices that are used only to perform sequential file processing will **not** permit

A. The use of a database structure.

B. Data to be edited in an offline mode.

C. Batch processing to be initiated from a terminal.

D. Data to be edited on a real-time basis.

Answer (D) is correct.
REQUIRED: The activity not permitted by devices used only for sequential file processing.
DISCUSSION: In an online, real-time system, direct (random), not sequential, access to files is required. As each transaction is entered, it is edited (validated). Files can then be immediately updated to reflect that transaction. Sequential file access is typical of (but not required in) batch processing.
Answer (A) is incorrect. A database can be used with direct or sequential file access. Answer (B) is incorrect. Separate conversion and editing runs are usually performed in an offline mode when sequential processing is used. Answer (C) is incorrect. Remote batch processing of sequential files is not unusual.

9. In traditional information systems, computer operators are generally responsible for backing up software and data files on a regular basis. In distributed or cooperative systems, ensuring that adequate backups are taken is the responsibility of

A. User management.

B. Systems programmers.

C. Data entry clerks.

D. Data librarians.

Answer (A) is correct.

REQUIRED: The persons responsible for ensuring that adequate backups are taken in distributed or cooperative systems.

DISCUSSION: In distributed or cooperative systems, the responsibility for ensuring that adequate backups are taken is the responsibility of user management. The systems are under the control of users, not a central information processing department.

Answer (B) is incorrect. Distributed environments have no systems programmers comparable to those at central sites for traditional systems. Answer (C) is incorrect. Distributed environments may not have data entry clerks. Users typically perform their own data entry. Answer (D) is incorrect. In distributed environments, there are no data librarians.

10. The system that permits the computers in a distributed network to share the use of another end-user's application program is

A. Electronic data interchange.

B. Interactive processing.

C. Executive support system.

D. Cooperative processing.

Answer (D) is correct.

REQUIRED: The system that permits the computers in a distributed processing network to share the use of another end-user's application program.

DISCUSSION: Cooperative processing is a system whereby computers in a distributed network can share the use of application programs belonging to another end user. The system assigns different machines the functions they perform best in executing a transaction-based application program. For example, a personal computer might be used to enter and validate data for the application, and a server might handle file input and output.

Answer (A) is incorrect. EDI is the communication of electronic documents directly from a computer in one entity to a computer in another entity. Answer (B) is incorrect. Interactive processing does not allow for the use of another end-user's application programs. Answer (C) is incorrect. An executive support system focuses on strategic objectives and gives immediate information about an organization's critical success factors.

11. An insurance company that has adopted cooperative processing is planning to implement new standard software in all its local offices. The new software has a fast response time, is very user friendly, and was developed with extensive user involvement. The new software captures, consolidates, edits, validates, and finally transfers standardized transaction data to the headquarters server. Local managers, who were satisfied with existing locally written personal computer applications, opposed the new approach because they anticipated

A. Increased workloads.

B. Centralization of all processing tasks.

C. More accountability.

D. Less computer equipment.

Answer (C) is correct.

REQUIRED: The reason for opposing introduction of new software.

DISCUSSION: Cooperative processing implies a tighter coupling than previously existed between the personal computers and the server. The result may threaten the managers' perceived autonomy by increasing the control exercised by headquarters and therefore the accountability of local managers.

Answer (A) is incorrect. Given that only existing systems would be converted, the transaction volume would likely remain relatively constant. Answer (B) is incorrect. In a cooperative processing environment, different computers execute different parts of an application. Answer (D) is incorrect. Compared with mainframe-only processing, cooperative processing typically requires more computer equipment at distributed locations.

11.3 Application Processing Phases

12. A file containing relatively long-term information used as a source of reference and periodically updated with detail is termed a

A. Transaction file.

B. Record layout.

C. Master file.

D. Dump.

Answer (C) is correct.
REQUIRED: The file containing relatively long-term information.
DISCUSSION: A master file containing relatively long-term information, such as an inventory file listing the part number, description, quantities on hand, quantities on order, etc., is used in a file processing run. Transactions are processed against the master file, thus periodically updating it.
Answer (A) is incorrect. A transaction file (detail file) contains current transaction information used to update the master file, such as the number of items shipped to be removed from inventory. Answer (B) is incorrect. A record layout is a representation of the format of the records on the file. It shows the position and length of the fields in the file. Answer (D) is incorrect. A dump is a listing of the contents of memory.

13. A commonly used measure of the activity in a master file during a specified time period is

A. Volatility.

B. The index ratio.

C. The frequency ratio.

D. The volume ratio.

Answer (A) is correct.
REQUIRED: The commonly used measure of the activity in a master file.
DISCUSSION: File volatility is the relative frequency with which records are added, deleted, or changed during a specified period.

14. At a remote computer center, management installed an automated scheduling system to load data files and execute programs at specific times during the day. The best approach for verifying that the scheduling system performs as intended is to

A. Analyze job activity with a queuing model to determine workload characteristics.

B. Simulate the resource usage and compare the results with actual results of operations.

C. Use library management software to track changes to successive versions of applications programs.

D. Audit job accounting data for file accesses and job initiation/termination messages.

Answer (D) is correct.
REQUIRED: The best approach for verifying that the scheduling system performs as intended.
DISCUSSION: Job accounting data analysis permits programmatic examination of job initiation and termination, record counts, and processing times. Auditing job accounting data for file accesses and job initiation/termination messages will reveal whether the right data files were loaded/dismounted at the right times and the right programs were initiated/terminated at the right times.
Answer (A) is incorrect. Analyzing job activity with a queuing model to determine workload characteristics gives information about resource usage but does not verify that the system actually functioned as intended. Answer (B) is incorrect. A simulation helps management characterize the workload but does not verify that the system actually functioned as intended. Answer (C) is incorrect. Using library management software to track changes to successive versions of application programs permits control of production and test versions but does not verify that the system actually functioned as intended.

15. Management is concerned that data uploaded from a personal computer to the company's server may be erroneous. Which of the following controls would best address this issue?

A. Server data should be backed up on a regular basis.

B. Two persons should be present at the personal computer when it is uploading data.

C. The data uploaded to the server should be subject to the same edits and validation routines that online data entry would require.

D. The users should be required to review a random sample of processed data.

Answer (C) is correct.
REQUIRED: The best control to prevent uploading erroneous data from a personal computer to the company's mainframe system in batch processing.
DISCUSSION: Data that are uploaded or downloaded are subject to significant risk. Personal computers are more vulnerable than servers to unauthorized access, and uploaded or downloaded data are subject to alteration on the personal computer. Furthermore, an uploaded file may replace an existing file without being subjected to standard edit and validation procedures.
Answer (A) is incorrect. This practice is a good control, but it does not address the issue of data-upload integrity. Backups cannot prevent or detect data-upload problems. They can only help correct data errors caused by a poor upload. Answer (B) is incorrect. This control may be somewhat helpful in preventing fraud in data uploads, but it is of little use in preventing errors. Answer (D) is incorrect. The error already could have caused erroneous reports and management decisions. Having users try to find errors in uploaded data is costly.

16. Using standard procedures developed by information center personnel, staff members download specific subsets of financial and operating data as they need it. The staff members analyze the data on their own personal computers and share results with each other. Over time, the staff members learn to modify the standard procedures to get subsets of financial and operating data that were not accessible through the original procedures. The greatest risk associated with this situation is that

   A. The data obtained might be incomplete or lack currency.

   B. The data definition might become outdated.

   C. The server data might be corrupted by staff members' updates.

   D. Repeated downloading might fill up storage space on staff members' personal computers.

Answer (A) is correct.
   REQUIRED: The risk associated with downloading additional subsets of financial data.
   DISCUSSION: Staff members may not be aware of how often they need to download data to keep it current, or whether their queries, especially the ones they modified, obtain all the necessary information. Users may employ faulty parameters or logic. Poorly planned queries may also use computing resources inefficiently.
   Answer (B) is incorrect. Downloading data does not affect the data definitions. Answer (C) is incorrect. Staff members are downloading, not uploading, so the staff members are unlikely to corrupt server data. Answer (D) is incorrect. The downloading procedures could replace previously downloaded files on the staff members' personal computers.

17. Advanced electronic point-of-sale (POS) systems allow instant capture and transmission of information for which purposes?

   I.   Instant updating of accounting records
   II. Accumulation of marketing information
   III. Tracking of information about specific customers
   IV. Facilitation of warehousing

   A. I and II only.

   B. III and IV only.

   C. I, II, and III only.

   D. I, II, III, and IV.

Answer (D) is correct.
   REQUIRED: The functions of an electronic POS system.
   DISCUSSION: An electronic POS system may update and analyze the perpetual inventory records for each outlet. It may also perform other accounting tasks, such as crediting revenue accounts and debiting cash, accounts receivable, and cost of goods sold. Moreover, a POS system may (1) provide marketing information to identify and respond to trends; (2) make sales forecasts; (3) determine which products are in demand; (4) improve customer service; (5) target products and promotions to customers with different demographic traits; and (6) evaluate the effects of promotions, including coupons. Another function of a POS system is to record personal and transactional information about specific customers, including tracking of warranties, deposits, rentals, progressive discounts, and special pricing. Still another function is use of bar coding in association with the stocking and warehousing functions to reduce the costs of data entry, including the effects of human error.

11.4 Systems that Support Routine Processes

18. An accounting information system (AIS) must include certain source documents in order to control purchasing and accounts payable. For a manufacturing organization, the best set of documents should include

   A. Purchase requisitions, purchase orders, inventory reports of goods needed, and vendor invoices.

   B. Purchase orders, receiving reports, and inventory reports of goods needed.

   C. Purchase orders, receiving reports, and vendor invoices.

   D. Purchase requisitions, purchase orders, receiving reports, and vendor invoices.

Answer (D) is correct.
   REQUIRED: The best set of documents to be included in an AIS to control purchasing and accounts payable.
   DISCUSSION: An AIS is a subsystem of a management information system that processes financial and transactional data relevant to managerial and financial accounting. The AIS supports operations by collecting and sorting data about an organization's transactions. An AIS is concerned not only with external parties but also with the internal activities needed for management decision making at all levels. An AIS is best suited to solve problems when reporting requirements are well defined. A manufacturer has well-defined reporting needs for routine information about purchasing and payables. Purchase requisitions document user department needs, and purchase orders provide evidence that purchase transactions were appropriately authorized. A formal receiving procedure segregates the purchasing and receiving functions and establishes the quantity, quality, and timeliness of goods received. Vendor invoices establish the liability for payment and should be compared with the foregoing documents.
   Answer (A) is incorrect. Receiving reports should be included. Answer (B) is incorrect. Requisitions and vendor invoices should be included. Answer (C) is incorrect. Purchase requisitions should be included.

19. Which one of the following statements about an accounting information system (AIS) is **false**?

A. AIS supports day-to-day operations by collecting and sorting data about an organization's transactions.

B. The information produced by AIS is made available to all levels of management for use in planning and controlling an organization's activities.

C. AIS is best suited to solve problems where there is great uncertainty and ill-defined reporting requirements.

D. AIS is often referred to as a transaction processing system.

Answer (C) is correct.
REQUIRED: The false statement about an accounting information system (AIS).
DISCUSSION: An AIS is a subsystem of a management information system that processes financial and transactional data relevant to managerial and financial accounting. The AIS supports operations by collecting and sorting data about an organization's transactions. An AIS is concerned not only with external parties, but also with the internal activities needed for management decision making at all levels. An AIS is best suited to solve problems when reporting requirements are well defined. A decision support system is a better choice for problems in which decision making is less structured.

20. An enterprise resource planning (ERP) system integrates the organization's computerized subsystems and may also provide links to external parties. An advantage of ERP is that

A. The reengineering needed for its implementation should improve business processes.

B. Customizing the software to suit the unique needs of the organization will facilitate upgrades.

C. It can be installed by organizations of all sizes.

D. The comprehensiveness of the system reduces resistance to change.

Answer (A) is correct.
REQUIRED: The advantage of ERP.
DISCUSSION: The benefits of ERP may significantly derive from the business process reengineering that is needed for its implementation. Using ERP software that reflects industry best practices forces the linked subunits in the organization not only to redesign and improve their processes but also to conform to one standard.
Answer (B) is incorrect. The disadvantages of ERP are its extent and complexity, which make customization of the software difficult and costly. Answer (C) is incorrect. ERP software is costly and complex. It usually is installed only by the largest enterprises. Answer (D) is incorrect. Implementing an ERP system is likely to encounter significant resistance because of its comprehensiveness.

21. In a traditional ERP system, the receipt of a customer order may result in

I. Customer tracking of the order's progress

II. Automatic replenishment of inventory by a supplier

III. Hiring or reassigning of employees

IV. Automatic adjustment of output schedules

A. I, II, and IV only.

B. I and III only.

C. III and IV only.

D. I, II, III, and IV.

Answer (C) is correct.
REQUIRED: The possible effects of receipt of a customer order by a traditional ERP system.
DISCUSSION: The traditional ERP system is one in which subsystems share data and coordinate their activities. Thus, if marketing receives an order, it can quickly verify that inventory is sufficient to notify shipping to process the order. Otherwise, production is notified to manufacture more of the product, with a consequent automatic adjustment of output schedules. If materials are inadequate for this purpose, the system will issue a purchase order. If more labor is needed, human resources will be instructed to reassign or hire employees. However, the subsystems in a traditional ERP system are internal to the organization. Hence, they are often called back-office functions. The information produced is principally (but not exclusively) intended for internal use by the organization's managers.
The current generation of ERP software (ERP II) has added front-office functions. Consequently, ERP II but not traditional ERP is capable of customer tracking of the order's progress and automatic replenishment of inventory by a supplier.

22. A principal advantage of an ERP system is

A. Program-data dependence.

B. Data redundancy.

C. Separate data updating for different functions.

D. Centralization of data.

Answer (D) is correct.
    REQUIRED: The principal advantage of an ERP system
    DISCUSSION: An advantage of an ERP system is the elimination of data redundancy through the use of a central database. In principle, information about an item of data is stored once, and all functions have access to it. Thus, when the item (such as a price) is updated, the change is effectively made for all functions. The result is reliability (data integrity).
    Answer (A) is incorrect. An ERP system uses a central database and a database management system. A fundamental characteristic of a database is that applications are independent of the physical structure of the database. Writing programs or designing applications to use the database requires only the names of desired data items, not their locations. Answer (B) is incorrect. An ERP system eliminates data redundancy. Answer (C) is incorrect. An ERP system is characterized by one-time data updating for all organizational functions.

23. The current generation of ERP software (ERP II) may include an advanced planning and scheduling system that

A. Determines the location of retail outlets.

B. Connects the organization with other members of a joint venture.

C. Controls the flow of a manufacturer's materials and components through the supply chain.

D. Permits tracking of orders by customers.

Answer (C) is correct.
    REQUIRED: The function of an advanced planning and scheduling system.
    DISCUSSION: An advanced planning and scheduling system may be an element of a supply chain management application for a manufacturer. It controls the flow of materials and components within the chain. Schedules are created given projected costs, lead times, and inventories.
    Answer (A) is incorrect. Customer relationship management applications in ERP II extend to customer service, finance-related matters, sales, and database creation and maintenance. Integrated data are helpful in better understanding customer needs, such as product preference or location of retail outlets. Answer (B) is incorrect. Partner relationship management applications connect the organization not only with such partners as customers and suppliers but also with owners, creditors, and strategic allies (for example, other members of a joint venture). Answer (D) is incorrect. An advanced planning scheduling system is used by a manufacturer to control flows through the supply chain. Other software permits customers to obtain information about order availability.

24. Enterprise resource planning (ERP) software packages, such as SAP R/3 and Oracle, are all-inclusive systems that attempt to provide entity-wide information. ERP systems provide advantages to an organization's auditors because they

A. Have proven difficult for some firms to install.

B. Typically require firms to reduce the division of duties and responsibilities found in traditional systems.

C. Typically have built-in transaction logs and ability to produce a variety of diagnostic reports.

D. Have been installed by smaller firms so, to date, few auditors have encountered them.

Answer (C) is correct.
    REQUIRED: The advantage of an ERP for the auditor.
    DISCUSSION: ERP systems have a variety of controls and report generation functions that allow auditors to abstract and monitor data collected and processed. Some ERP systems have built-in audit functions.
    Answer (A) is incorrect. The difficulty of installing ERP systems is a disadvantage for the auditors. Answer (B) is incorrect. ERP systems often require the client to depart from the traditional functional division of duties, such as accounting, finance, marketing, etc. The result is increased audit risk. Answer (D) is incorrect. ERP systems are very costly and therefore have been implemented only by large organizations. However, the trend is for more and more organizations to install these systems.

11.5 Systems that Support Decision Making

25. Which of the following is the best example of the use of a decision support system (DSS)?

A. A manager uses a personal-computer-based simulation model to determine whether one of the company's ships would be able to satisfy a particular delivery schedule.

B. An auditor uses a generalized audit software package to retrieve several purchase orders for detailed vouching.

C. A manager uses the query language feature of a database management system (DBMS) to compile a report showing customers whose average purchase exceeds $2,500.

D. An auditor uses a personal-computer-based word processing software package to modify an internal control questionnaire for a specific audit engagement.

Answer (A) is correct.

REQUIRED: The best example of the use of a decision support system.

DISCUSSION: A decision support system (DSS) assists middle- and upper-level managers in long-term, nonroutine, and often unstructured decision making. The system contains at least one decision model, is usually interactive, dedicated, and time-shared, but need not be real-time. It is an aid to decision making, not the automation of a decision process. The personal-computer-based simulation model is used to provide interactive problem solving (i.e., scheduling) assistance, the distinguishing feature of a DSS.

Answer (B) is incorrect. The generalized audit software package does not provide interactive problem solving assistance in retrieving the purchase orders and thus is not a DSS. Answer (C) is incorrect. The query feature of a DBMS does not provide interactive problem solving assistance in compiling the report and thus is not a DSS. Answer (D) is incorrect. The word processing software package does not provide interactive problem solving assistance to the auditor and thus is not a DSS.

26. Which one of the following terms best describes a decision support system (DSS)?

A. Management reporting system.

B. Formalized system.

C. Interactive system.

D. Accounting information system.

Answer (C) is correct.

REQUIRED: The best description of a DSS.

DISCUSSION: A decision support system is an interactive system that is useful in solving semistructured and unstructured problems, that is, those requiring a top-management or middle-management decision maker to exercise judgment and to control the process. A DSS does not automate a decision or provide structured information flows but rather provides tools for an end user to employ in applying insight and judgment. The system must be interactive to permit the user to explore the problem by using the computational capacities, models, assumptions, data resources, and display graphics of the DSS.

Answer (A) is incorrect. A management reporting system provides structured, routine information flows. Answer (B) is incorrect. The required flexibility of a DSS means that it cannot be highly formalized or structured. Answer (D) is incorrect. An accounting information system processes routine, highly structured financial and transactional data relevant for accounting purposes.

27. The processing in expert systems is characterized by

A. Algorithms.

B. Deterministic procedures.

C. Heuristics.

D. Simulations.

Answer (C) is correct.

REQUIRED: The characteristic of processing in knowledge-based systems.

DISCUSSION: Knowledge-based (expert) systems contain a knowledge base for a limited domain of human expertise and inference procedures for the solution of problems. They use symbolic processing based on heuristics rather than algorithms. A heuristic procedure is an exploratory problem-solving technique that uses self-education methods, e.g., the evaluation of feedback, to improve performance. These systems are often very interactive and provide explanations of their problem-solving behavior.

Answer (A) is incorrect. Algorithms are defined procedures used in typical computer programs. Answer (B) is incorrect. Deterministic procedures are procedures used in computer programs that permit no uncertainty in outcomes. Answer (D) is incorrect. Simulations are computer programs that permit experimentation with logical and mathematical models.

28. Which of the following features is classified as part of an expert system?

A. Use of electronic mail to route and approve purchase requisitions.

B. Automatic obligation of budget funds as soon as an order is issued.

C. Issuance of purchase requisition notices as soon as the on-hand balance reaches the reorder point.

D. Automatic placement of orders with suppliers who currently offer the best combination of price, freight cost, and delivery time.

Answer (D) is correct.
   REQUIRED: The feature classified as part of an expert system.
   DISCUSSION: The automatic placement of orders with the best combination of price, freight, and delivery time requires the maintenance of a database for all suppliers that is constantly changing as terms and conditions change. It simulates the decision process used by purchase managers.
   Answer (A) is incorrect. Use of electronic mail takes advantage of new software features but does not represent simulated thinking by the system. Answer (B) is incorrect. Automatic obligation of funds takes advantage of the real-time capability of the system but again does not represent simulated thinking by the system. Answer (C) is incorrect. Issuance of purchase requisition notices at the reorder point demonstrates a simple if/then decision but is not an example of an expert system feature.

29. For which of the following applications would the use of a fuzzy logic system be the most appropriate artificial intelligence (AI) choice?

A. Assigning airport gates to arriving airline flights.

B. Forecasting demand for spare auto parts.

C. Performing indoor climate control.

D. Diagnosing computer hardware problems.

Answer (C) is correct.
   REQUIRED: The most appropriate use for fuzzy logic.
   DISCUSSION: Fuzzy logic is a superset of conventional (Boolean) logic that has been extended to handle the concept of partial truth. Because they use nonspecific terms (membership functions) characterized by well-defined imprecision, fuzzy logic systems can create rules to address problems with many solutions. For example, applying fuzzy logic to indoor climate control may require defining in impressionistic terms and weighting functions such as indoor and outdoor temperature, humidity, and wind conditions. Thus, definitions (e.g., hot, warm, normal, cool, or cold, stated in temperature ranges) may overlap. The resulting rules describe actions to be taken when certain combinations of conditions exist. Fuzzy logic can be used when values are approximate or subjective, objects belong to multiple sets, membership in a set is a matter of degree, and data are incomplete or ambiguous.
   Answer (A) is incorrect. Assigning airport gates to arriving airline flights requires an expert system that uses precise data for quick and consistent decisions. Answer (B) is incorrect. Neural networks provide the technology to undertake sophisticated forecasting and analysis. They emulate the processing patterns of the brain and therefore can learn from experience. Answer (D) is incorrect. Diagnosing problems with computer hardware could be accomplished by an expert system.

30. Business intelligence (BI) has all of the following characteristics **except**

A. Focusing on strategic objectives.

B. Giving immediate information about an organization's critical success factors.

C. Displaying information in graphical format.

D. Providing advice and answers to top management from a knowledge-based system.

Answer (D) is correct.
   REQUIRED: The item that is not a characteristic of business intelligence (BI).
   DISCUSSION: BI serves the needs of top management for managerial control and strategic planning. BI focuses on strategic (long-range) objectives and gives immediate information about a firm's critical success factors. BI is not a program for providing top management with advice and answers from a knowledge-based (expert) system.
   Answer (A) is incorrect. BI does focus on strategic objectives. Answer (B) is incorrect. BI gives immediate information about an organization's critical (strategic) success factors. Answer (C) is incorrect. BI often displays information in graphical format.

**Page
Intentionally
Left Blank**

11.6 PRACTICE WRITTEN COMMUNICATION

Business Environment and Concepts
Testlet 4 of 4

Time Remaining
1 hour - 15 minutes

Unsplit   Split Horiz   Split Vertical   Exit

DIRECTIONS

Note: If you believe you have encountered a software malfunction, report it to the test center staff immediately.

Navigation

To navigate from task to task, use the controls at the bottom of the screen. Click on the **Next** button to advance to the next task, or the **Previous** button to go to the previous task. To go directly to any task, click on its number.

▼ = Reminder   Directions | 1 | 2 | 3 | 4 | 5 | 6 | 7 | ◀ Previous   Next ▶

If you would like a reminder to revisit a task, or want to indicate that you are finished with it, click on the reminder flag below the task number. To clear the flag, click on it again. Reminder flags are for your use only – they do not contribute to your score.

Tabs

In this part of the examination, you will be asked to complete various tasks. Every task has one or more **Work Tabs**. Every task also has a **Help** tab.

Written Communication   Help

Work tab   Help tab

Work Tabs:

- **Work Tabs** are identified with a pencil icon. This is where your responses are expected.
- Each task has one or more **Work Tabs**.
- **Work Tabs** contain directions for completing the task - be sure to read these directions carefully.
- The **Work Tab** name in the example above is for illustration only - yours will differ.
- You must complete all of the **Work Tabs** in each task to receive full credit.

Help Tab:

- The **Help Tab** provides assistance with the exam software that is used in this task. For example, if the task is to compose a memorandum, **Help** will provide information about the word processor.

The Toolbar

The toolbar at the top of the screen shows the amount of time remaining for you to complete the tasks. In addition, the following tools are available. Note that only the **Exit** button is displayed when Directions are visible - the others will appear when you begin the tasks.

Unsplit   Split Horiz   Split Vertical

Click on these buttons to split or unsplit the screen. You can split the screen vertically or horizontally.

Exit

Click on this button to go on to the next part of the examination. You must complete all of the tasks to receive full credit. Once you click on **Exit** and confirm the action, you will NOT be able to return to this testlet.

▼ = Reminder   Directions | 1 | ◀ Previous   Next ▶

Management is concerned about the potential effect of an aging work force on the company's pension plan. The human resources manager has recommended a defined benefit plan that awards employees retirement compensation based on the highest 10 years of earnings, excluding bonuses. Prepare the CFO's memo to management explaining the advantages and risks associated with the pension plan and what alternative might be available.

Type your communication below the line in the response area below.

REMINDER: Your response will be graded for both technical content and writing skills. Technical content will be evaluated for information that is helpful to the intended reader and clearly relevant to the issue. Writing skills will be evaluated for development, organization, and the appropriate expression of ideas in professional correspondence. Use a standard business memorandum or letter format with a clear beginning, middle, and end. Do not convey information in the form of a table, bullet point list, or other abbreviated presentation.

To: Management team
Re: Advantages and risks of the proposed pension plan

NOTE: Your Written Communications on the actual CPA exam may cover topics outside the scope of the BEC CSO (i.e., they may relate to topics from the AUD, FAR, and/or REG CSOs instead). Answer to the best of your ability, and remember that graders are mainly evaluating your writing ability and will overlook minor technical mistakes.

Unofficial Answer

Written Communication

To: Management team
Re: Advantages and risks of the proposed pension plan

A defined benefit pension plan is a type of retirement plan in which an employer promises a specified monthly benefit on retirement. This benefit is determined by a formula based on each employee's earnings history, period of service, and age. A defined benefit plan is defined in the sense that the benefit formula is defined and known in advance. This plan is attractive to employees because their retirement benefits are easily predicted. However, the cost to the employer is not as predictable, a major disadvantage for the employer.

Traditional defined benefit plans have a flat accrual rate and a decreasing time for interest discounting as employees near retirement age. Thus, the present value of benefits grows slowly early in an employee's career and accelerates significantly in mid-career. As a result, funding pensions is more costly for older employees than for younger ones. Given an aging work force, the accrual pattern of benefits is unfavorable for our company.

Furthermore, the investment risk of the recommended plan is borne by the employer, not the employees. The amount of contributions to be made to the plan is determined by market conditions. Accordingly, an economic downturn could greatly increase the amount of contributions to the plan. If investment returns are less than expected, additional contributions are required. However, the opposite is also true. If investment returns are greater than expected, smaller contributions are required, an advantage when the economy is doing well.

An alternative to a defined benefit plan is a defined contribution plan. This form of employee postretirement compensation predominates among large companies. Under a defined contribution plan, the employer does not guarantee the amount of retirement benefits. The employer's only obligation is to make periodic deposits defined by the plan's formula. Employees and the employer can contribute to the plan, and the employer's contributions are not affected by market conditions. As a result, investment risk is borne by employees.

The above depicts a Level 5 answer. Consult your booklet, *How to Pass the CPA Exam: A System for Success*, for a description of the three writing skills criteria. You may also access this booklet online by visiting www.gleim.com/PassCPA.

Self-Grade

Below, grade your response on technical content and writing skills. Bubble in the circle next to the appropriate score that you may receive based on the criteria given. Your **total** score is the sum of your scores on all six items. The maximum score is 19 points.

Technical Content Evaluation

Was your response on topic?	O No [0]	O Mostly [1]	O Yes [2]
Did your response have any *significant* errors?	O 0 errors [1]	O 1 major error [–1]	O 2 or more major errors [–2]
Did your response contain any illegal advice?	O No [1]	O Yes [0]	

Writing Skills Evaluation

	Poor	Below Average	Average	Above Average	Outstanding
Organization	O 1	O 2	O 3	O 4	O 5
Development	O 1	O 2	O 3	O 4	O 5
Expression	O 1	O 2	O 3	O 4	O 5

Disclaimer: This scoring schedule was developed by Gleim Publications as a guideline only. The AICPA has not released specific information on how the Written Communications are graded.

Practice even more Written Communications with the Gleim Mega Test Bank.

Learn more: gleim.com/CPAmega | 800.874.5346

STUDY UNIT TWELVE
IT SOFTWARE, DATA, AND CONTINGENCY PLANNING

(17 pages of outline)

A computer's software consists of the sets of instructions, often called programs, that are executed by the hardware. Programs and data are stored in a computer in a series of ones and zeros, called binary code. The binary code is grouped into larger units of fields, records, and files. Files can be integrated into a database. When an organization acquires a new system, either by buying it or by creating it internally, a series of steps must be carefully followed to ensure that the system is stable and cost-effective. Business information systems are crucial to the continued existence of the modern organization; therefore, every entity must plan how it will continue processing in the case of an interruption to normal processing.

12.1 SOFTWARE

1. **Overview**

    a. Software refers to the programs (i.e., sets of computer instructions) that are executed by the hardware.

    b. Software can be described from two perspectives: (1) systems vs. application software and (2) the programming language in which the software is written.

2. **Systems Software**

    a. Performs the fundamental tasks needed to manage computer resources. The two most common pieces of systems software are

    1) The **operating system**, which is the "traffic cop" of any computer system

        a) The operating system negotiates the conversation between the computer's hardware, the application the user is running, and the data that the application is working with.

        b) Examples are Linux, OS X, and Windows.

    2) **Utility programs**, which perform basic functions that are not particular to a certain application, such as file manipulation (copying, deleting, merging, and sorting data files) and file access control

3. **Application Software**

    a. Consists of programs that tell the computer what steps the user wants carried out. It may be purchased from vendors or developed internally.

    1) Examples of applications found on personal computers include word processors, spreadsheets, graphics, and small databases.

    2) Applications found on dedicated servers are payroll, human resources, purchasing, accounts payable, general ledger, treasury, etc.

4. Programming Languages

    a.   Software is written in languages that can be processed by the computer. The following is a description of types and development of computer languages.

    b.   **First-generation languages** (also called machine languages) are written in binary code (a combination of ones and zeros discussed in detail in Subunit 12.2) unique to each type of computer. Because they are in binary code, first-generation languages are understood directly by the computer.

    c.   **Third-generation languages** (many of which are termed procedural or programming languages) consist of English-like words and phrases that represent multiple machine language instructions, making these languages much easier to learn. These languages must be converted to machine language either by compilation (the whole program is converted at once, then executed) or interpretation (the program is converted and executed one line at a time). Third-generation languages have been deployed for decades with tremendous success. The following is a list of some of the better-known ones:

        1)   COBOL (COmmon Business-Oriented Language) was designed in 1959 to be easy to read and maintain, and the standard has been extensively revised and updated over the years. Vast quantities of lines of COBOL are still in use.

        2)   BASIC (Beginner's All-purpose Symbolic Instruction Code) was developed to teach programming but is not used in large business application processing. Visual BASIC provides a graphical user interface to develop Microsoft Windows applications from code written in BASIC.

        3)   C and C++ have been very popular languages since their introduction. C++ enhances C by adding features like support for object-oriented programming.

        4)   Java is a high-level, object-oriented programming language developed by Sun Microsystems that, among other things, is used to write programs embedded in World Wide Web documents.

            a)   Thus, software is stored on the network, and the user need not be concerned about compatibility of the software with the computer platform.

            b)   Java is platform independent because if each computer has it incorporated into a browser, it can run on the platform. Java programs that run in a web browser are called **applets**, and Java programs that run on a web server are called **servlets**.

    d.   **Fourth-generation languages** (also called problem-oriented or nonprocedural languages) provide still further simplification of programming. These interactive, English-like languages permit a nonspecialized user to describe the problem to, and receive guidance from, the computer instead of specifying a procedure.

        1)   Generalized audit software (GAS), also known as computer-assisted audit techniques (CAAT), involves the use of computer software packages that may allow not only parallel simulation but also a variety of other processing functions, such as extracting sample items, verifying totals, developing file statistics, and retrieving specified data fields. Audit Command Language (ACL) and Interactive Data Extraction and Analysis (IDEA) are the leading CAAT packages.

        2)   Hypertext markup language (HTML) is the authoring software language commonly used to create and link websites.

        3)   Extensible markup language (XML) is an open standard usable with many programs and platforms.

4) Extensible business reporting language (XBRL) is the specification developed by an AICPA-led consortium for commercial and industrial entities that report in accordance with U.S. GAAP. It is a variation of XML that is expected to decrease the costs of generating financial reports, reformulating information for different uses, and sharing business information using electronic media. The SEC allows firms to report using XBRL.

Stop and review! You have completed the outline for this subunit. Study multiple-choice questions 1 through 6 beginning on page 322.

12.2 NATURE OF BINARY DATA STORAGE

1. **Binary Storage**

   a. Digital computers store all information in binary format, that is, as a pattern of ones and zeros. This makes arithmetic operations and true/false decisions on the lowest level extremely straightforward.

   b. A **bit** is either 0 or 1 (off or on) in binary code. Bits can be strung together to form a binary (i.e., base 2) number.

EXAMPLE of a Bit

0

---

   c. A **byte** is a group of bits, most commonly eight. A byte can be used to signify a character (a number, letter of the alphabet, or symbol, such as a question mark or asterisk).

EXAMPLE of an 8-Bit Byte Representing the Capital Letter P

01010000

---

   1) Quantities of bytes are measured with the following units:

$$1{,}024 \ (2^{10}) \text{ bytes } = \textbf{1 kilobyte } = 1 \text{ KB}$$
$$1{,}048{,}576 \ (2^{20}) \text{ bytes } = \textbf{1 megabyte } = 1 \text{ MB}$$
$$1{,}073{,}741{,}824 \ (2^{30}) \text{ bytes } = \textbf{1 gigabyte } = 1 \text{ GB}$$
$$1{,}099{,}511{,}627{,}776 \ (2^{40}) \text{ bytes } = \textbf{1 terabyte } = 1 \text{ TB}$$

   Author's Note: Please do not memorize these numbers. Our intent is to demonstrate the difference in size for each unit to help you better grasp these terms.

   d. A **field**, also called a data item, is a group of bytes. The field contains a unit of data about some entity, e.g., a composer's name.

EXAMPLE of a Field

Paul Hindemith

---

   e. A **record** is a group of fields. All the fields contain information pertaining to an entity, e.g., a specific performance of an orchestral work.

EXAMPLE of a Record

Paul Hindemith	Violin Concerto	Chicago Symphony	Claudio Abbado	Josef Suk

---

1)   Some field or combination of fields on each record is designated as the **key**. The criterion for a key is that it contain enough information to uniquely identify each record; i.e., there can be no two records with the same key.

    a)   The designation of a key allows records to be sorted and managed with much greater efficiency. If all the records are sorted in the order of the key, searching for a particular one becomes much easier.

    b)   In the previous example, the key is the combination of the first two fields.

        i)   The first field alone is not enough because there could be several works by each composer. The second field alone is likewise not enough since there could be many pieces with the same title.

        ii)   The combination of the composer's name and title uniquely identify each piece of music.

f.   A **file** is a group of records. All the records in the file contain the same pieces of information about different occurrences, e.g., performances of several orchestral works.

EXAMPLE of a File				
Paul Hindemith	Violin Concerto	Chicago Symphony	Claudio Abbado	Josef Suk
Gustav Mahler	Das Lied von der Erde	New York Philharmonic	Leonard Bernstein	Dietrich Fischer-Dieskau
Bela Bartok	Piano Concerto No. 2	Chicago Symphony	Sir Georg Solti	Etsko Tazaki
Arnold Schoenberg	Gurrelieder	Boston Symphony	Seiji Ozawa	James McCracken
Leos Janacek	Sinfonietta	Los Angeles Philharmonic	Simon Rattle	None
Dmitri Shostakovich	Symphony No. 6	San Francisco Symphony	Kazuhiro Koizumi	None
Carl Orff	Carmina Burana	Berlin Radio Symphony	Eugen Jochum	Gundula Janowitz

Stop and review! You have completed the outline for this subunit. Study multiple-choice questions 7 through 9 beginning on page 323.

12.3 FILE ORGANIZATION AND DATABASES

1.   **Flat Files**

a.   The oldest file structure is the flat file, in which all records are stored continuously, one after the other, as on a reel of magnetic tape.

    1)   To find a certain record, every record on the tape has to be searched until the desired one is found.

    2)   Also, the ways in which a user can perform a search on a flat file are extremely limited.

b.   As computers became more powerful, new ways of storing data became possible that permitted much more flexibility in searching and updating.

    1)   Databases allow companies to save information (data) in one place instead of having hundreds of specific files with similar information.

2.   **Hierarchical Databases**

a.   The hierarchical, or tree, database model was a major development in file organization. Instead of the records being strung out one after the other, they form "branches" and "leaves" extending from a "root."

    1)   Note that the customer's address is stored only once; in a flat file, the address had to be stored every time the customer placed an order.

    2)   Another feature of the tree file structure is that every "parent" record can have multiple "child" records, but each child can have only one parent.

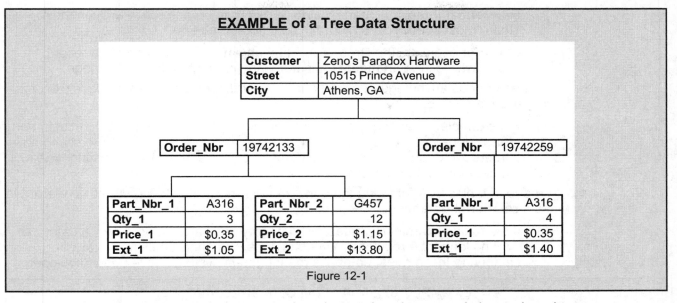

EXAMPLE of a Tree Data Structure

Customer	Zeno's Paradox Hardware
Street	10515 Prince Avenue
City	Athens, GA

Order_Nbr	19742133

Order_Nbr	19742259

Part_Nbr_1	A316
Qty_1	3
Price_1	$0.35
Ext_1	$1.05

Part_Nbr_2	G457
Qty_2	12
Price_2	$1.15
Ext_2	$13.80

Part_Nbr_1	A316
Qty_1	4
Price_1	$0.35
Ext_1	$1.40

Figure 12-1

    b.   One customer has many orders, but each order can only be assigned to one customer.

        1)   The tree structure improves speed and storage efficiency for related data; for example, a parent record consisting of a customer may directly index the child records containing the customer's orders.

        2)   However, adding new records is much more difficult than with a flat file. In a flat file, a new record is simply inserted whole in the proper place. In a tree structure, the relationships between the parent and child records must be maintained.

3.   **Relational Databases**

    a.   When a relational database is used, a file like the one depicted in the example on the next page is stored with every record in a single row and every column containing a value that pertains to that record.

        1)   In database terminology, a file stored this way is called a table, and the columns are called attributes.

    b.   Each data element is stored as few times as necessary. This reduction in data redundancy is accomplished through a process called **normalization**.

    c.   Two features that make the relational data structure stand out are cardinality and referential integrity.

        1)   **Cardinality** refers to how close a given data element is to being unique.

            a)   A data element that can only exist once in a given table has high cardinality. In Figure 12-2, Customer_Nbr has high cardinality in the Customer Table.

            b)   A data element that is not unique in a given table but that has a restricted range of possible values is said to have normal cardinality. Order_Nbr in the Order Table is an example.

            c)   A data element that has a very small range of values is said to have low cardinality. A field that can contain only male/female or true/false is an example.

2) **Referential integrity** means that for a record to be entered in a given table, there must already be a record in some other table(s).

   a) For example, the Order Table in Figure 12-2 cannot contain a record where the part number is not already present in the Parts Table.

d. The tremendous advantage of a relational data structure is that searching for records is greatly facilitated.

   1) For example, a user can specify a customer and see all the parts that customer has ordered, or the user can specify a part and see all the customers who have ordered it. Such queries were extremely resource-intensive, if not impossible, under older data structures.

e. A group of tables built following the principles of relational data structures is referred to as a **relational database**.

   1) If the rules of cardinality, referential integrity, etc., are not enforced, a database will no longer be relational. To aid in the exceedingly challenging task of enforcing these rules, database management systems have been developed.

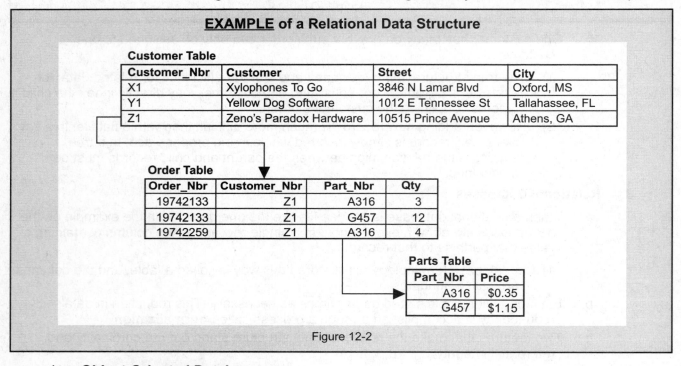

EXAMPLE of a Relational Data Structure

Customer Table

Customer_Nbr	Customer	Street	City
X1	Xylophones To Go	3846 N Lamar Blvd	Oxford, MS
Y1	Yellow Dog Software	1012 E Tennessee St	Tallahassee, FL
Z1	Zeno's Paradox Hardware	10515 Prince Avenue	Athens, GA

Order Table

Order_Nbr	Customer_Nbr	Part_Nbr	Qty
19742133	Z1	A316	3
19742133	Z1	G457	12
19742259	Z1	A316	4

Parts Table

Part_Nbr	Price
A316	$0.35
G457	$1.15

Figure 12-2

4. **Object-Oriented Databases**

a. An object-oriented database is a response to the need to store graphics and multimedia applications used by object-oriented programming languages such as C++ and Java.

   1) Translating this type of data into tables and rows is difficult. However, in an object-oriented database, the objects can be stored along with executable code that directs the behavior of the object.

Stop and review! You have completed the outline for this subunit. Study multiple-choice questions 10 through 14 beginning on page 324.

12.4 DATABASE MANAGEMENT SYSTEMS

1. **Overview**

   a. A **database management system** (DBMS) is an integrated set of software tools superimposed on the data files that helps maintain the integrity of the underlying database.

      1) Database management systems make the maintenance of vast relational databases practical. Without the sophisticated capabilities of database management systems, enforcing the rules that make the database relational would be overwhelmingly time-consuming.

   b. A DBMS allows programmers and designers to work independently of the physical and logical structure of the database.

      1) Before the development of DBMSs, programmers and systems designers needed to consider the logical and physical structure of the database with the creation of every new application. This was extremely time-consuming and therefore expensive.

      2) With a DBMS, the physical structure of the database can be completely altered without having to change any of the programs using the data items. Thus, different users may define their own views of the data (called subschemas).

   c. Those in the IT function responsible for dealing with the DBMS are called database administrators.

EXAMPLE

The three most prominent commercial relational database management systems are Oracle, IBM DB2, and Microsoft Access. A well-known open-source DBMS is MySQL.

---

2. **Aspects of a DBMS**

   a. A particular database's design, called its **schema**, consists of the layouts of the tables and the constraints on entering new records. To a great extent, a DBMS automates the process of enforcing the schema.

   b. Two vital parts of any DBMS are

      1) A **data definition language**, which allows the user to specify how the tables will look and what kinds of data elements they will hold

      2) A **data manipulation language**, with which the DBMS retrieves, adds, deletes, or modifies records and data elements

         a) Both of these roles are commonly fulfilled in the current generation of database management systems by Structured Query Language (SQL) or one of its many variants.

   c. The **data dictionary** contains the physical and logical characteristics of every data element in a database. The data dictionary contains the size, format, usage, meaning, and ownership of every data element as well as what persons, programs, reports, and functions use the data element.

   d. A DBMS can maintain a **distributed database**, meaning one that is stored in two or more physical sites.

      1) In the **replication**, or **snapshot**, technique, the DBMS duplicates the entire database and sends it to multiple locations. Changes are periodically copied and similarly distributed.

      2) In the **fragmentation**, or **partitioning**, method, specific records are stored where they are most needed. For example, a financial institution may store a particular customer's data at the branch where (s)he usually transacts his or her business. If the customer executes a transaction at another branch, the pertinent data are retrieved via communications lines.

Stop and review! You have completed the outline for this subunit. Study multiple-choice questions 15 through 19 beginning on page 325.

12.5 APPLICATION DEVELOPMENT AND MAINTENANCE

1.   **Organizational Needs Assessment**

   a.   The organizational needs assessment is a detailed process of study and evaluation of how information systems can be deployed to help the organization meet its goals. The steps in the assessment are as follows:

   1)   Determine whether current systems support organizational goals
   2)   Determine needs unmet by current systems
   3)   Determine capacity of current systems to accommodate projected growth
   4)   Propose path for information systems deployment to achieve organizational goals within budgetary constraints

2.   **Business Process Design**

   a.   A business process is a flow of actions performed on goods and/or information to accomplish a discrete objective.

   1)   Examples include hiring a new employee, recruiting a new customer, and filling a customer order.

   b.   Some business processes are contained entirely within a single functional area; e.g., hiring a new employee is performed by the human resources function.

   1)   Other processes cross functional boundaries. Filling a customer order requires the participation of the sales department, the warehouse, and accounts receivable.

   c.   In the early days of automated system deployment, hardware and software were very expensive. Systems tended to be designed to serve a single process or even a single functional area. Tremendous gains in processing power and storage capacity have made integrated systems, i.e., those that combine multiple processes, the norm.

   1)   The most advanced of these are enterprise resource planning (ERP) systems.

   d.   The automation of a process, or the acquisition of an integrated system, presents the organization with an opportunity for business process reengineering.

   1)   Business process reengineering involves a complete rethinking of how business functions are performed to provide value to customers, that is, radical innovation instead of mere improvement and a disregard for current jobs, hierarchies, and reporting relationships.

3.   **Participants in Business Process Design**

   a.   The everyday functioning of a business process affects multiple stakeholder groups.

   1)   Input from each group should be considered in the design of the process. However, some stakeholders will be more active participants.

   b.   End users are generally the drivers of a new or redesigned process.

   1)   For example, the customers of a multi-division business may have open accounts with several of the divisions. Whenever a customer calls, the customer relations department would like the most up-to-date customer balance information for all divisions to be accessible at once.

   2)   Although the motivation for the new process begins with the customer service department, personnel in the various divisions as well as the central IT function will be affected.

   c. Because IT pervades every aspect of operations in a modern organization, the IT steering committee must study each request for a new process and either approve or deny it.

      1) Typical members of the steering committee include, from the IT function, the chief information officer and the head of systems development. Executive management from each division is also represented.

      2) The committee members have an understanding of the interactions of the organization's current systems and how they will affect and be affected by new or redesigned business processes.

   d. Once a new process or system has been approved, a project team is assembled, consisting of representatives of the end users who requested it and the IT personnel who will design and build the software components that will support it.

   e. Upper management supports process design by making sufficient resources available to ensure successful implementation of the new process.

   f. If the new process or system crosses organizational boundaries, as is the case with EDI systems, external parties, such as representatives of the vendor or customer businesses, are participants.

4. **Build or Buy**

   a. When an organization acquires a new system by purchasing from an outside vendor, contract management personnel oversee the process. The future end-users of the system as well as IT personnel are also involved, drawing up specifications and requirements.

      1) However, when a new system is to be created in-house, planning and managing the development process is one of the IT function's most important tasks.

      2) The needs of the end users must be balanced with budget and time constraints; the decision to use existing hardware vs. the purchase of new platforms must be weighed.

   b. Extensive time and resources are devoted to the creation of a new application, and generally, the more important the business function being automated, the more complex the application is. Thus, having a well-governed methodology for overseeing the development process is vital.

   c. Both the end users who specified the new system's functionality and IT management who are overseeing the development process must approve progress toward the completion of the system at the end of each of the stages described below and on the following pages. This requirement for ongoing review and approval of the project is a type of implementation control.

5. **Systems Development Life Cycle (SDLC)**

   The AICPA has asked many questions concerning the systems development life cycle (SDLC). One of their favorite questions asks candidates to select the correct phase to which an activity belongs. Be sure you know each of the phases and the activities that occur in each.

   a. The systems development life-cycle approach is the traditional methodology applied to the development of large, highly structured application systems. A major advantage of the life-cycle approach is enhanced management and control of the development process.

b. Once the need for a new system has been recognized, the five phases (each with multiple steps) of the SDLC proceed as depicted in the diagram below (portions of the phases can overlap).

Systems Development Life-Cycle

Figure 12-3

c. Note that the feedback gathered during the maintenance of a system provides information for developing the next generation of systems, hence the name life **cycle**.

6. The **phases and component steps of the traditional SDLC** can be described as follows:

a. **Initiation, Feasibility, and Planning**

   1) The SDLC begins with recognizing there is a need for a new system, gaining an understanding of the situation to determine whether it is feasible to create a solution, and formulating a plan.

b. **Requirements Analysis and Definition**

   1) A formal proposal for a new system is submitted to the IT steering committee, describing the need for the application and the business function(s) that it will affect.

   2) Feasibility studies are conducted to determine

      a) What technology the new system will require
      b) What economic resources must be committed to the new system
      c) How the new system will affect current operations

   3) The steering committee gives its go-ahead for the project.

c. **System Design**

   1) Logical design consists of mapping the flow and storage of the data elements that will be used by the new system and the new program modules that will constitute the new system.

      a) Data flow diagrams and structured flowcharts are commonly used in this step.

      b) Some data elements may already be stored in existing databases. Good logical design ensures that they are not duplicated.

   2) Physical design involves planning the specific interactions of the new program code and data elements with the hardware platform (existing or planned for purchase) on which the new system will operate.

      a) Systems analysts are heavily involved in these two steps.

d. **Build and Development**

   1) The actual program code and database structures that will be used in the new system are written.

   2) Hardware is acquired and physical infrastructure is assembled.

e. **Testing and Quality Control**

   1) Testing is performed while the system is being built, and feedback obtained is used to improve performance and functionality.

      a) The programmers thoroughly test each new program module of the system, both alone and in concert with other modules.

           i)   The data used in testing new programs is never the organization's actual production data; such testing would be far too risky to the organization's business.

           ii)   Instead, a carefully designed test database is filled with both good and bad data to test how well the new system deals with bad input.

f.   **Acceptance, Installation, and Implementation**

   1)   User acceptance testing is the final step before placing the system in live operation.

      a)   IT must demonstrate to the user department that submitted the original request that the system performs the desired functionality.

      b)   Once the user department is satisfied with the new system, they acknowledge formal acceptance and implementation begins.

   2)   Four strategies for converting to the new system can be used.

      a)   With **parallel** operation, the old and new systems both are run at full capacity for a given period.

          i)   This strategy is the safest since the old system is still producing output (in case there are major problems with the new system), but it is also the most expensive and time-consuming.

      b)   With **cutover** conversion, the old system is shut down and the new one takes over processing at once.

          i)   This is the least expensive and time-consuming strategy, but it is also the riskiest.

      c)   Under **pilot** conversion, one branch, department, or division at a time is fully converted to the new system.

          i)   Experience gained from each installation is used to benefit the next one. One disadvantage of this strategy is the extension of the conversion time.

      d)   In some cases, **phased** conversion is possible. Under this strategy, one function of the new system at a time is placed in operation.

          i)   For instance, if the new system is an integrated accounting application, accounts receivable could be installed, then accounts payable, cash management, materials handling, etc.

          ii)   The advantage of this strategy is allowing the users to learn one part of the system at a time.

   3)   Training and documentation are critical.

      a)   The users must be made to feel comfortable with the new system and have plenty of guidance available, either hard copy or online.

      b)   Documentation consists of more than just operations manuals for the users. Layouts of the program code and database structures must also be available for the programmers who must modify and maintain the system.

g.   **Operations and Maintenance**

   1)   After a system becomes operational, the system should be monitored to ensure ongoing performance and continuous improvement.

   2)   Systems follow-up or post-audit evaluation is a subsequent review of the efficiency and effectiveness of the system after it has operated for a substantial time (e.g., 1 year).

7. **Program Change Control**

    a. Over the life of an application, users are constantly asking for changes. The process of managing these changes is referred to as systems maintenance, and the relevant controls are called **program change controls**.

    b. Once a change to a system has been approved, the programmer should save a copy of the production program in a test area of the computer, sometimes called a "sandbox."

        1) Only in emergencies, and then only under close supervision, should a change be made directly to the production version of a computer program.

        2) The IT function must be able to revert back to a prior version immediately if unexpected results are encountered during an emergency change.

    c. The programmer makes the necessary changes to this copy of the program's source code.

    d. The programmer transforms the changed program into a form that the computer can execute. The resulting machine-ready program is referred to as object code, or more precisely, executable code.

    e. Once the programmer has the executable version of the changed program, (s)he tests it to see if it performs the new task as expected.

        1) This testing process absolutely must not be run against production data. A special set of test data must be available for running test programs against.

    f. The programmer demonstrates the new functionality for the user who made the request.

        1) Either the user accepts the new program or the programmer goes back and makes further changes.

    g. Once the program is in a form acceptable to the user, the programmer moves it to a holding area.

        1) Programmers (except in emergencies) should never be able to put programs directly into production.

    h. The programmer's supervisor reviews the new program, approves it, and authorizes its move into production, which is generally carried out by operations personnel.

        1) The compensating control is that operators generally lack the programming knowledge to put fraudulent code into production.

8. **Application Development Tools**

    a. **Prototyping** is an alternative approach to application development. Prototyping involves creating a working model of the system requested, demonstrating it for the user, obtaining feedback, and making changes to the underlying code.

        1) This process repeats through several iterations until the user is satisfied with the system's functionality.

        2) Formerly, this approach was derided as being wasteful of resources and tending to produce unstable systems, but with vastly increased processing power and high-productivity development tools, prototyping can, in some cases, be an efficient means of systems development.

    b. **Computer-aided software engineering (CASE)** applies the computer to software design and development.

        1) It provides the capacity to maintain on the computer all of the system documentation, e.g., data flow diagrams, data dictionaries, and pseudocode (structured English); to develop executable input and output screens; and to generate program code in at least skeletal form.

        2) Thus, CASE facilitates the creation, organization, and maintenance of documentation and permits some automation of the coding process.

9. **End-User vs. Centralized Computing**

 a. End-user computing (EUC) involves user-created or user-acquired systems that are maintained and operated outside of traditional information systems controls.

  1) Certain environmental control risks are more likely in EUC. They include copyright violations that occur when unauthorized copies of software are made or when software is installed on multiple computers.

  2) Unauthorized access to application programs and related data is another concern. EUC lacks physical access controls, application-level controls, and other controls found in mainframe or networked environments.

  3) Moreover, EUC may not have adequate backup, recovery, and contingency planning. The result may be an inability to recreate the system or its data.

 b. Program development, documentation, and maintenance also may lack the centralized control found in larger systems.

  1) The risk of allowing end users to develop their own applications is decentralization of control. These applications may not be reviewed by independent outside systems analysts and are not created using a formal development methodology. They also may not be subject to appropriate standards, controls, and quality assurance procedures.

  2) When end users create their own applications and files, private information systems in which data are largely uncontrolled may proliferate. Systems may contain the same information, but EUC applications may update and define the data in different ways. Thus, determining the location of data and ensuring data consistency become more difficult.

  3) The auditors should determine that EUC applications contain controls that allow users to rely on the information produced. Identification of applications is more difficult than in a traditional centralized computing environment because few people know about and use them.

   a) The auditor's first concern is to discover their existence and their intended functions. One approach is to take an organization-wide inventory of major EUC applications. An alternative is for the auditors and the primary user (a function or department) to review major EUC applications.

   b) The next step is risk assessment. EUC applications that represent high-risk exposures are chosen for audit, for example, because they support critical decisions or are used to control cash or physical assets.

   c) The third step is to review the controls included in the applications chosen in the risk assessment.

 c. In a personal computer setting, the user is often the programmer and operator. Thus, the protections provided by segregation of duties are eliminated.

 d. The audit trail is diminished because of the lack of history files, incomplete printed output, etc.

 e. In general, available security features for stand-alone machines are limited compared with those in a network.

Stop and review! You have completed the outline for this subunit. Study multiple-choice questions 20 through 27 beginning on page 327.

12.6 CONTINGENCY PLANNING

1. **Overview**

   a. The information security goal of data availability is primarily the responsibility of the IT function.

   b. Contingency planning is the name commonly given to this activity.

      1) **Disaster recovery** is the process of resuming normal information processing operations after the occurrence of a major interruption.

      2) **Business continuity** is the continuation of business by other means during the period in which computer processing is unavailable or less than normal.

   c. Plans must be made for two major types of contingencies: those in which the data center is physically available and those in which it is not.

      1) Examples of the first type of contingency are (a) power failure, (b) random intrusions such as viruses, and (c) deliberate intrusions such as hacking incidents. The organization's physical facilities are sound, but immediate action is required to continue normal processing.

      2) The second type of contingency is much more serious. It is caused by disasters such as floods, fires, hurricanes, or earthquakes. An occurrence of this type requires an alternate processing facility.

2. **Backup and Rotation**

   a. Periodic backup and offsite rotation of computer files is the most basic part of any disaster recovery or business continuity plan.

   b. An organization's data are more valuable than its hardware.

      1) Hardware can be replaced for a price, but each organization's data are unique and indispensable to operations. If they are destroyed, they cannot be replaced. For this reason, periodic backup and rotation are essential.

   c. A typical backup routine duplicates all data files and application programs once a month. Incremental changes are then backed up and taken to an offsite location once a week. (Application files and data must be backed up because both change.)

      1) In case of an interruption of normal processing, the organization's systems can be restored such that, at most, 7 days of business information is lost. This is not ideal, but it is preferable to a complete loss of files that could bankrupt the organization.

   d. The offsite location must be temperature- and humidity-controlled and guarded against physical intrusion. Just as important, it must be far enough away from the site of main operations not to be affected by the same natural disaster. Adequate backup is useless if the files are not accessible or have been destroyed.

3. **Risk Assessment Steps**

   a. Identify and prioritize the organization's critical applications.

      1) Not all of an organization's systems are equally important. The firm must decide which vital applications it simply cannot do business without and in what order they should be brought back into operation.

   b. Determine the minimum recovery time frames and minimum hardware requirements.

      1) How long will it take to reinstall each critical application, and what platform is required? If the interruption has been caused by an attack, such as a virus or hacker, how long will it take to isolate the problem and eliminate it from the system?

   c. Develop a recovery plan.

4. **Disaster Recovery Plan (DRP)**

   a. Disaster recovery is the process of regaining access to data (e.g., hardware, software, and records), communications, work areas, and other business processes.

   b. Thus, a DRP that is established and tested must be developed in connection with the business continuity plan. It should describe IT recovery strategies, including details about procedures, vendors, and systems.

      1) Detailed procedures must be updated when systems and businesses change. The following are examples of items addressed by the DRP:

         a) Data center
         b) Applications and data needed
         c) Servers and other hardware
         d) Communications
         e) Network connections
         f) IT infrastructure (e.g., log-on services and software distribution)
         g) Remote access services
         h) Process control systems
         i) File rooms
         j) Document management systems

   c. The following are considerations for choosing DRP strategies:

      1) The DRP should be based on the business impact analysis.
      2) The recovery abilities of critical service providers must be assessed.
      3) The recovery of IT components often must be combined to recover a system.
      4) Service providers (internal and external) must furnish recovery information, such as their (a) responsibilities, (b) limitations, (c) recovery activities, (d) recovery time and point objectives, and (e) costs.
      5) Strategies for components may be developed independently. The objective is the best, most cost-effective solution that (a) allows user access and (b) permits components to work together, regardless of where systems are recovered.
      6) Security and compliance standards must be considered.

5. **Contingencies with Data Center Available**

   a. The purchase of backup electrical generators protects against power failures. These can be programmed to begin running automatically as soon as a dip in electric current is detected. This practice is widespread in settings such as hospitals, where 24-hour availability is crucial.

   b. Attacks such as viruses and denial-of-service require a completely different response. The system must be brought down "gracefully" to halt the spread of the infection. The IT staff must be well trained in the nature of the latest virus threats to know how to isolate the damage and bring the system back to full operation.

6. **Contingencies with Data Center Unavailable**

   a. The most extreme contingency is a disaster that makes the organization's main facility uninhabitable. To prepare for these cases, organizations contract for alternate processing facilities.

   b. An **alternate processing facility** is a physical location maintained by an outside contractor for the purpose of providing processing facilities for customers in case of disaster.

      1) The recovery center, like the off-site storage location for backup files, must be far enough away from the main facility that it is not affected by the same natural disaster. Usually, organizations contract for backup facilities in another city.
      2) Once processing is no longer possible at the principal site, the backup files are retrieved from the secure storage location and taken to the recovery center.

c.   Recovery centers take two basic forms. Organizations determine which facility is best by calculating the tradeoff between the cost of the contract and the cost of downtime.

1)   A **hot site** is a fully operational processing facility that is immediately available. The organization generally contracts with a service provider.

a)   For a fee, the service provider agrees to have a hardware platform and communications lines substantially identical to the organization's ready for use 24 hours a day, 365 days a year.

b)   This solution is the least risky and most expensive.

c)   Any contract for a hot site must include a provision for annual testing.

i)   The service provider agrees to a window of time in which the organization can declare a fake disaster, load its backup files onto the equipment at the hot site, and determine how long it takes to resume normal processing.

2)   A **warm site** is a compromise between a cold and hot site, combining features of both.

a)   Resources are available at the site but may need to be configured to support the production system.

b)   Some data may need to be restored.

c)   Typical recovery time ranges from 2 days to 2 weeks.

3)   A **cold site** is a shell facility with sufficient electrical power, environmental controls, and communications lines to permit the organization to install its own newly acquired equipment.

a)   On an ongoing basis, this solution is much less expensive.

b)   However, the time to procure replacement equipment can be weeks or months. Also, emergency procurement from equipment vendors can be very expensive.

7.   **Other Technologies for Restoration of Processing**

a.   Fault-tolerant computer systems (formerly called fail-soft systems) have additional hardware and software as well as a backup power supply. A fault-tolerant computer has additional chips and disk storage. This technology is used for mission-critical applications that cannot afford to suffer downtime.

1)   The technology that permits fault tolerance is the redundant array of inexpensive (or independent) disks, or RAID. It is a group of multiple hard drives with special software that allows for data delivery along multiple paths. If one drive fails, the other disks can compensate for the loss.

b.   High-availability computing is used for less critical applications because it provides for a short recovery time rather than the elimination of recovery time.

8.   **Business Continuity Management (BCM) Overview**

a.   The objective of BCM is to restore critical processes and to minimize financial and other effects of a disaster or business disruption.

b.   BCM is the third component of an emergency management program. Its time frame is measured in hours and days if not weeks. The other components are

1)   Emergency response, the goal of which is lifesaving, safety, and initial efforts to limit the effects of a disaster to asset damage. Its time frame is measured in hours if not minutes.

2)   Crisis management, the focus of which is managing communications and senior management activities. Its time frame is measured in days if not hours.

9. **Elements of BCM**

   a. **Management Support**

      1) Management must assign adequate resources to preparing, maintaining, and practicing a business continuity plan.

   b. **Risk Assessment and Mitigation**

      1) The entity must (a) define credible risk events (threats), (b) assess their effects, and (c) develop risk mitigation strategies.

   c. **Business Impact Analysis**

      1) This analysis identifies business processes necessary to functioning in a disaster and determines how soon they should be recovered.

      2) The organization (a) identifies critical processes, (b) defines the recovery time objective and the recovery point objective for processes and resources, and (c) identifies the other parties (e.g., vendors and other divisions of the organization) and physical resources (e.g., critical equipment and records) needed for recovery.

         a) A recovery time objective is the duration of time and service level within which a process must be restored. A recovery point objective is the amount of data the organization can afford to lose.

         b) The cost of a recovery solution ordinarily increases as either objective decreases.

   d. **Business Recovery and Continuity Strategy**

      1) A crucial element of business recovery is the existence of a comprehensive and current disaster recovery plan, which addresses the actual steps, people, and resources required to recover a critical business process. (Disaster recovery plans were discussed in greater detail earlier.)

      2) The organization plans for

         a) Alternative staffing (e.g., staff remaining at the site, staff at another site, or staff of another organization),

         b) Alternative sourcing (e.g., use of nonstandard products and services, use of diverse suppliers, outsourcing to organizations that provide standard services, or reciprocal agreements with competitors),

         c) Alternative work spaces (e.g., another organization facility, remote access with proper security, or a commercial recovery site), and

         d) The return to normal operations (e.g., entry of manually processed data, resolution of regulatory and financial exceptions, return of borrowed equipment, and replenishment of products and supplies).

   e. **Awareness, Exercises, and Maintenance**

      1) Education and awareness (including training exercises) are vital to BCM and execution of the business continuity plan.

      2) The BCM capabilities and documentation must be maintained to ensure that they remain effective and aligned with business priorities.

Stop and review! You have completed the outline for this subunit. Study multiple-choice questions 28 through 30 on page 329.

QUESTIONS

12.1 Software

1. Which of the following is a **false** statement about XBRL?

A. XBRL is freely licensed.

B. XBRL facilitates the automatic exchange of information.

C. XBRL is used primarily in the U.S.

D. XBRL is designed to work with a variety of software applications.

Answer (C) is correct.
    REQUIRED: The false statement about XBRL.
    DISCUSSION: XBRL (eXtensible Business Reporting Language) was developed for business and accounting applications. It is an XML-based application used to create, exchange, and analyze financial reporting information that was developed for worldwide use.
    Answer (A) is incorrect. The AICPA-led consortium that developed XBRL has promoted the language as a freely licensed product. Answer (B) is incorrect. XBRL facilitates the exchange of information, for example, for reporting to the SEC. Answer (D) is incorrect. XBRL allows exchange of data across many platforms and is being integrated into accounting software applications and products.

2. XML

A. Is focused on the content of the data.

B. Has become less important as new languages on the Internet are developed.

C. Uses standardized tags.

D. Is useful to display highly unstructured data.

Answer (A) is correct.
    REQUIRED: The true statement about XML.
    DISCUSSION: XML (eXtensible Markup Language) is useful for putting structured data into a text file. It can be used to extract and tag structured information from a database for transmission and subsequent use in other applications, e.g., display on the Internet or importation into a spreadsheet.
    Answer (B) is incorrect. XML has become very popular for use on the Internet. Information tagged in XML can be integrated into HTML and other presentations. Answer (C) is incorrect. XML is very flexible and allows the user to design customized (extensible) tags. Answer (D) is incorrect. The data must conform to a structure to be properly tagged.

3. C++, BASIC, FORTRAN, and COBOL are all examples of

A. Application programs.

B. Machine languages.

C. Procedural languages.

D. Operating systems.

Answer (C) is correct.
    REQUIRED: The proper classification of C++, BASIC, FORTRAN, and COBOL.
    DISCUSSION: A procedure-oriented or higher-level language allows specification of processing steps in terms of highly aggregated operations. They are ordinarily user-friendly. Translation to an object program is performed by a compiler program. COBOL (COmmon Business-Oriented Language) consists of a series of English-like statements. FORTRAN (FORmula TRANslation) is very effective for solving mathematics and engineering problems but is less so for business applications. BASIC (Beginner's All-purpose Symbolic Instruction Code) is a widely used language for personal computers but not for large business application processing. C++ is used extensively in the software industry.
    Answer (A) is incorrect. C++, BASIC, FORTRAN, and COBOL are languages, not application programs. Answer (B) is incorrect. Machine language is a programming language made up of instructions that a computer can directly recognize and execute. Answer (D) is incorrect. An operating system is a set of programs and routines to control the operations of the computer and its peripheral equipment.

4. A computer program processes payrolls. The program is a(n)

A. Operating system.

B. Application program.

C. Report generator.

D. Utility program.

Answer (B) is correct.
    REQUIRED: The term associated with a computer program used to perform a business function.
    DISCUSSION: Application programs are written to solve specific user problems; that is, they perform the ultimate computer functions required by system users. Thus, a program designed to process payroll is an application program.
    Answer (A) is incorrect. An operating system is a set of programs used by the CPU to control operations. Answer (C) is incorrect. A report generator is a component of a database management system that produces customized reports using data stored in the database. Answer (D) is incorrect. Utility programs are standardized subroutines that can be incorporated into other programs.

5. Fourth-generation computer programming languages are represented by

A. Procedure-oriented languages, which describe processing procedures.

B. Query languages, which allow direct access to a computer database.

C. Symbolic languages, which allow direct access to a stored database.

D. Machine languages, which describe processing procedures.

Answer (B) is correct.

REQUIRED: The fourth-generation computer programming languages.

DISCUSSION: Fourth-generation languages are intended to simplify programming. They are not intended to express a procedure as a specific algorithm. These interactive, English-like languages permit the user to describe the problem to and receive guidance from the computer. Query languages are most often used with databases. They permit reading and reorganization of data but not its alteration.

Answer (A) is incorrect. Procedure-oriented languages are third-generation languages that require translation into multiple machine-level instructions. Fourth-generation languages are nonprocedural languages. Answer (C) is incorrect. Symbolic languages are second-generation languages. Answer (D) is incorrect. Machine (first-generation) languages are far from the fourth-generation software development stage.

6. Which of the following programming languages supports object-oriented programming?

A. Pascal.

B. FORTRAN.

C. XBRL.

D. C++.

Answer (D) is correct.

REQUIRED: The programming language that supports object-oriented programming.

DISCUSSION: C++ was originally called "C with classes." As the name implies, C is its foundation. Classes provide a means of encapsulating the logical entities used by the program (which ordinarily represent the program's data) into a well-organized, modular format that is easy to reuse and maintain. Through a process called inheritance, new classes can be derived from existing classes by adding new elements to the existing class design. C++ was specifically designed with these features in mind. Because code segments can be reused in other programs, the time and cost of writing software is reduced.

Answer (A) is incorrect. Pascal traditionally emphasizes procedures rather than objects. Answer (B) is incorrect. FORTRAN traditionally emphasizes procedures rather than objects. Answer (C) is incorrect. XBRL is a problem-oriented or nonprocedural language. This is a type of language designed for use by non-technical individuals (i.e., not computer programmers). Object-oriented programming languages are what career computer programmers who have IT backgrounds use to program complex software applications.

12.2 Nature of Binary Data Storage

7. Based only on the database file excerpt presented below, which one of the fields or combinations of fields is eligible for use as a key?

Column I	Column II	Column III	Column IV	Column V	Column VI
Florida	Sopchoppy	G9441	6	02/06/2009	$1823.65
Georgia	Hahira	H5277	2	02/06/2009	$412.01
Iowa	Clear Lake	B2021	1	02/06/2009	$6606.53
Iowa	Clear Lake	C2021	14	02/06/2009	$178.90
Kansas	Lawrence	A1714	2	02/06/2009	$444.28
Georgia	Milledgeville	A1713	1	02/06/2009	$195.60

A. Column I and Column II in combination.

B. Column I and Column V in combination.

C. Column III alone.

D. Column IV and Column V in combination.

Answer (C) is correct.

REQUIRED: The field or combination thereof that could be used as a key.

DISCUSSION: Some field or combination of fields on each record is designated as the key. The essence of a key is that it contains enough information to uniquely identify each record; i.e., there can be no two records with the same key. Of the choices presented, only Column III by itself uniquely identifies each record.

Answer (A) is incorrect. Column I and Column II in combination do not uniquely identify each record. Answer (B) is incorrect. Column I and Column V in combination do not uniquely identify each record. Answer (D) is incorrect. Column IV and Column V in combination do not uniquely identify each record.

8. Computers understand codes that represent letters of the alphabet, numbers, or special characters. These codes require that data be converted into predefined groups of binary digits. Such chains of digits are referred to as

    A. Registers.

    B. ASCII code.

    C. Input.

    D. Bytes.

Answer (D) is correct.
    REQUIRED: The term for the chains of digits that a computer is capable of understanding.
    DISCUSSION: A byte is a grouping of bits that can define one unit of data, such as a letter or an integer.
    Answer (A) is incorrect. A register is a location within the CPU where data and instructions are temporarily stored. Answer (B) is incorrect. ASCII (American Standard Code for Information Interchange) is the coding convention itself. Answer (C) is incorrect. Input is the data placed into processing (noun) or the act of placing the data into processing (verb).

9. Which one of the following correctly depicts the hierarchy of storage commonly found in computerized databases, from least complex to most complex?

    A. Byte, field, file, record.

    B. Byte, field, record, file.

    C. Field, byte, record, file.

    D. Field, byte, file, record.

Answer (B) is correct.
    REQUIRED: The correct hierarchy in computerized databases.
    DISCUSSION: A byte is a group of bits (binary 1s and 0s). A field is a group of bytes. A record is a group of fields. A file is a group of records.
    Answer (A) is incorrect. A record is less complex than a file. Answer (C) is incorrect. A byte is less complex than a field. Answer (D) is incorrect. A byte is less complex than a field, and a record is less complex than a file.

12.3 File Organization and Databases

10. Of the following, the greatest advantage of a database (server) architecture is that

    A. Data redundancy can be reduced.

    B. Conversion to a database system is inexpensive and can be accomplished quickly.

    C. Multiple occurrences of data items are useful for consistency checking.

    D. Backup and recovery procedures are minimized.

Answer (A) is correct.
    REQUIRED: The greatest advantage of a database architecture.
    DISCUSSION: Data organized in files and used by the organization's various application programs are collectively known as a database. In a database system, storage structures are created that render the applications programs independent of the physical or logical arrangement of the data. Each data item has a standard definition, name, and format, and related items are linked by a system of pointers. The programs therefore need only specify data items by name, not by location. A database management system handles retrieval and storage. Because separate files for different application programs are unnecessary, data redundancy can be substantially reduced.
    Answer (B) is incorrect. Conversion to a database is often costly and time consuming. Answer (C) is incorrect. A traditional flat-file system, not a database, has multiple occurrences of data items. Answer (D) is incorrect. Given the absence of data redundancy and the quick propagation of data errors throughout applications, backup and recovery procedures are just as critical in a database as in a flat-file system.

11. A database is

    A. Essential for the storage of large data sets.

    B. A collection of related files.

    C. A real-time system.

    D. A network of computer terminals.

Answer (B) is correct.
    REQUIRED: The true statement about a database.
    DISCUSSION: The use of a database system significantly reduces redundancy of stored data in a system. Data in a standardized form are ideally entered once into integrated files and then used for any and all related applications. The database is usually built to serve multiple applications. Consequently, the data are independent of particular applications and greater flexibility in meeting unanticipated demands is possible. The database approach also allows for better access by users and for more rapid updating of information.
    Answer (A) is incorrect. The need for a database arises more from the multiplicity of applications than from the quantity of data stored. Answer (C) is incorrect. A database system need not provide immediate (real-time) responses. Answer (D) is incorrect. A database is an integrated, centralized group of files.

12. The primary purpose of a database system is to have a single storage location for each

- A. File.
- B. Record.
- C. Database.
- D. Item of data.

Answer (D) is correct.
    REQUIRED: The primary purpose of a database system.
    DISCUSSION: Databases allow companies to save data (information) in one place instead of having hundreds of specific files with similar data.
    Answer (A) is incorrect. Databases are not organized by file. Answer (B) is incorrect. Databases are not organized by records. Answer (C) is incorrect. The database is the collective result of organizing data in this way.

13. In an inventory system on a database, one stored record contains part number, part name, part color, and part weight. These individual items are called

- A. Fields.
- B. Stored files.
- C. Bytes.
- D. Occurrences.

Answer (A) is correct.
    REQUIRED: The term for the data elements in a record.
    DISCUSSION: A record is a collection of related data items (fields). A field (data item) is a group of characters representing one unit of information.
    Answer (B) is incorrect. A file is a group or set of related records ordered to facilitate processing. Answer (C) is incorrect. A byte is a group of bits (binary digits). It represents one character. Answer (D) is incorrect. "Occurrences" is not a meaningful term in this context.

14. A database has three record types: (1) for suppliers, a type that contains a unique supplier number, a supplier name, and a supplier address; (2) for parts, a type that contains a unique part number, a part name, a description, and a location; and (3) for purchases, a type that contains a unique supplier number referencing the supplier number in the supplier record, a part number referencing the part number in the part record, and a quantity. This database has a

- A. Single flat-file structure.
- B. Hierarchical structure.
- C. Relational structure.
- D. Network structure.

Answer (C) is correct.
    REQUIRED: The structure of the described database.
    DISCUSSION: A relational structure organizes data in conceptual tables. One relation (a table or file) can be joined with (related to) another by the DBMS without pointers or linked lists if each contains one or more of the same fields (also known as columns or attributes). This database has a relational structure because it includes no links that are not contained in the data records themselves.
    Answer (A) is incorrect. Each record type corresponds to a flat file, but there are multiple structures rather than a single flat-file structure. Answer (B) is incorrect. A hierarchical structure would have a tree structure with embedded links instead of explicit data values. Answer (D) is incorrect. A network structure would have bidirectional pointers instead of explicit data values.

12.4 Database Management Systems

15. One advantage of a database management system (DBMS) is

- A. Each organizational unit takes responsibility and control for its own data.
- B. The cost of the data processing department decreases as users are now responsible for establishing their own data handing techniques.
- C. A decreased vulnerability as the database management system has numerous security controls to prevent disasters.
- D. The independence of the data from the application programs, which allows the programs to be developed for the user's specific needs without concern for data capture problems.

Answer (D) is correct.
    REQUIRED: The advantage of a DBMS.
    DISCUSSION: A fundamental characteristic of databases is that applications are independent of the database structure; when writing programs or designing applications to use the database, only the name of the desired item is necessary. Programs can be developed for the user's specific needs without concern for data capture problems. Reference can be made to the items using the data manipulation language, after which the DBMS takes care of locating and retrieving the desired items. The physical or logical structure of the database can be completely altered without having to change any of the programs using the data items. Only the schema requires alteration.
    Answer (A) is incorrect. Each organizational unit develops programs to use the elements of a broad database. Answer (B) is incorrect. Data handling techniques are still the responsibility of the data processing department. It is the use of the data that is departmentalized. Answer (C) is incorrect. The DBMS is not necessarily safer than any other database system.

16. An overall description of a database, including the names of data elements, their characteristics, and their relationship to each other, is defined by using a

   A. Data definition language.

   B. Data control language.

   C. Data manipulation language.

   D. Data command interpreter language.

Answer (A) is correct.

REQUIRED: The language used to define a database.

DISCUSSION: The data definition language defines the database structure and content, especially the schema (the description of the entire database) and subschema (logical views of the database). The schema specifies characteristics such as the names of the data elements contained in the database and their relationship to each other. The subschema defines the logical data views required for applications, which limits the data elements and functions available to each application.

Answer (B) is incorrect. The data control language specifies the privileges and security rules governing database users. Answer (C) is incorrect. Data manipulation language provides application programs with a means of interacting with the database to add, retrieve, modify, or delete data or relationships. Answer (D) is incorrect. Data command interpreter languages are symbolic character strings used to control the current state of database management system operations.

17. Which of the following is a **false** statement about a database management system application environment?

   A. Data are used concurrently by multiple users.

   B. Data are shared by passing files between programs or systems.

   C. The physical structure of the data is independent of user needs.

   D. Data definition is independent of any one program.

Answer (B) is correct.

REQUIRED: The false statement about data in a DBMS environment.

DISCUSSION: In this kind of system, applications use the same database. There is no need to pass files between applications.

Answer (A) is incorrect. The advantage of a DBMS is that data can be used concurrently by multiple users. Answer (C) is incorrect. When a DBMS is used, the physical structure of the data is independent of user needs. Answer (D) is incorrect. When a DBMS is used, the data are defined independently of the needs of any one program.

18. The function of a data dictionary is to

   A. Mark the boundary between two consecutive transactions.

   B. Describe and share information about objects and resources.

   C. Specify systems users.

   D. Specify privileges and security rules for objects and resources.

Answer (B) is correct.

REQUIRED: The function of a data dictionary.

DISCUSSION: A data dictionary is an organized and shared collection of information about the objects and resources used by the information system (IS) organization to deliver or exchange information internally and externally.

Answer (A) is incorrect. The database management system log contains checkpoint records that mark the boundary between two consecutive transactions. Answer (C) is incorrect. Specification of system users is a function of the security features of a DBMS. Answer (D) is incorrect. The data control language specifies privileges and security rules for objects and resources.

19. The increased use of database processing systems makes managing data and information a major information service function. Because the databases of an organization are used for many different applications, they are coordinated and controlled by a database administrator. The functions of a database administrator are

   A. Data input preparation, database design, and database operations.

   B. Database design, database operation, and database security.

   C. Database design, database operation, and equipment operations.

   D. Database design, software support, and database security.

Answer (B) is correct.

REQUIRED: The functions of a database administrator.

DISCUSSION: A database administrator (DBA) is the person who has overall responsibility for developing, designing, controlling, and maintaining the database. The DBA manages all database functions including design and maintenance of the schema that describes the structure of the database. The DBA also assigns user passwords and establishes other security measures. Control of changes in data items and in the programs that use the database is another responsibility of the DBA.

Answer (A) is incorrect. The user is responsible for input preparation. Answer (C) is incorrect. The manager of the IT department is responsible for equipment (hardware) operations. Answer (D) is incorrect. The systems programming group is responsible for software support.

12.5 Application Development and Maintenance

20. An insurance firm that follows the systems development life cycle concept for all major information system projects is preparing to start a feasibility study for a proposed underwriting system. Some of the primary factors the feasibility study should include are

A. Possible vendors for the system and their reputation for quality.

B. Exposure to computer viruses and other intrusions.

C. Methods of implementation, such as parallel or cutover.

D. Technology and related costs.

Answer (D) is correct.
REQUIRED: The primary factors the feasibility study should include.
DISCUSSION: The feasibility study should consider the activity to be automated, the needs of the user, the type of equipment required, the cost, and the potential benefit to the specific area and the company in general. Thus, technical feasibility and cost are determined during this stage.
Answer (A) is incorrect. Possible vendors for the system and their reputation for quality would be determined after the feasibility study. Answer (B) is incorrect. Exposure to computer viruses and other intrusions is part of the information requirements phase. Answer (C) is incorrect. Methods of implementation, such as parallel or cutover, would be determined during the implementation and operations stage.

21. Ordinarily, the analysis tool for the systems analyst and steering committee to use in selecting the best system alternative is

A. Pilot testing.

B. User selection.

C. Decision tree analysis.

D. Cost-benefit analysis.

Answer (D) is correct.
REQUIRED: The analysis tool to use in selecting the best system alternative.
DISCUSSION: Feasibility studies should include an analysis of the cost-benefit ratio of any system alternatives. In many cases, the best possible system may not be cost effective. Thus, once the decision makers have determined that two or more systems alternatives are acceptable, the cost-benefit relationship should be used to select the best system for a particular application.
Answer (A) is incorrect. Pilot testing typically occurs after development of a system. Answer (B) is incorrect. Users may not have the necessary systems knowledge to make a decision. Answer (C) is incorrect. Decision tree analysis is probably more sophisticated than is necessary in choosing between a few systems alternatives.

22. The process of learning how the current system functions, determining the needs of users, and developing the logical requirements of a proposed system is referred to as

A. Systems maintenance.

B. Systems analysis.

C. Systems feasibility study.

D. Systems design.

Answer (B) is correct.
REQUIRED: The term referring to the process of learning how a system functions, determining the needs of users, and developing the logical requirements of a proposed system.
DISCUSSION: A systems analysis requires a survey of the existing system, the organization itself, and the organization's environment to determine (among other things) whether a new system is needed. The survey results determine not only what, where, how, and by whom activities are performed but also why, how well, and whether they should be done at all. Ascertaining the problems and informational needs of decision makers is the next step. The systems analyst must consider the entity's key success variables (factors that determine its success or failure), the decisions currently being made and those that should be made, the factors important in decision making (timing, relation to other decisions, etc.), the information needed for decisions, and how well the current system makes those decisions. Finally, the systems analysis should establish the requirements of a system that will meet user needs.
Answer (A) is incorrect. Maintenance is the final stage of the life cycle in that it continues throughout the life of the system; maintenance includes the redesign of the system and programs to meet new needs or to correct design flaws. Answer (C) is incorrect. The systems feasibility study does not involve the process of learning how the current system works. Answer (D) is incorrect. Systems design is the process of developing a system to meet specified requirements.

23. Two phases of systems planning are project definition and project initiation. All of the following are steps in the project initiation phase **except**

- A. Preparing the project proposal.
- B. Informing managers and employees of the project.
- C. Assembling the project team.
- D. Training selected personnel.

Answer (A) is correct.

REQUIRED: The step not a part of the project initiation phase of systems planning.

DISCUSSION: The project initiation phase includes promptly informing managers and employees about the project, assembling the project team (possibly including systems analysts, programmers, accountants, and users), training selected personnel to improve necessary skills and enhance communication among team members, and establishing project controls (e.g., by implementing a project scheduling technique such as PERT). Preparing the project proposal is a part of the project definition phase, as are conducting feasibility studies, determining project priority, and submitting the proposal for approval.

Answer (B) is incorrect. Informing managers and employees of the project is a component of the project initiation phase. Answer (C) is incorrect. Assembling the project team is a component of the project initiation phase. Answer (D) is incorrect. Training selected personnel is a component of the project initiation phase.

24. The **least** risky strategy for converting from a manual to a computerized accounts receivable system would be a

- A. Direct conversion.
- B. Parallel conversion.
- C. Pilot conversion.
- D. Database conversion.

Answer (B) is correct.

REQUIRED: The least risky strategy for converting from a manual to a computerized accounts receivable system.

DISCUSSION: The least risky strategy for converting from a manual to a computerized system is a parallel conversion in which the old and new systems are operated simultaneously until satisfaction is obtained that the new system is operating as expected. Slightly more risky is a pilot conversion in which the new system is introduced by module or segment.

Answer (A) is incorrect. A direct conversion is more risky than a parallel conversion. Answer (C) is incorrect. A pilot conversion is more risky than a parallel conversion. Answer (D) is incorrect. A database conversion is more risky than a parallel conversion.

25. The process of monitoring, evaluating, and modifying a system as needed is referred to as

- A. Systems analysis.
- B. Systems feasibility study.
- C. Systems maintenance.
- D. Systems implementation.

Answer (C) is correct.

REQUIRED: The term for the process of monitoring, evaluating, and modifying a system.

DISCUSSION: Systems maintenance must be undertaken by systems analysts and applications programmers continuously throughout the life of a system. Maintenance is the redesign of the system and programs to meet new needs or to correct design flaws. Ideally, these changes should be made as part of a regular program of preventive maintenance.

Answer (A) is incorrect. Systems analysis is the process of determining user problems and needs, surveying the organization's present system, and analyzing the facts. Answer (B) is incorrect. A feasibility study determines whether a proposed system is technically, operationally, and economically feasible. Answer (D) is incorrect. Systems implementation involves training and educating system users, testing, conversion, and follow-up.

26. An information system (IS) project manager is currently in the process of adding a systems analyst to the IS staff. The new systems analyst will be involved with testing the new computerized system. At which stage of the systems development life cycle will the analyst be primarily used?

- A. Cost-benefit analysis.
- B. Requirements definition.
- C. Flowcharting.
- D. Development.

Answer (D) is correct.

REQUIRED: The stage of the systems development life cycle involving testing of a new system.

DISCUSSION: The systems development life-cycle approach is the oldest methodology applied to the development of medium or large information systems. The cycle is analytically divisible into stages: definition, design, development, implementation, and maintenance. Testing is the most crucial step in the development stage of the life cycle.

Answer (A) is incorrect. Cost-benefit analysis is a part of the feasibility study conducted early in the life cycle. Answer (B) is incorrect. Requirements are defined during the analysis or systems study stage. Answer (C) is incorrect. Flowcharting is a necessary activity in all early stages of the life cycle.

27. A benefit of using computer-aided software engineering (CASE) technology is that it can ensure that

- A. No obsolete data fields occur in files.
- B. Users become committed to new systems.
- C. All programs are optimized for efficiency.
- D. Data integrity rules are applied consistently.

Answer (D) is correct.

REQUIRED: The benefit of CASE.

DISCUSSION: CASE is an automated technology (at least in part) for developing and maintaining software and managing projects. A benefit of using CASE technology is that it can ensure that data integrity rules, including those for validation and access, are applied consistently across all files.

Answer (A) is incorrect. Obsolete data fields must be recognized by developers or users. Once recognized, obsolete data fields can be treated consistently in CASE procedures. Answer (B) is incorrect. Using CASE will not ensure user commitment to new systems if they are poorly designed or otherwise do not meet users' needs. Answer (C) is incorrect. Although it has the potential to accelerate system development, CASE cannot ensure that all programs are optimized for efficiency. In fact, some CASE-developed modules may need to be optimized by hand to achieve acceptable performance.

12.6 Contingency Planning

28. Which of the following best describes the primary reason that organizations develop contingency plans for their computer-based information systems operations?

- A. To ensure that they will be able to process vital transactions in the event of a disaster.
- B. To ensure the safety of important records.
- C. To help hold down the cost of insurance.
- D. To plan for sources of capital for recovery from any type of disaster.

Answer (A) is correct.

REQUIRED: The primary reason that organizations develop contingency plans for their IS operations.

DISCUSSION: Contingency plans must be drafted so that the organization will be able to resume normal processing following a disaster.

Answer (B) is incorrect. The safety of records is a secondary reason. Answer (C) is incorrect. The reduction of insurance costs is a secondary reason. Answer (D) is incorrect. Planning for sources of capital is seldom included in disaster recovery planning.

29. Which of the following procedures would an entity most likely include in its computer disaster recovery plan?

- A. Develop an auxiliary power supply to provide uninterrupted electricity.
- B. Store duplicate copies of critical files in a location away from the processing facility.
- C. Maintain a listing of all entity passwords with the network manager.
- D. Translate data for storage purposes with a cryptographic secret code.

Answer (B) is correct.

REQUIRED: The most likely procedure to follow in a computer disaster recovery plan.

DISCUSSION: Off-site storage of duplicate copies of critical files protects them from a fire or other disaster at the computing facility. The procedure is part of an overall disaster recovery plan.

Answer (A) is incorrect. The use of an uninterruptible power supply ensures continued processing rather than recovery from a disaster. Answer (C) is incorrect. Maintaining a safeguarded copy of passwords protects against loss of passwords by personnel. Answer (D) is incorrect. Encrypting stored data files protects them from unauthorized use.

30. If High Tech Corporation's disaster recovery plan requires fast recovery with little or no downtime, which of the following backup sites should it choose?

- A. Hot site.
- B. Warm site.
- C. Cold site.
- D. Quick site.

Answer (A) is correct.

REQUIRED: The type of backup facility that has fast recovery and little or no downtime.

DISCUSSION: A company uses a hot site backup when fast recovery is critical. The hot site includes all software, hardware, and other equipment necessary for a company to carry out operations. Hot sites are expensive to maintain and may be shared with other organizations with similar needs.

Answer (B) is incorrect. A warm site provides an intermediate level of backup and causes more downtime than a hot site. Answer (C) is incorrect. A cold site is a shell facility suitable for quick installation of computer equipment. Disaster recovery would take more time in a cold site than a hot site. Answer (D) is incorrect. There is no backup site called a quick site.

12.7 PRACTICE WRITTEN COMMUNICATION

Business Environment and Concepts
Testlet 4 of 4

Time Remaining
1 hour - 15 minutes

Unsplit   Split Horiz   Split Vertical   Exit

DIRECTIONS

Note: If you believe you have encountered a software malfunction, report it to the test center staff immediately.

Navigation

To navigate from task to task, use the controls at the bottom of the screen. Click on the **Next** button to advance to the next task, or the **Previous** button to go to the previous task. To go directly to any task, click on its number.

▼ = Reminder   Directions   1 2 3 4 5 6 7   ◀ Previous   Next ▶

If you would like a reminder to revisit a task, or want to indicate that you are finished with it, click on the reminder flag below the task number. To clear the flag, click on it again. Reminder flags are for your use only — they do not contribute to your score.

Tabs

In this part of the examination, you will be asked to complete various tasks. Every task has one or more **Work Tabs**. Every task also has a **Help** tab.

✏ Written Communication | Help

Work tab   Help tab

Work Tabs:

- **Work Tabs** are identified with a pencil icon. This is where your responses are expected.
- Each task has one or more **Work Tabs**.
- **Work Tabs** contain directions for completing the task - be sure to read these directions carefully.
- The **Work Tab** name in the example above is for illustration only - yours will differ.
- You must complete all of the **Work Tabs** in each task to receive full credit.

Help Tab:

- The **Help Tab** provides assistance with the exam software that is used in this task. For example, if the task is to compose a memorandum, **Help** will provide information about the word processor.

The Toolbar

The toolbar at the top of the screen shows the amount of time remaining for you to complete the tasks. In addition, the following tools are available. Note that only the **Exit** button is displayed when Directions are visible - the others will appear when you begin the tasks.

Unsplit   Split Horiz   Split Vertical

Click on these buttons to split or unsplit the screen. You can split the screen vertically or horizontally.

Exit

Click on this button to go on to the next part of the examination. You must complete all of the tasks to receive full credit. Once you click on **Exit** and confirm the action, you will NOT be able to return to this testlet.

▼ = Reminder   Directions   1   ◀ Previous   Next ▶

Scott, a recent college graduate, has just begun his first year at Happy Accountants, LLP. He has been assigned to a client, Larry Co., whose financial statements have been audited by the firm for the past 3 years. Because Scott is inexperienced, he is unsure about certain documentation requirements. He is specifically confused about the auditor's responsibility with regard to fraud. He has asked you about the procedures and documentation requirements regarding the risk of material misstatement due to fraud.

In a memorandum to Scott, describe an auditor's documentation requirements regarding the consideration of the risk of material misstatement due to fraud in a financial statement audit.

Type your communication below the line in the response area below.

REMINDER: Your response will be graded for both technical content and writing skills. Technical content will be evaluated for information that is helpful to the intended reader and clearly relevant to the issue. Writing skills will be evaluated for development, organization, and the appropriate expression of ideas in professional correspondence. Use a standard business memorandum or letter format with a clear beginning, middle, and end. Do not convey information in the form of a table, bullet point list, or other abbreviated presentation.

To: Scott
Re: Documentation requirements for risk of material misstatement due to fraud

---

NOTE: Your Written Communications on the actual CPA exam may cover topics outside the scope of the BEC CSO (i.e., they may relate to topics from the AUD, FAR, and/or REG CSOs instead). Answer to the best of your ability, and remember that graders are mainly evaluating your writing ability and will overlook minor technical mistakes.

Unofficial Answer

Written Communication

To: Scott
Re: Documentation requirements for risk of material misstatement due to fraud

---

The auditor must document the consideration of the risks of material misstatement due to fraud in a financial statement audit. The documentation of planning-stage discussions should extend to (1) significant decisions made, (2) how and when the discussions were held, (3) the individuals involved, and (4) the identified risks at the financial statement and assertion levels. The auditor also documents (1) the overall responses to the assessed risks; (2) the nature, timing, and extent of audit procedures; (3) the connection between the assessed risks and the procedures performed at the assertion level; and (4) the results of those procedures.

Furthermore, a financial statement audit ordinarily is based on the presumption of a risk of material misstatement due to fraud related to revenue recognition. If the auditor has not identified such a risk, the reasons for that conclusion must be documented.

However, a risk of material misstatement due to fraud related to management override of controls is always assumed. Thus, the auditor must document the results of further addressing management override.

Other required documentation includes the nature of fraud communications to (1) management, (2) those charged with governance, (3) regulators, and (4) other parties.

The above depicts a Level 5 answer. Consult your booklet, *How to Pass the CPA Exam: A System for Success*, for a description of the three writing skills criteria. You may also access this booklet online by visiting www.gleim.com/PassCPA.

Self-Grade

Below, grade your response on technical content and writing skills. Bubble in the circle next to the appropriate score that you may receive based on the criteria given. Your **total** score is the sum of your scores on all six items. The maximum score is 19 points.

Technical Content Evaluation

Was your response on topic?	O No [0]	O Mostly [1]	O Yes [2]
Did your response have any *significant* errors?	O 0 errors [1]	O 1 major error [–1]	O 2 or more major errors [–2]
Did your response contain any illegal advice?	O No [1]	O Yes [0]	

Writing Skills Evaluation

	Poor	Below Average	Average	Above Average	Outstanding
Organization	O 1	O 2	O 3	O 4	O 5
Development	O 1	O 2	O 3	O 4	O 5
Expression	O 1	O 2	O 3	O 4	O 5

Disclaimer: This scoring schedule was developed by Gleim Publications as a guideline only. The AICPA has not released specific information on how the Written Communications are graded.

Practice even more Written Communications with the Gleim Mega Test Bank.

Learn more: gleim.com/CPAmega | 800.874.5346

STUDY UNIT THIRTEEN
IT NETWORKS AND ELECTRONIC COMMERCE

(12 pages of outline)

Huge gains in productivity have resulted from the networking of computers. The traditional ways of carrying on business have found new channels through electronic networking. Now, the use of encryption is required to make messages sent electronically secure. As a licensed CPA, you will need to know how computers communicate over networks so you can ascertain their vulnerability. This study unit introduces you to the types of communications between computers. The next study unit focuses on how to assess and quantify information risks.

13.1 NETWORKS AND THE INTERNET

1.   **Mainframe Communication**

   a.   Large mainframe computers dominated the electronic data processing field in its first decades. Mainframes were arranged so that all processing and data storage were done in a single, centralized location.

   b.   Communication with the mainframe was accomplished with the use of dumb terminals, simple keyboard-and-monitor combinations with no processing power (i.e., no CPU) of their own.

2.   **Increasing Decentralization**

   a.   Improvements in technology have led to increasing decentralization of information processing.

      1)   The mainframe-style computer was the only arrangement available in the early days of data processing. International Business Machines (now called IBM) dominated the marketplace.

      2)   Mainframes are still in use at large institutions, such as governments, banks, insurance companies, and universities. However, remote connections to them are usually through personal computers rather than through dumb terminals. This is known as terminal emulation.

      3)   As minicomputers evolved, the concept of distributed processing arose.

         a)   **Distributed processing** involves the decentralization of processing tasks and data storage and assigning these functions to multiple computers, often in separate locations.

         b)   This allowed for a drastic reduction in the amount of communications traffic because data needed locally could reside locally.

   b.   During the 1980s, personal computers and the knowledge needed to build information systems became widespread throughout the organization.

      1)   In the early part of this period, the only means of moving data from one computer to another was through the laborious process of copying the data to a diskette and physically carrying it to the destination computer.

      2)   It was clear that a reliable way of wiring office computers together would lead to tremendous gains in productivity.

Be sure you are able to describe distributed processing and the types of networks. Recent exams have included several questions on this topic.

3. **Local Area Networks (LANs)**

    a. The need to increase productivity led to the development of the local area network (LAN). A LAN is any interconnection between devices in a single office or building.

        1) Very small networks with few devices can be connected using a peer-to-peer arrangement, where every device is connected directly to every other. Peer-to-peer networks become increasingly difficult to administer with each added device.

    b. The most cost-effective and easy-to-administer arrangement for LANs uses the client-server model.

        1) Client-server networks differ from peer-to-peer networks in that the devices play more specialized roles. Client processes (initiated by the individual user) request services from server processes (maintained centrally).

        2) In a client-server arrangement, servers are centrally located and devoted to the functions that are needed by all network users.

            a) Examples include mail servers (to handle electronic mail), application servers (to run application programs), file servers (to store databases and make user inquiries more efficient), Internet servers (to manage access to the Internet), and web servers (to host websites).

            b) Whether a device is classified as a server is not determined by its hardware configuration, but rather by the function it performs. A simple personal computer can be a server.

        3) Technically, a client is any object that uses the resources of another object. Thus, a client can be either a device or a software program.

            a) In common usage, however, "client" refers to a device that requests services from a server. This understanding of the term encompasses anything from a powerful graphics workstation to a personal mobile device.

            b) A client device normally displays the user interface and enables data entry, queries, and the receipt of reports. Moreover, many applications, e.g., word processing and spreadsheet software, run on the client computer.

        4) The key to the client-server model is that it runs processes on the platform most appropriate to that process while attempting to minimize traffic over the network.

            a) This is commonly referred to as the three-tiered architecture of client, application, and database.

            b) Because of the specialized roles, client-server systems are often assembled with equipment from multiple vendors.

        5) Security for client-server systems may be more difficult than in a highly centralized system because of the numerous access points.

    c.   Along with the increased convenience and flexibility of decentralization came new security risks.

        1)   Unauthorized software can be easily installed on the network from a desktop computer. This exposes the organization to both viruses and liability for copyright violation.

        2)   Important files stored on a local computer may not be backed up properly by the user.

        3)   Applications written by users of local computers may not adhere to the standards of the organization, making data sharing difficult.

4.   **Classifying Networks by Geographical Extent and Function**

    a.   The range of networking has expanded from the earliest form (two computers in the same room) to the global reach of the Internet.

    b.   A **local area network (LAN)** connects devices within a single office or home or among buildings in an office park. The key aspect here is that a LAN is owned entirely by a single organization.

        1)   The LAN is the network familiar to office workers all over the world. In its simplest conception, it can consist of a few personal computers and a printer.

    c.   A **wide area network (WAN)** consists of a conglomerate of LANs over widely separated locations. The key aspect here is that a WAN can be either publicly or privately owned.

        1)   One advantage of a WAN is the possibility of spreading the cost of ownership among multiple organizations.

            a)   WANs come in many configurations. In its simplest conception, it can consist of a lone personal computer using a slow dial-up line to connect to an Internet service provider.

        2)   Publicly owned WANs, such as the public telephone system and the Internet, are available to any user with a compatible device. The assets of these networks are paid for by means other than individually imposed user fees.

            a)   Public-switched networks use public telephone lines to carry data. This arrangement is economical, but the quality of data transmission cannot be guaranteed and security is highly questionable.

        3)   Privately owned WANs are profit-making enterprises. They offer fast, secure data communication services to organizations that do not wish to make their own large investments in the necessary infrastructure.

            a)   **Value-added networks (VANs)** are private networks that provide their customers with reliable, high-speed secure transmission of data.

                i)   To compete with the Internet, these third-party networks add value by providing their customers with error detection and correction services, electronic mailbox facilities for EDI purposes, EDI translation, and security for email and data transmissions.

            b)   **Virtual private networks (VPNs)** emerged as a relatively inexpensive way to solve the problem of the high cost of leased lines.

                i)   A company connects each office or LAN to a local Internet service provider and routes data through the shared, low-cost public Internet.

                ii)   The success of VPNs depends on the development of secure encryption products that protect data while in transit.

    4)   Intranets and extranets are types of WANs.

        a)   An **intranet** permits sharing of information throughout an organization by applying Internet connectivity standards and Web software (e.g., browsers) to the organization's internal network.

            i)   An intranet addresses the connectivity problems faced by organizations that have many types of computers. Its use is restricted to those within the organization.

        b)   An **extranet** consists of the linked intranets of two or more organizations, for example, of a supplier and its customers. It typically uses the public Internet as its transmission medium but requires a password for access.

5. **The Internet**

    a.   The Internet is a network of networks all over the world.

Background

The Internet is descended from the original ARPANet, a product of the Defense Department's Advanced Research Projects Agency (ARPA), introduced in 1969. The idea was to have a network that could not be brought down during an enemy attack by bombing a single central location. ARPANet connected computers at universities, corporations, and government. In view of the growing success of the Internet, ARPANet was retired in 1990.

---

    b.   The Internet facilitates inexpensive communication and information transfer among computers, with gateways allowing servers to interface with personal computers.

        1)   Very high-speed Internet connections (termed the Internet backbone) carry signals around the world and meet at network access points.

    c.   Most Internet users obtain connections through **Internet service providers** (ISPs) that in turn connect either directly to a gateway or to a larger ISP with a connection to a gateway.

        1)   The topology of the backbone and its interconnections may once have resembled a spine with ribs connected along its length, but it is now more like a fishing net wrapped around the world with many circular paths.

    d.   TCP/IP (Transmission Control Protocol/Internet Protocol) is a term candidates should be familiar with. It is defined as a suite of communications protocols (rules or standards) used to connect computers to the Internet. It is also built into network operating systems.

6. **Aspects and Terminology of the Internet**

    a.   The Internet was initially restricted to email and text-only documents. **Hypertext markup language** (HTML) allows users to click on a word or phrase (a hyperlink) on their screens and have another document automatically be displayed.

    b.   **Hypertext transfer protocol** (HTTP) allows hyperlinking across the Internet rather than on just a single computer. A browser allows users to read HTML from any brand of computer. This system became known as the World Wide Web (often simply called "the Web").

        1)   As the use of HTML and its successor languages spread, it became possible to display rich graphics and stream audio and video in addition to text.

        2)   **Extensible markup language** (XML) was developed by an international consortium and released in 1998 as an open standard (e.g., not owned or controlled by any one entity) usable with many programs and platforms.

            a)   XML codes all information in such a way that a user can determine not only how it should be presented but also what it is; i.e., all computerized data may be tagged with identifiers.

        b)   Unlike HTML, XML uses extensible codes. Thus, if an industry can agree on a set of codes, software for that industry can be written that incorporates those codes.

    c.   Every resource on the Web has a unique address, made up of alphanumeric characters, periods, and forward slashes, called a **uniform resource locator** (URL). A URL is recognizable by any web-enabled device. An example is http://www.gleim.com/.

        1)   However, just because the address is recognizable does not mean its content is accessible to every user–security is a major feature of any organization's website.

7.   **Cloud Computing**

    a.   Cloud computing ("the cloud") is a popular term relating to on-demand access to resources that are accessed on the Internet and shared by others.

    b.   Advantages of using cloud computing include fast access to software, a reduced need for investment in IT infrastructure, and the ability to use "pay as you go" services.

    c.   IT security in the cloud is potentially more difficult due to the convenience and ease of access to sensitive data provided by cloud computing services.

    d.   There are four primary cloud services:

        1)   **Data-as-a-Service (DaaS)**
        2)   **Infrastructure-as-a-Service (IaaS)**
        3)   **Platform-as-a-Service (PaaS)**
        4)   **Software-as-a-Service (SaaS)**

    e.   Cloud computing has also benefited from the rise of smartphones and tablets.

        1)   Since these devices do not have unlimited memory, personal data (e.g., pictures, contacts, etc.) may be stored on the cloud to be retrieved later so that limited memory can be used for application software.

Stop and review! You have completed the outline for this subunit. Study multiple-choice questions 1 through 10 beginning on page 344.

13.2 ELECTRONIC COMMERCE

1.   **Overview**

    a.   **E-business** is an umbrella term referring to all methods of conducting business electronically.

        1)   This can include strictly internal communications as well as nonfinancial dealings with outside parties (e.g., contract negotiations).

    b.   **E-commerce** is a narrower term referring to the conduct of financial transactions with outside parties electronically (e.g., the purchase and sale of goods and services).

        1)   E-commerce introduces a new set of efficiencies into business relationships. Where orders previously were placed using a combination of phone calls and either mailed or faxed hard copy documents, e-commerce allows such transactions to take place entirely over the Internet.

        2)   E-commerce comes in two basic varieties: business-to-business (B2B) and business-to-consumer (B2C).

        3)   E-business and e-commerce are sometimes considered to be synonymous.

c. An extranet is one means of carrying on e-commerce.

    1) Extranets rely on the established communications protocols of the Internet. Thus, the expensive, specialized equipment needed for electronic data interchange (EDI) is unnecessary.

    2) Firewalls, which can be hardware- or software-based, provide security.

    3) The extranet approach is based on less formal agreements between the trading partners than in EDI and requires the sending firm to format the documents into the format of the receiving firm.

2. **Security and Reliability of E-Commerce**

  a. Because of the reduced level of human involvement in e-commerce, new security and reliability concerns arise.

  b. Specific concerns include the following (each issue is of greater or lesser relative importance depending on whether the application is B2B, B2C, or C2C):

    1) The transacting parties must be correctly identified, a process known as authentication. IDs and passwords are the most common tools for authentication.

    2) The circumstances in which a binding agreement can be made must be agreed to; in other words, who (or what system) is authorized to place (or promise to fill) an order? This is especially important in B2B applications, when entire production runs and large amounts of money are at stake.

    3) The confidentiality and integrity of information transmitted electronically must be maintained. Encryption is the most useful tool for this purpose.

    4) A reliable record of the transaction must be preserved such that disputes can be resolved and audits can be performed.

    5) Potential customers must be able to trust listed prices and discounts.

    6) Payment data must be verifiable.

    7) Both parties' systems must be robust; i.e., they are up and running at all times.

3. **Business-to-Business (B2B) E-Commerce**

  a. B2B can be used to speed up the order and fulfillment process.

    1) A manufacturer in need of raw materials can initiate the transaction with an email or by using the vendor's extranet.

    2) The process can be further automated by establishing an EDI arrangement, in which the buyer's purchasing system automatically places an order with the vendor when inventories reach a predetermined level.

      a) The partners must have (1) a common electronic document format and (2) a pre-existing agreement under which such orders will be accepted and filled without human intervention.

  b. **Benefits of B2B** include

    1) Reduced purchasing costs

      a) Purchasing products online saves time, and electronically processing an order simplifies the ordering process.

    2) Increased market efficiency

      a) By using the Internet, companies have easy access to price quotes from various suppliers. Buyers are more likely to get a better price, given the increased number of suppliers.

    3) Greater market intelligence

      a) B2B provides producers with better insights into the demand levels in any given market.

4) Decreased inventory levels

    a) Companies can make better use of their inventory and raw materials. The Internet allows companies using just-in-time (JIT) manufacturing techniques to achieve better control of their operations, for example, by more precise coordination of delivery of raw materials. It also allows companies to use less working capital to do the same amount of work, which allows those funds to be invested elsewhere.

c. The overriding principle of online B2B is that it can make companies more efficient.

    1) Increased efficiency means lower costs, which is a goal that interests every company. Thus, the potential of B2B online commerce is enormous.

4. **Business-to-Consumer (B2C) E-Commerce**

a. B2C is one of the fastest growing segments of the economy. Consumers can order a vast array of merchandise from the comfort of their homes or from mobile devices.

    1) B2C is almost exclusively conducted via the Internet.

    2) Traditional retailers have expanded their reach with B2C, and some firms, notably Amazon.com, use the Internet as their sole communication channel with customers.

b. Many of the same benefits accrue to businesses as in the B2B model with reduced costs and increased efficiency.

    1) Many of the same security issues, such as authorization, also apply, but on a smaller scale. Also, the vendor need not concern itself with the IT infrastructure on the customer's end.

5. **Social Media**

a. Social media is the interaction among people in virtual communities where they can share information and ideas.

    1) People access these virtual communities via platforms, apps, and websites that facilitate user interaction.

        a) Examples include Twitter, Facebook, and LinkedIn.

    2) The sharing and advancement of personal information over a virtual platform allows people to remain in contact, even if they are not physically close to each other.

b. The spread and advancement of mobile technology has allowed people to stay regularly connected to their social networks.

    1) By embracing social media, many companies have been able to connect with their customers and the market on a more personal basis, increasing the rate of growth of B2C.

        a) This can be done in the form of special coupons, promotional videos, etc.

    2) Social media has also facilitated the growth of **consumer-to-consumer (C2C)** e-commerce.

c. Laws and customs regarding privacy and ownership of material posted on social media websites are developing.

6. **Big Data**

a. Big data is the collection and analysis of large and complex data sets.

    1) Big data can be used in the fields of meteorology, genomics, and other disciplines.

b. Challenges include capturing, storing, analyzing, and securing this large amount of data.

    c.   As the amount of information people shared on social media sites grew, the operators of these sites began to see that this shared data had commercial value.

        1)   By analyzing information shared voluntarily by a person on a social media site, it is possible to profile customers so that certain ads can be targeted toward people that are more likely to be receptive to them.

        2)   For example, a person that shares that they live in a certain city and like a certain brand of clothes might begin to see ads with deals for that brand and similar brands in that location.

7.   **Electronic Funds Transfer (EFT)**

    a.   EFT is an e-commerce application provided by financial institutions worldwide that enables the transfer of funds via an access device, i.e., an electronic terminal (e.g., ATM or POS terminal), telephone, computer, or magnetic stripe (e.g., credit, debit, and check cards).

        1)   A typical consumer application of EFT is the direct deposit of payroll checks in employees' accounts or the automatic withdrawal of payments for cable and telephone bills, mortgages, etc.

        2)   EFT transaction costs are lower than for manual systems because documents and human intervention are eliminated from the transaction process. Moreover, transfer customarily requires less than a day.

        3)   Another significant advantage is that the opportunities for clerical errors are greatly reduced.

    b.   The most important application of EFT is check collection. To reduce the enormous volume of paper involved, the check-collection process has been computerized.

        1)   The result has been to reduce the significance of paper checks because EFT provides means to make payments and deposit funds without physical transfer of negotiable instruments. Thus, wholesale EFTs among financial institutions and businesses (commercial transfers) are measured in the trillions of dollars.

        2)   The two major systems for these "wire" or nonconsumer transfers are Fedwire (Federal Reserve wire transfer network) and CHIPS (Clearing House Interbank Payment System). Private systems also are operated by large banks.

8.   **EFT vs. Electronic Money**

    a.   EFT differs from the use of electronic money, which may someday supplant traditional currency and coins.

    b.   **Smart cards** contain computer chips rather than magnetized stripes. A smart card therefore can store data and security programs. It not only stores value but also authenticates transactions, such as by means of its digital signature.

    c.   A disadvantage of electronic money is that most types are not covered by the insurance offered by the Federal Deposit Insurance Corporation (FDIC). Federal Reserve rules concerning EFT also do not extend to electronic money.

    d.   Methods other than providing a credit card number or using electronic money may be used to make electronic payments.

        1)   One such method is an online payment system, such as PayPal. A buyer makes a payment by a customary method to the online payment system, which then notifies the seller that payment has been made. The final step is to transfer the money to the seller's account.

Stop and review! You have completed the outline for this subunit. Study multiple-choice questions 11 through 17 beginning on page 346.

13.3 ELECTRONIC DATA INTERCHANGE (EDI)

1. **Overview**

   a. Electronic data interchange (EDI) is the leading method of carrying on B2B e-commerce.

      1) EDI involves the communication of data in a format agreed to by the parties directly from a computer in one entity to a computer in another entity, for example, to order goods from a supplier or to transfer funds.

   b. EDI was the first step in the evolution of e-business.

      1) Successful EDI implementation begins with mapping the work processes and flows that support achievement of the organization's objectives.

      2) EDI was developed to enhance JIT inventory management.

   c. Advantages of EDI include the following:

      1) Reduction of clerical errors

      2) Increased speed of transactions

      3) Elimination of repetitive clerical tasks, such as document preparation, processing, and mailing

      4) Use of digital rather than physical record storage

   d. Disadvantages of EDI include the following:

      1) Information may be insecure.

         a) Thus, end-to-end data encryption should be used to protect data during EDI.

      2) Data may be lost.

      3) Transmissions to trading partners may fail.

      4) EDI is more complex and more costly than simpler B2B arrangements.

         a) In simpler B2B, each transaction is initiated over the Internet, with XML as the mediating language.

         b) EDI requires programming expertise and leased telephone lines or the use of a value-added or third-party network, whereas XML is simple and easy to understand.

2. **Costs of EDI**

   a. Specialized Software

      1) The software needed to convert data into the agreed-upon EDI format must be either purchased or developed in-house.

   b. Dedicated Hardware

      1) High-availability servers and high-speed communications devices must be installed. Another solution is to contract with a third party known as a VAN to provide this service, but this alternative has its own set of costs.

   c. Legal Costs

      1) Contracts with current trading partners must be renegotiated when entering into an EDI arrangement.

   d. Process Reengineering

      1) Since existing procedures are being replaced, EDI arrangements may require significant changes to current internal processes. This also involves the cost of employee retraining.

   e. Enhanced Security and Monitoring

      1) EDI transactions are subject to the same risks as all electronic communications that cross organizational boundaries.

3.   **Terms and Components of EDI**

    a.   Standards concern procedures to convert written documents into a standard electronic document-messaging format to facilitate EDI.

         1)   The current standards are ANSI X.12 in the U.S. or UN/EDIFACT in Europe and most of the rest of the world.

    b.   Conventions are the procedures for arranging data elements in specified formats for various accounting transactions, e.g., invoices, materials releases, and advance shipment notices.

    c.   A data dictionary prescribes the meaning of data elements, including specification of each transaction structure.

    d.   Transmission protocols are rules used to determine how each electronic envelope is structured and processed by the communications devices.

         1)   Normally, a group of accounting transactions is combined in an electronic envelope and transmitted into a communications network.

         2)   Rules are required for the separation and transmission of envelopes.

    e.   A crucial element of any EDI arrangement is the exchange of network and sender/recipient acknowledgment messages.

         1)   Acknowledgments serve as a nonrepudiation tool; i.e., one party cannot claim that a particular message was not received by a certain time or date.

4.   **Methods of Communication between EDI Computers**

    a.   A point-to-point system requires the use of dedicated computers by all parties.

         1)   Each computer must be designed to be compatible with the other(s). This system is very similar to a network within one company. Dedicated lines or modems are used.

    b.   Value-added networks (VANs) are private, third-party providers of common interfaces between organizations.

         1)   Subscribing to a VAN eliminates the need for one organization to establish direct computer communication with a trading partner. VANs also eliminate the need for dedicated computers waiting for incoming messages.

5.   **EDI Implications for Control**

    a.   EDI eliminates the paper documents, both internal and external, that are the traditional basis for many controls, including internal and external auditing.

    b.   Moreover, an organization that has reengineered its processes to take full advantage of EDI may have eliminated even the electronic equivalents of paper documents.

         1)   For example, the buyer's point-of-sale (POS) system may directly transmit information to the seller, which delivers on a JIT basis. Purchase orders, invoices, and receiving reports are eliminated and replaced with

             a)   A long-term contract establishing quantities, prices, and delivery schedules;

             b)   Evaluated receipts settlements (authorizations for automatic periodic payment);

             c)   Production schedules;

             d)   Advance ship notices; and

             e)   Payments by EFT.

The AICPA has frequently tested the topic of EDI on recent exams. Questions have addressed such areas as the advantages of EDI and internal control and security for EDI transactions.

Stop and review! You have completed the outline for this subunit. Study multiple-choice questions 18 through 24 beginning on page 348.

13.4 ELECTRONIC TRANSMISSION SECURITY

1. **Encryption Technology**

   a. Encryption technology is vital for the security and therefore the success of electronic commerce, especially with regard to transactions carried out over public networks.

      1) The sender's encryption program encodes the data prior to transmission. The recipient's program decodes it at the other end. Unauthorized users may be able to intercept the data, but without the encryption key, they will be unable to decode it.

   b. Encryption performed by physically secure hardware is inherently more secure than encryption performed by software.

   c. The use of encryption increases system overhead. A certain amount of system resources must be used to execute the machine instructions necessary to encrypt and decrypt data.

2. **Public-Key vs. Symmetric Encryption**

   a. With public-key (asymmetric) encryption, the communicating parties create mathematically related pairs of keys. One of the keys in the pair is made public, and the other is kept secret.

      1) The sending party uses the public key to encrypt the message. Since only the intended recipient has access to the private key that relates to that public key, only that party will be able to decrypt the message.

   b. With symmetric encryption, the communicating parties agree on a single (private) key for use in that session.

      1) Its strength comes from its length. The longer the key (measured in bits), the more resistant it is to decrypting by unauthorized parties.

      2) However, the parties must have a secure way of sharing the key.

3. **Digital Certificates**

   a. Digital certificates are data files created by trusted third parties called certificate authorities (e.g., VeriSign, Thawte, GoDaddy).

      1) An entity who wishes to engage in e-commerce first establishes a relationship with a certificate authority, who verifies that party's identity.

      2) The certificate authority then creates a coded electronic certificate that contains (a) the holder's name, (b) its public key, (c) a serial number, and (d) an expiration date. The certificate authority makes its own public key widely available.

      3) A party wishing to do business over the Internet with the certificate holder seeks the holder's certificate on the authority's server and uses the authority's public key to decrypt it.

      4) The sender obtains the recipient's public key from the certificate, encodes the message, and sends it. The recipient uses its private key to decrypt the message.

  b. This system, called the public-key infrastructure, relieves the parties from the need to establish their own pairs of keys when they want to communicate securely.

    1) The public-key infrastructure allows buyers to securely exchange credit card numbers with Internet vendors.

 4. **Digital Signatures**

  a. A digital signature is a means of authenticating an electronic document such as a purchase order, acceptance of a contract, or financial information.

    1) The sender uses its private key to encode all or part of the message, and the recipient uses the sender's public key to decode it. Hence, if that key decodes the message, the sender must have written it.

Stop and review! You have completed the outline for this subunit. Study multiple-choice questions 25 through 30 beginning on page 350.

QUESTIONS

13.1 Networks and the Internet

1. A local area network (LAN) is best described as a(n)

 A. Computer system that connects computers of all sizes, workstations, terminals, and other devices within a limited proximity.

 B. System to allow computer users to meet and share ideas and information.

 C. Electronic library containing millions of items of data that can be reviewed, retrieved, and analyzed.

 D. Method to offer specialized software, hardware, and data-handling techniques that improve effectiveness and reduce costs.

Answer (A) is correct.
 REQUIRED: The best description of a LAN.
 DISCUSSION: A LAN is a local distributed computer system, often housed within a single building. Computers, communication devices, and other equipment are linked by cable. Special software facilitates efficient data communication among the hardware devices.

2. The most distinguishing feature of the use of a client-server processing model over an old mainframe configuration is

 A. Digital processing over analog.

 B. Less need for data backup.

 C. Decentralization over centralization.

 D. Ability to connect remote locations.

Answer (C) is correct.
 REQUIRED: The distinguishing feature of a client-server system over a mainframe system.
 DISCUSSION: Mainframes were arranged so that all processing and data storage were done in a single, central location. Improvements in technology have led to increasing decentralization of information processing. The most cost-effective and easy-to-administer arrangement for local area networks (LANs) uses the client-server model.
 Answer (A) is incorrect. Both client-server configurations and mainframes use digital processing. Answer (B) is incorrect. Both client-server configurations and mainframes must employ data backup. Answer (D) is incorrect. Mainframes were able to connect to users in remote locations.

3. Which one of the following network configurations is distinguished by the possibility of spreading the cost of ownership among multiple organizations?

 A. Value-added network.

 B. Baseband network.

 C. Wide area network.

 D. Local area network.

Answer (C) is correct.
 REQUIRED: The network configuration that spreads its cost among multiple organizations.
 DISCUSSION: Wide area networks consist of a conglomerate of local area networks (LANs) over widely separated locations. The key aspect here is that a WAN can be either publicly or privately owned.
 Answer (A) is incorrect. A value-added network is a private network. Answer (B) is incorrect. Baseband refers to the signal-carrying capacity of a network, not the ownership of its hardware devices. Answer (D) is incorrect. All the equipment in a local area network (LAN) is owned by one organization.

4. Which of the following control risks is more likely with personal computers than in a mainframe environment with dedicated terminals?

- A. Copyright violations due to the use of unauthorized copies of purchased software.
- B. Applications written by one department that cannot share data with existing organization-wide systems.
- C. Lack of data availability due to inadequate data retention policies.
- D. All of the answers are correct.

Answer (D) is correct.
    REQUIRED: The environmental control risk(s) likely in a personal computer environment.
    DISCUSSION: When personal computers are used, likely control risks include copyright violations that occur when unauthorized copies of software are made or software is installed on multiple computers; locally written applications that do not adhere to the organization's standards; and inadequate backup, recovery, and contingency planning.
    Answer (A) is incorrect. Copyright violations are a common risk with personal computers. Answer (B) is incorrect. Locally written applications that do not adhere to the organization's standards are a common risk with personal computers. Answer (C) is incorrect. Failure to follow proper backup procedures is a common risk with personal computers.

5. Which of the following networks provides the **least** secure means of data transmission?

- A. Value-added.
- B. Public-switched.
- C. Local area.
- D. Private.

Answer (B) is correct.
    REQUIRED: The network that provides the least secure means of data transmission.
    DISCUSSION: Public-switched networks are wide area networks that use public telephone lines. This arrangement may be the most economical, but data transmission may be of lower quality, no connection may be available, and security measures may be ineffective.
    Answer (A) is incorrect. Value-added carriers provide data security and error detection and correction procedures. Answer (C) is incorrect. Local area networks inherently limit data transmission exposures. Answer (D) is incorrect. Private networks provide security through limited access and dedicated facilities.

6. Kelly Corporation needs an internal communication network that provides high speed communication among nodes. Which of the following is appropriate for Kelly?

- A. Wide area network (WAN).
- B. Local area network (LAN).
- C. File server.
- D. Value-added network (VAN).

Answer (B) is correct.
    REQUIRED: The network that provides the fastest communication.
    DISCUSSION: Local area networks are privately owned networks that provide high-speed communication among nodes. They are usually restricted to limited areas, such as a particular floor of an office building.
    Answer (A) is incorrect. Wide area networks provide lower-speed communication, owing to them being spread out among larger areas than LANs. Answer (C) is incorrect. A file server is hardware that acts as an access control mechanism in a local area network. Answer (D) is incorrect. A VAN is a privately owned telecommunications carrier that provides capacity to outside users. It does not provide high-speed communication among nodes.

7. Appropriate uses of an organization's internal communications network, or intranet, include all of the following **except**

- A. Making the human resources policy manual available to employees.
- B. Informing potential investors about company operations and financial results.
- C. Providing senior management with access to the executive support system.
- D. Enabling a project team that crosses departments to collaborate.

Answer (B) is correct.
    REQUIRED: The item not one of the basic purposes of an organization's internal communications network.
    DISCUSSION: An intranet permits sharing of information throughout an organization by applying Internet connectivity standards and Web software (e.g., browsers) to the organization's internal network. An intranet addresses the connectivity problems faced by organizations that have many types of computers. Its use is restricted to those within the organization.
    Answer (A) is incorrect. Making the human resources policy manual available to employees is an appropriate use of an organization's internal communications network. Answer (C) is incorrect. Providing senior management with access to the executive support system is an appropriate use of an organization's internal communications network. Answer (D) is incorrect. Enabling a project team that crosses departments to collaborate is an appropriate use of an organization's internal communications network.

8. Large organizations often have their own telecommunications networks for transmitting and receiving voice, data, and images. Small organizations, however, also can have remote locations that need to communicate. Such organizations are more likely to use

    A. Public-switched lines.

    B. Fast packet switches.

    C. Internet.

    D. A WAN.

Answer (C) is correct.
    REQUIRED: The telecommunications networks likely to be used by small organizations.
    DISCUSSION: Widespread use of the Internet has led to its becoming an efficient, low-cost transmission network.
    Answer (A) is incorrect. Public-switched lines have been eclipsed in efficiency by the Internet. Answer (B) is incorrect. Fast packet switching networks are typically installed by telecommunication utility companies and other large companies that have their own networks. Answer (D) is incorrect. Small organizations lack the capital necessary for investment in a wide area network (WAN).

9. A company has abandoned the large array of dedicated servers it formerly used to store and provide access to its database. The company has entered into a contract with a provider who will guarantee storage of the database at its own location along with access over the Internet. This arrangement is an example of

    A. Distributed computing.

    B. Cloud computing.

    C. Wide area network.

    D. Ethernet.

Answer (B) is correct.
    REQUIRED: The type of arrangement described in the question.
    DISCUSSION: Cloud computing is a popular term relating to on-demand access to resources that are accessed on the Internet and shared by others. The entity has the ability to choose and pay for only the applications needed from the array (cloud) of resources, reducing the need for a large investment in IT infrastructure.
    Answer (A) is incorrect. Distributed processing involves the decentralization of processing tasks and data storage and assigning these functions to multiple computers, often in separate locations. Answer (C) is incorrect. A wide area network (WAN) consists of a conglomerate of local area networks over widely separated locations. Answer (D) is incorrect. Ethernet is a local area network transmission protocol.

10. The Internet consists of a series of networks that include

    A. Gateways to allow networks to connect to each other.

    B. Bridges to direct messages through the optimum data path.

    C. Repeaters to physically connect separate local area networks (LANs).

    D. Routers to strengthen data signals between distant computers.

Answer (A) is correct.
    REQUIRED: The composition of the Internet.
    DISCUSSION: The Internet facilitates information transfer among computers. Gateways are hardware or software products that allow translation between two different protocol families. For example, a gateway can be used to exchange messages between different email systems.
    Answer (B) is incorrect. Bridges are used to connect segments of a LAN. Answer (C) is incorrect. Repeaters are used to strengthen data signals. Answer (D) is incorrect. Routers are used to determine the best path for data across the Internet.

13.2 Electronic Commerce

11. An employee uses her company-issued ID and password to log into her employer's human resources system from home and change her choices of benefits. This is an example of

    A. E-business.

    B. Data warehouse.

    C. Transmission protocol.

    D. Extensible markup language.

Answer (A) is correct.
    REQUIRED: The term for the transaction described.
    DISCUSSION: E-business is an umbrella term referring to all methods of conducting business electronically. This can include strictly internal communications as well as nonfinancial dealings with outside parties (e.g., contract negotiations).
    Answer (B) is incorrect. A data warehouse is a central database for transaction-level data from more than one of the organization's transaction processing systems. Answer (C) is incorrect. A transmission protocol is a necessary component of this transaction but does not describe the transaction itself. Answer (D) is incorrect. Extensible markup language (XML) is a way of coding information in such a way that a user can determine not only how it should be presented but also what it is; i.e., all computerized data may be tagged with identifiers.

12. Which of the following represents the greatest exposure to the integrity of electronic funds transfer data transmitted from a remote terminal?

A. Poor physical access controls over the data center.

B. Network viruses.

C. Poor system documentation.

D. Leased telephone circuits.

Answer (D) is correct.
    REQUIRED: The greatest exposure to the integrity of EFT data transmitted from a remote terminal.
    DISCUSSION: Leased telephone circuits represent a direct exposure to the risk of breached data integrity. They use public lines that can be easily identified and tapped.
    Answer (A) is incorrect. Poor physical access controls represent a secondary exposure for compromise of remote data communications lines. Answer (B) is incorrect. Network viruses represent a secondary exposure for compromise of remote data communications lines. Answer (C) is incorrect. Poor system documentation represent a secondary exposure for compromise of remote data communications lines.

13. A customer places an order for a sweater over the Internet using a mobile phone. This is an example of

A. Authentication.

B. Business intelligence.

C. Electronic funds transfer.

D. E-commerce.

Answer (D) is correct.
    REQUIRED: The term for the transaction described.
    DISCUSSION: E-commerce refers to the conduct of financial transactions with outside parties electronically, e.g., the purchase and sale of goods and services.
    Answer (A) is incorrect. Authentication is a necessary step to completing this transaction but does not describe the transaction itself. Answer (B) is incorrect. Business intelligence is a system that provides executive management immediate information about an organization's critical success factors. Answer (C) is incorrect. Electronic funds transfer is the electronic movement of monies from one financial institution to another.

14. Which of the following is **not** an advantage of business-to-business (B2B)?

A. Reduced purchasing costs.

B. Reduced information technology costs.

C. Increased market efficiency.

D. Decreased inventory levels.

Answer (B) is correct.
    REQUIRED: The factor that is not an advantage of B2B.
    DISCUSSION: Instituting a B2B system requires large initial outlays for equipment, software, and training.
    Answer (A) is incorrect. Purchasing products online saves time, and electronically processing an order simplifies the ordering process. Answer (C) is incorrect. By using the Internet, companies have easy access to price quotes from various suppliers. Buyers are more likely to get a better price, given the increased number of suppliers. Answer (D) is incorrect. Companies can make better use of their inventory and raw materials if they participate in B2B.

15. Which of the following risks is **not** greater in an electronic funds transfer (EFT) environment than in a manual system using paper transactions?

A. Unauthorized access and activity.

B. Duplicate transaction processing.

C. High cost per transaction.

D. Inadequate backup and recovery capabilities.

Answer (C) is correct.
    REQUIRED: The risk not greater in an EFT environment than in a manual system using paper transactions.
    DISCUSSION: EFT is a service provided by financial institutions worldwide that is based on EDI technology. EFT transaction costs are lower than for manual systems because documents and human intervention are eliminated from the transaction process.
    Answer (A) is incorrect. Unauthorized access and activity is a risk specific to EFT. Answer (B) is incorrect. Inaccurate transaction processing (including duplication) is a risk specific to EFT. Answer (D) is incorrect. Inadequate backup and recovery capabilities is a risk specific to EFT.

16. Which one of the following is **not** a reason for a company to use EFT with an EDI system?

A. To take advantage of the time lag associated with negotiable instruments.

B. To allow the company to negotiate discounts with EDI vendors based upon prompt payment.

C. To improve its cash management program.

D. To reduce input time and input errors.

Answer (A) is correct.
    REQUIRED: The item not a reason for using EFT.
    DISCUSSION: The time lag between transmittal of a check (a negotiable instrument) and its clearance through regular banking channels is called float. Float is eliminated by EFT.
    Answer (B) is incorrect. Payment schedules may be based on the time required to process invoices, prepare checks, and transmit checks. Using EFT, payment is instantaneous, and payment schedules can be based on other criteria, e.g., discounts for prompt payment. Answer (C) is incorrect. EFT allows for more effective control of payments and transfers among accounts. Answer (D) is incorrect. Integration of EDI and EFT eliminates manual input of transaction data, a process that introduces errors into the accounting system.

17. Which of the following significantly encouraged the development of electronic funds transfer (EFT) systems?

I.   Response to competition
II. Cost containment
III. Advances in information technology

    A.   I and II.

    B.   I and III.

    C.   II only.

    D.   I, II, and III.

Answer (D) is correct.
    REQUIRED: The items that most significantly encouraged the development of EFTs.
    DISCUSSION: Competition has been a strong motivator in the financial services industry in the development of EFT systems, which are an application of EDI. Furthermore, containing costs in a highly competitive industry can be aided by leveraging information technology. Finally, advances in information technology, especially the wide acceptance of telecommunications standards and protocols, have made EFT systems possible.
    Answer (A) is incorrect. Advances in information technology also significantly encouraged the development of EFT. Answer (B) is incorrect. Cost containment also significantly encouraged the development of EFT. Answer (C) is incorrect. Competitive forces and advances in information technology also significantly encouraged the development of EFT.

13.3 Electronic Data Interchange (EDI)

18. A system that permits suppliers and buyers to have direct access to portions of each others' databases, including inventory data, to enhance service and deliveries is

    A.   Electronic mail.

    B.   Interactive processing.

    C.   Electronic data interchange.

    D.   Distributed processing.

Answer (C) is correct.
    REQUIRED: The system giving suppliers and buyers direct access to portions of each others' databases.
    DISCUSSION: Electronic data interchange (EDI) is the communication of electronic documents directly from a computer in one entity to a computer in another entity. For example, a buyer's computer will issue a purchase order to a seller's computer. EDI was developed to enhance JIT inventory management. The advantages of EDI include reduction of clerical errors, speed, elimination of repetitive clerical tasks, and elimination of document preparing, processing, and mailing costs.
    Answer (A) is incorrect. Electronic mail is the computer-to-computer exchange of messages. Answer (B) is incorrect. Interactive processing does not permit access to another company's database. Answer (D) is incorrect. Distributed processing distributes work among computers linked by a communications network.

19. Companies now can use electronic transfers to conduct regular business transactions. Which of the following terms best describes a system in which an agreement is made between two or more parties to electronically transfer purchase orders, sales orders, invoices, and/or other financial documents?

    A.   Electronic mail (email).

    B.   Electronic funds transfer (EFT).

    C.   Electronic data interchange (EDI).

    D.   Electronic data processing (EDP).

Answer (C) is correct.
    REQUIRED: The term best describing electronic transfer of documents.
    DISCUSSION: Electronic data interchange is the electronic transfer of documents between businesses. EDI was developed to enhance just-in-time (JIT) inventory management. Advantages include speed, reduction of clerical errors, and elimination of repetitive clerical tasks and their costs.
    Answer (A) is incorrect. Email can send text or document files, but the term encompasses a wide range of transfers. EDI specifically applies to the system described in the question. Answer (B) is incorrect. EFT refers to the transfer of money. Answer (D) is incorrect. EDP is a generic term for computerized processing of transaction data within organizations.

20. Which of the following is an accepted example of electronic data interchange (EDI)?

    A.   Request for an airline reservation by a travel agent.

    B.   Withdrawal of cash from an automated teller by a bank's customer.

    C.   Transfer of summary data from a local area network to a centralized mainframe.

    D.   Placement of order entry transactions from a customer to its supplier.

Answer (D) is correct.
    REQUIRED: The accepted example of electronic data interchange.
    DISCUSSION: EDI is the communication of electronic documents directly from a computer in one entity to a computer in another entity. Placement of order entry transactions from a customer to its supplier is an accepted use of EDI between trading partners.
    Answer (A) is incorrect. A request for an airline reservation requires an online, real-time reservations system. Answer (B) is incorrect. Withdrawal of cash from an automated teller is accomplished via online transactions to copies of master files. Answer (C) is incorrect. The transfer of summary data to headquarters may be accomplished with point-to-point communications, known as distributed computing.

21. The emergence of electronic data interchange (EDI) as standard operating practice increases the risk of

A. Unauthorized third-party access to systems.

B. Systematic programming errors.

C. Inadequate knowledge bases.

D. Unsuccessful system use.

Answer (A) is correct.

REQUIRED: The risk increased by the emergence of EDI as standard operating practice.

DISCUSSION: EDI is the communication of electronic documents directly from a computer in one entity to a computer in another entity. EDI for business documents between unrelated parties has the potential to increase the risk of unauthorized third-party access to systems because more outsiders will have access to internal systems.

Answer (B) is incorrect. Systematic programming errors are the result of misspecification of requirements or lack of correspondence between specifications and programs. Answer (C) is incorrect. Inadequate knowledge bases are a function of lack of care in building them. Answer (D) is incorrect. A benefit of EDI is to improve the efficiency and effectiveness of system use.

22. Electronic data interchange (EDI) offers significant benefits to organizations, but it is not without certain major obstacles. Successful EDI implementation begins with which of the following?

A. Mapping the work processes and flows that support the organization's goals.

B. Purchasing new hardware for the EDI system.

C. Selecting reliable vendors for translation and communication software.

D. Standardizing transaction formats and data.

Answer (A) is correct.

REQUIRED: The initial phase of EDI implementation.

DISCUSSION: Marked benefits arise when EDI is tied to strategic efforts that alter, not mirror, previous practices. Applying EDI to an inefficient process results in continuing to do things the wrong way, only faster. Hence, the initial phase of EDI implementation includes understanding the organization's mission and an analysis of its activities as part of an integrated solution to the organization's needs.

Answer (B) is incorrect. The prerequisite for EDI success is an understanding of the mission of the business and the processes and flows that support its goals, followed by cooperation with external partners. Purchasing new hardware is a subsequent step. Answer (C) is incorrect. Before applying EDI technology to the business, EDI must be viewed as part of an overall integrated solution to organizational requirements. Answer (D) is incorrect. EDI is not a solution by itself. Instead of considering how to transmit and receive transactions, a company must first analyze the entire process.

23. After a company implements electronic data interchange (EDI) to communicate with its customers, an appropriate control for ensuring authenticity of the electronic orders it receives is to

A. Encrypt sensitive messages such as electronic payments for raw materials received.

B. Perform reasonableness checks on quantities ordered before filling orders.

C. Verify the identity of senders and determine whether orders correspond to contract terms.

D. Acknowledge receipt of electronic payments with a confirming message.

Answer (C) is correct.

REQUIRED: The control for ensuring the authenticity of the electronic orders the company receives.

DISCUSSION: An EDI system is subject not only to the usual risk exposures for computer systems but also to those arising from the potential ineffectiveness of control on the part of the trading partner and the third-party service provider. Accordingly, authentication of users and messages received is a major security concern.

Answer (A) is incorrect. Encrypting sensitive messages sent is an appropriate step but does not necessarily authenticate the transaction. Answer (B) is incorrect. Performing reasonableness checks on quantities ordered before placing orders is a control for ensuring the correctness of the company's own orders, not the authenticity of its customers' orders. Answer (D) is incorrect. Acknowledging receipt of electronic payments with a confirming message is good practice but will not authenticate orders from customers.

24. Before sending or receiving electronic data interchange (EDI) messages, a company should

A. Execute a trading partner agreement with each of its customers and suppliers.

B. Reduce inventory levels in anticipation of receiving shipments.

C. Demand that all its suppliers implement EDI capabilities.

D. Evaluate the effectiveness of its use of EDI transmissions.

Answer (A) is correct.

REQUIRED: The process to be performed before sending or receiving EDI messages.

DISCUSSION: Before sending or receiving EDI messages, a company should execute a trading partner agreement with its customers and suppliers. All parties should understand their responsibilities, the messages each will initiate, how they will interpret messages, the means of authenticating and verifying the completeness and accuracy of messages, the moment when the contract between the parties is effective, the required level of security, etc.

Answer (B) is incorrect. The company may intend to reduce inventory levels, but that intention is unrelated to the timing of its first EDI messages. Answer (C) is incorrect. The company may want to demand or encourage all its customers and suppliers to implement EDI capabilities, but that request is independent of sending and receiving messages. Answer (D) is incorrect. It is not possible to evaluate the effectiveness of EDI transmissions until after they occur.

13.4 Electronic Transmission Security

25. A client communicates sensitive data across the Internet. Which of the following controls will be most effective to prevent the use of the information if it were intercepted by an unauthorized party?

A. A firewall.

B. An access log.

C. Passwords.

D. Encryption.

Answer (D) is correct.

REQUIRED: The most effective control for preventing the use of intercepted information.

DISCUSSION: Encryption technology converts data into a code. Encoding data before transmission over communications lines makes it more difficult for someone with access to the transmission to understand or modify its contents.

Answer (A) is incorrect. A firewall prevents access from specific types of traffic to an internal network. After an unauthorized user has obtained information from the site, a firewall cannot prevent its use. Answer (B) is incorrect. An access log only records attempted usage of a system. Answer (C) is incorrect. Passwords prevent unauthorized users from accessing the system. If information has already been obtained, a password cannot prevent its use.

26. The use of message encryption software

A. Guarantees the secrecy of data.

B. Requires manual distribution of keys.

C. Increases system overhead.

D. Reduces the need for periodic password changes.

Answer (C) is correct.

REQUIRED: The effect of message encryption software.

DISCUSSION: The machine instructions necessary to encrypt and decrypt data constitute system overhead. As a result, processing speed may be slowed.

Answer (A) is incorrect. No encryption approach absolutely guarantees the secrecy of data. Answer (B) is incorrect. Keys may also be distributed electronically via secure key transporters. Answer (D) is incorrect. Periodic password changes are needed. Passwords are the typical means of validating users' access to unencrypted data.

27. Which of the following is an encryption feature that can be used to authenticate the originator of a document and ensure that the message is intact and has not been tampered with?

A. Heuristic terminal.

B. Perimeter switch.

C. Default settings.

D. Digital signatures.

Answer (D) is correct.

REQUIRED: The encryption feature used to authenticate the originator of a document and ensure that the original message is intact.

DISCUSSION: A digital signature is a means of authenticating an electronic document, such as a purchase order, acceptance of a contract, or financial information. Because digital signatures use public-key encryption, they are a highly secure means of ensuring security over the Internet.

Answer (A) is incorrect. The term "heuristic terminal" is not meaningful in this context. Answer (B) is incorrect. The term "perimeter switch" is not meaningful in this context. Answer (C) is incorrect. In a computer program, a default setting is a value that a parameter will automatically assume unless specifically overridden.

28. Which of the following IT developments poses the **least** risk to organizational security?

- A. Adoption of wireless technology.
- B. Use of public-key encryption.
- C. Outsourcing of the IT infrastructure.
- D. Enterprise-wide integration of functions.

Answer (B) is correct.

> **REQUIRED:** The least risky IT developments.
> **DISCUSSION:** Encryption is essential when electronic commerce is conducted over public networks, such as the Internet. Thus, the use of public-key encryption is a response to risk, not a source of risk.
> Answer (A) is incorrect. Adoption of wireless technology increases the risk that communications will be intercepted. Answer (C) is incorrect. Outsourcing of the IT infrastructure means that ineffective controls over the outside service provider's operations could compromise the security of the organization's information. Answer (D) is incorrect. Enterprise-wide integration of functions, for example, in an ERP system with an organization-wide database, increases the difficulty of assuring the integrity of information. In an organization with discrete, closed functional subsystems, compromising one subsystem does not affect the others. In an ERP system, however, a breach of security may affect the entire organization.

29. To ensure privacy in a public-key encryption system, knowledge of which of the following keys is required to decode the received message?

I.   Private
II.   Public

- A. I only.
- B. II only.
- C. Both I and II.
- D. Neither I nor II.

Answer (A) is correct.

> **REQUIRED:** The key(s) required to decode messages in a public-key system to ensure privacy.
> **DISCUSSION:** In a public-key system, the public key is used to encrypt the message prior to transmission. The private key is needed to decrypt (decode) the message.
> Answer (B) is incorrect. The private key, not the public key, is needed to decrypt (decode) the message. Answer (C) is incorrect. The public key is needed to encode, not decode, the message. Answer (D) is incorrect. The private key is needed to decrypt (decode) the message.

30. Which improvement in IT control specifically addresses the authentication issue?

- A. A digital certificate.
- B. A firewall.
- C. An intelligent router.
- D. Encryption.

Answer (A) is correct.

> **REQUIRED:** The improvement in IT control that specifically addresses the authentication issue
> **DISCUSSION:** A digital certificate is a data file created by trusted third parties called certificate authorities that verify an e-commerce participant's identity.
> Answer (B) is incorrect. A firewall is a configuration of hardware and software that intercepts and examines message packets sent to an internal network from an external network. Messages or access attempts that do not meet specified criteria are rejected. Answer (C) is incorrect. A router sends data packets from one LAN or WAN to another. It decides how to send packets based on the most expedient routine. Answer (D) is incorrect. Encryption converts data into a code that cannot be read by an unauthorized party who does not have the key required for decoding.

13.5 PRACTICE WRITTEN COMMUNICATION

DIRECTIONS

Note: If you believe you have encountered a software malfunction, report it to the test center staff immediately.

Navigation

To navigate from task to task, use the controls at the bottom of the screen. Click on the **Next** button to advance to the next task, or the **Previous** button to go to the previous task. To go directly to any task, click on its number.

If you would like a reminder to revisit a task, or want to indicate that you are finished with it, click on the reminder flag below the task number. To clear the flag, click on it again. Reminder flags are for your use only – they do not contribute to your score.

Tabs

In this part of the examination, you will be asked to complete various tasks. Every task has one or more **Work Tabs**. Every task also has a **Help** tab.

Written Communication | Help

Work tab   Help tab

Work Tabs:

- **Work Tabs** are identified with a pencil icon. This is where your responses are expected.
- Each task has one or more **Work Tabs**.
- **Work Tabs** contain directions for completing the task - be sure to read these directions carefully.
- The **Work Tab** name in the example above is for illustration only - yours will differ.
- You must complete all of the **Work Tabs** in each task to receive full credit.

Help Tab:

- The **Help Tab** provides assistance with the exam software that is used in this task. For example, if the task is to compose a memorandum, **Help** will provide information about the word processor.

The Toolbar

The toolbar at the top of the screen shows the amount of time remaining for you to complete the tasks. In addition, the following tools are available. Note that only the **Exit** button is displayed when Directions are visible - the others will appear when you begin the tasks.

   Click on these buttons to split or unsplit the screen. You can split the screen vertically or horizontally.

   Click on this button to go on to the next part of the examination. You must complete all of the tasks to receive full credit. Once you click on **Exit** and confirm the action, you will NOT be able to return to this testlet.

Dawn currently owns a home and uses it as her principal residence. She purchased the house and is considering moving to a more expensive home closer to her business. She has asked you to explain to her, in a memorandum-type format, the current tax law regarding sales of principal residences.

Type your communication below the line in the response area below.

REMINDER: Your response will be graded for both technical content and writing skills. Technical content will be evaluated for information that is helpful to the intended reader and clearly relevant to the issue. Writing skills will be evaluated for development, organization, and the appropriate expression of ideas in professional correspondence. Use a standard business memorandum or letter format with a clear beginning, middle, and end. Do not convey information in the form of a table, bullet point list, or other abbreviated presentation.

To: Dawn Early
Re: Sale of principal residence

NOTE: Your Written Communications on the actual CPA exam may cover topics outside the scope of the BEC CSO (i.e., they may relate to topics from the AUD, FAR, and/or REG CSOs instead). Answer to the best of your ability, and remember that graders are mainly evaluating your writing ability and will overlook minor technical mistakes.

Unofficial Answer

Written Communication

To: Dawn Early
Re: Sale of principal residence

IRC 121 allows taxpayers to exclude a portion of their gain upon the sale of a principal residence. The taxpayer can exclude up to $250,000 if filing single or $500,000 if married filing jointly. This exclusion may be used only once every 2 years. However, no loss may be recognized on the sale of such a residence.

The gain may only be excluded if the taxpayer owned and used the property as a principal residence for an aggregate of 2 years during the previous 5 years. The ownership and use times do not have to be concurrent. Short temporary absences for vacations or seasonal absences are counted for the period of use, even if the taxpayer rents out the residence during that time. An absence of an entire year is not considered a short temporary absence. Any portion of the gain that is allocable to a portion of the property that is separate from the principal residence and not used as the taxpayer's residence is not available for the exclusion. Gain must also be recognized to the extent of any depreciation adjustments with respect to the rental or business use of a principal residence after May 6, 1997.

In order for married individuals to exclude $500,000 of the gain, they must meet certain requirements. Either spouse may meet the ownership requirement, but both spouses must meet the use requirement. Additionally, neither spouse may be ineligible for the exclusion by virtue of a sale or an exchange of a residence within the last 2 years. However, if one spouse fails to meet these requirements, the other qualifying spouse is not prevented from claiming the $250,000 exclusion available to taxpayers filing single.

If the use and ownership tests are not met, or if the minimum 2-year period for claiming the full exclusion has not elapsed, the taxpayer may be able to claim a partial exclusion. However, the taxpayer's failure to meet one of the requirements must be due to either a change in the place of the taxpayer's employment, health reasons, or unforeseen circumstances. The partial exclusion is based on the ratio of months used to 24 months.

The above depicts a Level 5 answer. Consult your booklet, *How to Pass the CPA Exam: A System for Success*, for a description of the three writing skills criteria. You may also access this booklet online by visiting www.gleim.com/PassCPA.

Self-Grade

Below, grade your response on technical content and writing skills. Bubble in the circle next to the appropriate score that you may receive based on the criteria given. Your **total** score is the sum of your scores on all six items. The maximum score is 19 points.

Technical Content Evaluation

Was your response on topic?	O No [0]	O Mostly [1]	O Yes [2]
Did your response have any *significant* errors?	O 0 errors [1]	O 1 major error [–1]	O 2 or more major errors [–2]
Did your response contain any illegal advice?	O No [1]	O Yes [0]	

Writing Skills Evaluation

	Poor	Below Average	Average	Above Average	Outstanding
Organization	O 1	O 2	O 3	O 4	O 5
Development	O 1	O 2	O 3	O 4	O 5
Expression	O 1	O 2	O 3	O 4	O 5

Disclaimer: This scoring schedule was developed by Gleim Publications as a guideline only. The AICPA has not released specific information on how the Written Communications are graded.

Practice even more Written Communications with the Gleim Mega Test Bank.
Learn more: gleim.com/CPAmega | 800.874.5346

STUDY UNIT FOURTEEN
IT SECURITY AND CONTROLS

(17 pages of outline)

The goals of a business information system are the same regardless of whether the system is manual or computerized; the risks of a computer-based system, however, are quite different.

The material included in this study unit overlaps with the internal control and information technology study unit of the Auditing and Attestation (AUD) section of the exam. We have attempted to include here those issues that are more likely to be tested on the Business Environment and Concepts (BEC) section of the exam. However, if you have studied for AUD, many of these issues should be familiar. If you have not yet studied for AUD, this will be a good introduction to the material.

14.1 RISKS ASSOCIATED WITH BUSINESS INFORMATION SYSTEMS

1. **Overview**

   a. Organizations need to be aware of the unique risks associated with a computer-based business information system.

   b. IT security (or **cybersecurity**) is information security applied to computer hardware, software, and computer networks.

2. **System Availability**

   a. The ability to make use of any computer-based system is dependent on

      1) An uninterrupted flow of electricity

      2) Protection of computer hardware from environmental hazards (e.g., fire and water)

      3) Protection of software and data files from unauthorized alteration

      4) Preservation of functioning communications channels between devices

3. **Volatile Transaction Trails**

   a. In any computer-based environment, a complete trail useful for audit purposes might exist for only a short time or in only computer-readable form. In online and real-time systems, data are entered directly into the computer, eliminating portions of the audit trail traditionally provided by source documents.

4. **Decreased Human Involvement**

   a. Because employees who enter transactions may never see the final results, the potential for detecting errors is reduced. Also, output from a computer system often carries a mystique of infallibility, reducing the incentive of system users to closely examine reports and transaction logs.

5. **Uniform Processing of Transactions**

   a. Computer processing uniformly subjects like transactions to the same processing instructions, therefore virtually eliminating clerical error. Thus, it permits consistent application of predefined business rules and the performance of complex calculations in high volume.

   b. However, programming errors (or other similar systematic errors in either the hardware or software) will result in all like transactions being processed incorrectly.

6. **Unauthorized Access**

   a. When accounting records were kept in pen-and-ink format, physical access to them was the only way to carry out an alteration. Once they are computer-based, however, access may be gained by parties both internal and external to the organization.

   b. Security measures, such as firewalls and user ID-and-password combinations, are vital to maintaining security over data in an automated environment.

7. **Data Vulnerability**

   a. Destruction of a few hardware devices or units of storage media could have disastrous consequences if they contain the only copies of crucial data files or application programs.

   b. For this reason, it is vital that an organization's computer files be duplicated and stored offsite periodically.

8. **Reduced Segregation of Duties**

   a. Many functions once performed by separate individuals may be combined in an automated environment.

EXAMPLE

Receiving cash, issuing a receipt to the payor, preparing the deposit slip, and preparing the journal entry may once have been performed by separate individuals. In a computer-based system, the receipt, deposit slip, and journal entry may be automatically generated by the computer. If the same employee who receives the cash is also responsible for entering the relevant data into the system, the potential for fraud or error is increased.

---

9. **Reduced Individual Authorization of Transactions**

   a. Certain transactions may be initiated automatically by a computer-based system. This is becoming ever more widespread as an increasing number of business processes become automated.

   b. This reduced level of oversight for individual transactions requires careful coding to ensure that computer programs accurately reflect management's goals for business processes.

      1) Independent verification of transactions is an important compensating control in the absence of segregation of duties and reduced individual authorization. A third party performs the verification to ensure that the transactions were appropriately processed.

EXAMPLE

An enterprise resource planning system at a manufacturing concern may automatically generate a purchase order when raw materials inventory reaches a certain level. If the company shares an EDI system with the vendor, the purchase order may be sent to the vendor electronically without any human intervention.

---

10. **Malicious Software (Malware)**

    a. Malware is a term describing any program code that enters a computer system that has the potential to degrade that system. Common forms of malware include the following:

       1) A **Trojan horse** is an apparently innocent program (e.g., a spreadsheet) that includes a hidden function that may do damage when activated.

2) A **virus** is a program that copies itself from file to file. The virus may destroy data or programs. A common way of spreading a virus is by email attachments and downloads.

   a) **Logic bombs** are a type of virus triggered by a predetermined event (such as Friday the 13th, April Fool's day, etc.).

3) A **worm** copies itself not from file to file but from computer to computer, often very rapidly. Repeated replication overloads a system by depleting memory or overwhelming network traffic capacity.

4) A **denial-of-service (DOS) attack** is an attempt to overload a system (e.g., a network or Web server) with messages so that it cannot function (a system crash).

   a) A distributed DOS attack comes from multiple sources, for example, the machines of innocent parties infected by Trojan horses. When activated, these programs send messages to the target and leave the connection open.

5) **Phishing** is a method of electronically obtaining confidential information, such as a password or credit card number, through deceit. The perpetrator sets up a website that appears to be legitimate but actually serves no other purpose than to obtain the victim's information.

   a) Phishing scams are often initiated through email spoofing, in which the perpetrator sends out emails that appear to be from a real financial institution. When the victim clicks on the link to what (s)he thinks is the institution's website, the victim is unknowingly redirected to the perpetrator's website.

6) A **back door** is a program that allows unauthorized access to a system and bypasses the normal login procedures (front door).

Stop and review! You have completed the outline for this subunit. Study multiple-choice questions 1 through 7 beginning on page 371.

14.2 COBIT -- A FRAMEWORK FOR IT

1. **Overview**

   a. COBIT is the best-known control and governance framework that addresses information technology.

      1) In its original version, COBIT was focused on controls for specific IT processes.

      2) Over the years, information technology has gradually come to pervade every facet of the organization's operations. IT can no longer be viewed as a function distinct from other aspects of the organization.

         a) The evolution of COBIT has reflected this change in the nature of IT within the organization.

Background

When originally published in 1996, COBIT was an acronym for *Control Objectives for Information and Related Technology*. COBIT 5, the most recent version, was published in April 2012 by ISACA (formerly known as the Information Systems Audit and Control Association), located in Rolling Meadows, Illinois. The COBIT 5 framework document, which describes the five key principles for IT governance and management, is available as a free download at www.isaca.org/COBIT/Pages/Product-Family.aspx.

---

2.   **COBIT 5 -- Five Key Principles**

   a.   **Principle 1: Meeting Stakeholder Needs**

   1)   COBIT 5 asserts that value creation is the most basic stakeholder need. Thus, the creation of stakeholder value is the fundamental goal of any enterprise, commercial or not.

   a)   Value creation in this model is achieved by balancing three components:

   i)   Realization of benefits
   ii)   Optimization (not minimization) of risk
   iii)   Optimal use of resources

   2)   COBIT 5 also recognizes that stakeholder needs are not fixed. They evolve under the influence of both internal factors (e.g., changes in organizational culture) and external factors (e.g., disruptive technologies).

   a)   These factors are collectively referred to as stakeholder drivers.

   3)   In response to the identified stakeholder needs, enterprise goals are established.

   a)   COBIT 5 supplies 17 generic enterprise goals that are tied directly to the balanced scorecard model.

   4)   Next, IT-related goals are drawn up to address the enterprise goals.

   a)   COBIT 5 translates the 17 generic enterprise goals into IT-related goals.

   5)   Finally, enablers are identified that support pursuit of the IT-related goals. An enabler is broadly defined as anything that helps achieve objectives.

   6)   COBIT 5 refers to the process described above as the goals cascade. It can be depicted graphically as follows:

COBIT 5 Goals Cascade

Figure 14-1

b. **Principle 2: Covering the Enterprise End-to-End**

1) COBIT 5 takes a comprehensive view of all of the enterprise's functions and processes. Information technology pervades them all; it cannot be viewed as a function distinct from other enterprise activities.

   a) Thus, IT governance must be integrated with enterprise governance.

2) IT must be considered enterprise-wide and end-to-end, i.e., all functions and processes that govern and manage information "wherever that information may be processed."

c. **Principle 3: Applying a Single, Integrated Framework**

1) In acknowledgment of the availability of multiple IT-related standards and best practices, COBIT 5 provides an overall framework for enterprise IT within which other standards can be consistently applied.

2) COBIT 5 was developed to be an overarching framework that does not address specific technical issues; i.e., its principles can be applied regardless of the particular hardware and software in use.

d. **Principle 4: Enabling a Holistic Approach**

1) COBIT 5 describes seven categories of enablers that support comprehensive IT governance and management:

   a) Principles, policies, and frameworks
   b) Processes
   c) Organizational structures
   d) Culture, ethics, and behavior
   e) Information
   f) Services, infrastructure, and applications
   g) People, skills, and competencies

2) The last three of these enablers are also classified as resources, the use of which must be optimized.

3) Enablers are interconnected because they

   a) Need the input of other enablers to be fully effective and
   b) Deliver output for the benefit of other enablers.

e. **Principle 5: Separating Governance from Management**

1) The complexity of the modern enterprise requires governance and management to be treated as distinct activities.

   a) In general, governance is the setting of overall objectives and monitoring progress toward those objectives. COBIT 5 associates governance with the board of directors.

      i) Within any governance process, three practices must be addressed: evaluate, direct, and monitor.

   b) Management is the carrying out of activities in pursuit of enterprise goals. COBIT 5 associates these activities with executive management under the leadership of the CEO.

      i) Within any management process, four responsibility areas must be addressed: plan, build, run, and monitor.

Background

Besides the framework itself, the COBIT product family includes three other documents that can be purchased separately: enabler guides, which describe enabling processes (i.e., anything that can help to achieve enterprise objectives); professional guides, which provide guidance for the implementation of COBIT, as well as for such specific topics as information security, assurance, and risk; and an online environment allowing simultaneous participation and collaboration by interested parties.

Stop and review! You have completed the outline for this subunit. Study multiple-choice question 8 on page 373.

14.3 INFORMATION SECURITY

1. **Overview**

    a. Information security encompasses not only computer hardware and software but all of an organization's information, no matter what medium it resides on. It involves far more than just user IDs and passwords.

        1) The importance of a broad definition of information security becomes clear in light of recent incidents of firms accidentally disposing of documents containing confidential customer information with their regular trash.

    b. Organizations have three principal goals for their information security programs: data confidentiality, data availability, and data integrity.

        1) **Confidentiality** is protecting data from disclosure to unauthorized persons.

        2) **Availability** is ensuring that the organization's information systems are up and running so that employees and customers are able to access the data they need.

        3) **Integrity** is ensuring that data accurately reflect the business events underlying them and are not subject to tampering or destruction.

2. **Steps in Creating an Information Security Plan**

    a. Identify the threats to the organization's information, i.e., events that can potentially compromise an organization's information infrastructure.

        1) Threats to confidentiality include the previously mentioned improper disposal of customer records, threats to availability include viruses and denial-of-service attacks, and threats to integrity include employee errors and sabotage.

    b. Identify the risks that these threats entail.

        1) Risk analysis has two phases: determining the likelihood of the identified threats and the level of damage that could potentially be done should the threats materialize.

        2) For example, an organization may conclude that, while the potential damage from sabotage is very high, its likelihood may be quite low.

    c. Design the controls that will compensate for the risks.

        1) Controls are designed based on the combination of likelihood and potential damage determined in the risk analysis.

        2) Controls are of three major types: physical, logical, and policy.

    d. Incorporate the controls into a coherent, enterprise-wide information security plan.

        1) The plan lists the controls that will be put in place and how they will be enforced.

e. Policies set forth expectations of all persons, both employees and external users, with access to the organization's systems.

   1) The single most important policy is that which governs the information resources to which individuals have access and how the level of access will be tied to their job duties.

      a) Carrying out such a policy requires the organization's systems to be able to tie data and program access to individual system IDs.

      b) One provision of the policy must be for the immediate removal of access to the system by terminated employees.

3. **Generic Controls**

   a. IT controls can also be classified according to the traditional three-way division of internal controls.

   b. **Preventive controls** prevent errors from entering the system. Preventive controls are often highly visible and are considered better than other forms of control because they stop problems before they occur.

      1) Examples of physical preventive controls include fences, locked doors, security guards, and a segregation of duties policy.

      2) Examples of logical preventive controls are the input controls described later in this study unit.

   c. **Detective controls** call attention to errors that have already entered the system before an error causes a negative outcome.

      1) Examples of detective accounting controls are petty cash counts and physical inventories.

         a) An important detective control in IT is examination of system logs. These logs are reports automatically generated by the system of actions that require scrutiny, such as repeated failed login attempts and the use of powerful utility programs.

      2) Examples in an automated systems context are the output controls described later in this study unit.

   d. **Corrective controls** correct errors after they have been detected.

      1) Examples include correcting errors reported on error listings, isolating and removing viruses, and restarting from system crashes.

4. **Broad Controls**

   a. The two broad groupings of information systems control activities are **general controls** and **application controls**.

   b. **General controls** are the umbrella under which the IT function operates. They affect the organization's entire processing environment and commonly include controls over (1) data center and network operations; (2) systems software acquisition, change, and maintenance; (3) access security; and (4) application system acquisition, development, and maintenance.

      1) Controls over data center and network **operations** ensure efficient and effective operations of the computer activity. These include aspects of the control environment and risk assessment.

      2) Controls over **software acquisition, change, and maintenance** ensure that proper software is available for use.

      3) Controls over **access** encompass access to both computer hardware devices themselves (physical access) and to data and programs through the system (logical access).

c.   Application controls are particular to each of the organization's applications. Some features come built-in when applications are acquired from vendors. Software developed by the organization's own programmers must have appropriate controls incorporated in the design. Application controls may be further classified as follows:

1)   **Input controls** provide reasonable assurance that (a) data received for processing have been identified, properly authorized, and converted into machine-sensible form and (b) data (including data transmitted over communication lines) have not been lost, added to, suppressed, duplicated, or otherwise improperly changed. Input controls also relate to rejection, correction, and resubmission of initially incorrect data.

2)   **Concurrent update controls** regulate ongoing tasks to ensure that correct results for concurrent operations (operations happening at the same time) are generated.

3)   **Processing controls** provide reasonable assurance that processing has been performed as intended for the particular application. Thus, (a) all transactions should be processed as authorized, (b) no authorized transactions should be omitted, and (c) no unauthorized transactions should be added.

4)   **Output controls** ensure the accuracy of the processing result (such as account listings, reports, files, invoices, or disbursement checks) and the receipt of output by authorized personnel only.

5.   **General Controls**

a.   General controls relate to the organization's IT environment as a whole. They sustain the conditions under which application controls can function properly.

b.   IT Administration Controls Over Operations

1)   A modern organization should recognize information technology as a separate function with its own set of management and technical skills. An organization that allows every functional area to acquire and administer its own systems in isolation is not serious about proper control.

2)   Treating IT as a separate functional area of the organization involves the designation of a chief information officer (CIO) or chief technology officer (CTO) and the establishment of an information systems steering committee to set a coherent direction for the organization's systems and prioritize information technology projects.

c.   **Segregation of duties** is vital because a separation of functions (authorization, recording, and access to assets) may not be feasible in an IT environment. For example, a computer may print checks, record disbursements, and generate information for reconciling the account balance. These activities customarily are segregated in a manual system. Segregation of duties within the IT function is discussed in Subunit 14.5.

d.   Controls over software acquisition, change, and maintenance include:

1)   **Controls over systems software,** which ensure that operating systems, utilities, and database management systems are acquired and changed only under close supervision and that vendor updates are routinely installed.

2)   **Controls over application software,** which ensure that programs used for transaction processing (e.g., payroll and accounts receivable) are cost-effective and stable.

e.   **Hardware controls** are built into the equipment by the manufacturer. They ensure the proper internal handling of data as they are moved and stored.

1)   They include parity checks, echo checks, read-after-write checks, and any other procedure built into the equipment to ensure data integrity.

f. **Physical controls** limit physical access and environmental damage to computer equipment, data, and important documents.

   1) **Access Controls**

      a) Access controls prevent improper use or manipulation of data files and programs. They ensure that only those persons with a bona fide purpose and authorization have access.

      b) No persons except operators should be allowed unmonitored access to the processing facility. This can be accomplished through the use of a guard desk, a keypad, or a magnetic card reader.

      c) **Passwords and ID numbers.** The use of passwords and identification numbers (for example, a PIN used for an ATM) is an effective control in an online system to prevent unauthorized access to files. Lists of authorized persons are maintained online. To avoid unauthorized access, the entity may combine (1) the entry of passwords or identification numbers; (2) a prearranged set of personal questions; and (3) the use of badges, magnetic cards, or optically scanned cards.

      d) **Device authorization table.** This control grants access only to those physical devices that should logically need access. For example, because it is illogical for anyone to access the accounts receivable file from a manufacturing terminal, the device authorization table will deny access even when a valid password is used.

      e) **System access log.** This log records all uses and attempted uses of the system. The date and time, codes used, mode of access, data involved, and interventions by operators are recorded.

      f) **Encryption.** Encoding data before transmission over communication lines makes it more difficult for someone with access to the transmission to understand or modify its contents. Encryption technology converts data into a code. Unauthorized users may still be able to access the data but, without the encryption key, will be unable to decode the information.

      g) **Callback.** This feature requires the remote user to call, give identification, hang up, and wait for a call to an authorized number. This control ensures acceptance of data only from authorized modems. However, a call-forwarding device may thwart this control by transferring access from an authorized to an unauthorized number.

      h) **Controlled disposal of documents.** One method of enforcing access restrictions is to destroy data when they are no longer in use. Thus, paper documents may be shredded, and magnetic media may be erased.

      i) **Biometric technologies.** These are automated methods of establishing an individual's identity using physiological or behavioral traits. These characteristics include fingerprints, retina patterns, hand geometry, signature dynamics, speech, and keystroke dynamics.

      j) **Automatic log-off.** The disconnection of inactive data terminals may prevent the viewing of sensitive data on an unattended work station.

      k) **Security personnel.** An entity may hire security specialists. For example, (1) developing an information security policy for the entity, (2) commenting on security controls in new applications, and (3) monitoring and investigating unsuccessful access attempts are appropriate duties of the information security officer.

   2) **Environmental Controls**

      a) The processing facility should be equipped with both a cooling and heating system (to maintain a year-round constant level of temperature and humidity) and a fire-suppression system.

g. **Logical controls** are established to limit access in accordance with the principle that all persons should have access only to those elements of the organization's information systems that are necessary to perform their job duties. Logical controls have a double focus, authentication and authorization.

1) Authentication is the act of ensuring that the person attempting to access the system is in fact who (s)he says (s)he is. The most widespread means of achieving this is through the use of IDs and passwords.

2) The elements of user account management are as follows:

a) Anyone attempting access to one of the organization's systems must supply a unique identifier (e.g., the person's name or other series of characters) and a password that is known only to that person and is not stored anywhere in the system in unencrypted format.

i) Not even information security personnel should be able to view unencrypted passwords. Security personnel can change passwords, but the policy should require that the user immediately change it to something secret.

b) The organization's systems should force users to change their passwords periodically, e.g., every 90 days.

c) The policy should prohibit employees from leaving their IDs and passwords written down in plain view.

3) Authorization is the practice of ensuring that, once in the system, the user can only access those programs and data elements necessary for his or her job duties.

a) In many cases, users should be able to view the contents of some data fields but not be able to change them.

b) An example is an accounts receivable clerk who can view customers' credit limits but cannot change them. This same clerk can, however, change a customer's outstanding balance by entering or adjusting an invoice.

c) To extend the example, only the head of the accounts receivable department should be able to execute the program that updates the accounts receivable master balance file. An individual clerk should have no such power.

h. A **firewall** is a combination of hardware and software that separates an internal network from an external network (e.g., the Internet) and prevents passage of traffic deemed suspicious. Two principal types of firewalls are network firewalls and application firewalls.

1) Network firewalls regulate traffic to an entire network, such as an organization's LAN.

a) The firewall examines each query and, depending on the rules set up by the network security administrator, denies entry to the network based on the source, destination, or other data in the header.

b) Queries from a particular source address that repeatedly fail to gain access to the network might indicate a penetration attempt. The firewall can notify network security personnel who can then investigate.

      2)   Application firewalls regulate traffic to a specified application, such as email or file transfer.

          a)   An application firewall is based on proxy server technology. The firewall becomes a proxy, or intermediary, between the computer actually sending the packet and the application in question. This arrangement allows for a high level of security over the application but at the cost of slowing down communications.

          b)   Since an application firewall only provides security for a single application, it is not a substitute for a network firewall.

      3)   A firewall alone is not an adequate defense against computer viruses. Specialized antivirus software is a must.

Stop and review! You have completed the outline for this subunit. Study multiple-choice questions 9 through 16 beginning on page 373.

14.4 APPLICATION CONTROLS

 CPA exam questions concerning application controls often give a description of a control, then ask for the name of it.

1.   **Application Controls**

    a.   Application controls are built into each application (payroll, accounts payable, inventory management, etc.).

    b.   Application controls are designed to ensure that only correct, authorized data enter the system and that the data are processed and reported properly.

2.   **Input Controls**

    a.   Input controls provide reasonable assurance that data submitted for processing are (1) authorized, (2) complete, and (3) accurate. These controls vary depending on whether input is entered in online or batch mode.

    b.   The most basic input control is thus authorization; e.g., a batch of accounts payable transactions must be authorized by the AP supervisor before being submitted for recording.

    c.   Many input controls take the form of edit routines, i.e., controls programmed into the software that prevent certain types of errors from ever getting into the system.

        1)   Preformatting

           a)   To avoid data entry errors in online systems, a preformatted screen may be designed to look exactly like the corresponding paper document.

        2)   Edit (Field) Checks

           a)   Some data elements can only contain certain characters, and any transaction that attempts to use an invalid character is halted. A typical example is a Social Security number, which is not allowed to contain letters.

        3)   Limit (Reasonableness) and Range Checks

           a)   Based on known limits for given information, certain entries can be rejected by the system. For example, hours worked per week cannot exceed 80 without a special override by management, date of birth cannot be any date within the last 15 years, etc.

4) Validity Checks

    a) In order for a transaction to be processed, some other record must already exist in another file. For example, for the system to accept a transaction requesting payment of a vendor invoice, the vendor must already have a record on the vendor master file.

5) Sequence Checks

    a) Processing efficiency is greatly increased when files are sorted on some designated field(s), called the "key," before operations such as matching. For instance, the accounts payable transaction file and master file should both be sorted according to vendor number before the matching operation is attempted. If the system discovers a record out of order, it may indicate that the files were not properly prepared for processing.

6) Closed-Loop Verification

    a) Inputs by a user are transmitted to the computer, processed, and displayed back to the user for verification.

7) Check-Digit Verification (Self-Checking Digits)

    a) An algorithm is applied to, for instance, a product number and incorporated into the number. This reduces keying errors such as dropped and transposed digits.

EXAMPLE

A box of detergent has the product number 4187604. The last digit is actually a derived number, arrived at by applying the check-digit algorithm to the other digits.

The check digit is calculated by starting with the last position of the base product number and multiplying each successive digit to the left by 2, then by 1, then by 2, etc., and adding the results: $(0 \times 2) + (6 \times 1) + (7 \times 2) + (8 \times 1) + (1 \times 2) + (4 \times 1) = 0 + 6 + 14 + 8 + 2 + 4 = 34$. The last digit of this result becomes the check digit.

When the clerk enters 4187604 into the terminal, the system performs an immediate calculation and determines that this is a valid product number.

---

8) Zero-Balance Checks

    a) The system will reject any transaction or batch thereof in which the sum of all debits and credits does not equal zero.

d. **Batch input controls** can be used when data are grouped for processing.

1) **Management release.** A batch is not released for processing until a manager reviews and approves it.

2) **Record count.** A batch is not released for processing unless the number of records in the batch, as reported by the system, matches the number calculated by the user.

3) **Financial total.** A batch is not released for processing unless the sum of the dollar amounts of the individual items as reported by the system matches the amount calculated by the user.

4) **Hash total.** The arithmetic sum of a numeric field, which has no meaning by itself, can serve as a check that the same records that should have been processed were processed. An example is the sum of all Social Security numbers.

    a) This number is much too unwieldy to be calculated by the user, but once it is calculated by the system, it can follow the batch through subsequent stages of processing.

3. **Processing Controls**

    a.   Processing controls provide reasonable assurance that (1) all data submitted for processing are processed and (2) only approved data are processed. These controls are built into the application code by programmers during the systems development process.

    b.   Some processing controls repeat the steps performed by the **input controls**, such as limit checks and batch controls.

    c.   **Validation.** Identifiers are matched against master files to determine existence. For example, any accounts payable transaction in which the vendor number does not match a number on the vendor master file is rejected.

    d.   **Completeness.** Any record with missing data is rejected.

    e.   **Arithmetic controls.** Cross-footing compares an amount with the sum of its components. Zero-balance checking adds the debits and credits in a transaction or batch to ensure that their sum is zero.

    f.   **Sequence check.** Computer effort is expended most efficiently when data are processed in a logical order, such as by customer number. This check ensures the batch is sorted in the proper order before processing begins.

    g.   **Run-to-run control totals.** The controls associated with a given batch are checked after each stage of processing to ensure all transactions have been processed.

    h.   **Key integrity.** A record's key is the group of values in designated fields that uniquely identify the record. No application process should be able to alter the data in these key fields.

4. **Output Controls**

    a.   Output controls provide assurance that the processing result (such as account listings or displays, reports, files, invoices, or disbursement checks) is accurate and that only authorized personnel receive the output.

    b.   These procedures are performed at the end of processing to ensure that all transactions the user expected to be processed were actually processed.

        1)   Transaction Logs

            a)   Every action performed in the application is logged along with the date, time, and ID in use when the action was taken.

        2)   Error Listings

            a)   All transactions rejected by the system are printed and distributed to the appropriate user department for resolution.

        3)   Record Counts

            a)   The total number of records processed by the system is compared to the number the user expected to be processed.

        4)   Run-to-Run Control Totals

            a)   The new financial balance should be the sum of the old balance plus the activity that was just processed.

5. Specific Controls

 Recent CPA exams have contained questions regarding the duties and responsibilities of various IT personnel as well as the segregation of duties within the IT function. Understand the responsibilities of IT personnel from the standpoint of duty segregation.

a. **Information Security**

1) Information systems pervade every part of a modern organization's operations. Therefore, the area of security over information systems is a distinct function within the larger IT function.

2) The IT security officer is responsible for formulating and enforcing a formal information security policy for all employees and outside parties, such as EDI partners, who have access to the organization's systems.

3) Such a policy should, among other things, inform all those with access to the organization's systems that the organization's hardware, software, and network connections are purely for the benefit of the organization and not to be used for personal reasons.

4) In addition, the IT security function is responsible for ensuring that persons both inside and outside the organization can gain access only to those programs and data elements that are appropriate for their job duties. This requires that the IT security officer and his or her subordinates are well trained in the use of the organization's security software.

b. **Systems Development and Maintenance**

1) Users within the organization are constantly requesting the creation of new systems to help manage business processes and changes and enhancements to existing systems.

2) Systems analysts and applications programmers are responsible for designing, building, and maintaining the organization's applications.

3) Analysts and programmers should never be able to make changes directly to programs that are used in "live" production. A separate processing area devoted to development and testing should be set up and dedicated to the use of analysts and programmers.

4) In addition, analysts and programmers should never have access to live production data; the data used to test new or altered programs should be stored in the separate development area along with the programs.

c. **Computer operations**

1) Console operators are responsible only for the smooth running of the organization's medium- and large-scale computers, i.e., the scheduling of jobs and production of output.

2) Console operators should therefore have no access to make changes to applications programs. Ideally, computer operators should have no programming knowledge or access to documentation not strictly necessary for their work ("ignorance is a good internal control").

3) Librarians are responsible for "checking out" applications programs to analysts and programmers for modification and testing and for ensuring that the properly tested version gets "checked in" to production. Ideally, they too should have no programming knowledge.

d. **Data Administration**

    1) The totality of an organization's data is an extremely valuable asset. Hardware can be replaced for a price, but each organization's data bundle is unique and is indispensable to carrying on business. In large organizations, the task of organizing and storing data is often divided into two subfunctions.

    2) Data administrators determine how the organization's data should be stored and what relationships among the data best achieve the organization's business objectives.

        a) Confusingly, this function is also called database analyst.

    3) Database administrators (DBAs) keep the organization's databases running efficiently.

        a) Every database is a unique combination of

            i) The relationships among the data (the schema),
            ii) The database management system (the software), and
            iii) The equipment on which the database is stored (the hardware).

        b) Keeping a complex database "tuned" is a demanding task requiring a great deal of technical knowledge.

    4) Depending on the size of the organization, the functions of data administrator and database administrator are often combined in a single job.

        a) Because they have unfettered access to the organization's production data, employees in these functions should have no access to the application programs that process the data.

e. **End Users**

    1) In an organizational sense, the "owners" of data are the end user department (the accounting function is responsible for the accuracy of accounting data, the marketing function is responsible for the accuracy of marketing data, etc.). The IT function is merely the custodian of the data.

    2) User departments should be able to access and alter only the data pertaining to their job duties; e.g., credit managers should not be able to alter accounts payable data. End users should never be able to access the code underlying applications programs.

Stop and review! You have completed the outline for this subunit. Study multiple-choice questions 17 through 23 beginning on page 375.

14.5 ROLES AND RESPONSIBILITIES WITHIN THE IT FUNCTION

 In the early days of computing, maintaining a rigid segregation of duties was a simple matter because the roles surrounding a mainframe computer were so specialized. As IT became more and more decentralized over the years, clear lines that once separated jobs such as systems analyst and programmer became blurred and then disappeared. Candidates for the CPA exam must be aware of the evolving roles of IT personnel.

1. **Segregation of Duties -- IT Function**

    a. Organizational controls concern the proper segregation of duties and responsibilities within the information systems department.

    b. Controls should ensure the efficiency and effectiveness of IT operations. They include proper segregation of the duties within the IT environment. Thus, the responsibilities of systems analysts, programmers, operators, file librarians, the control group, and others should be assigned to different individuals, and proper supervision should be provided.

    c.   Segregation of duties is vital because a traditional segregation of responsibilities for authorization, recording, and access to assets may not be feasible in an IT environment.

        1)   For example, a computer may print checks, record disbursements, and generate information for reconciling the account balance, which are activities customarily segregated in a manual system.

            a)   If the same person provides the input and receives the output for this process, a significant control weakness exists. Accordingly, certain tasks should not be combined.

            b)   Thus, compensating controls may be necessary, such as library controls, effective supervision, and rational personnel. Segregating test programs makes concealment of unauthorized changes in production programs more difficult.

2.   **Responsibilities of IT Personnel**

    a.   **Database administrators** (DBAs) are responsible for developing and maintaining the organization's databases and for establishing controls to protect their integrity.

        1)   Thus, only the DBA should be able to update data dictionaries.

        2)   In small systems, the DBA may perform some functions of a database management system (DBMS). In larger applications, the DBA uses a DBMS as a primary tool.

    b.   **Network technicians** maintain the bridges, hubs, routers, switches, cabling, and other devices that interconnect the organization's computers. They are also responsible for maintaining the organization's connection to other networks, such as the Internet.

    c.   The **webmaster** is responsible for the content of the organization's website. (S)he works closely with programmers and network technicians to ensure that the appropriate content is displayed and that the site is reliably available to users.

    d.   **Computer operators** are responsible for the day-to-day functioning of the data center, whether the organization runs a mainframe, servers, or anything in between.

        1)   Operators load data, mount storage devices, and operate the equipment. Operators should not be assigned programming duties or responsibility for systems design. Accordingly, they also should have no opportunity to make changes in programs and systems as they operate the equipment.

            a)   Ideally, computer operators should not have programming knowledge or access to documentation not strictly necessary for their work.

    e.   **Librarians** maintain control over and accountability for documentation, programs, and data storage media.

    f.   **Systems programmers** maintain and fine-tune the operating systems on the organization's medium- and large-scale computers. The operating system is the core software that performs three of a computer's four basic tasks, i.e., input, output, and storage.

        1)   Programmers as well as analysts may be able to modify programs, data files, and controls. Thus, they should have no access to the data center operations or to production programs, or data.

    g.   **Applications programmers** design, write, test, and document computer programs according to specifications provided by the end users.

h.　A **systems analyst** uses his or her detailed knowledge of the organization's databases and applications programs to determine how an application should be designed to best serve the users' needs. These duties are often combined with those of applications programmers.

　　1)　Systems analysts should not have access to data center operations, production programs, or data files.

i.　**Help desk personnel** log problems reported by users, resolve minor difficulties, and forward more difficult problems to the appropriate person, such as a database administrator or the webmaster. Help desk personnel are often called on to resolve such issues as desktop computers crashing or problems with email.

j.　**Information security officers** are typically in charge of developing information security policies, commenting on security controls in new applications, and monitoring and investigating unsuccessful login attempts.

k.　**End users** must be able to change production data but not programs.

Stop and review! You have completed the outline for this subunit. Study multiple-choice questions 24 through 30 beginning on page 377.

QUESTIONS

14.1　Risks Associated with Business Information Systems

1. Your firm has recently converted its purchasing cycle from a manual process to an online computer system. Which of the following is a probable result associated with conversion to the new automatic system?

A.　Processing errors are increased.

B.　The firm's risk exposures are reduced.

C.　Processing time is increased.

D.　Traditional duties are less segregated.

Answer (D) is correct.

　　REQUIRED: The probable result associated with conversion to the new automatic system.

　　DISCUSSION: In a manual system with appropriate internal control, separate individuals are responsible for authorizing transactions, recording transactions, and having custody of assets. These checks and balances prevent fraud and detect inaccurate or incomplete transactions. In a computer environment, however, this segregation of duties is not always feasible. For example, a computer may print checks, record disbursements, and generate information for reconciling the account balance.

　　Answer (A) is incorrect. A computer system decreases processing errors. Answer (B) is incorrect. The conversion to a new system does not reduce the number of risk exposures. Answer (C) is incorrect. Processing time is decreased.

2. Which of the following statements most accurately describes the impact that automation has on the controls normally present in a manual system?

A.　Transaction trails are more extensive in a computer-based system than in a manual system because a one-for-one correspondence always exists between data entry and output.

B.　Responsibility for custody of information assets is more concentrated in user departments in a computer-based system than it is in a manual system.

C.　Controls must be more explicit in a computer-based system because many processing points that present opportunities for human judgment in a manual system are eliminated.

D.　The quality of documentation becomes less critical in a computer-based system than it is in a manual system because data records are stored in machine-readable files.

Answer (C) is correct.

　　REQUIRED: The impact that automation has on the controls normally present in a manual system.

　　DISCUSSION: Using a computer does not change the basic concepts and objectives of control. However, the use of computers may modify the control techniques used. The processing of transactions may be combined with control activities previously performed separately, or control functions may be combined within the information system activity.

　　Answer (A) is incorrect. The audit trail is less extensive in an information system. Combining processing and controls within the system reduces documentary evidence. Answer (B) is incorrect. Information assets are more likely to be under the control of the information system function. Answer (D) is incorrect. Documentation is more important in an information system. Information is more likely to be stored in machine-readable form than in hard copy.

3. Innovations in IT increase the importance of risk management because

   A. The objective of complete security is becoming more attainable.

   B. Information system security is continually subject to new threats.

   C. Closed private systems have proliferated.

   D. Privacy is a concern for only a very few users.

Answer (B) is correct.
   REQUIRED: The reason that IT innovations increase the importance of risk management.
   DISCUSSION: Advances in technology bring new capabilities and, along with them, new vulnerabilities. Because information system security is continually subject to new threats, that is, to new risks and exposures, risk assessment and management must be a continual process.
   Answer (A) is incorrect. Perfect security is not feasible. One reason is that system access cannot be eliminated. Answer (C) is incorrect. Internet connectivity has tended to reduce the prevalence of closed private systems. Answer (D) is incorrect. Privacy was an expectation of people everywhere before the innovations in IT led to the globalization of e-business via the Internet. Thus, risk management has increased in importance in part because those innovations created new threats to the privacy of personal information. As such, organizations must, for example, meet statutory requirements for safeguarding the personal information of customers.

4. As a result of technological developments facing businesses and CPAs,

   A. System boundaries are becoming less distinct.

   B. Computer programmers and operators have eliminated the need for accountants.

   C. Internet use has spread, and e-business control over user interaction has been simplified.

   D. Better controls have resulted in a reduction in threats.

Answer (A) is correct.
   REQUIRED: The effect of IT advances.
   DISCUSSION: Organizational system boundaries are becoming indistinct as electronic interactions with suppliers, customers, partners, and associates increase. Thus, CPAs have more difficulty in giving assurance about security, control, and privacy.
   Answer (B) is incorrect. Application of judgment and use of decision-making by accountants are still required regardless of the advancement of technology. Answer (C) is incorrect. As the Internet has spread globally, more products, services, languages, cultures, and political systems have become involved. Control over user interaction is therefore more difficult. Answer (D) is incorrect. Although IT may provide better controls, traditional threats remain, and new ones have emerged.

5. Attacks on computer networks may take many forms. Which of the following uses the computers of innocent parties infected with Trojan horse programs?

   A. A distributed denial-of-service attack.

   B. A man-in-the-middle attack.

   C. A brute-force attack.

   D. A password-cracking attack.

Answer (A) is correct.
   REQUIRED: The attack on a network that uses the computers of innocent parties infected with Trojan horse programs.
   DISCUSSION: A denial-of-service (DOS) attack is an attempt to overload a system (e.g., a network or Web server) with false messages so that it cannot function (a system crash). A distributed DOS attack comes from multiple sources, for example, the machines of innocent parties infected by Trojan horses.
   Answer (B) is incorrect. A man-in-the-middle attack takes advantage of network packet sniffing and routing and transport protocols to access packets flowing through a network. Answer (C) is incorrect. A brute-force attack uses password cracking software to try large numbers of letter and number combinations to access a network. Answer (D) is incorrect. Password-cracking software accesses a network by trying many letter and number combinations.

6. Spoofing is one type of malicious online activity. Spoofing is

   A. Trying large numbers of letter and number combinations to access a network.

   B. Eavesdropping on information sent by a user to the host computer of a website.

   C. Accessing packets flowing through a network.

   D. Identity misrepresentation in cyberspace.

Answer (D) is correct.
   REQUIRED: The nature of spoofing.
   DISCUSSION: Passwords, user account numbers, and other information may be stolen through spoofing. Spoofing is identity misrepresentation in cyberspace, for example, by using a false website to obtain information about visitors.
   Answer (A) is incorrect. A brute-force attack uses password cracking software to try large numbers of letter and number combinations to access a network. Answer (B) is incorrect. Sniffing is the use of software to eavesdrop on information sent by a user to the host computer of a website. Answer (C) is incorrect. A man-in-the-middle attack takes advantage of network packet sniffing and routing and transport protocols to access packets flowing through a network.

7. Which of the following is a computer program that appears to be legitimate but performs some illicit activity when it is run?

A. Hoax virus.

B. Web crawler.

C. Trojan horse.

D. Killer application.

Answer (C) is correct.
REQUIRED: The apparently legitimate computer program that performs an illicit activity.
DISCUSSION: A Trojan horse is a computer program that appears friendly, for example, a game, but that actually contains an application destructive to the computer system.
Answer (A) is incorrect. A hoax virus is a false notice about the existence of a computer virus. Answer (B) is incorrect. A web crawler (a spider or bot) is a computer program created to access and read information on websites. The results are included as entries in the index of a search engine. Answer (D) is incorrect. A killer application is one that is so useful that it may justify widespread adoption of a new technology.

14.2 COBIT -- A Framework for IT

8. Which of the following statements is **inconsistent** with the key principles of the COBIT 5 framework?

A. Enterprise governance and management are treated as the same activity.

B. The needs of stakeholders are the focus of all organizational activities.

C. Information technology controls are considered to be intertwined with those of the organization's everyday operations.

D. COBIT 5 can be applied even when other IT-related standards have been adopted.

Answer (A) is correct.
REQUIRED: The statement inconsistent with the key principles of the COBIT 5 framework.
DISCUSSION: Under the COBIT 5 framework, the complexity of the modern enterprise requires governance and management to be treated as distinct activities.
Answer (B) is incorrect. COBIT 5 asserts that the creation of stakeholder value is the fundamental goal of any enterprise. Answer (C) is incorrect. COBIT 5 takes a comprehensive view of all of the enterprise's functions and processes. Information technology pervades them all; it cannot be viewed as a function distinct from other enterprise activities. Answer (D) is incorrect. In acknowledgment of the availability of multiple IT-related standards and best practices, COBIT 5 provides an overall framework for enterprise IT within which other standards can be applied.

14.3 Information Security

9. A client installed the sophisticated controls using the biometric attributes of employees to authenticate user access to the computer system. This technology most likely replaced which of the following controls?

A. Use of security specialists.

B. Reasonableness tests.

C. Passwords.

D. Virus protection software.

Answer (C) is correct.
REQUIRED: The control most likely replaced by biometric technologies.
DISCUSSION: The use of passwords is an effective control in an online system to prevent unauthorized access to computer systems. However, biometric technologies are more sophisticated and difficult to compromise.
Answer (A) is incorrect. Biometric technologies do not eliminate the need for specialists who evaluate and monitor security needs. Answer (B) is incorrect. Reasonableness tests are related to input controls, not access controls. Answer (D) is incorrect. Virus protection software prevents damage to data in a system, not access to a system.

10. Authentication is the process by which the

A. System verifies that the user is entitled to enter the transaction requested.

B. System verifies the identity of the user.

C. User identifies himself or herself to the system.

D. User indicates to the system that the transaction was processed correctly.

Answer (B) is correct.
REQUIRED: The definition of authentication.
DISCUSSION: Identification is the process of uniquely distinguishing one user from all others. Authentication is the process of determining that individuals are who they say they are. For example, a password may identify but not authenticate its user if it is known by more than one individual.
Answer (A) is incorrect. Authentication involves verifying the identity of the user. This process does not necessarily confirm the functions the user is authorized to perform. Answer (C) is incorrect. User identification to the system does not imply that the system has verified the identity of the user. Answer (D) is incorrect. This procedure is an application control for accuracy of the transaction.

11. The two broad groupings of information systems control activities are general controls and application controls. General controls include controls

A. Relating to the correction and resubmission of faulty data.

B. For developing, modifying, and maintaining computer programs.

C. Designed to assure that only authorized users receive output from processing.

D. Designed to ensure that all data submitted for processing have been properly authorized.

Answer (B) is correct.
    REQUIRED: The general controls.
    DISCUSSION: General controls are policies and procedures that relate to the entity's overall IT environment. They support the effective functioning of application controls by helping to ensure the continued proper operation of information systems. General controls include controls over (1) data center and network operations; (2) systems software acquisition and maintenance; (3) access security; and (4) application systems acquisition, development, and maintenance.
    Answer (A) is incorrect. Control over correction of input errors is an application control. Answer (C) is incorrect. Control over report distribution (output) is an application control. Answer (D) is incorrect. Control over authorization of input is an application control.

12. The significance of hardware controls is that they

A. Ensure the proper execution of machine instructions.

B. Reduce the incidence of user input errors in online systems.

C. Ensure accurate programming of operating system functions.

D. Ensure that run-to-run totals in application systems are consistent.

Answer (A) is correct.
    REQUIRED: The significance of hardware controls.
    DISCUSSION: Hardware controls are built into the equipment by the manufacturer to detect and control errors arising from the use of the equipment. Examples include parity checks, read-after-write checks, and echo checks.
    Answer (B) is incorrect. Use of input screens, limit tests, self-checking digits, and other input controls can reduce the incidence of input errors in online systems. Answer (C) is incorrect. Programmers and/or analysts must correct errors in computer programs. Answer (D) is incorrect. Run-to-run totals ensure the completeness of update in an online system by accumulating separate totals for all transactions processed throughout a period. This total is compared with the total of items accepted for processing.

13. Which of the following is an important senior management responsibility with regard to information systems security?

A. Assessing exposures.

B. Assigning access privileges.

C. Identifying ownership of data.

D. Training employees in security matters.

Answer (A) is correct.
    REQUIRED: The senior management responsibility regarding information systems.
    DISCUSSION: Senior management is responsible for risk management, including identification of risks and consideration of their significance, the likelihood of their occurrence, and how they should be managed.
    Answer (B) is incorrect. Assignment of access privileges is the responsibility of security management. Answer (C) is incorrect. Determining ownership of data is the responsibility of security management. In this context, ownership of data or resources means responsibility for ultimate use or disposition. Answer (D) is incorrect. Training employees in security matters is the responsibility of security management.

14. An entity's database is modeled after a tree structure, with each record type having any number of lower-level dependent records. This is an example of which type of database model?

A. Relational.

B. Hierarchical.

C. Network.

D. Distributed.

Answer (B) is correct.
    REQUIRED: The type of database model described.
    DISCUSSION: A hierarchical database model uses a tree structure in which each record has one antecedent but may have an unlimited number of subsequent records.
    Answer (A) is incorrect. The data resemble sequential files and records, not an arrangement in conceptual tables with one or more fields in common. Answer (C) is incorrect. A network structure has many-to-many relationships, not one-to-many; such structures are very difficult to maintain. Answer (D) is incorrect. The data are not stored in a remote site as in a distributed system.

15. When a user enters a certain entity's system, a series of questions is asked of the user, including a name and mother's birth date. These questions are primarily intended to provide

    A. Authorization for processing.

    B. Access control to computer hardware.

    C. Authentication of the user.

    D. Data integrity control.

Answer (C) is correct.

    REQUIRED: The purpose of requiring a user to enter his or her name and mother's birth date.

    DISCUSSION: Requiring specified information allows the computer to identify the user. This access control is intended to limit access to data and programs and the nature of that access.

    Answer (A) is incorrect. Such names and questions are intended to identify the user entering the system. Answer (B) is incorrect. Access to the computer has already taken place. Questions and names do not prevent access to the hardware. Answer (D) is incorrect. Such questions have no effect on the integrity of data.

16. The headquarters' computer of a certain entity maintains a matrix of user names and the files/programs the user can access as well as what the user can do to/with the file or program. This matrix is primarily intended to provide

    A. Authorization for processing.

    B. Access control to computer hardware.

    C. Authentication of the user.

    D. Data integrity control.

Answer (A) is correct.

    REQUIRED: The purpose of the matrix of user names and file access and use data.

    DISCUSSION: Once the computer has identified the user, it should permit access to specified programs and data and limit what the user can do with that access. Thus, the matrix establishes the authorization for processing.

    Answer (B) is incorrect. Access to the computer hardware has already taken place. Answer (C) is incorrect. The matrix does not authenticate the user. Answer (D) is incorrect. Data integrity is not protected by the matrix.

14.4 Application Controls

17. An employee in the receiving department keyed in a shipment from a remote terminal and inadvertently omitted the purchase order number. The best systems control to detect this error is

    A. Completeness test.

    B. Sequence check.

    C. Reasonableness test.

    D. Compatibility test.

Answer (A) is correct.

    REQUIRED: The control to detect the omission of a purchase order number keyed in from a remote terminal.

    DISCUSSION: A completeness test checks that all data elements are entered before processing. An interactive system can be programmed to notify the user to enter the number before accepting the receiving report.

    Answer (B) is incorrect. A sequence check tests for the ordering, not omission, of records. Answer (C) is incorrect. A limit or reasonableness test checks the values of data items against established limits. Answer (D) is incorrect. A compatibility test (field check) determines whether characters are appropriate to a field.

18. Which one of the following input validation routines is **not** likely to be appropriate in a real-time operation?

    A. Sign check.

    B. Reasonableness check.

    C. Sequence check.

    D. Field check.

Answer (C) is correct.

    REQUIRED: The input validation routine not appropriate in a real-time operation.

    DISCUSSION: A sequence check tests to determine that records are in proper order. For example, a payroll input file can be sorted into Social Security number order. A sequence check can then be performed to verify record order. This control would not apply in a real-time operation because records are not processed sequentially.

    Answer (A) is incorrect. Sign checks test data for the appropriate arithmetic sign. For instance, hours worked in a payroll should always be a positive number. Answer (B) is incorrect. Reasonableness tests verify that amounts fall within predetermined limits. Answer (D) is incorrect. A field check tests a data item to determine if it has the expected type of characters; for example, a name field should have all alphabetic characters.

19. To ensure the completeness of update in an online system, separate totals are accumulated for all transactions processed throughout the day. The computer then agrees these totals to the total of items accepted for processing. This is an example of

A. Run-to-run totals.

B. Computer matching.

C. Computer sequence check.

D. One-for-one checking.

Answer (A) is correct.

    REQUIRED: The procedure that compares the total of all transactions processed with the total of items accepted.

    DISCUSSION: During each program run in a series, the computer accumulates the totals of transactions that have been processed. The run-to-run check reconciles them with the totals forwarded from the previous program run. Run-to-run totals thus ensure completeness of update.

    Answer (B) is incorrect. Computer matching compares transaction data with referenced fields or records. Answer (C) is incorrect. Computer sequence checks identify changes or breaks in a numerical sequence. Answer (D) is incorrect. One-for-one checking usually requires manual comparisons of input with processing results.

20. Which of the following computerized control procedures is most effective in ensuring that files of data uploaded from personal computers to a server are complete and that **no** additional data are added?

A. Self-checking digits to ensure that only authorized part numbers are added to the database.

B. Batch control totals, including control totals and hash totals.

C. Passwords that effectively limit access to only those authorized to upload the data to the server.

D. Field-level edit controls that test each field for alphanumerical integrity.

Answer (B) is correct.

    REQUIRED: The most effective computerized control procedure.

    DISCUSSION: Batch control totals for the data transferred can be reconciled with the batch control totals in the existing file. This comparison provides information on the completion of the data transfer. Batch totals may include record counts, totals of certain critical amounts, or hash totals. A hash total is a control total without a defined meaning, such as the total of employee numbers or invoice numbers, that is used to verify the completeness of data. Thus, the hash total for the employee listing by the personnel department could be compared with the total generated during the payroll run.

    Answer (A) is incorrect. Self-checking digits detect inaccurate identification numbers. They are an effective control to ensure that the appropriate part has been identified but not that data transfer is complete. Answer (C) is incorrect. Passwords help ensure that only authorized personnel make the transfer, not that data transfer is complete. Answer (D) is incorrect. Field checks are effective input controls, but they do not ensure completeness of data transfer.

21. In an automated payroll processing environment, a department manager substituted the time card for a terminated employee with a time card for a fictitious employee. The fictitious employee had the same pay rate and hours worked as the terminated employee. The best control to detect this action using employee identification numbers is a

A. Reasonableness test.

B. Record count.

C. Hash total.

D. Financial total.

Answer (C) is correct.

    REQUIRED: The best control technique to detect the action.

    DISCUSSION: A hash total is a control total without a defined meaning, such as the total of employee numbers or invoice numbers, that is used to verify the completeness of data. Thus, the hash total for the employee listing by the personnel department could be compared with the total generated during the payroll run.

    Answer (A) is incorrect. A reasonableness test is based on known limits for given information. Answer (B) is incorrect. A record count is a control total of the number of records processed during the operation of a program. Answer (D) is incorrect. Financial totals summarize dollar amounts in an information field in a group of records.

22. An online data entry program is used for original entry of vendor invoices. A batch check-writing program occasionally prepares a check for a vendor not yet included in the vendor file. Checks for such vendors contain nonsense characters in the payee field. The most effective programmed control to prevent this kind of error is to perform

A. A batch control total check on vendor payments.

B. A completeness test on fields in the check-writing program.

C. A verification of vendors in the check-writing program.

D. A record lookup for vendors during data entry.

Answer (D) is correct.

    REQUIRED: The most effective programmed control.

    DISCUSSION: Verifying valid vendors at the point of entry is the most cost-effective means of preventing incorrect data from entering the system.

    Answer (A) is incorrect. Control totals are used to reconcile computer input to the source document totals. Answer (B) is incorrect. Completeness tests are used to ensure that the input has the prescribed amount of data in all data fields. Answer (C) is incorrect. The most cost-effective point in a process to catch errors is the data entry point.

23. Certain payroll transactions were posted to the payroll file but were not uploaded correctly to the general ledger file on the main server. The best control to detect this type of error would be

    A. A standard method for uploading mainframe data files.

    B. An appropriate edit and validation of data.

    C. A record or log of items rejected during processing.

    D. Balancing totals of critical fields.

Answer (D) is correct.
    REQUIRED: The best control to detect failure to upload correctly to the general ledger certain payroll transactions.
    DISCUSSION: Balancing totals should be used to ensure completeness and accuracy of processing. For example, comparing totals of critical fields generated before processing with output totals for those fields tests for missing or improper transactions.
    Answer (A) is incorrect. A standard method for uploading data may not include the controls necessary to detect errors in the uploading process. Answer (B) is incorrect. Edit and validation checks are typically designed to identify errors in data entry rather than in processing. Answer (C) is incorrect. A record or log of rejected items is a control for monitoring the subsequent correction and processing of the items.

14.5 Roles and Responsibilities within the IT Function

24. Which one of the following represents a lack of internal control in a computer-based system?

    A. The design and implementation is performed in accordance with management's specific authorization.

    B. Any and all changes in application programs have the authorization and approval of management.

    C. Provisions exist to ensure the accuracy and integrity of computer processing of all files and reports.

    D. Programmers have access to change programs and data files when an error is detected.

Answer (D) is correct.
    REQUIRED: The example of a lack of internal control in a computer system.
    DISCUSSION: A functional separation of computer activities is necessary for internal control. A programmer designs program flowcharts and writes the computer programs as required by the system. Once the program has been debugged and the documentation has been prepared, the programmer should have no further access to it or to data files. A librarian is responsible for permitting only computer operators, not programmers, to have access to programs.
    Answer (A) is incorrect. The design and implementation should be authorized by management to maintain effective internal controls. Answer (B) is incorrect. Activities that involve making changes in application programs should be authorized and approved by management to maintain effective internal controls. Answer (C) is incorrect. Effective internal control ensures the reliability of records. A control group (clerk) should continuously supervise and monitor input, operations, and distribution of output.

25. A computer operator responsible for a particular job needed to know whether the job had already been run that day. The computer operator examined the

    A. Console log.

    B. Data control log.

    C. Job queue.

    D. Master run book.

Answer (A) is correct.
    REQUIRED: The source of information about execution of jobs.
    DISCUSSION: During processing, the operating system records in the console log the activities of the computer system and the actions taken by the computer operator. It should therefore contain entries for the work performed and provide a control over operator intervention.
    Answer (B) is incorrect. The data control log contains entries concerning jobs run and output distribution. However, recording is not concurrent with computer activity, and no entry may appear for some transactions already processed. Answer (C) is incorrect. The job queue is the list of jobs waiting to be processed, not those that have been executed. Answer (D) is incorrect. The master run book provides documentation of the system.

26. The risks created by rapid changes in IT have **not** affected which concepts of internal control?

I.   Cost-benefit analysis
II. Control environment
III. Reasonable assurance
IV. Management's responsibility

   A. I and II only.

   B. III and IV only.

   C. II, III, and IV only.

   D. I, II, III, and IV.

Answer (D) is correct.
   REQUIRED: The concepts of control not affected by rapid IT change.
   DISCUSSION: Internal control objectives remain essentially the same although technology, risks, and control methods change. Thus, many concepts of control (management's responsibility, the role of the control environment, reasonable assurance, monitoring, and cost-benefit analysis) are relevant regardless of IT changes.
   Answer (A) is incorrect. IT control processes and procedures must provide reasonable assurance that objectives are achieved and risks are reduced. Moreover, management continues to be responsible for control and for coordinating activities to achieve objectives. Answer (B) is incorrect. Cost-benefit analysis remains an essential tool for determining which controls mitigate identified risks at an acceptable cost. Furthermore, the control environment in an IT setting reflects the tone of the organization, influences control consciousness, and provides a foundation for the other components of control. Answer (C) is incorrect. Cost-benefit analysis remains an essential tool for determining which controls mitigate identified risks at an acceptable cost.

27. Robert is the data administrator (DA) for Big Time Corporation. An example of Robert's responsibilities as the DA is to monitor

   A. The database industry.

   B. The performance of the database.

   C. Database security.

   D. Backup of the system.

Answer (A) is correct.
   REQUIRED: The responsibilities of a data administrator.
   DISCUSSION: The DA handles administrative issues that arise regarding the database. The DA acts as an advocate by suggesting new applications and standards. One of the DA's responsibilities is to monitor the database industry for new developments. In contrast, the database administrator (DBA) deals with the technical aspects of the database.
   Answer (B) is incorrect. The performance of the database is an example of the database administrator's responsibilities. Answer (C) is incorrect. Database security is an example of the database administrator's responsibilities. Answer (D) is incorrect. Backup of the system is an example of the database administrator's responsibilities.

28. In the organization of the information systems function, the most important segregation of duties is

   A. Not allowing the data librarian to assist in data processing operations.

   B. Assuring that those responsible for programming the system do not have access to data processing operations.

   C. Having a separate information officer at the top level of the organization outside of the accounting function.

   D. Using different programming personnel to maintain utility programs from those who maintain the application programs.

Answer (B) is correct.
   REQUIRED: The most important segregation of duties.
   DISCUSSION: Segregation of duties is a general control that is vital in a computerized environment. Some segregation of duties common in noncomputerized environments may not be feasible in a computer environment. However, certain tasks should not be combined. Systems analysts and programmers should be segregate from computer operators. Both programmers and analysts may be able to modify programs, files, and controls, and should therefore have no access to those programs nor to computer equipment. Operators should not be assigned programming duties or responsibility for systems design, and should have no opportunity to make changes in programs and systems.
   Answer (A) is incorrect. Librarians maintain control over documentation, programs, and data files; they should have no access to equipment, but they can assist in data processing operations. Answer (C) is incorrect. A separate information officer outside of the accounting function would not be as critical a segregation of duties as that between programmers and processors Answer (D) is incorrect. Programmers usually handle all types of programs.

29. Which of the following should **not** be the responsibility of a database administrator?

    A. Design the content and organization of the database.

    B. Develop applications to access the database.

    C. Protect the database and its software.

    D. Monitor and improve the efficiency of the database.

Answer (B) is correct.
    REQUIRED: The choice not a responsibility of a database administrator.
    DISCUSSION: The database administrator (DBA) is the person who has overall responsibility for developing and maintaining the database. One primary responsibility is for designing the content of the database. Another responsibility of the DBA is to protect and control the database. A third responsibility is to monitor and improve the efficiency of the database. The responsibility of developing applications to access the database belongs to systems analysts and programmers.
    Answer (A) is incorrect. Designing the content and organization of the database is a responsibility of the database administrator. Answer (C) is incorrect. Protecting the database and its software is a responsibility of the database administrator. Answer (D) is incorrect. Monitoring and improving the efficiency of the database is a responsibility of the database administrator.

30. If a payroll system continues to pay employees who have been terminated, control weaknesses most likely exist because

    A. Procedures were not implemented to verify and control the receipt by the computer processing department of all transactions prior to processing.

    B. There were inadequate manual controls maintained outside the computer system.

    C. Programmed controls such as limit checks should have been built into the system.

    D. Input file label checking routines built into the programs were ignored by the operator.

Answer (B) is correct.
    REQUIRED: The reason control weaknesses most likely exist.
    DISCUSSION: The authorization to pay employees comes from outside the computer department. Thus, inadequate controls external to the computer processing department are most likely the cause of allowing the payments to terminated employees to continue without detection.
    Answer (A) is incorrect. Batch totals constitute adequate controls over properly authorized transactions but provide no control over unauthorized transactions. Answer (C) is incorrect. A limit check tests the reasonableness of a particular transaction but not whether it was authorized. Answer (D) is incorrect. Paying proper attention to input file labels (header labels) will not detect unauthorized transactions.

14.6 PRACTICE WRITTEN COMMUNICATION

| | Business Environment and Concepts
Testlet 4 of 4 | Time Remaining
1 hour - 15 minutes | Unsplit | Split Horiz | Split Vertical | Exit |

DIRECTIONS

Note: If you believe you have encountered a software malfunction, report it to the test center staff immediately.

Navigation

To navigate from task to task, use the controls at the bottom of the screen. Click on the **Next** button to advance to the next task, or the **Previous** button to go to the previous task. To go directly to any task, click on its number.

| ▼ = Reminder | | Directions | 1 2 3 4 5 6 7 | | Previous Next |

If you would like a reminder to revisit a task, or want to indicate that you are finished with it, click on the reminder flag below the task number. To clear the flag, click on it again. Reminder flags are for your use only – they do not contribute to your score.

Tabs

In this part of the examination, you will be asked to complete various tasks. Every task has one or more **Work Tabs**. Every task also has a **Help** tab.

| Written Communication | Help |
| Work tab | Help tab |

Work Tabs:

- **Work Tabs** are identified with a pencil icon. This is where your responses are expected.
- Each task has one or more **Work Tabs**.
- **Work Tabs** contain directions for completing the task - be sure to read these directions carefully.
- The **Work Tab** name in the example above is for illustration only - yours will differ.
- You must complete all of the **Work Tabs** in each task to receive full credit.

Help Tab:

- The **Help Tab** provides assistance with the exam software that is used in this task. For example, if the task is to compose a memorandum, **Help** will provide information about the word processor.

The Toolbar

The toolbar at the top of the screen shows the amount of time remaining for you to complete the tasks. In addition, the following tools are available. Note that only the **Exit** button is displayed when Directions are visible - the others will appear when you begin the tasks.

Click on these buttons to split or unsplit the screen. You can split the screen vertically or horizontally.

Click on this button to go on to the next part of the examination. You must complete all of the tasks to receive full credit. Once you click on **Exit** and confirm the action, you will NOT be able to return to this testlet.

| ▼ = Reminder | | Directions | 1 | | Previous Next |

You are a manager on the audit engagement for Wagner Corp., a manufacturer. This is your first year working on the engagement for this client. During the audit, you uncover suspicious paid invoices for material fixed assets. They are suspicious because the purchases were charged to an expense account instead of property, plant, and equipment. Accordingly, you communicate the possibility of fraud to the engagement partner.

Prepare a memorandum to the engagement partner discussing the possibility that the invoices are evidence of a misstatement arising from either fraudulent financial reporting, misappropriation of assets, or both. Recommend the next steps to be taken to determine what fraud, if any, may have been committed.

Type your communication below the line in the response area below.

REMINDER: Your response will be graded for both technical content and writing skills. Technical content will be evaluated for information that is helpful to the intended reader and clearly relevant to the issue. Writing skills will be evaluated for development, organization, and the appropriate expression of ideas in professional correspondence. Use a standard business memorandum or letter format with a clear beginning, middle, and end. Do not convey information in the form of a table, bullet point list, or other abbreviated presentation.

To: Engagement partner
Re: Fraud possibility -- Wagner Corp.

NOTE: Your Written Communications on the actual CPA exam may cover topics outside the scope of the BEC CSO (i.e., they may relate to topics from the AUD, FAR, and/or REG CSOs instead). Answer to the best of your ability, and remember that graders are mainly evaluating your writing ability and will overlook minor technical mistakes.

Unofficial Answer

Written Communication

To: Engagement partner
Re: Fraud possibility -- Wagner Corp.

Wagner Corp. has charged purchases of fixed assets to an expense account rather than to a fixed asset account. These entries may be evidence of either fraudulent financial reporting, misappropriation of assets, or both.

Fraudulent financial reporting involves intentional misstatements or omissions to deceive users of financial statements such as (1) altering accounting records or documents, (2) misrepresenting or omitting significant information, and (3) misapplying accounting principles. Recording an asset purchase as an expense is an example of misapplying an accounting principle.

Misappropriation of assets results from, for example, (1) theft of physical assets, (2) embezzlement (e.g., stealing collections of receivables), (3) an action that causes payment for items not received, or (4) using entity assets for personal reasons. Misappropriation is often most serious when management is involved. Managers are better able to conceal misappropriations effectively.

To determine whether fraud was committed, the audit team should test the existence assertion. The fixed assets should be located to determine that they were actually purchased by Wagner. Once the assets are identified, the audit trail should be followed to the paid invoices and the journal entries. In this way, the team will be able to determine who recorded the entries and whether a proper segregation of duties exists. The employee who authorized the purchase and payment should not also be making the related entries. If duties are not appropriately segregated, the risk of material misstatement due to fraud is increased. The employees will have an easy way of committing fraud in the books. In addition, the audit team should communicate with the company's management and those charged with governance about this discrepancy.

The above depicts a Level 5 answer. Consult your booklet, *How to Pass the CPA Exam: A System for Success*, for a description of the three writing skills criteria. You may also access this booklet online by visiting www.gleim.com/PassCPA.

Self-Grade

Below, grade your response on technical content and writing skills. Bubble in the circle next to the appropriate score that you may receive based on the criteria given. Your **total** score is the sum of your scores on all six items. The maximum score is 19 points.

Technical Content Evaluation

Was your response on topic?	o No [0]	o Mostly [1]	o Yes [2]
Did your response have any *significant* errors?	o 0 errors [1]	o 1 major error [−1]	o 2 or more major errors [−2]
Did your response contain any illegal advice?	o No [1]	o Yes [0]	

Writing Skills Evaluation

	Poor	Below Average	Average	Above Average	Outstanding
Organization	o 1	o 2	o 3	o 4	o 5
Development	o 1	o 2	o 3	o 4	o 5
Expression	o 1	o 2	o 3	o 4	o 5

Disclaimer: This scoring schedule was developed by Gleim Publications as a guideline only. The AICPA has not released specific information on how the Written Communications are graded.

Practice even more Written Communications with the Gleim Mega Test Bank.

Learn more: gleim.com/CPAmega | 800.874.5346

STUDY UNIT FIFTEEN
STRATEGIC PLANNING AND BUDGETING CONCEPTS

(18 pages of outline)

All organizations have a mission, that is, a reason for existing. Likewise, all organizations must have a plan for achieving that mission. Planning and managing progress toward the objectives stated in the resulting plans are the essence of strategic management.

Corporate objectives must be stated in concretely measurable terms. Thus, budgets are an essential part of any strategic plan. Budgeting has many purposes in the organization (one of which is motivating managers and employees), and a successful budgeting process requires careful planning. The appropriate budgeting method for an organization depends upon that organization's situation.

15.1 STRATEGIC MANAGEMENT

1. **Strategic Management**

   a. Strategic management sets overall objectives for an entity and guides the process of reaching those objectives. It is the responsibility of upper management.

      1) Strategic planning is the design and implementation of the specific steps and processes necessary to reach the overall objectives.

   b. Strategic management and strategic planning are thus closely linked. By their nature, strategic management and strategic planning have a long-term planning horizon.

2. **Steps in the Strategic Management Process**

   a. Strategic management is a five-stage process:

      1) The board of directors drafts the organization's mission statement.
      2) The organization performs a situational analysis, also called a SWOT analysis.
      3) Based on the results of the situational analysis, upper management develops a group of strategies describing how the mission will be achieved.
      4) Strategic plans are implemented through the execution of component plans at each level of the entity.
      5) Strategic controls and feedback are used to monitor progress, isolate problems, and take corrective action. Over the long term, feedback is the basis for adjusting the original mission and objectives.

Strategic Management

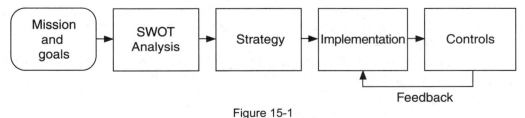

Figure 15-1

b.   The **mission statement** summarizes the entity's reason for existing. It provides the framework for formulation of the company's strategies.

   1)   Missions tend to be most effective when they consist of a single sentence.

      a)   For example, the mission of Starbucks Coffee Company is "to inspire and nurture the human spirit – one person, one cup and one neighborhood at a time."

   2)   Missions tend to be stated in general terms. Setting specific objectives in the mission statement can limit an entity's ability to respond to a changing marketplace.

c.   The **situational analysis** is most often called a SWOT analysis because it identifies the entity's strengths, weaknesses, opportunities, and threats.

   1)   **Strengths and weaknesses** are usually identified by considering the entity's capabilities and resources (its internal environment).

      a)   What the entity does particularly well or has in greater abundance are its core competencies. But many entities may have the same core competencies (cutting-edge IT, efficient distribution, etc.).

      b)   An entity gains a competitive advantage in the marketplace by developing one or more distinctive competencies, i.e., competencies that are unlike those of its competitors.

   2)   **Opportunities and threats** exist in the entity's external environment. They are identified by considering

      a)   Macroenvironment factors (economic, demographic, political, legal, social, cultural, and technical) and

      b)   Microenvironment factors (suppliers, customers, distributors, competitors, and other competitive factors in the industry).

d.   Based on the results of the situational analysis, upper management develops a **group of strategies** describing how the mission will be achieved. The strategies answer such questions as

   1)   "Which lines of business will we be in?"

   2)   "How do we penetrate and compete in the international marketplace?"

   3)   "How will this line of business reach its objectives that contribute to achievement of the overall entity's mission?"

   4)   "How do we perform each strategic business unit's basic processes (materials handling, assembly, shipping, human resources, customer relations, etc.) as efficiently as possible?"

e.   **Implementing** the chosen strategies involves every employee at every level of the entity. Incentive systems and employee performance evaluations must be designed so that they encourage employees to focus their efforts on achieving the entity's objectives.

   1)   This approach requires communication among (a) senior managers, who devise strategies; (b) middle managers, who supervise and evaluate employees; (c) and human resources managers, who must approve evaluation and compensation plans.

f.   As plans are executed at each organizational level, **strategic controls and feedback** allow management to determine the degree of progress toward the stated objectives.

   1)   For controls to be effective, standards against which performance can be measured must be established. Then, the results of actual performance must be measured against the standards and reported to the appropriate managers. If performance is unsatisfactory, managers take corrective action.

2) Results are sent to higher-level management for continual refinement of the strategies.

3. **Porter's Five Competitive Forces**

a. Business theorist Michael E. Porter has developed a model of the structure of industries and competition. It includes an analysis of the five competitive forces that determine long-term profitability as measured by long-term return on investment.

1) This analysis includes an evaluation of the basic economic and technical characteristics that determine the strength of each force and the attractiveness of the industry. The competitive forces are depicted in the following diagram and discussed in detail below and on the following pages:

Porter's Five Competitive Forces

Figure 15-2

b. **Rivalry among existing firms** will be intense when an industry contains many strong competitors. Price-cutting, large advertising budgets, and frequent introduction of new products are typical. The intensity of rivalry and the threat of entry vary with the following factors:

1) The stage of the industry life cycle, e.g., rapid growth, growth, maturity, decline, or rapid decline

a) Thus, growth is preferable to decline. In a declining or even a stable industry, a firm's growth must come from winning other firms' customers, thereby strengthening competition.

2) The distinctions among products (product differentiation) and the costs of switching from one competitor's product to another

a) Less differentiation tends to heighten competition based on price, with price cutting leading to lower profits. But high costs of switching suppliers weaken competition.

    3)   Whether fixed costs are high in relation to variable costs

        a)   High fixed costs indicate that rivalry will be intense. The greater the cost to generate a given amount of sales revenues, the greater the investment intensity and the need to operate at or near capacity. Hence, price cutting to sustain demand is typical.

    4)   Capacity expansion

        a)   If the size of the expansion must be large to achieve economies of scale, competition will be more intense. The need for large-scale expansion to achieve production efficiency may result in an excess of industry capacity over demand.

c.   The prospects of long-term profitability depend on the industry's **barriers to entry**.

    1)   Factors that increase the threat of entry are the following:

        a)   Economies of scale (and learning curve effects) are not significant.

        b)   Brand identity of existing products is weak.

        c)   Costs of switching suppliers are low.

        d)   Existing firms do not have the cost advantages of vertical integration.

        e)   Product differences are few.

        f)   Access to existing suppliers is not blocked, and distribution channels are willing to accept new products.

        g)   Capital requirements are low.

        h)   Exit barriers are low.

        i)   The government's policy is to encourage new entrants.

    2)   The most favorable industry condition is one in which entry barriers are high and exit barriers are low.

        a)   When the threat of new entrants is minimal and exit is not difficult, returns are high, and risk is reduced in the event of poor performance.

        b)   Low entry barriers keep long-term profitability low because new firms can enter the industry, increasing competition and lowering prices and the market shares of existing firms.

d.   The **threat of substitutes** limits price increases and profit margins. The greater the threat, the less attractive the industry is to potential entrants.

    1)   Substitutes are types (not brands) of goods and services that have the same purposes, for example, plastic and metal or minivans and SUVs. Thus, a change in the price of one such product (service) causes a change in the demand for its substitutes.

    2)   Structural considerations affecting the threat of substitutes are

        a)   Relative prices,
        b)   Costs of switching to a substitute, and
        c)   Customers' inclination to use a substitute.

e.   As the **threat of buyers' bargaining power** increases, the appeal of an industry to potential entrants decreases. Buyers seek lower prices, better quality, and more services. Moreover, they use their purchasing power to obtain better terms, possibly through a bidding process. Thus, buyers affect competition.

    1)   Buyers' bargaining power varies with the following factors:

        a)   When purchasing power is concentrated in a few buyers or when buyers are well organized, their bargaining power is greater. This effect is reinforced when sellers are in a capital-intensive industry.

        b)   High (low) switching costs decrease (increase) buyers' bargaining power.

c) The threat of backward (upstream) vertical integration, that is, the acquisition of a supply capacity, increases buyers' bargaining power.

d) Buyers are most likely to bargain aggressively when their profit margins are low and a supplier's product accounts for a substantial amount of their costs.

e) Buyers are in a stronger position when the supplier's product is undifferentiated.

f) The more important the supplier's product is to buyers, the less bargaining power they have.

f. As the **threat of suppliers' bargaining power** increases, the appeal of an industry to potential entrants decreases. Accordingly, suppliers affect competition through pricing and the manipulation of the quantity supplied.

1) Suppliers' bargaining power is greater when

a) Switching costs are substantial.

b) Prices of substitutes are high.

c) They can threaten forward (downstream) vertical integration.

d) They provide something that is a significant input to the value added by the buyer.

e) Their industry is concentrated, or they are organized.

2) Buyers' best responses are to develop favorable, mutually beneficial relationships with suppliers or to diversify their sources of supply.

4. **Generic Competitive Strategies Model**

a. Strategies with a Broad Competitive Scope

1) **Cost leadership** is the generic strategy of entities that seek competitive advantage through lower costs and that have a broad competitive scope.

2) **Differentiation** is the generic strategy of entities that seek competitive advantage through providing a unique product and that have a broad competitive scope.

b. Strategies with a Narrow Competitive Scope

1) **Cost focus** is the generic strategy of entities that seek competitive advantage through lower costs and that have a narrow competitive scope (a regional or smaller market).

2) **Focused differentiation** is the generic strategy of entities that seek competitive advantage through providing a unique product and that have a narrow competitive scope (a regional or smaller market).

Competitive Advantage

Competitive Scope	Low Cost	Product Uniqueness
Broad (Industry wide)	Cost Leadership Strategy	Differentiation Strategy
Narrow (Market segment)	Focused Strategy: Cost	Focused Strategy: Differentiation

Figure 15-3

5.   **Five Operations Strategies**

a.   A **cost strategy** is successful when the entity is the low-cost producer. However, the product (e.g., a commodity) tends to be undifferentiated in these cases, the market is often very large, and the competition tends to be intense because of the possibility of high-volume sales.

b.   A **quality strategy** involves competition based on product quality or process quality. Product quality relates to design, for example, the difference between a luxury car and a subcompact. Process quality concerns the degree of freedom from defects.

c.   A **delivery strategy** may permit an entity to charge a higher price when the product is consistently delivered rapidly and on time. An example is UPS.

d.   A **flexibility strategy** involves offering many different products. This strategy also may reflect an ability to shift rapidly from one product line to another. An example is a publisher that can write, edit, print, and distribute a book within days to exploit the public's short-term interest in a sensational event.

e.   A **service strategy** seeks to gain a competitive advantage and maximize customer value by providing services, especially post-purchase services such as warranties on automobiles and home appliances.

6.   **Strategies for Product Life Cycle Stages**

a.   The strategy in the **precommercialization** (product development) stage is to innovate by conducting R&D, marketing research, and production tests. During product development, the entity has no sales, but it has high investment costs.

b.   The **introduction stage** is characterized by slow sales growth and lack of profits because of the high expenses of promotion and selective distribution to generate awareness of the product and encourage customers to try it. Thus, the per-customer cost is high.

   1)   Competitors are few, basic versions of the product are produced, and higher-income customers (innovators) are usually targeted. Cost-plus prices are charged. Prices may be set either high so that development costs can be recovered quickly or low to encourage widespread adoption.

   2)   The strategy is to (a) infiltrate the market, (b) plan for financing to cope with losses, (c) build supplier relations, (d) increase production and marketing efforts, and (e) plan for competition.

c.   In the **growth stage**, (1) sales and profits increase rapidly, (2) cost per customer decreases, (3) customers are early adopters, (4) new competitors enter an expanding market, (5) new product models and features are introduced, and (6) promotion spending declines or remains stable.

   1)   The entity enters new market segments and distribution channels and attempts to build brand loyalty and achieve the maximum share of the market. Thus, (a) prices are set to penetrate the market, (b) distribution channels are extended, and (c) the mass market is targeted through advertising.

   2)   The strategy is to advance by these means and by achieving economies of productive scale.

d.   In the **maturity stage**, (1) sales peak but growth declines, (2) competitors are most numerous but may begin to decline in number, and (3) per-customer cost is low.

   1)   Profits are high for large market-share entities. For others, profits may fall because of competitive price-cutting and increased R&D spending to develop improved versions of the product.

   2)   The strategy is to defend market share and maximize profits through (a) diversification of brands and models to enter new market segments; (b) still more intensive distribution, cost cutting, advertising and promotions to encourage brand switching; and (c) emphasizing customer service.

e. During the **decline stage**, sales and profits drop as prices are cut, and some entities leave the market. Customers include late adopters (laggards), and per-customer cost is low.

   1) Weak products and unprofitable distribution media are eliminated, and advertising budgets are pared to the level needed to retain the most loyal customers. The strategy is to withdraw by reducing production, promotion, and inventory.

f. **Graphical Depiction**

Product Life Cycle

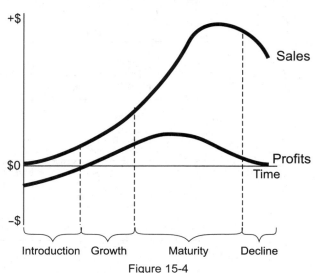

Figure 15-4

7. **Value-Chain Analysis**

   a. A **value-added cost** is the cost of an activity that increases the value of a product or service to the customer. Any reduction in value-added costs decreases (1) the utility of the product and (2) the amount customers are willing to pay. Examples of value-added costs are

      1) Standard costs of direct materials and direct labor necessary to produce the product and
      2) Product-specific features desired by customers.

   b. A **nonvalue-added cost** is the cost of an activity that does not increase the value of a product or service to the customer. The reduction of these costs does not affect the customer's valuation of the product. Examples of nonvalue-added costs are

      1) Costs of moving, handling, and storage of inventory and
      2) Rework of defective products.

   c. Some costs may relate to activities that include both value-added and nonvalue-added aspects. Examples of such costs are

      1) Costs of indirect labor and indirect materials that cannot be traced to any individual product and
      2) Testing and inspection costs.

   d. The **value chain** depicts the way in which every function in an entity adds value to the final product. Costs and customer value accumulate along a chain of activities that lead to an end product or service.

      1) A value chain consists of the following internal processes and activities: (a) R&D, (b) design, (c) production, (d) marketing, (e) distribution, and (f) customer service.

2)   Another definition is that the value chain consists of all value-creating activities leading to the ultimate end-use product delivered into the final consumers' hands.

a)   Thus, a value chain is an overall chain of value-creating (value-added) processes.

3)   Primary activities apply directly to the product. Support activities assist the primary activities. The value chain can be graphically depicted as follows:

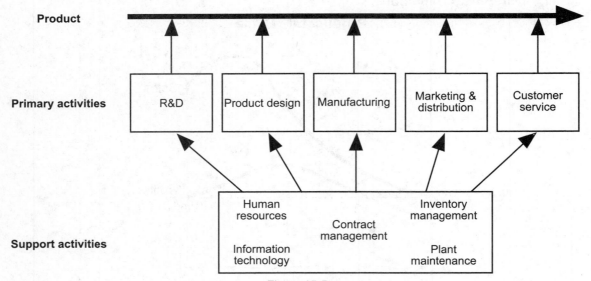

Figure 15-5

e.   **Value-chain analysis** is a strategic tool that allows an entity to emphasize activities that are consistent with its overall strategy.

1)   Value-chain analysis determines the parts of the value chain in which the entity can increase its competitive advantage by adding customer value or by reducing costs.

2)   Because the value chain identifies and connects strategic activities, the analysis improves knowledge of relations with customers, suppliers, and competitors. It also facilitates the strategic determination of the phase(s) of the industry's value chain in which the entity should operate.

a)   The first step is to identify value-creating activities.

b)   The second step is to determine how each value-creating activity can produce a competitive advantage. The entity should identify

i)   Its competitive advantages (e.g., cost reduction or product differentiation) so that its position in the industry's value chain can be clarified.

ii)   The ways in which value-creating activities can generate additional customer value.

iii)   Activities with costs that can be reduced.

iv)   Activities that provide noncore competencies that can be outsourced.

v)   Value-adding ways in which other activities can be linked.

3)   Value-chain analysis is a team effort that integrates strategic planning and management accounting.

a)   Management accountants collaborate with engineering, production, marketing, distribution, and customer service professionals to address the strengths, weaknesses, opportunities, and threats identified.

8. **Customer Value and Satisfaction as Strategic Issues**

   a. A market analysis must identify potential customers and determine their needs. A marketer responds to customer needs by stating a **value proposition**, that is, the benefits offered to satisfy those needs. The value proposition is an attempt to affect customer wants (needs focused on particular satisfiers). It becomes tangible in an offering, which may consist of products, services, and other things that are intended to satisfy the needs of target buyers.

      1) Value is a combination of the elements of the **customer value triad**: quality, service, and price. Value increases as quality and service increase and price decreases.

   b. **Customer satisfaction** is the relation between the offering's perceived performance and the customer's expectations. High customer satisfaction tends to create high customer loyalty that results in repurchases. However, at lower satisfaction levels, customers are more likely to switch when a superior alternative becomes available.

      1) Expectations are a function of a customer's experience, marketing information, and other factors. Marketers should not raise expectations above the level at which they can be satisfied. However, some superior entities have had great success by adopting a total customer satisfaction approach, that is, by elevating expectations and then satisfying them.

      2) **High customer loyalty** is an emotional as well as rational bond that develops when an entity provides high customer value. To obtain such loyalty, the entity needs to develop a value proposition that has superior competitiveness in the target market segment. Crucially, it must be supported by an effective value delivery system, the accumulation of all the experiences the customer has with the offering. Thus, brand value must be supported by core business processes that actually deliver the promised customer value.

      3) Customer satisfaction information is gathered by

         a) Complaint and suggestion systems, such as websites and hotlines

         b) Customer surveys

         c) Lost customer analysis (e.g., exit interviews and determination of the customer loss rate)

         d) Testing of the treatment customers receive when purchasing the entity's (or competitors') products (ghost shopping)

      4) Customer satisfaction must be balanced against the satisfaction level of the entity's other stakeholders (e.g., shareholders, employees, suppliers, and retailers). Thus, raising customer satisfaction at the expense of profit or other stakeholders' interests may not be appropriate.

   c. To sustain customer value, the entity must seek continuous improvement of value-creating activities. **Benchmarking** the best attributes of top performers and adopting their best practices is a key method of continuous improvement.

   d. Effective coordination of the following core business processes is crucial:

      1) Market sensing consists of obtaining, distributing, and acting upon market intelligence.

      2) New offering realization should be timely and efficient. It involves R&D and the launch of products, services, and other elements of offerings.

      3) Customer acquisition defines target markets and researches customers.

      4) Customer relationship management seeks to increase the value of the customer base by developing long-term relationships with individual customers by such methods as customer service, customized (if not personalized) offerings, and choice of marketing messages and media.

      5) Fulfillment management relates to order processing, on-time delivery, and collection.

    e.   The value-delivery network is another source of competitive advantage. Partner relationship management involves coordinating with suppliers and distributors in this network (the supply chain) to provide better customer value.

9.   **Customer Relationship Management (CRM)**

    a.   Customer relationship management can be defined as "the process of managing detailed information about individual customers and carefully managing all the customer 'touchpoints' with the aim of maximizing customer loyalty." Its purpose is to create optimal customer equity. CRM is an attempt to tie together three traditionally separate functions: marketing, sales, and service. It employs large databases and integrated information systems to link the three customer relationship functions.

        1)   Marketing seeks unfulfilled customer needs and customer groups who might be interested in the entity's existing products.

        2)   Sales brings the products to the attention of the targeted customers and closes the sale.

        3)   Customer service provides after-the-sale support, such as product help and account information.

    b.   **Customer retention** through customer satisfaction is a key to profitability. Thus, the entity should seek to minimize customer churn (customer loss).

        1)   High customer satisfaction means a longer relationship with the entity, repeat purchases of new offerings and upgrades, favorable word-of-mouth, and less concern about price and competitors' offerings.

            a)   Moreover, the highly satisfied repeat customer is less costly than a new customer and is more likely to provide helpful feedback.

        2)   The listening process plays a major role in customer retention. Accordingly, the entity should (a) measure customer satisfaction frequently, (b) facilitate complaints and suggestions, and (c) act rapidly on the results.

        3)   The entity should emphasize customer retention because the customer base is an important intangible asset.

            a)   Loss of some customers is unavoidable. For example, a customer may cease operations.

            b)   Customer retention is far less costly than customer attraction.

            c)   Increasing the retention rate increases profits exponentially.

            d)   The longer the customer relationship, the more profitable it is.

    c.   An entity should estimate **customer lifetime value**, the net present value of the cash flows (purchases – costs of acquiring, selling to, and serving the customer) related to a particular customer.

    d.   An entity may be able to regain lost customers more cheaply than it could attract new ones using existing information and the results of surveys and exit interviews. An entity must determine the appropriate investment in building customer relationships.

    e.   Customer profitability analysis determines all revenues and all costs assignable to specific customers. The following classification of customers is possible:

        1)   Platinum – most profitable (highest investment)

        2)   Gold – profitable (high investment, with objective of converting to platinum)

        3)   Iron – low profit but desirable (lower investment with objective of converting to gold)

        4)   Lead – not profitable or desirable (drop or provide low investment while raising prices or lowering costs of serving)

10.　**General Pricing Approaches**

a.　**Cost-Based Pricing**

1)　This process begins with a cost determination followed by setting a price that will recover the value chain costs and provide the desired return on investment.

2)　When an industry is characterized by significant product differentiation, e.g., the automobile industry, cost-based and market-based pricing approaches are combined.

a)　Basing prices on cost assumes that costs can be correctly determined. Thus, cost-behavior patterns, cost traceability, and cost drivers become important determinants of profitability.

3)　A cost-plus price equals the cost plus a markup. Cost may be defined in many ways. Most companies use either absorption manufacturing cost or total cost when calculating the price. Variable costs may be used as the basis for cost, but then fixed costs must be covered by the markup.

b.　**Market-Based Pricing**

1)　This approach involves basing prices on the product's perceived value and competitors' actions rather than on the seller's cost. Nonprice variables in the marketing mix augment the perceived value. Market comparables, which are assets with similar characteristics, are used to estimate the price of a product.

a)　For example, a cup of coffee may have a higher price at an expensive restaurant than at a fast-food outlet.

2)　Market-based pricing is typical when many competitors exist, and the product is undifferentiated, as in many commodities markets, e.g., agricultural products or natural gas.

c.　**Competition-Based Pricing**

1)　Going-rate pricing bases price largely on competitors' prices.

2)　Sealed-bid pricing bases price on the perception of competitors' prices.

d.　**New Product Pricing**

1)　Price skimming sets an introductory price relatively high to (a) attract buyers who are not concerned about price and (b) recover research and development costs.

2)　Penetration pricing sets an introductory price relatively low to gain deep market penetration quickly.

e.　**Pricing by Intermediaries**

1)　Using markups tied closely to the price paid for a product

2)　Using markdowns -- a reduction in the original price set on a product

f.　**Price Adjustments**

1)　Geographical Pricing

a)　FOB-origin pricing charges each customer its actual freight costs.

b)　A seller that uses uniform delivered pricing charges the same price, inclusive of shipping, to all customers regardless of their location.

i)　This policy is easy to administer, permits the company to advertise one price nationwide, and facilitates marketing to faraway customers.

c)　Zone pricing sets differential freight charges for customers on the basis of their location. Customers are not charged actual average freight costs.

2)   Discounts and Allowances

a)   Cash discounts encourage prompt payment, improve cash flows, and avoid bad debts.

b)   Quantity discounts encourage large volume purchases.

c)   Trade (functional) discounts are offered to other members of the marketing channel for performing certain services, such as selling.

d)   Seasonal discounts are offered for sales out of season. They help smooth production.

e)   Allowances (e.g., trade-in and promotional allowances) reduce list prices.

3)   Discriminatory pricing adjusts for differences among customers, the forms of a product, or locations.

4)   Promotional pricing temporarily reduces prices below list or even cost to stimulate sales.

5)   Value pricing involves redesigning products to improve quality without raising prices or offering the same quality at lower prices.

6)   International pricing adjusts prices to local conditions.

g.   **Illegal Pricing**

1)   Certain pricing tactics are illegal. For example, pricing products below cost to harm competitors (predatory pricing) is illegal.

a)   The U.S. Supreme Court has held that a price is predatory if (1) it is below an appropriate measure of costs, and (2) the seller has a reasonable prospect of recovering its losses in the future through higher prices or greater market share.

2)   Price discrimination among customers also is illegal. Pricing is illegal if it has the effect of lessening competition.

3)   Another improper form of pricing is collusive pricing. Conspiracies to restrict output and set artificially high prices violate antitrust laws.

4)   Still another inappropriate pricing tactic is selling below cost in other countries (dumping), which may trigger retaliatory tariffs and other sanctions.

h.   **Target pricing** is the expected market price for a product or service, given knowledge of consumers' perceptions of value and competitors' responses.

Stop and review! You have completed the outline for this subunit. Study multiple-choice questions 1 through 9 beginning on page 401.

15.2 STRATEGIC PLANNING

1.   **Planning**

a.   Planning is the determination of what is to be done and of how, when, where, and by whom it is to be done. Plans direct the activities that all organizational members must perform successfully for the organization to accomplish its objectives.

1)   However, no transactions occur during the planning cycle that must be recorded in the general ledger.

b.   Planning must be completed before undertaking any other managerial function.

1)   Forecasting is the basis of planning because it projects the future.

c.   Planning establishes the means to reach organizational ends (objectives).

1)   This means-end relationship extends throughout the organization so that the various means emphasize the same ends.

2)   One organizational level's ends are the next higher level's means.

EXAMPLE

Management by objectives (MBO) identifies relationships between an individual's job objectives (ends) and the immediate superior's objectives (ends). Thus, the subordinate can understand how his or her job is the means by which the superior's job is accomplished. This will be discussed in more detail later in this subunit.

---

2. **The Planning Process**

   a.   Long-range (strategic) planning includes **strategic budgeting**. It has a horizon of 1 to 10 years or more. Such planning is difficult because of uncertainty about future events and conditions.

   1)   Thus, strategic plans tend to be general and exclude operational detail.

   2)   The strategic plan must be completed before specific budgeting can begin. The strategic plan states the means by which an entity expects to achieve its stated mission.

   b.   Strategic planning reflects the intentions of senior management. It is based on a strategic analysis that includes the following:

   1)   Identifying and specifying organizational objectives

   2)   Evaluating the strengths (competitive advantages) and weaknesses of the organization and its competitors

   3)   Assessing risks

   4)   Identifying and forecasting the effects of external (environmental) factors relevant to the organization.

   a)   For example, (1) market trends, (2) changes in technology, (3) international competition, and (4) social change may provide opportunities, impose limitations, or represent threats.

   b)   Forecasting is the basis of planning because it projects the future. Many quantitative methods are used in forecasting.

   5)   Deriving the best strategy for reaching the objectives, given the organization's strengths and weaknesses and the relevant future trends

   6)   Capital budgeting, a planning process for choosing and financing long-term projects and programs

   7)   Capacity planning, an element of planning closely related to capital budgeting that includes, among other things, consideration of business combinations or divestitures

   c.   Strategic plans are translated into measurable and achievable intermediate and operational plans. Thus, intermediate and operational plans must be consistent with, and contribute to achieving, strategic objectives.

3. **Premises**

   a.   Assumptions must be made because perfect information is impossible to acquire.

   1)   Premises are the underlying assumptions about the expected environment in which the strategic plan will be implemented.

   a)   Premises should be limited to those crucial to the success of the plans.

   b.   Managers should determine the internal and external factors that could influence the actions of the organization. Moreover, premises must be considered at all levels of the organization.

   1)   Thus, capital budgeting plans should be premised on assumptions (forecasts) about economic cycles, price movements, etc.

   a)   For example, a supply department's plans might be premised on stability of parts prices or on forecasts that prices will rise.

EXAMPLES

- The economy will be in recession next year.
- Our closest competitor's new model will provide greater competition for potential sales.
- Union negotiations will result in a general wage increase.
- Over the next 5 years, the cost of materials will increase by 30%.
- The elasticity of demand for our products is 1.2.

---

4. **Organizational Objectives**

   a. Organizations may have contradictory objectives.

      1) The objectives of maximizing profit and growth could be mutually exclusive. Maximizing short-term profit might preclude future growth.

      2) Conflict among an organization's objectives is common.

   b. Objectives vary with the organization's type and stage of development.

5. **Management Objectives**

   a. The primary task of management is to direct operations effectively and efficiently.

      1) **Effectiveness** is the degree to which an objective is accomplished. **Efficiency** is maximizing the output for a given quantity of input.

         a) Trade-offs are frequently made between efficiency and effectiveness.

   b. Objectives should be clearly and specifically stated, communicated to all relevant parties, and accepted by those affected.

6. **Means-End Hierarchy**

   a. Objectives should be established at the top and retranslated in more specific terms as they are communicated downward in the means-end hierarchy.

EXAMPLE

- An entity has a socioeconomic purpose, such as providing food.
- The entity's mission is the accomplishment of its socioeconomic purpose through the production of breakfast cereal.
- The entity develops long-range or strategic objectives with regard to profitability, growth, or survival.
- A more specific overall objective might be to provide investors with an adequate return on their investment.
- Divisional objectives can be developed, e.g., to increase the sales of a certain kind of cereal.
- Departmental objectives are developed, e.g., to reduce waste in the packaging department.
- Low-level managers and supervisors then develop personal performance and development objectives.

---

7. **Policies, Procedures, and Rules**

   a. After premises and objectives are formulated, the next step in the planning process is the development of policies, procedures, and rules. These elements are necessary at all levels of the organization and overlap both in definition and in practice.

      1) Intermediate and operational plans are translated into policies, procedures, and rules, which are standing plans for repetitive situations.

   b. Policies and procedures provide **feedforward control** because they anticipate and prevent problems and provide guidance on how an activity should be performed to best ensure that an objective is achieved.

      1) **Policies** are general statements that guide thinking and action in decision making. Policies may be explicitly published by, or implied by the actions of, management.

         a) A strong organizational culture means that its key values are intensely held and widely shared.

2) **Procedures** are specific directives that define how work is to be done.

3) **Rules** are specific, detailed guides that restrict behavior.

8. **Management by Objectives (MBO)**

    a. MBO is a comprehensive, behavioral, communications-oriented, responsibility approach to management and employee self-direction. It is therefore relevant to planning and control.

    b. MBO is based on the philosophy that employees

        1) Want to work hard if they know what is expected.

        2) Like to understand what their jobs actually involve.

        3) Are capable of self-direction and self-motivation.

    c. MBO requires

        1) Senior management participation and commitment to the program. These managers must

            a) Determine the overall direction and objectives of the organization.

            b) Communicate these effectively in operational or measurable terms.

            c) Coordinate subordinates' objectives with overall objectives.

            d) Follow up at the end of the MBO cycle period to reward performance and review problems.

        2) Integration of objectives for all subunits into a compatible, balanced system directed toward accomplishment of the overall objectives.

        3) Provisions for regular periodic reporting of performance toward attainment of the objectives.

        4) Free and honest communication between supervisor and subordinate.

        5) A commitment to taking the ideas of subordinates seriously on the part of supervisors.

        6) An organizational climate that encourages mutual trust and respect.

    d. Steps necessary to implement an MBO program include establishing objectives and action plans (the planning steps) and periodic review and final appraisal (the control steps).

Stop and review! You have completed the outline for this subunit. Study multiple-choice questions 10 through 16 beginning on page 403.

15.3 ELEMENTS OF BUDGETING

1. **Four Uses**

    a. The budget is used for **planning**.

        1) A budget is a written plan for the future. Preparing a budget compels management to evaluate the assumptions used and the objectives identified in the budgetary process.

        2) Organizations that prepare budgets anticipate problems before they occur.

EXAMPLE

A shortage of a material may cause a work stoppage that results in the incurrence of high freight costs for an emergency shipment. An organization with a budgetary process may have anticipated the shortage and planned for it.

b.   The budget is used for **control**.

1)   A budget helps an entity control costs by setting cost standards.

2)   Efficient or inefficient use of resources can be determined by analysis of variances from the standards.

3)   Budgets also can identify highly effective managers. Consequently, employees should not fear budgets.

a)   Managers may use a budget as a self-evaluation tool.

4)   For the budgetary process to be an effective control, it must be integrated with the accounting system and the organizational structure. Integration enhances control by transmitting data and assigning variances to the proper organizational subunits.

c.   The budget is used for **motivation**.

1)   A budget must be perceived as realistic by employees before it can become a good motivator.

2)   Some managers regard a budget as a restriction.

3)   Employees are more likely to accept a budget if some flexibility is allowed.

d.   The budget is a means of **communication and coordination**.

1)   A budget communicates the objectives of the organization.

2)   A budget is an aid to efficient resource allocation.

3)   A budget promotes consistency of subunit objectives with those of other subunits and of the organization.

4)   Senior management must be involved in the budgetary process. This involvement does not extend to formulating the numbers in the budget. Senior management lacks a detailed knowledge of daily operations.

EXAMPLE

The sales department may want a large inventory so that sales are not lost because of a shortage. But the CFO may want a small inventory to conserve cash. If the budget specifies the amount of inventory, all employees can work toward the same objectives.

---

2.   **Quantification of Plans**

a.   Businesses have objectives for market share, profitability, growth, dividend payout, etc. Not-for-profit organizations also have objectives, such as those for fundraising and service efforts.

1)   These objectives cannot be achieved without planning for the allocation of resources and the expected results.

b.   A budget quantifies expectations about the consumption of resources and the resulting outcomes.

c.   A budget requires a significant commitment of internal resources. The most important factor in ensuring its success is for senior managers to demonstrate their commitment.

3.   **Role in Planning and Evaluation**

a.   Planning is the process by which an organization sets specific objectives for itself.

b.   To evaluate progress toward achievement of objectives, quantification is necessary.

1)   The budget is therefore a strategic control.

4.   **Effects of External Factors**

a.   Decisions about an organization's strategy and its budget are dependent on general economic conditions, their expected trends, and the availability of financial resources.

EXAMPLE

If the economy is entering a period of lower demand, a manufacturer will not project increased sales. If costs are not changeable, losses may be budgeted for the short-term to retain market share.

---

  b. The state of the industry includes the organization's current market share, governmental regulatory measures, the labor market, and the activities of competitors.

EXAMPLE

If input costs are rising in the industry, the budget must reflect that reality. Profit margins and cash flows will not be the same as in prior years. Also, an organization in or near bankruptcy faces a financial situation different from that of the market leader.

---

5. **Short-Term Objectives**

    a. The budget states the specific revenue targets and expense limitations for each functional area and department of the organization on a month-by-month basis.

        1) Incremental objectives must be achieved each month or week, especially in seasonal businesses, such as agricultural supply.

6. **Characteristics of Successful Budgeting**

    a. **Sufficient lead time.** For a budget to be useful, it must be complete when the fiscal year begins.

        1) The preparation of an organizational budget usually takes several months. Given a calendar year end, the budget process may start in September.

        2) The **budget planning calendar** is the schedule of activities for the development and adoption of the budget. It includes a list of dates indicating when specific information is to be provided to others by each information source.

            a) Because departmental budgets are based on forecasts prepared by others and the budgets of other departments, a planning calendar is essential to integrate the process.

        3) The budget department is responsible for compiling the budget and managing the process. However, the budget director and department are not responsible for developing the estimates on which the budget is based.

    b. **Budget manual.** Everyone involved in preparing the budget must be educated on the detailed procedures for preparing and submitting their sections of the overall budget.

        1) Because budgets have many components, they must be prepared in a standard format.

        2) Distribution instructions are vital because the components of the organizational budget are interrelated and must be coordinated.

            a) One department's budget may be dependent on another's, and a budget for a function must be aggregated from its constituent departmental budgets.

    c. **Buy-in at all levels.**

        1) Participative budgeting increases the chance of acceptance by those affected and the acheivement of objectives.

        2) The most important factor in ensuring the success of a budget process is for senior managers to demonstrate that they consider it vital to the organization's future.

7. **Revisions of the Budget**

    a. Assumptions underlying may change during the year. A policy must be established to guide revisions to the budget resulting from these changes.

        1) Accommodation of change is a characteristic of successful budgeting. Without such a policy, morale may suffer if managers believe they will be evaluated using an unachievable standard.

    b. Reported results and variances are a basis for corrective action. The following are the steps in a control loop:

        1) Establishing standards of performance (the budget)
        2) Measuring actual performance
        3) Analyzing and comparing performance with standards
        4) Devising and implementing corrective actions
        5) Reviewing and revising the standards

Stop and review! You have completed the outline for this subunit. Study multiple-choice questions 17 through 23 beginning on page 405.

15.4 BUDGETING AND MOTIVATION

1. **Measuring Performance**

    a. A budget provides standards for assessing individual managers and functions.
    b. Revenues, expenses, and other measures can be compared with the budget to determine whether organizational performance is meeting expectations.

2. **Authoritative vs. Participative Budgeting**

    a. Authoritative budgeting is a top-down approach to budgeting.
    b. Participative budgeting uses input from middle- and lower-level employees. It also is called grass-roots or bottom-up budgeting.

	Advantages	**Disadvantages**
Authoritative	• Ensures consistency across all functions • Is less complex and time-consuming than coordinating input from the middle and lower levels	• Less likely to promote commitment
Participative	• Encourages employees to have a sense of ownership of the output of the process, resulting in acceptance of, and commitment to, objectives expressed in the budget • Enables employees to relate performance to rewards or penalties • Provides a broader information base (middle- and lower-level managers often are far better informed about operational realities than senior managers)	• Higher costs in time and money • Quality of participation is affected by the objectives, values, beliefs, and expectations of those involved • Creation of budgetary slack

    c. Budgetary slack (overestimation of expenses or underestimation of revenues) must be avoided if a budget is to have its desired effects. The natural tendency of a manager is to negotiate for a less stringent measure of performance so as to avoid unfavorable variances from expectations. A manager who expects his or her request to be reduced may inflate the amount. If a budget is to be used as a performance evaluator, a manager asked for an estimate may provide one that is easily attained.

Stop and review! You have completed the outline for this subunit. Study multiple-choice questions 24 through 30 beginning on page 407.

QUESTIONS

15.1 Strategic Management

1. A firm's statement of broad objectives or mission statement should accomplish all of the following **except**

    A. Outlining strategies for technological development, market expansion, and product differentiation.

    B. Defining the purpose of the company.

    C. Providing an overall guide to those in high-level, decision-making positions.

    D. Stating the moral and ethical principles that guide the actions of the firm.

Answer (A) is correct.
    REQUIRED: The purpose not achieved by a mission statement.
    DISCUSSION: The determination of organizational objectives is the first step in the planning process. A mission statement is a formal, written document that defines the organization's purpose in society, for example, to produce and distribute certain goods of high quality in a manner beneficial to the public, employees, shareholders, and other constituencies. Thus, a mission statement does not announce specific operating plans. It does not describe strategies for technological development, market expansion, or product differentiation because these are tasks for operating management.
    Answer (B) is incorrect. A mission statement defines the purpose of the company (some writers differentiate between purpose and mission). Answer (C) is incorrect. Broad objectives provide guidance to those in high-level positions who are responsible for long-range planning. Answer (D) is incorrect. Mission statements increasingly are concerned with ethical principles.

2. Intensity of rivalry among existing firms in an industry increases when

    I.   Products are relatively undifferentiated
    II. Consumer switching costs are low

    A. I only.

    B. II only.

    C. Both I and II.

    D. Neither I nor II.

Answer (C) is correct.
    REQUIRED: The condition(s), if any, that increase(s) the intensity of rivalry in an industry.
    DISCUSSION: The degree of product differentiation and the costs of switching from one competitor's product to another increase the intensity of rivalry and competition in an industry. Less differentiation tends to heighten competition based on price, with price cutting leading to lower profits. Low costs of switching products also increase competition.
    Answer (A) is incorrect. Low consumer switching costs also increase rivalry. Answer (B) is incorrect. A low degree of product differentiation also increases rivalry. Answer (D) is incorrect. Both low consumer switching costs and a low degree of product differentiation increase rivalry.

3. A manufacturing company produces plastic utensils for a particular segment at the lowest possible cost. The company is pursuing a cost

    A. Leadership strategy.

    B. Focus strategy.

    C. Differentiation strategy.

    D. Containment strategy.

Answer (B) is correct.
    REQUIRED: The cost strategy of manufacturer.
    DISCUSSION: Cost focus is the generic strategy that seeks competitive advantage through lower costs but with a narrow competitive scope (e.g., a regional market or a specialized product line). The reason for a cost-focus strategy is that the narrower market can be better served because the firm knows it well.
    Answer (A) is incorrect. A cost leader is the lowest cost producer in the industry as a whole. Answer (C) is incorrect. Cost differentiation aims at providing a product at different costs in different market segments. Answer (D) is incorrect. Cost containment aims at controlling costs related to a particular product or market but not necessarily producing at the lowest possible cost.

4. What operations strategy is most likely to be adopted when the product sold by an organization is a commodity and the market is large?

    A. Flexibility strategy.

    B. Quality strategy.

    C. Service strategy.

    D. Cost strategy.

Answer (D) is correct.
    REQUIRED: The strategy most likely to be adopted when the product sold is a commodity and the market is large.
    DISCUSSION: An operations strategy formulates a long-term plan for using entity resources to reach strategic objectives. A cost strategy is successful when the entity is the low-cost producer. However, the product (e.g., a commodity) tends to be undifferentiated in these cases, the market is often very large, and the competition tends to be intense because of the possibility of high-volume sales.
    Answer (A) is incorrect. A flexibility strategy involves offering many different products. Answer (B) is incorrect. A quality strategy involves competition based on product quality or process quality. Answer (C) is incorrect. Service is not an issue in a sale of commodities.

5. In the <List A> stage of the product life cycle, <List B> tend to be highest.

	List A	List B
A.	Introduction	Sales
B.	Growth	Profits
C.	Maturity	Profits
D.	Decline	Cash flows

Answer (C) is correct.
    REQUIRED: The stages in the product life cycle.
    DISCUSSION: The product life cycle has five stages: (1) product development, (2) introduction, (3) growth, (4) maturity, and (5) decline. In the maturity stage, profits level off or begin to decline.
    Answer (A) is incorrect. In the introduction stage, sales are low. Answer (B) is incorrect. In the growth stage, profits are increasing, but they do not usually peak until the maturity stage. Answer (D) is incorrect. In the decline stage, sales and profits drop, and cash flows are low.

6. In the value creation chain model, the primary activities include

    A. Logistics, operations, marketing and sales, and service.

    B. Procurement, infrastructure, operations, and service.

    C. Procurement, infrastructure, operations, and technology development.

    D. Procurement, infrastructure, human resources, and technology development.

Answer (A) is correct.
    REQUIRED: The primary activities in the value creation chain.
    DISCUSSION: The model consists of primary and supporting activities. The primary activities are (1) inbound logistics, (2) operations, (3) outbound logistics, (4) marketing and sales, and (5) service. Inbound logistics activities involve the firms' capture of materials to be processed. Operations activities are conversion processes. Outbound logistics activities include shipment of products. Marketing and sales activities are the promotion and sale of final products. Service activities provide customer service. The four support activities are (1) infrastructure (e.g., administration, finance, and planning), (2) procurement, (3) human resources, and (4) technology development.

7. Customer relationship management is best defined as

    A. Coordination with members of the firm's supply chain.

    B. Maximizing short-term sales to customers.

    C. Market sensing.

    D. Maximizing customer loyalty by managing customer "touchpoints."

Answer (D) is correct.
    REQUIRED: The best definition of customer relationship management.
    DISCUSSION: Customer relationship management can be defined as "the process of managing detailed information about individual customers and carefully managing all the customer 'touchpoints' with the aim of maximizing customer loyalty." Its purpose is to create optimal customer equity. Thus, the process involves more than merely attracting customers (through media advertising, direct mail, etc.) and satisfying them (something competitors also may do).
    Answer (A) is incorrect. Coordination with members of the firm's supply chain is partner relationship management. Answer (B) is incorrect. Customer relationship management seeks to increase the value of the customer base by developing long-term relationships with individual customers by such methods as customer service, customized (if not personalized) offerings, and choice of marketing messages and media. Answer (C) is incorrect. Market sensing consists of obtaining, distributing, and acting upon market intelligence.

8. The firm should emphasize customer retention

   A. By creating low switching costs.

   B. By maximizing customer churn.

   C. Although new customers are less costly than old customers.

   D. Because the customer base is an intangible asset.

Answer (D) is correct.
   REQUIRED: The true statement about customer retention.
   DISCUSSION: Customer retention through customer satisfaction is a key to profitability. The firm should emphasize customer retention because the customer base is an important intangible asset.
   Answer (A) is incorrect. High switching costs tend to increase customer retention. Answer (B) is incorrect. The firm should minimize customer churn (customer loss). Answer (C) is incorrect. Customer retention is less costly than customer attraction.

9. While auditing a marketing department, the internal auditor discovered that the product life cycle model was used to structure the marketing mix. The manager has asked the auditor for advice about increasing advertising of the few, basic products being sold. During which stage of the life cycle is the strategy to begin increasing marketing efforts for these products?

   A. Introduction stage.

   B. Growth stage.

   C. Maturity stage.

   D. Decline stage.

Answer (A) is correct.
   REQUIRED: The stage of the life cycle when marketing efforts should begin to increase.
   DISCUSSION: During the introduction stage, only a few, basic products are produced, and the strategy is to increase marketing efforts.
   Answer (B) is incorrect. During the growth stage, the entity enters many new market segments and marketing has already begun. Answer (C) is incorrect. During the maturity stage, the strategy is to maximize products through diversification of brands and models to enter new market segments. Answer (D) is incorrect. During the decline stage, sales and profits drop while prices are cut. Marketing efforts are not as great in this stage.

15.2 Strategic Planning

10. The budget that describes the long-term position and objectives of an entity within its environment is the

   A. Capital budget.

   B. Operating budget.

   C. Cash management budget.

   D. Strategic budget.

Answer (D) is correct.
   REQUIRED: The budget that describes the long-term position and objectives of an entity.
   DISCUSSION: Strategic budgeting is a form of long-range planning based on identifying and specifying organizational objectives. The strengths and weaknesses of the organization are evaluated, and risk levels are assessed. The influences of environmental factors are forecast to derive the best strategy for reaching the organization's objectives.
   Answer (A) is incorrect. Capital budgeting involves evaluating specific long-term investment decisions. Answer (B) is incorrect. The operating budget is a short-range management tool. Answer (C) is incorrect. Cash management is a short-range consideration related to liquidity.

11. Which of the following is an example of an outcome of strategic planning?

   A. A formal statement of the organization's definition of the fundamental truths that guide its actions.

   B. A broad statement of concepts that emphasizes the implementation of organizational objectives over the long term.

   C. A set of general guides for action that channel thinking and allow a certain amount of discretion in execution.

   D. A document specifying a sequence of steps detailing the exact manner in which a certain activity must be accomplished.

Answer (B) is correct.
   REQUIRED: The outcome of strategic planning.
   DISCUSSION: The strategic plan states the means by which an entity expects to achieve its stated mission. Achieving the mission is predicated on implementing long-term objectives.
   Answer (A) is incorrect. Truths that guide an organization's actions are principles. Answer (C) is incorrect. General guides for action are policies. Answer (D) is incorrect. A detailed sequence of steps for accomplishing a certain activity is a procedure.

12. Which one of the following management considerations is usually addressed first in strategic planning?

- A. Outsourcing.
- B. Overall objectives of the firm.
- C. Organizational structure.
- D. Recent annual budgets.

Answer (B) is correct.
    REQUIRED: The management consideration usually addressed first in strategic planning.
    DISCUSSION: Strategic planning sets overall organizational objectives and drafts strategic plans. Setting ultimate objectives for the firm is necessary to develop strategies for achieving those objectives. Plans and budgets then are needed to implement those strategies.
    Answer (A) is incorrect. Outsourcing is a shorter-term operating decision. Answer (C) is incorrect. Organizational structure, although important in strategic planning, is based upon the firm's overall objectives. Answer (D) is incorrect. Recent annual budgets are a basis for short-term planning.

13. Strategy is a broad term that usually means the selection of overall objectives. Strategic analysis ordinarily **excludes** the

- A. Trends that will affect the entity's markets.
- B. Target product mix and production schedule to be maintained during the year.
- C. Forms of organizational structure that would best serve the entity.
- D. Best ways to invest in research, design, production, distribution, marketing, and administrative activities.

Answer (B) is correct.
    REQUIRED: The item ordinarily excluded from the process of strategic analysis.
    DISCUSSION: Strategic analysis is long-range planning. Such tasks as setting the target product mix and production schedule for the current year are short-term activities.
    Answer (A) is incorrect. Strategic analysis includes examining marketing trends. Answer (C) is incorrect. Strategic analysis evaluates organizational structure. Answer (D) is incorrect. Strategic analysis includes evaluation of the best ways to invest in research, design, etc.

14. Strategic planning, as practiced by most modern organizations, includes all of the following **except**

- A. Top-level management participation.
- B. A long-term focus.
- C. Strategies that will help in achieving long-range goals.
- D. Analysis of the current month's actual variances from budget.

Answer (D) is correct.
    REQUIRED: The item not an element of strategic planning.
    DISCUSSION: Strategic planning sets overall organizational objectives. It is a long-term process aimed at determining the future course of the organization. Analysis of the current month's budget variances is a short-term activity.
    Answer (A) is incorrect. Top-level management participation is an element of strategic planning. Answer (B) is incorrect. A long-term focus is an element of strategic planning. Answer (C) is incorrect. Strategies that will help in achieving long-range goals are elements of strategic planning.

15. An organization's policies and procedures are part of its overall system of internal controls. The control function performed by policies and procedures is

- A. Feedforward control.
- B. Implementation control.
- C. Feedback control.
- D. Application control.

Answer (A) is correct.
    REQUIRED: The control function of policies and procedures.
    DISCUSSION: Feedforward control anticipates and prevents problems. Policies and procedures serve as feedforward controls because they provide guidance on how an activity should be performed to best ensure that an objective is achieved.
    Answer (B) is incorrect. Implementation controls are controls applied during systems development. Answer (C) is incorrect. Policies and procedures provide primary guidance before and during the performance of some task rather than give feedback on its accomplishment. Answer (D) is incorrect. Application controls apply to specific applications, e.g., payroll or accounts payable.

16. Formal written policies are normally recommended. However, the presence of certain conditions in an organization minimizes the need for written policies. One condition that minimizes the need for written policies is a

A. High division of labor.

B. Strong organizational culture.

C. Large span of control.

D. Strict unity of command.

Answer (B) is correct.

    REQUIRED: The condition minimizing the need for written policies.

    DISCUSSION: If the culture is strong, the organization's key values are intensely held and widely shared. Substantial training has been expended to achieve this high degree of acceptance, minimizing the need for formal, written policies.

    Answer (A) is incorrect. High specialization of labor indicates a higher need for supervision and a correspondingly strong need for formal policies and procedures. Answer (C) is incorrect. Large spans of control minimize the ability of a manager to provide direct supervision. They increase the need for the indirect supervision provided by formalized policies and procedures. Answer (D) is incorrect. An organization with strict unity of command also most likely requires strict adherence to policies and procedures. Formalization of those policies and procedures promotes adherence.

15.3 Elements of Budgeting

17. Each organization plans and budgets its operations for slightly different reasons. Which one of the following is **not** a significant reason for budgeting?

A. Providing a basis for controlling operations.

B. Forcing managers to consider expected future trends and conditions.

C. Ensuring profitable operations.

D. Checking progress toward the objectives of the organization.

Answer (C) is correct.

    REQUIRED: The item not a significant reason for budgeting.

    DISCUSSION: A budget is a realistic plan for the future that is expressed in quantitative terms. It is a planning, control, motivational, and communications tool. A budget promotes consistency of objectives at all levels of the organization and coordination among operating units. Unfortunately, a budget does not ensure profitable operations.

    Answer (A) is incorrect. Control of operations is a goal of planning. Answer (B) is incorrect. Forcing managers to consider expected future trends and conditions is a goal of planning. Answer (D) is incorrect. Checking progress toward objectives is a goal of planning.

18. One of the primary advantages of budgeting is that it

A. Does not take the place of management and administration.

B. Bases the profit plan on estimates.

C. Is continually adapted to fit changing circumstances.

D. Requires departmental managers to make plans in conjunction with the plans of other interdependent departments.

Answer (D) is correct.

    REQUIRED: The primary advantage of budgeting.

    DISCUSSION: A budget is a quantitative model of a plan of action developed by management. A budget functions as an aid to planning, coordination, and control. Thus, a budget helps management to allocate resources efficiently and to ensure that subunit objectives are consistent with those of other subunits and of the organization.

    Answer (A) is incorrect. Budgeting, far from taking the place of management and administration, makes them even more important. Answer (B) is incorrect. Basing the profit plan on estimates is a necessity, not an advantage. Answer (C) is incorrect. Adaptation to changing circumstances is a commitment that upper management must make. It is not inherent in a budget.

19. All of the following are advantages of the use of budgets in a management control system **except** that budgets

A. Force management planning.

B. Provide performance criteria.

C. Promote communication and coordination within the organization.

D. Limit unauthorized expenditures.

Answer (D) is correct.

    REQUIRED: The item not an advantage of using budgets in a management control system.

    DISCUSSION: Budgets force management to plan, communicate organizational goals throughout the organization, and provide criteria for future performance evaluations. However, they cannot prevent departments from overspending.

    Answer (A) is incorrect. Forcing management planning is an advantage of using budgets. Answer (B) is incorrect. Providing performance criteria is an advantage of using budgets. Answer (C) is incorrect. Promoting communication and coordination within the organization is an advantage of using budgets.

20. When developing a budget, an external factor to consider in the planning process is

   A. A change to a decentralized management system.

   B. The implementation of a new bonus program.

   C. New product development.

   D. The merger of two competitors.

Answer (D) is correct.
   REQUIRED: The external factor considered during the budget planning process.
   DISCUSSION: External factors that must be considered in the planning process include (1) general economic conditions and their expected trend; (2) current market share; (3) governmental regulatory measures; (4) the labor market in the locale of facilities; and (5) activities of competitors, including the effects of mergers.
   Answer (A) is incorrect. A change in management is an internal factor. Answer (B) is incorrect. Employee compensation is an internal factor. Answer (C) is incorrect. A new product line is an internal factor.

21. A planning calendar in budgeting is the

   A. Calendar period covered by the budget.

   B. Schedule of activities for the development and adoption of the budget.

   C. Calendar period covered by the annual budget and the long-range plan.

   D. Sales forecast by months in the annual budget period.

Answer (B) is correct.
   REQUIRED: The definition of a budget planning calendar.
   DISCUSSION: The preparation of a master budget usually takes several months. The budget planning calendar is the schedule of activities for the development and adoption of the budget. It should include a list of dates indicating when specific information is to be provided by each information source to others.
   Answer (A) is incorrect. The period covered by the budget precedes the events in the planning calendar. Answer (C) is incorrect. The period covered by the budget precedes the events in the planning calendar. Answer (D) is incorrect. The planning calendar is not associated with sales.

22. A budget manual, which enhances the operation of a budget system, is most likely to include

   A. A chart of accounts.

   B. Distribution instructions for budget schedules.

   C. Employee hiring policies.

   D. Documentation of the accounting system software.

Answer (B) is correct.
   REQUIRED: The item normally included in a budget manual.
   DISCUSSION: A budget manual describes how a budget is to be prepared. Items usually included in a budget manual are a planning calendar and distribution instructions for all budget schedules.
   Answer (A) is incorrect. A chart of accounts is included in the accounting manual. Answer (C) is incorrect. Employee hiring policies are not needed for budget preparation. They are already available in the human resources manual. Answer (D) is incorrect. Software documentation is not needed in the budget preparation process.

23. Which one of the following is most important to a successful budgeting effort?

   A. Experienced analysts.

   B. Integrated budget software.

   C. Reliable forecasts and trend analyses.

   D. Top management support.

Answer (D) is correct.
   REQUIRED: The most important factor in successful budgeting.
   DISCUSSION: An organizational budget requires a significant commitment of internal resources. The single most important factor in ensuring its success is for senior managers to demonstrate that they consider it vital to the organization's future.
   Answer (A) is incorrect. Experienced analysts are not crucial to success of a budget. Understanding the business is as important as training in budget preparation. Answer (B) is incorrect. Integrated budget software is not the most important factor in budget success. Large and sophisticated budgets can be prepared with ordinary spreadsheets. Answer (C) is incorrect. Although important, reliable forecasts and trend analyses are not the most important factor. A budget must be flexible enough to adapt to changing circumstances.

15.4 Budgeting and Motivation

24. All of the following are advantages of top-down budgeting as opposed to participatory budgeting **except** that it

A. Increases coordination of subunit objectives.

B. Reduces the time required for budgeting.

C. May limit the acceptance of proposed objectives.

D. Facilitates implementation of strategic plans.

Answer (C) is correct.
    REQUIRED: The item not an advantage of top-down budgeting.
    DISCUSSION: Because a top-down budget is imposed by upper management, it has less chance of acceptance (buy-in) by those on whom the budget is imposed.
    Answer (A) is incorrect. A top-down budget is imposed by upper management, so coordinating the objectives of separate divisions is simplified. Answer (B) is incorrect. A top-down budget is coordinated from above. Thus, it is less time-consuming than obtaining lower-level input. Answer (D) is incorrect. Because a top-down budget is coordinated from above, the implementation of strategic plans is centralized and simplified.

25. The following sequence of steps is employed by a company to develop its annual profit plan:

- Planning guidelines are disseminated downward by upper-level management after receiving input from all levels of management.

- A sales budget is prepared by individual sales units reflecting the sales targets of the various segments. This provides the basis for departmental production budgets and other related components by the various operating units. Communication is primarily lateral with some upward communication possible.

- A profit plan is submitted to upper-level management for coordination and review. Upper-level management's recommendations and revisions are acted upon by middle management. A revised profit plan is resubmitted for further review to upper-level management.

- Upper-level management grants final approval and distributes the formal plan downward to the various operating units.

This outline of steps best describes which one of the following approaches to budget development?

A. Imposed budgeting by upper-level management.

B. Participative approach.

C. Top-down approach.

D. Total justification of all activities by operating units.

Answer (B) is correct.
    REQUIRED: The described approach to budget development.
    DISCUSSION: A participative approach is characterized by general guidance from the highest levels of management, followed by extensive input from middle and lower management. This sequence of steps aptly describes this process.
    Answer (A) is incorrect. Upper-level management has received extensive input and cooperation from lower levels through performing these steps. Answer (C) is incorrect. These steps describe the opposite of a top-down approach. Answer (D) is incorrect. Upper-level management is not demanding justification of all activities in the steps described. Such a demand would be consistent with a system known as zero-based budgeting.

26. All of the following are disadvantages of top-down budgeting as opposed to participatory budgeting **except** that it

A. May result in a budget that is not possible to achieve.

B. May limit the acceptance of proposed objectives.

C. Reduces the communication between employees and management.

D. Reduces the time required for budgeting.

Answer (D) is correct.
    REQUIRED: The item not a disadvantage of top-down budgeting.
    DISCUSSION: Because a top-down budget is coordinated from above, it is less time-consuming than obtaining lower-level input.
    Answer (A) is incorrect. A budget established without lower-level input may set unrealistic objectives. Answer (B) is incorrect. Because a top-down budget is imposed by upper management, it has less chance of acceptance (buy-in) by those on whom the budget is imposed. Answer (C) is incorrect. Reduced communication between employees and management is a disadvantage of top-down budgeting.

27. In developing the budget for the next year, which approach is most likely to produce positive motivation and consistency of objectives?

- A. Permit the subunit manager to develop the objectives for the subunit that, in the manager's view, will generate the greatest profit.
- B. Have senior management develop overall objectives and permit the subunit manager to determine how they will be met.
- C. Have the subunit manager and senior management jointly develop objectives and operational plans.
- D. Have the subunit manager and senior management jointly develop objectives and the subunit manager develop operational plans.

Answer (D) is correct.
REQUIRED: The approach most likely to produce positive motivation and consistency of objectives.
DISCUSSION: Participative development of objectives has a positive effect on motivation. Lower-level managers are more likely to accept and be committed to the result.
Answer (A) is incorrect. Allowing subunit managers to develop their objectives does not promote consistency of organizational objectives with those of all levels of the entity. Answer (B) is incorrect. Allowing the subunit manager to participate in the development of objectives has a positive effect on motivation. Answer (C) is incorrect. A further advantage of participation is that it provides a broader information base. Middle- and lower-level managers often are far better informed about operations than senior managers.

28. Marietta Thomas, Amador Corporation's vice president of planning, has seen and heard it all. She has told the corporate controller that she is ". . . very upset with the degree of slack that veteran managers have in the budgets they prepare." Thomas has considered implementing some of the following activities during the budgeting process:

1. Develop the budgets by top management and issue them to lower-level operating units.
2. Study the actual revenues and expenses of previous periods in detail.
3. Have the budgets developed by operating units and accept them as submitted by a company-wide budget committee.
4. Share the budgets with all employees as a means to reach company objectives.
5. Use a budgeting process that proceeds through several stages with changes initiated by operating units or senior managers.

Which of these activities should Amador implement to best remedy Thomas's concerns, help eliminate the problems experienced by Amador, and motivate personnel?

- A. 1 only.
- B. 2 and 3.
- C. 2 and 4.
- D. 2, 4, and 5.

Answer (D) is correct.
REQUIRED: The activity or activities to implement during the budgeting process.
DISCUSSION: Steps 2, 4, and 5 are appropriate for alleviating the budget problems. Step 1 should not be performed because a budget imposed from the top is more likely to encounter resistance. Step 3 should not be performed because operating units tend to consider only their own interests when preparing budgets.
Answer (A) is incorrect. A budget imposed from the top is more likely to encounter resistance. Answer (B) is incorrect. Operating units tend to consider only their own interests when preparing budgets. Answer (C) is incorrect. Studying previous periods and sharing the budget with all employees are important steps to correcting problems. But incrementally improving the budget through a multistage process is also crucial.

29. Budgeting problems arise when subunit objectives are too easy or too difficult to achieve. Such problems are minimized by establishing

- A. Preventive controls.
- B. A policy that allows managers to build slack into the budget.
- C. Participative budgeting to encourage managers to pursue objectives consistent with those set by senior management.
- D. Better communication that permits managers to discuss budget matters daily with their superiors.

Answer (C) is correct.
REQUIRED: The approach used to minimize budget problems.
DISCUSSION: Participative budgeting is a feasible way to set realistic, achievable budgetary objectives.
Answer (A) is incorrect. The term "preventive controls" is too vague in this context. Answer (B) is incorrect. A policy allowing budgetary slack makes the problem worse. Answer (D) is incorrect. Simply discussing budget matters more often does not improve the process.

30. The budgeting process should motivate managers and employees to work toward organizational objectives. Which one of the following is **least** likely to motivate managers?

A. Setting budget targets at attainable levels.

B. Participation by subordinates in the budgetary process.

C. Use of management by exception.

D. Having upper-level management set budget levels.

Answer (D) is correct.

REQUIRED: The item least likely to motivate managers.

DISCUSSION: A budget is potentially an effective motivational tool. If lower-level managers have participated in preparing the budget instead of simply receiving a budget imposed by upper-level management, they are more likely to understand and share the objectives of upper-level management and to work to keep costs within the budget. Participation and understanding also are likely to result in budgets that are reasonably attainable and viewed as realistic. However, a budget also is a motivator in the sense that managers are accountable for variances in controllable costs but are rewarded for good performance. Moreover, budgeting coupled with analysis of variances tends to improve motivation by allowing upper-level managers to concentrate on problems (exceptions) rather than engaging in routine supervision of subordinates, which may be viewed as unnecessarily intrusive and unwelcome.

Answer (A) is incorrect. Setting budget targets at attainable levels is a means of increasing manager motivation. Answer (B) is incorrect. Participation by subordinates in the budgetary process is a means of increasing manager motivation. Answer (C) is incorrect. Use of management by exception is a means of increasing manager motivation.

What our customers are saying

15.5 PRACTICE WRITTEN COMMUNICATION

DIRECTIONS

Note: If you believe you have encountered a software malfunction, report it to the test center staff immediately.

Navigation

To navigate from task to task, use the controls at the bottom of the screen. Click on the **Next** button to advance to the next task, or the **Previous** button to go to the previous task. To go directly to any task, click on its number.

If you would like a reminder to revisit a task, or want to indicate that you are finished with it, click on the reminder flag below the task number. To clear the flag, click on it again. Reminder flags are for your use only – they do not contribute to your score.

Tabs

In this part of the examination, you will be asked to complete various tasks. Every task has one or more **Work Tabs**. Every task also has a **Help** tab.

Work Tabs:

- **Work Tabs** are identified with a pencil icon. This is where your responses are expected.
- Each task has one or more **Work Tabs**.
- **Work Tabs** contain directions for completing the task - be sure to read these directions carefully.
- The **Work Tab** name in the example above is for illustration only - yours will differ.
- You must complete all of the **Work Tabs** in each task to receive full credit.

Help Tab:

- The **Help Tab** provides assistance with the exam software that is used in this task. For example, if the task is to compose a memorandum, **Help** will provide information about the word processor.

The Toolbar

The toolbar at the top of the screen shows the amount of time remaining for you to complete the tasks. In addition, the following tools are available. Note that only the **Exit** button is displayed when Directions are visible - the others will appear when you begin the tasks.

Click on these buttons to split or unsplit the screen. You can split the screen vertically or horizontally.

Click on this button to go on to the next part of the examination. You must complete all of the tasks to receive full credit. Once you click on **Exit** and confirm the action, you will NOT be able to return to this testlet.

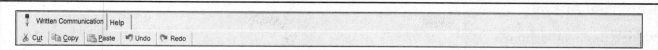

Mr. and Mrs. Robinson have been your tax clients for many years now. They received the following notice from the Internal Revenue Service and have sent it to you, asking for your assistance. As your clients' CPA, write a letter to them explaining the significance of the notice and telling them what information you need in order to respond to the IRS.

Department of the Treasury	Date of Notice: Oct. 9, Year 3
Internal Revenue Service	Form: 1020
	Tax Period: Dec. 31, Year 4

Mr. and Mrs. Robinson
42 Chestnut Street
Anytown, USA

WE CHANGED THE INCOME REPORTED ON YOUR TAX RETURN
YOU HAVE AN AMOUNT DUE

We changed your Year 3 return. As a result of these changes, you owe $500. Our records show that you received a Form 1099-DIV from First Investors Brokerage showing ordinary dividend income in the amount of $2,000. If you think we made a mistake, please reply to this letter no later than October 30, Year 4.

Type your communication below the line in the response area below.

REMINDER: Your response will be graded for both technical content and writing skills. Technical content will be evaluated for information that is helpful to the intended reader and clearly relevant to the issue. Writing skills will be evaluated for development, organization, and the appropriate expression of ideas in professional correspondence. Use a standard business memorandum or letter format with a clear beginning, middle, and end. Do not convey information in the form of a table, bullet point list, or other abbreviated presentation.

To: Mr. and Mrs. Robinson
Re: IRS Notice of Amount Due

NOTE: Your Written Communications on the actual CPA exam may cover topics outside the scope of the BEC CSO (i.e., they may relate to topics from the AUD, FAR, and/or REG CSOs instead). Answer to the best of your ability, and remember that graders are mainly evaluating your writing ability and will overlook minor technical mistakes.

Unofficial Answer

Written Communication

To: Mr. and Mrs. Robinson
Re: IRS Notice of Amount Due

We are writing to explain the significance of the IRS notice you received last week and the information we need to respond to the IRS on your behalf.

The IRS notice is about an additional dividend income of $2,000 that the IRS thinks should be reported on your Year 3 tax return. Based on a 25% marginal ordinary tax rate, there would be an additional $500 income tax due on your Year 3 return. If you agree with the notice, you need to make a payment of $500 within 30 days of the notice. Otherwise, there will be additional interest and penalty charges. You can make the payment by filling out the payment voucher enclosed with the notice to ensure proper application of your payment.

If you do not agree with the notice and want us to represent you before the IRS, we need the following documents from you: (1) a signed statement explaining why you do not agree; (2) supporting documents, such as original transaction documents; and (3) a signed response form with indication of disagreement with the amount due.

Please do not hesitate to contact us if you have any questions or concerns.

The above depicts a Level 5 answer. Consult your booklet, *How to Pass the CPA Exam: A System for Success*, for a description of the three writing skills criteria. You may also access this booklet online by visiting www.gleim.com/PassCPA.

Self-Grade

Below, grade your response on technical content and writing skills. Bubble in the circle next to the appropriate score that you may receive based on the criteria given. Your **total** score is the sum of your scores on all six items. The maximum score is 19 points.

Technical Content Evaluation

Was your response on topic?	O No [0]	O Mostly [1]	O Yes [2]
Did your response have any *significant* errors?	O 0 errors [1]	O 1 major error [−1]	O 2 or more major errors [−2]
Did your response contain any illegal advice?	O No [1]	O Yes [0]	

Writing Skills Evaluation

	Poor	Below Average	Average	Above Average	Outstanding
Organization	O 1	O 2	O 3	O 4	O 5
Development	O 1	O 2	O 3	O 4	O 5
Expression	O 1	O 2	O 3	O 4	O 5

Disclaimer: This scoring schedule was developed by Gleim Publications as a guideline only. The AICPA has not released specific information on how the Written Communications are graded.

Practice even more Written Communications with the Gleim Mega Test Bank.
Learn more: gleim.com/CPAmega | 800.874.5346

STUDY UNIT SIXTEEN
BUDGET COMPONENTS

(11 pages of outline)

A modern organization needs an integrated, entity-wide budget. To be effective, a budget must be based on carefully chosen standards. The preparation of a comprehensive budget has two stages: the operating budget and the financial budget. A flexible budget is prepared for better analysis of budget variances.

16.1 THE MASTER BUDGET AND ITS COMPONENTS

1. **The Master Budget Process -- Sequence**

   a. The master budget, also called the comprehensive budget, static budget, or annual profit plan, encompasses the organization's operating and financial plans for a specified period (ordinarily a year or single operating cycle).

   b. The master budget consists of the operating budget and the financial budget. Both consist of inputs from interrelated sub-budgets.

      1) For example, the production budget cannot be prepared until after completion of the sales budget. The direct materials budget and the direct labor budget cannot be prepared until after completion of the production budget.

2. **The Operating Budget**

   a. In the operating budget, the emphasis is on obtaining and using current resources. It contains the following components:

      1) Sales budget
      2) Production budget
      3) Direct materials budget
      4) Direct labor budget
      5) Manufacturing overhead budget
      6) Cost of goods sold budget
      7) Nonmanufacturing budget

         a) Research and development budget
         b) Selling and administrative budget

            i) Design budget
            ii) Marketing budget
            iii) Distribution budget
            iv) Customer service budget
            v) Administrative budget

      8) Pro forma income statement

3. The Financial Budget

    a.   In the financial budget, the emphasis is on obtaining the funds needed to purchase operating assets. It contains the following components:

        1)   Capital budget

        2)   Cash budget

            a)   Projected cash disbursement schedule

            b)   Projected cash collection schedule

        3)   Pro forma balance sheet

        4)   Pro forma statement of cash flows

4. Master Budget Process -- Graphical Depiction

Figure 16-1

  * PCDS = projected cash disbursements schedule
 ** PCCS = projected cash collection schedule

Stop and review! You have completed the outline for this subunit. Study multiple-choice questions 1 through 8 beginning on page 424.

16.2 STANDARD COSTS

1. **Standard Costs**

   a. Standard costs are predetermined expectations about how much a unit of input, a unit of output, or a given activity should cost.

      1) The use of standard costs in budgeting allows the standard-cost system to alert management when the actual costs of production differ significantly from the standard.

$$\text{Standard cost of input per unit of output} = \text{Units of input per single unit of output} \times \text{Price per unit of input}$$

   b. A standard cost is not just an average of past costs but is an objectively determined estimate of what a cost should be. Standards may be based on accounting, engineering, or statistical quality control studies.

 Standard costs have been tested by asking for the calculation of a cost for a standard unit of input. You may be asked to explain the use of standard costs.

---

2. **Theoretical vs. Practical Standards**

   a. Ideal (theoretical) standards are standard costs that are set for production under optimal conditions. For this reason, they also are called perfection or maximum efficiency standards.

      1) They are based on the work of the most skilled workers with no allowance for spoilage, waste, machine breakdowns, or other downtime.

      2) Often called tight standards, they can have positive behavioral effects if workers are motivated to strive for excellence. However, they are not in wide use because they can have negative effects if the standards are impossible to attain.

      3) Ideal standards ordinarily are replaced by currently attainable (practical) standards for cash budgeting, product costing, and budgeting departmental performance. Otherwise, accurate financial planning is impossible.

   b. Currently attainable (practical) standards are the results expected to be achieved by reasonably well-trained workers with an allowance for normal spoilage, waste, and downtime.

      1) An alternative interpretation is that practical standards represent possible but difficult-to-attain results.

3. **Activity Analysis**

   a. Activity analysis identifies, describes, and evaluates the activities and resources needed to produce a particular output. This process aids in the development of standard costs.

   b. Each operation requires a unique set of inputs and preparations. Activity analysis describes what these inputs are and who performs these preparations.

      1) Inputs include the amounts and kinds of equipment, facilities, materials, and labor. Engineering analysis, cost accounting, time-and-motion study, and other approaches may be useful.

   c. Historical data may be used to set standards if an entity lacks the resources to engage in the complex task of activity analysis.

Stop and review! You have completed the outline for this subunit. Study multiple-choice questions 9 through 11 on page 426.

16.3 THE OPERATING BUDGET

1. **Sales Budget**

   a. The sales budget, also called the revenue budget, is the starting point for the cycle that produces the annual profit plan (the master budget).

   b. The sales budget is based on the sales forecast. The forecast reflects (1) recent sales trends, (2) overall conditions in the economy and industry, (3) market research, (4) activities of competitors, and (5) credit and pricing policies.

   c. The sales budget must specify both projected unit sales and dollar revenues.

EXAMPLE of a Sales Budget

	April	Ref.
Projected sales in units	1,000	SB1
Selling price	× $400	
Projected total sales	$400,000	SB2

---

2. **Production Budget**

   a. The production budget follows directly from the sales budget. The production budget is stated in units only. Product pricing is ignored because the purpose is only to plan output and inventory levels and the necessary manufacturing activity.

   b. To minimize finished goods carrying costs and obsolescence, the levels of production are dependent upon the projections in the sales budget.

EXAMPLE of a Production Budget

Finished goods beginning inventory consists of 100 units at $125 cost per unit, a total of $12,500, and the desired finished goods ending inventory is 120 units.

	Source	April	Ref.
Projected sales in units	SB1	1,000	
Plus: desired ending inventory		120	
Minus: beginning inventory		(100)	
Units to be produced		1,020	PB

---

   c. The **purchases budget** for a retailer is prepared after projected sales are estimated.

   1) It is prepared on a monthly or even a weekly basis.

   2) Purchases can be planned so that stockouts are avoided.

   3) Inventory should be at an appropriate level to avoid unnecessary carrying costs.

   4) It is similar to the production budget example above. However, the units are purchased rather than produced.

Questions asked by the AICPA about budgeting often require calculations. Always read and think through the scenario very carefully. For example, you may encounter a question regarding budgeted materials required for a time period. If it asks for the budgeted number of legs necessary for tables produced, be sure to calculate the amount using the appropriate number of legs per table.

3. **Direct Materials Budget**

    a. The direct materials budget reflects both units and input prices.

        1) Two dollar amounts are calculated in the direct materials budget: the cost of materials actually used in production and the total cost of materials purchased.

EXAMPLE of a Direct Materials Budget

Materials beginning inventory is 1,000 units at $18 cost per unit, and the desired materials ending inventory is 980 units.

Materials Used (Quantity)	Source	April	Ref.
Finished units to be produced	PB	1,020	
Times: materials per finished product		× 4	
Total units needed for production		4,080	DMB1

Materials Purchased	Source	April	Ref.
Units needed for production	DMB1	4,080	
Plus: desired units in ending inventory		980	
Minus: beginning inventory		(1,000)	
materials to be purchased		4,060	
Times: materials cost per unit		× $20	
Cost of materials to be purchased		$81,200	DMB2

Materials Used ($)	Source	April	Ref.
Beginning inventory (1,000 × $18)		$18,000	
Plus: purchases of material	DMB2	81,200	
Minus: desired ending inventory (980 × $20)		(19,600)	
Cost of materials used in production		$79,600	DMB3

---

4. **Direct Labor Budget**

    a. The direct labor budget depends on wage rates, amounts and types of production, numbers and skill levels of employees to be hired, etc.

    b. In addition to the regular wage rate, the total direct labor cost per hour also may include employer FICA taxes, health insurance, life insurance, and pension contributions.

EXAMPLE of a Direct Labor Budget

The Human Resources department has determined that the total cost per labor hour is $18.

	Source	April	Ref.
Units to be produced	PB	1,020	
Times: direct labor hours per unit		× 2	
Projected total direct labor hours		2,040	DLB1
Times: direct labor cost per hour		× $18	
Total projected direct labor cost		$36,720	DLB2

---

5. **Manufacturing Overhead Budget**

    a. The manufacturing overhead budget has variable and fixed components because overhead is a mixed cost. (Mixed costs are defined in Study Unit 18.)

    b. Variable overhead contains elements that vary with the level of production.

        1) Indirect materials

        2) Some indirect labor

        3) Variable factory operating costs (e.g., electricity)

EXAMPLE of a Variable Overhead Budget

Variable overhead is applied to production on the basis of direct labor hours.

	Source	April	Ref.
Projected total direct labor hours	DLB1	2,040	
Variable OH rate per direct labor hour		× $3	
Projected variable overhead		$6,120	MOB1

---

c.   Fixed overhead contains elements that do **not** change regardless of the level of production.

1)   Real estate taxes
2)   Insurance
3)   Depreciation

EXAMPLE of a Fixed Overhead Budget

	April	Ref.
Projected fixed overhead	$9,000	MOB2

---

6.   **Cost of Goods Sold Budget**

a.   The cost of goods sold budget combines the projections for the three major inputs (materials, labor, and overhead). The result directly affects the pro forma income statement. Cost of goods sold is the largest cost for a manufacturer.

EXAMPLE of a Cost of Goods Sold Budget

	Source	April		Ref.
Beginning finished goods inventory			$ 12,500	
Manufacturing costs:				
Direct materials used	DMB3	$79,600		
Direct labor used	DLB2	36,720		
Variable overhead	MOB1	6,120		
Fixed overhead	MOB2	9,000		
Cost of goods manufactured			131,440	
Cost of goods available for sale			$143,940	
Ending finished goods inventory				
(120 units × $130)			(15,600)	
Cost of goods sold			$128,340	CGSB

---

7.   **Nonmanufacturing Budget**

a.   The nonmanufacturing budget consists of the individual budgets for (1) R&D, (2) design, (3) marketing, (4) distribution, (5) customer service, and (6) administrative costs. The development of separate budgets for these functions is based on a value chain approach.

1)   An alternative is to prepare a single budget for selling and administrative (S&A) costs of nonproduction functions.

b.   The variable and fixed portions of selling and administrative costs must be treated separately.

1)   Some S&A costs vary directly and proportionately with the level of sales. As more products are sold, sales representatives must travel more miles and serve more customers.

2)   Other S&A expenses, such as sales support staff, are fixed. They must be paid at any level of sales.

8. **Pro Forma Income Statement**

   a. The pro forma income statement is the end of the operating budget process.

      1) Financial statements are pro forma when they report projected, not actual, results.

   b. The pro forma income statement is used to decide whether the budgeted activities will result in an acceptable level of income. If the initial projection is a loss or otherwise unacceptable, adjustments can be made to the components of the master budget.

EXAMPLE of a Pro Forma Income Statement

Manufacturing Company
Pro Forma Statement of Income
Month of April

Sales		$400,000
Beginning finished goods inventory	$ 12,500	
Plus: cost of goods manufactured	131,440	
Goods available for sale	$143,940	
Minus: ending finished goods inventory	(15,600)	
Cost of goods sold		(128,340)
Gross margin		$271,660
Minus: selling and administrative expenses		(82,000)
Operating income		$189,660
Minus: other revenues, expenses, gains, and losses		(15,000)
Earnings before interest and taxes		$174,660
Minus: interest expense		(45,000)
Earnings before income taxes		$129,660
Minus: income taxes (40%)		(49,200)
Net income		$ 80,460

Stop and review! You have completed the outline for this subunit. Study multiple-choice questions 12 through 17 beginning on page 426.

16.4 THE FINANCIAL BUDGET

1. **Capital Budget**

   a. The preparation of the capital budget is separate from the operating budget cycle.

   b. The capital budget, which often must be approved by the board of directors, addresses financing of major expenditures for long-term assets. It therefore must have a multi-year perspective. Productive assets must be acquired to enable the entity to achieve its projected levels of output.

   c. A procedure for ranking projects according to their risk and return characteristics is necessary because every organization has finite resources. [These procedures (net present value, internal rate of return, payback method, etc.) are covered in Study Unit 9, Subunits 3 through 6.]

   d. The capital budget is a direct input to the cash budget and the pro forma balance sheet and statement of cash flows.

      1) Principal and interest on debt acquired to finance capital purchases require regular cash outflows. The acquired debt also appears in the liabilities section of the pro forma balance sheet.

      2) The output produced by new productive assets generates regular cash inflows. The new assets also appear in the assets section of the pro forma balance sheet.

2.   **Cash Budget**

a.   The cash budget is the part of the financial budget cycle that connects all the schedules from the operating budget. A cash budget projects cash flows for planning and control purposes. Thus, it helps prevent not only cash emergencies but also excessive idle cash.

  1)   A cash budget is vital because an organization must have adequate cash at all times. Almost all organizations, regardless of size, prepare a cash budget.

    a)   Even with plenty of other assets, an organization with a temporary shortage of cash can become bankrupt.

  2)   Proper planning can help prevent financial difficulty. Thus, cash budgets are prepared not only for annual and quarterly periods but also for monthly and weekly periods.

    a)   They are particularly important for organizations operating in seasonal industries.

    b)   The factors needed to prepare a cash forecast include all other elements of the budget preparation process plus consideration of (1) collection policies, (2) bad debt estimates, and (3) changes in the economy.

  3)   Credit and purchasing policies directly affect the cash budget.

    a)   Loose customer credit policies delay cash receipts.
    b)   Use of purchase discounts accelerates cash payments.

b.   The cash budget process begins with preparation of a **projected cash collection schedule**. It forecasts the inflows of cash from customer payments.

EXAMPLE of a Cash Collection Schedule for April

Sales are made on credit.

	February Sales (Actual)	March Sales (Actual)	Source	April Sales (Projected)	Totals	Ref.
Sales	$180,000	$220,000	SB2	$400,000		
Projection of collection in April	× 30%	× 50%		× 15%		
From 2nd prior-month sales	$ 54,000				$ 54,000	
From prior-month sales		$110,000			110,000	
From current-month sales				$ 60,000	60,000	
Total cash collections from sales					$224,000	PCCS

---

c.   The next step is preparation of a **projected cash disbursements schedule**.

EXAMPLE of a Cash Disbursements Schedule for April

Materials purchases are the only purchases made on credit.

	March Purchases (Actual)	Source	April Purchases (Projected)	Totals	Ref.
Cost of materials purchased	$72,000	DMB2	$81,200		
Projection of payments in April	× 40%		× 60%		
For prior-month purchases	$28,800			$28,800	
For current-month purchases			$48,720	48,720	
Total cash disbursements for materials				$77,520	PCDS

d. The **cash budget** is the key element of the financial budget.

1) A comprehensive statement of the sources and uses of the entity's cash flows combines the operating budget and the cash flow schedules.

2) The cash budget can be used to plan financing activities. For example, if the budget projects a cash deficit, the entity can plan to borrow the necessary funds or sell stock.

3) Dividend policy also can be planned using the cash budget. For example, dividend payment dates should correspond to a time when the entity has excess cash.

EXAMPLE of a Cash Budget

The bottom line is the expected cash surplus or the financing required.

	Source	April
Beginning cash balance		$100,000
Cash collections from sales	PCCS	224,000
Cash available for disbursement		$324,000
Cash disbursements:		
For materials	PCDS	$ 77,520
For direct labor	DLB2	36,720
For variable overhead	MOB1	6,120
For fixed overhead	MOB2	9,000
For nonmanufacturing costs		26,000
For equipment purchases		110,000
Total disbursements		(265,360)
Excess of cash available over disbursements		$ 58,640
Desired ending cash balance		100,000
Short-term financing required		$ 41,360

---

3. **Pro Forma Balance Sheet and Cash Flow Statement**

a. The **pro forma balance sheet** is prepared using the cash and capital budgets and the pro forma income statement.

1) The pro forma balance sheet is the beginning-of-the-period balance sheet updated for projected changes in cash, receivables, payables, inventory, etc.

2) If the balance sheet indicates that a contract may be breached, the budgeting process must be repeated.

a) For example, some loan agreements require that (1) owners' equity be maintained at some percentage of total debt or (2) current assets be maintained at a given multiple of current liabilities.

b. The **pro forma statement of cash flows** classifies cash flows depending on whether they are from operating, investing, or financing activities.

c. The pro forma statements are interrelated. For example, the pro forma cash flow statement includes anticipated borrowing. The interest on this borrowing appears in the pro forma income statement.

Stop and review! You have completed the outline for this subunit. Study multiple-choice questions 18 through 23 beginning on page 429.

16.5 FLEXIBLE BUDGETING

1. **Flexible Budget**

    a. A flexible budget is an annual profit plan prepared for various levels of production or sales. It reports the operating income for each level.

        1) A flexible budget can be used for any component of the budget process that varies with the level of activity. Examples are (a) sales revenue, (b) direct labor and materials, (c) marketing expenses, and (d) sales and administrative expenses.

2. **Static vs. Flexible Budgeting**

    a. The **static (master) budget** is prepared before the period begins and is not changed. The static budget is based on only one level of expected activity (output planned at the beginning of the period).

EXAMPLE of a Static Budget

The following static (master) budget for the upcoming month is based on production and sales of 1,000 units:

Sales revenue ($400 per unit)	$400,000
Minus: variable costs ($160 per unit)	(160,000)
Contribution margin	$240,000
Minus: fixed costs	(200,000)
Operating income	$ 40,000

---

b. The flexible budget is prepared

    1) Based on the actual output sold (produced) during the period.
    2) Using the same drivers as those used to prepare the master budget.
    3) After the end of the period when all actual results are known.

EXAMPLE of a Flexible Budget

	Flexible Budget Based on 800 Units	Static Budget Based on 1,000 Units	Flexible Budget Based on 1,200 Units
Sales revenue ($400 per unit)	$320,000	$400,000	$480,000
Minus: variable costs ($160 per unit)	(128,000)	(160,000)	(192,000)
Contribution margin	$192,000	$240,000	$288,000
Minus: fixed costs	(200,000)	(200,000)	(200,000)
Operating income	$ (8,000)	$ 40,000	$ 88,000

---

3. **Variance Analysis Using Flexible Budgeting**

    a. The most common use of the flexible budget is for analysis of budget variances.

        1) Variance analysis helps management in monitoring and measuring performance.

    b. A variance is the difference between the actual results for the period and a budgeted amount for the period.

        1) A favorable variance (F) occurs when actual revenues are greater than standard (budgeted) or actual costs are less than standard (budgeted).
        2) An unfavorable variance (U) occurs when actual revenues are less than standard (budgeted) or actual costs are greater than standard (budgeted).

EXAMPLE of Budget Variances

Actual results for the month were as follows:

Sales revenue	$342,000 (800 units × $427.50 price per unit)
Variable costs	$153,000
Fixed costs	$220,000

	Actual Results	Budget Variances	Master Budget
Sales revenue	$342,000	$(58,000) U	$400,000
Minus: variable costs	(153,000)	7,000 F	(160,000)
Contribution margin	$189,000	$(51,000) U	$240,000
Minus: fixed costs	(220,000)	(20,000) U	(200,000)
Operating income (loss)	$ (31,000)	$(71,000) U	$ 40,000

c. To analyze performance for the period, the budget variances should be subdivided into sales-volume variances and flexible budget variances.

1) Sales-volume variances result from inaccurate forecasting of the output sold for the period. They are measured as the difference between the flexible budget and the static (master) budget amounts.

2) Flexible budget variances report the differences between (a) the actual revenues and costs for the period and (b) the amounts that should have been earned and expended given the achieved level of production.

   a) Flexible budget variances are measured as the difference between the actual results and the flexible budget. More extensive analysis of flexible budget variances can be made by using standard costing. (This topic is covered in detail in Study Unit 20.)

EXAMPLE of a Flexible Budget and Sales-Volume Variances

	Actual Results	Flexible Budget Variances	Flexible Budget Based on Actual Sales of 800 Units	Sales-Volume Variances	Master (Static) Budget
Sales revenue	$342,000	$ 22,000 F	$320,000	$(80,000) U	$400,000
Minus: variable costs	(153,000)	(25,000) U	(128,000)	32,000 F	(160,000)
Contribution margin	$189,000	$ (3,000) U	$192,000	$(48,000) U	$240,000
Minus: fixed costs	(220,000)	(20,000) U	(200,000)	– –	(200,000)
Operating income (loss)	$ (31,000)	$(23,000) U	$ (8,000)	$(48,000) U	$ 40,000

The net of the two variances equals the difference between the master budget and the actual results, the static budget variance.

Flexible budget variance	$(23,000) U	Actual results	$(31,000)
Sales volume variance	(48,000) U	Master (static) budget	40,000
Static budget variance	$(71,000) U	Static budget variance	$(71,000) U

Stop and review! You have completed the outline for this subunit. Study multiple-choice questions 24 through 28 beginning on page 430.

QUESTIONS

16.1 The Master Budget and Its Components

1. In an organization that plans by using comprehensive budgeting, the master budget is

A. A compilation of all the separate operational and financial budget schedules of the organization.

B. The booklet containing budget guidelines, policies, and forms to use in the budgeting process.

C. The current budget updated for operations for part of the current year.

D. A budget of a not-for-profit organization after it is approved by the appropriate authoritative body.

Answer (A) is correct.
    REQUIRED: The nature of the master budget.
    DISCUSSION: The overall budget, often called the master or comprehensive budget, encompasses the organization's operating and financial plans for a specified period (ordinarily a year). Thus, all other budgets are subsets of the master budget.
    Answer (B) is incorrect. The booklet containing budget guidelines, policies, and forms to use in the budgeting process is the budget manual. Answer (C) is incorrect. The current budget updated for operations for part of the current year is a continuous budget. Answer (D) is incorrect. A master budget may be prepared by a for-profit entity.

2. Pro forma financial statements are part of the budgeting process. Normally, the **last** pro forma statement prepared is the

A. Capital expenditure plan.

B. Income statement.

C. Statement of cost of goods sold.

D. Statement of cash flows.

Answer (D) is correct.
    REQUIRED: The last pro forma financial statement prepared.
    DISCUSSION: The statement of cash flows is usually the last of the listed items prepared. All other elements of the budget process must be completed before it can be developed.
    Answer (A) is incorrect. The capital expenditure plan must be prepared before the cash budget. Cash may be needed to pay for capital purchases. Answer (B) is incorrect. The income statement must be prepared before the statement of cash flows, which reconciles net income and net operating cash flows. Answer (C) is incorrect. Cost of goods sold is included in the income statement, which is an input to the statement of cash flows.

3. The preparation of a comprehensive master budget culminates with the preparation of the

A. Production budget.

B. Capital investment budget.

C. Cash budget.

D. Strategic budget.

Answer (C) is correct.
    REQUIRED: The final step in the preparation of the comprehensive master budget.
    DISCUSSION: Apart from the pro forma balance sheet and statement of cash flows, the cash budget is the culmination of the master budget process.
    Answer (A) is incorrect. The production budget must precede the capital investment and cash budgets. Answer (B) is incorrect. A capital investment budget is prepared before a cash budget. Answer (D) is incorrect. A strategic budget is a long-range planning tool that is prepared before the master budget.

4. Wilson Company uses a comprehensive planning and budgeting system. The proper order for Wilson to prepare certain budget schedules would be

A. Cost of goods sold, balance sheet, income statement, and statement of cash flows.

B. Income statement, balance sheet, statement of cash flows, and cost of goods sold.

C. Statement of cash flows, cost of goods sold, income statement, and balance sheet.

D. Cost of goods sold, income statement, balance sheet, and statement of cash flows.

Answer (D) is correct.
    REQUIRED: The order in which budget schedules should be prepared.
    DISCUSSION: The cost of goods sold budget is an input for the pro forma income statement. The entire operating budget process must be completed before the pro forma balance sheet and statement of cash flows can be prepared.
    Answer (A) is incorrect. The balance sheet should not precede the income statement. Answer (B) is incorrect. The income statement cannot precede cost of goods sold. Answer (C) is incorrect. The statement of cash flows cannot precede the cost of goods sold. The latter is an input of the former.

5. Which one of the following best describes the order in which budgets should be prepared when developing the annual master operating budget?

A. Production budget, direct material budget, revenue budget.

B. Production budget, revenue budget, direct material budget.

C. Revenue budget, production budget, direct material budget.

D. Revenue budget, direct material budget, production budget.

Answer (C) is correct.
   REQUIRED: The order in which budgets should be prepared when developing the annual master operating budget.
   DISCUSSION: The components of the operating budget are prepared in the following order: (1) sales (revenue) budget, (2) production budget, (3) direct materials budget, (4) direct labor budget, (5) manufacturing overhead budget, (6) ending finished goods inventory budget, (7) cost of goods sold budget, and (8) nonmanufacturing budget.
   Answer (A) is incorrect. The revenue budget must be completed before the other two can be prepared. Answer (B) is incorrect. The revenue budget must be completed before the production budget can be prepared. Answer (D) is incorrect. The production budget must be completed before the direct material budget can be prepared.

6. The cash budget must be prepared before completing the

A. Capital expenditure budget.

B. Sales budget.

C. Forecasted balance sheet.

D. Production budget.

Answer (C) is correct.
   REQUIRED: The budget element prepared after the cash budget.
   DISCUSSION: The pro forma balance sheet is the balance sheet for the beginning of the period updated for projected changes in cash, receivables, inventories, payables, etc. Accordingly, it cannot be prepared until after the cash budget is completed because cash is a current asset reported on the balance sheet.
   Answer (A) is incorrect. The capital expenditure budget is an input necessary for the preparation of a cash budget. Answer (B) is incorrect. The sales budget is usually the first budget prepared. Answer (D) is incorrect. A production budget is normally prepared before the cash budget is started.

7. Which of the following is normally included in the financial budget of a firm?

A. Direct materials budget.

B. Selling expense budget.

C. Budgeted balance sheet.

D. Sales budget.

Answer (C) is correct.
   REQUIRED: The item normally included in the financial budget.
   DISCUSSION: The financial budget normally includes (1) the capital budget, (2) the cash budget, (3) the budgeted balance sheet, and (4) the budgeted statement of cash flows.
   Answer (A) is incorrect. The direct materials budget is included in the production budget. Answer (B) is incorrect. The selling expense budget is included in the operating budget. Answer (D) is incorrect. The sales budget is included in the operating budget.

8. Many companies use comprehensive budgeting in planning for the next year's activities. When both an operating budget and a financial budget are prepared, which one of the following is correct concerning the financial budget?

	Included in the Financial Budget		
	Capital Budget	Pro Forma Balance Sheet	Cash Budget
A.	Yes	No	Yes
B.	No	Yes	No
C.	Yes	Yes	Yes
D.	No	No	No

Answer (C) is correct.
   REQUIRED: The true statement concerning the financial budget.
   DISCUSSION: In the financial budget, the emphasis is on obtaining the funds needed to purchase operating assets. It contains the capital budget, projected cash disbursement schedule, projected cash collection schedule, cash budget, pro forma balance sheet, and pro forma statement of cash flows.
   Answer (A) is incorrect. The pro forma balance sheet is part of the financial budget. Answer (B) is incorrect. The capital budget and cash budget are part of the financial budget. Answer (D) is incorrect. The capital budget, pro forma balance sheet, and cash budget are part of the financial budget.

16.2 Standard Costs

9. The best basis upon which cost standards should be set to measure controllable production inefficiencies is

    A. Engineering standards based on ideal performance.

    B. Normal capacity.

    C. Recent average historical performance.

    D. Engineering standards based on attainable performance.

Answer (D) is correct.
    REQUIRED: The best basis upon which cost standards should be set.
    DISCUSSION: Standards must be accepted by those who will carry them out if they are to have maximum effectiveness. Subordinates should believe that standards are both fair and achievable. Otherwise, they may tend to sabotage, ignore, or circumvent them.
    Answer (A) is incorrect. Employees may not cooperate with standards based on ideal performance. Attainable standards are usually better for motivational purposes. Answer (B) is incorrect. Normal capacity may not suffice to control production inefficiencies. Answer (C) is incorrect. Historical performance may not always be a guide to future performance, and standards should be based on anticipated future conditions.

10. When compared with ideal standards, practical standards

    A. Produce lower per-unit product costs.

    B. Result in a less desirable basis for the development of budgets.

    C. Incorporate very generous allowance for spoilage and worker inefficiencies.

    D. Serve as a better motivating target for manufacturing personnel.

Answer (D) is correct.
    REQUIRED: The correct statement regarding practical standards when compared to ideal standards.
    DISCUSSION: Practical standards, also called attainable standards, are more likely to be accepted by workers than standards based on an unachievable ideal.
    Answer (A) is incorrect. The effect of one type of standard over another cannot guarantee lower costs. Answer (B) is incorrect. Practical standards are more appropriate in most cases than ideal standards in the development of budgets. Answer (C) is incorrect. An acceptance of high levels of spoilage and worker inefficiencies cannot be overcome through the use of standards.

11. After performing a thorough study of Michigan Company's operations, an independent consultant determined that the firm's labor standards were too tight. Which of the following is **inconsistent** with the consultant's conclusion?

    A. A review of performance reports revealed the presence of many unfavorable efficiency variances.

    B. Michigan's budgeting process was based on a top-down (authoritative) philosophy.

    C. Management noted that minimal incentive bonuses have been paid in recent periods.

    D. Production supervisors found several significant fluctuations in manufacturing volume, with short-term increases in output being followed by rapid, sustained declines.

Answer (D) is correct.
    REQUIRED: The statement inconsistent with the consultant's conclusion.
    DISCUSSION: The situation described is indicative of rush jobs being too common, which is a result of poor production planning, not tight labor standards.
    Answer (A) is incorrect. Many unfavorable efficiency variances indicate standards are too tight. Answer (B) is incorrect. A budgeting process based on a top-down (authoritative) philosophy is more likely than a bottom-up approach to set standards that are too tight. Answer (C) is incorrect. The widespread failure to earn expected bonuses indicates standards are too tight.

16.3 The Operating Budget

12. When budgeting, the items to be considered by a manufacturing firm in going from a sales quantity budget to a production budget would be the

    A. Expected change in the quantity of work-in-process inventories.

    B. Expected change in the quantity of finished goods and work-in-process inventories.

    C. Expected change in the quantity of finished goods and raw material inventories.

    D. Expected change in the availability of raw material without regard to inventory levels.

Answer (B) is correct.
    REQUIRED: The items to be considered in developing a production budget from a sales quantity budget.
    DISCUSSION: Production quantities are not identical to sales because of changes in inventory levels. Both finished goods and work-in-process inventories may change during a period, necessitating an analysis of both inventory levels before the production budget can be set.
    Answer (A) is incorrect. Finished goods inventories cannot be ignored. Answer (C) is incorrect. Work-in-process inventory should be considered. Answer (D) is incorrect. Existing inventories determine production levels.

Questions 13 and 14 are based on the following information. Paradise Company budgets on an annual basis for its fiscal year. The following beginning and ending inventory levels (in units) are planned for the fiscal year of July 1 through June 30:

	July 1	June 30
Direct material*	40,000	50,000
Work-in-process	10,000	20,000
Finished goods	80,000	50,000

* Two units of direct material are needed to produce each unit of finished product.

13. If Paradise Company plans to sell 480,000 units during the fiscal year, the number of units it will have to manufacture during the year is

A. 440,000 units.

B. 480,000 units.

C. 510,000 units.

D. 450,000 units.

Answer (D) is correct.
REQUIRED: The number of units to be manufactured at a given sales level.
DISCUSSION: If 480,000 units are sold with an ending finished goods inventory of 50,000 units, 530,000 units must be available. Given that 80,000 units are in beginning inventory, production must be 450,000 units (530,000 – 80,000).
Answer (A) is incorrect. The calculation need not be adjusted for the change in work-in-process. Only finished goods are being discussed. Answer (B) is incorrect. The amount to be sold is 480,000 units. Answer (C) is incorrect. The number of 510,000 units equals sales, plus beginning inventory, minus ending inventory.

14. If 500,000 complete units were to be manufactured during the fiscal year by Paradise Company, the number of units of direct materials to be purchased is

A. 1,000,000 units.

B. 1,020,000 units.

C. 1,010,000 units.

D. 990,000 units.

Answer (C) is correct.
REQUIRED: The number of units of materials to be purchased at a given production level.
DISCUSSION: The total materials needed for production will be 1,000,000 units (500,000 units × 2 units of materials). In addition, materials inventory is expected to increase by 10,000 units. Thus, materials purchases will be 1,010,000.
Answer (A) is incorrect. The total needed for production is 1,000,000 units. Answer (B) is incorrect. The number of units in materials is not doubled. Answer (D) is incorrect. The number of 990,000 units is less than the amount used in production.

15. Superior Industries' sales budget shows quarterly sales for the next year as follows:

Quarter	Units
1	10,000
2	8,000
3	12,000
4	14,000

Company policy is to have a finished goods inventory at the end of each quarter equal to 20% of the next quarter's sales. Budgeted production for the second quarter of the next year would be

A. 7,200 units.

B. 8,000 units.

C. 8,800 units.

D. 8,400 units.

Answer (C) is correct.
REQUIRED: The budgeted production for the second quarter given ending inventory for each quarter.
DISCUSSION: The finished units needed for sales (8,000), plus the units desired for ending inventory (12,000 units to be sold in the third quarter × 20% = 2,400), minus the units in beginning inventory (8,000 units to be sold in the second quarter × 20% = 1,600) equals budgeted production for the second quarter of 8,800 units.
Answer (A) is incorrect. Subtracting the beginning inventory twice results in 7,200 units. Answer (B) is incorrect. Assuming no change in inventory results in 8,000 units. Answer (D) is incorrect. Including the beginning inventory for the first quarter, not the second quarter, in the calculation results in 8,400 units.

Questions 16 and 17 are based on the following information. Superflite expects April sales of its deluxe model airplane, the C-14, to be 402,000 units at $11 each. Each C-14 requires three purchased components shown below.

	Purchase Cost	Number Needed for Each C-14 Unit
A-9	$ .50	1
B-6	.25	2
D-28	1.00	3

Manufacturing direct labor and variable overhead per unit of C-14 totals $3.00. Fixed manufacturing overhead is $1.00 per unit at a production level of 500,000 units. Superflite plans the following beginning and ending inventories for the month of April and uses standard absorption costing for valuing inventory.

Part No.	Units at April 1	Units at April 30
C-14	12,000	10,000
A-9	21,000	9,000
B-6	32,000	10,000
D-28	14,000	6,000

16. Superflite's C-14 production budget for April should be based on the manufacture of

A. 390,000 units.

B. 400,000 units.

C. 402,000 units.

D. 424,000 units.

Answer (B) is correct.
REQUIRED: The number of units upon which the production budget should be based.
DISCUSSION: Sales are expected to be 402,000 units in April. The beginning inventory is 12,000 units, and the ending inventory is expected to be 10,000 units, a decline in inventory of 2,000 units. Thus, the budget should be based on production of 400,000 units (402,000 units to be sold – 12,000 units BI + 10,000 units EI).
Answer (A) is incorrect. Not considering the need to produce for ending inventory results in 390,000 units. Answer (C) is incorrect. Sales for the month equals 402,000 units. A portion of these sales will come from the beginning inventory. Answer (D) is incorrect. The sum of sales and beginning and ending inventories is 424,000 units.

17. Assume Superflite plans to manufacture 400,000 units in April. Superflite's April budget for the purchase of A-9 should be

A. 379,000 units.

B. 388,000 units.

C. 402,000 units.

D. 412,000 units.

Answer (B) is correct.
REQUIRED: The purchases budget for component A-9.
DISCUSSION: Each of the 400,000 units to be produced in April will require one unit of A-9, a total requirement of 400,000 units. In addition, ending inventory is expected to be 9,000 units. Thus, 409,000 units must be supplied during the month. Of these, 21,000 are available in the beginning inventory. Subtracting the 21,000 beginning inventory from 409,000 leaves 388,000 to be purchased.
Answer (A) is incorrect. The number of 379,000 units fails to consider the 9,000 units in the ending inventory. Answer (C) is incorrect. Sales for the month equals 402,000 units. Answer (D) is incorrect. Adding the decline in inventory of 12,000 to production needs instead of subtracting it results in 412,000.

16.4 The Financial Budget

18. Which one of the following is the best characteristic concerning the capital budget? The capital budget is a(n)

A. Plan to ensure that there are sufficient funds available for the operating needs of the company.

B. Exercise that sets the long-range goals of the company including the consideration of external influences caused by others in the market.

C. Plan that results in the cash requirements during the operating cycle.

D. Plan that assesses the long-term needs of the company for plant and equipment purchases.

Answer (D) is correct.
   REQUIRED: The true statement about the capital budget.
   DISCUSSION: Capital budgeting is the process of planning expenditures for long-lived assets. It involves choosing among investment proposals using a ranking procedure. Evaluations are based on various measures involving the rate of ROI.
   Answer (A) is incorrect. Capital budgeting involves long-term investment needs, not immediate operating needs. Answer (B) is incorrect. Establishing long-term goals in the context of relevant factors in the environment is strategic planning. Answer (C) is incorrect. Cash budgeting determines operating cash flows. Capital budgeting evaluates the rate of return on specific investment alternatives.

19. The cash receipts budget includes

A. Funded depreciation.

B. Operating supplies.

C. Extinguishment of debt.

D. Loan proceeds.

Answer (D) is correct.
   REQUIRED: The item included in a cash receipts budget.
   DISCUSSION: A cash budget may be prepared monthly or even weekly to facilitate cash planning and control. The purpose is to anticipate cash needs while minimizing the amount of idle cash. The cash receipts section of the budget includes all sources of cash. One such source is the proceeds of loans.
   Answer (A) is incorrect. Funded depreciation involves cash outlays. Answer (B) is incorrect. Purchases of supplies involves cash outlays. Answer (C) is incorrect. The extinguishment of debt involves cash outlays.

20. Which one of the following items would have to be included for a company preparing a schedule of cash receipts and disbursements for Calendar Year 1?

A. A purchase order issued in December Year 1 for items to be delivered in February Year 2.

B. Dividends declared in November Year 1 to be paid in January Year 2 to shareholders of record as of December Year 1.

C. The amount of uncollectible customer accounts for Year 1.

D. The borrowing of funds from a bank on a note payable taken out in June Year 1 with an agreement to pay the principal and interest in June Year 2.

Answer (D) is correct.
   REQUIRED: The item included in a cash budget for Year 1.
   DISCUSSION: A schedule of cash receipts and disbursements (cash budget) should include all cash inflows and outflows during the period without regard to the accrual accounting treatment of the transactions. Thus, it should include all checks written and all sources of cash, including borrowings. A borrowing from a bank in June Year 1 should appear as a cash receipt for Year 1.
   Answer (A) is incorrect. The cash disbursement presumably will not occur until Year 2. Answer (B) is incorrect. The cash flow will not occur until dividends are paid in Year 2. Answer (C) is incorrect. Bad debt expense is a noncash item.

21. Which one of the following may be considered an independent item in the preparation of the annual master budget?

A. Ending inventory budget.

B. Capital investment budget.

C. Pro forma income statement.

D. Pro forma statement of financial position.

Answer (B) is correct.
   REQUIRED: The independent item in the preparation of the annual master budget.
   DISCUSSION: The capital investment budget may be prepared more than a year in advance, unlike the other elements of the master budget. Because of the long-term commitments that must be made for some types of capital investments, planning must be done far in advance and is based on needs in future years as opposed to the current year's needs.
   Answer (A) is incorrect. The ending inventory budget is based on the current production budget. Answer (C) is incorrect. The pro forma income statement is based on the sales budget, expense budgets, and all other elements of the current master budget. Answer (D) is incorrect. The pro forma balance sheet is based on the other elements of the current master budget.

22. Trumbull Company budgeted sales on account of $120,000 for July, $211,000 for August, and $198,000 for September. Collection experience indicates that 60% of the budgeted sales will be collected the month after the sale, 36% will be collected the second month, and 4% will be uncollectible. The cash receipts from accounts receivable that should be budgeted for September would be

A. $169,800

B. $147,960

C. $197,880

D. $194,760

Answer (A) is correct.
  REQUIRED: The budgeted cash receipts for September.
  DISCUSSION: The budgeted cash collections for September are $169,800 [($120,000 July sales × 36%) + ($211,000 August sales × 60%)].

23. Whopper, Inc., budgeted sales on account of $150,000 for July, $210,000 for August, and $198,000 for September. Collection experience indicates that 60% of the budgeted sales will be collected the month after the sale, 36% the second month, and 4% will be uncollectible. The cash receipts from accounts receivable that should be budgeted for September equal

A. $180,000

B. $165,600

C. $194,400

D. $198,000

Answer (A) is correct.
  REQUIRED: The budgeted cash receipts from sales on account for September.
  DISCUSSION: The budgeted cash collections for September equal $180,000.

July:	$150,000 × .36	=	$ 54,000
August:	210,000 × .60	=	126,000
			$180,000

  Answer (B) is incorrect. Reversing the percentages for July and August results in $165,600. Answer (C) is incorrect. Budgeted collections for October equal $194,400. Answer (D) is incorrect. The amount of $198,000 equals September sales.

16.5 Flexible Budgeting

24. A static budget

A. Drops the current month or quarter and adds a future month or a future quarter as the current month or quarter is completed.

B. Presents a statement of expectations for a period but does not present a firm commitment.

C. Presents the plan for only one level of activity and does not adjust to changes in the level of activity.

D. Presents the plan for a range of activity so that the plan can be adjusted for changes in activity.

Answer (C) is correct.
  REQUIRED: The definition of a static budget.
  DISCUSSION: A static budget plans for only one level of activity and does not provide for changed levels of activity.
  Answer (A) is incorrect. Budgets dropping the current month or quarter and adding a future month or quarter as the current month or quarter is completed are continuous budgets. Answer (B) is incorrect. A statement of expectations for a period is a forecast. Answer (D) is incorrect. A budget planning for a range of activities so the plan can be adjusted for a change in activity level is a flexible budget.

25. The use of the master budget throughout the year as a constant comparison with actual results signifies that the master budget is also a

A. Flexible budget.

B. Capital budget.

C. Zero-based budget.

D. Static budget.

Answer (D) is correct.
  REQUIRED: The type of budget that is used throughout the year for comparison with actual results.
  DISCUSSION: If an unchanged master budget is used continuously throughout the year for comparison with actual results, it must be a static budget, that is, one prepared for just one level of activity.
  Answer (A) is incorrect. A flexible budget can be used in conjunction with standard costs to provide budgets for different activity levels. Answer (B) is incorrect. A capital budget addresses only long-term investments. Answer (C) is incorrect. A zero-based budget is one that requires its preparer to fully justify every item in the budget for each period.

26. Which one of the following statements regarding the difference between a flexible budget and a static budget is true?

A. A flexible budget primarily is prepared for planning purposes, while a static budget is prepared for performance evaluation.

B. A flexible budget provides cost allowances for different levels of activity, whereas a static budget provides costs for one level of activity.

C. A flexible budget includes only variable costs, whereas a static budget includes only fixed costs.

D. A flexible budget is established by operating management, while a static budget is determined by top management.

Answer (B) is correct.
REQUIRED: The difference between a flexible and a static budget.
DISCUSSION: A flexible budget provides cost allowances for different levels of activity, but a static budget provides costs for only one level of activity. Thus, a flexible budget conceptually is a series of budgets prepared for many different levels of activity.
Answer (A) is incorrect. Both budgets are prepared for both planning and performance evaluation purposes. Answer (C) is incorrect. Both budgets include both fixed and variable costs. Answer (D) is incorrect. Either budget can be established by any level of management.

27. RedRock Company uses flexible budgeting for cost control. RedRock produced 10,800 units of product during October, incurring indirect materials costs of $13,000. Its master budget for the year reflected indirect materials costs of $180,000 at a production volume of 144,000 units. A flexible budget for October production would reflect indirect materials costs of

A. $13,000

B. $13,500

C. $13,975

D. $11,700

Answer (B) is correct.
REQUIRED: The flexible budget amount of indirect materials cost for the month.
DISCUSSION: The cost of indirect materials for 144,000 units was expected to be $180,000. Consequently, the unit cost of indirect materials is $1.25 ($180,000 ÷ 144,000). Multiplying the $1.25 unit cost times the 10,800 units produced results in an expected total indirect materials cost of $13,500.
Answer (A) is incorrect. The actual cost of indirect materials in October is $13,000. Answer (C) is incorrect. The amount of $13,975 is not the flexible budget cost for indirect materials. Answer (D) is incorrect. The amount of $11,700 is not the flexible budget cost for indirect materials.

28. Flexible budgets

A. Provide for external factors affecting company profitability.

B. Are used to evaluate capacity use.

C. Are budgets that project costs based on anticipated future improvements.

D. Accommodate changes in activity levels.

Answer (D) is correct.
REQUIRED: The true statement about flexible budgets.
DISCUSSION: A flexible budget conceptually is a series of budgets prepared for various levels of activity. A flexible budget adjusts the master budget for changes in activity so that actual results can be compared with meaningful budget amounts.
Answer (A) is incorrect. Flexible budgets address external factors only to the extent that activity is affected. Answer (B) is incorrect. A flexible budget essentially restates variable costs for different activity levels within the relevant range. Thus, a flexible budget variance does not address capacity use. An output level (production volume) variance is a fixed cost variance. Answer (C) is incorrect. By definition, flexible budgets address differences in activity levels only within the relevant range.

16.6 PRACTICE WRITTEN COMMUNICATION

Business Environment and Concepts
Testlet 4 of 4

Time Remaining
1 hour - 15 minutes

Unsplit   Split Horiz   Split Vertical   Exit

DIRECTIONS

Note: If you believe you have encountered a software malfunction, report it to the test center staff immediately.

Navigation

To navigate from task to task, use the controls at the bottom of the screen. Click on the **Next** button to advance to the next task, or the **Previous** button to go to the previous task. To go directly to any task, click on its number.

▼ = Reminder   Directions   1 2 3 4 5 6 7   ◄ Previous   Next ►

If you would like a reminder to revisit a task, or want to indicate that you are finished with it, click on the reminder flag below the task number. To clear the flag, click on it again. Reminder flags are for your use only – they do not contribute to your score.

Tabs

In this part of the examination, you will be asked to complete various tasks. Every task has one or more **Work Tabs**. Every task also has a **Help** tab.

Written Communication   Help

Work tab   Help tab

Work Tabs:

- **Work Tabs** are identified with a pencil icon. This is where your responses are expected.
- Each task has one or more **Work Tabs**.
- **Work Tabs** contain directions for completing the task - be sure to read these directions carefully.
- The **Work Tab** name in the example above is for illustration only - yours will differ.
- You must complete all of the **Work Tabs** in each task to receive full credit.

Help Tab:

- The **Help Tab** provides assistance with the exam software that is used in this task. For example, if the task is to compose a memorandum, **Help** will provide information about the word processor.

The Toolbar

The toolbar at the top of the screen shows the amount of time remaining for you to complete the tasks. In addition, the following tools are available. Note that only the **Exit** button is displayed when Directions are visible - the others will appear when you begin the tasks.

Unsplit   Split Horiz   Split Vertical

Click on these buttons to split or unsplit the screen. You can split the screen vertically or horizontally.

Exit

Click on this button to go on to the next part of the examination. You must complete all of the tasks to receive full credit. Once you click on **Exit** and confirm the action, you will NOT be able to return to this testlet.

▼ = Reminder   Directions   1   ◄ Previous   Next ►

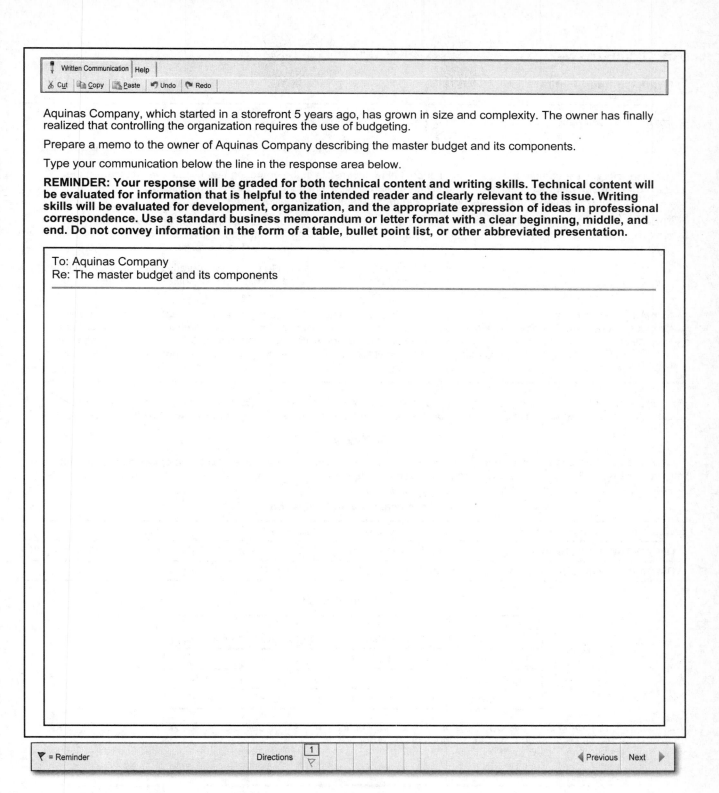

To: Aquinas Company
Re: The master budget and its components

NOTE: Your Written Communications on the actual CPA exam may cover topics outside the scope of the BEC CSO (i.e., they may relate to topics from the AUD, FAR, and/or REG instead). Answer to the best of your ability, and remember that graders are mainly evaluating your writing ability and will overlook minor technical mistakes.

Unofficial Answer

Written Communication

> To: Aquinas Company
> Re: The master budget and its components
>
> ---
>
> A master budget is a comprehensive, annual budget plan. It consists of the operating budget and the financial budget. Each of these sub-budgets consists of several interrelated component budgets. Thus, it is necessary to identify the elements of the operating and financial budgets and to understand their relationships.
>
> The operating budget focuses on obtaining and using current resources. The budgets that track this use are the sales, production, direct materials, direct labor, manufacturing overhead, ending finished goods inventory, cost of goods sold, and nonmanufacturing budgets. The data provided by these budgets are inputs to the pro forma income statement.
>
> The financial budget emphasizes the process of obtaining the funds needed to purchase operating assets. It contains the capital budget, the projected cash disbursement schedule, the projected cash collection schedule, and the cash budget. These items are inputs to the pro forma balance sheet and statement of cash flows.
>
> Identifying the components of the master budget is required to establish the budget calendar. Accordingly, a higher-level budget must be created before work can begin on the next level. For example, the production budget cannot be prepared until the sales budget is completed, and a projected cash collection schedule must be completed prior to preparing the cash budget. For this reason, the components of the operating and financial budgets must be understood before a master budget is prepared.

The above depicts a Level 5 answer. Consult your booklet, *How to Pass the CPA Exam: A System for Success*, for a description of the three writing skills criteria. You may also access this booklet online by visiting www.gleim.com/PassCPA.

Self-Grade

Below, grade your response on technical content and writing skills. Bubble in the circle next to the appropriate score that you may receive based on the criteria given. Your **total** score is the sum of your scores on all six items. The maximum score is 19 points.

Technical Content Evaluation

Was your response on topic?	O No [0]	O Mostly [1]	O Yes [2]
Did your response have any *significant* errors?	O 0 errors [1]	O 1 major error [–1]	O 2 or more major errors [–2]
Did your response contain any illegal advice?	O No [1]	O Yes [0]	

Writing Skills Evaluation

	Poor	Below Average	Average	Above Average	Outstanding
Organization	O 1	O 2	O 3	O 4	O 5
Development	O 1	O 2	O 3	O 4	O 5
Expression	O 1	O 2	O 3	O 4	O 5

Disclaimer: This scoring schedule was developed by Gleim Publications as a guideline only. The AICPA has not released specific information on how the Written Communications are graded.

Practice even more Written Communications with the Gleim Mega Test Bank.

Learn more: gleim.com/CPAmega | 800.874.5346

STUDY UNIT SEVENTEEN
PERFORMANCE MEASUREMENT AND PROCESS MANAGEMENT

(17 pages of outline)

Responsibility accounting allows each component of the organization to be judged based on the achievement of its own objectives. The performance of a responsibility center must be evaluated using appropriate criteria. Marketing incentives and executive compensation must be designed to inspire improvement in these criteria. The balanced scorecard is a tool for ensuring that the organization does not neglect some objectives in favor of others.

Much practical and theoretical innovation has occurred in business processes and the ways of monitoring their efficiency. Quality is a special area of management scrutiny. Its costs can be quantified, and frameworks have been developed for systematizing the pursuit of quality.

One of a manager's most important tasks is the monitoring of progress toward the completion of an individual project.

17.1 RESPONSIBILITY CENTERS

1. **Decision Making and Decentralization**

    a. The primary distinction between centralized and decentralized organizations is in the degree of freedom of decision making by managers.

    1) In a centralized organization, decision making is consolidated so that activities may be more effectively coordinated from the top.

    2) In a decentralized organization, decision making is at the lowest level possible. The premise is that the local manager can make more informed decisions than a manager farther from the decision.

2. **Responsibility Centers**

    a. A decentralized organization is divided into **responsibility centers** (also called **strategic business units**, or SBUs) to facilitate local decision making. Four types of responsibility centers generally are recognized.

    1) A **cost center**, e.g., a maintenance department, is responsible for costs only.

        a) Cost drivers are the relevant performance measures.

        b) A disadvantage of a cost center is the potential for cost shifting, for example, replacement of variable costs for which a manager is responsible with fixed costs for which (s)he is not.

        i) Another disadvantage is that long-term issues may be disregarded when the emphasis is on, for example, annual costs.

        c) Allocation of service department costs to cost centers is another issue. Service centers provide specialized support to other organizational subunits. They usually are operated as cost centers.

      2) A **revenue center**, e.g., a sales department, is responsible for revenues only.

         a) Revenue drivers are the relevant performance measures. They are factors that influence unit sales, such as (1) changes in prices and products, (2) customer service, (3) marketing efforts, and (4) delivery terms.

      3) A **profit center**, e.g., an appliance department in a retail store, is responsible for revenues and expenses.

      4) An **investment center**, e.g., a branch office, is responsible for revenues, expenses, and invested capital.

         a) The performance of an investment center can be compared with that of other responsibility centers or other potential investments on a return on investment basis. ROI measures the effectiveness of asset usage.

3. **Performance Measures and Manager Motivation**

    a. In a responsibility center, a logical group of operations is directed by one manager.

      1) Measures are designed for every responsibility center to monitor performance.

    b. **Controllability.** The performance measures on which the manager's compensation is based should be, to the extent practicable, under the manager's influence.

      1) Controllable factors are those a manager can influence in a given period.

         a) But some costs, for example, the costs of central administration, cannot be traced to particular activities or responsibility centers.

         b) Most costs, revenues, etc., are not wholly controlled by one manager. They may be influenced by (1) factors external to the organization (e.g., prices of materials), (2) a team of managers, or (3) a person with no authority over incurrence of the cost (e.g., a purchasing manager with expert knowledge of price changes).

      2) Controllable cost is not synonymous with variable cost. Often, this classification depends on the level of the organization.

         a) For example, the fixed cost of depreciation may not be controllable by the manager of a revenue center. But it is controllable by the division vice president to which that manager reports.

    c. **Goal congruence.** Performance measures must be designed so that they relate directly to accomplishment of the organization's goals.

      1) Suboptimization results when the goals of segments of the organization differ from the organization's goals.

4. **Common Costs**

    a. Common costs are the costs of products, activities, facilities, services, or operations shared by two or more cost objects. Joint costs are the common costs of a single process that yields two or more joint products.

      1) The costs of service centers and central administration are examples.

    b. Because common costs are indirect, identification of a direct cause-and-effect relationship with the actions of the cost object to which it is allocated can be difficult.

      1) Such a relationship promotes acceptance of common cost allocation by managers who perceive the fairness of the procedure.

5. **Management Reporting**

    a. Relevance is the most important attribute of management reporting. Relevance is determined by whether a revenue or cost element depends on a manager's decision.

Stop and review! You have completed the outline for this subunit. Study multiple-choice questions 1 through 4 beginning on page 451.

17.2 PERFORMANCE MEASURES, INCENTIVES, AND THE BALANCED SCORECARD

1. **Financial vs. Nonfinancial Measures**

   a. The appropriate financial performance measures vary with the type of responsibility center.

      1) Cost centers -- Variable costs, total costs
      2) Revenue centers -- Gross sales, net sales
      3) Profit centers -- Sales, gross margin, operating income
      4) Investment centers

         a) Return on investment, residual income
         b) Return on assets, return on common equity, economic rate of return on common stock, economic value added

   b. Nonfinancial performance measures are not standardized and thus can take any appropriate form.

2. **Effect of Marketing on Performance**

   a. Performance measurement should be consistent with marketing goals.

      1) Sales is the typical performance measure for a revenue center.
      2) For a profit center, sales, gross margin, and operating income should be evaluated.

      Calculation of Profit Center Operating Income

Net sales	$1,000,000
Cost of goods sold	(650,000)
Gross margin	$ 350,000
Controllable expenses	(200,000)
Operating income	$ 150,000

   b. If an overall goal is to increase market share, prices and gross margins are likely to be cut. Thus, profit center managers should be evaluated based on sales results, not margins.

      1) But if profits have the highest priority, operating income is a more appropriate measure. The manager is responsible for balancing sales, cost of goods sold, and controllable expenses.

   c. Choices among marketing practices also must be considered.

      1) The flexibility granted to salespeople in matters of price affects margins and operating income.
      2) Highly centralized marketing, such as advertising to improve brand awareness, increases the difficulty of tracing marketing costs to profit centers.

3. **Incentive Compensation**

   a. Management compensation generally has three components: (1) annual salary, (2) fringe benefits, and (3) annual bonus.

      1) Ideally, these components should motivate the manager to achieve the goals of the responsibility center. They in turn should be aligned with those of the organization.

   b. Salary is base pay, i.e., contractually obligated to be paid for effort and not affected by outcomes.

    c.   Fringe benefits for most employees include medical insurance, life insurance, and paid vacation.

        1)   However, managers must motivate all employees of a responsibility center to achieve goals. The incentive provided to a manager therefore should be proportional to the effort required.

        2)   Benefits for upper management may include use of a vehicle, travel by airplane, use of a resort home, etc.

    d.   The annual bonus ordinarily relates to the main performance measure for the responsibility center.

        1)   Bonuses for upper management often relate to the stock price. Return on investment and residual income also may be considered.

        2)   For profit centers, operating income (segment contribution) is the most appropriate basis for the annual bonus.

4.   **Balanced Scorecard -- Critical Success Factors (CSFs)**

    a.   The trend in performance evaluation is the balanced scorecard approach to managing the implementation of the firm's strategy.

        1)   The balanced scorecard is an accounting report that connects the firm's CSFs with measurements of its performance.

    b.   The balanced scorecard is a goal congruence tool that informs managers about the nonfinancial factors that upper management believes to be important.

        1)   Measures on the balanced scorecard may be financial or nonfinancial, internal or external, and short-term or long-term.

        2)   The balanced scorecard facilitates best practice analysis. Best practices are methods of performing a business function that are superior to all other known methods.

    c.   CSFs are specific, measurable financial and nonfinancial, internal and external, short-term and long-term elements of performance that are vital to competitive advantage.

        1)   Multiple measures of performance determine whether a manager is achieving certain objectives but not others that may be more important. For example, an improvement in operating results at the expense of new product development is apparent using a balanced scorecard.

5.   **SWOT Analysis**

    a.   A firm identifies its CSFs by means of a SWOT analysis that addresses internal factors (its strengths and weaknesses) and external factors (its opportunities and threats).

        1)   An outline of SWOT analysis is in Study Unit 15, Subunit 1.

6.   **Balanced Scorecard -- Measures**

    a.   Specific measures for each CSF should be relevant to the success of the firm and reliably stated.

        1)   Thus, the balanced scorecard varies with the strategy adopted by the firm.

    b.   The scorecard should include **lagging** indicators (such as output and financial measures) and **leading** indicators (such as many types of nonfinancial measures).

        1)   The latter should be used only if they are predictors of ultimate financial performance.

   c.　The scorecard should permit a determination of whether certain objectives are being achieved at the expense of others.

   1)　For example, reduced spending on customer service may improve short-term financial results at a significant cost that is revealed by a long-term decline in customer satisfaction measures.

7.　**Possible CSFs and Measures**

   a.　A typical balanced scorecard classifies objectives into one of four perspectives:

   1)　**Financial**

Possible CSF	Possible Measure
Sales	New Product Sales
FV of Firm's Stock	Price-Earnings Ratio
Profits	Return on Investment
Liquidity	Quick Ratio

   2)　**Customer Satisfaction**

CSF	Financial Measure	Nonfinancial Measure
Customer Satisfaction	Trends in dollar amounts of returns	Market share
Dealer and Distributor Relationships	Trends in dollar amounts of discounts taken	Lead time
Marketing and Selling Performance	Trends in dollar amounts of sales	Market research results
Prompt Delivery	Trends in delivery expenses	On-time delivery rate
Quality	Dollar amounts of defects	Rate of defects

   3)　**Internal Business Processes**

CSF	Financial Measure	Nonfinancial Measure
Quality	Scrap costs	Rate of scrap and rework
Productivity	Change in company revenue/ change in company costs	Units produced per machine hour
Flexibility of Response to Changing Conditions	Cost to re-purpose machine for new use	Time to repurpose machine for new use
Operating Readiness	Set-up costs	Downtime
Safety	Dollar amount of injury claims	Number of injury claims

   4)　**Learning and Growth**

CSF	Financial Measure	Nonfinancial Measure
Development of New Products	R&D costs	Number of new patents applied for
Promptness of Their Introduction	Lost revenue (from slow introduction of new product to market)	Length of time to bring a product to market
Human Resource Development	Recruiting costs	Personnel turnover
Morale	Orientation/team-building costs	Personnel complaints
Competence of Work Force	Training/retraining costs	Hours of training

8.   **Development**

   a.   The active participation of senior management is essential.

      1)   This involvement ensures the cooperation of lower-level managers in the identification of objectives, appropriate measures, targeted results, and methods of achieving the results.

   b.   The scorecard should contain measures at the detail level that permits everyone to understand how his or her efforts affect the firm's results.

      1)   The scorecard and the strategy it represents must be communicated to all managers and used as a basis for compensation decisions.

9.   **Functionality**

   a.   Each objective is associated with one or more measures that permit the organization to measure progress toward the objective.

      1)   The organization should identify a cause-and-effect relationship between an action taken (or avoided), that affects a CSF.

         a)   For example, if the R&D budget increases, the number of new patents applied for increases.

      2)   Achievement of the objectives in one perspective makes it possible to achieve the objectives in other perspectives.

      3)   A **strategy map** relates objectives and perspectives.

   b.   To achieve its objectives, the organization must establish relevant

      1)   Criteria to measure outcomes
      2)   Performance drivers

The AICPA has tested the balanced scorecard approach by asking for the perspective related to either measures or CSFs.

EXAMPLE of a Balanced Scorecard

OBJECTIVES	PERFORMANCE MEASURES	TARGETS	INITIATIVES
PERSPECTIVE: Financial			
Increase sales	Gross revenues	Increase 15%	• Expand into new markets • Improve same-store sales
PERSPECTIVE: Customer Satisfaction			
Reduce returns	Number of returns	Decrease 10%	• Reduce number of defects • Determine customer needs prior to sale
PERSPECTIVE: Internal Business Processes			
Reduce scrap	Costs of scrap	Decrease 5%	• Employee training • Seek higher quality materials
PERSPECTIVE: Learning and Growth			
Reduce personal turnover	Length of time employed	Increase 50%	• Improve hiring practices • Reevaluate compensation plan

Stop and review! You have completed the outline for this subunit. Study multiple-choice questions 5 through 8 beginning on page 452.

17.3 PROCESS MANAGEMENT

1. **Performance-Improving Processes**

   a. The Process-Management-Driven Business

      1) Management emphasizes the effective and efficient performance of predefined business processes.

      2) Well-designed processes lead to the accomplishment of the organization's goals.

   b. Shared Services

      1) Shared services are centralized but with a nontraditional focus.

      2) The shared services model involves designing the service center so that its employees are motivated to be flexible and responsive to customer needs.

      3) Centralizing a firm's internal services at a single location may delay services.

   c. Outsourcing

      1) Processes such as human resources, payroll, and information services may not be core competencies of an organization.

         a) Contracting with outside service providers who specialize in these functions may result in cost savings. The organization also is not affected by knowledge loss when key employees leave.

      2) Potential disadvantages include (a) loss of core knowledge, (b) loss of control over the outsourced function, (c) unexpected costs, and (d) the challenges of contract management.

   d. Off-Shore Operations

      1) Cost advantages (lower taxes, lower wages, and less strict environmental and occupational safety regulations) can be gained by moving operations to foreign countries.

      2) The effects of currency exchange rate fluctuations and the possibility of political instability must be considered.

2. **Business Process Reengineering (BPR)**

   a. BPR is the complete, bottom-up revision of the way an organization performs a business process.

   b. Organizations undertaking BPR ignore how the process currently is performed.

   c. BPR is **not**

      1) A gradual, incremental streamlining of existing procedures (kaizen);
      2) Computerization of manual processes (automation); or
      3) A change in the nature of the business itself (paradigm shift).

   d. The goals of BPR are usually stated in terms of increased efficiency or elimination of redundant jobs. These goals eventually can be stated in terms of cost savings.

   e. But BPR often does not provide the promised benefits.

      1) Business processes routinely cross organizational boundaries.

         a) Redesigning the process of one department often requires the cooperation of other departments that may be reluctant to reduce their autonomy.

      2) Upper management may have begun other strategic initiatives, such as total quality management or Six Sigma, that conflict with either the goals of, or the resources necessary for, BPR.

         a) Any BPR program must be closely aligned with the overall organizational strategy.

3. **Lean Operation**

    a.   The ultimate goal of lean operation is a smooth, rapid flow of work through the system. To achieve this ultimate goal, three supporting goals are constantly pursued.

        1)   Elimination of Disruptions

            a)   A disruption is anything that interrupts the smooth flow of work, e.g., line stoppages, materials shortages, and excessive defects.

        2)   System Flexibility

            a)   A flexible system can be adapted to changes in product mix or quantities without creating a disruption.

        3)   Elimination of Waste

            a)   Waste is any unproductive use of resources. In accordance with a just-in-time philosophy, inventory is considered waste.

4. **Demand Flow Technology (DFT)**

    a.   Demand flow technology is a mathematically based approach devised in the 1980s by operations management expert John Costanza.

    b.   DFT combines knowledge of materials and work-in-process inventory levels with customer demand to maximize use of the firm's productive capacity, i.e., to maintain continuous production flow.

        1)   In contrast with the forecast-push model used by MRP described in Study Unit 8, Subunit 8, DFT is a pull system driven by customer demand.

5. **Theory of Constraints (TOC)**

    a.   The theory of constraints is a system to improve human thinking about problems. It has been greatly extended to include manufacturing operations.

        1)   The basic premise of TOC as applied to business is that improving any process is best done not by trying to maximize efficiency in every part of the process but by focusing on a limiting factor, called the constraint (or bottleneck operation).

EXAMPLE

During the early days of the American Civil War, several units calling themselves legions were formed, consisting of combined infantry, artillery, and cavalry. This arrangement did not last because the entire unit could only maneuver as fast as the slowest part. The artillery was the constraint.

---

        2)   Increasing the efficiency of processes that are not constraints merely creates backup in the system.

    b.   The following are the steps in a TOC analysis:

        1)   Identify the constraint.
        2)   Determine the most profitable product mix given the constraint.
        3)   Maximize the flow through the constraint.
        4)   Increase capacity at the constraint.
        5)   Redesign the manufacturing process for greater flexibility and speed.

    c.   A basic principle of TOC analysis is that short-term profit maximization requires maximizing the contribution margin through the constraint (throughput contribution).

        1)   Thus, the product with the highest output should be the one with the highest throughput contribution per unit, not necessarily the highest contribution margin per unit.

d. To determine the most profitable use of the bottleneck operation, a manager calculates the throughput contribution per unit of time spent in the constraint.

1) Profits are maximized by maximizing the flow through the bottleneck operation of the product with the highest throughput contribution per unit of time.

6. **Six Sigma**

a. Six Sigma is a quality improvement approach. The goal is to reduce the number of defects in a mass-production process.

1) The name Six Sigma (sometimes written 6σ) is derived from statistics and probability theory. In a normal distribution (i.e., a bell curve), six standard deviations encompass 99.99966% of the items in the distribution.

2) Because of the importance of statistical analysis in any Six Sigma program, accurate and verifiable data are a necessity.

b. A Six Sigma program also involves role-filling by specific individuals in the organization.

1) The executive level must demonstrate its commitment to the Six Sigma program and must empower those in the other roles with enough authority and resources to implement the program successfully.

2) Champions have responsibility for oversight of the implementation of the Six Sigma program across the organization.

3) Master black belts assist the champions in implementing the program.

4) Black belts, like champions and master black belts, devote all of their time to the Six Sigma program. They oversee specific projects.

5) Green belts and yellow belts do Six Sigma work in addition to their regular duties. They are closest to the production processes to be improved.

Stop and review! You have completed the outline for this subunit. Study multiple-choice questions 9 through 12 beginning on page 453.

17.4 TOOLS FOR PROCESS MEASUREMENT

 Past exam questions have asked for identification of the methods used to measure process performance.

1. **Statistical Process Control (SPC)**

a. SPC is a method of quality control that uses statistical methods.

b. Results of an operation are monitored to determine whether it is within certain limits or at certain capacities.

c. SPC can be applied to any process in which a conforming product can be measured.

d. The information learned from SPC should be used in planning and budgeting.

2. **Statistical Control Charts**

a. Statistical control charts are graphic aids for monitoring the status of any process subject to acceptable or unacceptable variations during repeated operations.

1) They also have applications of direct interest to auditors and accountants, for example, (a) unit cost of production, (b) direct labor hours used, (c) ratio of actual expenses to budgeted expenses, (d) number of calls by sales personnel, or (e) total accounts receivable.

b.   A control chart consists of three lines plotted on a horizontal time scale.

1)   The center line represents the overall mean or average range for the process being controlled. The other two lines are the upper control limit (UCL) and the lower control limit (LCL).

2)   The processes are measured periodically, and the values (X) are plotted on the chart.

a)   If the value falls within the control limits, no action is taken.

b)   If the value falls outside the limits, the result is abnormal, the process is considered out of control, and an investigation is made for possible corrective action.

c.   Another advantage of the chart is that it makes trends and cycles visible.

1)   A disadvantage of the chart is that it does not indicate the cause of the variation.

EXAMPLE

The chart below depicts 2 weeks of production by a manufacturer who produces a single precision part each day. To be salable, the part can vary from the standard by no more than +/– 0.1 millimeter.

Figure 17-1

The part produced on the 20th had to be scrapped, and changes were made to the equipment to return the process to the controlled state for the following week's production.

---

3.   **Pareto Diagrams**

a.   A Pareto diagram is a bar chart that assists managers in quality control analysis.

1)   In the context of quality control, managers optimize their time by focusing their effort on the relatively few sources of the most defects.

a)   The independent variable, plotted on the x axis, is the factor selected by the manager as the subject of interest, e.g., a department, time period, or geographical location. The frequency of occurrence of the defect (dependent variable) is plotted on the y axis.

b)   The occurrences of the independent variable are ranked from highest to lowest, allowing the manager to observe the sources of the most defects.

EXAMPLE

The chief administrative officer wants to know which departments are generating the most travel vouchers that have to be returned to the submitter because of incomplete documentation.

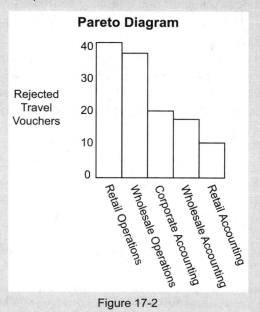

Figure 17-2

4. Histograms

a. A histogram is similar to a Pareto diagram. The major distinction is that histograms display a continuum for the independent variable.

EXAMPLE

The CAO wants to know the amount of a typical rejected travel voucher.

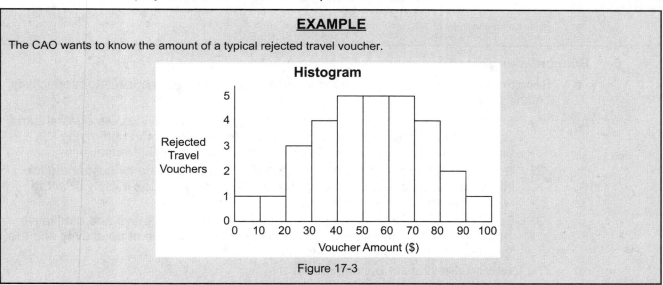

Figure 17-3

5. **Fishbone Diagrams**

    a. A fishbone diagram (also called a cause-and-effect diagram) is a total quality management process improvement method that is useful in studying causation (why the actual and desired situations differ).

        1) The diagram organizes the analysis of causation and helps to identify possible interactions among causes.

        2) The head of the skeleton represents the statement of the problem.

        3) The principal classifications of causes are represented by lines (bones) drawn diagonally from the heavy horizontal line (the spine).

        4) Smaller horizontal lines are added in their order of probability in each classification.

EXAMPLE

Fishbone Diagram

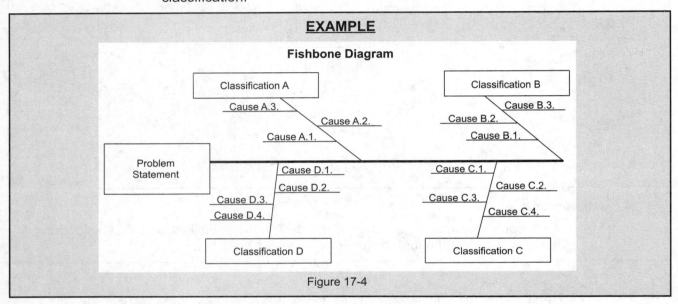

Figure 17-4

---

6. **Benchmarking**

    a. Benchmarking is a primary tool used in quality management. It applies to productivity management and business process analysis.

        1) Benchmarking involves analysis and measurement of key outputs against those of the best organizations. This procedure also identifies the underlying key actions and causes that contribute to the performance difference.

        2) Best practices are recognized by authorities in the field and by customers for their outstanding results. They generally are innovative technically or in the management of human resources.

        3) Benchmarking is an ongoing process that requires quantitative and qualitative measurement of the difference between the performance of an activity and the performance by the benchmark.

    b. The following are kinds of benchmarking:

        1) Competitive benchmarking studies an organization in the same industry.

        2) Process (function) benchmarking studies operations of organizations with similar processes regardless of industry. Thus, the benchmark need not be a competitor or even a similar entity.

            a) This method may introduce new ideas that provide a significant competitive advantage.

        3) Strategic benchmarking is a search for successful competitive strategies.

        4) Internal benchmarking is the application of best practices in one part of the organization to its other parts.

7. **Gamification**

    a.   This method of problem solving involves thinking of business goals as if they were goals in a game, such as achieving a higher return on investment.

        1)   Rewards are given to players who achieve certain goals.

            a)   **Scores** can be published so that players are encouraged to compete.

            b)   Due to the possibility that increased competition could lead to unethical behavior, the game should be monitored.

EXAMPLE

A team from an airline company charged with improving its aircraft ground turnaround time (refueling, maintenance, and service) might consider the benchmark of auto racing's pit stops and determine the applicability of their best practices.

Stop and review! You have completed the outline for this subunit. Study multiple-choice questions 13 through 16 beginning on page 454.

17.5 COSTS OF QUALITY

1. **Costs of Quality**

    a.   The costs of quality must be assessed in terms of relative costs and benefits. Thus, an organization should attempt to minimize its total cost of quality.

        1)   Moreover, nonquantitative factors also must be considered. For example, an emphasis on quality improves competitiveness, enhances employee expertise, and generates goodwill.

2. **Categories**

    a.   **Conformance costs** include costs of prevention and costs of appraisal, which are financial measures of internal performance.

        1)   **Prevention** attempts to avoid defective output. These costs include (a) preventive maintenance, (b) employee training, (c) review of equipment design, and (d) evaluation of suppliers.

        2)   **Appraisal** includes such activities as statistical quality control programs, inspection, and testing.

    b.   **Nonconformance costs** include internal failure costs (a financial measure of internal performance) and external failure costs (a financial measure of customer satisfaction).

        1)   **Internal failure costs** occur when defective products are detected before shipment. Examples are scrap, rework, tooling changes, and downtime.

        2)   **External failure costs**, e.g., warranty costs, product liability costs, and loss of customer goodwill, result when problems occur after shipment.

            a)   Environmental costs also are external failure costs, e.g., fines for nonadherence to environmental law and loss of customer goodwill.

EXAMPLE

Conformance costs:	
Prevention costs	$35,000
Appraisal costs	5,000
Nonconformance costs:	
Internal failure costs	17,500
External failure costs	9,500
Total costs of quality	**$67,000**

Stop and review! You have completed the outline for this subunit. Study multiple-choice questions 17 through 22 beginning on page 455.

17.6 TQM AND THE ISO FRAMEWORK

1. **Total Quality Management (TQM) Defined**

    a. TQM is the continuous pursuit of quality in every aspect of organizational activities through (1) a philosophy of doing it right the first time, (2) employee training and empowerment, (3) promotion of teamwork, (4) improvement of processes, and (5) attention to satisfaction of internal and external customers.

    1) TQM emphasizes the supplier's relationship with the customer and identifies customer needs. It also recognizes that everyone in a process is at some time a customer or supplier of someone else, either within or outside the organization.

    2) Thus, TQM (a) begins with external customer requirements, (b) identifies internal customer-supplier relationships and requirements, and (c) establishes requirements for external suppliers.

    3) Organizations tend to be vertically organized, but TQM requires strong horizontal linkages.

Background

TQM was developed in the mid-1940s by statistician W. Edwards Deming, who aided Japanese industry in its recovery from World War II. The Deming Prize is awarded by the Union of Japanese Scientists and Engineers for outstanding contributions to the study or application of TQM (www.juse.or.jp/deming_en). While Deming was praised and deeply respected in Japan, it took 30 years for his principles to be applied in the U.S.

---

    b. TQM treats the pursuit of quality as a basic organizational function that is as important as production or marketing.

    c. TQM recognizes that quality improvement can increase revenues and decrease costs significantly. The following are TQM's core principles or critical factors:

    1) Emphasis on the customer

        a) Satisfaction of external customers
        b) Satisfaction of internal customers
        c) Requirements for external suppliers
        d) Requirements for internal suppliers

    2) Continuous improvement as a never-ending process, not a destination

    3) Engaging every employee in the pursuit of total quality

        a) Avoidance of defects in products or services and satisfaction of external customers requires that all internal customers be satisfied.

    d. The management of quality is not limited to quality management staff, engineers, and production personnel. It extends to everyone in the organization.

2. **Implementation**

    a. Implementation of TQM cannot be accomplished by application of a formula, and the process is lengthy and difficult. The following phases are typical:

    1) Establishing an executive-level quality council of senior managers with strong involvement by the CEO.

    2) Providing quality training programs for senior managers.

    3) Conducting a quality audit to evaluate the success of the process for gathering background information to develop the strategic quality improvement plan.

        a) The quality audit also may identify the best improvement opportunities and the organization's strengths and weaknesses compared with its benchmarked competitors.

4) Preparing a gap analysis to determine what is necessary to close the gap between the organization and the quality leaders in its industry and to establish a database for the development of the strategic quality improvement plan.

5) Developing strategic quality improvement plans for the short and long term.

6) Conducting employee communication and training programs.

7) Establishing quality teams, which ensure that goods and services conform to specifications.

8) Creating a measurement system and setting goals.

9) Revising compensation, appraisal, and recognition systems.

10) Reviewing and revising the entire effort periodically.

3. **The ISO Standards**

   a. In 1987, the International Organization for Standardization (ISO) introduced ISO 9000, a group of 11 standards and technical reports that provide guidance for establishing and maintaining a **quality management system** (QMS). The ISO's rules specify that its standards be revised every 5 years to reflect technological and market developments.

Background

ISO is not an acronym. It means equal, suggesting that entities certified under ISO standards have equal quality. For specific and up-to-date information, see the ISO's website (www.iso.org).

---

   b. The intent of the standards is to ensure the quality of the process, not the product. The marketplace determines whether a product is good or bad.

   1) For this reason, the ISO deems it unacceptable for phrases referring to ISO certification to appear on individual products or packaging.

   c. Basic Requirements of an ISO QMS

   1) Key processes affecting quality must be identified and included.

      a) A process management approach must be used. It manages the entity as a set of linked processes that are controlled for continuous improvement.

   2) General requirements. The entity must have a quality policy and quality goals. It also must design a QMS to control process performance. Quality goals are measurable and specific.

      a) The QMS is documented in the (1) quality policy, (2) quality manual, (3) procedures, (4) work instructions, and (5) records.

   3) Management responsibility. Management (a) reviews the quality policy, (b) analyzes data about QMS performance, and (c) assesses opportunities for improvement and the need for change.

      a) Management ensures that systems exist to determine and satisfy customer requirements.

   4) Resource management. The resources needed to improve the QMS and satisfy customer requirements must be provided.

   5) Product realization processes result in products or services received by customers. These processes must be planned and controlled. Issues are (a) means of control, (b) objectives, (c) documentation and records needed, and (d) acceptance criteria.

   6) Measurement, analysis, and improvement. The entity must have processes for (a) inspection, (b) testing, (c) measurement, (d) analysis, and (e) improvement.

Stop and review! You have completed the outline for this subunit. Study multiple-choice questions 23 through 26 beginning on page 457.

17.7 PROJECT MANAGEMENT

1. **Project Management**

   a. A project is a temporary undertaking with specified objectives that often involves a cross-functional team and working outside customary organizational lines. Thus, interpersonal skills are required in project management because a manager may not have line authority over some team members.

      1) Examples include (a) building construction, (b) R&D projects, (c) new product planning, (d) feasibility studies, (e) audit studies, (f) movie production, and (g) conversion to a new computer information system.

      2) Project management aids the planning and control of large-scale projects having many interrelated activities.

   b. Four distinct roles for those participating in the project can be identified:

      1) The steering committee consists of the managers who decide which projects should be undertaken. Once a project is approved, the committee's function is to demand accountability regarding the project's progress.

      2) The project sponsor (project champion) defines the project and provides the business justification for it to the steering committee. The project sponsor is vested with sufficient authority by upper management to allocate the resources to ensure successful completion. The sponsor's mandate includes compelling cooperation across departmental boundaries to achieve the project's goals.

      3) The project manager oversees the day-to-day activities of the project team and ensures that project deliverables are ready for the sponsor to present to the steering committee on time.

      4) Project team members often must continue performing their regular job duties while simultaneously committing some portion of their time to the project. Obtaining cooperation from the project members' immediate supervisors is therefore crucial to the success of a project.

   c. Project management consists of the following five principal tasks:

      1) Authorization establishes through the project charter the scope, objectives, and stakeholders in a project and defines the responsibilities and authority of the project manager.

      2) Planning determines goals and their due dates and schedules available resources.

      3) Implementation puts the plan into effect and directs resources to the proper activities.

      4) Monitoring corrects, meets expectations, and finishes the project within the time and budgetary limits.

      5) Closing confirms the completion of the project to the satisfaction of the relevant stakeholders.

   d. The risk of an unsuccessful project can be analyzed in terms of the following:

      1) Ensuring resources. Resources consist of personnel, equipment, computer processing time, and sometimes cash.

      2) Maintaining scope. **Scope creep** often affects projects in organizations. The temptation is to continue adding functions to a new system or process. Keeping project members focused on the approved goals (and timetable) of the project is a crucial responsibility of the project manager.

      3) Controlling cost. The cost of a project must be measured in the opportunity cost of employee time and cash spent on new equipment.

      4) Providing deliverables. A deliverable may be as simple as a one-page written report or as complex as an installation of enterprise-wide software. Most large-scale projects have deliverables at the completion of each stage of the project to ensure that the process remains on schedule.

e. Project management is the process of managing the trade-off between the two major inputs (time and cost) and the major output (quality). The project management triangle graphically depicts this relationship.

Project Management Triangle

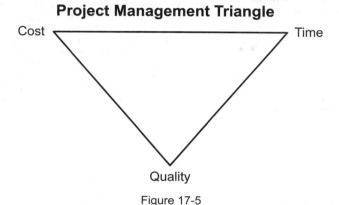

Figure 17-5

1) The implication is that a high-quality deliverable can be achieved only by (a) devoting a large number of employee hours to a project or (b) spending a lot of money.

EXAMPLE

In the days before widespread computer use, old-fashioned job-order print shops used to display signs saying, "You Want It Fast -- Cheap -- Correct. Pick Two."

Designers of submarines often speak of their classic trade-off of depth, speed, and stealth. A vessel with sufficient shielding to be silent and to survive at great depths is too heavy to go very fast.

---

f. Project management software is available. Among other things, it should

1) Specify and schedule required activities
2) Provide the ability to do sensitivity analysis of the effects of changes in plans
3) Calculate a project's critical path
4) Establish priorities
5) Be able to modify or merge plans
6) Manage all types of project resources
7) Monitor progress, including adherence to time budgets for activities

Stop and review! You have completed the outline for this subunit. Study multiple-choice questions 27 through 30 beginning on page 458.

QUESTIONS

17.1 Responsibility Centers

1. If a manufacturing company uses responsibility centers, which one of the following items is **least** likely to appear in a performance report for a manager of an assembly line?

A. Supervisory salaries.

B. Materials.

C. Repairs and maintenance.

D. Equipment depreciation.

Answer (D) is correct.

REQUIRED: The item least likely to appear in a performance report for the manager of an assembly line.

DISCUSSION: Responsibility centers hold managers responsible for factors they can influence. The depreciation of equipment will probably not appear on the performance report of an assembly-line manager because the manager usually has no influence over the investment in the equipment.

Answer (A) is incorrect. The manager of an assembly line is likely to be responsible for the salaries of supervisors, which are to some degree influenced by the manager. Answer (B) is incorrect. The manager of an assembly line is likely to be responsible for materials, which are to some degree influenced by the manager. Answer (C) is incorrect. The manager of an assembly line is likely to be responsible for repairs and maintenance, which are to some degree influenced by the manager.

2. A segment of an organization is referred to as a profit center if it has

    A. Authority to make decisions affecting the major determinants of profit including the power to choose its markets and sources of supply.

    B. Authority to make decisions affecting the major determinants of profit including the power to choose its markets and sources of supply and significant control over the amount of invested capital.

    C. Authority to make decisions over the most significant costs of operations including the power to choose the sources of supply.

    D. Authority to provide specialized support to other units within the organization.

Answer (A) is correct.
    REQUIRED: The definition of a profit center.
    DISCUSSION: A profit center is responsible for both revenues and expenses. For example, the perfume department in a department store is a profit center. The manager of a profit center usually has the authority to make decisions affecting the major determinants of profit, including the power to choose markets (revenue sources) and suppliers (costs).
    Answer (B) is incorrect. An investment center, not a profit center, has control over invested capital. Answer (C) is incorrect. A cost center manager has authority over all significant costs but not of revenues or investments. Answer (D) is incorrect. A service center supports other organizational units.

3. Managers are most likely to accept allocations of common costs based on

    A. Cause and effect.

    B. Ability to bear.

    C. Percent of revenues earned.

    D. Top management decisions.

Answer (A) is correct.
    REQUIRED: The criterion most likely to result in acceptable allocations of common costs.
    DISCUSSION: The difficulty with common costs is that they are indirect costs whose allocation may be arbitrary. A direct cause-and-effect relationship between a common cost and the actions of the cost object to which it is allocated is desirable. Such a relationship promotes acceptance of the allocation by managers who perceive the fairness of the procedure, but identification of cause and effect may not be feasible.
    Answer (B) is incorrect. Allocation using an ability-to-bear criterion punishes successful managers and rewards underachievers. Answer (C) is incorrect. Allocations based on the percentage of revenues earned use an ability-to-bear approach. Answer (D) is incorrect. Top management decisions on cost allocation tend to be arbitrary.

4. Which criterion for allocation of common costs most likely promotes acceptance of the allocation?

    A. Direct cause-and-effect relationship.

    B. Benefit-received relationship.

    C. Ability-to-bear relationship.

    D. Arbitrary allocation.

Answer (A) is correct.
    REQUIRED: The criterion for allocation of common costs most likely to promote acceptance of the allocation.
    DISCUSSION: Establishment of a direct cause-and-effect relationship often is the most accepted allocation by managers because of the perceived fairness of the procedure.
    Answer (B) is incorrect. The benefit-received criterion lacks the clear cause-and-effect relationship that many managers desire. However, the benefit-received criterion is still likely to be accepted because of the equitable treatment of the costs allocated. Answer (C) is incorrect. The ability-to-bear criterion rewards underachievers and penalizes successful managers and is likely be perceived as unfair. Answer (D) is incorrect. Managers often do not perceive arbitrary allocation to be fair. Arbitrary allocation is considered the least desired form of allocation by managers.

17.2 Performance Measures, Incentives, and the Balanced Scorecard

5. Management of a company is attempting to build a reputation as a world-class manufacturer of quality products. Which of the following measures would **not** be used by the firm to measure quality?

    A. The percentage of shipments returned by customers because of poor quality.

    B. The number of parts shipped per day.

    C. The number of defective parts per million.

    D. The percentage of products passing quality tests the first time.

Answer (B) is correct.
    REQUIRED: The item not used for quality measurement.
    DISCUSSION: The number of parts shipped per day is most likely to be used as a measure of the effectiveness and efficiency of shipping procedures, not the quality of the product. This measure does not consider how many of the parts are defective.
    Answer (A) is incorrect. The percentage of shipments returned is a very useful direct measure of the number of unacceptable products. Answer (C) is incorrect. The number of defective parts per million, a simple and direct measure of poor quality, is likely to be used. Answer (D) is incorrect. The percentage of products passing quality tests the first time measures quality by the number of nondefective products.

6. In evaluating an investment center, top management should concentrate on

    A. Dollar sales.

    B. Net income.

    C. Profit percentages.

    D. Return on investment.

Answer (D) is correct.
    REQUIRED: The focus of management when evaluating an investment center.
    DISCUSSION: Each investment center of a business should be evaluated based upon return on investment to judge operating performance. ROI is comparable to calculations made both within and outside a particular organization. Management may review the investment opportunities available. In essence, net income is stated as a proportion of investment capital (resources required).
    Answer (A) is incorrect. Dollar sales do not give a measure of operating performance based on resources required. Answer (B) is incorrect. Net income does not give a measure of operating performance based on resources required. Answer (C) is incorrect. Profit percentages do not give a measure of operating performance based on resources required.

7. Using the balanced scorecard approach, an organization evaluates managerial performance based on

    A. A single ultimate measure of operating results, such as residual income.

    B. Multiple financial and nonfinancial measures.

    C. Multiple nonfinancial measures only.

    D. Multiple financial measures only.

Answer (B) is correct.
    REQUIRED: The nature of the balanced scorecard approach.
    DISCUSSION: The trend in managerial performance evaluation is the balanced scorecard approach. Multiple measures of performance permit a determination as to whether a manager is achieving certain objectives at the expense of others that may be equally or more important. These measures may be financial or nonfinancial and usually include items with four perspectives: (1) financial; (2) customer; (3) internal business processes; and (4) learning, growth, and innovation.

8. On a balanced scorecard, which is more of an internal process measure than an external-based measure?

    A. Cycle time.

    B. Profitability.

    C. Customer satisfaction.

    D. Market share.

Answer (A) is correct.
    REQUIRED: The measure more internal-process related on a balanced scorecard.
    DISCUSSION: Cycle time is the manufacturing time to complete an order. Thus, cycle time is strictly related to internal processes. Profitability is a combination of internal and external considerations. Customer satisfaction and market share are related to how customers perceive a product and how competitors react.
    Answer (B) is incorrect. Profitability is a measure that includes external considerations. Answer (C) is incorrect. Customer satisfaction is a measure that includes external considerations. Answer (D) is incorrect. Market share is a measure that includes external considerations.

17.3 Process Management

9. System flexibility, elimination of waste, and elimination of disruptions are characteristic goals of which business process?

    A. Lean operation.

    B. Six Sigma.

    C. Delphi technique.

    D. Monte Carlo technique.

Answer (A) is correct.
    REQUIRED: The business process with the characteristic goals of system flexibility, elimination of waste, and elimination of disruptions.
    DISCUSSION: The three supporting goals of lean operation are (1) elimination of disruptions, (2) system flexibility, and (3) elimination of waste. Inventory is considered a waste.
    Answer (B) is incorrect. The goal of Six Sigma is to reduce the number of defects per million opportunities in a mass-production process to 3.4. Answer (C) is incorrect. The Delphi technique is a system for forecasting based on identifying a consensus among experts. Answer (D) is incorrect. Monte Carlo is a system for using random variables for forecasting in an environment of uncertainty.

10. Champions, yellow belts, and master black belts are associated with which business process?

A. Business process reengineering.

B. Six Sigma.

C. Demand flow technology.

D. Kanban.

Answer (B) is correct.
REQUIRED: The business process associated with champions, yellow belts, and master black belts.
DISCUSSION: A Six Sigma program involves role-filling by specific individuals in the organization. Champions are responsible for overseeing the implementation of the Six Sigma program across the organization. Master black belts assist the champions in implementing the program. Green belts and yellow belts are the ones closest to the production processes that are being improved.
Answer (A) is incorrect. Champions, yellow belts, and master black belts are not associated with business process reengineering. Answer (C) is incorrect. Champions, yellow belts, and master black belts are not associated with demand flow technology. Answer (D) is incorrect. Champions, yellow belts, and master black belts are not associated with kanban.

11. Increasing the efficiency of all phases of a given process is specifically discouraged by which of the following models?

A. Lean operation.

B. Theory of constraints.

C. Six Sigma.

D. Demand flow technology.

Answer (B) is correct.
REQUIRED: The business process model that specifically discourages increasing the efficiency of all phases.
DISCUSSION: Under the theory of constraints, increasing the efficiency of processes that are not constraints (bottlenecks) merely creates backup in the system.
Answer (A) is incorrect. Lean operation does not specifically discourage increasing the efficiency of all phases. Answer (C) is incorrect. Six Sigma does not specifically discourage increasing the efficiency of all phases. Answer (D) is incorrect. Demand flow technology does not specifically discourage increasing the efficiency of all phases.

12. Which of the following is a characteristic of business process reengineering?

A. Gradual, incremental streamlining of existing procedures.

B. The movement of manual processes to computers.

C. A change in the nature of the business itself.

D. The bottom-up revision of the way the organization carries out a particular business process.

Answer (D) is correct.
REQUIRED: The characteristic of business process reengineering.
DISCUSSION: Business process reengineering (BPR) is the complete, bottom-up revision of the way an organization carries out a particular business process. Organizations undertaking BPR totally rethink how a particular business function should be carried out, without regard to how it is currently performed.
Answer (A) is incorrect. Gradual, incremental streamlining of existing procedures (kaizen) is specifically rejected by business process reengineering. Answer (B) is incorrect. Simply moving manual processes to computers (automation) is not a characteristic of business process engineering. Answer (C) is incorrect. A change in the nature of the business itself (paradigm shift) is not a characteristic of business process reengineering.

17.4 Tools for Process Measurement

13. The director of sales asks for a count of customers grouped in descending numerical rank by (1) the number of orders they place during a single year and (2) the dollar amounts of the average order. The visual format of these two pieces of information is most likely to be a(n)

A. Fishbone diagram.

B. Cost of quality report.

C. Kaizen diagram.

D. Pareto diagram.

Answer (D) is correct.
REQUIRED: The appropriate process measurement tool.
DISCUSSION: A Pareto diagram displays the values of an independent variable such that managers can quickly identify the areas most in need of attention.
Answer (A) is incorrect. A fishbone diagram is useful for determining the unknown causes of problems, not for stratifying quantifiable variables. Answer (B) is incorrect. The contents of a cost of quality report are stated in monetary terms. This report is not helpful for determining when to adjust machinery. Answer (C) is incorrect. Kaizen diagram is not a meaningful term in this context.

14. Which of the following statements regarding benchmarking is **false**?

A. Benchmarking involves continuously evaluating the practices of best-in-class organization and adapting processes to incorporate the best of these practices.

B. Benchmarking, in practice, usually involves formation of benchmarking teams.

C. Benchmarking is an ongoing process that involves quantitative and qualitative measurement of the difference between the organization's performance of an activity and the performance by the best in the world or the best in the industry.

D. The benchmarked organization against which a firm is comparing itself must be a direct competitor.

Answer (D) is correct.
    REQUIRED: The false statement about benchmarking.
    DISCUSSION: Benchmarking is an ongoing process that involves quantitative and qualitative measurement of the difference between the organization's performance of an activity and the performance by a best-in-class organization. The benchmarked organization need not be a direct competitor. The important consideration is that it be an outstanding performer in its industry.
    Answer (A) is incorrect. Benchmarking involves continuously evaluating the practices of best-in-class organization and adapting company processes to incorporate the best of these practices. Answer (B) is incorrect. Benchmarking, in practice, usually involves a formation of benchmarking teams. Answer (C) is incorrect. Benchmarking is an ongoing process that involves quantitative and qualitative measurement of the difference between the organization's performance of an activity and the performance by the best in the world or the best in the industry.

15. An example of an internal nonfinancial benchmark is

A. The labor rate of comparably skilled employees at a major competitor's plant.

B. The average actual cost per pound of a specific product at the company's most efficient plant.

C. A $50,000 limit on the cost of employee training programs at each of the company's plants.

D. The percentage of customer orders delivered on time at the company's most efficient plant.

Answer (D) is correct.
    REQUIRED: The internal nonfinancial benchmark.
    DISCUSSION: Benchmarking is a continuous evaluation of the practices of the best organizations in their class and the adaptation of processes to reflect the best of these practices. It requires analysis and measurement of key outputs against those of the best organizations. This procedure also involves identifying the underlying key actions and causes that contribute to the performance difference. The percentage of orders delivered on time at the most efficient plant is an example of an internal nonfinancial benchmark.
    Answer (A) is incorrect. The labor rate of a competitor is a financial benchmark. Answer (B) is incorrect. The cost per pound of a product at the most efficient plant is a financial benchmark. Answer (C) is incorrect. The cost of a training program is a financial benchmark.

16. A company, which has many branch stores, has decided to benchmark one of its stores for the purpose of analyzing the accuracy and reliability of branch store financial reporting. Which one of the following is the most likely measure to be included in a financial benchmark?

A. High turnover of employees.

B. High level of employee participation in setting budgets.

C. High amount of bad debt write-offs.

D. High number of suppliers.

Answer (C) is correct.
    REQUIRED: The most likely measure to be included in a financial benchmark.
    DISCUSSION: High bad debt write-offs could indicate fraud, which compromises the accuracy and reliability of financial reports. Bad debt write-offs may result from recording fictitious sales.
    Answer (A) is incorrect. Turnover of employees is not a financial benchmark. Answer (B) is incorrect. Employee participation in setting budgets is not a financial benchmark. Answer (D) is incorrect. The number of suppliers is not a financial benchmark.

17.5 Costs of Quality

17. An example of an internal failure cost is

A. Maintenance.

B. Inspection.

C. Rework.

D. Product recalls.

Answer (C) is correct.
    REQUIRED: The example of an internal failure cost.
    DISCUSSION: In a quality management system, one of the costs of product nonconformance is internal failure cost, the cost of discovering, after appraisal but before shipment, that a completed product does not meet quality standards. An example is the cost of reworking the product.
    Answer (A) is incorrect. A maintenance cost is a prevention cost. Answer (B) is incorrect. Inspection is an appraisal cost. Answer (D) is incorrect. Product recalls are external failure costs.

18. The cost of statistical quality control in a product quality cost system is categorized as a(n)

    A. Internal failure cost.

    B. Training cost.

    C. External failure cost.

    D. Appraisal cost.

Answer (D) is correct.

    REQUIRED: The cost category that includes statistical quality control.

    DISCUSSION: The four categories of quality costs are (1) prevention, (2) appraisal, (3) internal failure, and (4) external failure (lost opportunity). Appraisal costs include quality control programs, inspection, and testing. However, some authorities regard statistical quality and process control as preventive activities. They not only detect faulty work but also allow for adjustment of processes to avoid future defects.

    Answer (A) is incorrect. Internal failure costs are incurred after poor quality has been found before shipment. Statistical quality control is designed to detect quality problems. Answer (B) is incorrect. Statistical quality control is not a training cost. Answer (C) is incorrect. External failure costs are incurred after the product has been shipped, including the costs associated with (1) warranties, (2) product liability, and (3) loss of customer goodwill.

19. The cost of scrap, rework, and tooling changes in a product quality cost system are categorized as a(n)

    A. External failure cost.

    B. Internal failure cost.

    C. Prevention cost.

    D. Appraisal cost.

Answer (B) is correct.

    REQUIRED: The cost category that includes scrap, rework, and tooling changes.

    DISCUSSION: The four categories of quality costs are (1) prevention, (2) appraisal, (3) internal failure, and (4) external failure (lost opportunity). Internal failure costs are incurred when detection of defective products occurs before shipment. Examples include (1) scrap, (2) rework, (3) tooling changes, and (4) downtime.

    Answer (A) is incorrect. External failure costs are incurred for quality reasons after the product has reached the customer. For example, warranty and product liability costs are external failure costs. Answer (C) is incorrect. Scrap and rework costs are incurred after a product has been manufactured. They are not prevention costs. Answer (D) is incorrect. Appraisal costs are incurred to discover quality problems. Scrap and rework occur after the discovery of a quality problem.

20. Listed below are selected line items from the cost of quality report for Watson Products for last month.

Category	Amount
Rework	$ 725
Equipment maintenance	1,154
Product testing	786
Product repair	695

What is Watson's total prevention and appraisal cost for last month?

    A. $786

    B. $1,154

    C. $1,940

    D. $2,665

Answer (C) is correct.

    REQUIRED: The total prevention and appraisal costs.

    DISCUSSION: The costs of prevention and appraisal are conformance costs that serve as financial measures of internal performance. Prevention costs are incurred to prevent defective output. These costs include (1) preventive maintenance, (2) employee training, (3) review of equipment design, and (4) evaluation of suppliers. Appraisal costs are incurred to detect nonconforming output. They include such activities as (1) statistical quality control programs, (2) inspection, and (3) testing. The equipment maintenance cost of $1,154 is a prevention cost. The product testing cost of $786 is an appraisal cost. Their sum is $1,940.

    Answer (A) is incorrect. The amount of $786 is the appraisal cost. Answer (B) is incorrect. The amount of $1,154 is the prevention cost. Answer (D) is incorrect. The amount of $2,665 includes rework, an internal failure cost.

21. The four categories of costs associated with product quality costs are

A. External failure, internal failure, prevention, and carrying.

B. External failure, internal failure, prevention, and appraisal.

C. Warranty, product liability, training, and appraisal.

D. Warranty, product liability, prevention, and appraisal.

Answer (B) is correct.
REQUIRED: The categories of product quality costs.
DISCUSSION: The four categories of quality costs are (1) prevention, (2) appraisal, (3) internal failure, and (4) external failure. Costs of prevention include attempts to avoid defective output, such as (1) employee training, (2) review of equipment design, (3) preventive maintenance, and (4) evaluation of suppliers. Appraisal includes quality control programs, inspection, and testing. Internal failure costs are incurred when detection of defective products occurs before shipment. They include costs of (1) scrap, (2) rework, (3) tooling changes, and (4) downtime. External failure costs are incurred after the product has been shipped. They include costs of the costs associated with warranties, product liability, and loss of customer goodwill.
Answer (A) is incorrect. Carrying cost is an inventory cost. Answer (C) is incorrect. All training costs are not quality control related. Also, internal failure costs should be included. Answer (D) is incorrect. Internal failure costs should be included.

22. Which of the following quality costs are nonconformance costs?

A. Systems development costs.

B. Costs of inspecting in-process items.

C. Environmental costs.

D. Costs of quality circles.

Answer (C) is correct.
REQUIRED: The nonconformance costs.
DISCUSSION: Nonconformance costs include internal and external failure costs. External failure costs include environmental costs, e.g., fines for violations of environmental laws and loss of customer goodwill.
Answer (A) is incorrect. Systems development costs are prevention (conformance) costs. Answer (B) is incorrect. Costs of inspecting in-process items are appraisal (conformance) costs. Answer (D) is incorrect. Costs of quality circles are prevention (conformance) costs.

17.6 TQM and the ISO Framework

23. Which statement best describes total quality management (TQM)?

A. TQM emphasizes reducing the cost of inspection.

B. TQM emphasizes participation by all employees in the decision-making process.

C. TQM implementation is quick and easy.

D. TQM is the continuous pursuit of quality.

Answer (D) is correct.
REQUIRED: The best description of TQM.
DISCUSSION: TQM is the continuous pursuit of quality in every aspect of organizational activities through (1) a philosophy of doing it right the first time, (2) employee training and empowerment, (3) promotion of teamwork, (4) improvement of processes, and (5) attention to satisfaction of customers, both internal and external.
Answer (A) is incorrect. Reducing the cost of inspection helps achieve the lowest overall business cost. Answer (B) is incorrect. Participative management emphasizes participation by all employees in the decision-making process. Answer (C) is incorrect. TQM implementation is often lengthy and difficult.

24. Total quality management (TQM) in a manufacturing environment is best exemplified by

A. Identifying and reworking production defects before sale.

B. Designing the product to minimize defects.

C. Performing inspections to isolate defects as early as possible.

D. Making machine adjustments periodically to reduce defects.

Answer (B) is correct.
REQUIRED: The activity characteristic of TQM.
DISCUSSION: TQM emphasizes quality as a basic organizational function. TQM is the continuous pursuit of quality in every aspect of organizational activities. One of the basic principles of TQM is doing it right the first time. Thus, errors should be caught and corrected at the source, and quality should be built in (designed in) from the start.

25. If a company is customer-centered, its customers are defined as

A. Only people external to the company who have purchased something from the company.

B. Only people internal to the company who directly use its product.

C. Anyone external to the company and those internal who rely on its product to get their job done.

D. Everybody external to the company who is currently doing, or may in the future do, business with the company.

Answer (C) is correct.
REQUIRED: The definition of customers if a firm is customer-centered.
DISCUSSION: One of the principles of TQM is customer orientation, whether the customer is internal or external. An internal customer is a member of the organization who relies on another member's work to accomplish his or her task.

26. Which statement best describes the emphasis of total quality management (TQM)?

A. Reducing the cost of inspection.

B. Implementing better statistical quality control techniques.

C. Doing each job right the first time.

D. Encouraging cross-functional teamwork.

Answer (C) is correct.
REQUIRED: The emphasis of TQM.
DISCUSSION: The basic principles of TQM include (1) doing each job right the first time, (2) being customer-oriented, (3) committing the organizational culture to continuous improvement, and (4) promoting teamwork and employee empowerment.
Answer (A) is incorrect. Reducing the cost of inspection is a detail of the TQM emphasis. Answer (B) is incorrect. Implementing better statistical quality control is a detail of the TQM emphasis. Answer (D) is incorrect. Encouraging cross-functional teamwork is a detail of the TQM emphasis.

17.7 Project Management

27. Which of the following personnel has primary responsibility for allocating sufficient resources to ensure successful completion of a project?

A. Project manager.

B. Project sponsor.

C. Project team members.

D. Steering committee.

Answer (B) is correct.
REQUIRED: The person charged with the responsibility to allocate resources to a project.
DISCUSSION: The project sponsor is vested with sufficient authority by executive management to allocate the resources that will ensure successful completion.
Answer (A) is incorrect. The project manager typically is not vested with sufficient authority to allocate resources. Answer (C) is incorrect. Project team members rarely have sufficient authority to allocate organizational resources. Answer (D) is incorrect. The steering committee provides guidance and demands accountability. Allocating resources is a day-to-day management function in which the steering committee does not normally participate.

28. Which of the following personnel has primary responsibility for ensuring that project deliverables are ready on time?

A. Project manager.

B. Project sponsor.

C. Project team members.

D. Steering committee.

Answer (A) is correct.
REQUIRED: The person charged with the responsibility for project deliverables.
DISCUSSION: The project manager oversees the day-to-day activities of the project team members and ensures that project deliverables are ready for the sponsor to present to the steering committee on time.
Answer (B) is incorrect. The project sponsor is not responsible for such day-to-day oversight activities as monitoring progress on project deliverables. Answer (C) is incorrect. Project team members must complete the deliverables, but they are not responsible for day-to-day oversight of the project as a whole. Answer (D) is incorrect. The steering committee reviews and approves the project deliverables. It does not present them.

29. The project management triangle depicts

   A. The degree of shared responsibility between the participants in a project.

   B. The decision process used to determine which projects should be undertaken.

   C. The interrelation of the component tasks that make up the overall project.

   D. The tradeoff between the time spent on a project, the cost of the project, and the quality of the final deliverable.

Answer (D) is correct.
   REQUIRED: The elements of the project management triangle.
   DISCUSSION: The project management triangle depicts the tradeoff between (1) the time spent on a project, (2) the cost of the project, and (3) the quality of the final deliverable.

30. During which of the following tasks of a project is the satisfaction of the stakeholders confirmed?

   A. Authorization.

   B. Implementation.

   C. Monitoring.

   D. Closing.

Answer (D) is correct.
   REQUIRED: The project task that includes stakeholder satisfaction.
   DISCUSSION: The closing phase consists of confirming that completion of the project to the satisfaction of the stakeholders.
   Answer (A) is incorrect. Authorization is carried out at the beginning of the project. Answer (B) is incorrect. During implementation, the detailed steps to achieve the project's goals are carried out. Answer (C) is incorrect. Ongoing monitoring, which is parallel with implementation, ensures that efforts are directed toward achieving the project's goals.

17.8 PRACTICE WRITTEN COMMUNICATION

| | Business Environment and Concepts
Testlet 4 of 4 | Time Remaining
1 hour - 15 minutes | Unsplit | Split Horiz | Split Vertical | Exit |

DIRECTIONS

Note: If you believe you have encountered a software malfunction, report it to the test center staff immediately.

Navigation

To navigate from task to task, use the controls at the bottom of the screen. Click on the **Next** button to advance to the next task, or the **Previous** button to go to the previous task. To go directly to any task, click on its number.

| ▼ = Reminder | | Directions | 1 2 3 4 5 6 7 ▽ ▽ ▽ ▽ ▽ ▽ ▽ | | ◀ Previous | Next ▶ |

If you would like a reminder to revisit a task or want to indicate that you are finished with it, click on the reminder flag below the task number. To clear the flag, click on it again. Reminder flags are for your use only – they do not contribute to your score.

Tabs

In this part of the examination, you will be asked to complete various tasks. Every task has one or more **Work Tabs**. Every task also has a **Help** tab.

✏ Written Communication   Help

Work tab   Help tab

Work Tabs:

- **Work Tabs** are identified with a pencil icon. This is where your responses are expected.
- Each task has one or more **Work Tabs**.
- **Work Tabs** contain directions for completing the task - be sure to read these directions carefully.
- The **Work Tab** name in the example above is for illustration only - yours will differ.
- You must complete all of the **Work Tabs** in each task to receive full credit.

Help Tab:

- The **Help Tab** provides assistance with the exam software that is used in this task. For example, if the task is to compose a memorandum, **Help** will provide information about the word processor.

The Toolbar

The toolbar at the top of the screen shows the amount of time remaining for you to complete the tasks. In addition, the following tools are available. Note that only the **Exit** button is displayed when Directions are visible - the others will appear when you begin the tasks.

Click on these buttons to split or unsplit the screen. You can split the screen vertically or horizontally.

Click on this button to go on to the next part of the examination. You must complete all of the tasks to receive full credit. Once you click on **Exit** and confirm the action, you will NOT be able to return to this testlet.

| ▼ = Reminder | | Directions | 1 ▽ | | ◀ Previous | Next ▶ |

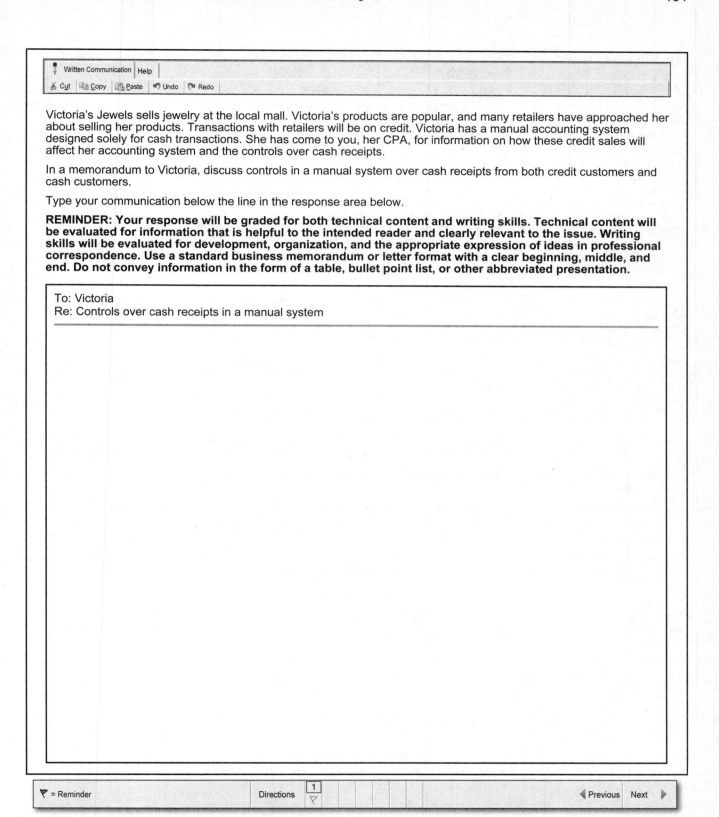

To: Victoria
Re: Controls over cash receipts in a manual system

NOTE: Your Written Communications on the actual CPA exam may cover topics outside the scope of the BEC CSO (i.e., they may relate to topics from the AUD, FAR, and/or REG CSOs instead). Answer to the best of your ability, and remember that graders are mainly evaluating your writing ability and will overlook minor technical mistakes.

Unofficial Answer

Written Communication

To: Victoria
Re: Controls over cash receipts in a manual system

The controls over cash receipts from credit customers in a manual system begin in the mail room. Two clerks should be present in the mail room during the opening and recording of receipts. The checks received are then endorsed "For Deposit Only into Account Number XXXX" immediately upon opening the mail. All cash is deposited intact daily. This procedure ensures that the cash received and recorded on the daily remittance list can be reconciled with the deposit ticket validated by the bank. Periodic reconciliation of the accounts receivable subsidiary ledger and the accounts receivable control account in the general ledger establishes agreement of the total amounts posted. However, the reconciliation cannot determine whether an amount was posted to the wrong account in the subsidiary ledger. Moreover, application of such a control will be ineffective if sales were not recorded in the books of original entry, e.g., the sales journal.

Other controls include sending monthly statements to customers and bonding employees. Monthly statements ensure that failure to receive or record payments made by customers is detected. Employees responsible for handling cash are bonded. Because the bonding company investigates employees before providing the bond, some assurance is provided about their integrity. Also, the bond provides insurance against losses.

A cash sales environment often lacks the segregation of duties necessary for a proper framework of control. For example, the sales clerk often authorizes sales (e.g., acceptance of a check), records sales (i.e., enters it on a terminal), and has custody of the assets related to sales.

One of the compensating controls in a cash sales environment is the use of a cash register or sales terminal to record the sale. The terminal makes a permanent record of the event that the clerk cannot erase.

Another compensating control is the assignment of one clerk to be responsible for sales recording and cash receipts during a work period. The cash drawer can be reconciled with the record of sales and accountability assigned to the clerk.

Increased supervision also is a compensating control. For example, the manager's office may be positioned to observe the clerks' sales recording and cash collection activities.

A fourth compensating control is the customer audit of the transaction. Displaying the recorded transaction and providing a receipt to the customer provide some assurance that the clerk accomplished the recording process appropriately.

The above depicts a Level 5 answer. Consult your booklet, *How to Pass the CPA Exam: A System for Success*, for a description of the three writing skills criteria. You may also access this booklet online by visiting www.gleim.com/PassCPA.

Self-Grade

Below, grade your response on technical content and writing skills. Bubble in the circle next to the appropriate score that you may receive based on the criteria given. Your **total** score is the sum of your scores on all six items. The maximum score is 19 points.

Technical Content Evaluation

Was your response on topic?	O No [0]	O Mostly [1]	O Yes [2]
Did your response have any *significant* errors?	O 0 errors [1]	O 1 major error [–1]	O 2 or more major errors [–2]
Did your response contain any illegal advice?	O No [1]	O Yes [0]	

Writing Skills Evaluation

	Poor	Below Average	Average	Above Average	Outstanding
Organization	O 1	O 2	O 3	O 4	O 5
Development	O 1	O 2	O 3	O 4	O 5
Expression	O 1	O 2	O 3	O 4	O 5

Disclaimer: This scoring schedule was developed by Gleim Publications as a guideline only. The AICPA has not released specific information on how the Written Communications are graded.

STUDY UNIT EIGHTEEN
COSTING FUNDAMENTALS

(11 pages of outline)

Management accounting has specialized terminology that should be understood before the other outlines are read. This study unit also covers the most fundamental cost calculations and measurements. It also addresses decisions involving marginal (incremental or differential) costs. The final subunits in this Study Unit apply to cost-volume-profit analysis, a method for determining the effects of changes in unit sales, sales price, unit variable cost, fixed cost, and product mix.

18.1 COST MEASUREMENT TERMINOLOGY

1. **Manufacturing vs. Nonmanufacturing**

   a. The costs of manufacturing a product can be classified as one of three types:

      1) **Direct materials** are tangible inputs to the manufacturing process that can feasibly be traced to the product, e.g., sheet metal welded together for a piece of heavy equipment.

         a) All costs of bringing materials to the production line, e.g., transportation-in, are included in the cost of direct materials.

      2) **Direct labor** is the cost of human labor that can feasibly be traced to the product, e.g., the wages of the welder.

      3) **Manufacturing overhead** consists of all costs of manufacturing that are not direct materials or direct labor.

         a) Indirect materials are tangible inputs to the manufacturing process that cannot feasibly be traced to the product, e.g., the welding compound used to put together a piece of heavy equipment.

         b) Indirect labor is the cost of human labor connected with the manufacturing process that cannot feasibly be traced to the product, e.g., the wages of assembly line supervisors and janitorial staff.

         c) Other operating costs of manufacturing include utilities expense, real estate taxes, insurance, and depreciation on factory equipment.

   b. Manufacturing costs also may be classified as follows:

      1) **Prime cost** equals direct materials plus direct labor, costs directly attributable to a product.

      2) **Conversion cost** equals direct labor plus manufacturing overhead, costs of converting materials into the finished product.

   c. A manufacturer incurs nonmanufacturing costs.

      1) Selling (marketing) costs are incurred while getting the product to the consumer, e.g., sales personnel salaries and product transportation.

      2) Administrative expenses are not directly related to producing or marketing the product, e.g., executive salaries and depreciation on the administration building.

2.   **Direct vs. Indirect**

    a.   Costs can be classified by how they are assigned to cost objects.

        1)   Direct costs can be traced to a cost object in an economically feasible way.

            a)   Examples are direct materials and direct labor inputs.

        2)   Indirect costs, such as indirect materials and indirect labor, cannot be traced to a cost object in an economically feasible way. Thus, they must be allocated.

            a)   To simplify allocation, indirect costs often are collected in cost pools.

                i)   A cost pool is an account in which similar cost elements with a common cause are accumulated.

                ii)   Manufacturing overhead is a commonly used cost pool in which various untraceable costs of manufacturing are accumulated prior to allocation.

3.   **Product vs. Period**

    a.   An important issue in management accounting is whether to capitalize costs in finished goods inventory or to expense them as incurred.

        1)   Product costs (inventoriable costs) are capitalized as part of finished goods inventory. They eventually become components of cost of goods sold.

        2)   Period costs are expensed as incurred and are therefore excluded from cost of goods sold.

    b.   This distinction is crucial because of the required treatment of manufacturing costs for external financial reporting purposes.

        1)   Under GAAP, all manufacturing costs (direct materials, direct labor, variable overhead, and fixed overhead) must be recognized as product costs. All selling and administrative (S&A) costs are period costs.

            a)   This approach is **absorption costing** (full costing).

        2)   For internal reporting, operational planning and control may be facilitated by treating only variable manufacturing costs as product costs. All other costs (variable S&A and the fixed portion of both production and S&A expenses) are period costs.

            a)   This approach is **variable costing** (direct costing).
            b)   Variable costing is covered in Study Unit 19, Subunit 1.

        3)   The following table summarizes absorption and variable costing:

	Absorption Costing (Required under GAAP)	Variable Costing (For Internal Reporting Only)
Product Costs (Included in Cost of Goods Sold)	Variable production costs	
	Fixed production costs	
Period Costs		Fixed production costs
	Variable S&A expenses	
(Excluded from Cost of Goods Sold)	Fixed S&A expenses	

    c.   **Gross profit** (gross margin) is an intermediate component of operating income under absorption (full) costing. It is the excess of sales over cost of goods sold that consists of variable and fixed manufacturing costs.

        1)   Only costs directly associated with manufacturing the product may be subtracted.

        2)   GAAP require this calculation.

Gross profit percentage = Gross profit ÷ Sales

    d. **Contribution margin** is the intermediate component under variable costing. It is the excess of sales over the sum of variable manufacturing and selling and administrative costs.

        1) Contribution margin is the amount available to cover fixed costs.

        2) This calculation often is used for internal (managerial) reporting purposes.

Stop and review! You have completed the outline for this subunit. Study multiple-choice questions 1 through 5 beginning on page 474.

18.2 BASIC COST CALCULATIONS

1. **Cost of Goods Sold and Cost of Goods Manufactured**

    a. Cost of goods sold is a straightforward computation for retailers because they have only one class of inventory.

```
  Beginning inventory
+ Purchases
- Ending inventory
= Cost of goods sold
```

    b. The calculation is more complex for manufacturers because they have three classes of inventory.

        1) Cost of goods manufactured is an intermediate component of cost of goods sold. It is similar to a retailer's purchases account.

```
  Beginning work-in-process inventory
+ Total manufacturing costs
- Ending work-in-process inventory
= Cost of goods manufactured
```

    c. A comparison of these computations in full is as follows:

Cost of goods sold for a retailer:

Beginning inventory		$10,000
Plus: purchases	$15,000	
Minus: returns and discounts	(1,000)	
Net purchases	**$14,000**	
Plus: freight-in	1,000	15,000
Goods available for sale		**$25,000**
Minus: ending inventory		(5,000)
Costs of goods sold		**$20,000**

Cost of goods sold for a manufacturer:

Beginning direct materials inventory		$ 2,000	
Plus: purchases	$ 4,000		
Minus: returns and discounts	(1,000)		
Net purchases	$ 3,000		
Plus: freight-in	1,000	4,000	
Direct materials available for use		$ 6,000	
Minus: ending direct materials inventory		(1,000)	
Direct materials used in production			$ 5,000
Direct labor costs			5,000
Manufacturing overhead costs			4,000
Total manufacturing costs for the period			**$14,000**
Plus: beginning work-in-process inventory			5,000
Minus: ending work-in-process inventory			(4,000)
Costs of goods manufactured			**$15,000**
Plus: beginning finished goods inventory			6,000
Goods available for sale			**$21,000**
Minus: ending finished goods inventory			(11,000)
Costs of goods sold			**$10,000**

2. **Relevant vs. Sunk**

    a.   Relevant costs are future costs that vary depending on the action taken. All other costs are assumed to be constant and are irrelevant to the decision.

        1)   An example is tuition that must be spent to attend a fourth year of college.

    b.   Sunk costs already have been incurred or irrevocably committed to be incurred. Because they are unavoidable and do not vary with the option chosen, they are not relevant to future decisions.

        1)   An example is 3 years of tuition already paid. The previous 3 years of tuition do not affect the decision to attend a fourth year.

3. **Additional Cost Concepts**

    a.   **Value-adding costs** cannot be eliminated without reducing the quality, responsiveness, or quantity of the output required.

    b.   **Incremental (differential) cost** is the difference in total cost between two decisions. Incremental cost never includes fixed costs or sunk costs.

    c.   **Opportunity cost** is the maximum benefit forgone by using a scarce resource for a given purpose.

Stop and review! You have completed the outline for this subunit. Study multiple-choice questions 6 through 10 beginning on page 475.

18.3 OTHER COST MEASUREMENT CONCEPTS

1. **Variable vs. Fixed**

    a.   Variable cost per unit is constant in the short run regardless of the level of production. But variable costs in total vary directly and proportionally with changes in volume. Typical variable costs are direct materials, direct labor, and manufacturing supplies.

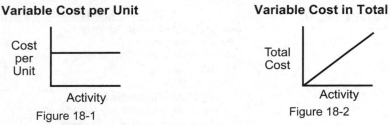

Variable Cost per Unit	**Variable Cost in Total**
Figure 18-1	Figure 18-2

EXAMPLE

One unit of direct materials is to be used in each unit of a finished good.

Number of Units Produced		Cost per Unit		Total Cost of Units
0	×	$10	=	$ 0
100	×	$10	=	$ 1,000
1,000	×	$10	=	$ 10,000
5,000	×	$10	=	$ 50,000
10,000	×	$10	=	$100,000

b. Fixed costs in total are unchanged in the short run regardless of production level. Accordingly, the amount paid for an assembly line is the same even if nothing is produced. But fixed cost per unit varies indirectly with the activity level. Typical fixed costs are rent, depreciation, and insurance.

Fixed Costs in Total

Figure 18-3

Fixed Cost per Unit

Figure 18-4

EXAMPLE

The historical cost of an assembly line is fixed, but its cost per unit decreases as production increases.

Cost of Assembly Line		Number of Units Produced		Per-Unit Cost of Assembly Line
$1,000,000	÷	1	=	$1,000,000
$1,000,000	÷	100	=	$ 10,000
$1,000,000	÷	1,000	=	$ 1,000
$1,000,000	÷	5,000	=	$ 200
$1,000,000	÷	10,000	=	$ 100

---

c. **Mixed (semivariable) costs** combine fixed and variable elements, e.g., rental of a car for a flat fee per month plus an additional fee for each mile driven.

Mixed Cost

Figure 18-5

EXAMPLE

A piece of machinery is rented to improve the efficiency of a production line. The rent is $150,000 per year plus $1 for every unit produced.

Number of Units Produced	Fixed Cost of Extra Machine		Variable Cost of Extra Machine		Total Cost of Extra Machine
0	$150,000	+	$ 0	=	$150,000
100	$150,000	+	$ 100	=	$150,100
1,000	$150,000	+	$ 1,000	=	$151,000
5,000	$150,000	+	$ 5,000	=	$155,000
10,000	$150,000	+	$ 10,000	=	$160,000

---

1) The fixed and variable portions of a mixed cost can be estimated using the high-low method.

2. **Relevant Range**

a. Within the relevant range, per-unit variable costs and fixed costs do not change. It is synonymous with the **short run** because all costs are variable in the long run.

1) The relevant range is established by the efficiency of current manufacturing operations, agreements with labor unions and suppliers, etc.

a) Investment in more efficient equipment may result in higher total fixed costs and lower total and per-unit variable costs.

3.   **Spoilage and Scrap**

a.   **Normal spoilage** occurs under normal, efficient operating conditions. It is essentially uncontrollable in the short run. Thus, it is accounted for as a product cost and included in the cost of the good output.

b.   **Abnormal spoilage** is not expected to occur under normal, efficient operating conditions. It is accounted for as a period cost (a loss).

c.   **Scrap** consists of materials left over from making a product. No cost is recognized for scrap, and it is not classified as normal or abnormal. If scrap is common to all jobs or process costing is used, the proceeds of sale reduce manufacturing overhead. If job costing is used, the proceeds reduce work-in-process. Scrap also may be reused or discarded.

Stop and review! You have completed the outline for this subunit. Study multiple-choice questions 11 through 15 beginning on page 477.

18.4 DECISION COSTING

1.   **Relevant vs. Irrelevant Factors**

a.   Decision making should focus only on relevant revenues and costs. To be relevant, they must

1)   Be expected to be earned or incurred, respectively, in the future.

a)   Costs already incurred or to which the organization is committed (sunk costs) do not affect current decisions.

b)   EXAMPLE: A manufacturer is considering the purchase of new equipment. The amounts paid for the existing equipment are sunk costs. They are irrelevant to the purchase decision.

c)   EXAMPLE: A union contract may require 6 months of wage continuance after a plant shutdown. Thus, 6 months of wages must be paid regardless of whether the plant is closed.

2)   Differ among the possible decisions.

b.   Only avoidable costs are relevant.

1)   A cost is avoidable if it can be eliminated by choosing a specific option. Avoidable costs may include variable materials costs or direct labor costs.

2)   An unavoidable cost must be incurred regardless of whether a specific option is chosen.

a)   For example, rent under a long-term lease on a building is not eliminated by closing the business in that building. Thus, the rent is an unavoidable cost.

c.   Marginal (incremental or differential) analysis relates to relevance.

1)   For example, throughout the relevant range, the marginal cost of an additional unit of output is the same. However, beyond a certain output, current production capacity is insufficient and additional fixed costs must be incurred.

EXAMPLE

The following unit costs of a product are incurred:

Direct materials	$2.00
Direct labor	3.00
Variable overhead	.50
Fixed overhead	.50
Total cost	$6.00

The product normally sells for $10 per unit. Marginal analysis is necessary if a buyer, who has never before been a customer, offers to pay $5.60 per unit for a special order of the product. One possibility is to reject the offer because the selling price is less than the average cost of production.

However, marginal analysis results in a different decision. Assuming idle capacity is available, the only marginal costs are for direct materials, direct labor, and variable overhead. No additional fixed overhead costs are incurred. Because marginal revenue (the $5.60 selling price) exceeds marginal costs ($2 materials + $3 labor + $.50 variable OH = $5.50 per unit), accepting the special order is profitable.

---

2. **Add-or-Drop-a-Segment Decisions**

    a. Disinvestment decisions involve discontinuing an operation, product or product line, business segment, branch, or major customer.

        1) In general, if the marginal cost of a project exceeds the marginal revenue, the firm should disinvest.

    b. A firm making a disinvestment decision should

        1) Identify fixed costs that will be eliminated, e.g., insurance on equipment used.

        2) Determine the revenue that justifies continuing operations. In the short run, this amount should at least equal the variable cost of production or continued service.

        3) Establish the opportunity cost of funds that will be received (e.g., salvage value).

        4) Determine whether the carrying amount of the assets equals their economic value. If not, the decision should be evaluated using current fair value.

    c. When a firm disinvests, excess capacity may exist unless it is used immediately by another project. The cost of idle capacity is a relevant cost.

3. **Special Orders When Excess Capacity Exists**

    a. When a manufacturer has excess production capacity, accepting a special order has no opportunity cost.

        1) The order should be accepted if the minimum price for the product equals the variable costs.

        2) A special order might be rejected if acceptance affects the price of regular sales.

EXAMPLE

The following price and cost data are available for two products:

	X		Z	
Selling price		$250		$300
Variable costs:				
Direct materials	$110		$125	
Direct labor	20		25	
Variable overhead	55		50	
Variable S&A	5	(190)	5	(205)
Contribution margin		$ 60		$ 95

A special, one-time order for 2,000 units of X has been received. Sufficient unused capacity exists. The order can be accepted at a price of at least $190 (unit variable cost) per unit of X.

---

4. **Special Orders in the Absence of Excess Capacity**

   a. When a manufacturer lacks excess production capacity, the marginal costs of accepting the order must be considered.

      1) Besides the variable costs of the production run, the firm must consider the opportunity cost of redirecting productive capacity away from (possibly more profitable) products.

EXAMPLE

A special order for 2,000 units of X has been received, but the firm is operating at full capacity. All 24,000 machine hours available to produce Z are being used.

Each unit of X requires 4 hours to produce, and each unit of Z requires 6 hours. The firm must divert 8,000 hours (2,000 units of X × 4 hours per unit) to produce the special order.

The opportunity cost of these hours is the contribution margin (CM) earned by producing Z. X has a CM of $15 per machine hour ($60 ÷ 4 hours), and Z has a CM of $15.83 per machine hour ($95 ÷ 6 hours).

Hours needed	8,000	Z's UCM	$ 95
Hours per unit of Z	÷ 6	Units of Z forgone	× 1,333
Units of Z forgone	1,333	Opportunity cost	$126,635

For the special order to be profitable, the firm must recover (1) the opportunity cost of not producing 1,333 units of Z and (2) the variable costs of the production run.

Z's total CM forgone	$ 126,635
Variable costs of special order (2,000 units × $190)	380,000
Total cost to be recovered	$ 506,635
Units in the special order	÷ 2,000
Minimum price per unit	$253.3175

Stop and review! You have completed the outline for this subunit. Study multiple-choice questions 16 through 20 beginning on page 478.

18.5 COST-VOLUME-PROFIT ANALYSIS -- BASICS

1. Cost-volume-profit (CVP) analysis (also called breakeven analysis) explains the effects of changes in assumptions about cost behavior and the relevant ranges in which those assumptions are valid. These changes may affect the relationships among revenues, variable costs, and fixed costs at different output levels.

   a. Thus, CVP analysis determines the probable effects of changes in unit sales, sales price, unit variable cost, fixed cost, and product mix.

2. **Simplifying Assumptions**

   a. Cost and revenue relationships are predictable and linear. They are true over the relevant range of activity and specified time span.

   b. Unit selling prices and market conditions are constant.

   c. Changes in inventory are insignificant in amount. Thus, production equals sales.

   d. Total variable costs change proportionally with volume, but unit variable costs are constant over the relevant range.

      1) Direct materials and direct labor are variable costs.

   e. Fixed costs are constant over the relevant range, but unit fixed costs vary indirectly with activity.

3. **Breakeven Point in Units**

    a. The **breakeven point** is the output at which all fixed costs and cumulative variable costs have been covered. It is the output at which operating income is zero.

        1) Each additional unit produced above the breakeven point generates operating profit.

    b. The simplest calculation for breakeven in units is to divide fixed costs by the unit contribution margin (UCM). UCM equals unit selling price minus unit variable cost.

$$Breakeven\ point\ in\ units\ =\ \frac{Fixed\ costs}{UCM}$$

EXAMPLE

A product has a unit sales price of $0.60 and a unit variable cost of $0.20. Fixed costs are $10,000.

Unit selling price	$0.60	Breakeven point in units = Fixed costs ÷ UCM
Minus: unit variable costs	(0.20)	= $10,000 ÷ $0.40
Unit contribution margin (UCM)	$0.40	= 25,000 units

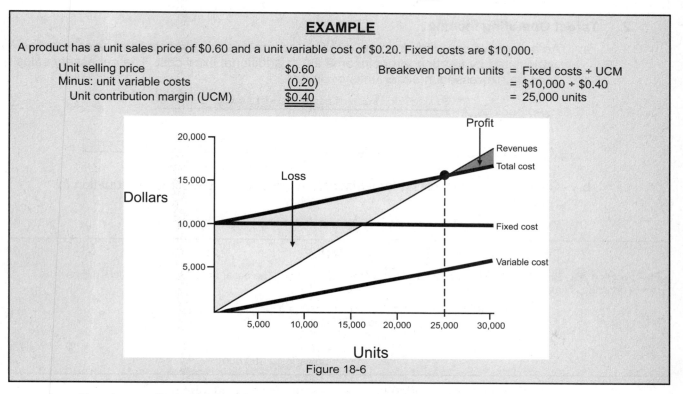

Figure 18-6

---

4. **Breakeven Point in Dollars**

    a. The breakeven point in sales dollars equals fixed costs divided by the contribution margin ratio (CMR). CMR is the ratio of contribution margin to sales price on either a total or per-unit basis.

$$Breakeven\ point\ in\ dollars\ =\ \frac{Fixed\ costs}{CMR}$$

    b. The breakeven point in sales dollars also equals the breakeven point in units multiplied by the selling price.

EXAMPLE

The contribution margin ratio is 66.667% ($0.40 ÷ $0.60).

        Breakeven point in dollars = Fixed costs ÷ CMR
                             = $10,000 ÷ .66667
                             = $15,000

Stop and review! You have completed the outline for this subunit. Study multiple-choice questions 21 through 25 beginning on page 479.

18.6 COST-VOLUME-PROFIT ANALYSIS -- APPLICATIONS

1. **Margin of Safety**

   a. The margin of safety is the excess of sales over breakeven sales. It is the amount by which sales can decline before losses occur.

   b. The margin of safety can be expressed as either a dollar amount or a percentage of sales.

$$Margin\ of\ safety\ in\ dollars = Total\ sales\ in\ dollars - Breakeven\ point\ in\ dollars$$

$$Margin\ of\ safety\ (\%) = \frac{Margin\ of\ safety\ (in\ dollars)}{Total\ sales\ (in\ dollars)}$$

2. **Target Operating Income**

   a. An amount of operating income, either in dollars or as a percentage of sales, can be calculated by treating target income as an additional fixed cost. The necessary sales can be expressed in either units or dollars.

$$Target\ units = \frac{Fixed\ costs + Target\ operating\ income}{UCM}$$

$$Target\ sales\ in\ dollars = \frac{Fixed\ costs + Target\ operating\ income}{Contribution\ margin\ ratio}$$

   b. Other problems involving target income require use of the standard equation for operating income.

$$Sales - Variable\ costs - Fixed\ costs = Operating\ income$$

EXAMPLE

Fixed costs are $150,000, and variable costs are 85% of the selling price. The dollar amount of sales needed for a 10% return on sales is calculated as follows:

$$Sales - Variable\ costs - Fixed\ costs = Operating\ income$$
$$Sales - (.85)Sales - \$150,000 = (.1)Sales$$
$$(.15)Sales - \$150,000 = (.1)Sales$$
$$(.05)Sales = \$150,000$$
$$Sales = \$3,000,000$$

---

   1) The unit selling price is not necessary for this calculation.

EXAMPLE

Assuming that target operating income is $25,000, unit sales are calculated as follows:

$$Target\ units = (Fixed\ costs + Target\ operating\ income) \div UCM$$
$$= (\$10,000 + \$25,000) \div \$0.40$$
$$= \$35,000 \div \$.40$$
$$= 87,500\ units$$

---

3. **Target Net Income**

   a. A problem may ask for net income (an after-tax amount) instead of operating income (a pretax amount).

$$Net\ income = Operating\ income - (Operating\ income \times Tax\ rate)$$
$$= Operating\ income \times (1 - Tax\ rate)$$
$$Operating\ income = Net\ income \div (1 - Tax\ rate)$$

1) The calculation of unit sales or sales dollars for a given target net income is based on the same equations used for target operating income. The difference is that net income is substituted for target operating income.

$$Target\ units = \frac{Fixed\ costs + [Target\ net\ income \div (1.0 - tax\ rate)]}{UCM}$$

EXAMPLE

Assuming that target net income is $30,000 and the effective tax rate is 40%, unit sales are calculated as follows:

Target units = {Fixed costs + [Target net income ÷ (1.0 − .40)]} ÷ UCM
= [$10,000 + ($30,000 ÷ .60)] ÷ $.40
= 150,000 units

---

4. **Multiple Products**

a. CVP analysis can be adapted to problems involving multiple products. The assumption is that the product mix is constant over the relevant range.

1) The UCM is the weighted average of the UCMs of the products.

EXAMPLE

Two products have the following selling prices and variable costs:

	Q	Y
Unit selling price	$100.00	$130.00
Unit variable cost	85.00	95.00

Five units of Q are sold for every four units of Y. Total annual fixed costs are $80,600. The problem is to determine how many units of each product must be sold to earn $100,000 of operating income.

The UCMs of the two products are $15 ($100 − $85) and $35 ($130 − $95), respectively. The sales mix consists of a composite unit of five units of Q and four units of Y. Thus, the number of composite units that must be sold is calculated using the composite (weighted-average) UCM.

Target units = (Target operating income + Fixed costs) ÷ Composite (weighted-average) UCM
= ($100,000 + $80,600) ÷ [(5 × $15) + (4 × $35)]
= $180,600 ÷ ($75 + $140)
= $180,600 ÷ $215
= 840 composite units

840 × 9 = 7,560 total units of Q and Y sold
Q: 7,560 × (5 ÷ 9) = 4,200 units
Y: 7,560 × (4 ÷ 9) = 3,360 units

Total contribution margin of $180,600 [(4,200 × $15) + (3,360 × $35)] equals the sum of fixed costs ($80,600) and target operating income ($100,000).

 Proficiency in using the CVP equations is needed to determine the information required by questions. The multiple-choice questions in the Gleim materials give you the opportunity to practice and improve your proficiency in working with these equations.

Stop and review! You have completed the outline for this subunit. Study multiple-choice questions 26 through 30 beginning on page 481.

QUESTIONS

18.1 Cost Measurement Terminology

1. If a product required a great deal of electricity to produce, and crude oil prices increased, which of the following costs most likely increased?

    A. Direct materials.

    B. Direct labor.

    C. Prime costs.

    D. Conversion costs.

Answer (D) is correct.
    REQUIRED: The costs that most likely increase if overhead increases.
    DISCUSSION: Conversion costs consist of direct labor and manufacturing overhead. Overhead includes the costs of utilities, such as electricity. An increase in the price of crude oil, which is used to generate electricity, therefore is likely to increase conversion costs.
    Answer (A) is incorrect. Direct materials are tangible inputs to the manufacturing process that can practicably be traced to the product. Electricity is not a direct material. Answer (B) is incorrect. Direct labor is the cost of labor that can feasibly be traced to the product. Electricity is not direct labor. Answer (C) is incorrect. Prime costs equal direct materials plus direct labor. Because electricity is neither a direct material nor direct labor, electricity is not a prime cost.

2. Which one of the following best describes direct labor?

    A. A prime cost.

    B. A period cost.

    C. A product cost.

    D. Both a product cost and a prime cost.

Answer (D) is correct.
    REQUIRED: The best description of direct labor.
    DISCUSSION: Direct labor is a product cost and a prime cost. Product costs are incurred to produce units of output and are deferred to future periods to the extent that output is not sold. Prime costs are the direct cost of manufacturing, for example, direct materials and direct labor.
    Answer (A) is incorrect. Direct labor also is a product cost. Answer (B) is incorrect. A period cost is expensed when incurred. Direct labor cost is inventoriable. Answer (C) is incorrect. Direct labor also is a prime cost.

3. Inventoriable costs

    A. Include only the prime costs of manufacturing a product.

    B. Include only the conversion costs of manufacturing a product.

    C. Are expensed when products become part of finished goods inventory.

    D. Are regarded as assets before the products are sold.

Answer (D) is correct.
    REQUIRED: The true statement about inventoriable costs.
    DISCUSSION: Product (inventoriable) costs are capitalized as part of finished goods inventory. But period costs are expensed as they are incurred and are not capitalized as assets. Under an absorption costing system, inventoriable costs include variable and fixed costs of production. Under variable costing, inventoriable costs include only variable production costs.
    Answer (A) is incorrect. Overhead costs and prime costs (direct materials and labor) are included in inventory. Answer (B) is incorrect. Materials costs also are included. Answer (C) is incorrect. Inventory costs are expensed when the goods are sold, not when they are transferred to finished goods.

4. The unit costs for direct materials, machining, and assembly of a manufactured product represent

    A. Conversion costs.

    B. Separable costs.

    C. Committed costs.

    D. Prime costs.

Answer (D) is correct.
    REQUIRED: The type of cost represented by direct materials, machining, and assembly.
    DISCUSSION: Prime costs are a manufacturer's direct cost. Direct materials and direct labor (such as machining and assembly) are examples.
    Answer (A) is incorrect. Conversion costs consist of direct labor and overhead. Answer (B) is incorrect. Separable costs are incurred beyond the point at which jointly produced items become separately identifiable. Answer (C) is incorrect. Committed costs result when an entity holds fixed assets. Examples of committed costs include long-term lease payments and depreciation.

5. In cost terminology, conversion costs consist of

   A. Direct and indirect labor.

   B. Direct labor and direct materials.

   C. Direct labor and factory overhead.

   D. Indirect labor and variable factory overhead.

Answer (C) is correct.
   REQUIRED: The components of conversion costs.
   DISCUSSION: Conversion costs consist of direct labor and manufacturing overhead. They are the costs of converting materials into a finished product.
   Answer (A) is incorrect. All manufacturing overhead is included in conversion costs, not just indirect labor. Answer (B) is incorrect. Direct materials are not an element of conversion costs. They are a prime cost. Answer (D) is incorrect. Direct labor is also an element of conversion costs.

18.2 Basic Cost Calculations

Questions 6 and 7 are based on the following information. The estimated unit costs for Cole Co. using absorption (full) costing and planning to produce and sell at a level of 12,000 units per month are as follows:

Cost Item	Estimated Unit Cost
Direct materials	$32
Direct labor	20
Variable manufacturing overhead	15
Fixed manufacturing overhead	6
Variable selling	3
Fixed selling	4

6. Cole's estimated conversion costs per unit are

   A. $35

   B. $41

   C. $48

   D. $67

Answer (B) is correct.
   REQUIRED: The estimated conversion costs per unit.
   DISCUSSION: Conversion costs are incurred in transforming direct materials into finished products. They include direct labor and manufacturing overhead. Thus, unit conversion costs equal $41 ($20 direct labor + $15 variable overhead + $6 fixed overhead).
   Answer (A) is incorrect. Direct labor plus variable manufacturing overhead equals $35. It does not include the $6 of fixed overhead. Answer (C) is incorrect. Including $3 in variable selling costs and $4 in fixed selling costs results in $48. Answer (D) is incorrect. The amount of $67 includes $32 in direct materials and excludes $6 fixed overhead.

7. Cole's estimated prime costs per unit are

   A. $73

   B. $32

   C. $67

   D. $52

Answer (D) is correct.
   REQUIRED: The estimated prime costs per unit.
   DISCUSSION: The direct costs of manufacturing, also called prime costs, are the costs of direct materials and direct labor. They are costs that can be directly associated with the finished product. Thus, direct manufacturing costs per unit are $52 ($32 direct materials + $20 direct labor).
   Answer (A) is incorrect. The amount of $73 includes $15 variable manufacturing overhead and $6 fixed manufacturing overhead. Answer (B) is incorrect. Not including $20 direct labor results in $32. Answer (C) is incorrect. Including $15 variable manufacturing overhead results in $67.

Questions 8 and 9 are based on the following information.

Jackson Products
Schedule of Cost of Goods Manufactured
For the Year Ended December 31 (in thousands)

Direct materials:		
Beginning inventory	$17,000	
Purchases of direct materials	70,000	
Cost of direct materials available for use	$87,000	
Ending inventory	(9,000)	
Direct materials used		$ 78,000
Direct manufacturing labor		9,000
Indirect manufacturing costs:		
Indirect manufacturing labor	$ 8,000	
Supplies	1,000	
Heat, light, and power	4,000	
Depreciation -- plant building	2,000	
Depreciation -- plant equipment	3,000	
Miscellaneous	2,000	20,000
Manufacturing costs incurred during the period		$107,000
Add beginning work-in-process inventory		11,000
Total manufacturing costs to account for		$118,000
Deduct ending work-in-process inventory		(7,000)
Cost of goods manufactured (to Income Statement)		$111,000

8. What are Jackson's direct manufacturing costs for the year?

A. $20,000

B. $79,000

C. $87,000

D. $98,000

Answer (C) is correct.
    REQUIRED: The total of prime costs.
    DISCUSSION: Prime costs are all direct manufacturing costs. They equal the direct materials cost ($78,000) plus direct manufacturing labor cost ($9,000), or $87,000.
    Answer (A) is incorrect. Overhead is $20,000. Answer (B) is incorrect. Using the cost of material purchases instead of materials used results in $79,000. Answer (D) is incorrect. Using overhead instead of labor results in $98,000.

9. What are Jackson's conversion costs for the year?

A. $4,000

B. $20,000

C. $29,000

D. $98,000

Answer (C) is correct.
    REQUIRED: The total conversion costs.
    DISCUSSION: Conversion costs are all manufacturing costs other than direct material costs. Conversion costs equal direct manufacturing labor cost ($9,000) plus indirect manufacturing costs ($20,000), or $29,000.
    Answer (A) is incorrect. The difference between the beginning and ending work-in-process inventories is $4,000. Answer (B) is incorrect. The amount of $20,000 excludes direct labor. Answer (D) is incorrect. Including materials and excluding labor results in $98,000.

10. During the month just ended, Nale Co. used $300,000 of direct materials. At month end, Nale's direct materials inventory was $50,000 more than it was at the beginning of the month. Direct material purchases during the month amounted to

A. $0

B. $250,000

C. $300,000

D. $350,000

Answer (D) is correct.
    REQUIRED: The amount of direct materials purchases for the month.
    DISCUSSION: Direct materials costs are the costs of new materials included in finished goods that can be feasibly traced to those goods. The beginning direct materials inventory, plus direct material purchases, minus ending direct materials inventory equals the direct materials used. Because the direct materials inventory increased during the month, the increase can be added to the direct materials used to determine the amount of purchases. Thus, the direct materials purchases for the month equal $350,000 ($300,000 + $50,000).
    Answer (A) is incorrect. Direct materials must have been purchased if materials were used and the inventory increased. Answer (B) is incorrect. The amount of $250,000 results from subtracting the increase in direct materials inventory. Answer (C) is incorrect. The amount of $300,000 results from excluding the increase in direct materials inventory.

18.3 Other Cost Measurement Concepts

Questions 11 and 12 are based on the following information. The estimated unit costs for Cole Co. using absorption (full) costing and planning to produce and sell at a level of 12,000 units per month are as follows:

Cost Item	Estimated Unit Cost
Direct materials	$32
Direct labor	20
Variable manufacturing overhead	15
Fixed manufacturing overhead	6
Variable selling	3
Fixed selling	4

11. Cole's estimated total variable costs per unit are

A. $38

B. $70

C. $52

D. $18

Answer (B) is correct.
  REQUIRED: The estimated total variable costs per unit.
  DISCUSSION: Variable costs vary in direct proportion to production. Total unit variable costs are $70 ($32 direct materials + $20 direct labor + $15 variable overhead + $3 variable selling costs).
  Answer (A) is incorrect. The amount of $38 does not include $32 direct materials. Answer (C) is incorrect. The amount of $52 does not include $15 variable overhead and $3 variable selling costs. Answer (D) is incorrect. The amount of $18 does not include $32 direct materials and $20 direct labor.

12. Estimated total costs that Cole would incur during a month with a production level of 12,000 units and a sales level of 8,000 units are

A. $692,000

B. $960,000

C. $948,000

D. $932,000

Answer (C) is correct.
  REQUIRED: The estimated total costs incurred during a month with given production and sales levels.
  DISCUSSION: Manufacturing costs at a production level of 12,000 units are $73 per unit ($32 + $20 + $15 + $6). Total estimated manufacturing costs are therefore $876,000 (12,000 units × $73). Fixed selling costs are expected to be $48,000 (12,000 units × $4). The anticipated total variable selling costs are $24,000 (8,000 units × $3). Thus, the total estimated costs are $948,000 ($876,000 + $48,000 + $24,000).
  Answer (A) is incorrect. Total estimated costs are $948,000 [(12,000 × $73) + (12,000 × $4) + (8,000 × $3)]. Answer (B) is incorrect. Using 12,000 units to determine variable selling costs instead of 8,000 results in $960,000. Answer (D) is incorrect. Using 8,000 units to determine fixed selling costs instead of 12,000 results in $932,000.

13. Data from the duplicating department of a company for the last 2 months are as follows:

	Number of Copies Made	Duplicating Department's Costs
January	100,000	$8,500
February	150,000	9,500

What is total variable cost at 110,000 copies?

A. $1,100

B. $2,200

C. $5,500

D. $7,920

Answer (B) is correct.
  REQUIRED: The total variable cost.
  DISCUSSION: The fixed and variable portions of mixed costs can be estimated using the high-low method. Unit variable cost can be determined by dividing the $1,000 cost increase for the additional copies made in February by the increase in copies made. Thus, total variable cost for 110,000 copies is $2,200 {110,000 × [$1,000 ÷ (150,000 – 100,000)]}.
  Answer (A) is incorrect. Total variable cost would be $1,100 if 200,000 copies were made in February. Answer (C) is incorrect. Variable cost per unit would have to be $.05 to total $5,500. Answer (D) is incorrect. Calculating an average cost per copy for January and February and then multiplying by 110,000 copies results in $7,920.

14. In manufacturing its products for the month just ended, Elk Co. incurred normal spoilage of $10,000 and abnormal spoilage of $12,000. How much spoilage cost should Elk charge as a period cost for the month?

    A. $22,000

    B. $12,000

    C. $10,000

    D. $0

Answer (B) is correct.
    REQUIRED: The spoilage charged as a period cost.
    DISCUSSION: Normal spoilage occurs under efficient operating conditions and is therefore a product cost. Abnormal spoilage is not expected to occur under efficient operating conditions. It is accounted for as a period cost. Thus, the amount of spoilage charged as a period cost is the $12,000 related to abnormal spoilage.
    Answer (A) is incorrect. The amount of $22,000 includes the normal spoilage ($10,000), which is a product cost. Answer (C) is incorrect. The $10,000 normal spoilage is a product cost. Answer (D) is incorrect. The abnormal spoilage ($12,000) is a period cost.

15. Dahl Co. uses a standard costing system in connection with the manufacture of a "one size fits all" article of clothing. Each unit of finished product contains 2 yards of direct materials. However, a 20% direct materials spoilage calculated on input quantities occurs during the manufacturing process. The cost of the direct materials is $3 per yard. The standard direct materials cost per unit of finished product is

    A. $4.80

    B. $6.00

    C. $7.20

    D. $7.50

Answer (D) is correct.
    REQUIRED: The standard direct materials cost per unit of finished product.
    DISCUSSION: If 2 yards remain in each unit after spoilage of 20% of the direct materials input, the total per unit input must have been 2.5 yards (2.0 ÷ 80%). The standard unit direct materials cost is therefore $7.50 (2.5 yards × $3).
    Answer (A) is incorrect. The 2 yards of good output should be divided (not multiplied) by 80% to determine the standard yards of material per unit. Answer (B) is incorrect. The cost per unit before spoilage is added is $6.00. Answer (C) is incorrect. Adding 20% of the materials of the finished product as spoilage and then multiplying by the $3.00 cost per yard results in $7.20 [(2.00 × 1.20) × $3.00].

18.4 Decision Costing

16. Clay Co. has considerable excess manufacturing capacity. A special job order's cost sheet includes the following applied manufacturing overhead costs:

Fixed costs	$21,000
Variable costs	33,000

The fixed costs include a normal $3,700 allocation for in-house design costs, although no in-house design will be done. Instead, the job will require the use of external designers costing $7,750. What is the total amount to be included in the calculation to determine the minimum acceptable price for the job?

    A. $36,700

    B. $40,750

    C. $54,000

    D. $58,050

Answer (B) is correct.
    REQUIRED: The total amount to be included in the calculation to determine the minimum acceptable price.
    DISCUSSION: Given excess capacity, neither increased fixed costs nor opportunity costs are incurred by accepting the special order. Thus, the marginal cost of the order (the minimum acceptable price) is $40,750 ($33,000 variable costs + $7,750 cost of external design).
    Answer (A) is incorrect. The amount of $36,700 equals variable costs plus the in-house design costs. Answer (C) is incorrect. The amount of $54,000 equals the fixed costs plus the variable costs. Answer (D) is incorrect. The amount of $58,050 equals the fixed costs, plus the variable costs, minus the in-house design costs, plus the external design costs.

17. When considering a special order that will enable a company to make use of currently idle capacity, which of the following costs is irrelevant?

    A. Materials.

    B. Depreciation.

    C. Direct labor.

    D. Variable overhead.

Answer (B) is correct.
    REQUIRED: The irrelevant cost when a special order permits use of idle capacity.
    DISCUSSION: Because depreciation is expensed whether or not the the special order is accepted, it is irrelevant to the decision. Only the variable costs are relevant.
    Answer (A) is incorrect. Materials are relevant to a decision whether to accept a special order. Answer (C) is incorrect. Direct labor is relevant to a decision whether to accept a special order. Answer (D) is incorrect. Variable overhead is relevant to a decision whether to accept a special order.

18. When only differential manufacturing costs are taken into account for special-order pricing, an essential assumption is that

A. Manufacturing fixed and variable costs are linear.

B. Selling and administrative fixed and variable costs are linear.

C. Acceptance of the order will not affect regular sales.

D. Acceptance of the order will not cause unit selling and administrative variable costs to increase.

Answer (C) is correct.
REQUIRED: The assumption when only differential manufacturing costs are considered for special-order pricing.
DISCUSSION: Granting a lower-than-normal price for a special order has potential effects on regular sales. Other customers may demand the same price. Thus, the decision to consider only differential (marginal) manufacturing costs should be based on a determination that all other costs are not relevant. The other costs should not vary with the option chosen.
Answer (A) is incorrect. Manufacturing costs need not be linear. The analysis of a special order considers total marginal costs. Consequently, the unit variable costs and total fixed costs need not be constant, and any changes need not be in direct proportion to the measure of activity. Answer (B) is incorrect. The assumption is that selling and administrative costs are not relevant. Thus, whether they are linear also is irrelevant. Answer (D) is incorrect. The assumption is that acceptance of the order will not cause total selling and administrative costs to change.

19. Based on potential sales of 500 units per year, a new product has estimated traceable costs of $990,000. What is the target price to obtain a 15% profit margin on sales?

A. $2,329

B. $2,277

C. $1,980

D. $1,935

Answer (A) is correct.
REQUIRED: The target price.
DISCUSSION: Costs of the product must be 85% of sales to achieve a 15% profit on sales. Thus, sales must be $1,164,706 ($990,000 ÷ .85). The price per unit is $2,329 ($1,164,706 ÷ 500).
Answer (B) is incorrect. The amount of $2,277 results from multiplying $990,000 by 1.15 and dividing by 500 units. Answer (C) is incorrect. The cost per unit is $1,980. Answer (D) is incorrect. The amount of $1,935 is 85% of $2,277.

20. Mili Co. plans to discontinue a division with a $20,000 contribution to overhead. Overhead allocated to the division is $50,000, of which $5,000 cannot be eliminated. The effect of this discontinuance on Mili's pretax income would be an increase of

A. $5,000

B. $20,000

C. $25,000

D. $30,000

Answer (C) is correct.
REQUIRED: The effect of discontinuing a division.
DISCUSSION: This disinvestment decision eliminates $45,000 of overhead ($50,000 – $5,000) and the $20,000 contribution to overhead. The net effect on pretax income is therefore a $25,000 increase ($45,000 – $20,000).
Answer (A) is incorrect. The overhead allocated to the division, which cannot be eliminated, is $5,000. The net effect is a $25,000 increase in pretax income ($45,000 overhead that can be eliminated – $20,000 contribution to overhead). Answer (B) is incorrect. The contribution to overhead is $20,000. Answer (D) is incorrect. The $5,000 of overhead that cannot be eliminated from the $50,000 overhead allocated should be subtracted.

18.5 Cost-Volume-Profit Analysis -- Basics

21. The breakeven point in units increases when unit costs

A. Increase and sales price remains unchanged.

B. Decrease and sales price remains unchanged.

C. Remain unchanged and sales price increases.

D. Decrease and sales price increases.

Answer (A) is correct.
REQUIRED: The event that causes the breakeven point in units to increase.
DISCUSSION: A BEP ratio can be increased either by raising the numerator or lowering the denominator. The breakeven point in units is calculated by dividing fixed costs by the unit contribution margin. If selling price is constant and costs increase, the unit contribution margin decreases. The effect is to decrease the denominator and increase the ratio.
Answer (B) is incorrect. A decrease in costs decreases the breakeven point. The unit contribution margin increases. Answer (C) is incorrect. An increase in the selling price also increases the unit contribution margin, resulting in a lower breakeven point. Answer (D) is incorrect. The unit contribution margin is increased by a cost decrease and a sales price increase, resulting in a lower breakeven point.

22. The breakeven point in units sold for Tierson Corporation is 44,000. If fixed costs for Tierson are equal to $880,000 annually and variable costs are $10 per unit, what is the contribution margin per unit for Tierson Corporation?

A. $0.05

B. $20.00

C. $44.00

D. $88.00

Answer (B) is correct.
    REQUIRED: The contribution margin per unit.
    DISCUSSION: The breakeven point in units is equal to the fixed costs divided by the unit contribution margin (UCM).

$$\text{Fixed costs} \div \text{UCM} = \text{Breakeven point in units}$$
$$\$880,000 \div \text{UCM} = 44,000 \text{ units}$$
$$\text{UCM} = \$20$$

    Answer (A) is incorrect. The amount of $.05 results from inverting the numerator and denominator in the calculation. Answer (C) is incorrect. The amount of $44.00 results from using variable cost as part of the calculation. Answer (D) is incorrect. The amount of $88.00 results from dividing by an erroneous denominator.

Questions 23 and 24 are based on the following information. Oradell Company sells its single product at a price of $60 per unit and incurs the following variable costs per unit of product:

Direct material	$16
Direct labor	12
Manufacturing overhead	7
Variable manufacturing costs	$35
Selling expenses	5
Total variable costs	$40

Oradell's annual fixed costs are $880,000, and Oradell is subject to a 30% income tax rate.

23. The number of units of product that Oradell Company must sell annually to break even is

A. 22,000 units.

B. 44,000 units.

C. 35,200 units.

D. 30,800 units.

Answer (B) is correct.
    REQUIRED: The breakeven point in units.
    DISCUSSION: The breakeven point in units equals fixed costs divided by the unit contribution margin (UCM). At a selling price of $60 per unit and with variable costs of $40 per unit, the unit contribution margin is $20. Thus, the breakeven point is 44,000 units ($880,000 ÷ $20).

24. If prime costs increased by 20% and all other values remained the same, Oradell Company's contribution margin (to the nearest whole percent) would be

A. 30%

B. 76%

C. 20%

D. 24%

Answer (D) is correct.
    REQUIRED: The contribution margin ratio after an increase in prime costs.
    DISCUSSION: Prime costs are direct materials and direct labor. Because their total was $28 ($16 + $12) before the increase, the new total is $33.60 ($28 × 1.2). Thus, prime costs increase by $5.60, and total variable costs increase to $45.60. Subtracting $45.60 from the $60 selling price leaves a contribution margin of $14.40. The contribution margin percentage thus becomes 24% ($14.40 ÷ $60).

25. The following information pertains to Sisk Co.:

Sales (25,000 units)	$500,000
Direct materials and direct labor	150,000
Factory overhead:	
Variable	20,000
Fixed	35,000
Selling and general expenses:	
Variable	5,000
Fixed	30,000

Sisk's breakeven point in number of units is

A. 4,924

B. 5,000

C. 6,250

D. 9,286

Answer (B) is correct.

REQUIRED: The breakeven point in units.

DISCUSSION: The breakeven point in units equals the fixed costs divided by the unit contribution margin (UCM). The fixed costs are $65,000 ($35,000 manufacturing overhead + $30,000 SG&A). The UCM is calculated as follows:

	Dollars	Units		Per Unit
Sales	$500,000 ÷	25,000	=	$20.00
Variable costs:				
Prime costs	$150,000			
Variable overhead	20,000			
Variable SG&A	5,000			
Total var. costs	$175,000 ÷	25,000	=	(7.00)
Contribution margin				$13.00

Thus, the breakeven point in units is 5,000 ($65,000 fixed costs ÷ $13 UCM).

Answer (A) is incorrect. The amount of 4,924 does not include the variable selling and general expenses in the unit contribution margin calculation. Answer (C) is incorrect. The amount of 6,250 includes the unit fixed manufacturing overhead and unit fixed selling and general expenses in the unit contribution margin. Answer (D) is incorrect. The amount of 9,286 results from using the total variable costs of $7 rather than the contribution margin of $13.

18.6 Cost-Volume-Profit Analysis -- Applications

26. The following information pertains to Clove Co. for the month just ended:

Budgeted sales	$1,000,000
Breakeven sales	700,000
Budgeted contribution margin	600,000
Cash flow breakeven	200,000

Clove's margin of safety is

A. $300,000

B. $400,000

C. $500,000

D. $800,000

Answer (A) is correct.

REQUIRED: The margin of safety.

DISCUSSION: The margin of safety measures the amount by which sales may decline before losses occur. It is the excess of budgeted or actual sales over the breakeven sales. Given that the budgeted sales are $1,000,000 and the breakeven sales are $700,000, the margin of safety is $300,000 ($1,000,000 – $700,000).

Answer (B) is incorrect. The budgeted sales minus the budgeted contribution margin is $400,000. Answer (C) is incorrect. The breakeven sales minus the cash flow breakeven is $500,000. Answer (D) is incorrect. The budgeted sales minus the cash flow breakeven is $800,000.

27. In using cost-volume-profit analysis to calculate expected unit sales, which of the following should be added to fixed costs in the numerator?

A. Predicted operating loss.

B. Predicted operating income.

C. Unit contribution margin.

D. Variable costs.

Answer (B) is correct.

REQUIRED: The addition to fixed costs when calculating expected unit sales.

DISCUSSION: CVP analysis can be used to restate the equation for target net income to determine the required level of unit sales.

$$Target\ unit\ volume = \frac{Fixed\ costs + Target\ operating\ income}{UCM}$$

Answer (A) is incorrect. Predicted operating loss is subtracted from fixed costs, not added. Answer (C) is incorrect. Unit contribution margin is the denominator. Answer (D) is incorrect. Variable costs are a component of unit contribution margin.

28. During Year 1, Thor Lab supplied hospitals with a comprehensive diagnostic kit for $120. At a volume of 80,000 kits, Thor had fixed costs of $1 million and a profit before income taxes of $200,000. Because of an adverse legal decision, Thor's Year 2 liability insurance increased by $1.2 million over Year 1. Assuming the volume and other costs are unchanged, what should the Year 2 price be if Thor is to make the same $200,000 profit before income taxes?

A. $120.00

B. $135.00

C. $150.00

D. $240.00

Answer (B) is correct.

REQUIRED: The price charged to earn a specified pretax profit.

DISCUSSION: CVP analysis can be used to restate the equation for operating income to determine the required level of unit sales:

$$Target\ unit\ volume = \frac{Fixed\ costs\ +\ Target\ operating\ income}{UCM}$$

Thor's Year 1 unit variable cost (UVC) can thus be calculated as follows:

$$80,000\ units = (\$1,000,000 + \$200,000) \div (\$120 - UVC)$$
$$80,000 \times (\$120 - UVC) = \$1,200,000$$
$$\$120 - UVC = \$15$$
$$UVC = \$105$$

The Year 2 unit selling price (USP) can now be derived:

$$80,000\ units = (\$1,000,000 + \$200,000 + \$1,200,000) \div (USP - \$105)$$
$$80,000 \times (USP - \$105) = \$2,400,000$$
$$USP - \$105 = \$30$$
$$USP = \$135$$

Answer (A) is incorrect. The Year 1 unit price was $120.00. Answer (C) is incorrect. The amount of $150.00 assumes that the unit variable cost is $120. Answer (D) is incorrect. The amount of $240.00 assumes that the price must double, given that the sum of fixed costs and targeted profit has doubled.

29. Wren Co. manufactures and sells two products with selling prices and variable costs as follows:

	A	B
Selling price	$18.00	$22.00
Variable costs	12.00	14.00

Wren's total annual fixed costs are $38,400. Wren sells four units of A for every unit of B. If operating income last year was $28,800, what was the number of units Wren sold?

A. 5,486

B. 6,000

C. 9,600

D. 10,500

Answer (D) is correct.

REQUIRED: The number of units sold.

DISCUSSION: The contribution margins of the two products are $6 and $8, respectively ($18 – $12 and $22 – $14). The units sold can be calculated as follows:

$$Target\ unit\ volume = (Fixed\ costs + Target\ operating\ income) \div Weighted\ UCM$$
$$= (\$38,400 + \$28,800) \div (\$6A + \$8B)$$
$$\$6A + \$8B = \$67,200$$
$$\$6(4B) + \$8B = \$67,200$$
$$\$32B = \$67,200$$
$$B = 2,100\ units$$

Because 4 units of A are sold for every unit of B, the volume of A was 8,400 units (2,100 × 4). Thus, the total number of units sold was 10,500 (8,400A + 2,100B).

Answer (A) is incorrect. The amount of 5,486 units equals the fixed costs divided by the contribution margin from product B. Answer (B) is incorrect. The amount of 6,000 units does not include the operating income of $28,800 in the calculation. Answer (C) is incorrect. The operating income plus the fixed costs are divided by the contribution margin for product B, giving the number of units sold of 9,600.

Question 30 is based on the following information.
Oradell Company sells its single product at a price
of $60 per unit and incurs the following variable
costs per unit of product:

Direct material	$16
Direct labor	12
Manufacturing overhead	7
Variable manufacturing costs	$35
Selling expenses	5
Total variable costs	$40

Oradell's annual fixed costs are $880,000, and
Oradell is subject to a 30% income tax rate.

30. The annual sales revenue required by Oradell
Company in order to achieve after-tax net income of
$224,000 for the year is

A. $3,600,000

B. $3,312,000

C. $1,656,000

D. $3,110,400

Answer (A) is correct.
REQUIRED: The annual sales revenue needed to earn a
given after-tax net income.
DISCUSSION: CVP analysis can be used to restate the
equation for net income and determine the required level of unit
sales.

$$\text{Target unit volume} = \{\text{Fixed costs} + [\text{Target net income} \div (1.0 - \text{tax rate})]\} \div \text{UCM}$$
$$= [\$880,000 + (\$224,000 \div .70)] \div (\$60 - \$40)$$
$$= \$1,200,000 \div \$20$$
$$= 60,000 \text{ units}$$

At a unit selling price of $60, the total revenue is $3,600,000
(60,000 units × $60).
Answer (B) is incorrect. The annual sales revenue that
results when the $96,000 of income tax is ignored is $3,312,000.
Answer (C) is incorrect. The amount of $1,656,000 is the annual
sales revenue when the $96,000 of income tax is ignored and the
sum of the fixed costs and net income ($1,104,000 = $880,000
fixed costs + $224,000 net income) is divided by the variable unit
cost of $40 (instead of the contribution margin of $20).
Answer (D) is incorrect. The annual sales revenue when the
$96,000 of income is subtracted from (instead of added to) the
$224,000 is $3,110,400.

18.7 PRACTICE WRITTEN COMMUNICATION

| | Business Environment and Concepts Testlet 4 of 4 | Time Remaining 1 hour - 15 minutes | | | | |

DIRECTIONS

Note: If you believe you have encountered a software malfunction, report it to the test center staff immediately.

Navigation

To navigate from task to task, use the controls at the bottom of the screen. Click on the **Next** button to advance to the next task, or the **Previous** button to go to the previous task. To go directly to any task, click on its number.

If you would like a reminder to revisit a task, or want to indicate that you are finished with it, click on the reminder flag below the task number. To clear the flag, click on it again. Reminder flags are for your use only – they do not contribute to your score.

Tabs

In this part of the examination, you will be asked to complete various tasks. Every task has one or more **Work Tabs**. Every task also has a **Help** tab.

Work tab   Help tab

Work Tabs:

- **Work Tabs** are identified with a pencil icon. This is where your responses are expected.
- Each task has one or more **Work Tabs**.
- **Work Tabs** contain directions for completing the task - be sure to read these directions carefully.
- The **Work Tab** name in the example above is for illustration only - yours will differ.
- You must complete all of the **Work Tabs** in each task to receive full credit.

Help Tab:

- The **Help Tab** provides assistance with the exam software that is used in this task. For example, if the task is to compose a memorandum, **Help** will provide information about the word processor.

The Toolbar

The toolbar at the top of the screen shows the amount of time remaining for you to complete the tasks. In addition, the following tools are available. Note that only the **Exit** button is displayed when Directions are visible - the others will appear when you begin the tasks.

Click on these buttons to split or unsplit the screen. You can split the screen vertically or horizontally.

Click on this button to go on to the next part of the examination. You must complete all of the tasks to receive full credit. Once you click on **Exit** and confirm the action, you will NOT be able to return to this testlet.

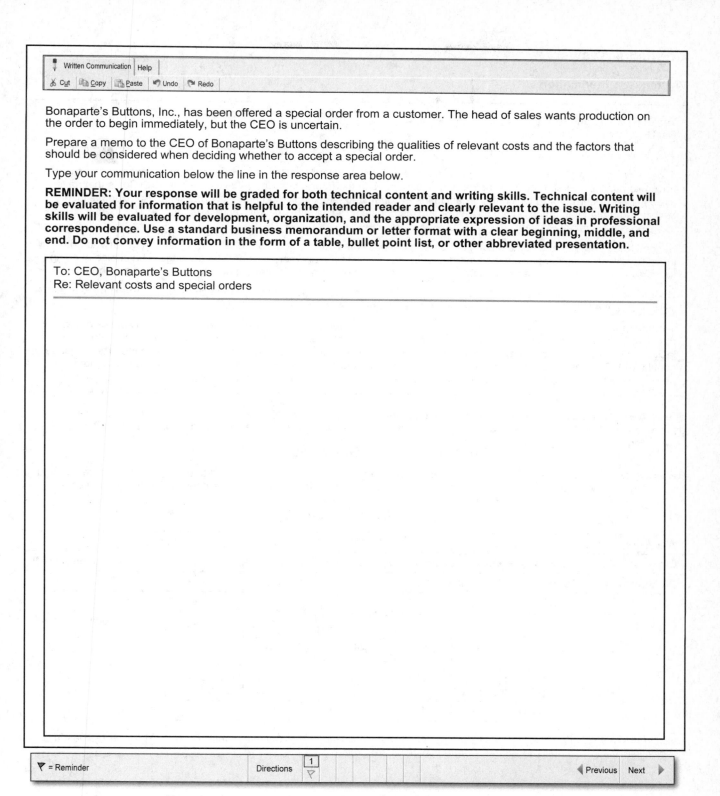

Bonaparte's Buttons, Inc., has been offered a special order from a customer. The head of sales wants production on the order to begin immediately, but the CEO is uncertain.

Prepare a memo to the CEO of Bonaparte's Buttons describing the qualities of relevant costs and the factors that should be considered when deciding whether to accept a special order.

Type your communication below the line in the response area below.

REMINDER: Your response will be graded for both technical content and writing skills. Technical content will be evaluated for information that is helpful to the intended reader and clearly relevant to the issue. Writing skills will be evaluated for development, organization, and the appropriate expression of ideas in professional correspondence. Use a standard business memorandum or letter format with a clear beginning, middle, and end. Do not convey information in the form of a table, bullet point list, or other abbreviated presentation.

To: CEO, Bonaparte's Buttons
Re: Relevant costs and special orders

NOTE: Your Written Communications on the actual CPA exam may cover topics outside the scope of the BEC CSO (i.e., they may relate to topics from the AUD, FAR, and/or REG CSOs instead). Answer to the best of your ability, and remember that graders are mainly evaluating your writing ability and will overlook minor technical mistakes.

Unofficial Answer

Written Communication

To: CEO, Bonaparte's Buttons
Re: Relevant costs and special orders

In decision making, an organization emphasizes relevant revenues and costs. To be relevant, revenues and costs must have two qualities. First, they must be earned or expended in the future. Only future costs are relevant. Costs that have already been incurred or to which the organization is committed (sunk costs) do not affect decisions. An example is the decision to replace an aging automobile that requires constant repair with a newer, more reliable one. The money already spent on repairs is not relevant.

Second, the revenues and costs must differ among the possible courses of action. Cash flows that do not vary do not affect decisions. An example is a gym membership that is debited every month regardless of usage. The choice of going to a movie or to the gym on a given night depends on the cost of the movie ticket but not that of the gym membership.

Only avoidable costs are relevant. A cost is unavoidable if it is incurred regardless of the action taken. An example is a 12-month lease liability that is due to a landlord, even if a new job in another city is accepted.

When a manufacturer has excess production capacity, no opportunity cost is involved when accepting a special order. The entity should accept the order if the minimum price for the product is equal to the variable costs. When a manufacturer lacks excess production capacity, however, the differential (marginal or incremental) costs of accepting the order must be considered. Besides the variable costs of the production run, the entity must consider the opportunity cost of redirecting productive capacity away from (possibly more profitable) products. management, control, and governance processes.

The above depicts a Level 5 answer. Consult your booklet, *How to Pass the CPA Exam: A System for Success*, for a description of the three writing skills criteria. You may also access this booklet online by visiting www.gleim.com/PassCPA.

Self-Grade

Below, grade your response on technical content and writing skills. Bubble in the circle next to the appropriate score that you may receive based on the criteria given. Your **total** score is the sum of your scores on all six items. The maximum score is 19 points.

Technical Content Evaluation

Was your response on topic?	O No [0]	O Mostly [1]	O Yes [2]
Did your response have any *significant* errors?	O 0 errors [1]	O 1 major error [−1]	O 2 or more major errors [−2]
Did your response contain any illegal advice?	O No [1]	O Yes [0]	

Writing Skills Evaluation

	Poor	Below Average	Average	Above Average	Outstanding
Organization	O 1	O 2	O 3	O 4	O 5
Development	O 1	O 2	O 3	O 4	O 5
Expression	O 1	O 2	O 3	O 4	O 5

Disclaimer: This scoring schedule was developed by Gleim Publications as a guideline only. The AICPA has not released specific information on how the Written Communications are graded.

Practice even more Written Communications with the Gleim Mega Test Bank.

Learn more: gleim.com/CPAmega | 800.874.5346

STUDY UNIT NINETEEN
COSTING METHODS

(10 pages of outline)

The difference between absorption and variable costing is in the treatment of the fixed portion of manufacturing overhead. **Absorption costing** includes all costs of manufacturing, variable and fixed, in product cost. This method is required under GAAP. **Variable costing** assigns only variable manufacturing costs to products. It is not permitted for external reporting but is useful for managerial purposes.

Cost allocation is necessary when separate products are produced by a manufacturing process from a common input. The outputs are **joint products**. Joint costs must be allocated to the various products but normally are not allocated to by-products. **By-products** are of relatively small total value and are produced simultaneously from a common process with products of greater value and quantity (joint products).

Job-order costing and process costing are the fundamental methods for assigning costs to products. **Job-order costing** assigns costs to specific units, lots, or batches. It is appropriate when products have unique characteristics, such as custom-made furniture. **Process costing** assigns costs to large numbers of homogeneous products with costs accumulated by processes, departments, or cost centers. Process costing is covered in Study Unit 20.

Overhead consists of indirect costs that cannot be traced feasibly to final products. They consist primarily of indirect materials, indirect labor, and indirect operating costs such as utilities and depreciation. Overhead is accumulated in one or more cost pools and applied using a standard rate.

19.1 ABSORPTION COSTING AND VARIABLE COSTING -- THEORY

1. **Absorption Costing**

   a. Absorption (full) costing includes the fixed portion of manufacturing overhead in product cost.

      1) Product cost includes all manufacturing costs (fixed and variable).

      2) Sales minus absorption-basis cost of goods sold equals **gross profit** (gross margin).

      3) **Operating income** equals gross profit minus total selling and administrative expenses (fixed and variable).

      4) This method is required under GAAP for external reporting purposes and under the Internal Revenue Code for tax purposes. The justification is that, for external reporting, product cost should include all manufacturing costs.

2. **Variable Costing**

   a. Variable costing includes only variable manufacturing costs in product cost. Variable costing is preferable for internal reporting. It better satisfies management's needs for operational planning and control information because it excludes arbitrary allocations of fixed costs.

      1) Furthermore, variable-costing net income varies directly with sales and is not affected by changes in inventory levels.

b. **Contribution margin** equals sales minus variable cost of goods sold and the variable portion of selling and administrative expenses.

1) This amount (sales – total variable costs) is an important element of the variable costing income statement. It is the amount available for covering fixed costs (fixed manufacturing, fixed selling, and administrative).

EXAMPLE

Beginning inventory is 0, 100 units are produced, and 80 units are sold. The following costs were incurred:

Direct materials	$1,000
Direct labor	2,000
Variable overhead	1,500
Manufacturing costs for variable costing	$4,500
Fixed overhead	3,000
Manufacturing costs for absorption costing	$7,500

The following are the effects on the financial statements of using absorption or variable costing:

	Manufacturing costs	Divided by: Units produced	Equals: Per-unit cost	Times: Units in ending inventory	Equals: Cost of ending inventory
Absorption costing	$7,500	100	$75	20	$1,500
Variable costing	4,500	100	45	20	900

The per-unit selling price of the finished goods was $100, and $200 of variable selling and administrative expenses and $600 of fixed selling and administrative expenses were incurred.

The following are partial income statements prepared using the two methods:

		Absorption Costing (Required under GAAP)		Variable Costing (Internal reporting only)	
	Sales		$ 8,000		$ 8,000
	Beginning inventory	$ 0		$ 0	
Product Costs	Plus: variable manufacturing costs	4,500 (a)		4,500 (a)	
	Plus: fixed manufacturing costs	3,000 (b)			
	Goods available for sale	$7,500		$4,500	
	Minus: ending inventory	(1,500)		(900)	
	Cost of goods sold		$(6,000)		$(3,600)
	Minus: variable S&A expenses				(200) (c)
	Gross profit (abs.) or contribution margin (var.)		$ 2,000		$ 4,200
Period Costs	Minus: fixed manufacturing costs				(3,000) (b)
	Minus: variable S&A expenses		(200) (c)		
	Minus: fixed S&A expenses		(600) (d)		(600) (d)
	Operating income		$ 1,200		$ 600

Given no beginning inventory, the difference in operating income ($1,200 – $600 = $600) is the difference between the ending inventory amounts ($1,500 – $900 = $600).

Under the absorption method, 20% of the fixed overhead costs ($3,000 × 20% = $600) is recorded as an asset because 20% of the month's production (100 units available – 80 units sold = 20 units) is still in inventory.

---

3. **Effects on Operating Income**

CPA candidates must know how to calculate the various income statement components under the absorption and variable costing methods. The AICPA has frequently tested this topic, focusing especially on the differences between the amounts, such as operating income, determined by each method.

a. As production and sales change, the two methods have varying effects on operating income.

b. When production and sales are equal for a period, the two methods report the same operating income.

1) Total fixed costs for the period are expensed during the period under both methods.

c. When production and sales are not equal for a period, the two methods report different operating incomes as illustrated below:

When production	**When production**
△△△△△△△	△△△
exceeds sales,	**is less than sales,**
△△△	△△△△△△△
ending inventory increases.	**ending inventory decreases.**
↑↑↑↑↑↑↑↑↑↑↑↑↑↑↑	↓↓↓↓↓↓
Under absorption costing, some fixed manufacturing costs are included in ending inventory.	**Under absorption costing,** fixed manufacturing costs included in beginning inventory are expensed.
Under variable costing, all fixed costs of the current period are expensed. No fixed costs are included in ending inventory.	**Under variable costing,** all fixed costs of the current period are expensed. No fixed costs are included in ending inventory.
Operating income is higher under <u>absorption</u> costing.	**Operating income is higher under <u>variable</u> costing.**

Figure 19-1

Stop and review! You have completed the outline for this subunit. Study multiple-choice questions 1 through 6 beginning on page 497.

19.2 ABSORPTION COSTING AND VARIABLE COSTING -- CALCULATIONS

CPA candidates can expect questions that require quantifying the difference between absorption and variable costing. This subunit consists entirely of such questions. Please review Subunit 19.1 before answering these questions.

Stop and review! You have completed the outline for this subunit. Study multiple-choice questions 7 through 12 beginning on page 498.

19.3 JOINT PRODUCT AND BY-PRODUCT COSTING

1. **Joint Product Costing**

a. Joint products are separate products resulting from a common manufacturing process. They have high sales values compared with the sales values of other outputs.

1) **Joint costs** are incurred up to the split-off point where the products become separately identifiable. They include direct materials, direct labor, and manufacturing overhead.

a) Because joint costs are incurred before products can be identified separately, they must be allocated.

b.   Costs incurred after split-off are separable costs.

1)   Separable costs can be identified with a specific joint product.

Figure 19-2

c.   The decision to **sell or process further** is made based on whether the incremental revenue from further processing exceeds the incremental cost. The joint cost of the product is irrelevant because it is a sunk cost.

2.   **By-Product Costing**

a.   By-products are one or more products of relatively small total value that are produced simultaneously from a common manufacturing process with products of greater value.

1)   Whether the benefits of further processing and sale exceed the costs must be determined.

Selling price
– Additional processing costs
– Selling costs
= **Net realizable value**

2)   If the net realizable value is zero or negative, the by-products should be sold at the split-off point or discarded as scrap if they cannot be sold.

b.   The value of a by-product may be recognized initially either at the time

1)   Production is completed. The amount equals the expected net proceeds from its sale (or its expected NRV if the by-product is subject to further processing to be salable). Thus, by-product inventory is recognized.

2)   The by-product is sold.

c.   Any proceeds (revenue) from the sale of a by-product are recognized either as (1) a reduction of the cost of goods sold of the joint products or (2) a revenue.

1)   Cost of goods sold is not recognized for by-products.

d.   Regardless of the timing of their recognition in the accounts, by-products usually do not receive an allocation of joint costs. The cost of this accounting treatment ordinarily exceeds the benefit.

Stop and review! You have completed the outline for this subunit. Study multiple-choice questions 13 through 19 beginning on page 501.

19.4 JOINT COST ALLOCATION METHODS

1. **Physical-Quantity Method**

   a. The physical-quantity method uses a physical measure such as volume or weight.

      1) Joint production costs are allocated to each product based on its relative proportion of the measure selected.

EXAMPLE

Processing 1,000 barrels of crude oil costs $100,000. The process results in the following outputs:

	Barrels	Selling price per barrel at a split-off point	Separable costs	Selling price per barrel after additional process
Asphalt	300	$ 60	$1,000	$ 70
Fuel oil	300	180	1,000	200
Diesel fuel	200	160	1,000	180
Kerosene	100	80	2,000	90
Gasoline	100	180	2,000	190

Under the physical-quantity method, the joint costs up to split-off are allocated as follows:

Asphalt	$100,000 × (300 barrels ÷ 1,000 barrels) =	$ 30,000
Fuel oil	$100,000 × (300 barrels ÷ 1,000 barrels) =	30,000
Diesel fuel	$100,000 × (200 barrels ÷ 1,000 barrels) =	20,000
Kerosene	$100,000 × (100 barrels ÷ 1,000 barrels) =	10,000
Gasoline	$100,000 × (100 barrels ÷ 1,000 barrels) =	10,000
Joint costs allocated		$100,000

---

   b. The physical-quantity method's simplicity is an advantage, but it does not match costs with the individual products' revenues.

2. **Allocating Joint Costs -- Market-Based Approach**

   a. A market-based approach assigns a proportionate amount of the total cost to each product on a quantitative basis. These allocations are **not** based on units sold because the joint costs were incurred for all units produced, not just those sold. The following are common methods of allocation:

      1) The **sales-value at split-off method** is based on the relative sales values of the separate products at split-off.

EXAMPLE

The five outputs can be sold for the following prices at split-off:

Asphalt	300 barrels × $ 60 per barrel	=	$ 18,000
Fuel oil	300 barrels × $180 per barrel	=	54,000
Diesel fuel	200 barrels × $160 per barrel	=	32,000
Kerosene	100 barrels × $ 80 per barrel	=	8,000
Gasoline	100 barrels × $180 per barrel	=	18,000
Total sales value at split-off			$130,000

The total sales value for the production run at split-off is $130,000. For each product, total joint cost to be allocated is multiplied by the proportion of the sales of each product:

Asphalt	$100,000 × ($18,000 ÷ $130,000) =	$ 13,846
Fuel oil	$100,000 × ($54,000 ÷ $130,000) =	41,538
Diesel fuel	$100,000 × ($32,000 ÷ $130,000) =	24,616
Kerosene	$100,000 × ($ 8,000 ÷ $130,000) =	6,154
Gasoline	$100,000 × ($18,000 ÷ $130,000) =	13,846
Joint costs allocated		$100,000

---

2)   The **estimated net realizable value (NRV) method** allocates joint costs based on the relative market values of the products after additional processing.

    a)   Net realizable value (NRV) at split-off equals the sale price at the point of sale minus the cost to complete after split-off (separable costs).

    b)   Under the estimated NRV method, all separable costs necessary to make the product salable are subtracted before the allocation.

EXAMPLE

The following are the final estimated sales prices:

Asphalt	300 barrels × $ 70 per barrel =	$21,000
Fuel oil	300 barrels × $200 per barrel =	60,000
Diesel fuel	200 barrels × $180 per barrel =	36,000
Kerosene	100 barrels × $ 90 per barrel =	9,000
Gasoline	100 barrels × $190 per barrel =	19,000

From these amounts, separable costs are subtracted (these costs are given):

Asphalt	$21,000 – $1,000 =	$ 20,000
Fuel oil	$60,000 – $1,000 =	59,000
Diesel fuel	$36,000 – $1,000 =	35,000
Kerosene	$ 9,000 – $2,000 =	7,000
Gasoline	$19,000 – $2,000 =	17,000
Total net realizable value		$138,000

The total NRV for the production run is $138,000. For each product, total joint cost to be allocated is multiplied by the proportion of the NRV of each product:

Asphalt	$100,000 × ($20,000 ÷ $138,000) =	$ 14,493
Fuel oil	$100,000 × ($59,000 ÷ $138,000) =	42,754
Diesel fuel	$100,000 × ($35,000 ÷ $138,000) =	25,362
Kerosene	$100,000 × ($ 7,000 ÷ $138,000) =	5,072
Gasoline	$100,000 × ($17,000 ÷ $138,000) =	12,319
Joint costs allocated		$100,000

Stop and review! You have completed the outline for this subunit. Study multiple-choice questions 20 through 24 beginning on page 503.

19.5 JOB-ORDER COSTING AND OVERHEAD APPLICATION

1.   **Uses of Job-Order Costing**

    a.   Job-order costing is used when each end product is unique. Because the end products are few, tracking their costs is relatively simple.

    b.   Manufacturers that use job-order costing include construction and shipbuilding. Service industries include software design and plumbing.

2.   **Accumulation of Direct Costs**

    a.   The accumulation of costs in a job-order system can best be described in terms of the flow of manual documents in the process. (These functions currently are performed most often with computers rather than physical documents.)

    b.   The accounting process begins when a sales order is received from a customer. Because products are custom made, no finished goods inventory is held, but production cannot begin until an order is placed. After the sales order is approved, a production order is issued.

c. The physical inputs required for production are obtained from suppliers.

   1) For example, $100,000 of direct materials are purchased on account. The journal entry is

Materials control	$100,000	
Accounts payable		$100,000

d. A subsidiary account is created within the work-in-process ledger to track the costs for each job. The accumulation of direct costs (direct materials and direct labor) is simple.

e. Materials requisition forms request direct materials to be sent from the warehouse to the production line.

   1) For example, the production line submits a materials requisition to the warehouse for $60,000 of direct materials for Job 1015. The journal entry is

Work-in-process -- Job 1015	$60,000	
Materials control		$60,000

f. Time tickets track the direct labor by workers on various jobs.

   1) For example, workers accrue $45,000 in salaries on Job 1015. The journal entry is

Work-in-process -- Job 1015	$45,000	
Wages payable		$45,000

g. Direct costs are recorded in the general ledger at their actual amounts. Job-order costing facilitates tracing the direct costs incurred for a given job.

3. **Accumulation of Indirect Costs**

   a. Accounting for overhead costs is more difficult because they are indirect costs. It is not feasible to trace them to final products. Thus, they must be accumulated in one or more indirect cost pools and allocated based on an appropriate cost driver.

   1) When one indirect cost pool is used, it is commonly called manufacturing overhead control. (Some manufacturers require a higher degree of accuracy in indirect cost assignment and use two overhead control accounts, one for variable overhead and one for fixed. For simplicity, the following examples use one pool.)

   b. Manufacturing overhead consists of three main categories of costs:

   1) Indirect materials are tangible inputs to the manufacturing process that cannot feasibly be traced to the product, e.g., the welding compound used to assemble a piece of heavy equipment.

      a) For example, the production department requisitions $4,500 of lubricating oil for a machine that was due maintenance. The journal entry is

Manufacturing overhead control	$4,500	
Materials control		$4,500

   2) Indirect labor is the cost of human labor used in the manufacturing process that cannot feasibly be traced to the product, e.g., the wages of assembly line supervisors and janitorial staff.

      a) For example, $2,000 in wages are accrued for the janitorial staff. The journal entry is

Manufacturing overhead control	$2,000	
Wages payable		$2,000

3)   Other overhead operating costs include such items as utility expense, real estate taxes, insurance, and depreciation of equipment. The actual total of these costs is not known until the end of the period.

a)   For example, $8,500 of property taxes are accrued, $1,600 of insurance costs are prepaid, and $12,000 of depreciation expense is recognized. The journal entry is

Manufacturing overhead control	$8,500	
Property taxes payable		$8,500
Manufacturing overhead control	$1,600	
Prepaid insurance		$1,600
Manufacturing overhead control	$12,000	
Accumulated depreciation -- equipment		$12,000

c.   When an overhead control account is used, actual overhead costs do not affect work-in-process when they are incurred. The total actual overhead incurred is the debit balance in the control account.

4.   **Allocation of Indirect Costs**

a.   Indirect costs are allocated to production using an overhead allocation rate. The first step is to estimate the total indirect costs for the next period.

1)   The overhead application rate is best derived using estimated annual totals rather than on a monthly basis. Many overhead costs are fixed and must be incurred every month regardless of the level of production. Calculating a new rate every month may cause large variations in product costs even though the underlying cost structure does not change.

b.   The following is the equation for the rate:

$$Overhead\ application\ rate = \frac{Estimated\ annual\ total\ overhead\ costs}{Estimated\ total\ units\ of\ allocation\ base}$$

(If more than one indirect cost pool is used, a different rate is used for each pool.)

1)   The numerator is estimated from annual budget data.
2)   The denominator (the allocation base) must be a cost driver that has a direct cause-and-effect relationship with the incurrence of overhead costs. When overhead costs change, the units of the allocation base also should change. Common allocation bases for one indirect cost pool are direct labor hours and machine hours.

a)   For example, an estimated $350,000 in overhead costs will be incurred during the year. The best way to allocate these costs is by machine hours (budgeted at 10,000 hours). The allocation rate is determined as follows:

Overhead application rate ($350,000 ÷ 10,000) = $35 per machine hour

c.   At the end of each month, the number of units of the allocation base expended is multiplied by the application rate to determine the amount of overhead to be applied to that month's production.

1)   For example, Job 1015 has used 900 machine hours this month. The calculation is

Overhead applied = Units of overhead driver × Application rate
= 900 machine hours for Job 1015 × $35 per hour
= $31,500

2) This amount ordinarily is not credited to the control account. Instead, it is credited to manufacturing overhead applied (a contra account). The two accounts track actual and applied costs separately.

    a) For example, overhead is applied to Job 1015. The journal entry is

Work-in-process -- Job 1015	$31,500	
Manufacturing overhead applied		$31,500

3) Separate tracking retains actual overhead amounts in the debit balance of the control account. It also permits comparison of actual and applied costs. The closer they are, the better the estimate.

5. **Completion of Job**

  a. When a job order is completed, all costs are transferred to finished goods.

    1) For example, when work on Job 1015 is completed, the product is prepared for sale. Total costs accrued for Job 1015 are $136,500. The journal entry is

Finished goods	$136,500	
Work-in-process -- Job 1015		$136,500

  b. When the output is sold, the sale is recorded and the appropriate portion of the cost is transferred to cost of goods sold.

    1) For example, the product created in Job 1015 is sold for $200,000 on account. The journal entry is

Accounts receivable	$200,000	
Sales		$200,000
Cost of goods sold	$136,500	
Finished goods		$136,500

6. **Job-Order Cost Flows**

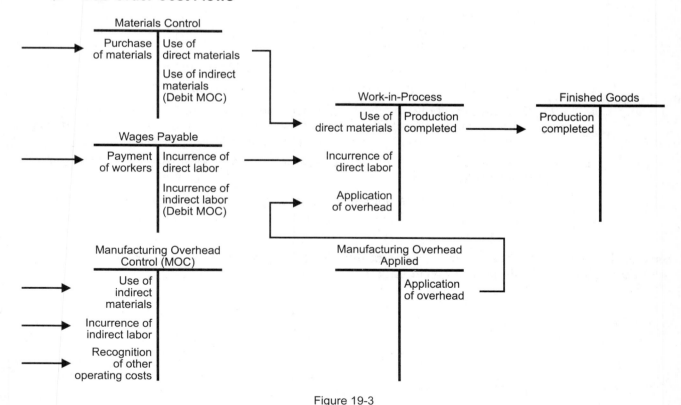

Figure 19-3

7. Over- and Underapplied Overhead

a. At the end of the period, if the balance in the overhead control account is less than that in the overhead applied account, overhead was overapplied. If the balance in the overhead applied account is lower, overhead was underapplied.

    1) For example, overhead applied was $331,500 during the period, but the amount accrued was only $328,600.

    2) Total indirect costs were less than expected ($328,600 < $350,000). Furthermore, the number of machine hours was only 9,471.4 ($331,500 ÷ $35) instead of the 10,000 estimated.

    3) Given that more overhead was applied than was actually incurred, overhead was overapplied by $2,900.

        a) If the variance is immaterial, it may be closed directly to cost of goods sold.

            i) Overhead applied is debited and manufacturing overhead control is credited. The balancing credit is to cost of goods sold. The journal entry is

Manufacturing overhead applied (balance)	$331,500	
Cost of goods sold (difference)		$ 2,900
Manufacturing overhead control (balance)		328,600

            (If overhead is underapplied, cost of goods sold is debited.)

        b) If the variance is material, it should be allocated based on the relative values of work-in-process, finished goods, and cost of goods sold.

            i) For example, the amount overapplied has a 20:20:60 cost relationship. The journal entry is

Manufacturing overhead applied (balance)	$331,500	
Work-in-process (difference × 20%)		$ 580
Finished goods (difference × 20%)		580
Cost of goods sold (difference × 60%)		1,740
Manufacturing overhead control (balance)		328,600

    4) Actual overhead costs for the period eventually become product costs.

b. The reason for the foregoing procedure is to identify **variance**.

    1) The variance between the control and applied amounts indicates whether production for the period sufficed to spread overhead costs among as many units as were expected when the annual budget was completed.

c. A variance results from factors that affect the numerator or the denominator of the application rate.

    1) Factors affecting the numerator cause higher or lower costs than estimated.

    2) Factors affecting the denominator cause the activity level to vary from the estimate.

Stop and review! You have completed the outline for this subunit. Study multiple-choice questions 25 through 30 beginning on page 505.

QUESTIONS

19.1 Absorption Costing and Variable Costing -- Theory

1. The change in period-to-period operating income when using variable costing can be explained by the change in the

A. Unit sales level multiplied by the unit sales price.

B. Finished goods inventory level multiplied by the unit sales price.

C. Unit sales level multiplied by a constant unit contribution margin.

D. Finished goods inventory level multiplied by a constant unit contribution margin.

Answer (C) is correct.
REQUIRED: The factor explaining the change in period-to-period operating income when using variable costing.
DISCUSSION: In a variable costing system, only the variable costs are recorded as product costs. All fixed costs are expensed in the period incurred. Because changes in the relationship between production levels and sales levels do not cause changes in the amount of fixed manufacturing cost expensed, profits more directly follow the trends in sales, especially when the UCM (selling price per unit – variable costs per unit) is constant. Unit sales times the UCM equals the total CM, and operating income (a pretax amount) equals the CM minus fixed costs of operations. If the UCM is constant and fixed costs are stable, the change in operating income will approximate the change in the CM (unit sales × UCM).

2. Which of the following statements is true for a firm that uses variable costing?

A. The cost of a unit of product changes because of changes in number of units manufactured.

B. Profits fluctuate with sales.

C. An idle facility variation is calculated.

D. Product costs include variable administrative costs.

Answer (B) is correct.
REQUIRED: The true statement about variable costing.
DISCUSSION: In a variable costing system, only the variable costs are recorded as product costs. All fixed costs are expensed in the period incurred. Because changes in the relationship between production levels and sales levels do not cause changes in the amount of fixed manufacturing cost expensed, profits more directly follow the trends in sales.
Answer (A) is incorrect. Changing unit costs based on different levels of production is a characteristic of absorption costing systems. Answer (C) is incorrect. An idle facility variation is calculated in absorption costing. Answer (D) is incorrect. Neither variable nor absorption costing includes administrative costs in inventory.

3. In the application of variable costing as a cost-allocation process in manufacturing,

A. Variable direct costs are treated as period costs.

B. Nonvariable indirect costs are treated as product costs.

C. Variable indirect costs are treated as product costs.

D. Nonvariable direct costs are treated as product costs.

Answer (C) is correct.
REQUIRED: The true statement about variable costing.
DISCUSSION: Variable costing considers only variable manufacturing costs to be product costs. Variable indirect costs included in variable overhead are therefore treated as inventoriable. Fixed costs are considered period costs and are expensed as incurred.
Answer (A) is incorrect. Variable manufacturing costs, whether direct (direct materials and direct labor) or indirect (variable overhead), are accounted for as product costs, not period costs. Answer (B) is incorrect. Nonvariable indirect costs are treated as period costs in direct costing. Answer (D) is incorrect. In direct costing, nonvariable direct costs are treated as period costs, not product costs.

4. Which method of inventory costing treats direct manufacturing costs and manufacturing overhead costs, both variable and fixed, as inventoriable costs?

A. Direct costing.

B. Variable costing.

C. Absorption costing.

D. Conversion costing.

Answer (C) is correct.
REQUIRED: The method of inventory costing that treats direct manufacturing costs and all manufacturing overhead as inventoriable.
DISCUSSION: Absorption (full) costing considers all manufacturing costs to be inventoriable as product costs. These costs include variable and fixed manufacturing costs, whether direct or indirect. The alternative to absorption is variable (direct) costing.
Answer (A) is incorrect. Direct costing does not inventory fixed manufacturing overhead. Answer (B) is incorrect. Variable costing does not inventory fixed manufacturing overhead. Answer (D) is incorrect. Conversion costs include direct labor and manufacturing overhead but not direct materials.

5. The management of a company computes net income using both absorption and variable costing. This year, the net income under the variable-costing approach was greater than the net income under the absorption-costing approach. This difference is most likely the result of

A. A decrease in the variable marketing expenses.

B. An increase in the finished goods inventory.

C. Sales volume exceeding production volume.

D. Inflationary effects on overhead costs.

Answer (C) is correct.
REQUIRED: The reason net income is greater under variable costing than absorption costing.
DISCUSSION: Absorption costing (full costing) is the accounting method that considers all manufacturing costs as product costs. These costs include variable and fixed manufacturing costs, whether direct or indirect. However, variable costing treats fixed manufacturing overhead as a period cost instead of charging it to the product (inventory). Thus, when sales exceed production, the absorption costing method recognizes fixed manufacturing overhead inventoried in a prior period. Direct costing does not. Accordingly, net income under variable costing is greater than net income under absorption costing.
Answer (A) is incorrect. A change in a variable period cost will affect absorption and variable costing in the same way. Answer (B) is incorrect. If the beginning inventory is less than the ending finished goods inventory, absorption costing assigns more fixed overhead costs to the balance sheet and less to the cost of goods sold on the income statement than does variable costing. Answer (D) is incorrect. Inflationary effects usually affect both absorption and variable costing in the same way.

6. When a firm prepares financial reports by using absorption costing,

A. Profits will always increase with increases in sales.

B. Profits will always decrease with decreases in sales.

C. Profits may decrease with increased sales even if there is no change in selling prices and costs.

D. Decreased output and constant sales result in increased profits.

Answer (C) is correct.
REQUIRED: The profit relationship between output and sales under absorption costing.
DISCUSSION: In an absorption costing system, fixed overhead costs are included in inventory. When sales exceed production, more overhead is expensed under absorption costing because fixed overhead is carried over from the prior inventory. If sales exceed production, more than one period's fixed overhead is recognized as expense. Accordingly, if the increase in fixed overhead expensed is greater than the contribution margin of the increased units sold, less profit may result from an increased level of sales.
Answer (A) is incorrect. Profit is a function of both sales and production, so profit may not increase with increases in sales. Answer (B) is incorrect. Profit is a function of both sales and production, so profit may not decrease with decreases in sales. Answer (D) is incorrect. Decreased output will increase the unit cost of items sold. Fixed overhead per unit will increase.

19.2 Absorption Costing and Variable Costing -- Calculations

Questions 7 and 8 are based on the following information. At the end of its fiscal year, C.G. Manufacturing recorded the data below:

Prime cost	$800,000
Variable manufacturing overhead	100,000
Fixed manufacturing overhead	160,000
Variable selling and other expenses	80,000
Fixed selling and other expenses	40,000

7. If C.G. uses variable costing, the inventoriable costs for the fiscal year are

A. $800,000

B. $900,000

C. $980,000

D. $1,060,000

Answer (B) is correct.
REQUIRED: The inventoriable costs using variable costing.
DISCUSSION: The only costs capitalized are the variable costs of manufacturing. Prime costs (direct materials and direct labor) are variable.

Prime costs, direct materials, and direct labor	$800,000
Variable manufacturing overhead	100,000
Total inventoriable costs	$900,000

Answer (A) is incorrect. Prime costs equal $800,000. Answer (C) is incorrect. The amount of $980,000 includes the variable selling and other expenses. Answer (D) is incorrect. Inventoriable costs under absorption costing equal $1,060,000.

8. Using absorption (full) costing, C.G.'s inventoriable costs are

A. $800,000

B. $900,000

C. $1,060,000

D. $1,080,000

Answer (C) is correct.
REQUIRED: The inventoriable costs using absorption costing.
DISCUSSION: Absorption costing is required by GAAP. It charges all costs of production to inventories. The prime costs ($800,000), variable manufacturing overhead ($100,000), and the fixed manufacturing overhead ($160,000) are included. They total $1,060,000.
Answer (A) is incorrect. Prime costs equal $800,000. Answer (B) is incorrect. Inventoriable costs under variable costing equal $900,000. Answer (D) is incorrect. The amount of $1,080,000 includes the fixed and variable selling and other expenses.

Questions 9 and 10 are based on the following information. Presented are Valenz Company's records for the current fiscal year ended November 30:

Direct materials used	$300,000
Direct labor	100,000
Variable manufacturing overhead	50,000
Fixed manufacturing overhead	80,000
Selling and admin. costs -- variable	40,000
Selling and admin. costs -- fixed	20,000

9. If Valenz Company uses variable costing, the inventoriable costs for the fiscal year are

A. $400,000

B. $450,000

C. $490,000

D. $530,000

Answer (B) is correct.
REQUIRED: The inventoriable costs using the variable costing.
DISCUSSION: Under variable costing, the only costs that are capitalized are the variable costs of manufacturing. These include

Direct materials used	$300,000
Direct labor	100,000
Variable overhead	50,000
Total inventoriable costs	$450,000

Answer (A) is incorrect. The amount of $400,000 does not include $50,000 of variable overhead. Answer (C) is incorrect. The $40,000 of variable selling and administrative costs should not be included in the inventoriable costs. Answer (D) is incorrect. The inventoriable cost under absorption (full) costing is $530,000.

10. Using absorption (full) costing, inventoriable costs for Valenz are

A. $400,000

B. $450,000

C. $530,000

D. $590,000

Answer (C) is correct.
REQUIRED: The inventoriable costs using the absorption costing.
DISCUSSION: The absorption method is required for financial statements prepared according to GAAP. It charges all costs of production to inventories. The variable cost of materials ($300,000), direct labor ($100,000), variable overhead ($50,000), and fixed overhead ($80,000) are included. They total $530,000.
Answer (A) is incorrect. Not including $80,000 of fixed overhead and $50,000 of variable overhead results in $400,000. Answer (B) is incorrect. The inventoriable cost under variable costing is $450,000. Answer (D) is incorrect. Selling and administrative costs are not inventoriable using absorption (full) costing.

Questions 11 and 12 are based on the following information. Osawa, Inc., planned and actually manufactured 200,000 units of its single product during its first year of operations. Variable manufacturing costs were $30 per unit of product. Planned and actual fixed manufacturing costs were $600,000, and selling and administrative costs totaled $400,000. Osawa sold 120,000 units of product at a selling price of $40 per unit.

11. Osawa's operating income using absorption (full) costing is

A. $200,000

B. $440,000

C. $600,000

D. $840,000

Answer (B) is correct.
　REQUIRED: The operating income under absorption costing.
　DISCUSSION: Because production equaled planned output, and fixed costs equaled the budgeted amount, fixed overhead was not over- or under-applied. Also, planned fixed overhead equaled the actual amount. Thus, no fixed overhead variances had to be accounted for. Osawa applied $600,000 of fixed overhead, or $3 per unit ($600,000 ÷ 200,000 units), to its output. The unit cost of the 80,000 (200,000 – 120,000 sold) units in ending inventory is therefore $33 ($30 VC + $3 FC). Absorption costing net income is computed as follows:

Sales (120,000 units × $40)		$4,800,000
Variable production costs		
(200,000 units × $30)	$6,000,000	
Fixed production costs	600,000	
Total production costs	$6,600,000	
Ending inventory		
(80,000 units × $33)	(2,640,000)	
Cost of goods sold		(3,960,000)
Gross profit		$ 840,000
Selling and administrative expenses		(400,000)
Operating income		$ 440,000

　Answer (A) is incorrect. The amount of $200,000 is the operating income under variable costing. Answer (C) is incorrect. The amount of $600,000 is the operating income that results from capitalizing $240,000 fixed manufacturing costs and $160,000 of selling and administrative costs (the $160,000 is incorrect as all selling and administrative costs should be expensed). Answer (D) is incorrect. The amount of $840,000 is the gross profit under absorption costing, i.e., before selling and administrative expenses.

12. Osawa's operating income for the year using variable costing is

A. $200,000

B. $440,000

C. $800,000

D. $600,000

Answer (A) is correct.
　REQUIRED: The operating income under variable costing.
　DISCUSSION: The contribution margin from manufacturing (sales – variable costs) is $10 ($40 – $30) per unit sold, or $1,200,000 (120,000 units × $10). The fixed costs of manufacturing ($600,000) and selling and administrative costs ($400,000) are deducted from the contribution margin to arrive at an operating income of $200,000. The difference between the absorption income of $440,000 and the $200,000 of variable costing income is attributable to capitalization of the fixed manufacturing costs under the absorption method. Because 40% of the goods produced are still in inventory (80,000 ÷ 200,000), 40% of the $600,000 in fixed costs, or $240,000, was capitalized under the absorption method. That amount was expensed under the variable costing method.
　Answer (B) is incorrect. The amount of $440,000 is the operating income under absorption costing. Answer (C) is incorrect. The amount of $800,000 is the operating income if fixed costs of manufacturing are not deducted. Answer (D) is incorrect. The amount of $600,000 is the operating income that results from capitalizing 40% of both fixed manufacturing costs and selling and administrative costs.

19.3 Joint Product and By-Product Costing

13. For the purposes of cost accumulation, which of the following are identifiable as different individual products before the split-off point?

	By-Products	Joint Products
A.	Yes	Yes
B.	Yes	No
C.	No	No
D.	No	Yes

Answer (C) is correct.
REQUIRED: The products identifiable before the split-off point.
DISCUSSION: In a joint production process, at the split-off point, neither by-products nor joint products are separately identifiable as individual products. Joint costs up to the split-off point are usually related to both joint products and by-products. After split-off, additional (separable) costs can be traced and charged to the individual products. By-products usually do not receive an allocation of joint costs.
Answer (A) is incorrect. Neither by-products nor joint products are separately identifiable until split-off. Answer (B) is incorrect. By-products are also not separately identifiable until split-off. Answer (D) is incorrect. Joint products are also not separately identifiable until split-off.

14. Kode Co. manufactures a major product that gives rise to a by-product called May. May's only separable cost is a $1 selling cost when a unit is sold for $4. Kode accounts for May's sales by deducting the $3 net amount from the cost of goods sold of the major product. There are no inventories. If Kode were to change its method of accounting for May from a by-product to a joint product, what would be the effect on Kode's overall gross margin?

A. No effect.

B. Gross margin increases by $1 for each unit of May sold.

C. Gross margin increases by $3 for each unit of May sold.

D. Gross margin increases by $4 for each unit of May sold.

Answer (B) is correct.
REQUIRED: The effect on gross margin (gross profit) of treating a product as a joint product rather than a by-product.
DISCUSSION: Gross margin is the difference between sales and the cost of goods sold. Subtracting the $3 net amount from cost of goods sold does not have the same effect on overall gross margin as recording the $4 sales revenue and subtracting the $1 cost. In the latter case, the $1 unit selling cost is not subtracted in arriving at the gross margin. Thus, gross margin increases by $1 for each unit of May sold.
Answer (A) is incorrect. Net income, not gross margin, is unaffected. Answer (C) is incorrect. The amount of $3 is the per-unit increase in net income using either by-product or joint-product costing. Answer (D) is incorrect. The amount of $4 is the per-unit increase in sales when switching to joint-product from by-product costing.

15. In accounting for by-products, the value of the by-product may be recognized at the time of

	Production	Sale
A.	Yes	Yes
B.	Yes	No
C.	No	No
D.	No	Yes

Answer (A) is correct.
REQUIRED: The timing of recognition of by-products.
DISCUSSION: Practice with regard to recognizing by-products in the accounts is not uniform. The most cost-effective method for the initial recognition of by-products is to account for their value at the time of sale as a reduction in the joint cost or as a revenue. The alternative is to recognize the net realizable value at the time of production, a method that results in the recording of by-product inventory.
Answer (B) is incorrect. By-products also may be recognized initially at the time of sale. Answer (C) is incorrect. By-products may be initially recognized at the time of sale or at the time of production. Answer (D) is incorrect. By-products may also be recorded in the accounts when produced.

16. In joint-product costing and analysis, which one of the following costs is relevant when deciding the point at which a product should be sold to maximize profits?

A. Separable costs after the split-off point.

B. Joint costs to the split-off point.

C. Sales salaries for the period when the units were produced.

D. Purchase costs of the materials required for the joint products.

Answer (A) is correct.
REQUIRED: The cost relevant to deciding when a joint product should be sold.
DISCUSSION: Joint products are created from processing a common input. Joint costs are incurred prior to the split-off point and cannot be identified with a particular joint product. As a result, joint costs are irrelevant to the timing of sale. However, separable costs incurred after the split-off point are relevant because, if incremental revenues exceed the separable costs, products should be processed further, not sold at the split-off point.
Answer (B) is incorrect. Joint costs have no effect on the decision when to sell a product. Answer (C) is incorrect. Sales salaries for the production period do not affect the decision. Answer (D) is incorrect. Purchase costs are joint costs.

17. A joint process is a manufacturing operation yielding two or more identifiable products from the resources employed in the process. The two characteristics that identify a product generated from this type of process as a joint product are that it

A. Is identifiable as an individual product only upon reaching the split-off point, and it has relatively minor sales value when compared to the other products.

B. Is identifiable as an individual product before the production process, and it has relatively significant physical volume when compared with the other products.

C. Is identifiable as an individual product only upon reaching the split-off point, and it has relatively significant sales value when compared with the other products.

D. Has relatively significant physical volume when compared with the other products, and it can be sold immediately without any additional processing.

Answer (C) is correct.
REQUIRED: The two characteristics of a joint product.
DISCUSSION: Joint products are two or more separate products generated by a common process from a common input that are not separable prior to the split-off point. Moreover, in contrast with by-products, they have significant sales values in relation to each other either before or after additional processing.
Answer (A) is incorrect. A joint product has relatively significant sales value when compared with the other products. A by-product is identifiable as an individual product only upon reaching the split-off point, and it has relatively minor sales value when compared to the other products. Answer (B) is incorrect. Products that are separately identifiable before the production process are not classified as joint products. Furthermore, physical volume has nothing to do with determining a joint product. Some joint products with significant physical volume may not have significant sales value. Answer (D) is incorrect. Products do not have to be salable at the split-off point to be considered joint products. Many joint products must be processed after the split-off point before they can be sold.

18. A lumber company produces two-by-fours and four-by-eights as joint products and sawdust as a by-product. The packaged sawdust can be sold for $2 per pound. Packaging costs for the sawdust are $.10 per pound and sales commissions are 10% of sales price. The by-product net revenue serves to reduce joint processing costs for joint products. Joint products are assigned joint costs based on board feet. Cost and production data are:

Joint processing costs	$ 50,000
Two-by-fours produced (board feet)	200,000
Four-by-eights produced (board feet)	100,000
Sawdust produced (pounds)	1,000

What is the cost assigned to two-by-fours?

A. $32,000

B. $32,133

C. $32,200

D. $33,333

Answer (C) is correct.
REQUIRED: The cost assigned to a joint product when joint products and a by-product are produced.
DISCUSSION: The net revenue from sale of the by-product is $1,700 [(1,000 lb. × $2 price) − (1,000 lb. × $.10) − (1,000 lb. × $2 × .1)]. Joint processing costs to be allocated to joint products are therefore $48,300 ($50,000 − $1,700 net by-product revenue). Of this amount, $32,200 should be assigned to the two-by-fours [$48,300 × (200,000 board feet of two-by-fours ÷ 300,000 total board feet)].
Answer (A) is incorrect. The net revenue from the sale of the by-product is $1,700, not $2,000. The costs related to the packaging and selling of the by-product must be deducted. Answer (B) is incorrect. The $.10-per-pound packaging cost for the sawdust must be subtracted from the by-product revenue. Answer (D) is incorrect. The net revenue of $1,700 [1,000 lb. × ($2 sale price − $.10 packaging − $.20 sales cost)] from the by-product should be subtracted from the joint processing costs before the joint processing costs are allocated.

19. Copeland, Inc., produces X-547 in a joint manufacturing process. The company is studying whether to sell X-547 at the split-off point or upgrade the product to become Xylene. The following information has been gathered:

I. Selling price per pound of X-547
II. Variable manufacturing costs of upgrade process
III. Avoidable fixed costs of upgrade process
IV. Selling price per pound of Xylene
V. Joint manufacturing costs to produce X-547

Which items should be reviewed when making the upgrade decision?

A. I, II, and IV.

B. I, II, III, and IV.

C. All items.

D. I, II, IV, and V.

Answer (B) is correct.
REQUIRED: The items reviewed for a sell-or-process further decision.
DISCUSSION: Common, or joint, costs cannot be identified with a particular joint product. By definition, joint products have common costs until the split-off point. Costs incurred after the split-off point are separable costs. The decision to continue processing beyond split-off is made separately for each product. The costs relevant to the decision are the separable costs because they can be avoided by selling at the split-off point. They should be compared with the incremental revenues from processing further. Thus, items I (revenue from selling at split-off point), II (variable costs of upgrade), III (avoidable fixed costs of upgrade), and IV (revenue from selling after further processing) are considered in making the upgrade decision.
Answer (A) is incorrect. The affordable fixed costs of the upgrade process also should be considered. Answer (C) is incorrect. The joint manufacturing costs are irrelevant. Answer (D) is incorrect. The affordable fixed costs of the upgrade process should be reviewed, and the joint manufacturing costs should be ignored.

19.4 Joint Cost Allocation Methods

Questions 20 and 21 are based on the following information.

Petro-Chem, Inc., is a small company that acquires high-grade crude oil from low-volume production wells owned by individuals and small partnerships. The crude oil is processed in a single refinery into Two Oil, Six Oil, and impure distillates. Petro-Chem does not have the technology or capacity to process these products further and sells most of its output each month to major refineries. There were no beginning inventories of finished goods or work-in-process on November 1. The production costs and output of Petro-Chem for November are shown in the next column.

Crude oil acquired and placed in production	$5,000,000
Direct labor and related costs	2,000,000
Manufacturing overhead	3,000,000

Production and sales

- Two Oil, 300,000 barrels produced; 80,000 barrels sold at $20 each
- Six Oil, 240,000 barrels produced; 120,000 barrels sold at $30 each
- Distillates, 120,000 barrels produced and sold at $15 each

20. The portion of the joint production costs assigned to Two Oil based upon the relative sales value of output is

A. $4,800,000

B. $4,000,000

C. $2,286,000

D. $2,500,000

Answer (B) is correct.
REQUIRED: The joint production costs assigned to a product based on relative sales value.
DISCUSSION: The total production costs incurred are $10,000,000, consisting of crude oil of $5,000,000, direct labor of $2,000,000, and overhead of $3,000,000. The total value of the output is as follows:

Two Oil (300,000 × $20)	$ 6,000,000
Six Oil (240,000 × $30)	7,200,000
Distillates (120,000 × $15)	1,800,000
Total sales value	$15,000,000

Because Two Oil composes 40% of the total sales value ($6,000,000 ÷ $15,000,000), it will be assigned 40% of the $10,000,000 of joint costs, or $4,000,000.
Answer (A) is incorrect. The amount of $4,800,000 is the amount that would be assigned to Six Oil. Answer (C) is incorrect. The amount of $2,286,000 is based on the relative sales value of units sold. Answer (D) is incorrect. The amount of $2,500,000 is based on the physical quantity of barrels sold.

21. The portion of the joint production costs assigned to Six Oil based upon physical output is

A. $3,636,000

B. $3,750,000

C. $1,818,000

D. $7,500,000

Answer (A) is correct.
REQUIRED: The joint production costs assigned to a product based on physical output.
DISCUSSION: The total production costs incurred are $10,000,000, consisting of crude oil of $5,000,000, direct labor of $2,000,000, and overhead of $3,000,000. The total physical output was 660,000 barrels, consisting of 300,000 barrels of Two Oil, 240,000 barrels of Six Oil, and 120,000 barrels of distillates. Thus, the allocation (rounded) is $3,636,000 {$10,000,000 × [240,000 ÷ (300,000 + 240,000 + 120,000)]}.
Answer (B) is incorrect. The amount of $3,750,000 is based on the physical quantity of units sold, not units produced. Answer (C) is incorrect. The amount of $1,818,000 is the amount that would be assigned to distillates. Answer (D) is incorrect. Six Oil does not compose 75% of the total output in barrels.

Questions 22 through 24 are based on the following information.

Atlas Foods produces the following three supplemental food products simultaneously through a refining process costing $93,000.

The joint products, Alfa and Betters, have a final selling price of $4 per pound and $10 per pound, respectively, after additional processing costs of $2 per pound of each product are incurred after the split-off point. Morefeed, a by-product, is sold at the split-off point for $3 per pound.

Alfa	10,000 pounds of Alfa, a popular but relatively rare grain supplement having a caloric value of 4,400 calories per pound
Betters	5,000 pounds of Betters, a flavoring material high in carbohydrates with a caloric value of 11,200 calories per pound
Morefeed	1,000 pounds of Morefeed, used as a cattle feed supplement with a caloric value of 1,000 calories per pound

22. Assuming Atlas Foods inventories Morefeed, the by-product, the joint cost to be allocated to Alfa using the net realizable value method is

A. $3,000

B. $30,000

C. $31,000

D. $60,000

Answer (B) is correct.

REQUIRED: The joint cost allocated to a joint product based on net realizable values if the by-product is inventoried.

DISCUSSION: The NRV at split-off for each of the joint products must be determined. Given that Alfa has a $4 selling price and an additional $2 of processing costs, the value at the split-off is $2 per pound. The total value at split-off for 10,000 pounds is $20,000. Betters has a $10 selling price and an additional $2 of processing costs. Thus, the value at split-off is $8 per pound. The total value of 5,000 pounds of Betters is therefore $40,000. The 1,000 pounds of Morefeed has a split-off value of $3 per pound, or $3,000. Assuming that Morefeed (a by-product) is inventoried (recognized in the accounts when produced) and treated as a reduction of joint costs, the allocable joint cost is $90,000 ($93,000 – $3,000). The total net realizable value of the main products is $60,000 ($20,000 Alfa + $40,000 Betters). The allocation to Alfa is $30,000 [$90,000 × ($20,000 ÷ $60,000)].

Answer (A) is incorrect. The value of the by-product is $3,000. Answer (C) is incorrect. Failing to adjust the joint processing cost for the value of the by-product results in $31,000. Answer (D) is incorrect. The amount allocated to Betters is $60,000.

23. Assuming Atlas Foods inventories Morefeed, the by-product, and that it incurs no additional processing costs for Alfa and Betters, the joint cost to be allocated to Alfa using the gross sales value method is

A. $36,000

B. $40,000

C. $41,333

D. $50,000

Answer (B) is correct.

REQUIRED: The joint cost allocated to a joint product using the gross sales value method if the by-product is inventoried.

DISCUSSION: The gross sales value of Alfa is $40,000 (10,000 pounds × $4), Betters has a total gross sales value of $50,000 (5,000 pounds × $10), and Morefeed has a split-off value of $3,000. If the value of Morefeed is inventoried and treated as a reduction in joint cost, the allocable joint cost is $90,000 ($93,000 – $3,000). The total gross sales value of the two main products is $90,000 ($40,000 + $50,000). Of this total, $40,000 should be allocated to Alfa [$90,000 × ($40,000 ÷ $90,000)].

Answer (A) is incorrect. The amount of $36,000 is based on 40%, not 4/9. Answer (C) is incorrect. Failing to adjust the joint cost by the value of the by-product results in $41,333. Answer (D) is incorrect. The joint cost allocated to Betters is $50,000.

24. Assuming Atlas Foods does not inventory Morefeed, the by-product, the joint cost to be allocated to Betters using the net realizable value method is

A. $30,000

B. $31,000

C. $52,080

D. $62,000

Answer (D) is correct.

REQUIRED: The joint cost allocated to a joint product based on net realizable values if the by-product is not inventoried.

DISCUSSION: The NRV of Alfa is $20,000, and the NRV of Betters is $40,000. If the joint cost is not adjusted for the value of the by-product, the amount allocated to Betters is $62,000 {$93,000 × [$40,000 ÷ ($20,000 + $40,000)]}.

Answer (A) is incorrect. The amount allocated to Alfa when the by-product is inventoried is $30,000. Answer (B) is incorrect. The amount allocated to Alfa when the by-product is not inventoried is $31,000. Answer (C) is incorrect. Assuming that a weighting method using caloric value is used results in $52,080.

19.5 Job-Order Costing and Overhead Application

25. Felicity Corporation manufactures a specialty line of dresses using a job-order cost system. During January, the following costs were incurred in completing job J-1:

Direct materials	$27,400
Direct labor	9,600
Administrative costs	2,800
Selling costs	11,200

Overhead was applied at the rate of $50 per direct labor hour, and job J-1 required 400 direct labor hours. If job J-1 resulted in 4,000 good dresses, the cost of goods sold per unit is

A. $9.25

B. $14.25

C. $14.95

D. $17.75

Answer (B) is correct.

REQUIRED: The cost of goods sold per unit.

DISCUSSION: Cost of goods sold is based on the manufacturing costs incurred in production. It does not include selling or general and administrative expenses. Manufacturing costs consist of direct materials ($27,400), direct labor ($9,600), and overhead (400 direct labor hours × $50 per hour = $20,000). The total of these cost elements is $57,000. Dividing the $57,000 of total manufacturing costs by the 4,000 units produced results in a per-unit cost of $14.25.

Answer (A) is incorrect. Failing to include overhead results in $9.25. Answer (C) is incorrect. Including administrative costs results in $14.95. Answer (D) is incorrect. The amount of $17.75 includes selling and administrative costs.

26. Lucy Sportswear manufactures a specialty line of T-shirts using a job-order cost system. During March, the following costs were incurred in completing Job ICU2: direct materials, $13,700; direct labor, $4,800; administrative, $1,400; and selling, $5,600. Overhead was applied at the rate of $25 per machine hour, and Job ICU2 required 800 machine hours. If Job ICU2 resulted in 7,000 good shirts, the cost of goods sold per unit would be

A. $6.50

B. $6.30

C. $5.70

D. $5.50

Answer (D) is correct.

REQUIRED: The cost of goods sold per unit.

DISCUSSION: Cost of goods sold is based on the manufacturing costs incurred in production but does not include selling or general and administrative expenses. Manufacturing costs equal $38,500 [$13,700 DM + $4,800 DL + (800 hours × $25) OH]. Thus, per-unit cost is $5.50 ($38,500 ÷ 7,000 units).

Answer (A) is incorrect. The amount of $6.50 includes selling and administrative expenses. Answer (B) is incorrect. Including selling costs results in cost of goods sold per unit of $6.30. Answer (C) is incorrect. Including administrative expenses results in cost of goods sold per unit of $5.70.

27. Worley Company has underapplied overhead of $45,000 for the year. Before disposition of the underapplied overhead, selected year-end balances from Worley's accounting records were

Sales	$1,200,000
Cost of goods sold	720,000
Direct materials inventory	36,000
Work-in-process inventory	54,000
Finished goods inventory	90,000

Under Worley's cost accounting system, over- or underapplied overhead is assigned to appropriate inventories and COGS based on year-end balances. In its year-end income statement, Worley should report COGS of

A. $682,500

B. $684,000

C. $757,500

D. $765,000

Answer (C) is correct.

REQUIRED: The amount of cost of goods sold after allocation of underapplied overhead.

DISCUSSION: The assignment of underapplied overhead increases COGS. The underapplied overhead of $45,000 for the year should be assigned on a pro rata basis to work-in-process ($54,000), finished goods ($90,000), and COGS ($720,000). The sum of these three items is $864,000. Thus, $37,500 should be assigned to COGS [($720,000 ÷ $864,000) × $45,000]. COGS after assignment is $757,500 ($37,500 + $720,000). The remaining $7,500 should be assigned proportionately to work-in-process and finished goods.

Answer (A) is incorrect. The appropriate COGS balance if overhead was overapplied by $45,000 and $37,500 was assigned to COGS is $682,500. Answer (B) is incorrect. The COGS balance if overhead was overapplied by $45,000 and direct materials inventory was incorrectly included in the denominator of the ratio used to assign overhead is $684,000. Answer (D) is incorrect. Debiting the full amount of underapplied overhead ($45,000) to COGS results in $765,000.

Questions 28 and 29 are based on the following information. Hamilton Company uses job-order costing. Manufacturing overhead is applied to production at a predetermined rate of 150% of direct labor cost. Any over- or underapplied overhead is closed to the cost of goods sold account at the end of each month. Additional information is available as follows:

- Job 101 was the only job in process at January 31, with accumulated costs as follows:

Direct materials	$4,000
Direct labor	2,000
Applied manufacturing overhead	3,000
Total manufacturing costs	$9,000

- Jobs 102, 103, and 104 were started during February.
- Direct materials requisitions for February totaled $26,000.
- Direct labor cost of $20,000 was incurred for February.
- Actual manufacturing overhead was $32,000 for February.
- The only job still in process on February 28 was Job 104, with costs of $2,800 for direct materials and $1,800 for direct labor.

28. The cost of goods manufactured for February was

A. $77,700

B. $78,000

C. $79,700

D. $85,000

Answer (A) is correct.
REQUIRED: The cost of goods manufactured (COGM).
DISCUSSION: COGM is the sum of the costs in BWIP and all the costs incurred during the period minus the costs in EWIP. The calculation of COGM uses applied overhead ($30,000 = $20,000 DL cost × 150%). The $7,300 in EWIP includes $2,800 for direct materials, $1,800 for direct labor, and $2,700 for applied overhead (at 150% of DL cost).

BWIP	$ 9,000
Direct labor	20,000
Applied OH	30,000
Direct materials	26,000
EWIP	(7,300)
COGM	$77,700

Answer (B) is incorrect. The amount of $78,000 does not reflect BWIP and EWIP and is based on actual manufacturing OH. Answer (C) is incorrect. Actual manufacturing OH of $32,000 was used. Answer (D) is incorrect. EWIP was not subtracted.

29. Over- or underapplied manufacturing overhead should be closed to the cost of goods sold account at February 28 in the amount of

A. $700 overapplied.

B. $1,000 overapplied.

C. $1,700 underapplied.

D. $2,000 underapplied.

Answer (D) is correct.
REQUIRED: The amount of over- or underapplied manufacturing overhead closed to COGS.
DISCUSSION: The amount of over- or underapplied overhead is the difference between the actual overhead incurred and the overhead applied. The amount of overhead applied was $30,000 ($20,000 DL cost ×150%). The amount of overhead incurred was $32,000. Consequently, underapplied overhead of $2,000 ($32,000 actual – $30,000 applied) should be closed to COGS.
Answer (A) is incorrect. The amount of $700 overapplied equals applied overhead in EWIP minus the difference between actual February overhead and overhead applied in February. Answer (B) is incorrect. The $3,000 of applied manufacturing overhead in BWIP should not be used in determining the current month's over- or underapplied overhead. Answer (C) is incorrect. The amounts of applied overhead in BWIP and EWIP should not be used in calculating the current month's over- or underapplied overhead.

30. Merry Co. has two major categories of manufacturing overhead: material handling and quality control. The costs expected for these categories for the coming year are as follows:

Material handling	$120,000
Quality inspection	200,000

The plant currently applies overhead based on direct labor hours. The estimated direct labor hours are 80,000 per year. The plant manager is asked to submit a bid and assembles the following data on a proposed job:

Direct materials	$4,000
Direct labor (2,000 hours)	6,000

What is the estimated product cost on the proposed job?

A. $8,000

B. $10,000

C. $14,000

D. $18,000

Answer (D) is correct.
  REQUIRED: The estimated product cost for the proposed job.
  DISCUSSION: Product costs (also called inventoriable costs) are capitalized as part of finished goods inventory, and eventually become a component of cost of goods sold. All manufacturing costs (direct materials, direct labor, and manufacturing overhead) must be treated as product costs. The plant applies overhead based on direct labor hours. The manufacturing overhead costs for the coming year equal $320,000 ($120,000 Material handling + $200,000 Quality inspection). Thus, overhead per direct labor hour equals $4.00 ($320,000 manufacturing overhead costs ÷ 80,000 direct labor hours). For the proposed job, direct materials and direct labor costs equal $10,000 ($4,000 + $6,000). Overhead applied to the job equals $8,000 (2,000 direct labor hours × $4.00 per hour). Thus, the estimated product cost on the proposed job equals $18,000 ($10,000 direct materials and labor + $8,000 overhead).
  Answer (A) is incorrect. The amount of $8,000 equals only the overhead applied to the proposed job. It does not consider the direct materials and direct labor. Answer (B) is incorrect. The amount of $10,000 equals the direct materials and direct labor for the proposed job, and omits the applied overhead. Answer (C) is incorrect. The amount of $14,000 does not add the correct amount of applied overhead to the direct materials and direct labor for the proposed job.

19.6 PRACTICE WRITTEN COMMUNICATION

| Business Environment and Concepts Testlet 4 of 4 | Time Remaining 1 hour - 15 minutes | | | | |

DIRECTIONS

Note: If you believe you have encountered a software malfunction, report it to the test center staff immediately.

Navigation

To navigate from task to task, use the controls at the bottom of the screen. Click on the **Next** button to advance to the next task, or the **Previous** button to go to the previous task. To go directly to any task, click on its number.

| ▼ = Reminder | | Directions | 1 ▽ | 2 ▽ | 3 ▽ | 4 ▽ | 5 ▽ | 6 ▽ | 7 ▽ | | ◀ Previous | Next ▶ |

If you would like a reminder to revisit a task, or want to indicate that you are finished with it, click on the reminder flag below the task number. To clear the flag, click on it again. Reminder flags are for your use only – they do not contribute to your score.

Tabs

In this part of the examination, you will be asked to complete various tasks. Every task has one or more **Work Tabs**. Every task also has a **Help** tab.

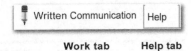

Work tab   **Help tab**

Work Tabs:

- **Work Tabs** are identified with a pencil icon. This is where your responses are expected.
- Each task has one or more **Work Tabs**.
- **Work Tabs** contain directions for completing the task - be sure to read these directions carefully.
- The **Work Tab** name in the example above is for illustration only - yours will differ.
- You must complete all of the **Work Tabs** in each task to receive full credit.

Help Tab:

- The **Help Tab** provides assistance with the exam software that is used in this task. For example, if the task is to compose a memorandum, **Help** will provide information about the word processor.

The Toolbar

The toolbar at the top of the screen shows the amount of time remaining for you to complete the tasks. In addition, the following tools are available. Note that only the **Exit** button is displayed when Directions are visible - the others will appear when you begin the tasks.

Click on these buttons to split or unsplit the screen. You can split the screen vertically or horizontally.

Click on this button to go on to the next part of the examination. You must complete all of the tasks to receive full credit. Once you click on **Exit** and confirm the action, you will NOT be able to return to this testlet.

| ▼ = Reminder | | Directions | 1 ▽ | | | | | | | | ◀ Previous | Next ▶ |

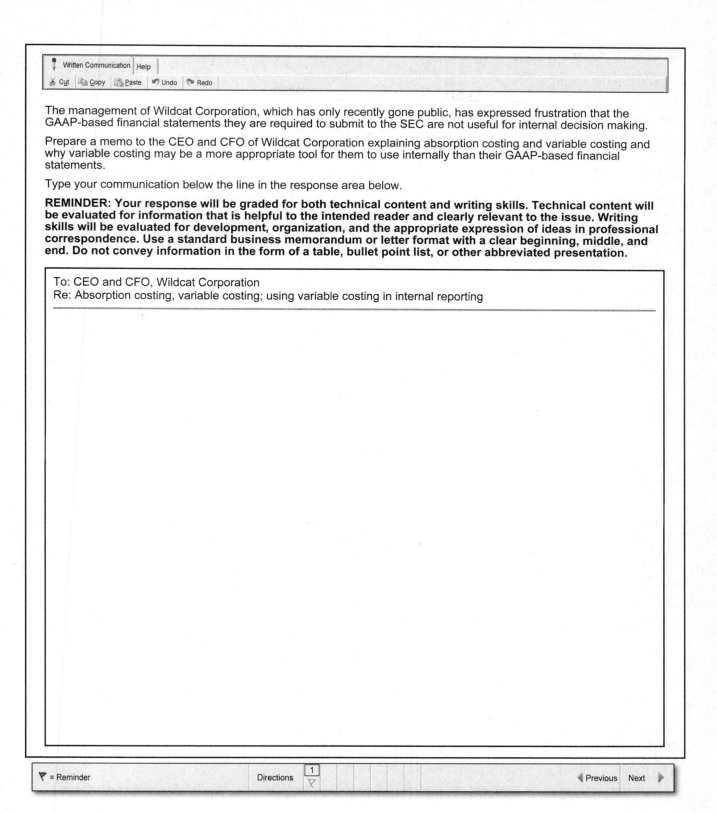

The management of Wildcat Corporation, which has only recently gone public, has expressed frustration that the GAAP-based financial statements they are required to submit to the SEC are not useful for internal decision making.

Prepare a memo to the CEO and CFO of Wildcat Corporation explaining absorption costing and variable costing and why variable costing may be a more appropriate tool for them to use internally than their GAAP-based financial statements.

Type your communication below the line in the response area below.

REMINDER: Your response will be graded for both technical content and writing skills. Technical content will be evaluated for information that is helpful to the intended reader and clearly relevant to the issue. Writing skills will be evaluated for development, organization, and the appropriate expression of ideas in professional correspondence. Use a standard business memorandum or letter format with a clear beginning, middle, and end. Do not convey information in the form of a table, bullet point list, or other abbreviated presentation.

To: CEO and CFO, Wildcat Corporation
Re: Absorption costing, variable costing; using variable costing in internal reporting

NOTE: Your Written Communications on the actual CPA exam may cover topics outside the scope of the BEC CSO (i.e., they may relate to topics from the AUD, FAR, and/or REG CSOs instead). Answer to the best of your ability, and remember that graders are mainly evaluating your writing ability and will overlook minor technical mistakes.

Unofficial Answer

Written Communication

To: CEO and CFO, Wildcat Corporation
Re: Absorption costing, variable costing; using variable costing in internal reporting

---

Although GAAP require absorption (full) costing for external reporting, and the IRS requires it for tax purposes, variable costing is preferred for internal reporting purposes. First, an understanding of the differences between absorption and variable costing needs to be developed. Next, it is important to understand the benefit of using variable costing in internal reporting despite statutory requirements to use absorption costing for external reporting.

Absorption costing reports unit costs that include the portion of total manufacturing cost attributable to that unit or group of units. It is more inclusive than variable costing, which only includes variable manufacturing costs in the determination of unit costs. Thus, absorption costing is required for external reporting and for tax purposes.

Nevertheless, variable costing, or contribution margin reporting, is an important internal measure because it is an immediate response to the informational needs of management. Management requires a knowledge of cost behavior under various operating conditions. For planning and control, management is more concerned about treating fixed and variable costs separately than with calculating full costs. Full costs are usually of little value because they contain arbitrary allocations of fixed cost. Also, profit planning and decision making are easier under variable costing. It does not require auxiliary records and supplementary analysis for the fixed manufacturing portion of product costs. Accordingly, although absorption costing responds to the needs of external users, managers within the organization have different informational needs.

The above depicts a Level 5 answer. Consult your booklet, *How to Pass the CPA Exam: A System for Success*, for a description of the three writing skills criteria. You may also access this booklet online by visiting www.gleim.com/PassCPA.

Self-Grade

Below, grade your response on technical content and writing skills. Bubble in the circle next to the appropriate score that you may receive based on the criteria given. Your **total** score is the sum of your scores on all six items. The maximum score is 19 points.

Technical Content Evaluation

Was your response on topic?	O No [0]	O Mostly [1]	O Yes [2]
Did your response have any *significant* errors?	O 0 errors [1]	O 1 major error [−1]	O 2 or more major errors [−2]
Did your response contain any illegal advice?	O No [1]	O Yes [0]	

Writing Skills Evaluation

	Poor	Below Average	Average	Above Average	Outstanding
Organization	O 1	O 2	O 3	O 4	O 5
Development	O 1	O 2	O 3	O 4	O 5
Expression	O 1	O 2	O 3	O 4	O 5

Disclaimer: This scoring schedule was developed by Gleim Publications as a guideline only. The AICPA has not released specific information on how the Written Communications are graded.

Practice even more Written Communications with the Gleim Mega Test Bank.

Learn more: gleim.com/CPAmega | 800.874.5346

STUDY UNIT TWENTY
COSTING SYSTEMS AND VARIANCE ANALYSIS

(17 pages of outline)

Process costing is used when relatively homogeneous products are mass produced on a continuous basis (Subunits 20.1 and 20.2). Activity-based costing is used when indirect costs are high (Subunit 20.3).

A standard cost is an estimate of what a cost should be under normal operating conditions based on accounting and engineering studies. Standard costs are used to assign costs to products and control actual costs. Comparing actual and standard costs permits evaluation of managerial performance using variance analysis (Subunits 20.4 and 20.5). This analysis also can be applied to revenue amounts (Subunit 20.6).

20.1 PROCESS COSTING -- PRINCIPLES

1. **Uses of Process Costing**

   a. Process cost accounting assigns costs to inventoriable goods or services. It applies to relatively homogeneous products that are mass produced on a continuous basis (e.g., petroleum products, thread, and computer monitors).

   b. Instead of using subsidiary ledgers to track specific jobs, process costing typically uses a work-in-process account for each department through which the production of output passes.

   c. Process costing calculates the average cost of all units as follows:

      1) Costs are accumulated for a cost object that consists of a large number of similar units of goods or services,

      2) Work-in-process is stated in terms of equivalent units, and

      3) Unit costs are established.

2. **Accumulation of Costs**

   a. The accumulation of costs under a process costing system is by department to reflect the continuous, homogeneous nature of the process.

   b. The physical inputs required for production are obtained from suppliers.

   | Materials | $XXX | |
   | Accounts payable | | $XXX |

   c. Direct materials are added by the first department in the process.

   | Work-in-process -- Department A | $XXX | |
   | Materials | | $XXX |

d. Conversion costs are the sum of direct labor and manufacturing overhead. The nature of process costing makes this accounting treatment more efficient. (Section 4 contains an outline of equivalent units.)

Work-in-process -- Department A	$XXX	
Wages payable (direct and indirect labor)		$XXX
Manufacturing overhead		XXX

e. Products move from one department to the next.

Work-in-process -- Department B	$XXX	
Work-in-process -- Department A		$XXX

f. The second department adds more direct materials and more conversion costs.

Work-in-process -- Department B	$XXX	
Materials		$XXX

Work-in-process -- Department B	$XXX	
Wages payable (direct and indirect labor)		$XXX
Manufacturing overhead		XXX

g. When processing is finished in the last department, all costs are transferred to finished goods.

Finished goods	$XXX	
Work-in-process -- Department B		$XXX

h. As products are sold, sales are recorded and the costs are transferred to cost of goods sold.

Accounts receivable	$XXX	
Sales		$XXX
Cost of goods sold	$XXX	
Finished goods		$XXX

i. The changes in these accounts during the period can be summarized as follows:

Materials Inventory (MI)	Work-in-Progress Inventory (WIP)	Finished Goods Inventory (FG)
Beginning MI	Beginning WIP	Beginning FG
Purchases of MI	Conversion Costs	Cost of Goods Manufactured
(Ending MI)	Materials Used	(Ending FG)
	(Ending WIP)	
Materials Used	Cost of Goods Manufactured	Cost of Goods Sold

Figure 20-1

3. Process Cost Flows

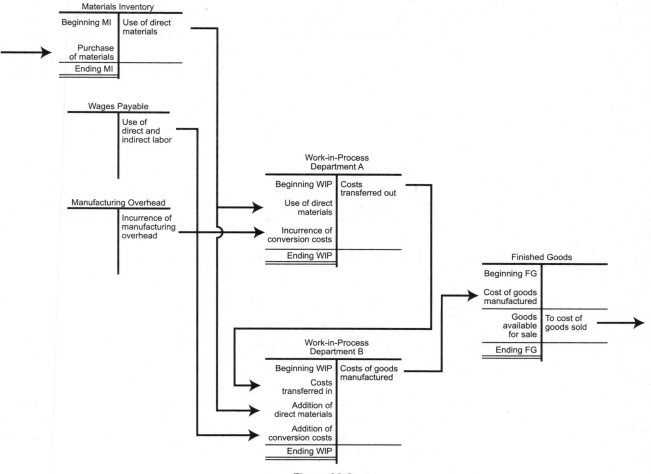

Figure 20-2

4. Equivalent Units of Production (EUP)

a. Some units are unfinished at the end of the period. To account for their costs, the units are restated in terms of equivalent units of production (EUP). EUP equal the number of finished goods that could have been produced using the inputs consumed during the period. EUP for direct materials or conversion costs is the amount required to complete one physical unit of production.

EXAMPLE

One thousand work-in-process units, 80% complete for direct materials and 60% for conversion costs, equal 800 EUP of direct materials (1,000 × 80%) and 600 EUP of conversion costs (1,000 × 60%).

1) Determining the costs of unfinished units requires (a) determining the EUP and (b) calculating the per-unit cost.

2) The two calculations are made separately for direct materials and conversion costs. Conversion costs are assumed to be uniformly incurred.

    a) Transferred-in costs are by definition 100% complete. The units (costs) transferred in from the previous department should be included in the computation of the EUP of the second department.

        i) These costs are treated the same as direct materials added at the beginning of the period.

3) The actual production quantity flow is based on the following relationship:

$$\begin{matrix} Beginning \\ work\text{-}in\text{-}process \end{matrix} + \begin{matrix} Units\ started \\ this\ period \end{matrix} = \begin{matrix} Units\ transferred \\ out\ (completed) \end{matrix} + \begin{matrix} Ending \\ work\text{-}in\text{-}process \end{matrix}$$

4) Two methods of calculating EUP are common: weighted-average and FIFO.

b. Under the **weighted-average** method, units in beginning work-in-process (WIP) are treated the same as units started and completed during the current period. This method averages the costs of beginning WIP with the costs of current-period production.

1) The calculation of EUP under the weighted-average method is as follows:

> Total units completed (transferred out) this period
> \+ Ending work-in-process × Percent completed
> EUP under weighted-average

2) The cost per EUP under the weighted-average method is calculated as follows:

$$Cost\ per\ EUP = \frac{Beginning\ WIP\ costs + Current\text{-}period\ costs}{EUP}$$

c. Under the **first-in, first-out (FIFO)** method, the EUP in beginning work-in-process (work done in the prior period) must be excluded from the calculation. Only the costs incurred in the current period are considered. The EUP produced during the current period are based only on the work done during the current period.

1) The calculation of EUP under the FIFO method is as follows:

> Beginning work-in-process (WIP) × Percent left to complete
> \+ Units started and completed during the current period
> \+ Ending work-in-process (WIP) × Percent completed
> EUP under FIFO

NOTE: Units started and completed during the current period are equal to units started minus ending WIP.

Another version of this equation is below:

> Total units completed this period
> \+ Ending work-in-process (WIP) × Percent completed
> − Beginning work-in-process × Percent completed in previous periods
> EUP under FIFO

2) The cost per EUP under FIFO is calculated as follows:

$$Cost\ per\ EUP = \frac{Current\text{-}period\ costs}{EUP}$$

EXAMPLE

Cost reports are being prepared for the month. The first step is to prepare a quantity schedule.

	Units	Completed for Direct Materials	Completed for Conversion Costs
Beginning work-in-process	2,000	80%	40%
Units started during period	8,000		
Units to account for	10,000		
Units completed	9,000		
Ending work-in-process	1,000	90%	70%
Units accounted for	10,000		

The next step is to calculate the EUP. This table illustrates the different outcomes of the two methods. The EUP in beginning work-in-process (work done in the prior period) are included in the weighted-average calculation but not the FIFO calculation.

	Weighted-Average		FIFO	
	Direct Materials	Conversion Costs	Direct Materials	Conversion Costs
Units completed	9,000	9,000	9,000	9,000
Plus: ending work-in-process EUP				
Direct materials: 1,000 units × 90%	900		900	
Conversion costs: 1,000 units × 70%		700		700
Minus: beginning work-in-process EUP				
Direct materials: 2,000 units × 80%			(1,600)	
Conversion costs: 2,000 units × 40%				(800)
Equivalent units of production	9,900	9,700	8,300	8,900

The costs to be allocated are presented in this table:

	Direct Materials	Conversion Costs
Beginning work-in-process	$25,000	$10,000
Added during the month	55,000	50,000
Totals	$80,000	$60,000

d. After the EUP have been calculated, the per-unit costs for each method can be determined.

   1) Under the weighted-average method, all direct materials and conversion costs incurred in the current period and in beginning work-in-process are averaged.

EXAMPLE

Direct materials cost per EUP: $\dfrac{\$80,000}{9,900 \text{ EUP}}$ = $ 8.08

Conversion costs per EUP: $\dfrac{\$60,000}{9,700 \text{ EUP}}$ = $ 6.19

Total cost of a completed unit under
the weighted-average method: $14.27

   2) Under the FIFO method, only the costs incurred in the current period are included in the calculation.

EXAMPLE

Direct materials cost per EUP: $\dfrac{\$55,000}{8,300 \text{ EUP}}$ = $ 6.63

Conversion costs per EUP: $\dfrac{\$50,000}{8,900 \text{ EUP}}$ = $ 5.62

Total cost of a completed unit
under the FIFO method: $12.25

e.   When beginning work-in-process is zero, the two methods have the same results.

 Beginning inventory is subtracted in the EUP calculation only when applying FIFO. The weighted-average method treats units in beginning inventory as if they had been started and completed during the current period.

Stop and review! You have completed the outline for this subunit. Study multiple-choice questions 1 through 4 beginning on page 527.

20.2 PROCESS COSTING -- CALCULATIONS

Process costing questions on the CPA exam test the understanding of principles and the ability to perform detailed calculations. This subunit consists entirely of the second type of question. Please review Subunit 20.1 before answering these questions.

Stop and review! You have completed the outline for this subunit. Study multiple-choice questions 5 through 10 beginning on page 528.

20.3 ACTIVITY-BASED COSTING (ABC)

1.   **Disadvantages of Volume-Based Systems**

a.   ABC is a response to the significant increase in the incurrence of indirect costs resulting from the rapid advance of technology. ABC is a refinement of an existing costing system (job-order or process).

1)   Under a **traditional (volume-based)** system, overhead is accumulated in one cost pool and allocated to all end products using one allocation base, such as direct labor hours or direct machine hours used.

2)   Under **ABC**, indirect costs are assigned to activities and then rationally allocated to end products.

3)   ABC may be used by manufacturing, service, or retailing firms.

4)   ABC may be used in a job-order system or a process cost system.

b.   The inaccurate averaging or spreading of indirect costs over products or service units that use different amounts of resources is called **peanut-butter costing**. Peanut-butter costing results in product-cost cross-subsidization. It miscosts one product and, as a result, miscosts other products.

c.   The peanut-butter effect of using a volume-based system can be summarized as follows:

1)   Direct labor and direct materials are traced to products or service units.

2)   One pool of indirect costs (overhead) is accumulated for a given organizational unit.

3)   Indirect costs from the pool are assigned using an allocative (rather than a tracing) procedure, such as using a single overhead rate for an entire department, e.g., $3 of overhead for every direct labor hour.

a)   The effect is an averaging of costs that may result in significant inaccuracy when products or service units do not use similar amounts of resources.

EXAMPLE

The effect of product-cost cross-subsidization can be illustrated as follows:

1.   Two products are produced. Both require 1 unit of direct materials and 1 hour of direct labor. Materials costs are $14 per unit, and direct labor is $70 per hour. Also, the manufacturer has no beginning or ending inventories.

2.   During the month just ended, production equaled 1,000 units of Product A and 100 units of Product B. Manufacturing overhead for the month was $20,000.

3.   Using direct labor hours as the overhead allocation base, per-unit costs and profits are calculated as follows:

	Product A	Product B	Total
Direct materials	$ 14,000	$ 1,400	
Direct labor	70,000	7,000	
Overhead {$20,000 × [1,000 ÷ (1,000 + 100)]}	18,182		
Overhead {$20,000 × [100 ÷ (1,000 + 100)]}		1,818	
Total costs	$102,182	$ 10,218	$112,400
Selling price	$ 119.99	$ 139.99	
Cost per unit	(102.18)	(102.18)	
Profit per unit	$ 17.81	$ 37.81	

4.   Overhead consists almost entirely of production line setup costs, and the two products require equal setup times. Allocating overhead on this basis has different results.

	Product A	Product B	Total
Direct materials	$14,000	$ 1,400	
Direct labor	70,000	7,000	
Overhead ($20,000 × 50%)	10,000		
Overhead ($20,000 × 50%)		10,000	
Total costs	$94,000	$18,400	$112,400
Selling price	$119.99	$139.99	
Cost per unit	(94.00)	(184.00)	
Profit (loss) per unit	$ 25.99	$ (44.01)	

5.   Under volume-based costing, Product B appeared to be profitable. But ABC revealed that high-volume Product A has been subsidizing the setup costs for the low-volume Product B.

d.   The example above assumed a single component of overhead for clarity. In reality, overhead consists of many components. The peanut-butter effect of traditional overhead allocation is illustrated in the following diagram:

Overhead Allocation in Volume-Based Costing

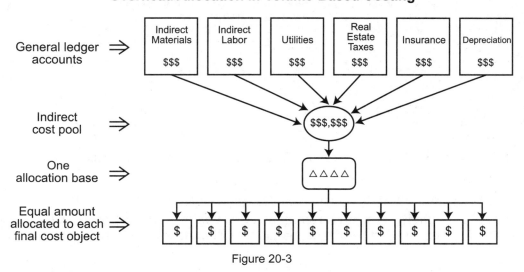

Figure 20-3

2. **Volume-Based vs. Activity-Based**

    a.   Volume-based systems are appropriate when most manufacturing costs are homogeneously consumed. In these cases, one volume-based cost driver can be used to allocate the overhead costs. However, overhead costs do not always fluctuate with volume. ABC addresses the increasing complexity and variety of overhead costs.

    b.   Activity-based systems involve

        1)   Identifying organizational activities that result in overhead.

        2)   Assigning the costs of resources consumed by the activities.

        3)   Assigning the costs of the activities by appropriate cost drivers to final cost objects.

3. **Step 1: Activity Analysis**

    a.   An activity is a set of work actions undertaken, and a cost pool is established for each activity.

    b.   Analysis identifies value-adding activities, which contribute to customer satisfaction. Nonvalue-adding activities should be reduced or eliminated.

    c.   Activities are classified in a hierarchy according to the level of the production process where they occur.

4. **Step 2: Assign Resource Costs to Activities**

    a.   After activities are identified, the next step is to assign the costs of resources to the activities, a **first-stage allocation**.

    b.   Identifying resource costs is not as simple as in volume-based overhead allocation, which designates general ledger accounts to be combined in one general ledger cost pool.

        1)   A separate accounting system may be necessary to track resource costs separately from the general ledger.

    c.   After resources have been identified, resource drivers are designated to allocate resource costs to **activity cost pools**.

        1)   **Resource drivers** are measures of the resources consumed by an activity.

EXAMPLE

A job-order system accumulates costs for a product made in various models. But given increasing reliance on robots in the production process and computers for monitoring and control, overhead is now a greater percentage of total costs, and direct labor costs have decreased. Thus, implementation of an activity-based costing system has begun.

The following resources are used by the indirect cost processes:

Resource	Driver
Computer processing	CPU cycles
Production line	Machine hours
Materials management	Hours worked
Utilities	Square footage

---

5. **Step 3: Allocate Costs in Activity Cost Pools to Final Cost Objects**

    a.   This final step is a **second-stage allocation**.

    b.   Costs are reassigned to final-stage cost objects on the basis of activity cost drivers.

        1)   **Activity cost drivers** are measures of the demands on an activity by next-stage cost objects, such as the number of parts in a product used to measure an assembly activity.

        2)   A driver is a factor that causes a change in a cost. **Cost drivers** are cost assignment bases that are used in the allocation of manufacturing overhead costs to cost objects.

c. Drivers (both resource and activity) must be chosen on the basis of a **cause-and-effect** relationship with the resource or activity cost allocated. A high positive correlation does not suffice.

EXAMPLE

The following cost drivers have a cause-and-effect relationship with their corresponding activities:

Activity	Cost driver
Product design	Number of products
Production setup	Number of setups
Machining	Number of units produced
Inspection and testing	Number of units produced
Production orders	Number of orders

EXAMPLE

The following information pertains to current-month activities regarding the manufacture of X and Z:

Manufacturing overhead costs		Cost driver
Plant utilities and real estate taxes	$150,000	Square footage
Materials handling	40,000	Pounds of direct materials used
Inspection and testing	10,000	Number of units produced
	$200,000	

Current month activity level

	X	Z	Total
Direct labor hours	20,000	5,000	25,000
Plant square footage	400	600	1,000
Pounds of direct materials used	10,000	6,000	16,000
Number of units produced	15,000	3,000	18,000

Using direct labor hours as the overhead allocation base (volume-based system), the manufacturing overhead costs are allocated as follows:

X: $200,000 × (20,000 ÷ 25,000) = $160,000
Z: $200,000 × (5,000 ÷ 25,000) = $40,000

Manufacturing overhead costs per unit of X: $160,000 ÷ 15,000 = $10.67
Manufacturing overhead costs per unit of Z: $40,000 ÷ 3,000 = $13.33

Under an ABC system, the manufacturing overhead costs are allocated as follows:

	X		Z	
Plant utilities and real estate taxes	$150,000 × (400 ÷ 1,000)	= $60,000	$150,000 × (600 ÷ 1,000)	= $ 90,000
Materials handling	$40,000 × (10,000 ÷ 16,000)	= $25,000	$40,000 x (6,000 ÷ 16,000)	= $ 15,000
Inspection and testing	$10,000 × (15,000 ÷ 18,000)	= $ 8,333	$10,000 × (3,000 ÷ 18,000)	= $ 1,667
		$93,333		$106,667

Manufacturing overhead costs per unit of X = $93,333 ÷ 15,000 = $6.22
Manufacturing overhead costs per unit of Z = $106,667 ÷ 3,000 = $35.56

Stop and review! You have completed the outline for this subunit. Study multiple-choice questions 11 through 17 beginning on page 530.

20.4 VARIANCE ANALYSIS -- MATERIALS AND LABOR

The AICPA frequently tests variance analysis. Be certain to learn how to calculate the different variances. However, variance analysis is complex, and the terminology is not standardized.

1.   **Use of Variance Analysis**

a.   Variance analysis is the basis of performance evaluation using standard costs.

1)   A favorable variance **(F)** occurs when actual costs are **less** than standard.

2)   An unfavorable variance **(U)** occurs when actual costs are **greater** than standard.

b.   Variance analysis enables management by exception, the practice of emphasizing significant deviations from expectations (whether favorable or unfavorable). A variance alerts management that corrective action may be needed.

2.   **Framework for Variance Calculation**

a.   Variable inputs (direct materials and direct labor) can be analyzed in terms of a price (rate) variance and an efficiency (quantity usage) variance.

1)   **Price (rate) variances** result from a difference between (a) the actual price of resources used in production and (b) the standard price if quantity is constant.

2)   **Efficiency (quantity) variances** result from differences between (a) the actual resources used in production and (b) the standard amount if price is constant.

b.   The following abbreviations are used in the calculation of variances:

AQP = Actual quantity of materials purchased
AQ = Actual quantity of materials or hours
AP = Actual price (rate) of materials or hours
SQ = Standard quantity of materials or hours
SP = Standard price (rate) of materials or hours

3.   **Direct Materials**

a.   The total direct materials variance is the difference between (1) the actual materials cost of the actual units of output and (2) the standard materials cost of that output. Direct materials variances have price and quantity components.

1)   The **materials price variance** equals the actual quantity of input purchased during the period times the difference between (a) the standard price of materials and (b) the actual price.

$$\begin{array}{c} \textit{Direct materials} \\ \textit{price variance} \end{array} = \begin{array}{c} \textit{Actual quantity} \\ \textit{purchased (AQP)} \end{array} \times \left(\begin{array}{c} \textit{Standard materials} \\ \textit{price (SP)} \end{array} - \begin{array}{c} \textit{Actual materials} \\ \textit{price (AP)} \end{array} \right)$$

2)   The **materials quantity variance** (also called usage or efficiency variance) equals the standard price times the difference between (a) the standard quantity of materials and (b) the actual quantity used in production.

$$\begin{array}{c} \textit{Direct materials} \\ \textit{quantity variance} \end{array} = \left(\begin{array}{c} \textit{Standard quantity of} \\ \textit{input allowed (SQ)} \end{array} - \begin{array}{c} \textit{Actual quantity} \\ \textit{consumed (AQ)} \end{array} \right) \times \begin{array}{c} \textit{Standard materials} \\ \textit{price (SP)} \end{array}$$

EXAMPLE of Direct Materials Variances

Budgeted use is 980 tons of materials at a cost of $54 per ton. The actual amounts purchased and used during the month were 1,150 tons and 1,078 tons, respectively. The actual cost for the period was $50 per ton. If the materials price variance is recognized at purchase, variances for direct materials are calculated as follows:

AQP × AP	AQP × SP	AQ × SP	SQ × SP
1,150 tons × $50	1,150 tons × $54	1,078 tons × $54	980 tons × $54
$57,500	$62,100	$58,212	$52,920

Materials Price Variance
$4,600 F

Materials Quantity Variance
$5,292 U

Materials price variance	= AQP × (SP − AP)	Materials quantity variance	= (SQ − AQ) × SP
	= 1,150 × ($54 − $50)		= (980 − 1,078) × $54
	= 1,150 × $4		= −98 × $54
	= $4,600 favorable		= $5,292 unfavorable

4. **Direct Labor**

   a. The total variance for direct labor is the sum of the two components below:

      1) The **labor rate variance** equals the actual number of hours worked times the difference between (a) the standard hourly wage rate and (b) the actual hourly rate.

$$\text{Direct labor rate variance} = \text{Actual hours worked (AQ)} \times \left(\text{Standard hourly rate (SP)} - \text{Actual hourly rate (AP)} \right)$$

      2) The **labor efficiency variance** equals the difference between (a) the standard number of hours allowed and (b) the actual number of hours worked, times the standard hourly wage rate.

$$\text{Direct labor efficiency variance} = \left(\text{Standard number of hours allowed (SQ)} - \text{Actual number of hours worked (AQ)} \right) \times \text{Standard hourly rate (SP)}$$

AQ × AP	AQ × SP	SQ × SP

Labor Rate Variance   Labor Efficiency Variance

Figure 20-4

EXAMPLE of Direct Labor Variances

Standard direct labor use was 882 hours at $17 per hour. However, 932 direct labor hours were actually worked at $18 per hour. The variances for direct labor are calculated as follows:

AQ × AP	AQ × SP	SQ × SP
932 hours × $18	932 hours × $17	882 hours × $17
$16,776	$15,844	$14,994

Labor Rate Variance
$932 U

Labor Efficiency Variance
$850 U

Labor rate variance	= AQ × (SP − AP)	Labor efficiency variance	= (SQ − AQ) × SP
	= 932 × ($17 − $18)		= (882 − 932) × $17
	= $932 unfavorable		= $850 unfavorable

5. **Mix and yield** variances for interchangeable inputs are beyond the scope of this outline.

Stop and review! You have completed the outline for this subunit. Study multiple-choice questions 18 through 23 beginning on page 533.

20.5 VARIANCE ANALYSIS -- OVERHEAD

1.   **Variable Overhead**

   a.   The amount of variable overhead (VOH) **under- or overapplied** for the period is the variable overhead flexible budget variance.

   1)   Overhead is applied based on the expected quantity (EQ) rather than the standard quantity. EQ is the standard number of driver units (e.g., direct machine hours) allowed given the achieved output.

   2)   For simplicity, assume that the variable overhead is applied based on direct machine hours used.

$$VOH\ flexible\ budget\ variance = Actual\ VOH\ costs\ incurred\ -\ (EQ \times SP)$$

$$VOH\ over\text{-}\ or\ underapplied = Actual\ VOH\ costs\ incurred\ -\ VOH\ applied$$

$$\begin{matrix}Actual\ unit \\ output\end{matrix} - \left(\begin{matrix}Actual\ VOH \\ incurred\end{matrix} \times \begin{matrix}Standard\ hours\ allowed \\ per\ unit\ of\ output\end{matrix} \times Standard\ VOH\ rate \right)$$

   b.   This variance has a spending component and an efficiency component.

   1)   The **VOH spending variance** is the difference between (a) the actual VOH incurred and (b) the actual number of driver units (e.g., machine hours) times the standard VOH rate.

$$VOH\ spending\ variance = Actual\ VOH\ -\ (Actual\ number\ of\ hours\ used \times Standard\ VOH\ rate)$$

$$= Actual\ VOH\ -\ (AQ \times SP)$$

   2)   The **VOH efficiency variance** is the difference between (a) the standard number of hours allowed for actual unit output (EQ) and (b) the actual number of hours used, times the standard VOH rate.

$$VOH\ efficiency\ variance = (EQ\ -\ AQ)\ \times SP$$

Variable Overhead Variances

Figure 20-5

<u>EXAMPLE</u> of Variable Overhead Variances

Variable overhead is applied at the rate of $4 per machine hour. The use of 10 machine hours is budgeted for each unit produced. The planned output was 90 units. Actual output is 98 units. The number of machine hours used was 900, and actual variable overhead was $4,000. The variances for variable overhead are calculated as follows:

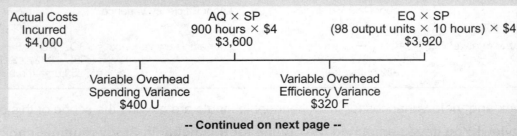

-- **Continued on next page** --

EXAMPLE -- Continued

These calculations can be reconciled with the following equation:

Amount applied – Actual costs incurred = VOH flexible budget variance
= VOH spending variance + VOH efficiency variance
$3,920 – $4,000 = $400 U + $320 F
$80 underapplied = $80 U

---

2. **Fixed Overhead**

    a. The amount of fixed overhead (FOH) that was under- or overapplied for the period consists of a spending component and a volume component.

$$\text{FOH over- or underapplied} = \text{Actual FOH incurred} - \text{FOH applied}$$

$$= \begin{matrix} \text{Actual FOH} \\ \text{incurred} \end{matrix} - \left(\begin{matrix} \text{Actual unit} \\ \text{output} \end{matrix} \times \begin{matrix} \text{Standard hours allowed} \\ \text{per unit of output} \end{matrix} \times \begin{matrix} \text{Standard} \\ \text{FOH rate} \end{matrix} \right)$$

   1) The **FOH spending variance** is the difference between (a) the actual costs incurred and (b) the amount budgeted.

$$\text{FOH spending variance} = \text{Actual FOH incurred} - \text{Amount budgeted}$$

$$= \begin{matrix} \text{Actual FOH} \\ \text{incurred} \end{matrix} - \left(\begin{matrix} \text{Budgeted} \\ \text{unit output} \end{matrix} \times \begin{matrix} \text{Standard hours allowed} \\ \text{per unit of output} \end{matrix} \times \begin{matrix} \text{Standard} \\ \text{FOH rate} \end{matrix} \right)$$

   2) The **FOH volume variance** is the difference between (a) the amount of fixed overhead budgeted and (b) the amount applied.

$$\text{FOH volume variance} = \text{Amount budgeted} - \text{FOH applied}$$

    b. Fixed overhead has a volume variance instead of an efficiency variance.

   1) Fixed costs by definition do not change within the relevant range of the budgeting cycle. The same amount of fixed cost is budgeted regardless of the number of driver units actually used or the actual unit output.

       a) For the same reason, the sum of the fixed overhead spending and volume variances is not flexible budget variance.

Fixed Overhead Variances

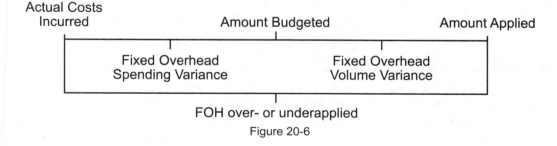

Figure 20-6

EXAMPLE of Fixed Overhead Variances

The budget for fixed overhead during the period is $1,440 based on budgeted output of 90 units. The fixed overhead allocation rate is $1.60 per machine hour, and 10 hours are required per output unit. Actual fixed overhead for the period is $1,600.

These calculations can be reconciled with the following equation:

Amount applied – Actual costs incurred = FOH spending variance + VOH volume variance
$1,568 – $1,600 = $160 U + $128 F
$32 underapplied = $32 U

3.   **Integrated Overhead Variance Analysis**

   a.   **Three-way overhead variance analysis** combines the variable and fixed spending variances ($400 U + $160 U = $560 U) and reports the other two variances separately.

EXAMPLE

Three-Way Analysis	Spending Variance	Efficiency Variance	Volume Variance
Total overhead	$560 U	$320 F	$128 F

   b.   **Two-way overhead variance analysis** combines the spending and efficiency variances into one budget variance ($560 U + $320 F = $240 U) and reports the volume variance separately.

EXAMPLE

Two-Way Analysis	Budget Variance	Volume Variance
Total overhead	$240 U	$128 F

   1)   The budget variance in two-way analysis also is called the **controllable variance**. It is the portion of the total not attributable to the volume variance.

   c.   The **net overhead variance** (one-way overhead variance analysis) combines all the components into one amount ($240 U + $128 F = **$112 U**).

   1)   The net overhead variance equals the difference between (a) the total actual overhead incurred of $5,600 ($4,000 actual VOH + $1,600 actual FOH) and (b) the total overhead applied of $5,488 [(98 × 10) standard hours applied to actual output produced × ($4 + $1.6) standard total overhead rate].

$5,600 – $5,488 = $112 U

4.   Comprehensive Example

	STANDARD COSTS	ACTUAL COSTS (AC)
DIRECT MATERIALS	600,000 units of materials at $2.00 each	700,000 units purchased and used at $1.90
DIRECT LABOR	60,000 hours allowed for actual output at $7 per hour	65,000 hours at $7.20
OVERHEAD	$8.00 per direct labor hour on normal capacity of 50,000 direct labor hours:	
	$6.00 for variable overhead	$396,000 variable
	$2.00 for fixed overhead	$130,000 fixed

MATERIALS VARIANCES

Price

$$
\begin{aligned}
AQ \times (SP - AP) &= \text{Actual quantity} \times (\text{Standard price} - \text{Actual price}) \\
&= 700{,}000 \text{ units} \times (\$2.00 - \$1.90) \\
&= 700{,}000 \times \$0.10 \\
&= \$70{,}000 \text{ F}
\end{aligned}
$$

Quantity

$$
\begin{aligned}
(SQ - AQ) \times SP &= (\text{Standard quantity} - \text{Actual quantity}) \times \text{Standard price} \\
&= (600{,}000 \text{ units} - 700{,}000 \text{ units}) \times \$2.00 \\
&= -100{,}000 \times \$2.00 \\
&= \$200{,}000 \text{ U}
\end{aligned}
$$

LABOR VARIANCES

Rate

$$
\begin{aligned}
AQ \times (SP - AP) &= \text{Actual hours} \times (\text{Standard rate} - \text{Actual rate}) \\
&= 65{,}000 \text{ hours} \times (\$7.00 - \$7.20) \\
&= 65{,}000 \times -\$0.20 \\
&= \$13{,}000 \text{ U}
\end{aligned}
$$

Efficiency

$$
\begin{aligned}
(SQ - AQ) \times SP &= (\text{Standard hours} - \text{Actual hours}) \times \text{Standard rate} \\
&= (60{,}000 \text{ hours} - 65{,}000 \text{ hours}) \times \$7.00 \\
&= -5{,}000 \times \$7.00 \\
&= \$35{,}000 \text{ U}
\end{aligned}
$$

VARIABLE OVERHEAD VARIANCES

Spending

$$
\begin{aligned}
(AQ \times SP) - AC &= (\text{Actual hours} \times \text{Standard rate}) - \text{Actual costs incurred} \\
&= (65{,}000 \times \$6.00) - \$396{,}000 \\
&= \$390{,}000 - \$396{,}000 \\
&= \$6{,}000 \text{ U}
\end{aligned}
$$

Efficiency

$$
\begin{aligned}
(SQ - AQ) \times SP &= (\text{Standard hours allowed for actual production} - \text{Actual hours}) \times \text{Standard rate} \\
&= (60{,}000 - 65{,}000) \times \$6.00 \\
&= -5{,}000 \times \$6.00 \\
&= \$30{,}000 \text{ U}
\end{aligned}
$$

Total VOH Variance

$$
\begin{aligned}
&= \text{Actual VOH incurred} - \text{VOH applied} \\
&= \$396{,}000 - (60{,}000 \times \$6.00) \\
&= \$36{,}000 \text{ U}
\end{aligned}
$$

FIXED OVERHEAD VARIANCES

Spending

Flexible/Static budget – Actual costs incurred = (50,000 hours × $2.00) – $130,000
= $30,000 U

Volume

(Standard hours allowed for actual output × Standard rate) – Flexible/Static budget
= (60,000 hours × $2.00) – (50,000 hours × $2.00)
= $120,000 – $100,000
= $20,000 F

Total FOH Variance

= FOH incurred – FOH applied
= $130,000 – (60,000 hours × $2.00)
= $10,000 U

Stop and review! You have completed the outline for this subunit. Study multiple-choice questions 24 through 29 beginning on page 535.

20.6 SALES VARIANCES

1. **Sales, Contribution Margin, and Operating Income**

   a. Variance analysis is useful for evaluating not only the production function but also the selling function.

      1) If sales differ from the amount budgeted, the difference could consist of a **sales price variance**, a **sales volume variance**, or both.

      2) The analysis of these variances concentrates on **contribution margins** because fixed costs are assumed to be constant.

<table>
<tr><th colspan="5">EXAMPLE</th></tr>
<tr><td colspan="5">Budgeted sales of a product are 10,000 units at $17 per unit. Variable costs are expected to be $10 per unit, and fixed costs are budgeted at $50,000. The following compares budgeted and actual results:</td></tr>
<tr><th></th><th>Budget Computation</th><th>Budget Amount</th><th>Actual Computation</th><th>Actual Amount</th></tr>
<tr><td>Sales</td><td>10,000 units × $17 per unit</td><td>$170,000</td><td>11,000 units × $16 per unit</td><td>$176,000</td></tr>
<tr><td>Variable costs</td><td>10,000 units × $10 per unit</td><td>(100,000)</td><td>11,000 units × $10 per unit</td><td>(110,000)</td></tr>
<tr><td>Contribution margin</td><td></td><td>$ 70,000</td><td></td><td>$ 66,000</td></tr>
<tr><td>Fixed costs</td><td></td><td>(50,000)</td><td></td><td>(50,000)</td></tr>
<tr><td>Operating income</td><td></td><td>$ 20,000</td><td></td><td>$ 16,000</td></tr>
<tr><td>Unit contribution margins</td><td>$70,000 ÷ 10,000 units</td><td>$ 7</td><td>$66,000 ÷ 11,000 units</td><td>$ 6</td></tr>
</table>

2. **Sales Variances**

   a. In the example above, sales were greater than budgeted, but the contribution margin is lower. The difference can be analyzed in terms of the sales price variance and the sales volume variance.

      1) The **sales price variance** is the change in the contribution margin attributable solely to the change in selling price (if quantity is constant).

$$\textit{Sales price variance} = \textit{Actual units sold} \times \left(\begin{array}{c} \textit{Actual selling} \\ \textit{price per unit} \end{array} - \begin{array}{c} \textit{Budgeted selling} \\ \textit{price per unit} \end{array} \right)$$

      2) In the example, the actual selling price of $16 per unit is $1 less than expected. Thus, the sales price variance is $11,000 U (11,000 actual units sold × $1).

b.   The **sales volume variance** is the change in the contribution margin attributable solely to the difference between the actual and budgeted unit sales (if price is constant).

$$\text{Sales volume variance} = \frac{\text{Budgeted contribution}}{\text{margin per unit}} \times \left(\frac{\text{Actual units}}{\text{sold}} - \frac{\text{Budgeted units}}{\text{sold}} \right)$$

1)   In the example, it equals $7,000 F (1,000 unit increase in sales × $7).

c.   The sales price variance ($11,000 U) plus the sales volume variance ($7,000 F) equals the total change in the contribution margin ($4,000 U).

Stop and review! You have completed the outline for this subunit. Study multiple-choice question 30 on page 536.

QUESTIONS

20.1 Process Costing -- Principles

1. The units transferred in from the first department to the second department should be included in the computation of the equivalent units for the second department under which of the following methods of process costing?

	FIFO	Weighted-Average
A.	Yes	Yes
B.	Yes	No
C.	No	Yes
D.	No	No

Answer (A) is correct.
  REQUIRED: The cost flow method(s) that include(s) transferred-in costs in EUP calculations.
  DISCUSSION: The units transferred from the first to the second department should be included in the computation of EUP for the second department regardless of the cost flow assumption used. The transferred-in units are considered materials added at the beginning of the period.
  Answer (B) is incorrect. Units transferred in also should be included in the EUP computation under the weighted-average method. Answer (C) is incorrect. Units transferred in also should be included in the EUP computation under the FIFO method. Answer (D) is incorrect. Units transferred in should be included in the EUP computation under both methods.

2. Purchased direct materials are added in the second department of a three-department process. This addition does **not** increase the number of units produced in the second department and will

A.   Not change the dollar amount transferred to the next department.

B.   Decrease total ending work-in-process inventory.

C.   Increase the factory overhead portion of the ending work-in-process inventory.

D.   Increase total unit cost.

Answer (D) is correct.
  REQUIRED: The effect of adding direct materials in a subsequent department given constant production.
  DISCUSSION: Adding materials to a production process without changing the number of units produced increases the unit cost. The numerator (total cost) increases while the denominator (total units) remains the same.
  Answer (A) is incorrect. If purchased materials are added to the process, the cost will be added to the total cost transferred to the next department. Answer (B) is incorrect. The unit cost, and therefore the cost of EWIP, increases when materials are added. Answer (C) is incorrect. Materials cost is separate from overhead.

3. Assuming no beginning work-in-process (BWIP) inventory, and that the ending work-in-process (EWIP) inventory is 50% complete as to conversion costs, the number of equivalent units as to conversion costs would be

A.   The same as the units completed.

B.   The same as the units placed in process.

C.   Less than the units completed.

D.   Less than the units placed in process.

Answer (D) is correct.
  REQUIRED: The number of EUP as to conversion costs.
  DISCUSSION: Given no BWIP, it is immaterial whether the FIFO or weighted-average method is used. Thus, conversion cost EUP equal the units that were started and completed this period plus the EUP in EWIP. Because the units in EWIP are 50% complete as to conversion costs, they will not be fully counted for purposes of determining EUP.
  Answer (A) is incorrect. Given no BWIP, the only units completed were those started in the current period. Total EUP include these units plus the EUP in EWIP. Answer (B) is incorrect. Given no BWIP, conversion cost EUP equals units started if no EWIP exists. Answer (C) is incorrect. Conversion cost EUP include units completed plus work in EWIP.

4. Assuming no beginning work-in-process inventory, and that the ending work-in-process inventory is 100% complete as to materials costs, the number of equivalent units as to materials costs is

A. The same as the units placed in process.

B. The same as the units completed.

C. Less than the units placed in process.

D. Less than the units completed.

Answer (A) is correct.
REQUIRED: The number of EUP as to materials costs.
DISCUSSION: Given no BWIP, whether the FIFO or weighted-average method is used is immaterial. Because EWIP is 100% complete as to materials costs, the EUP for materials costs are equal to the number of units placed in process (units in EWIP + units transferred to finished goods).
Answer (B) is incorrect. The number of EUP is equal to the units completed only if there is no EWIP. Answer (C) is incorrect. The number of EUP is less than the units placed in process when EWIP is less than 100% complete as to materials costs. Answer (D) is incorrect. The EUP must at least equal the number of units completed.

20.2 Process Costing -- Calculations

5. The following data pertain to a company's cracking-department operations in December:

	Units	Completion
Work-in-process, December 1	20,000	50%
Units started	170,000	
Units completed and transferred to the distilling department	180,000	
Work-in-process, December 31	10,000	50%

Materials are added at the beginning of the process, and conversion costs are incurred uniformly throughout the process. Assuming use of the FIFO method of process costing, the equivalent units of production (EUP) with respect to conversion performed during December were

A. 170,000

B. 175,000

C. 180,000

D. 185,000

Answer (B) is correct.
REQUIRED: The EUP for conversion.
DISCUSSION: Under the FIFO method, EUP are determined based only on work performed during the current period. Thus, units in beginning work-in-process must be excluded.

	Conversion
Units transferred out	180,000
Add: EWIP (10,000 × 50%)	5,000
Total completed units	185,000
Less: BWIP (20,000 × 50%)	(10,000)
Equivalent units of production	175,000

Answer (A) is incorrect. The number of EUP of materials for the period is 170,000. Answer (C) is incorrect. The total amount of work done on the completed units is 180,000. Answer (D) is incorrect. The amount determined using the weighted-average method is 185,000.

6. A company employs a process cost system using the first-in, first-out (FIFO) method. The product passes through both Department 1 and Department 2 in order to be completed. Units enter Department 2 upon completion in Department 1. Additional direct materials are added in Department 2 when the units have reached the 25% stage of completion with respect to conversion costs. Conversion costs are added proportionally in Department 2. The production activity in Department 2 for the current month was as follows:

Beginning work-in-process inventory (40% complete with respect to conversion costs)	15,000
Units transferred in from Department 1	80,000
Units completed and transferred to finished goods	85,000
Ending work-in-process inventory (20% complete with respect to conversion costs)	10,000

How many equivalent units for direct materials were added in Department 2 for the current month?

A. 70,000 units.

B. 80,000 units.

C. 85,000 units.

D. 90,000 units.

Answer (A) is correct.
REQUIRED: The EUP for direct materials added in Department 2 for the current month.
DISCUSSION: Beginning inventory is 40% complete. Thus, direct materials have already been added. Ending inventory has not reached the 25% stage of completion, so direct materials have not yet been added to these units. Thus, the EUP for direct materials calculated on a FIFO basis are equal to the units started and completed in the current period (85,000 units completed – 15,000 units in BWIP = 70,000 units started and completed).
Answer (B) is incorrect. The amount transferred in from Department 1 was 80,000 total units. Answer (C) is incorrect. The EUP for direct materials calculated on a weighted-average basis equals 85,000. Answer (D) is incorrect. The sum of units transferred in from Department 1 and ending work-in-process inventory equals 90,000 units.

Questions 7 and 8 are based on the following information. A sporting goods manufacturer buys wood as a direct material for baseball bats. The Forming Department processes the baseball bats, and the bats are then transferred to the Finishing Department, where a sealant is applied. The Forming Department began manufacturing 10,000 "Casey Sluggers" during the month of May. There was no beginning inventory. Costs for the Forming Department for the month of May were as follows:

Direct materials	$33,000
Conversion costs	17,000
Total	$50,000

A total of 8,000 bats were completed and transferred to the Finishing Department; the remaining 2,000 bats were still in the forming process at the end of the month. All of the Forming Department's direct materials were placed in process, but, on average, only 25% of the conversion cost was applied to the ending work-in-process inventory.

7. The cost of the units transferred to the Finishing Department is

A. $50,000

B. $40,000

C. $53,000

D. $42,400

Answer (D) is correct.

REQUIRED: The cost of the units transferred to the Finishing Department.

DISCUSSION: The total EUP for materials equal 10,000 because all materials for the ending work-in-process had already been added to production. Thus, the materials cost per unit was $3.30 ($33,000 ÷ 10,000). For conversion costs, the total EUP equal 8,500 [8,000 completed + (2,000 in EWIP × 25%)]. Thus, the conversion cost was $2.00 per unit ($17,000 ÷ 8,500). The total cost transferred was therefore $42,400 [8,000 units × ($3.30 + $2.00)].

Answer (A) is incorrect. A portion of the total costs is still in work-in-process. Answer (B) is incorrect. The amount of $40,000 assumes that work-in-process is 100% complete as to conversion costs. Answer (C) is incorrect. The amount of $53,000 exceeds the actual costs incurred during the period. Given no beginning inventory, the amount transferred out cannot exceed the costs incurred during the period.

8. The cost of the work-in-process inventory in the Forming Department at the end of May is

A. $10,000

B. $2,500

C. $20,000

D. $7,600

Answer (D) is correct.

REQUIRED: The cost of the work-in-process inventory.

DISCUSSION: The EUP for materials equal 10,000 (8,000 + 2,000) because the work-in-process is 100% complete as to materials. Thus, dividing the $33,000 by 10,000 units results in a unit cost for materials of $3.30. The EUP for conversion costs equal 8,500 units [8,000 + (2,000 units × .25)]. Dividing the $17,000 of conversion costs by 8,500 EUP results in a unit cost of $2 per bat, and the total cost of goods transferred out is $5.30, consisting of $3.30 for materials and $2 for conversion costs. Multiplying $5.30 by the 8,000 bats completed results in a total transfer of $42,400. Consequently, the cost of the ending work-in-process must have been $7,600 ($50,000 total costs incurred – $42,400).

Answer (A) is incorrect. The amount of $10,000 assumes that work-in-process inventory is 100% complete as to conversion costs. Answer (B) is incorrect. The amount of $2,500 assumes that work-in-process inventory is 100% complete as to conversion costs and that 500 bats are in inventory. Answer (C) is incorrect. The amount of $20,000 assumes that work-in-process is 100% complete as to conversion costs and that 6,000 units were transferred out.

9. A company manufactures a product that passes through two production departments: molding and assembly. Direct materials are added in the assembly department when conversion is 50% complete. Conversion costs are incurred uniformly. The activity in units for the assembly department during April is as follows:

	Units
Work-in-process inventory, April 1 (60% complete as to conversion costs)	5,000
Transferred in from molding department	32,000
Defective at final inspection (within normal limits)	2,500
Transferred out to finished goods inventory	28,500
Work-in-process inventory, April 30 (40% complete as to conversion costs)	6,000

The number of equivalent units for direct materials in the assembly department for April calculated on the weighted-average basis is

A. 26,000 units.

B. 28,500 units.

C. 31,000 units.

D. 34,000 units.

Answer (C) is correct.

REQUIRED: The EUP for direct materials on the weighted-average basis.

DISCUSSION: The weighted-average approach averages the costs in beginning work-in-process with those incurred during the period. Accordingly, the degree of completion of the BWIP is ignored in computing the EUP for direct materials. Direct materials EUP therefore consist of units transferred to finished goods (28,500) and units that failed inspection (2,500), or 31,000. Ending work-in-process inventory has not reached the point at which materials are added.

Answer (A) is incorrect. The number of direct materials EUP calculated using the FIFO method is 26,000 (31,000 weighted-average EUP – 5,000 EUP in BWIP). Answer (B) is incorrect. The number of units transferred out to finished goods inventory is 28,500. Answer (D) is incorrect. The number of physical units minus the conversion work previously done on the BWIP is 34,000 [5,000 units in BWIP + 32,000 units transferred in – (5,000 units in BWIP × 60%)].

10. A company uses weighted-average process costing for the product it manufactures. All direct materials are added at the beginning of production, and conversion costs are applied evenly during production. The following data apply to the past month:

Total units in beginning inventory (30% complete as to conversion costs)	1,500
Total units transferred to finished goods inventory	7,400
Total units in ending inventory (60% complete as to conversion costs)	2,300

Assuming no spoilage, equivalent units of production (EUP) with respect to conversion costs total

A. 8,330

B. 8,780

C. 9,230

D. 9,700

Answer (B) is correct.

REQUIRED: The equivalent units of production for conversion costs.

DISCUSSION: The weighted-average method averages the work performed in the prior period with the work done in the current period. Thus, beginning work-in-process is left in the calculation (unlike FIFO).

	Conversion
Units transferred out	7,400
Add: EWIP (2,300 × 60%)	1,380
EUP	8,780

Answer (A) is incorrect. The EUP for conversion costs are 8,330 [8,780 weighted-average EUP – (1,500 units in BWIP × 30%)] if the FIFO method were used. Answer (C) is incorrect. Including 30% of BWIP in the total results in 9,230. Answer (D) is incorrect. The sum of the physical, not equivalent, units completed and in EWIP is 9,700.

20.3 Activity-Based Costing (ABC)

11. A company is considering the implementation of an activity-based costing and management program. The company

A. Should focus on manufacturing activities and avoid implementation with service-type functions.

B. Would probably find a lack of software in the marketplace to assist with the related recordkeeping.

C. Would normally gain added insights into causes of cost.

D. Would likely use fewer cost pools than it did under more traditional accounting methods.

Answer (C) is correct.

REQUIRED: The most likely result of an ABC and ABM program.

DISCUSSION: One of the benefits of activity-based costing is the discovery of cost relationships that are unnoticed using traditional accounting methods.

Answer (A) is incorrect. Activity-based costing is suitable for service-type functions. Answer (B) is incorrect. Software exists to help firms implement activity-based management. Answer (D) is incorrect. Activity-based costing generally results in many more cost pools than under traditional accounting methods.

Question 12 is based on the following information.

Zeta Company is preparing its annual profit plan. As part of its analysis of the profitability of individual products, the controller estimates the amount of overhead that should be allocated to the individual product lines from the information given in the next column:

	Wall Mirrors	Specialty Windows
Units produced	25	25
Material moves per product line	5	15
Direct labor hours per unit	200	200
Budgeted materials handling costs		$50,000

12. Under a costing system that allocates overhead on the basis of direct labor hours, Zeta Company's materials handling costs allocated to one unit of wall mirrors would be

A. $1,000

B. $500

C. $2,000

D. $5,000

Answer (A) is correct.

REQUIRED: The amount of materials handling costs allocated to one unit of wall mirrors when direct labor hours is the activity base.

DISCUSSION: If direct labor hours are used as the allocation base, the $50,000 of costs is allocated over 400 hours of direct labor. Multiplying the 25 units of each product times 200 hours results in 5,000 labor hours for each product, or a total of 10,000 hours. Dividing $50,000 by 10,000 hours results in a cost of $5 per direct labor hour. Multiplying 200 hours times $5 results in an allocation of $1,000 of overhead per unit of product.

Answer (B) is incorrect. The amount of $500 is the allocation based on number of material moves. Answer (C) is incorrect. The amount of $2,000 assumes that all the overhead is allocated to the wall mirrors. Answer (D) is incorrect. The amount of $5,000 assumes overhead of $250,000.

13. Pelder Products Company manufactures two types of engineering diagnostic equipment used in construction. The two products are based on different technologies, x-ray and ultrasound, but are manufactured in the same factory. Pelder has computed the manufacturing cost of the x-ray and ultrasound products by adding together direct materials, direct labor, and overhead cost applied based on the number of direct labor hours. The factory has three overhead departments that support the single production line that makes both products. Budgeted overhead spending for the departments is as follows:

Department			
Engineering design	Material handling	Setup	Total
$6,000	$5,000	$3,000	$14,000

Pelder's budgeted manufacturing activities and costs for the period are as follows:

	Product	
Activity	X-Ray	Ultrasound
Units produced and sold	50	100
Direct materials used	$5,000	$8,000
Direct labor hours used	100	300
Direct labor cost	$4,000	$12,000
Number of parts used	400	600
Number of engineering changes	2	1
Number of product setups	8	7

The budgeted cost to manufacture one ultrasound machine using the activity-based costing method is

A. $225

B. $264

C. $293

D. $305

Answer (B) is correct.

REQUIRED: The ABC cost of a single ultrasound machine.

DISCUSSION: Charges for direct materials and direct labor are traceable to each type of machine ($8,000 and $12,000 respectively for the ultrasound). The departmental costs must be allocated based on each machine's proportional driver level. Engineering design costs can be allocated to the ultrasound machine at a rate of 33.3% [1 ÷ (1 + 2)], material handling at a rate of 60% [600 ÷ (600 + 400)], and setup at a rate of 46.7% [7 ÷ (7 + 8)]. Pelder's cost for a single ultrasound machine can thus be calculated as follows:

	For 100 Units
Direct materials ($8,000)	$ 80
Direct labor ($12,000)	120
Engineering changes ($6,000 × 33.3%)	20
Materials handling ($5,000 × 60%)	30
Setup ($3,000 × 46.7%)	14
Total	$264

Answer (A) is incorrect. The amount of $225 results from using x-ray direct labor rather than ultrasound direct labor. Answer (C) is incorrect. The amount of $293 results from improperly using the units of production to allocate the engineering, handling, and setup costs. Answer (D) is incorrect. The amount of $305 results from improperly using direct labor hours to allocate the engineering, handling, and setup costs.

14. All of the following are likely to be used as a cost allocation base in activity-based costing **except** the

   A. Number of different materials used to manufacture the product.

   B. Units of materials used to manufacture the product.

   C. Number of vendors supplying the materials used to manufacture the product.

   D. Cost of materials used to manufacture the product.

Answer (D) is correct.
   REQUIRED: The item not an appropriate allocation base in activity-based costing.
   DISCUSSION: Activity-based costing is founded on the idea that drivers for indirect cost assignment should be based on some level of activity. Cost of materials does not directly reflect a level of a given activity.
   Answer (A) is incorrect. The number of different materials used to manufacture a product can be a cost driver. Different materials often require different setups and thus a proportional amount of employee time. Answer (B) is incorrect. The units of materials used to manufacture a product can be a cost driver. Units of material used directly reflects the amount of employee time spent on the production process. Answer (C) is incorrect. The number of vendors supplying materials used to manufacture the product can be a cost driver. Each supplier requires servicing by buyers and other personnel, and thus the number of suppliers directly reflects the level of production activity.

15. The Chocolate Baker specializes in chocolate baked goods. The firm has long assessed the profitability of a product line by comparing revenues to the cost of goods sold. However, Barry White, the firm's new accountant, wants to use an activity-based costing system that takes into consideration the cost of the delivery person. Listed below are activity and cost information relating to two of Chocolate Baker's major products.

	Muffins	Cheesecake
Revenue	$53,000	$46,000
Cost of goods sold	26,000	21,000
Delivery activity:		
Number of deliveries	150	85
Average length of delivery	10 minutes	15 minutes
Cost per hour for delivery	$20.00	$20.00

Using activity-based costing, which one of the following statements is correct?

   A. The muffins are $2,000 more profitable.

   B. The cheesecakes are $75 more profitable.

   C. The muffins are $1,925 more profitable.

   D. The muffins have a higher profitability as a percentage of sales and therefore are more advantageous.

Answer (C) is correct.
   REQUIRED: The true statement given activity-based costing.
   DISCUSSION: The first step is to calculate the gross margin on the two products:

	Muffins	Cheesecake
Revenues	$53,000	$46,000
Cost of goods sold	(26,000)	(21,000)
Gross margin	$27,000	$25,000

The next step is to calculate total delivery cost for each product:

	Muffins	Cheesecake
Number of deliveries	150	85
Times: minutes per delivery	× 10	× 15
Total delivery minutes	1,500	1,275
Divided by: minutes per hour	÷ 60	÷ 60
Total delivery hours	25.00	21.25
Times: delivery cost per hour	× $20	× $20
Total delivery cost	$500	$425

The operating profits on these two products, and the difference between them, can now be determined:

Muffins	($27,000 − $500)	$26,500
Cheesecake	($25,000 − $425)	(24,575)
Excess		$ 1,925

   Answer (A) is incorrect. Muffins exceed cheesecake by $2,000 only at the gross margin, not the total profitability, level. Answer (B) is incorrect. The total delivery cost for muffins exceeds that of cheesecake by $75. Answer (D) is incorrect. Muffins ($26,500 ÷ $53,000 = 50.0%) have a lower profitability percentage than cheesecake ($24,575 ÷ $46,000 = 53.4%).

16. A company with three products classifies its costs as belonging to five functions: design, production, marketing, distribution, and customer services. For pricing purposes, all company costs are assigned to the three products. The direct costs of each of the five functions are traced directly to the three products. The indirect costs of each of the five business functions are collected into five separate cost pools and then assigned to the three products using appropriate allocation bases. The allocation base that will most likely be the best for allocating the indirect costs of the distribution function is

   A. Number of customer phone calls.

   B. Number of shipments.

   C. Number of sales persons.

   D. Dollar sales volume.

Answer (B) is correct.
   REQUIRED: The allocation base that will most likely be the best for allocating the indirect costs of the distribution function.
   DISCUSSION: The number of shipments is an appropriate cost driver. A cause-and-effect relationship may exist between the number of shipments and distribution costs.
   Answer (A) is incorrect. The number of customer phone calls has little relation to distribution. It is probably more closely related to customer service. Answer (C) is incorrect. The number of sales persons is not related to distribution. It is more closely related to marketing. Answer (D) is incorrect. The dollar sales volume is not necessarily related to distribution. It is more likely related to marketing.

17. Cost allocation is the process of assigning indirect costs to a cost object. The indirect costs are grouped in cost pools and then allocated by a common allocation base to the cost object. The base that is employed to allocate a homogeneous cost pool should

A. Have a cause-and-effect relationship with the cost items in the cost pool.

B. Assign the costs in the pool uniformly to cost objects even if the cost objects use resources in a nonuniform way.

C. Be a nonfinancial measure (e.g., number of setups) because a nonfinancial measure is more objective.

D. Have a high correlation with the cost items in the cost pool as the sole criterion for selection.

Answer (A) is correct.
REQUIRED: The characteristic of a base used to allocate a homogeneous cost pool.
DISCUSSION: A cost allocation base is the common denominator for systematically correlating indirect costs and a cost object. The cost driver of the indirect costs is ordinarily the allocation base. In a homogeneous cost pool, all costs should have the same or a similar cause-and-effect relationship with the cost allocation base.
Answer (B) is incorrect. If an allocation base uniformly assigns costs to cost objects when the cost objects use resources in a nonuniform way, the base is smoothing or spreading the costs. Smoothing can result in undercosting or overcosting of products, with adverse effects on product pricing, cost management and control, and decision making. Answer (C) is incorrect. Financial measures (e.g., sales dollars and direct labor costs) and nonfinancial measures (e.g., setups and units shipped) can be used as allocation bases. Answer (D) is incorrect. High correlation between the cost items in a pool and the allocation base does not necessarily mean that a cause-and-effect relationship exists. Two variables may move together without such a relationship. The perceived relationship between the cost driver (allocation base) and the indirect costs should have economic plausibility and high correlation.

20.4 Variance Analysis -- Materials and Labor

18. Tub Co. uses a standard cost system. The following information pertains to direct labor for product B for the month of October:

Standard hours allowed for actual production	2,000
Actual rate paid per hour	$8.40
Standard rate per hour	$8.00
Labor efficiency variance	$1,600 U

What were the actual hours worked?

A. 1,800

B. 1,810

C. 2,190

D. 2,200

Answer (D) is correct.
REQUIRED: The actual hours worked.
DISCUSSION: The labor efficiency variance is the difference between the standard hours and the actual hours worked, times the standard wage rate.

$$(SQ - AQ) \times SP = \text{Labor efficiency variance}$$
$$(2{,}000 \text{ hours} - AQ) \times \$8 = -\$1{,}600$$
$$\$16{,}000 - \$8AQ = -\$1{,}600$$
$$-\$8AQ = -\$17{,}600$$
$$AQ = 2{,}200 \text{ hours}$$

19. In a standard cost system, the materials price variance is obtained by multiplying the

A. Actual price by the difference between actual quantity used and standard quantity used.

B. Actual quantity purchased by the difference between standard price and actual price.

C. Standard price by the difference between expected quantity and budgeted quantity.

D. Standard quantity used by the difference between actual price and standard price.

Answer (B) is correct.
REQUIRED: The method used to compute the materials price variance.
DISCUSSION: The materials price variance is the portion of the flexible budget variance attributable entirely to a difference in purchased input unit cost. If it is recognized at the time of purchase, it is calculated by multiplying the actual quantity purchased (AQP) by the difference between standard price (SP) and actual price (AP) [AQP × (SP – AP)].
Answer (A) is incorrect. The product of actual price and the difference between actual quantity used and standard quantity used is not a defined variance. Answer (C) is incorrect. The product of standard price and the difference between expected quantity and budgeted quantity is the sales volume variance. Answer (D) is incorrect. The materials price variance is the actual quantity of input purchased times the difference between the standard price of materials and the actual price.

20. The standard unit cost is used in the calculation of which of the following variances?

	Materials Price Variance	Materials Usage Variance
A.	No	No
B.	No	Yes
C.	Yes	No
D.	Yes	Yes

Answer (D) is correct.
 REQUIRED: The variance(s) using standard unit costs.
 DISCUSSION: The materials price variance is isolated at either the time of purchase or use in production. It is calculated by multiplying the actual quantity of units purchased (or used) by the difference between actual price and standard price. The materials quantity (usage) variance is calculated by multiplying the difference between (1) the standard quantity of units (the actual output times the standard number of inputs per unit of output) and (2) the actual quantity of units consumed, times standard price. Thus, the standard unit cost is used to compute both the materials price variance and the materials quantity variance.
 Answer (A) is incorrect. Standard unit cost is used in the calculation of materials price variance and materials quantity variance. Answer (B) is incorrect. Standard unit cost also is used in the calculation of the materials price variance. Answer (C) is incorrect. Standard unit cost also is used in the calculation of the materials quantity variance.

21. Which of the following unfavorable variances is directly affected by the relative position of a production process on a learning curve?

A. Materials mix.

B. Materials price.

C. Labor rate.

D. Labor efficiency.

Answer (D) is correct.
 REQUIRED: The variance affected by the learning curve.
 DISCUSSION: The efficiency of employees varies with how long they have been performing the particular task. Thus, more experienced employees are expected to be more efficient, which affects the labor efficiency variance.
 Answer (A) is incorrect. The learning curve has little correlation with materials mix variances. Answer (B) is incorrect. A materials price variance is primarily the result of external factors. Answer (C) is incorrect. The labor rate variance should not be affected by the learning curve.

22. The difference between the actual labor rate multiplied by the actual hours worked and the standard labor rate multiplied by the standard labor hours is the

A. Total labor variance.

B. Labor rate variance.

C. Labor usage variance.

D. Labor efficiency variance.

Answer (A) is correct.
 REQUIRED: The variance defined by the difference between total actual labor costs and total standard costs allowed.
 DISCUSSION: The total actual labor cost equals the actual labor rate times the actual labor hours. The total standard cost for good output equals the standard rate times the standard hours allowed. The total labor rate variance is the difference between the total actual labor costs and the total standard labor costs.
 Answer (B) is incorrect. The labor rate variance is AQ × (SP – AP). Answer (C) is incorrect. The labor usage variance is (SQ – AQ) × SP. Answer (D) is incorrect. The labor efficiency variance is the same as the labor usage variance: (SQ – AQ) × SP.

23. Information on Hanley's direct labor costs for the month of January is as follows:

Actual direct labor rate	$7.50
Standard direct labor hours allowed	11,000
Actual direct labor hours	10,000
Direct labor rate variance -- favorable	$5,500

The standard direct labor rate in January was

A. $6.95

B. $7.00

C. $8.00

D. $8.05

Answer (D) is correct.
 REQUIRED: The standard direct labor rate for the month.
 DISCUSSION: The labor rate variance, actual hours, and actual rate are given. Thus, the standard rate can be derived by substituting into the following formula:

$$AQ \times (SP - AP) = \text{Labor rate variance}$$
$$10,000 \times (SP - \$7.50) = \$5,500 \text{ F}$$
$$10,000SP - \$75,000 = \$5,500$$
$$10,000SP = \$80,500$$
$$SP = \$8.05$$

Answer (A) is incorrect. The amount of $6.95 treats the $.55 variance per unit as unfavorable. Answer (B) is incorrect. Actual hours, not standard hours, are used to determine the standard rate. Furthermore, the favorable variance should be added, not subtracted, in calculating the standard rate. Answer (C) is incorrect. Actual hours, not standard hours, should be used in determining the standard rate.

20.5 Variance Analysis -- Overhead

24. During the month just ended, a department's fixed overhead standard costing system reported unfavorable spending and volume variances. The activity level selected for allocating overhead to the product was based on 80% of practical capacity. If 100% of practical capacity had been selected instead, how would the reported unfavorable spending and volume variances be affected?

	Spending Variance	Volume Variance
A.	Increased	Unchanged
B.	Increased	Increased
C.	Unchanged	Increased
D.	Unchanged	Unchanged

Answer (C) is correct.
REQUIRED: The effects on unfavorable spending and volume variances of increasing the budgeted activity level.
DISCUSSION: The fixed overhead spending variance equals the actual costs incurred minus the budgeted amount. Thus, the spending variance is not affected by the denominator level of the overhead application driver. However, the volume variance equals the budgeted amount minus the amount applied. Because the fixed overhead applied depends on the activity level of the driver used for application, a change in the denominator affects the volume variance. If the denominator increases, the application rate and the amount applied decrease, causing the variance to increase.

25. Which of the following variances would be useful in calling attention to a possible short-term problem in the control of overhead costs?

	Spending Variance	Volume Variance
A.	No	No
B.	No	Yes
C.	Yes	No
D.	Yes	Yes

Answer (C) is correct.
REQUIRED: The variance(s) useful for controlling overhead costs.
DISCUSSION: The volume variance is the difference between fixed overhead applied and fixed overhead budgeted. Thus, the volume variance has no relation to cost control because the amount of fixed costs is constant. The variance results only from a change in the level of the application base. However, the spending variance is simply a price variance for manufacturing overhead. Consequently, it is the spending variance, not the volume variance, that is useful in detecting problems in the control of overhead costs.
Answer (A) is incorrect. The spending variance is a price variance. Answer (B) is incorrect. The spending variance, not the volume variance, is useful for calling attention to a possible short-term problem in the control of overhead costs. Answer (D) is incorrect. The volume variance does not indicate whether problems exist in the control of costs.

26. The fixed factory overhead application rate is a function of a predetermined activity level. If standard hours allowed for good output equal this predetermined activity level for a given period, the volume variance will be

A. Zero.

B. Favorable.

C. Unfavorable.

D. Either favorable or unfavorable, depending on the budgeted overhead.

Answer (A) is correct.
REQUIRED: The volume variance when standard hours allowed for good output equal the predetermined activity.
DISCUSSION: The volume variance is the difference between the amount of fixed overhead applied and the amount budgeted. Thus, given no difference between the predetermined activity level and the standard input allowed for the actual output, no variance occurs.
Answer (B) is incorrect. A favorable volume variance means standard input allowed for the actual output exceeds the predetermined (budgeted) amount. Answer (C) is incorrect. An unfavorable volume variance means that standard input allowed for the actual output is less than the amount budgeted. Answer (D) is incorrect. No variance occurs.

27. Under the three-variance method for analyzing factory overhead, the difference between the actual factory overhead and the factory overhead applied to production is the

A. Net factory overhead variance.

B. Controllable variance.

C. Efficiency variance.

D. Spending variance.

Answer (A) is correct.
REQUIRED: The difference between the actual manufacturing overhead and the manufacturing overhead applied.
DISCUSSION: Three-way analysis calculates spending, efficiency, and volume variances. However, regardless of whether two-, three-, or four-way analysis is used, the net manufacturing overhead variance is the difference between actual overhead and the amount applied to production.
Answer (B) is incorrect. The controllable (budget) variance is calculated in two-way analysis. Answer (C) is incorrect. No single efficiency variance is calculated in overhead variance analysis. Answer (D) is incorrect. In three-way analysis, the spending variance is the sum of the variable overhead spending variance and the fixed overhead spending variance.

28. Union Company uses a standard cost accounting system. The following factory overhead and production data are available for August:

Standard fixed overhead rate per DLH	$1
Standard variable overhead rate per DLH	$4
Budgeted monthly DLH	40,000
Actual DLH worked	39,500
Standard DLH allowed for actual production	39,000
Overall overhead variance – favorable	$2,000

The applied factory overhead for August should be

A. $195,000

B. $197,000

C. $197,500

D. $199,500

Answer (A) is correct.
REQUIRED: The applied manufacturing overhead for the month.
DISCUSSION: The applied overhead equals the standard direct hours allowed for actual production multiplied by the total standard overhead rate per hour.

$$39,000 \times (\$4\ VOH + \$1\ FOH) = \$195,000$$

Answer (B) is incorrect. The amount of $197,000 includes the $2,000 favorable overhead variance. This variance should not be added to the $195,000 applied overhead. Answer (C) is incorrect. The actual DLH worked were used to determine the applied FO when the standard DLH allowed for actual production should have been used. Answer (D) is incorrect. The actual DLH worked were used instead of the standard DLH allowed. Furthermore, the $2,000 favorable overhead variance should not be included.

29. Jones, a department manager, exercises control over the department's costs. The following is selected information relating to the department for July:

Variable factory overhead
Budgeted based on standard hours allowed	$80,000
Actual	85,000

Fixed factory overhead
Budgeted	25,000
Actual	27,000

In a three-way analysis of variance, the department's unfavorable spending variance for July was

A. $7,000

B. $5,000

C. $2,000

D. $0

Answer (A) is correct.
REQUIRED: The amount of unfavorable spending variance.
DISCUSSION: In three-way analysis, the spending variance is the sum of the variable overhead spending variance and the fixed overhead spending variance. The variable overhead spending variance equals the actual number of units of the overhead driver consumed times the application rate minus the amount actually incurred ($80,000 – $85,000 = $5,000 unfavorable). The fixed overhead spending variance equals the budgeted amount minus the actual amount incurred ($25,000 – $27,000 = $2,000 unfavorable). The department's total unfavorable spending variance for July is thus $7,000 ($5,000 + $2,000).
Answer (B) is incorrect. The variable overhead spending variance is $5,000. Answer (C) is incorrect. The fixed overhead spending variance is $2,000. Answer (D) is incorrect. The department incurred an unfavorable spending variance for the month.

20.6 Sales Variances

30. The following data are available for July:

	Budget	Actual
Sales	40,000 units	42,000 units
Selling price	$6 per unit	$5.70 per unit
Variable cost	$3.50 per unit	$3.40 per unit

What is the sales volume variance for July?

A. $5,000 favorable.

B. $4,600 favorable.

C. $12,000 unfavorable.

D. $12,600 unfavorable.

Answer (A) is correct.
REQUIRED: The sales volume variance for a particular month.
DISCUSSION: The sales volume variance is the difference between the actual volume and the budgeted volume in units, times the budgeted contribution margin per unit.

= (Actual volume – Budgeted volume) ×
   (Selling price – Unit variable cost)
= (42,000 – 40,000) × ($6 – $3.50)
= $5,000 F

Answer (B) is incorrect. The budgeted selling price and budgeted variable cost must be used to determine the sales volume variance, not the actual selling price and actual variable cost. Answer (C) is incorrect. The budgeted variable cost must be subtracted from the selling price before multiplying by the 2,000 difference in units actually sold from budgeted sales. Answer (D) is incorrect. The sales volume variance is found by multiplying the 2,000 unit difference between actual and budgeted sales by the $2.50 budgeted contribution margin.

*Page
Intentionally
Left Blank*

20.7 PRACTICE WRITTEN COMMUNICATION

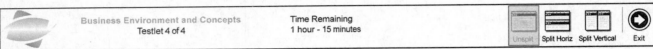

Business Environment and Concepts	Time Remaining		
Testlet 4 of 4	1 hour - 15 minutes		

DIRECTIONS

Note: If you believe you have encountered a software malfunction, report it to the test center staff immediately.

Navigation

To navigate from task to task, use the controls at the bottom of the screen. Click on the **Next** button to advance to the next task, or the **Previous** button to go to the previous task. To go directly to any task, click on its number.

▽ = Reminder		Directions	1 2 3 4 5 6 7	◄ Previous	Next ►

If you would like a reminder to revisit a task, or want to indicate that you are finished with it, click on the reminder flag below the task number. To clear the flag, click on it again. Reminder flags are for your use only – they do not contribute to your score.

Tabs

In this part of the examination, you will be asked to complete various tasks. Every task has one or more **Work Tabs**. Every task also has a **Help** tab.

| Work tab | Help tab |

Work Tabs:

- **Work Tabs** are identified with a pencil icon. This is where your responses are expected.
- Each task has one or more **Work Tabs**.
- **Work Tabs** contain directions for completing the task - be sure to read these directions carefully.
- The **Work Tab** name in the example above is for illustration only - yours will differ.
- You must complete all of the **Work Tabs** in each task to receive full credit.

Help Tab:

- The **Help Tab** provides assistance with the exam software that is used in this task. For example, if the task is to compose a memorandum, **Help** will provide information about the word processor.

The Toolbar

The toolbar at the top of the screen shows the amount of time remaining for you to complete the tasks. In addition, the following tools are available. Note that only the **Exit** button is displayed when Directions are visible - the others will appear when you begin the tasks.

Click on these buttons to split or unsplit the screen. You can split the screen vertically or horizontally.

Click on this button to go on to the next part of the examination. You must complete all of the tasks to receive full credit. Once you click on **Exit** and confirm the action, you will NOT be able to return to this testlet.

▽ = Reminder		Directions	1	◄ Previous	Next ►

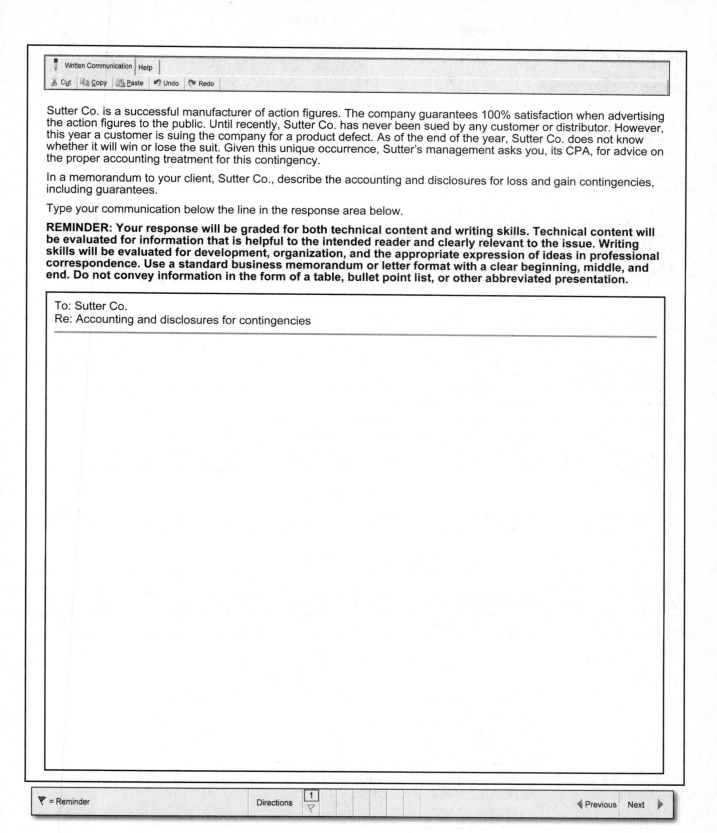

To: Sutter Co.
Re: Accounting and disclosures for contingencies

NOTE: Your Written Communications on the actual CPA exam may cover topics outside the scope of the BEC CSO (i.e., they may relate to topics from the AUD, FAR, and/or REG CSOs instead). Answer to the best of your ability, and remember that graders are mainly evaluating your writing ability and will overlook minor technical mistakes.

Unofficial Answer

Written Communication

> To: Sutter Co.
> Re: Accounting and disclosures for contingencies
>
> ---
>
> A contingent loss must be accrued when two conditions are met: It must be probable that an asset has been impaired or a liability has been incurred, and the entity must be able to make a reasonable estimate of the loss.
>
> If the loss is probable and can be reasonably estimated, it should be accrued if the amount is material. If the estimate is stated within a given range, and no amount appears to be a better estimate than any other, the minimum of the range should be accrued. Required disclosures include the nature of the contingency, any additional loss exposure, and possibly the amount accrued.
>
> If both conditions are not met, but the probability of the loss is at least reasonably possible, the nature of the contingency should be described. Also, an estimate of the amount or the range of loss must be disclosed, or a statement should be included indicating that an estimate cannot be made.
>
> Normally, loss contingencies are not disclosed when their probability of occurrence is remote. For a direct or indirect debt guarantee, however, disclosure must be made of a remote loss contingency.
>
> A guarantee is a noncontingent obligation to be ready to perform after the occurrence of a triggering event. It is coupled with a contingent obligation to make payments if such an event occurs. Thus, recognition of a liability at the inception of a guarantee is required even when it is not probable that payments will be made. The initial measurement ordinarily is at fair value. If a contingent loss and liability also are required to be recognized, the liability recognized is the greater of the fair value measurement or the contingent liability amount.
>
> Gain contingencies should be disclosed but not recognized until they are realized.

The above depicts a Level 5 answer. Consult your booklet, *How to Pass the CPA Exam: A System for Success*, for a description of the three writing skills criteria. You may also access this booklet online by visiting www.gleim.com/PassCPA.

Self-Grade

Below, grade your response on technical content and writing skills. Bubble in the circle next to the appropriate score that you may receive based on the criteria given. Your **total** score is the sum of your scores on all six items. The maximum score is 19 points.

Technical Content Evaluation

Was your response on topic?	O No [0]	O Mostly [1]	O Yes [2]
Did your response have any *significant* errors?	O 0 errors [1]	O 1 major error [–1]	O 2 or more major errors [–2]
Did your response contain any illegal advice?	O No [1]	O Yes [0]	

Writing Skills Evaluation

	Poor	Below Average	Average	Above Average	Outstanding
Organization	O 1	O 2	O 3	O 4	O 5
Development	O 1	O 2	O 3	O 4	O 5
Expression	O 1	O 2	O 3	O 4	O 5

Disclaimer: This scoring schedule was developed by Gleim Publications as a guideline only. The AICPA has not released specific information on how the Written Communications are graded.

Practice even more Written Communications with the Gleim Mega Test Bank.
Learn more: gleim.com/CPAmega | 800.874.5346

APPENDIX A
AICPA CONTENT SPECIFICATION OUTLINES (CSOs) WITH GLEIM CROSS-REFERENCES

The AICPA has indicated that the content specification outlines have several purposes, including

1. *Ensure that the testing of entry-level knowledge and skills that are important to the protection of the public interest is consistent across examination administrations*

2. *Determine what kinds of questions should be included on the CPA Examination so that every version of the examination reflects the required distribution and balance of knowledge and skill components*

3. *Provide candidates preparing for the examination with information about the subject matter that is eligible to be tested*

For your convenience, we have reproduced verbatim the AICPA's BEC CSOs. We also have provided cross-references to the study units and subunits in this book that correspond to the CSOs' coverage. If one entry appears above a list, it applies to all items.

AICPA CONTENT SPECIFICATION OUTLINE

Business Environment and Concepts

I. **Corporate Governance (18%)**

    A. Rights, Duties, Responsibilities, Authority, and Ethics of the Board of Directors, Officers, and Other Employees

        1. Financial and non-financial reporting - 1.1
        2. Internal control (including COSO or similar framework) - 1.2-1.3
        3. Enterprise risk management (including COSO or similar framework) - 1.4

    B. Entity-Level Controls - 1.3

        1. Tone at the top – establishing control environment
        2. Monitoring control effectiveness
        3. Change control process

II. **Economic Concepts and Analysis (18%)**

    A. Changes in Economic and Business Cycles – Economic Measures/Indicators - SU 2-SU 3

    B. Globalization and Local Economies

        1. Impacts of globalization on companies - 4.1, 4.3
        2. Shifts in economic balance of power (e.g., capital) to/from developed from/to emerging markets - 4.2

    C. Market Influences on Business Strategies - SU 2-SU 3

    D. Financial Risk Management

        1. Market, interest rate, currency, liquidity, credit, price, and other risks - 4.2, 5.1-5.3
        2. Means for mitigating/controlling financial risks - 4.3, 5.4

III. **Financial Management (21%)**

    A. Financial Modeling, Projections, and Analysis

        1. Forecasting and trends - SU 6
        2. Financial and risk analysis - 1.5, 8.2-8.3, 9.2-9.6
        3. Impact of inflation/deflation - 3.5, 4.2

    B. Financial Decisions

        1. Debt, equity, leasing - 7.1-7.3
        2. Asset and investment management - SU 5, SU 8

    C. Capital Management, including Working Capital

        1. Capital structure - 7.1-7.2, 7.4-7.5, 10.5
        2. Short-term and long-term financing - 7.1-7.2, 8.1, 9.1
        3. Asset effectiveness and/or efficiency - SU 8, SU 10

   D. Financial Valuations (e.g., Fair Value)

     1. Methods for calculating valuations - 5.3, 9.3, 10.3-10.5
     2. Evaluating assumptions used in valuations - 5.3, 9.3-9.4, SU 10

   E. Financial Transaction Processes and Controls - 11.2, 11.4

IV. **Information Systems and Communications (17%)**

   A. Organizational Needs Assessment

     1. Data capture - 11.1-11.3
     2. Processing - 11.2-11.3
     3. Reporting - 11.3
     4. Role of information technology in business strategy - SU 11

   B. Systems Design and Other Elements - 12.1-12.2

     1. Business process design (integrated systems, automated, and manual interfaces) - 12.3-12.5
     2. Information Technology (IT) control objectives - 14.1-14.4
     3. Role of technology systems in control monitoring - 12.6, 14.1-14.4
     4. Operational effectiveness - 14.1
     5. Segregation of duties - 14.5
     6. Policies - 14.1

   C. Security - 13.4, 14.3

     1. Technologies and security management features
     2. Policies

   D. Internet – Implications for Business

     1. Electronic commerce - 13.2-13.4
     2. Opportunities for business process reengineering - 12.5, 17.3
     3. Roles of Internet evolution on business operations and organization cultures - SU 13

   E. Types of Information System and Technology Risks - 12.1-12.4, 14.1

   F. Disaster Recovery and Business Continuity - 12.6

V. **Strategic Planning (12%)**

   A. Market and Risk Analysis - 15.1-15.2
   B. Strategy Development, Implementation, and Monitoring - 15.1-15.2
   C. Planning Techniques

     1. Budget and analysis - 15.3-15.4, SU 16
     2. Forecasting and projection - SU 6, SU 16
     3. Coordinating information from various sources for integrated planning - 15.2, 16.1, 16.3

VI. **Operations Management (14%)**

   A. Performance Management and Impact of Measures on Behavior

     1. Financial and nonfinancial measures - 10.3-10.4, 17.2
     2. Impact of marketing practices on performance - 15.1, 17.1-17.2
     3. Incentive compensation - 17.2

   B. Cost Measurement Methods and Techniques - SU 18-SU 20

   C. Process Management

     1. Approaches, techniques, measures, and benefits to process-management-driven businesses - 17.3

     2. Roles of shared services, outsourcing, and off-shore operations, and their implications on business risks and controls - 17.3

     3. Selecting and implementing improvement initiatives - 17.3-17.6

     4. Business process reengineering - 17.3

     5. Management philosophies and techniques for performance improvement such as Just in Time (JIT), Quality, Lean, Demand Flow, Theory of Constraints, and Six Sigma - 17.3

   D. Project Management - 17.7

     1. Project planning, implementation, and monitoring
     2. Roles of project managers, project members, and oversight or steering groups
     3. Project risks, including resource, scope, cost, and deliverables

INDEX